SHARPEVILLE

THE MAKING OF THE MODERN WORLD

This group of narrative histories focuses on key moments and events in the twentieth century to explore their wider significance for the development of the modern world.

PUBLISHED:

The Fall of France: The Nazi Invasion of 1940, Julian Jackson
A Bitter Revolution: China's Struggle with the Modern World, Rana Mitter
Dynamic of Destruction: Culture and Mass Killing in the First World War, Alan Kramer

FORTHCOMING:

Algeria: The Undeclared War, Martin Evans

SERIES ADVISERS:

PROFESSOR CHRIS BAYLY, University of Cambridge
PROFESSOR RICHARD J. EVANS, University of Cambridge
PROFESSOR DAVID REYNOLDS, University of Cambridge

SHARPEVILLE

AN APARTHEID MASSACRE
AND ITS CONSEQUENCES

TOM LODGE

OXFORD
UNIVERSITY PRESS

OXFORD

UNIVERSITY PRESS

Great Clarendon Street, Oxford OX2 6DP

Oxford University Press is a department of the University of Oxford.
It furthers the University's objective of excellence in research, scholarship,
and education by publishing worldwide in

Oxford New York

Auckland Cape Town Dar es Salaam Hong Kong Karachi
Kuala Lumpur Madrid Melbourne Mexico City Nairobi
New Delhi Shanghai Taipei Toronto

With offices in

Argentina Austria Brazil Chile Czech Republic France Greece
Guatemala Hungary Italy Japan Poland Portugal Singapore
South Korea Switzerland Thailand Turkey Ukraine Vietnam

Oxford is a registered trade mark of Oxford University Press
in the UK and in certain other countries

Published in the United States
by Oxford University Press Inc., New York

© Tom Lodge 2011

The moral rights of the author have been asserted
Database right Oxford University Press (maker)

First published 2011

British Library Cataloguing in Publication Data

Data available

Library of Congress Cataloging in Publication Data

Data available

Typeset by SPI Publisher Services, Pondicherry, India
Printed in Great Britain
on acid-free paper by
Clays Ltd, St Ives plc

ISBN 978-0-19-280185-2

1 3 5 7 9 10 8 6 4 2

Preface and Acknowledgements

> A quarter of a century after the police opened fire on a crowd of demonstrators at Sharpeville the meaning of that event—or series of events, for 'Sharpeville' soon came to denote the general crisis that resulted—still remains elusive. It has different meanings for different people, some trying to understand it by looking at consequences, others more concerned with its symbolic significance ... Last September, when new violence at Sharpeville brought that township once more into the news, an editorial writer in the *Cape Times* wrote as follows: 'Not until blacks are acknowledged as South African citizens will a lasting peace return to this country. If this truth again is evaded, there will be more Sharpevilles until South Africa slides into civil war. As that happens or does not happen in the next quarter century, the true meaning of "Sharpeville 1960" will become clear.'[1]

This book joins a small body of writing that address the causes, the consequences, and the 'meaning' of the Sharpeville massacre of 21 March 1960. Given the event's generally received status as an historical dividing point, it is quite surprising how infrequently people have tried to answer questions about how the killings at Sharpeville happened and why they mattered.

For a long time, the only full-length study of the massacre was a popular book by Bishop Ambrose Reeves, published in 1961. The volume relied heavily on the testimony offered at the official Commission of Inquiry. Supported by the inclusion within the volume of a full sequence of the superb photographs Ian Berry took before, during, and after the shooting, Reeves' text supplied a powerful and politically influential indictment of both the police and the South African authorities more generally. However it contained very little explanatory detail to illuminate why the killing happened, where it did, and when it did. From the conventional perspective of anti-apartheid politics, in which movement Reeves was an important early spokesman, brutalities of the order of Sharpeville did not really need to be explained, they were what apartheid-fascism did reflexively, automatically. In Reeves' account, low wages and high rents may have accentuated popular grievances in Sharpeville, otherwise 'one of the best planned and most reasonably conducted locations in the Transvaal' but the local dynamics of political confrontation were in his analysis unimportant: the shootings were the product of an inevitable 'pattern of events' imposed by apartheid's architects.[2]

My own doctoral research, undertaken in the late 1970s and early 1980s, addressed the local settings in which during the 1950s and early 1960s South African nationalist movements were successful in mobilizing large followings prepared to engage in militant kinds of collective protest. My hypothesis at that time was in order to explain such successes we needed to do more than look at leaders, organizations, strategies, and ideologies, that up until then had been the chief emphases in earlier studies of black South African politics. The most effective political challenges were those that brought together the high culture of nationalist elites with the concerns and preoccupations of everyday life, animating people around tangible and sometimes parochial grievances. This did not happen very easily or very frequently until the 1950s, and to understand the instances when and where it did, what was needed was intimate local knowledge. Without the insights resulting from such knowledge it would be impossible to explain relationships between political leaders and the people they led, I believed.

In developing these assumptions I was influenced by my own training as a historian at a time when 'history from below', based on the study of the experiences of ordinary people, was helping to transform the discipline and nowhere more so than in South Africa. In 1978 I arrived in Johannesburg to take up a post in the Political Studies Department, teaching 'African Government', at the University of the Witwatersrand just at the time when a 'History Workshop' was being established by my new colleagues. Heavily influenced by British Marxist traditions and models, the overriding concern of the Workshop was to 'pursue the study of South African society from the point of view of those ordinary people who inhabit it' and to explore 'the cultural and structural matrix in which the consciousness of ordinary South Africans is forged'.[3] In particular the Workshop established a powerful lineage of urban social history that developed at South African universities during the 1970s and 1980s and which continues to flourish today.

In their explorations of this world of 'ordinary' South Africans, the Wits social historians were working in a self-consciously revisionist mode, hoping to find alternative explanations to those offered by earlier schools of radical, liberal, and nationalist historiography. I published part of my doctoral work in 1983 in *Black Politics in South Africa since 1945*.[4] This volume included a chapter on the Sharpeville crisis, a chapter containing two very localized studies of the conditions and circumstances that generated popular political tumult in Sharpeville itself and in Cape Town, where African opposition to the pass laws also generated a major confrontation with the authorities.

For the research on Sharpeville at that time, that is in the late 1970s, I was unable to interview any of the key local activists. However I was able to obtain access to a considerable body of archival material, including the transcript of the Commission of Inquiry, a rare carbon copy that was held at the University of York's library. I was also allowed to consult the relevant records at the Vereeniging municipality, concentrating on the deliberations of the Non-European Affairs Committee. Until 1970, African townships were administered by white local government and hence their records were not kept in the state archives where they would have been subject to the normal restrictions. In the case of Cape Town, I was able to interview participants, and I could also draw upon a rich collection of private papers that included diaries of events, the Patrick Duncan collection. Indeed it was my initial apprenticeship as a researcher working as an assistant to C. J. Driver, when he was writing his biography of Pat Duncan, that brought me my first introductions to the Pan-Africanists and the world they inhabited. These kinds of sources allowed me to identify the considerations that helped to especially predispose particular groups within local communities to constitute themselves into a following for the Pan-Africanists: unemployed school-leavers in the case of Sharpeville and semi-urbanized migrants inhabiting the 'bachelor' quarters of Langa township in Cape Town.

In addition to influencing my own research at that time, the Wits History Workshop through the 1980s also shaped the training of successive cohorts of graduate students across particularly the disciplines of history, politics, sociology, and social anthropology. In his research for his master's dissertation, Matthew Chaskalson explored a much wider range of records at the Vereeniging local archive than I had used in my own work. In particular he obtained from this documentation fresh perceptions about the planning preoccupations that helped to determine the pace and nature of the resettlement of the city's African residents from the older Top Location to Sharpeville through the 1950s.[5] Terri Shakinovsky's History honours dissertation on the 'Shaping of the Black Working Class' in Vereeniging and

Ian Jeffrey's study of the Sharpetown Swingsters jazz band also embody the extraordinarily ambitious junior post-graduate research that, at that time, was helping to chart the local evolution of South Africa's industrial heartland.[6]

Aside from its academic objectives, a key goal for the History Workshop was the popularization of historical consciousness both through nurturing a wider readership outside universities and through stimulating 'history from below' in the sense of encouraging working-class people writing their own histories. This effort did help to nurture a new vein of first-person autobiographical accounts of local history that were published by Ravan Press, an agency that supplied indispensable support and encouragement to the Workshop and its writers. This book draws upon two of these narratives, the trade unionist Petrus Tom's memoir about life and work in and around Sharpeville between the 1950s and 1980s and Johannes Rantete's vivid eyewitness reportage on the Sebokeng uprising, written while he was a first-year politics student at Wits University.[7] Both represent key sources for the quality of lived experience they communicate as well as the more reflective perceptions interpreting this experience that they contain.

More recently, newly accessible source materials have prompted a fresh generation of scholarship focused on Sharpeville. Written and researched at the end of the century, several years after South Africa's democratic transition, Philip Frankel's monograph on the Sharpeville massacre[8] was animated by quite different analytical considerations from the concerns of the History Workshop movement. Frankel took his conceptual framework of reference from systematic investigations of the forensics of mass murder. In his work the analytical programme is constituted by the considerations that arise from this framework: the delivery point, the trigger catalysts, the mode of killing, the dispersal of dying, and, finally of course, the reconstruction of bureaucratic order. Fortunately, Frankel is too good and too humane a writer to rely upon the clinically dispassionate vocabulary that accompanies this macabre academic genre. In any case, as important a source of inspiration in his investigation of Sharpeville is the work of Primo Levi. Like Levi, Frankel is interested in the gradations of moral responsibility, in the moral complicities, and in the personal idiosyncrasies of the actors in the event that shaped history. In particular his study focuses on the police and upon local officials. For this purpose he located and interviewed elderly surviving policemen who were present at the massacre. He was also able to find hitherto unused local records. As importantly, he was conducting his

research at a time when South African archives were undergoing reorgani-
zation and certain repositories were unusually open, allowing him free
access to unsorted files in the Department of Justice. The most important
revelations in his study are about the motivations and the psychology of the
policemen who were facing the crowd on 21 March 1960, showing how
both circumstances and ideology helped to dehumanize the killers and
'encase' them in an 'explosive mixture of fear, frustration, rage and isolation'. Frankel's remarkable study of Sharpeville's policemen is likely to
remain the definitive work in this genre not least because very few of his
informants are alive today.

What will my book add to our existing knowledge? It was originally
commissioned by its publishers to join a range of monographs assembled in a
series about historical junctures and starting points, 'key moments for the
development of the modern world'. Almost immediately after it occurred,
the Sharpeville massacre became invested with epoch-making importance
and it has continued to be characterized as historically decisive. Indeed,
perhaps because of the atmosphere of political crisis that the massacre
precipitated there have been very few efforts to consider just what changed
after Sharpeville, in which ways South African political, social, and economic life were altered and whether these changes were irrevocable. This
book is the first sustained analysis of the long-term consequences of the
Sharpeville crisis. The later chapters address the effects of the crisis within
South Africa and its impact upon South Africa's relationship with the
outside world, and finally, of course, the local legacy of the massacre, the
extent to which it still configures the daily experience of Sharpeville's
residents. The book's concerns are not limited to consequences, though.
It seeks to offer fresh arguments about causes as well. To do this it has
exploited new or at least more recently accessible sources.

The chapter that immediately follows this Preface details the political
background to the massacre. In doing this it addresses topics neglected in
earlier writing about the Sharpeville crisis. The Wits urban history school's
foregrounding of the preoccupations of 'ordinary people' may help to
explain the rather cursory treatment in existing studies of the events afforded
to the Pan-Africanists' organization, leadership, and ideas. Here I have been
able to draw upon materials that were in any case not available to the earlier
South African researchers. These include the collection of Robert Sobukwe's papers that are now held at the University of the Witwatersrand.
The Sobukwe archive was assembled by the PAC's founding president's

biographer and friend, Benjamin Pogrund. Pogrund was a reporter working for the *Rand Daily Mail*. For several years he had been assigned with special responsibilities for covering African politics, at that time, for most of the *Mail*'s readers, a remote field. He was trusted and liked amongst the disaffected 'Africanist' group who were preparing to secede from the ANC. Pogrund kept careful notes of all his conversations and interviews with the Africanists and typed them up afterwards. Many of these notes are preserved in the Sobukwe papers and they supply us with contemporary insights into the Pan-Africanists' strategic thinking in the years, months, and days leading up to the crisis. Later, during Robert Sobukwe's imprisonment and subsequent confinement on Robben Island, he and Benjamin Pogrund corresponded frequently and copiously: by this time the two men were close friends. Sobukwe's papers preserve this correspondence. Pogrund's notes on his conversations with Sobukwe and Robert Sobukwe's own letters both offer rewarding seams of reflective thinking and confessional writing by this compelling and attractive man. As we shall see, Sobukwe's ideas and the words he used to express them shaped events profoundly.

A second invaluable source in illuminating the Pan-Africanists is a wonderfully comprehensive set of interviews with PAC officials by the American researcher, Gail Gerhart, which she conducted in various African countries through the 1960s to the 1980s. These interviews were part of her contribution to the monumental South African documentation project initially mounted by Thomas Karis and Gwendoline Carter and later sustained and led by Gail Gerhart herself with the support of the Ford Foundation and the American National Endowment for the Humanities. Some of these interviews Gail originally undertook for her own doctoral research. With typical generosity she has made the records of these interviews generally accessible, both online and in South African archives. As with the Pogrund-Sobukwe papers, the Gerhart transcripts offer reminiscences and commentaries by key personalities who were rarely interviewed by anyone else and many of whom have since died.

My own interviews with Pan-Africanists and other survivors of events in Sharpeville and elsewhere have also helped me to change my mind about the causes and courses of events around Vereeniging and Cape Town since I first wrote about them in the early 1980s. I now have a clearer sense of what kinds of people supplied leadership in Sharpeville and Cape Town and why it was that over a few momentous days they were capable of imposing their will over so many people. Taking my cue from Philip Frankel's findings, I have also paid more attention than hitherto to the dynamics of policing and public order: as we shall see, the political predispositions of particular policemen was a critical variable in shaping the course of events in different localities during the Sharpeville crisis. Since the 1980s a range of published and unpublished autobiographical writing has become available, participant and insider narratives which help both to complicate and clarify our understandings of the ways things happened. In this vein, I have drawn extensively upon memoirs by Philip Kgosana, Mxolise Mgxashe, and Zolile Hamilton Keke.

In writing this book, then, I could draw upon generations of earlier scholarship by other people and collections of primary data that other researchers have placed in the public domain. I also have a more personal set of debts to people who have more knowingly helped me.

A number of people allowed me to interview them in the course of my research for this book. Without their words this book would be very substantially the poorer. I hope I have used their testimony in ways that do justice to their trust and generosity. For this I am very grateful to Paul Arthur in Derry, Northern Ireland, Philip Kgosana in Pretoria, Piet Swanepoel in Pretoria, Lydia Mahabuke, Ikabot Makiti, Mary Mantsho, Johannes Sefatsa, Michael Thekiso, Samuel Tshabalala, and Gideon Tsolo in Sharpeville, Hugh Bayley in York and Randolph Vigne in Cape Town. I was also able to find fresh insights in a number of interviews that I had conducted with earlier informants and I owe much to their kindness and candour: Brian Bunting, Peter Hjul, Abednego Ngcobo, Matthew Nkoana, Peter Raboroko, David Sibeko, and Neshtadi Sidzamba.

I have other debts. Jonty Driver supplied me with a vivid pen portrait of Patrick Duncan which reminded me of how much I had learned from him about writing when I worked as his research assistant. Hermann Giliomee asked and answered questions for me about Hendrik Verwoerd's behaviour during the Sharpeville crisis. In different ways, Randolph Vigne has guided me through the events, the personalities, and the developments in Cape Town during the crisis: he has unusual authority acquired both as a committed participant and later as a more dispassionate historian. A number of colleagues and friends have helped me in all sorts of ways through suggesting sources or authorities or by giving me copies of documents they found themselves: Bob Edgar discovered an essay by Philip Kgosana in an archive in Chicago, Gail Gerhart told me about people she had interviewed, Marcus Makhari shared with me his collection of Pan-Africanist memorabilia.

Randolph Vigne drew my attention to Zolile Hamilton Keke's unpublished autobiography and Hamilton himself allowed me to use it freely. It is a superb memoir and it should be published and I hope that one day it can find its own readership.

In writing this book I have received many kinds of help and encouragement. My first thanks are to members of my family: Carla, Kim, and Guy. I am grateful to the Khulumani Support Group's Sharpeville executive generally and in particular to Mrs Mary Mantsho, the branch secretary for helping me to arrange interviews with Sharpeville residents. Michelle Pickover and Carol Archibald navigated me through the shoals of relevant archival records in the Historical Papers section of the University of the Witwatersrand Library. I must also express my thanks to Andre Landman and Lesley Hart of the archival section of the University of Cape Town Library, to Sipho Khumalo and his colleagues who manage the archive collection at the Vaal Teknorama Museum in Vereeniging, to Mariki Victor, Andre Mohammed, and Babalwa Solwandle at the University of Western Cape's Mayibuye Archives, and to Gail Berman who organized the copying of films held at the Apartheid Museum as well as the to the curators at the museum for allowing me access to the film. Lucy McCann at Rhodes House identified relevant files in the Anti-Apartheid Archive and Cíara Ní Nualláin read and made copies of these for me.

In the University of Limerick I found a sympathetic and generous setting in which to write this book. Research grants from the Department of Politics and Public Administration and the Faculty of Arts, Humanities, and Social Sciences paid for my travel costs. All my colleagues at one time or another have helped me in important ways. I am particularly indebted to Neil Robinson for being the best kind of critical reader, identifying lapses and errors while it was not too late to put them right. To Noam and Eleanor Pines in Johannesburg I owe more than thanks for their hospitality during the research for this book: for nearly thirty years their friendship helped me make South Africa my home.

My final acknowledgment is to Sekwati Sekoane, curator of the exhibition at the Sharpeville Memorial. More than anyone else he has helped me to find my way through Sharpeville and no visitor could wish for a wiser interpreter or a kinder companion.

Contents

List of Plates

List of Maps

List of Acronyms and Abbreviations

AABN	Anti-Apartheid Beweging Nederland
AAC	All African Convention
AAM	(British) Anti-Apartheid Movement
ACOA	American Committee on Africa
AFL–CIO	American Federation of Labour and Congress of Industrial Organizations
ANC	African National Congress
APLA	Azanian People's Liberation Army
ASSOCOM	Association of South African Chambers of Commerce
AUEW	Amalgamated Union of Engineering Workers
AZANYU	Azanian National Youth Unity
BC	Black Consciousness
BCP	Basotho Congress Party
CND	Campaign for Nuclear Disarmament
COD	Congress of Democrats
CODESA	Conference for a Democratic South Africa
COREMO	Comite Revolucionario de Mocambique
COSAS	Congress of South African Students
CPP	Convention Peoples' Party
CYL	Congress Youth League
CZA	Comite Zuid-Afrika
EAWU	Engineering and Allied Workers' Union
FCWU	Food and Canning Workers' Union
FNLA	Frente Nationale de Libertacao de Angola
FOFATUSA	Federation of Free Trade Unions of South Africa
Frelimo	Frente de Libertacao de Mocambique
GNU	Government of National Unity
IAAM	Irish Anti-Aparheid Movement
ICFTU	International Confederation of Free Trade Unions
IDA	(Irish) Industrial Development Association

IDAF	International Defence and Aid Fund
IDATU	Irish Distributive Administrative Workers' Union
IFP	Inkatha Freedom Party
IRFU	Irish Rugby Football Union
IRRC	Investors' Responsibility Research Centre
ITGWU	Irish Transport and General Workers' Union
KZA	Komittee Zuidelijk Afrika
ICCL	Irish Council for Civil Liberties
ITN	Independent Television News
LTC	Lekoa Town Council
MAWU	Metal and Allied Workers' Union
MPLA	Movimento Popular de Libertacao de Angola
NALGO	National and Local Government Officers' Association
NBC	National Broadcasting Corporation
NGK	Nederduitsch Gereformeerde Kerk
NICRA	Northern Irish Civil Rights Association
NUS	National Union of Students
NUSAS	National Union of South African Students
OAU	Organisation of African Unity
PAC	Pan-Africanist Congress
PASO	Pan-Africanist Students' Organisation
PRWM	Polaroid Revolutionary Workers' Movement
SABC	South African Broadcasting Corporation
SACP	South African Communist Party
SACTU	South African Congress of Trade Unions
SALP	South African Liberal Party
SANDF	South African National Defence Force
SAP	South African Police
SARC	Sharpeville Anti-Rent Committee
SASM	South African Students' Movement
SASO	South African Students' Organisation
SASPU	South African Students' Press Union
SAUF	South African United Front
SCA	Sharpeville Civic Association
SDLP	(Northern Irish) Social Democratic Labour Party
SDS	Students for a Democratic Society
SFS	Swedish Forenader Studentkarer

SOYA	Society of Young Africa
SRC	Students' Representative Council
STST	Stop the Seventies' Tour
SWAPO	South West Africa People's Organisation
SDU	Special Defence Unit
TRC	Truth and Reconciliation Commission
UDF	United Democratic Front
UNICEF	United Nations' Children's Fund
UNITA	Uniao Nacional para a Independencia Total de Angola
VCA	Vaal Civic Association
VE	Victory in Europe
YCW	Young Christian Workers
YMCA	Young Christian Men's Association
ZANLA	Zimbabwe African National Liberation Army
ZANU	Zimbabwe African National Union

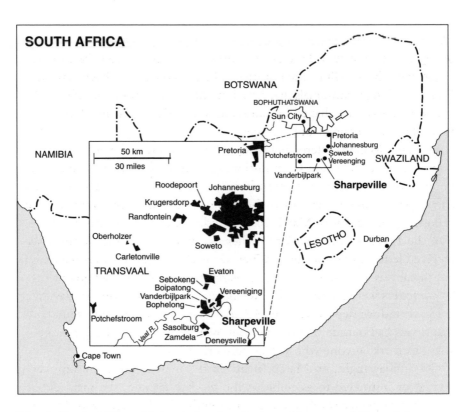

Map 1. South Africa with inset showing the townships around Vereeniging

I

Voices from a Massacre

Over the last two decades, the survivors of the Sharpeville massacre have been telling their stories. Their recollections have remained fresh and vivid, testimonials that for a long time they could not offer freely. These narratives are shaped by emotions and feelings that for thirty years needed to be contained and curtailed.

Elizabeth Mabona offered her first public testimony at the hearings of the Truth and Reconciliation Commission, in August 1996. In 1960 she was a young woman, married very recently, sharing a new house with her husband and eagerly looking forward to bringing up a family. She remembered waking up on Friday 18 March 1960 to discover an unexpected summons: 'On the Friday of the 18 March when we woke up in the morning we received letters in our postbox. When we looked at those letters we found out that it was written that on the 21 March 1960 we should not go to work. These letters were telling us that. We never went to work on that day. We got back and we slept. Later, on Monday when we woke up we found out that it was bad outside. People were all over in the streets saying no one is going to work, anyone who will go to work will be killed.'[1]

On Sunday night, 20 March, many of the men in the township were invited or instructed to assemble at the football ground, the main public space in Sharpeville. Only the men apparently, for the organizers discouraged women from attending. Frederick Batkani was interviewed in 1999 at the age of seventy-eight.

At Sunday night we gathered at the football ground. All the men were there. Women were not allowed. It was the middle of the night, around midnight, when the police came. They said: 'What are you doing here?' The leaders of the Pan-Africanist Congress answered: 'We're here to talk about the bad rules of the passes.' That wasn't the right answer, because moments later the officers started to hit us with whips. We ran away, some of us badly hurt. There were also shots. I don't know if they were aimed at the people or not. It was dark, I couldn't see.[2]

Ruben Rapoetsoe was also present at this gathering; he was aged nineteen at the time.

> I was present at the gathering on Sunday evening at the football ground. The men were there to talk about giving away the passes. In the crowd there was a policeman in disguise, who was there to see what it was all about. He left, and a little while later returned with reinforcements. The police started beating us up, trying to stop the meeting. They succeeded in that. Some of the men were heavily bleeding, and were brought to hospital. So, you see, the violence already started on the 20th.[3]

Not everybody who lived in Sharpeville would be a willing participant in the planned protest. The activists, though, were keen to include all local residents, irrespective of their backgrounds, even locally resident police-men. George Myubu was a police constable, living in Sharpeville, though commuting every day to the main police station in Vereeniging.

> On the evening of the 20th, people came round to my house. They woke me and when I looked through the window I saw a lot of them. I mustn't be scared, so I unlocked the door and went out. I joined a large group, marching to the police station. A crowd was already standing there. They were shouting they'd tackle the police. It seemed almost like a rehearsal. I wasn't happy about this, so left the crowd and locked myself in my home.[4]

★

For Segametsi Makhanya, Monday 21 March began as a normal day. She rose early before dawn, and ate a hurried breakfast before leaving home to catch the first bus to Vereeniging so she would arrive in time to cook and clean for her employer. 'As on every Monday morning I wanted to go to my work. But once outside I was stopped by a group of people and told to come with them to the police station to protest against the pass laws.'[5]

The organizers from the Pan-Africanist Congress (PAC) had begun their work well before daybreak. Groups of young men constituted as Task Forces worked the streets, visiting houses door to door:

> In the early morning everyone got lifted from their beds by PAC people and was summoned to come outside and join the march. It was meant to protest against the pass laws. We were told to leave our passes at home, and turn ourselves in at the police station. It was to be a peaceful protest, absolutely no violence. They specifically emphasized on that.[6]

There were no buses to catch because bus drivers failed to arrive at the Vereeniging Transport Company depot. Task Forcers had abducted the Sharpeville drivers from their homes the previous evening, compelling them to spend the night in guarded premises. At the age of nineteen, Sam Poletsi was still a schoolboy, keen on his lessons and ambitious to do well in life, an attitude instilled into him by his parents who themselves had obtained no education but who had moved to Vereeniging specially so that their children could attend secondary school. At that time he really 'wasn't involved in politics' for he was more interested in succeeding at school, the first stage in fulfilling his ambition to become a businessman. However: 'On the morning of the 21st we didn't go to school, even if we wanted to, there was no transport anyway. Us teenagers were excited: what was going to happen? I cycled to the police station at about 8.30 am to see what was happening. I got blocked by all the crowds and couldn't get through, so decided to go home and eat a bowl of porridge.'[7]

Lebitsa Ramohoase was on his way to his factory job that Monday morning. He had heard about the plans for the impending protest but had ignored them. At that time he was in his mid-thirties, 'not so involved in politics' for he had a family to maintain. He knewthat some people were staying away from work but he believed that most people would ignore the strike call.

> On that day, as stories have been told, we didn't believe that this would happen but when this happened we were stopped on our way and we realized that it was true, the story that has been told. We tried to go back but those who were stopping us on the roads said no, we have to go to the police station, we want to resolve this issue about the pass. They asked me where my pass was. I said no I don't have it with me, I left it at home, but truly it was in my pocket. We jumped on our bicycles and we went off. I realized that I wouldn't make it with the bicycle. I took it back home and then I walked. When we got to the scene a large group of people was there. It was between the police station and the clinic. I wanted to be at the forefront of the crowd but I couldn't force my way through and that is where I decided to stand.[8]

Lydia Mahabuke was better informed that Lebitsa Ramohoase. Still in her teens, she wasn't an activist but the Pan-Africanists seem to have engaged her sympathy. She woke up that morning with a sense of expectation:

> On that day we were going to get an answer to the effect the passes were going to done away with. I knew about the PAC but I didn't know exactly what kind of organization it was. We then went to the police station and gathered

there. While we were gathered there white police officers arrived with Saracens and guns. We were gathered there singing, nothing very hostile. We were very happy. Very excited. My six-year-old sister was with me. Earlier we had followed the Saracens because we were curious.[9]

Meanwhile Elizabeth Mabona and her husband decided they would venture out onto the streets to join the protest, despite feeling somewhat apprehensive.

We went and we were standing by the corner. That is when we saw the police vehicles. There were six cars approaching and there were policemen also. When they got there they saw smoke at the corner and realizing that they decided to turn. While they were still standing there they made another U-turn, the last car to pass us belonged to a policeman, a white police man who pointed a gun at us and he said you are going to [indistinct] today and then we took off in different directions.

Undeterred by this discouraging experience, the Mabonas decided that they would make a second attempt to join their neighbours in participating in the demonstration:

When we arrived at home, no one was available at home. We left, we went to the police station and at the police station we sat down, we were singing hymns, you know it was a jolly atmosphere. Everybody was taking his feelings out. We spent that whole time at the police station until the jets arrived. We didn't mind, the sirens went off and we just ignored them. Now the people from the PAC approached and when they came that is where they said we should disperse, we should go home and at about dinner time we should come back so that there can be another meeting.

As a sociable young man, Simon Mkutau was keen to join the crowd assembling in Zwane Street, next to the police station:

I went to the police station like all the others. The atmosphere was cheerful, people were happy, singing and dancing. While the people were marching through the streets, policemen were chasing them and using tear gas to try and separate them. Despite this we marched straight to the police station, still singing and shouting. Once we were there, we kind of waited for police to come and take our passes and arrest us. I was standing at the main gate, and had a clear view of what was going on inside. I actually saw the officers loading their guns. Then a commander told the crowd to go to the football ground and wait there. I didn't want to, but we started moving anyway. Then an old man started to shout to us that we had to go back, that we were going to be killed if we went to the football pitch. So the whole crowd went to stand by the police station again.

At this stage he began to have second thoughts: 'Then the whole situation started to look threatening, fighter planes were circling in the air, really low. I recall getting thirsty, it was hot, but I couldn't get out. Because the crowd was so big, and I stood in front.'[10]

Mrs and Mrs Mguni were another couple who decided they would accompany each other to the protest. First of all, though, there was house-work to complete: 'On the morning of the shootings I was busy cooking lunch. My husband left the house to go see what was happening outside, what all the noise was about and why all those people were walking around. A while later he came back and told me there was a protest against the pass laws going on. We decided to eat first and then join in.'[11]

In the meantime Constable Myubu was determined that this day would be like any other. He put on his uniform and left home in time to walk the short distance to the place where he was normally collected by the official transport despatched from Vereeniging's police station:

> In the morning I got dressed for work, as usual. Even though it was very early, the township was already full of people. Finding this strange, I went out on the street. When I got to the square we were usually picked up to go to Vereeniging but there was no transport.

He decided to make enquiries to his Sharpeville colleagues and while on his way to the station became an involuntary participant in the PAC's demon-stration: 'Trying to find out why there was no transport I followed a group of people to Sharpeville police station. I felt very uncomfortable in my police outfit. A couple of young men from the PAC came up to me and forced me to do their sign, "Izwe Lethu". Meanwhile more and more and more policemen got off trucks and went inside the precinct.'

Vincent Leutsoa belonged to Sharpeville's middle-class elite, managing its public library, an unusual amenity in a black South African township at that time. Though his own political predispositions predisposed him to sympathize with the Pan-Africanists' call to action, Leutsoa decided that the library would remain open that day, all the same. Then noise outside the building became increasingly tumultuous, for the library was located next to the open space where the PAC's followers were assembling:

> I worked as a librarian in 1960, one of the only black librarians in South Africa at that time. By sheer coincidence the library was located right opposite the police station. Like every normal day I went to work and when in the library I saw a big crowd gathering in front of the police station. Determined to find

out what was going on, I locked the door and went to see. I stood in front
of the gate, waiting to hear what the police had to say. The crowd, at that time,
I feel I must add, wasn't violent. They were singing and generally noisy,
but not intent on any violence. At around 8.30 am reinforcements arrived
from Johannesburg. I became quite scared. What was going to happen?
The shouting and chanting intensified. Our leaders called: 'Our land!' We
responded: 'Our land!'.[12]

Despite his alarming escapade at the football ground the night before,
Frederick Batkani had joined the multitude that had assembled itself outside
Vincent Leutsoa's library:

> The next morning we were told to go to the police station and turn our passes
> in. A big crowd gathered, there were at least 30,000 people there. Between 10
> and 1 in the morning three Saracens moved into the area. Around midday a
> policeman on top of one of the Saracens said that the Commissioner of Police
> from Pretoria was to come at 14.00 pm. He also said that he wanted everyone
> to go to the football ground to hear the answer from Pretoria. We answered as
> one man: 'We're not going there.'

Taking his cue from his brother, Lebitsa, father-of-five David Ramohoase
also decided that he would disregard the Pan-Africanists' summons and
travel to work that day. Once out on the street, though, he did not require
persuasion to alter his plans. After all, he hated carrying his pass, 'it was just a
misery', with all the restrictions that it imposed:

> In 1960 we were on our way to work and people stopped us. You know they just
> stopped us from going to work and we asked them what to do. They said no, we
> are heading for the police station today. We asked them what are you going to
> do there, they said no we are going to enquire about our pass. And after a few
> minutes we decided to go to the police station. I wanted to go and listen to this
> issue about passes. When we arrived there we spend some few minutes sitting,
> you know there was a large crowd of people going just up and down . . . It was a
> very sunny day. Many young men were gathering holding their umbrellas in
> their hands, they were singing Nkosi Sikileli and the other one that I can't
> remember . . . Not even one person was armed. I saw men and women and
> young men just holding their umbrellas because it was a hot day. Those who
> might have had guns, maybe they were hidden somewhere but I didn't see
> anyone carrying any weapon, not even a stick and knobkerrie, not even a
> knobkerrie. I only saw umbrellas. If one of them had a weapon or you know
> like a knobkerrie or a spear or a gun I didn't see any. Because I believe the people
> wanted to know something about the passes. They were not going there to fight.
> They were peaceful. They didn't have anything in their hands.[13]

Segametsi Makhanya did not need to be bullied into attending either. After all, everywhere she looked, people were in the streets, making their way to the police station. Once she arrived she was keen to see what was going on and she pushed her way through the crowd so that she found herself near the main gate, by the entrance to the station:

> More of these crowds were gathering all around the township. Once we got to the police station it was already packed. White policemen then ordered us to go to the football stadium where we would get an explanation from them. But we had barely started moving there, or the crowd was already heading back to the precinct. In all the pushing and moving I ended up right in front, almost pressed against the gate. I could clearly see what was happening on the other side. Policemen were trying to push people back, but because of the big crowd this was impossible. Also there was a white man with a camera taking pictures of the events. On the side there was Saracen armoured car. A fellow climbed up on it, and started directing the cannon, aiming it at the crowd. At that point I started to become thirsty—it was a very hot day—and together with a friend we tried to leave the crowd to go and get a drink. Police tried to push us back, but we managed to navigate our way out of it.

Notwithstanding their determination to remain outside the police station and defy the injunctions to move to the football field, members of the crowd seem to have been in a relaxed mood and, as Segametsi's recollections suggest, there was no compulsion to stay: people remained of their own volition sometimes choosing to leave the assembly to obtain refreshments before rejoining it. Several witnesses attest to the good-natured tone of the gathering, despite the grievances that had prompted it. Puselato Malelo was three months pregnant when she made her journey along Zeane Street to the station. As an expectant mother she wouldn't have attended any event that might have appeared threatening:

> I remember going to the police station to hand in our reference books. You had to take them everywhere to show where you lived and to go from here to there. Anyway Saracens were brought in and aside from that nothing much was happening. We, the crowd, were singing African songs and waiting for things to come. By no means were we threatening anyone.[14]

Carlton Monnakgotla was standing near Segametsi Makhanya when the Saracens arrived at the station bringing with them substantial reinforcements. Despite the appearance of the armoured personnel vehicles, each armed with a heavy Browning machine gun, the overall mood amongst the people around him remained tranquil, Monnakgotla confirms, and though initially willing to obey the instruction to walk over to the football stadium, they were quickly dissuaded from doing so:

> I was standing in the crowd in front of the police station when the Saracens came driving in. There were about ten of these armoured cars, and some hundred policemen. The crowd was then ordered to march to the football stadium where the police would address us. While walking we were chanting hymns like God Bless Africa. On the way there the late reverend told us to turn back. If we'd go to the football grounds they would shoot us all, he said. So we turned back and went to stand in front of and around the police station once more.

As far as garage mechanic Isaac Moeung was concerned, once it became evident that travel to work that day would be impossible, the Pan-Africanists' call afforded residents a welcome break from routine. A holiday mood prevailed and, as much as anything else, curiosity prompted people to follow the Saracens as they drove down Seeiso Street on their way to the police station:

> I worked at a garage called Leo's Motors' Place at the time and wanted to go to work as usual. But once outside there was no transport and I joined in the march to the police station. There was tension in the air, something was going to happen. I saw two Saracens driving down the street, people were running after them, wondering what those vehicles were doing in Sharpeville. Just for your information, it was a very hot day, people wore as little clothing as possible. That morning, there was a happy atmosphere at the police station. Us protestors were in a joyous mood, singing freedom songs and dancing. The policemen were at first not aggressive at all, they seemed happy as well.[15]

★

The crowd grew steadily through the morning. Shortly after lunchtime, around 1.30 pm, despite the fierce heat from the midday sun the numbers of demonstrators and onlookers assembled around the station seemed to have reached a peak. At this juncture the atmosphere swiftly shifted register, at least amongst people in the front ranks of the crowd. Police had been ordered to load their weapons and were lining up on their side of the fence. Though initially sitting down at the edge of the crowd, David Ramohoase had moved forwards, obtaining a better position where he could watch what was happening just in front of the station:

> Between one and two o'clock, after a long time that we have been there, there drove in a very small car. It drove into the police station premise but the armoured vehicles, the Saracens, had already been there. Two of them

approached from the south, they got into the police station premises and they faced to the west. This is the site where most of the people were gathered. They faced towards the people. Most of the people were just behind the fence. This white car drove in and a man jumped out of the car, a white person, and he had a very short stick in his hand and then he had band on his head. He had this stick, you know he just dropped his stick and then he said 'Shoot'.

For David's brother Lebitsa, at this moment, the important activity seemed to be taking place around one of the Saracen armoured cars:

> I can't remember whether it was two o'clock or not because I didn't have a watch but now the soldiers were now present in the police station yard. There was a Saracen parking there and the soldiers were right behind the Saracen pointing their guns at us. We saw a white person jumping over the Saracen. He got inside and then he pulled to the door above him.

Ruben Rapoetsoe was watching the aeroplanes that had been flying over the township at intervals during the morning. He remembers the Harvard trainers returning at 1.30 and was certain that their appearance at this juncture was decisive:

> We waited until about 1.30 pm. In the air about four planes were flying around. I noticed one red plane flying very, very low over the police station. Immediately after, the commander of the police went into the station. Five minutes later the shooting started. I think the plane must've somehow given an order to the policemen in Sharpeville. The order for them to shoot.

Notwithstanding the bowl of mealie meal porridge he had consumed for breakfast that morning at one o'clock Sam Poletsi had felt hungry again and decided to visit home quickly to eat lunch. He too saw the aeroplanes flying low over the township: 'When I got home, three fighter planes surprised me, circling in the air. I found it quite threatening: what were they doing? I took a chair and sat down on the porch, because it was such a hot day.'

Trapped inside the increasingly dense crowd gathered on the west side of the station, Simon Mkutau found himself being pushed forward, closer and closer to the front rows. At this stage people were pressing against the wire fence surrounding the station and police officers were becoming visibly agitated:

> Then a commander shouted to the people clutched to the gate: 'Go away!' We couldn't, of course, there were way too many people behind us. Maybe it was because of the refusal of the crowd to move back, or maybe something else, but a few minutes later the police started to shoot.

At least one of these witnesses, Frederick Batkani, heard a police officer order the constables to fire their weapons: 'This memory is hard for me. At about 13.45 pm one officer gave the order to shoot . . . I'm sorry . . . I can't tell any more . . . so they started firing. People began running in all directions.' For Constable George Myubu, still standing in the crowd in his uniform, it was difficult to see clearly: 'Outside it was very dusty with reddish smoke.' What happened next seemed unprompted by any preceding portents or developments: 'And then, without any warning, I heard the gunfire.'

Lydia Mahabuke was near the front of the crowd and she watched the police take up their firing positions. She was still holding her little sister's hand and joining in with the hymn singing. She heard no order and saw no signal.

> While we were standing there singing we suddenly saw the police in a row pointing their guns at us. Whilst we were still singing, without any word, without any argument, we just heard the guns being fired. I then tried to run towards the open space where the post office is now. While I was running something was hitting me in the back. After having felt this I tried to look back. People were falling, scattered. There was blood streaming down my leg. I tried to hobble. I struggled to get home.

The police standing by the main gate on the west side of the station discharged their weapons first into the crowd vanguard, pressed up against the fence. Puselato Malelo had been close enough to the main gate to watch the police escort the Pan-Africanist leaders inside the station. She was standing by the west fence when the firing began, close enough to the gunmen to take two bullets from the first volley: 'I stood right in front, against the fence, and I was badly hurt. The bullet went straight through my leg and ripped a large part of the flesh away. Another clip hit me in the thigh.' Most of the first casualties, dead and wounded, were among the people who had moved or been pushed into the front rows Both the Ramohoase brothers were shot in the legs, and had fallen to the ground. David found himself unable to move: 'I don't know what happened because it was now chaos. People were lying on the ground. At the time while I was on the ground a person who was shot lying next to me said things are bad please lie down, don't raise your head otherwise they are going to shoot you.' Meanwhile Lebitsa succeeded in struggling to his feet but was knocked over again: 'After that I heard gunshots. I don't what happened but I was on the ground and I decided I would run but I didn't know what happened. People were just trampling on me. I tried to push them off but I couldn't and now this leg was troubling me.' Mrs Mguni had only joined the crowd recently after eating lunch with her husband at home. Shortly after arriving at the station she became separated from her husband and found herself progressively drawn into the crowd's embrace, driven forward by other new arrivals into its vulnerable front ranks: 'When we went into the crowd I lost my husband in all the people. I was pushed farther and farther forward. Then all of a sudden I heard gunfire and a moment later felt great pain and dizziness. I was shot.'

Amongst these witnesses, Isaac Moeung was a fifth casualty, brought down a few seconds later. Before he was hit he had already had time to respond to the first volley of gunfire by turning and beginning to run. As with the majority of dead and wounded, Isaac was shot from behind in a second round of gunfire: 'Then I was shot. It felt like somebody had hit me with a brick on my buttock. I couldn't stand up, my leg was bleeding. I tried to crawl, everywhere I looked I saw bleeding people, dead bodies, shouting.'

Ruben Rapoetsoe was luckier than Isaac Moeung. Though quite close to the front he was unhurt by the gunfire. He was able to turn and run. He succeeded in reaching the shopping centre where he found refuge in a toilet: 'I wasn't hit in the shootings. Like most of the crowd, I started running. I found one of the public toilets that were all around Sharpeville and locked myself in.'

When the shooting began, Sam Poletsi was still eating his porridge, sitting in the sunshine on his step in Seeiso Street. His house was close enough to the police station for him to hear what was happening. To him it seemed as if the shooting continued for a protracted period for he could still hear the sound of gunfire when he saw the first wounded people running down the street towards him:

> Just as I was starting to eat my porridge, I heard the sound of gunfire. Ratatataatatatta!!! I couldn't believe it. And I saw Saracens driving into town towards the police station. It wasn't until then that I fully realized what was happening. Moments later, I saw people running through the street, some of them wounded. And all the while the shooting continued with a 'gagagaga-gaga' sound.

Segametsi Makhanya had also decided to leave the crowd temporarily, in her case to visit her friend's house to drink some water. She seems also to have sensed premonitions of an impending tragedy. Her friend lived very close by, close enough for Segametsi to watch through the window as people fell down and died:

> On my way to my friend's house I said to her: 'these people are going to die, this is not good'. She said she didn't believe this, the police wouldn't do such a thing. Just as we got to her house, the shooting commenced. I felt deeply sad and very scared but watched through the window. People lied down, some were dead, others wounded. There was panic, the people on the ground were trampled by others fleeing.

At half past one, Carlton Monnakgotla also took himself out of range from the police's gunfire, for he too needed refreshment. He was just emerging from the shopping precinct with his soft drink when the Saracens opened fire:

> While standing there I felt thirsty, and decided to leave the crowd for a moment to buy a can of Coke at the shops down the street. When I left the store with my Coke, I suddenly heard TRMMM ..., TRMMM ..., the sound of machine guns firing. I stood frozen, couldn't belive what was happening. Then I saw the bodies and people fleeing. Right in front of me a pregnant woman was shot. Her unborn baby fell out of her stomach and the next bullet got her. Horrible.

Vincent Leutsoa had locked the library and joined the crowd outside the police station. He too had begun to feel very thirsty. 'I'm a lover of tea and together with a friend we went to his house to make some. As we arrived at his place we heard BANG! Shots were fired!'. Meanwhile, Elizabeth Mabona had returned to her house shortly after midday; PAC officials had advised her to go home and revisit the police station later in the day. Her husband seems to have remained at the police station. Once she had arrived back at her home it wasn't long before she became concerned. She walked back to the police station to begin searching for her husband:

> On our arrival I couldn't remain in that situation not knowing what was happening. And I searched for the people I know. I wanted my mother, where she was, and I found her. I went on to search for my husband and when I couldn't find him. And I wanted to go back to the people, which of course I did. I searched all over for him and I couldn't find him. And I met his friend and I asked him where my husband was, because they were together. He said no he is around, please go. Why do you involve yourself in issues involving men? After listening to those words I decided to leave then but when I was at home I had a running stomach and I wanted to urinate. I went to the toilet but there was nothing coming out and I went back. On my way

I could feel this heavy burden in my heart. I went back to the people. I was so uncomfortable . . . Every time I would turn back. When I looked at the police station I saw a Saracen parked, this armoured vehicle. A white person was busy working the Saracen. I asked another woman to accompany me but she refused. But I didn't know what to do. We got into our street. As we were walking we heard gun shots. I ran. I opened the door at my house and I opened all the doors until the kitchen door. I came back again. I was confused. I didn't know what was happening. I felt something that was right on my chest and I said to myself where is my husband at this moment. As I was wondering another gentleman came and he said the whites are killing people in a very brutal way. I said to him are you talking about guns. He said, yes they are using guns.

★

After the shooting stopped, there seemed to be a complete silence for several minutes. Before long, however, the police were busy, inspecting the dead, and beginning their efforts to gather and create exculpatory evidence to excuse their actions. Segametsi left her friend's dwelling to join other people who were trying to assist their wounded neighbours. The police were offering no such help, she remembers. Instead: 'I saw police officers putting stones and knives in the dead people's hands, to make it look like they were armed and violent. Bodies were loaded onto trucks, on top of each other, then transported to unknown destinations.' As the constables used their guns and knobkerries to turn over and check the bodies of the dead and dying they mocked those people whom they found alive. Ruben Rapoetsoe had returned from the shopping centre to the killing ground:

> . . . when I passed the police station again I heard officers shouting: 'Where is your land now, *kaffirs*? Where is your land now?' Oh, I forgot one thing. During the shooting, there was a man who, despite the bullets, ran straight towards the police station, shouting: 'It's enough, you've shot enough!' He was shot moments later.

Several witnesses were convinced that the police were continuing to kill people, butchering wounded survivors as they lay on the ground. Albert Mbongo had accompanied his friend Frederick Batkani to the protest. He managed to escape unharmed when the shooting started and ran back home, but only to collect his Red Cross insignia before returning to the site of the massacre: 'I went to my house. When I got there I took a Red Cross belt and put it on my arm. Back in the streets, I tried to help the injured. Suddenly a policeman appeared. He wanted to shoot me, but didn't after he saw my belt. That saved me. After that, trucks and lorries came, bodies were loaded into them. In between all the bodies policemen were finishing off those still living. People were lying there like flies.'[16] Carlton Monnakgotla is another witness who believes the police murdered live casualties:

> After about ten minutes the shooting stopped. The scene was heartbreaking. Bodies were loaded in trucks and taken away to unknown destinations. Policemen were walking in between the corpses finishing off all those who were alive. Wounded people were brought to hospital, senseless arrests were being made.

Vincent Leutsoa's recollections do not refer to the police killing or molesting survivors but he does remember that they continued to behave very aggressively: 'Right after that, policemen were all over the street, pushing people away, threatening them.' With his companion he walked back to the police station: 'Despite them, we managed to reach the police station and take a look at what happened. It shook me deeply. So many bodies, dead and wounded. And then I realized: if I had not gone for tea, I would've been a dead man, because we were standing in front. Later on I went to check on the library. To my horror, three bullets had gone right through the window. If I had stayed there I would have been a dead man as well.' That was the limit of his good fortune, though: 'Things got even worse. I found out that two of my family members were killed. I was alive but it didn't feel that way. I was alone.'

About half an hour after the shooting stopped ambulances began to arrive to carry away the wounded. Among the first to be picked up was Isaac Moeung. He thinks the ambulances arrived with suspicious-seeming alacrity: 'Later, I was loaded into an ambulance and taken to a hospital in Vereeniging. I was barely conscious by then, but it struck me there were so many ambulances so quickly. As if they already knew they were needed.' Mrs Mguni was also among the wounded people who were collected by the first ambulances and taken to Vereeniging. Though quite seriously hurt she would not stay in hospital for very long for the police had other plans: 'Barely conscious I was taken to the hospital in Vereeniging. What happened there I still cannot understand. I was arrested and taken to the Boksburg prison. After being questioned they released me. I was on medication for almost a year, I can't remember exactly. The bullet hit me in the leg and ripped away a great part of flesh. It missed my bone by mere inches. If it had hit it, I would have lost my leg. So I was extremely lucky.'

Three months pregnant Puselato Malelo was taken to Baragwanath Hospital, fifty miles away, for after the first ambulance transfers there were to be no spare beds in the wards at Vereeniging. She seems to have received more considerate treatment, the closest approximation in these narratives to a comforting conclusion. 'As soon as it was safe for the ambulances I was taken to a hospital in Soweto. I stayed there for fifteen months and even gave birth to my son there. Here, let me show you this newspaper clipping. That's me in the photograph, giving birth to what they called a "Sharpeville baby" in a Johannesburg hospital. Thank the Almighty God that my son was healthy and happily born. He has two children of his own now.'

As the ambulances departed a thunderstorm completed the cleansing of the killing ground, a fortuitous event that several these witnesses invested with symbolic meaning. Simon Mkutau: 'On the way to my house, I saw some terrible things. I most vividly remember a man who was shot in the head and a part of his skull was shredded off. When I got to my house, I locked myself in. After that, God washed the streets. That's all.' Vincent Leutsoa: 'In the beginning of the afternoon it started drizzling and not much later a great thunderstorm washed the blood off the streets.' Ruben Rapoet-soe: 'Immediately after the massacre, the rain came and cleaned the despair from the streets.'

For Elizabeth Mabona, though, the rain would offer no solace. Through the afternoon she would continue her frantic search for her husband:

Now our neighbour three houses from mine came and the neighbour was coming with another Mr Matsela and the neighbour had been shot and we realized he had been badly injured and when seeing this I said oh my God what is happening to my husband. And I was crying, I was hitting myself on the ground. Now the women came, they took me to the house next door, they said be calm, there is nothing wrong happening, your husband will come home. Why do you have to do this. Don't you think you are bringing him bad luck. Please be quiet. While we were sitting another gentleman came and he called another woman. The woman went to him and they spoke for a few minutes and they went around the corner but this feeling inside me got worse. I felt something was just wrong. I cried continually. They tried to console me. They said no come, let's have a cup of tea. And this other woman who had been called by the gentleman said to me come here I want to talk to you and she said to me please don't cry, there is nothing happening. She took me into the house and she let me sit down and another woman came. When I saw the two men getting into their house I realize there was trouble and they said to me your husband is dead, please don't get worried, he is now in town. When we were still talking a car stopped outside. This car took me—it was the car belonging to my brother-in-law. He said can we please go and check the hospital whether he is not there. We drove off with him. That time it had already rained. You know after the first shots the first drops fell. Now it had rained and we are now driving off to the police station. When we arrived there they said do you want to die further. We said no, we don't want Africa, we are just here to search for our loved ones. We checked the hospital, my husband was not there. When we saw that he was not there one of the women said it is better if we go to the police station. When we arrived there we saw that everybody at the police station, I mean the people that had been taken to the police station were all dead. They said to me please don't have a look, we will look. After that we went back home . . . My husband was shot behind the shoulders. Just in the middle.

★

In the days that followed, anybody who had been present outside the police station became a target for official recrimination. A major preoccupation for the police seems to haven been to discourage residents from offering evidence at the official investigation. Even respected local personalities such as Vincent Leutsoa were vulnerable. 'When the inquiry into the shootings started later, I found out how mean man can be. I was arrested and questioned, accused of being a communist. They didn't like me. I was lucky I wasn't jailed.'

Mrs Mguni's experience was not unique. Many of the people whose wounds were so severe that they had to stay in hospital had their convalescence cut short when they too were arrested and taken to prison. Most would not be charged with any crime. It soon became clear that the main purpose of these detentions was to silence witnesses. The detainees would include women as well as men, as Lydia Mahabuke would discover:

When I was discharged from hospital and when I was coming out of the building we saw a number of trucks waiting outside. They took us back to Sharpeville police station. That's where they took statements from us. After they had taken statements the same trucks took us to Leeukop prison or Boksburg prison or a female prison. From there we would be taken to Vereeniging in cars for our case. It was not clear to us whether it was a trial or an inquest because it kept on being postponed. I was in prison for three months. After the three months we were told never to say anything. They were looking for ringleaders. I was released on bail of R60. They fetched me and brought me home. The case eventually fizzled out.

Isaac Moeung would spend a year in prison before the police withdrew charges against him.

I was in the hospital for four weeks when some police officers came into the ward, asking us patients if we wanted to go home. They had trucks waiting outside, everything was taken care of, no problem. Of course we bought it, we wanted to see our families and try to get our lives back on track. Guess what. The trucks were not going to Sharpeville. They were going straight to jail. Then the ordeal really started . . . There were four buckets in each cell. One for piss, the other for shit, one for food, and one for drinking water. Impossible! They made me feel lower than a pig. Bugs were every-where and if you got ill, don't think you received treatment. We slept on the hard stone floor with only small and thin blankets. Almighty God, this story pains me. In prison we were waiting for trial. Innocent people like me had to live in those inhuman conditions for a year to wait for an unfair trial. In the end I was lucky I wasn't a PAC member. They were all sentenced to jail periods ranging from a couple of months to five years. Me and the others were released . . . And even after I got back to Sharpeville it wasn't over. The police used to raid houses of people that had been arrested in the past. Almost everyday they came in my house in full force, armed and ready, just to see if I was still there. They wanted to check if I was a communist. Yeah, of course. To annoy us, they came mostly in the middle of the night. This continued for five to six months.

As Albert Mbongo remembers, the arrests had wider effects, helping to discourage any public discussion of the tragedy: 'In the days after the shootings, nothing happened. Nobody dared say anything, because if you did you were arrested. I couldn't even attend the burial, because only women and children were allowed there.'

Normal social life was further inhibited by a climate in which people could no longer trust their neighbours, as Sam Poletsi discovered: 'It took a long time for me to pick up my normal life, also because of the situation in the township after the shootings. It was not good. There was a strict curfew, and there were a lot of arrests. A lot of people acted as spies for the police. Because they were so poor, they needed those few Rands they were paid. As a result you couldn't say anything anymore because those sell-outs would get you arrested.' Resident local policemen were obvious targets for any remaining activists at liberty. Even so, Constable Myubu was allowed to join the domestic rituals of mourning that families arranged within the privacy of their homes:

In the days after the shootings the young men directed their anger towards black policemen like myself. They called us sell-outs and some of our houses were burned down. There were a lot of funerals later on, and before each one we held night vigils. People close to the deceased would sit down for an entire night and speak about the lost one, honour his or her memory, sing hymns and pray all night.

★

Decades later, for survivors, there are daily reminders of the ways their lives were damaged that day. Puselato Malelo's baby was unharmed but today she is still disabled with a serious limp: 'I still suffer from the shootings. Walking is hard, I have enormous scars on my leg. See my left leg here? The flesh that was ripped out by the bullet has never grown back, and it's just a gap in my leg now. When I finally got out of hospital I resumed working. What else could I do? There was no alternative but to forget about it. But during this time of the year, when the 21st is so close, I remember it, I do.' Mrs Mguni was also pregnant when she attended the protest and she is convinced that her then unborn child should be counted among the casualties:

> When the shootings happened I was three months pregnant. When I gave birth to my child I was still under medication. And that showed. To this day she's been mentally retarded. I'm sure it's because of my trauma and all the medicine I took. I shall never forget what happened that day, nor forgive anyone. I cannot. I lost family there, my child was affected. Those wrongs cannot be forgotten. I even named my child after it: Cannon.

For many years Sharpeville's residents felt it was impossible to speak about these events, even to each other. Sam Kolisang was chairman of the township's Advisory Board, a person who interacted regularly with authority, continuing to serve as an officially acknowledged civic leader in the years after the shootings. 'We were forced to forget about the shootings', he told his interviewer in 1999, 'because if you spoke about them you were arrested. As simple as that. The Special Branch of the South African Police was all over the township, looking for "communists" or "those intent on overthrowing the government". It went so far that parents hardly dared to tell their children about 1960.'[17]

Since 1994, in a very different political climate, the survivors of the Sharpeville massacre have been encouraged to speak about their experiences. Many, however, do not find any comfort in doing so. Though he offered in his interview a very detailed narrative, Vincent Leutsoa was a reluctant witness when he spoke in 1999: 'I never liked repeating this story. It hurts me deeply. Even now it does.' For George Myubu, speaking to researchers was also emotionally taxing: 'These days I don't think about it anymore. I try to suppress it. But I know that others are thinking about it even today.' When Carlton Monnakgotla was interviewed he had very mixed feelings. He still relived the events of that day in his dreams and would have prefered not to remember them. On the other hand he felt the public memory of the massacre should be kept alive: 'I have had some nightmares about the massacre since and am now trying to forget. It's hard but we have to. Although it is important that the truth be known.' Segametsi Makhanya, too would have liked to put the past behind her but she found this very difficult to accomplish: 'Nowadays I try and forget and reconcile. It isn't going well.'

★

Excerpts from several of these interviews appear on placards displayed in the museum that now occupies the site of the massacre. Elizabeth Mabona's narrative together with the recollections of the Ramohoase brothers supplied the authoritative sources for the analysis of the event that appears in the *Report* of the South African Truth and Reconciliation Commission. Knitted together, these first-person accounts help to constitute a local folk history of the tragedy: they are probably a representative enough sampling of the ways in which most people in Sharpeville who were alive at the time remember the event today.

The speakers can be categorized into two groups, people who joined the crowd outside the police station because they wished to participate in the protest and those who arrived as onlookers. Most of these witnesses were prompted to attend out of curiosity or they made the short journey from their homes to the station because they had been told to do so. Several of these survivors were evidently sympathetically predisposed to the organization that led the protest, the Pan-Africanist Congress—Lydia Mahabuke, Simon Mkutau, and Vincent Leutsoa, perhaps—but not one of these people was a deeply committed political activist. With the exception of George Myubu, the policeman, once they had arrived to join the gathering assembled outside the police station, they remained there because they found the experience engaging, exhilarating even. Their testimony does not suggest that they were compelled to stay and indeed four of them, Sam Poletsi, Segametsi Makhanya, Carlton Monnakgotla, and Vincent Leutsoa may owe their lives to their decision to leave the crowd to seek refreshment. All of them insist that the crowd was a convivial and good-natured assembly and that initially, at least, as Isaac Moeung's testimony indicates, its mood was infectious, affecting even some of the policemen.

Police reinforcements may have helped to alter the attitude of the constables, especially after the deployment on the station perimeter of the Saracen armoured vehicles, each of which was conspicuously equipped with a Browning heavy machine gun. Witnesses in the front rows were able to observe a flurry of activity among the policemen before the shooting, including the arrival of a senior officer, the loading of their weapons, and the arrangement of the men into a firing line. At this juncture, the front ranks of the crowd began pressing against the gate, forced towards the police line by pressure from behind, a dynamic that Simon Mkutau experienced as he was thrust forward into the gathering's vanguard. His narrative indicates that it may have been an involuntary surge forward by people pressing against the main gate that panicked the police commanders. Certain witnesses heard an order to fire. For others, the detonations discharged by the .303 rifles were preceded by no warning or command. All the testimony confirms that the firing continued well after people began to turn and run, and the recollections of the way that the crowd dispersed suggests that all or most of the police on each of the three sides of the building fired their weapons, so that in effect there were three fields of fire, prompting people to flee in different directions, colliding with each other, as the assembly became transformed into a melee.

For these people, their presence outside the police station was transformative for it changed their lives profoundly. For some of them, fifty years later they live with constant reminders of the fear, pain and heartbreak they experienced that day and in the days and weeks that followed. Decisive as it was in their lives, few of these witnesses can find consolation from their own participation in a confrontation that changed history; indeed several of the people interviewed in 1999 seemed to feel that their world at least had not changed. To repeat the phraseology used by Sam Kolisang, 'nothing will change in Sharpeville. Ever.' Indeed, for many of the people who lived through the Sharpeville massacre, their daily existence will always be configured by a history that has never turned course.

These intimate personal histories had consequences that fulfilled or exceeded political expectations that to most South Africans living in 1960 must have seemed wildly improbable. The men and women who for one reason or another joined the processions the Pan-Africanists that led to police stations on 21 March 1960 would indeed change history. They would help shape profoundly the future actions and policies of the apartheid state, its international allies and opponents, and the route of liberatory politics in South

Africa. The people who assembled in these processions, the people whose voices supply the narrative in the first part of this chapter, people like Elizabeth Mabona, Ruben Rapoetsoe, Frederick Batkani, George Myubu, Segametsi Makhanya, Sam Poletsi, Lebitsa Ramohoase, Lydia Mahabuke and all the rest, they represent unusual protagonists in an academic analysis of grand politics: ordinary people who made history 'from below'. This study has been reinforced again and again by their memories and their voices.

Notwithstanding their power, in these testimonials certain voices are absent. In particular if we are seeking a comprehensive set of explanations about the causes and consequences of the events in Sharpeville that day we need other witnesses and other kinds of evidence. At the time the police began firing, many of the most assertive Pan-Africanist Congress activists were standing in the front rows near the main gate and they died in the opening volley of the police fusillade. Before the shooting started the key local leaders were in police detention. They were imprisoned subsequently and few of them returned to Sharpeville. Unlike most of the witnesses whose stories we have just documented they were certainly attempting to change the world around them and we need their evidence if we are to explore the ways in which Sharpeville's residents behaved as historical agents, actively altering the course of their country's political evolution. Official voices are also silent in this communal narrative for aside from the evidence they submitted to the commission that investigated the shootings shortly afterwards, none of the policemen who were present on the other side of the fence have spoken in public about their actions. As we shall see, though, even the selective and tendentious explanations of their conduct offered by the police to the official inquiry would turn out to be very helpful. We can draw upon this kind of evidence to explain the policemen's extraordinarily bellicose deployment, in illuminating their reactions to the crowd, and in projecting the nature of the threat that they perceived in the apparently joyous multitude that assembled outside their station.

There are other questions in which the perspective of distance is more useful in seeking answers, in which the foregrounding of eyewitness experience may be an obstruction. The lethal combination of such an enthusiastic, determined, and well-attended protest and, equally, such heavily armed, badly led and aggressively-predisposed policemen was an exceptional event. To be sure, the police had a history of discharging their weapons into crowds but the extent of their firepower and the way they used it at Sharpeville was hardly routine in South Africa in 1960. It was the product of circumstances that nobody present at the time could have been fully conscious. These considerations included a local social structure in which for a number of reasons young African men were unusually ready to assert authority over older people, a predisposition generated by a peculiarly constrained labour market.

This book is about consequences as well as causes. In particular it addresses the question of whether the massacre, as well as the associated events it brought in its train, represented an epoch-making juncture in South African history. Was the tragedy at Sharpeville a momentous event about which we can conclude with certainty, that afterwards, large sections of society and important social institutions behaved in new ways? Would South Africa's political gestation have been different if the Sharpeville massacre had not happened; was it in this sense a turning point? Was it really, to use the words employed by the British Liberal Party's leader Jo Grimond in the House of Commons in 1960, 'a dividing line in history'?[18]

To answer these questions, it is not enough to discover how people understood events as they were happening. Indeed such perceptions may be misleading for they may offer false pointers about the significance of events. At the time, in the hours and days that followed the massacre, it is true that many South Africans did believe they were living through historically decisive developments. Such perceptions can be wrong, though, even when, as they did here, they inspired significant numbers of people to undertake actions they otherwise might not have conceived of as practical. Shortly after the Soweto student uprising of 1976, John Kane-Berman compared that eruption to the events after Sharpeville, concluding that both represented fairly inconsequential insurrectionary adventures. They were, he maintained, 'turning points where South Africa did not turn', when history in fact remained on course. For Kane-Berman and other influential authorities writing in the same vein, South Africa at that time was an authoritarian state that rather than being weakened by insurgent challenges, was becoming increasingly unassailable. New technology and in particular computers had 'open[ed] up possibilities of regulation, surveillance, and control that few regimes in history would have dreamed of'.[19] In the late 1970s, for many South African liberals, the best prospects for change would be through the reforms that sooner or later would accompany South Africa's developmental path of industrial capitalism.[20] From such a perspective, insurgent politics represented momentary diversions from an entrenched trajectory.

The argument in this book is different. To be sure, Sharpeville did not represent a staging point on the road to revolutionary transformation nor did it prompt the kind of unsuccessful liberalization and modernization that can bring about social disintegration. But Sharpeville and associated happenings certainly constituted a political crisis, creating an atmosphere in which serious weaknesses in the state's authority could become apparent even to senior officials and amongst privileged citizens. Following on from this an entire echelon of black political leadership committed itself both strategically and philosophically to doctrines of revolutionary political change. Just because such strategies eventually proved elusive does not mean that these commitments were inconsequential, for in various fashions they continue today to shape South African political life. However the political developments precipitated by the massacre followed opposed trajectories. Sharpeville's sacrifice elicited compassion and empathy worldwide, feelings that helped mobilize a powerful movement of international solidarity, a movement that had it not been for the massacre may well have remained a limited concern of informed minorities and special interests. The various anti-apartheid organizations within this movement certainly enlisted in their leadership and followings people who were committed to revolutionary change in South Africa but their most important effect was quite different. In the long-term their main achievement would be to help ensure that South Africa's political transition was through a relatively orderly process of negotiation.

The scope and the intensity of political reactions to the Sharpeville massacre themselves need to be explained. This was not the first time in South Africa that armed police had fired into crowds of protestors, nor was the brutality of the event unparalleled by events elsewhere in imperial Africa in the preceding decade of African decolonization.

The Bulhoek massacre remains today the largest mass killing on a single occasion by South African policemen. On 24 May 1921, 800 police fired into a crowd of members of the millenarian Israelite sect. They had assembled on Ntabelanga Hill, twenty-five miles from Queenstown in the Eastern Cape to await the Second Coming, defying various injunctions to move off the white-owned farmland they were occupying. One hundred and eighty-three members of the sect were killed and 100 more wounded. The police claimed subsequently that members of the assembly had attacked first, using knives and knobkerries and indeed one policeman was stabbed. Surviving Israelites maintained that the police assault was unprovoked by any preceding violence.[21]

In the first decades of the Union police and soldiers would also turn their guns on white workers, on a occasion in 1913 firing into a gathering of striking white miners killing a hundred workers and bystanders. Nine years later, in the 1922 mineworkers' rebellion, police and soldiers would kill eighty-one civilians. This was a true insurrection though, in which forty-three soldiers and twenty-nine police lost their lives. The same year, however, there could be no such justifications for the way in which the Union Defence Force (UDF) reacted to the Bondelswarts rebellion in Namibia in which 115 fatal casualties included women and children.

During the 1930s and 1940s armed police confrontations with unarmed groups of protestors or strikers became regular or at least unremarkable events. During a day of anti-pass demonstrations organized by the Communist Party of South Africa, on 16 December 1930, police fired into a pass-burning meeting in central Durban fatally wounding the local Communist leader Johannes Nkosi and three of his companions. When their bodies arrived at the morgue it was discovered that they had been mutilated with knives or pangas, violations that at the time were attributed to the African constabulary who had joined in the dispersal of the meeting after the gunfire from the white officers.[22] The use of lethal force in suppressing protest was not confined to confrontations with political radicals. Well-armed police were beginning to be deployed rather frequently in dealing with even quite minor and fairly unthreatening local protests within the boundaries of black townships. For example, in Germiston's municipal location in 1933 police used their weapons in retaliation to protests against official raidsto arrest illegal lodgers and subtenants. On this occasion an elderly woman died later from gunshot wounds.

In Marabastad in 1943, one of the main African residential neighbourhoods in Pretoria at the time, municipal workers mutinied after officials announced that a new scheme of weekly rather than monthly wage payments would be deferred. Again the police restored order by using their weapons, on this occasion killing fifteen rioters and wounding another eleven. Three years later, in another major confrontation between the authorities and mineworkers (on this occasion African mineworkers) during a five-day strike between 12–16 August 1946, on various occasions police shot into groups of miners outside compounds across the Witwatersrand, again killing a total of thirteen men and wounding 1,250. Soldiers were also called out during this strike.

During the Durban riots over the weekend of 14–16 January 1949, when Africans clashed with their Indian neighbours killing around fifty people, in restoring order, both soldiers and policemen were mobilized and the eighty-seven Africans that died during the riots were mainly shot by the police or army.

Through the 1950s, constabulary deployed in riot-control duties were equipped and prepared as a paramilitary force, towards the end of the decade frequently armed with automatic weapons. Eighteen people died in confrontations between demonstrators and the police around Johannesburg on 1 May 1950 during a protest against the banning of the Communist Party. That same year on 27 October 1950 police killed fourteen 'Tribesmen' in Witzieshoek Reserve while breaking up an assembly during opposition to cattle culling. On this occasion the police also took casualties: two dead and sixteen wounded. On 18 January 1957, police fired upon a crowd of bus boycott supporters in Lady Selborne, Pretoria: they fired over the heads of the crowd but one bullet went astray and hit and killed a cyclist returning home from work. The officers were members of the Police Mobile Unit, a group specially constituted to deal with severe instances of political or social unrest. That year the Unit would impose its authority on a cluster of villages around Dinokane near Zeerust. Here opposition to the issue of women's passes acquired a particular intensity as it coincided with communal antipathy to official efforts to replace an uncooperative local chief. Through March, fatalities from police-instigated violence ran into double figures. The following year in Sekhukhuneland in the Northern Transvaal the police killed four people who were attempting to prevent the arrest of another recalcitrant chief opposed to the new Bantu Authorities. On 17 June 1959 the police shot dead three people during riots in Cato Manor outside Durban: the riots were precipitated by protests against official 'raids' to arrest illegal brewers and distillers. In February the following year during a similar liquor raid, nine police officers were killed, an event that influenced the predispositions of the constabulary deployed outside Sharpeville police station. To round off this catalogue of carnage, on 10 December 1959, eleven people died while taking part in a demonstration outside the municipal beerhall in Old Location outside Windhoek. The meeting was called in support of a wider boycott of municipal facilities to protest against the impending enforced resettlement of the Location's residents to a new township, Katatura. Shooting continued for over two hours. The police first opened fire, convinced, apparently, that they were about to be attacked, a perceptionthat may have been prompted by the rupture of telephone wires connecting the municipal office where they were stationed.[23] Similar developments would help to ratchet up police predispositions to use their firepower in the events described in this book.

The Sharpeville massacre happened in a national setting in which the authorities had already repeatedly demonstrated a propensity to suppress with armed force even fairly peaceful kinds of collective protest. As we shall see, the way the police were deployed in Sharpeville still needs to be explained for it was by no means a given that in 1960 police would always use guns to impose their will upon even militant assembles. Even so, what was different about Sharpeville from these preceding events was not so much the scale or ferocity of violence. South African police had fired into large assemblies before and at least on one occasion had killed more people. What was truly singular about the Sharpeville massacre was the political reaction the massacre elicited, both within South Africa and beyond its borders.

Why the Sharpeville massacre engendered these reactions is one of the major questions that this book addresses. As we shall see, to explain international responses to the Sharpeville shootings we need to understand the social and cultural changes that helped to set the agenda for such widespread indignation in response to the killings outside South Africa. Agenda-setting was an indispensable requirement before public outrage. In Europe and North America, public reactions to comparably violent events elsewhere in Africa and even within Europe were relatively muted and confined. For example, in the English-speaking world, French repression directed at Algerian civilians rarely generatedwidespread public criticism. This was strikingly evident in 1961, when between about fifty and possibly as many as 200 Algerians were killed in Paris during or after participation in a 30,000-strong protest against a curfew that had been imposed in those sections of the city that accommodated North African immigrants. Under the direction of Maurice Papon, a wartime collaborator with the German occupation and a former police prefect who had directed counter insurgency operations in Constantine in Algeria during the 1950s, the police were instructed to treat the demonstrators harshly and many of those who were killed were murdered after their arrest. Despite the availability of plenty of eyewitness accounts of the suppression of the protestors while they were still in the streets, most press reportage in Britain and the United States was restrained and low-key, influenced by French official denials that the deaths had exceeded single figures, and using disdainful language about the 'rabble'-

like behaviour of the Algerian 'mob'.[24] Such journalism was in sharp contrast to treatment accorded by the same newspapers to the Sharpeville massacre. As we shall see, though, for a range of reasons, among significant sections of the general public as well as within their political elites in certain European countries and in the United States, by 1960 there was a readiness to empathize with the experiences of black South Africans. Similar predispositions did not exist amongst ordinary people with respect to Muslim Algerians in France or in North Africa or with respect to other groups subjected to brutalities of post-war imperial pacification: the Kikuyu in Kenya for instance, or the Makonde in northern Mozambique.[25] Later in this book we will explore the international cultural shifts that created the social setting in which this empathy with black South Africans could exist in Europe and North America.First, though we need to understand why the Sharpeville massacre happened where it did, when it did.

2

Pan-Africanist Preparations

During the 1950s, the South African government's main extra parliamentary political opponent was the African National Congress. Just after the National Party's accession to power, in 1949, the ANC had adopted a Programme of Action, committing itself to using a range of militant tactics, including strikes, civil disobedience, boycotts, and stay-at-homes in pursuit of the goals of 'national freedom', 'political independence', and 'self determination'. The adoption of this programme reflected the ascendancy within the ANC of its Youth League, a body formed in 1944 by a group who were mainly teachers or university students and whose members felt that within the Congress there was a need 'for vigilance against communists and other groups that foster non-African interests'. Leaguers were heavily critical of the ANC's past efforts to seek to influence government decisions by cultivating close relationships with liberal intermediaries including parliamentary 'native representatives'. Africans should not rely on anyone else to help them, they maintained, 'only African nationalism or Africanism [could] save the African people'. In particular Africans should not expect to benefit from any cross-racial class solidarity and therefore Youth Leaguers were opposed to any cooperation between the ANC and the Communist Party. Africans were engaged in 'a national fight against oppression' and they hence needed to 'reject foreign leadership'.[1] Indeed for certain Youth Leaguers, African identity was ascriptive and racially constituted. Their first president, Anton Lembede, believed that races were constituted by unique collective psychologies. No foreigner, Lembede proposed, could ever truly interpret the African spirit. All Africans, throughout the continent, Lembede maintained, constituted a single nation and inhabited 'a blackman's country'.[2]

Not all the Youth Leaguers agreed with this view and in its 'Basic Policy', the League itself rejected a racially exclusive future. The Youth League's 'Africanism' was to be moderate, it insisted:

> We of the Youth League take account of the concrete situation in South Africa and realize that the different groups have come to stay. But we insist that a condition for inter-racial peace and progress is the abandonment of white domination and such a change in the basic structure of South African society that those relations which breed exploitation and human misery disappear.[3]

Such a society could be achieved, many Youth Leaguers believed, if African cultural predispositions were allowed free rein in any reconstitution of the social order. Zolile Hamilton Keke learned his Africanist doctrine from veteran Youth Leaguers while he was a political prisoner. In his autobiography he recalls that:

> It was commonly said by members of the Congress Youth League that the African way of life was not individualistic and that personal power, success and fame was no absolute measure of values. Africans are inclined towards unity and aggregation, toward greater social responsibility and the harmonious corporate culture where communal contentment was the absolute measure of values. Language ties, psychological inclinations, institutions like tribal democracy and our past rural life linked the Africans in the south to their brethren north of the Limpopo. Africa has her own contribution to make to the sum total of human civilization and culture.[4]

The Programme of Action did not address the issue of how the ANC should work with other groups within the South African population or indeed whether it should. Its phraseology, though, suggested that Africans were engaged in a racially exclusive nationalist struggle for self-determination, as did even the Leaguers' half-humorous usage of such forms of address as 'son of the soil' as in 'Good morning, son of the soil' in their encounters with each other.[5] Youth Leaguers believed that with their parent movement's adoption of their programme, their views would prevail in the organization's leadership. After all, along with the adoption of the programme, the 1949 ANC conference elected several Youth Leaguers into important leadership positions.

It is quite true that the Programme did influence the ANC to embrace more militant forms of protest in 1950. On the whole, though, most ANC leaders would resist Africanist urgings that they should adopt racial 'self determination' as their goal. As the ANC's president general, Albert Luthuli, would remind conference delegates in 1958, the ANC's aim was to establish 'a democratic majority' rather than a 'racial majority' within the government of the country.[6] Accordingly, through the decade the ANC would in fact work more closely then ever with Communists, white 'democrats', and leaders of the Natal and Transvaal Indian Congresses. This was not surprising. Communists were in fact well-represented within the ANC leadership through the 1940s and the Communist Party itself had developed a well-organized branch-based organization in certain African townships—particularly in Port Elizabeth and in the industrial centres of the East Witwatersrand—and in these places local Communist activists asserted themselves within the ANC's local structures as well. The government's prohibition of the Communist Party in mid-1950 encouraged Communists to invest even more effort into consolidating their influence within the ANC. Youth Leaguers such as Oliver Tambo and Nelson Mandela, who joined the ANC's top leadership at the beginning of the decade, soon dropped their early objections to working with Communists and with leaders of sympathetic Indian organizations. On 1 May 1950, the ANC joined the Communist Party in calling for a general 'stay-away' strike in protesting against the impending Suppression of Communism Act. At this juncture, Mandela and Tambo opposed the ANC's support for this venture; they were still keen to curtail Communist influence within the ANC. However they were impressed by the extent of participation the strike call elicited and Mandela was present when police baton-charged a well-attended Communist Party 'Freedom Day' meeting in Orlando. The police killed eighteen people at similar gatherings elsewhere on the Rand. Subsequently Mandela and other Youth League leaders shifted position, agreeing to support 'joint action' with the Indian Congresses for a second stay-away, on 26 June, to mark a 'Day of Mourning' for the people killed on May Day. The Transvaal Youth League issued a fiery statement supporting the protest and stirringly concluding it with 'Up you mighty race.'

The first fully planned implementation of the civil disobedience called for in the Programme of Action was the Defiance Campaign, led by a Joint Planning Council of three Indian Congress officials and four ANC leaders. Though jointly led, the campaign was a mainly African affair, with fewer than one hundred Indians serving as volunteers. Ostensibly the campaign sought the abolition of 'five unjust laws' that represented the first phase of the government's apartheid programme. These laws elaborated urban segregation, imposed passes on African women, banned the Communist Party, removed coloured people from the voters' roll, and accorded to rural chiefs new authoritarian powers to implement highly unpopular land conservation measures. The Joint Planning Council appointed a 'volunteer-in-chief', Nelson Mandela, and an Indian deputy, Yusuf Cachalia, to lead three stages of civil disobedience—beginning in June with small bands of resisters in the main towns, broadening the movement to embrace smaller centers and larger groups, and then extending the movement into the countryside. In the second and third phases the intention was to support passive resistance with general strikes. Action began in June 1952 with Mandela leading a group of senior ANC and Indian Congress members in violation of Johannesburg curfew regulations. Subsequent civil disobedience mainly targeted 'petty apartheid' regulations in railway stations and post offices as well as the rules governing non-residents' entry into African 'locations'.

Over 8,000 people were arrested in the Defiance Campaign, nearly 6,000 of them in the Eastern Cape, where ANC organization had historically been facilitated by relatively liberal local government, a concentration of educational institutions, and the development of especially strong trade union organizations. In Port Elizabeth, a one-day strike in November to protest curfews and a ban on meetings closed the docks and brought armoured cars onto the streets. Thousands of African dock-workers lost their jobs afterwards. But protest was not confined to urban workers. In parts of the Ciskei the campaign attracted peasant support.

Reaching a peak in August, the movement lost impetus after violent riots in its two main centres, Port Elizabeth and East London. But in December 1952, just before the campaign's end, a particularly well-publicized act of defiance took place in Germiston when forty volunteers entered the African township without the required permits. The group included seven whites and was led by Mohandas Gandhi's son, Manilal, and by Patrick Duncan, the son of a wartime governor-general. We will encounter Patrick Duncan again later in this narrative. The seven white volunteers served prison sentences, the first white South Africans to be convicted for civil disobedience. Their engagement was an unusually radical expression of dissent from the prevalent political predispositions amongst most white South Africans. Despite some expressions of sympathy for African grievances in English-language newspapers (most of the defiance was reported very dismissively), within the white community the campaign elicited either hostility or indifference. In early 1953, the Criminal Law Amendment

Act was passed. The new law prescribed a maximum prison term of three years with fines and whipping for 'offences committed by way of protest'. Young volunteers had already been subjected to lashings in several towns. Most activists were unprepared for such severity. For ANC leaders, their following now swollen to 120,000, civil disobedience no longer seemed a practical option.

African women thought differently, however. Beginning in 1955, a series of protests against the extension of passes to women were mobilized by the Federation of South African Women, an umbrella body to which the ANC's Women's League, various trade unions, and left-wing white and coloured organizations were affiliated. Demonstrations began in October 1955 outside the Union Buildings in Pretoria and a series of local protests in many smaller centres followed the travelling 'mobile units' that issued the new passes. In Winburg, in the Free State, in March 1956, women recalled an earlier local tradition of pass protests and burned the passes that had just been distributed. The Federation collected money for their defence but it counselled against outright law-breaking. Refusing to accept the passes was not illegal (they were not made compulsory for women until 1963), but burning them was. A second massive demonstration in Pretoria took place in August, at which time 20,000 women assembled outside the Union Buildings to sing their bellicose anthem: 'Strijdom you have tampered with the women, you have struck a rock.' Unfortunately, Prime Minister J. G. Strijdom was absent from his office that day.

The movement acquired fresh momentum in Johannesburg. Here in 1958 township branches of the ANC's Women's League persuaded large numbers of women to deliberately court arrest by taking part in meetings and marches in the city centre, which were then prohibited. Twelve hundred women were charged under the Criminal Law Amendment Act before an alarmed ANC leadership overruled the Federation and directed that the women should not in future break the law. In return, the ANC undertook to launch a national campaign against passes in general. Despite the ANC's strictures, though, women's protest spread outside the boundaries of organized politics. In mid-1959, anger about the passes and grievances arising from soil conservation regulations helped to generate a series of revolts led by women in the Natal countryside. Mostly, participants concentrated on destroying cattle-dipping tanks, but they also set fire to sugar cane fields and marched on police stations and magistrates' courts. About 20,000 women were involved in these events and nearly 1,000 were arrested before the demoralizing effects of heavy fines and prison sentences took their toll.

After 1952, up to 1960, given the penalties associated with civil disobedience, ANC leaders sought instead to mobilize their following through boycotts and through demonstrative 'stay-at-home' strikes. Boycotts were not a new tactic in African opposition. For example, in 1922 women's *manyanos* (self-help organizations developed around church congregations) organized a remarkably cohesive boycott of rural trading stores in the Herschel district of the Eastern Cape in protest against high commodity prices. In 1994, in Brakpan on the East Rand, parents withdrew nine hundred children from a mission school in protest against the Department of Native Affairs, which had organized the dismissal of a popular teacher who had belonged to the Communist Party. Proposals for electoral boycotts began in 1936 with the introduction of a separate voting roll and token parliamentary representation for Africans. Despite their earlier objections to these electoral arrangements, the leaders of a specially formed All African Convention (AAC) stood for election in the now advisory Native Representative Council and endorsed white 'native' parliamentary representatives.

During the 1950s, black political organizations were divided over the merits of electoral boycotts. The ANC was committed to electoral abstention by its 1949 Programme of Action, but in fact, through the decade, ANC candidates contested township Advisory Board elections while its white allies in the (clandestine) Communist Party and the Congress of Democrats attempted to attract coloured common-roll voters and African native representative voters to secure seats in parliament. The ANC was more forthrightly engaged in two kinds of anti-apartheid boycott in the 1950s. In 1955, it tried to counter the introduction of a demeaning syllabus of 'Bantu Education' in primary schools by mounting a class boycott. The organization's initial resolve, however, was eroded by the reluctance of many Congress leaders to withdraw their own children from school. In the end, the boycott was launched and sustained in the two areas in which ANC organization was strongest and most proletarian in social ethos, Port Elizabeth and the East Rand. In these places 12,000 children stayed out of school for up to six months, attending special schools run by the Congress's African Education Movement. Eventually the children returned to official classes, but in the context of the times, this was an impressive undertaking.

Consumer boycotts, which had hitherto been directed at particular enterprises to bring down prices or support industrial actions, began in

1959 to assume a more politically assertive character with an ANC campaign to 'Boycott Nationalist Products'. The boycott achieved some improvements in the treatment of workers in vineyards and potato farms, and it also helped to inspire the opening of an international campaign of trading sanctions initiated in London the same year by Christian Action and the Africa Bureau. Adding impetus to the boycott movement was a series of bus boycotts: twenty-three of these protests were reported in the press between 1948 and 1961. Most of these boycotts were provoked by fare increases, but they often became invested with broader political concerns as ANC activists moved into their leadership committees. In the 1950s, however, consumer boycotts of any type by Africans could only make a limited impact, except in those services or enterprises in which Africans dominated consumption, in public transport, for example. Electoral boycotts in an era in which government was in any case concerned mainly to limit African political representation were also a weak weapon. Generally, South Africa's rulers during the 1950s were indifferent as to whether Africans chose to vote in elections, and in 1959 even the indirect 1936 franchise arrangements were abolished. As far as education was concerned, most parents tended to take the view that even 'Bantu' education was better for their children than no education at all, and from 1956 onwards the ANC concentrated its energies in this sphere in trying to win control of the newly-elected school boards, which originally it had intended to embargo.

Similar constraints in the political structure limited the ANC's attempts to mobilize African workers in demonstrative general strikes. To be sure, the ANC's growth through the decade, peaking at around 100,000 members and probably with an informal following rather greater, represented a mass political movement unprecedented in its size and duration in South African history. This was certainly a reflection of important social changes: the doubling of African urban population during the 1940s and the accompanying movement of Africans into secondary industry as well as the expansion of an African urban middle class, which from 1950 would be confronted by government policies with new threats to its security, status, and aspirations. Reflecting these developments, during the 1950s the ANC was able to draw upon the support of an increasingly tightly knit trade union movement. However, African working-class presence in manufacturing was uneven and much of the work its members contributed more generally was unskilled and easily replaceable: this meant that even strong unions exercised only limited leverage. In the metal industries of the East Rand, for example, the introduction of the new technology that heralded the takeover by Africans of most stages of production was only just beginning in the mid-1950s. Africans only joined the vehicle industry's assembly lines in Port Elizabeth in the 1960s. White workers were supplanted much earlier in textiles and food processing and not surprisingly it was here that African labour organization proceeded most swiftly. But in the case of many townships during the 1950s, the number of industrial workers would have been greatly exceeded by those working as delivery men, servants, cleaners, watchmen, and in similar capacities in shops, offices, and households. African trade unionism through the decade was especially concentrated in three branches of light industry—food, textiles, and clothing—as well as in services, laundry and dry-cleaning establishments especially. As Julius Lewin pointed out in 1959, 'even if trade unions were much stronger and more wisely led, it is difficult to see what vital industries or essential services could be brought to a standstill'.[7]

The ANC organized four stay-at-home strikes through the decade, two in 1950, one in 1957, and one in 1958. South Africa's racial urban geography facilitated the organization of these protests, as most Africans lived in densely built townships, enclosed and isolated from other suburban communities, with relatively few points of outside communication. With quite small groups of picketers outside railway and bus stations, a determined leadership could quite easily control departures from a township. Picketing certainly played a role in stay-away strikes. On the whole, though, ANC leaders disliked the coercion implicit in such picketing— which in any case was illegal as were the strikes themselves—and preferred to rely on exhortation and mass meetings to engender participation in such protests. Trade union support for such protests was decisive. In June 1957 a Congress call for a 'Day of Protest, Prayer and Demonstration' included strike calls for workers concentrated around Johannesburg and Port Elizabeth and, on this occasion, organizational work was concentrated in factories with leafleting outside gates and meetings between ANC officials and shop stewards. Though nationally the Day of Protest was directed at a range of issues including passes, amongst workers propaganda emphasized calls for a national minimum wage of a pound a day, a demand adopted by the 55,000-strong South African Congress of Trade Unions (SACTU) at a National Workers' Conference. Organizers claimed a 70 per cent turnout in the two centres. In 1957 a relatively high number of industrial strikes succeeded in prompting a succession of wage determinations supported by the government that resulted in 1958 in a general rise in real wages.

That year an attempt to repeat the success of the 1957 protest with a call for a three-day protest, timed to coincide with general elections, was less successful. Though initially called at a second National Workers' Conference to back the pound a day demand, the call became conflated with more general political concerns: by the beginning of April according to SACTU's official history, 'the strike call had become less and less a SACTU-oriented campaign and more and more one focusing on the white elections'.[8] The main focus of preparation shifted from the factories to the townships and the ANC ruled out picketing. In the days before, the strike police mounted a succession of pass raids in the centres and on the dawn of election day large groups of armed constables moved into the townships. Turnout was disappointing for the organizers, less than ten per cent on the Witwatersrand, and to the chagrin of trade unionists the ANC's National Working Committee called off the protest at the end of its first day. Though it is likely that the government's and employers' intimidation discouraged participation, trade unionists also believed that people had been mobilized around the wrong issues: 'the slogan led a considerable section of the people to believe that the Congresses were in favour of the United Party coming to power'.[9]

★

Dissenting Africanists within the ANC agreed with the view that the ANC was addressing the wrong issues. Through the decade, within the Youth League a residual group of more doctrinaire 'African nationalists' or 'Africanists' remained who maintained their objections to the increasingly close collaboration between the ANC and its 'multiracial' allies, blaming them for any setbacks the organization experienced and accusing them of exercising a disproportionate influence over strategic decisions. These dissenters were clustered in a group of ANC branches in Johannesburg, especially in Orlando, though there were several Africanist-led ANC branches in Cape Town and there was a busy group of Africanists in East London's Duncan Village.

Africanists were often comparatively well-educated and many of them were employed as secondary school teachers as well as in other liberal professions, including, importantly, journalism, writing for the *Bantu World*, *Drum*, and later *Golden City Post*. Africanist-affiliated journalists included Peter Molotsi and Matthew Nkoana. This concentration of teachers among the Africanists helps to explain their geographic concentration in and around Orlando and the way in which they were sidelined in the ANC during the early 1950s.

Soweto's first and most prestigious high school was situated in Orlando and several members of its staff were drawn to the Africanists. Teachers were barred from political activism and were very vulnerable to dismissal. Those former Youth Leaguers who began to achieve national leadership status within the ANC at the beginning of the 1950s—Nelson Mandela and Oliver Tambo were cases in point—had obtained the professional qualifications that enabled them to move into independent livelihoods, as lawyers or doctors, for example.

A significant number of Orlando Africanists struggled and failed to find rewarding alternatives to teaching, frustrated in their efforts to find work that made them 'independent of government salary'.[10] Peter Raboroko, for example, one of the early principals in the faction and a founding member of the Youth League, enrolled for a year of pre-medical training at Wits University before dropping out and trying to secure articles with an attorney's office before returning to his classroom. Most of the people who belonged to the Africanist faction during the 1950s confined their political activity to discussion meetings and polemical writing, using pseudonyms, though several of the Africanists had volunteered and served prison sentences during the Defiance Campaign. The Orlando Youth Leaguers also published a mimeographed journal, *The Africanist*.

Most of the Soweto-based Africanists were not involved in the ANC's organization-building after the Defiance Campaign nor did they participate in its campaigning activity. At this stage their numbers were small. In 1968 Gail Gerhart interviewed Potlake Leballo, the chairman of the Orlando East Youth League branch after his election in 1953. Leballo told Gerhart that 'when I founded the Africanist movement ... we were about three there when we gave opposition to the mother body'. Leballo's observations during this interview suggests that the movement remained tiny—in Orlando the Africanists used to assemble in his house—though larger, more public meetings for 'the indoctrination of youth' took place in the Bantu Men's Social Centre in Johannesburg.[11]

From 1954, an Africanist Central Committee (Cencom) attempted to develop a structured organization of 'branches and cells'. There is no evidence that such an organization was established in the Transvaal though leading Africanists believed there were clusters of Africanist disaffections in each of the ANC's eighty-odd provincial branches.[12] The Eastern Cape ANC's 'volunteer in chief', Elliot Mfaxa was an enthusiastic Africanist. He recalled later that 'there were cells of Africanists organized all over [in the province], two, three or ten people in each' who would assemble for secret night-time meetings 'from six o'clock in the evening to six in the morning'.[13] Africanist-inclined Youth Leaguers had led the Defiance Campaign in East London, one of strongest areas of civil disobedience in 1952. Their ascendancy there was partly a consequence of the contacts that developed between young ANC activists and nationalist students at Fort Hare. However the ANC's local organization was seriously damaged in the aftermath of police action against the Defiance Campaign. In November 1952, riots followed the police's dispersal of a meeting with a baton charge. Eight people died in the subsequent disorder, including a white Dominican nun, killed and mutilated by rioters, many of them young teenagers. Prompted by fear of reprisals, 5,000 residents left the East London townships, and the ANC's—and hence the Africanists'—popular base collapsed. For the remainder of the decade, East London's Africanist Youth Leaguers had to content themselves with private discussion groups and the production of roneod bulletins under the imprint of their 'Bureau of African Nationalism'.[14]

In the Transvaal, Cencom did expect its younger adherents 'to travel on the trains and buses, mingle with the people, and read them papers'.[15] This was an unlikely stratagem for broadening the movement's popular base if the goal was to achieve structured organization. In any case not all the Africanist principals at this stage were keen to encourage popular engagement with their movement, for them the priority was to win a politically dominant position among well-educated Africans, the 'intelligentsia'.[16] Nevertheless, Potlake Leballo was convinced that the core group of dedicated Africanists enjoyed wider support. In 1954, the Youth League's Transvaal provincial leaders tried to rescind Leballo's election and expel him from the organization but they failed, he told Gerhart, because he enjoyed local backing from people who 'in fact didn't like my ideas as such, but they liked me because I was a great organizer myself'. As we shall see, Leballo was indeed a compelling figure who could quite well have acquired a personal following, though he was probably overstating the case when he claimed that in Soweto by the middle of the decade the Africanists 'had taken over all the branches'.[17] The effort by the Transvaal Youth League executive to expel Leballo was divisive and three of its officials resigned.

As his biographer notes, Potlake Kitchener Leballo 'lived to dramatize, to command the centre of attention, [and] to captivate listeners with impassioned stories'.[18] Even after allowing for this tendency to self-aggrandizement, his life history suggests a strikingly unruly and assertive personality. He was born in Lesotho in 1924, near Mafeteng, the youngest of fourteen children, the son of an Anglican catechist and mission school teacher. His father served in the First World War and another former warrior, his father's brother, helped bring him up. Leballo's uncle was an early object of the youngster's hero worship. He was a veteran of the Gun War in 1880 and was subsequently often in jail for disobeying the colonial administration. Potlake was educated first at a mission primary school, St Saviours, from which he was expelled after undergoing initiation—*leballo*—at his uncle's behest. Then he attended the Masite Institution, Morija, before enrolling at Lovedale in 1940 to train as a teacher. Here he was inspired by an address by Minister Jan Hofmeyr to enlist in the Union Defence Force. He travelled to Krugersdorp for this purpose in October, so as to avoid any unwelcome attention from the school authorities, enlisting in the Native Military Corps, and training as a lorry driver.

Leballo's military service began well with an early promotion in February 1941 to corporal. He served first in Abyssinia and then in Egypt with the 8th army in its Motorized Transport Company. According to army records, in November 1943, though, Corporal Leballo was returned to the Union as 'undesirable'. He was then stationed for the remainder of the war in Pretoria in Non European Armed Services. He was promoted to sergeant at end of 1945 and demobilized in January 1946. Later, Leballo embellished his record claiming that he had been on board a ship that had been sunk on the way to Alexandra, and that he was then rescued by Turkish soldiers. Military files indicate that in Egypt he spent his service mainly in Cairo. Leballo also maintained that he had led a revolt against discrimination in the South African encampment and that he had been taken prisoner and then escaped. He also told people that he had served in the British Army bearing arms— and indeed he did demonstrate a persuasively accurate knowledge of the region around Tobruk where he said he had fought. Less plausibly, he also insisted that he had been imprisoned in a POW camp in Germany. All this seems to have been fictional though it is possible that Leballo may have attributed to his own story experiences he had heard about from other African soldiers. The army records disclose no details about the reason for Leballo's repatriation to South Africa, though the date, just after mutiny in 1943 may not be coincidental.

In January 1946, Leballo re-enrolled at Lovedale. Here he seems to have played a lead role in the Lovedale food riot—a tumultuous rebellion in which students set fire to buildings, smashed 600 windows, and severed electrical power and telephone lines. Leballo was among the 157 students arrested. Most of those arrested were convicted for public violence and caned if they were under eighteen years of age or otherwise imprisoned briefly or fined. The subsequent inquiry found that some of the rioters were armed and that ex-servicemen had led the planning. Along with many of the other ringleaders Leballo was expelled. He then moved in with relatives living in Lady Selbourne in Pretoria. Here he began a still-preserved correspondence with the Lovedale authorities seeking readmission and support for payment of an army grant. In his letters he insisted upon his innocence in playing any command role in the events and he supplied additional information on the main inciters of the riot, noting that during the tumult, 'Satan defeated me unconditionally'. Leballo also claimed that he had hidden in a teacher's house when rioting began, but Lovedale's principal, Robert Shepherd, investigated this claim and found it to be untrue. Leballo was refused readmission and the school returned Leballo's UDF cheques to the army.

He managed to secure a teaching post at an Anglican mission school in Lady Selbourne before undergoing further teacher training at the Wilberforce Institute in Evaton. During this time he lived in Orlando West and attended Youth League meetings. By his own account he was also involved in a brawl with members of the Afrikaner nationalist *Stormjaars*, a paramilitary group.[19] By April 1948, though, Wilberforce's principal, B. Rajuili, was writing to Shepherd of Lovedale complaining about Leballo as 'a very bad student indeed'—who was leading 'a passive sit down kind of strike'. According to an interview he gave to Gail Gerhart, Leballo completed his training and then returned to the school in Lady Selbourne and served as an Anglican church counsellor. In this capacity he had a confrontation with the Reverend John Arrowsmith Maund whom he accused of fathering an illegitimate child with a schoolteacher. The diocesal authorities found the accusation baseless and Maund subsequently became bishop of Lesotho. At about this time Leballo joined the Africanist core group that first assembled in Orlando East in July 1950. That year he was dismissed from his teaching post and he returned to Lesotho to take up a post with the Basutoland High School. He also engaged in Basuto politics, apparently helping to establish the Basuto Congress Party that would be led by his high school colleague, Ntsu Mokhehle. Leballo returned to South Africa in 1952 moving into a house in Orlando in Soweto in 1952. He retained his membership of the Basuto Congress Party (BCP), serving as its Transvaal secretary, active in attempting to build its membership within the Basuto migrant community, which indeed was to supply the party's largest following.[20]

Leballo may have served in the ANC's Defiance Campaign: he was certainly imprisoned that year, though the sources suggest different reasons for his imprisonment.[21] Instead of teaching he drove a lorry for one of the mining companies as well as taking fees as a ballroom dancing instructor. Afterwards he sold insurance policies for Soweto's leading businessman, Paul Mosaka, as well as undertaking motor-scooter deliveries for Mosaka's African Chamber of Commerce. By 1953 he had become the most conspicuous personality among the Orlando Africanists, already attracting censure from the ANC's senior echelons because of his denunciation as 'Eastern functionaries' the Youth Leaguers who had accepted invitations to the World Youth Festival in Bucharest.[22]

For the Orlando Africanists who actively opposed the 1958 strike call, the ANC's decision to time their protest so that it would influence the outcome of white elections simply confirmed their belief that non-African outsiders had superseded the ANC's leadership. Campaigning failures to mobilize sufficient numbers of people were attributable, they believed, to the influence of ostensible sympathizers from 'minority groups' who 'present us with programmes which protect their sectional interests'.[23] Nor was this feeling confined to the relatively urbane group of schoolteachers and middle-class professionals who predominated within the Africanist faction in Orlando. The ANC's own national organizer, T. E. Tshunungwa, after a visit to the Western Cape warned the National Executive of the 'extreme confusion that resulted when people discovered that the white Congress of Democrat men are taking a lead in ANC meetings . . . a politically raw African who has been much oppressed, exploited and victimized by the European sees red when a white face appears'.[24] Meanwhile for the Africanists the damaging impact of sectional interests in diverting the ANC from its proper nationalist orientation was particularly evident in the ANC's adoption of a Freedom Charter in the year following a multi-racial Congress of the People.

In 1954, a 'National Action Council' established by the ANC and its allies began undertaking preparations for a Congress of the People. The council recruited an army of Freedom Volunteers, many of them trade unionists, to collect nationwide popular 'demands' for inclusion in a Freedom Charter. From the thousands of suggestions and petitions that the volunteers collected, a group appointed by the council distilled a draft document. The ANC's leadership reviewed this document on the day before a specially summoned Congress of the People at which delegates from a range of invited organizations were supposed to debate the draft. It was compiled and written mainly by Lionel Bernstein, though the charter's authorship was not public knowledge at the time. Bernstein was a member of the white Congress of Democrats as well as of the clandestine South African Communist Party. In the event, the proceedings at the Congress of the People, held at Kliptown on the borders of Soweto, were halted by the police at the end of the first day. However there had been sufficient time for the 3,000 or so delegates to approve through acclamation an unaltered draft. In April 1956, the ANC adopted the document as its own programme at a specially convened meeting, despite objections from Africanists present. Meanwhile a 'million signature' campaign collected 100,000 names to represent popular endorsement of the charter's contents. The charter contained a list of rights, entitlements, and freedoms as well as calling for nationalization of the mines and 'monopoly industry' and the redistribution of the land 'amongst those that work it'. For the Africanists, though, the most contentious sections of the document were its opening clauses that reaffirmed the multi-racial character of South African society ('South Africa belongs to all who live in it, black and white') and its pledge that a free South Africa would accord equal status for all 'national groups'.

These commitments prompted mimeographed expressions of outrage in the pages of *The Africanist*. 'To whom does Afrika belong', a correspondent writing under the name of 'Africanus' asked. 'Do stolen goods belong to a thief and not to their owner? Those Africans who renounce their claims over Afrika should not stand in the way of the people, for they will be crushed with oppression.' Africans had 'an unalienable claim on every inch of the African soil'. Non-Africans were 'guests of the Africans'. 'No sane man can come into your home and claim as his the chamber or the room you are occupying.'[25] Africanists believed that in their expression of such sentiments they were voicing views that were widely shared, especially amongst recently urbanized people with experience of a rural upbringing in which oral traditions would draw upon still-vivid memories of primary resistance to white settlement. As Z. B. Molete later reflected in a conversation with the American researcher Gail Gerhart, the most effective way of communicating politically with many township residents was through evocation of such recollections:

'What can you do with a white man?' That's what they would tell you. 'The white man is all right; there is nothing we can do.' They would also use some of the texts from the Bible, some of them, in order to show how God dictated things to be; there's nothing to be done about them. But here you would have to use methods of persuasion. You draw examples from as many sources as you can, show the fight that went on in our country . . . The question of land for instance, touches on the African to the core of his heart. Now if you draw from the fights of Moshesh in defence of his land, every Mosotho respects Moshesh very much. Once you talk of Moshesh . . . he is bound to listen. Or you talk of Hintsa, you talk of other heroes, Sekhukhuni and Tshaka and his warriors, that the land is the central point. Let us get back to the land that was given to us by our forefathers.[26]

Instead of depicting the struggle for what it was, an anti-colonial movement against the historic dispossession of Africans of their land by settlers, the 'Kliptown Charter', the Africanists maintained, substituted an anodyne conception of a generalized people's offensive against an abstractly presented 'system'. The truth was, the Africanists insisted, 'the African people have been robbed by the European people'. From this perspective, the ANC's failure to project this message, indeed its eagerness to 'water-down' its polemics 'in order to accommodate all Anti-Nat elements in this country' was the one major reason for its inability to expand its active support during the 1950s beyond the following achieved in the Defiance Campaign. 'Europeans' were to blame, Africanists believed, for the ANC's substitution of the Programme of Action's core principle of self determination with the rights-based prospectus offered in the Freedom Charter. 'We say we do not want the milk, we want the cow', Josias Madzunya explained to supporters in Alexandra. 'Hence we do not want freedom, we want independence. We do not want to have the vote but we want to rule ourselves in this country and make our own laws. In terms of African nationality we want independence and freedom.'[27]

Aside from its ideological turnabout, the other major reason for the ANC's failure to build its following, the Africanists and other critics insisted, was that its leaders were too cautious. During the Defiance Campaign, for example, 'the President of the ANC betrayed his followers leaving many of them in prison'.[28] Indeed, Jordan Ngubane suggested, the 1953 Criminal Law Amendment Act that imposed such severe penalties on civil disobedience succeeded in intimidating ANC leaders through the remainder of the 1950s.[29] Philip Kgosana was certainly projecting a widespread contention amongst his fellow PAC leaders when he told an interviewer in 1963 that 'the weakness of the ANC and other past movements was that the leaders put the people up to something and then abandoned them and failed to follow through with action on their own part'.[30] This was probably an unfair perception and an explanation of the ANC's record that did not acknowledge the very real difficulties posed by the coercive resources at the disposal of the authorities as well as the limits of what any movement might achieve in poor and vulnerable communities. It is also possible that 'The white man is all right, there is nothing we can do' sentiment encountered by Molete might have reflected, in the main industrial centres and amongst the most urbanized Africans, the ameliorating effects of a phase of economic expansion. As one contemporary observer noted:

> ... the long-continued economic prosperity, which is shared to a significant extent by Africans, and the rising standards of living generally, tend to compensate people for the sense of personal frustration induced by the colour bars. Only a small minority think otherwise, and even their actions commonly belie their fears.[31]

Even so, notwithstanding the challenges to activists arising from these environmental considerations, in the late 1950s, inside the activist community contained within the ANC's following, opportunities were opening up for the Africanists to exploit significant sources of tension between leadership and rank and file. By the end of 1957, most of the senior ANC leadership was on trial charged with treason and much of their energy and attention was engaged in time-consuming court proceedings, first in Johannesburg and later in Pretoria. In October at its provincial elections, the Transvaal ANC leadership secured a unanimous en-bloc reelection, arguing that the involvement of many of them in the Treason Trial had meant that they were unable to fulfill all the commitments undertaken at their previous election. They maintained their retention of office would represent a powerful rank and file endorsement of the 'We stand by our leaders' exhortation that the ANC had used to mobilize solidarity and fundraising after the beginning of the trial.

Between these provincial improprieties in October and the ANC's annual national conference in December a Transvaal 'petitioner' movement emerged. Disgruntled branch officials constituted the petitioner group. They complained that the October meeting had been inquorate because outlying branches had not been invited and hence were not represented with delegates. They had various other grievances as well. At the ANC's

December conference Africanists, hoping to ride the more broadly based disaffection at the meeting, moved for a vote of no confidence but failed to obtain sufficient support. ANC leaders offered a concession to the petitioners: a special conference would be held on 23 February 1958 in Orlando to consider their grievances. On this occasion Africanists succeeded in joining forces with the petitioners. The meeting began with a brawl as 'Freedom Volunteers' loyal to the embattled provincial executive tried to check the credentials of delegates entering the hall. What followed was equally divisive. After several hours of abusive tumult, Leballo managed to focus the meeting's attention on a motion for fresh leadership elections. However the chairman pre-empted any calls for voting by announcing that time had run out, the booking period for the hall hire had expired, he explained. As might be expected, many delegates challenged this ruling and the meeting ended with the executive still claiming an authority that was now widely contested.

Several weeks later the National Executive intervened, dismissing the provincial leadership but also expelling Potlake Leballo from the ANC. Until the next provincial conference, scheduled for November, national leaders would manage the provincial organization directly. Their task was facilitated by a government ban on meetings imposed to inhibit protest during the general elections. Even so, in August 1958, Peter Raboroko announced the formation of an 'Anti-Charterist Council' that would seek to coordinate the various strands of opposition to the Transvaal ANC leadership. The council proposed its own candidate for the top post in the impending provincial organizational elections, nominating Josias Madzunya, a rather surprising choice. In 1957 Madzunya had emerged as a conspicuous personality during the Alexandra bus boycott, associating himself with Africanist opposition to top ANC leadership but hitherto not counted among the inner circle of the movement. Known in the press as 'The man in an overcoat', in Alexandra Madzunya enjoyed popular stature. Born in Muletane near Sibasa in Vendaland in 1909, since the late 1930s Madzunya had made a living in Johannesburg salvaging and selling cardboard boxes. He had started attending ANC meetings in 1937. He served as a branch secretary for the ANC in 1952 but fell out with the hierarchy over the Freedom Charter and identified himself with the Africanists. His personal base was sufficiently strong for him to obtain election to the vice-chairmanship of the Coordinating Committee that united various political factions in the leadership of the bus boycott. Journalists paid him more attention than any of the other boycott leaders not least because of his habit of wearing a dark woollen overcoat in all weathers. He owned five such coats, apparently. He had always worn a coat, ever since 1937, he recalled thirty years later, in fact, he owned five of them because they had become his 'uniform of struggle'.[32]

As things turned out, the Africanists were unable to test the extent of Madzunya's popularity among delegates attending the Transvaal ANC's conference. The meeting opened on 1 November. The ANC's president, Chief Albert Luthuli, addressed the assembly, warning them of the pitfalls of a 'dangerously narrow African nationalism which itself tends to encourage us to go back to a tribal narrative'. This reproof engendered a derisive clamour from the floor. Indeed Chief Luthuli had to struggle to make himself heard over the noise of stamping feet and chants of 'Afrika'. According to reporters, a group of a hundred or so Africanists grouped at the back of the hall constituted the main chorus of hecklers. In preparation for the meeting, both the provincial leadership and the Africanists had each recruited their own strong-arm groups of 'volunteers'. The Africanists had obtained some of their volunteers from the ex-patriate Basuto community in Newclare and Evaton and from members of the Basuto Congress Party. Several of the more noisy PAC supporters were wearing Basuto blankets, leading to press reports that the PAC's bodyguard was constituted by 'Russian' gangsters.[33] This partisan chorus then supplied a supportive accompaniment to Zephania Mothopeng, the first of the Africanist speakers to offer a dissenting view. South Africa's people were divided into two communities, the oppressed and the oppressors, Mothopeng told the assembly. There could be no cooperation between them, he insisted. 'Let us cease to believe the people that they can get friendship from the whites—they are the oppressors. Africa is for the Africans, and the whites must go back to Europe.'[34] It was left to Robert Sobukwe, a lecturer at Wits in African languages, to offer a calmer perspective from the Africanist camp. Sobukwe spoke in Sotho, through an interpreter:

> Let us listen to each other's point of view and we shall disagree as we go along. The president has divided nationalism into left, right, and centre. He said we are going back to tribalism. But we are wearing European clothes and we are not going back to tribalism. When we speak of nationalism, there is no point of connection with tribalism. When the ANC was born in 1912 a Zulu nation and the other tribes were completely buried. No one says today I am a Zulu, a Sotho, etc. We all say we are Africans. Nationalism made us say this and this is

far from tribalism. It is nationalism which will carry us forward. We are against nobody. We demand freedom. We cannot forget our history [reference to tribal wars—translation unclear]—we cannot pretend this did not happen. This is an African land. We were born here. This is our national heritage. After freedom, whoever will stay will enjoy human rights. There will be no *baas* [master] here. Other nationalists will respect us when we are a united group.[35]

This exchange was then followed by a protracted disagreement over which delegates were accredited and which were not, because in a large number of cases rival groups claimed to represent their respective branches. Eventually the officials on the rostrum ordained that the next day's programme would be open to properly accredited delegates only. On the following day, however, the entrance to the Orlando Community Hall was picketed by a large band of loyalist 'Freedom Volunteers', a hundred or so young men, many of them carrying wooden clubs or metal bars. A similarly equipped group of Africanists found their passage into the hall blocked. A specially elected credentials committee had been chosen at the end of the previous night's proceedings, after several of the key Africanists had left the hall. Africanists believed that because they had dominated in the rhetorical exchanges that had continued through the day they had succeeded in winning over most of the people present in the hall. The journalist Benjamin Pogrund was present, covering the meeting for *Contact* and his employer, the *Rand Daily Mail*. Pogrund was not unsympathetic to the Africanists but he felt that the concerted aggression the Africanists directed at the platform merely antagonized most delegates. 'My purely subjective impression', Pogrund conceded, 'was that the Africanists lost more in debate than they gained.'[36]

At midday the credentials committee was ready to announce its findings as to which delegates were properly accredited. Most of the Africanist representatives found themselves excluded. After a tense standoff, the Africanist group walked away, leaders telling those journalists in attendance that they were seceding from the organization 'as custodians of the ANC policy as it was formulated in 1912 and pursued up to the time of the Congress Alliance'.

A few weeks later Africanist groups broke away in the Cape and Natal provincial organizations. The Natal faction was very small indeed partly because of the provincial popularity of Chief Luthuli. In Cape Town two groups claimed executive authority: they had jostled for influence through 1958 and here as we shall see later the Africanists succeeded in winning over a substantial following in the branches around the city though not so much in the outlying areas where local ANC organization was well integrated with the Food and Canning Workers' Union activity.

On 6 April 1959, once again the Africanists assembled at Orlando's Community Hall, this time to hold their founding convention as a new political organization, the Pan-Africanist Congress. The date was chosen, intentionally, to coincide with Van Riebeeck's Day, the anniversary of 'the arrival in South Africa of the first group of settlers'. The opening preliminaries included an address from the Reverend Walter Dimba, leader of a federation of independent African churches who reminded his listeners about 'a black man, Simon of Arabia, who carried Jesus from the cross'[37] and a homily from Reverend N. B. Tantsi:

> In his short sermon, Reverend Mr Tantsi, observing the Special Branch of the South African police around the Orlando community hall . . . equated the birth of the PAC with the birth of Jesus Christ. He said the Special Branch was taking the role of Herod, the Tetrach of Judea who ordered the murder of all infants and babies, hoping to murder Jesus after the wise men from the East had inquired from him where the king who would restore the house of David would be born.[38]

These theological preliminaries were followed with the reading out of telegrams from Kwame Nkrumah and Sekou Toure, an impressive signal triumph for the PAC, for no other South African organization had hitherto solicited such courtesies from African statesmen. Subsequently, the meeting adopted a constitution, a manifesto, and a disciplinary code and elected its first national executive committee. Predictably enough, delegates chose Potlake Leballo as the movement's new organizational secretary but to the surprise of journalists in attendance, they turned down the presidential candidature of Josias Madzunya and opted instead to vote unanimously for a hitherto relatively unknown figure, Robert Sobukwe. To insiders present, though, Sobukwe was an obvious choice for the presidential position. Indeed Potlake Leballo had nominated him. Leballo later explained 'that he realized the need for an intellectual for the post of party president, and he made sure that he himself was not put forward when nomination time came'.[39] Robert Sobukwe would impress his personality profoundly on the new movement's early history and for this reason his background merits exploration in some detail.

Robert Mangaliso ('It is wonderful') Sobukwe was born in 1924 in Graaff-Reinet where 'even the dogs bark in Afrikaans',[40] one of four surviving children of the household of Hubert Sobukwe, a municipal labourer and part-time woodcutter. His mother cooked for the local hospital and also worked as a domestic servant. His father was Sesotho-speaking, whereas Angelina Sobukwe was Mpondo. Notwithstanding the strong Christian ethos of the Sobukwes' home—Hubert was a conspicuous local Method-ist—Robert underwent 'tribal initiation ceremonies':[41] circumcision and three weeks in the bush smeared with ochre-coloured clay. In 1940, two years after outgrowing the local primary schools, Robert enrolled at the Healdtown Institute, the biggest Methodist school in South Africa. Here Sobukwe encountered sympathetic teachers. In one interview he remem-bered a Mrs Scott 'who encouraged my reading' and helped to instill within him 'a love of literature, especially poetry and drama'.[42] He spent six years at Healdtown, rising to be head boy, distinguishing himself according to fellow students for 'his brilliance and command of the English language',[43] surviv-ing an attack of tuberculosis, and securing financial support from bursaries and the private generosity of Healdtown's headmaster George Caley.

His matriculation and entry to university at the age of twenty-two con-solidated a remarkable record of family achievement. The Sobukwes were poor—they celebrated Christmas with a new suit of clothes for each child, the only ones they purchased through the year. Angelina could not read but she brought back home cast-off books from her employers and joined her husband in encouraging their children to obtain the education that had been denied to them. When Robert began attending high school he became one of less than 6,000 African secondary school students nationwide. All three Sobukwe brothers graduated from high school and the oldest, Ernest, went on to train as a priest and later was ordained as a Methodist bishop.

Robert Sobukwe began his studies at Fort Hare in 1947. For the first year he concentrated on his books, sustaining a reputation for zealous good conduct, which he had earned as a Healdtown prefect by lying on the roof to catch junior pupils urinating in the open. From the days of his enrolment, though, he was assertively independent-minded and resistant to the corporate culture of the institution. At a 'Fresher's Social' he delivered what he later called a 'venomous attack' on the group camaraderie fostered by the college's halls of residence, what Sobukwe termed 'its aggravated spirit of hostelism and the un-intellectual nature of discussion'. Incensed senior students decreed that he should be 'sent to Coventry' for a month.[44] In his second year, though, prompted by a course on native administration, a growing consciousness of racial discrimination 'of which he was a victim only in his mid-20s',[45] and the influence of one of his teachers, Cecil Ntloko, a follower of the All African Convention (AAC), Sobukwe became more engaged politically, helping to prepare a daily commentary on current issues, called 'Beware'; its favourite topic was 'non collaboration'.

At that stage, the AAC was considered 'more advanced in thought'[46] by Fort Hare students than the African National Congress. The initiative to start a branch of the ANC Youth League was taken in August 1948 by Godfrey Pitje, a lecturer in the Department of African Studies. Sobukwe and his classmates were at first sceptical and had to be urged to become founder members; for them the ANC was compromised by its continuing participation in the Native Representative Council and the township Advisory Boards. Sobukwe rapidly attracted the attention of more senior Youth Leaguers, beginning in 1948 a regular correspondence with the CYL's president, A. P. Mda. He also 'read all that was available on Africa', supplementing the library's resources by subscribing to Nnamdi Azikiwe's *West African Pilot*.[47] At Fort Hare, the League seems mainly to have functioned as a discussion club though it played a significant role in the lobbying leading up to the ANC's adoption of Mda's militant Programme of Action at its 1949 national conference. In Pitje's words, Sobukwe 'towered over' his peers and mentors alike; some of the intellectual grounds for his ascendancy are evident in the text of an extraordinary speech Sobukwe made as outgoing Student Representative Council (SRC) president at the 1949 'Completers' Social'.

The speech was 'quoted for years by students'[48] and in the context of its time it was remarkable, anticipating the political perceptions and rhetoric of several successive generations. It included a closely argued critique of liberal gradualism: 'if you see any signs of "broadmindedness" or "reasonableness" in us, or if you hear us talk of practical experience as a modifier of man's views, denounce us as traitors'. Its depiction of 'the second rape of Africa' by 'financial and economic imperialism under the guise of a tempting slogan, 'the development of backward areas and people'[49] was also of a different order of sophistication to most of the anti-colonial polemics then in vogue. As his friend and biographer Benjamin Pogrund observes, the speech 'contained much of what was to be Sobukwe's later political philosophy'.[50] Above all it emphasized the transcendent power of ideas, whether in constructing social identity—for example, Europeans and other 'minorities' could secure 'mental and spiritual freedom' in South Africa by learning to breath, dream, and live Africa—or in mobilizing popular revolt—'show the light and the masses will find the way'.

For Sobukwe, the 'choice' of an appropriate 'ideology' by leadership was the key to building an effective political movement—then and later he was demonstrably unconcerned with the more technical and pragmatic considerations of activism and organization. Revealingly, when the nurses at nearby Victoria Hospital went on strike and Fort Hare students began raising support, Sobukwe, then SRC president, remained aloof at first: 'He said he was busy with his studies.' His fellow students 'had to persuade him that the nurses were his sisters and he had a duty to help them . . . for days he remained with his books'.[51] The speech confirmed Sobukwe's rising reputation 'as a major standard bearer for African nationalism':[52] in December 1949 Sobukwe was selected by Godfrey Pitje as the Youth League's national secretary. The 1949 speech was one of several incidents that persuaded the college authorities to ban the Youth League at Fort Hare, another was a protest connected to the nurses' strike. As Godfrey Pitje reported in a letter to Jordan Ngubane dated 9 November 1949: 'The European staff . . . is altogether opposed to the League . . . even when a student who is not a Leaguer . . . cheeks a member of staff or a warden, his cheekiness is attributed to the influence of the League.' In the same letter, Pitje praised Sobukwe as 'by far the most brilliant fellow we have at college at the moment'.[53]

With the inception of the new decade, though, Sobukwe withdrew to the political margins; accepting a teaching post in Standerton and appearing as a lay preacher at the Methodist church,[54] and under his and Pitje's stewardship the League stagnated. He remained on the sidelines during the Defiance Campaign, though he courageously put his teaching job in jeopardy by addressing a public meeting convened by the local ANC branch of which he was secretary, offering his listeners a revisionist interpretation of the great Xhosa cattle killing in which George Grey 'through his agents . . . deceived Africans into killing their animals'.[55] Otherwise his public activities were confined to writing articles for a cyclostyled newsletter distributed by the East London 'Bureau of African Nationalism'. He was critical of the Defiance Campaign, dismissing it as a 'communist stunt', professing distrust of its intentions because African Nationalists 'had not had a hand in planning it and the decision-making was not theirs'.[56]

Two years later, Sobukwe married Victoria Mathe, one of the nurses who had participated in the Victoria Hospital strike, and moved to Johannesburg to take up a post at the University of the Witwatersrand as a Zulu language instructor on a salary of £550 a year.[57] In the course of his work at Wits he also completed an honours dissertation, an analysis of Xhosa riddles, later published in *African Studies*.[58] In Soweto, he joined the Mofolo branch of the ANC and cautiously emerged 'from the hibernation of Standerton',[59] writing articles for the *Africanist*, a bulletin issued from neighbouring Orlando by disgruntled members of the Youth League. Sobukwe published his contributions under a pseudonym as was common practice with Africanist contributors, most of whom were teachers and therefore barred by the authorities from participation in the ANC. Sobukwe had a different reason for discretion; he believed that if his views were known publicly, Communists might seek his dismissal from his university post. To Benjamin Pogrund, who first met Sobukwe in late 1957, this fear seemed 'far-fetched', though 'it did indicate the depth of anxiety among those in the ANC who were opposed to communists'.[60] In fact, if anything, Sobukwe's antipathy to Communists would have been a commendation to his employers had they known his views. And Sobukwe's first-hand experience of Communists within the ANC could not have been extensive; during this time he was not a vigorous participant in the ANC's activities preferring, as even his friends noted, to 'remain behind the scenes; being at the university he found it difficult to get in touch with people'.[61] His antipathy to Communists was in any case philosophical and shaped by his reading: predictably enough George Padmore's *Pan-Africanism or Communism* was for him a formative authority[62] though he also included Arthur Koestler among his favourite authors.[63] Though he shared the Africanist conviction that Communists subverted the ANC and 'diluted' the force of its nationalist inspiration he was also opposed to Communism 'as a creed, believing it to bear its own oppression'.

The leadership crisis in 1958 within the Transvaal ANC persuaded Sobukwe to abandon circumspection; he played a central role in the Africanists' efforts to take over the provincial proceedings though privately he doubted the likelihood of their succeeding. The Africanists had anticipated a violent rupture at this meeting and in the days before the meeting conspiratorial rumours helped to ratchet up their excited expectations. Sobukwe's own recollections reflect the exaggerated sense of drama with which the Africanists perceived their conflict with the ANC leadership; Sobukwe himself was certain that Oliver Tambo and his colleagues had assigned killers to three of the leading dissenters.[64] In fact, gently predisposed Tambo was hardly the personality who would have sanctioned any such assignment, though as we have seen ANC leaders were quite ready to use strong-arm tactics to exclude the Africanists from a meeting at which they might well have succeeded in winning leadership positions. When the

Africanists were forced to withdraw, it was Sobukwe who drafted the letter that announced their 'parting of the ways' and in the weeks that followed the secession he would exercise a predominant influence in the way the new movement would formally define its purpose and character.

★

At their inaugural conference, as well as electing their main leaders, the Pan-Africanists adopted a manifesto, a constitution, and a disciplinary code. Robert Sobukwe delivered an address in which he presented a fluent condensation of the PAC's politics.

Sobukwe began his oration by noting that he and his audience were 'living today in an era pregnant with untold possibilities for good and evil'. However, he noted, 'amazing discoveries in the fields of medicine, science, and physics' notwithstanding, mankind's progress was threatened by its inability 'to solve the problem of social relations'. 'We see the world split today into two large hostile blocks', Sobukwe continued. So the question arose, where should Africa fit into this picture? 'Our answer', Sobukwe insisted, was readily available in the words of Africa's leaders. Africa should embrace Nkrumah's policy of 'positive neutrality', borrowing the best from East and West and rejecting the excesses of both, while maintaining 'our distinctive personality'. The days of independent small countries were over. To assert their independent and distinctive personality, Africans needed to unite: 'We regard it as the sacred duty of every African state to strive ceaselessly and energetically for the creation of a United States of Africa, striving from the Cape to Cairo, Morocco to Madagascar.' In South Africa, Pan-Africanists should 'admire, bless and identify ourselves with the entire nationalist movement in Africa'. 'Africanists', Sobukwe declared:

> ... do not all subscribe to the fashionable doctrine of South African excep-tionalism. Our contention is that South Africa is an integral part of the indivisible whole that is Afrika. She cannot solve her problems in isolation from and with utter disregard of the rest of the continent.

Within South Africa, white supremacy prevented the establishment of true democracy, not just within its own borders by throughout the continent, given the indivisibility of Africa's peoples. South African politics was complicated by the existence of 'national groups which are the result of geographical origin'. There were three such groups—Europeans, a foreign minority, Indians, an oppressed minority but led by a 'merchant class' that

'identifies itself by and large with the oppressor', and Africans, 'the indigenous group'. Coloured people were also Africans, Sobukwe believed, a
position that would not be understood by all his followers. Accordingly, it
was the 'illiterate and semi-literate African masses' that constituted 'the key
and centre of any struggle for true democracy'. And these people, Sobukwe
maintained, could 'be organized only under the banner of African nationalism
in an All-African Organization where they themselves formulate policies and
programmes without interference from either so-called left-wing or right-
wing groups of the minorities'. The Pan-Africanists were not racists, though.
'In our vocabulary', Sobukwe explained, 'the word "race" as applied to man
has no plural form'. In a democratic South Africa, all would be free, 'the
European included', everybody would have equal rights of citizenship.
Indeed all citizens would be considered as Africans, for be an African would
be anyone 'who owes his only loyalty to Afrika and who is prepared to accept
the democratic rule of an African majority'.[65]

The PAC's manifesto presented a more elaborate version of these arguments and it also included a much more sharply worded attack on the ANC,
whose leadership, it argued had been 'captured'. This 'captured' leadership
claimed to be fighting for freedom, but in fact it was 'tooth and nail against
the Africans gaining effective control of their country'. 'Charterists' were
'fighting for the maintenance of the status quo . . . for the "constitutional
guarantees" or "national rights" for our alien nationals.' Meanwhile, in line
with the Pan-Africanist characterization of itself as a force for African self-
determination, a 'Disciplinary Code' committed the PAC's members to 'a
struggle in this country for national independence'. In a 'democratic cen-
tralist' system of leadership, the president would wield 'unquestioned
power' in enacting decisions 'democratically arrived at'. As we shall see,
this explicit commitment to centralized executive authority would have
important consequences. Further buttressing the president's power was an
oath of allegiance to the leadership that new members had to pledge
themselves which included acceptance of 'death as a punishment' if they
failed to honour its undertakings.[66]

Both Sobukwe's address and the PAC's foundation protocols represented
the new movement's ideas in a much more intellectually systematic way
than any earlier attempts to summarize its arguments. This sort of exposition
certainly enhanced its attractions for the educated intelligentsia from
which the PAC drew so many of its leaders, providing a reassuring tone
of dispassionate restraint. This was intentional. Pan-Africanists, their code

commanded, 'should be armed with theory', capable of 'vanquish[ing] the other man with arguments, and not with a knuckleduster.' Robert Sobukwe in particular was keen to refute the view 'that the Africanists were a wild "cowboy" crew, undisciplined and confused',[67] an impression that was fostered by media emphasis on the more excitable language used in public by many of the Africanists, including Josias Madzunya, characterized by the Communist-edited New Age as the 'wild man of the Africanist group'.[68] Madzunya 'didn't grasp the full import of our philosophy', Sobukwe recalled in 1970, 'His thinking was rather primitive—he wanted to put spears and shields on our flag.'[69] Gerhart suggests that for well-educated Africans, though many might in their day to day life speak or think in very similar ways to more racially aggressive Pan-Africanists, they rather expected public personalities to behave in a more restrained and decorous fashion than people in their private everyday lives. Indeed, the PAC's leadership code devoted an entire section to 'Personal Habits', enjoining members to 'maintain an exemplary standard of cleanliness', to keep appointments punctually, and to 'show a true respect for African womanhood and demonstrate in practice the theory of sex equality'. In a letter to the writer Bessie Head, written in 1972, Robert Sobukwe conceded that when the PAC was established, 'many of our intellectuals' were 'sceptical of the Africanists', not least because of the arguments 'we propounded, which, I admit, did have some racialist undertones then'.[70]

At this stage the PAC was unwilling to jettison its prospects of support from 'respectable' middle-class Africans, nor did it want to alienate possible external allies. In general the leaders it elected at its foundation meeting embodied an 'educated elite'.[71] A decade or so later, Peter Molotsi recalled in an interview with Gail Gerhart a discussion among the PAC leaders about whether their new organization should embrace calls to 'drive the white man into the sea'. People 'liked it privately', he remembered, 'but we didn't want it to go down on paper'. In any case, it would have attracted attention, 'the police would come in' and 'we would have been destroyed in a day'.[72] The conversations within Molotsi's social circle may not have been very representative of beliefs within the wider milieu of the 'respectable' community. Gerhart's contention that conciliatory racial attitudes reflected prevalent public norms among middle-class Africans are supported by the findings from a pioneering effort to solicit African public opinion. In November 1960 Teddy Brett undertook a survey for the Institute of Race Relations, interviewing a cross-section of Africans with a middle-class background, 150 in all, professionals, ministers, teachers, clerks, and students at university and high school. He found that of his sample, the largest share, eighty-six, 'felt they would like to see a community developing in South Africa in which all races would be able to live in an equal basis'. He probed this issue further to ensure that members of this group were not merely voicing 'pious protestations' but concluded that his respondents held these views sincerely. When it came to political affiliations, amongst this sample, the same proportion favoured the PAC, though Brett also found that the PAC supporters included the small minority of his respondents who felt that the prospects for racial harmony were unlikely and even undesirable, so that, as one teacher expressed it, 'the majority who are African, should be above'.[73] In reasoning their position, PAC leaders tended to settle for a logical compromise. As Mlami Makwetu, a prominent Cape Town Africanist explained, 'we accept the concept of one human race' but this acceptance did not require 'sacrificing our birthright to Africa'.[74]

So, the Pan-Africanists had to maintain a balance between keeping a degree of genteel respectability while continuing to project messages that would appeal to a more down-to-earth constituency among the 'illiterate and semi-literate African masses'. As Sobukwe observed at the beginning of 1959, 'In every struggle, whether national or class, the masses do not fight an abstraction. They do not hate oppression or capitalism.' Instead, 'they concretize these and hate the oppressor ... in South Africa, the white man'. Sobukwe believed optimistically that in a free society, there would be no longer any reason for such hatred[75] and generally Sobukwe himself avoided using language that 'concretized' such antipathies. For the time being, though, even for PAC leaders who may not have shared such feelings, 'anti-white' sentiment was politically and morally compelling, an emotional base for mass political assertion too potent to repudiate. The PAC's slogan, *Izwe Lethu*, echoed the words of an old political anthem:

Thina sizwe esintsundu,	We the black nation,
Sikhalela izwe lethu,	We cry for our land,
Elathathwa ngabamhlophe;	Which was taken by the whites
Mabauyeke umhlaba wethu.	Let them leave our land.
Abantwana be-Afrika,	The children of Africa,
Bakhalela izwe labo,	Cry for their land,
Elathatthwa ngabamhlophe,	Which was taken by the whites
Mabauyeke umhlaba wethu.	Let them leave our land.[76]

As Gail Gerhart has shown, the language used by the PAC in their public meetings was generally of the kind that accorded with the masses' 'concretizing' predispositions. 'There is no room for Europeans in Africa' a PAC speaker announced to a crowd in Nyanga, outside Cape Town. In Naledi near Johannesburg, a PAC orator told his listeners that 'I want the Europeans to become our boys, and they will be our boys from next year.' When Potlake Leballo visited Naledi, he had no inhibitions in castigating 'White foreign dogs in our continent.' 'The white people must surrender to the rule of Africa by the Africans', he added. In a similar vein, Josias Madzunya was recorded in Alexandra as telling residents that Nkrumah was deporting whites from Ghana. 'I will demand to be Minister of Justice. I will send all the police to demand the permits from the whites for about two months', he promised.[77]

The PAC's foundation meeting agreed on no specific campaigning activity. The first task, after all, was to build an organized following for the new movement. The code instructed members 'to spread the ideas of our cause':

> .... In the streets, in house to house campaigns, in the trains, in the restaurants, at state functions, cinemas, on the sports fields, at railway platforms, in social gatherings, tea parties, dance parties, in church, in school and at orations by the graveside.[78]

In two areas, in the townships around the steel-making town of Vereeniging, fifty miles south of Johannesburg, and in the Western Cape, there is evidence that members of the original core-group of Africanist dissenters who had broken away from the ANC did indeed try to bring new members into the organization using the opportunities and approaches alluded to in the code. We will be considering the effects of their activities in the next two chapters. Elsewhere, though, there is not much evidence to suggest that the four hundred or so delegates who attended the PAC's founding convention invested much effort in systematic recruitment initiatives. In any case, even by the standards of time, the organization was starved of resources. Robert Sobukwe paid for its rent of rooms in Mylur House, a office building in Jeppe Street and other office expenses out of his own pocket as well as the wages for a part-time stenographer and secretary, William Jolobe, and an allowance to support Leballo's family.[79] Originally the intention was that Leballo would receive a salary of £50 a month but this remained an aspiration. Though the Pan-Africanists managed to raise

£900 from delegate contributions at their foundation convention they were
unable to maintain this level of fundraising subsequently. As national secretary, Potlake Leballo used his Chamber of Commerce scooter to make his
visits to the PAC's branches.[80]

Four months after its foundation, the PAC's national leadership published a
relatively impressive set of membership statistics, well short of the 100,000 that
had been predicted for July in the columns of the *Africanist*, but suggesting a
substantial achievement all the same. The organization claimed a total of 101
branches and a membership of 24,664, more than half of these, 13,324 in forty-
seven branches in the Transvaal and 7,427 in the Cape, 3,612 in Natal, and 301
in the Orange Free State. Such statistics do not tell us very much, though. The
organization's informal support garnered through the widespread press publicity it received or through the mass meetings it held in certain centres may
well have been much wider. On the other hand, the figures probably represented overestimates of committed disciplined membership: nothing like the
nearly fifty branches with on average each of 300 members claimed here was
going to be in evidence in the PAC's subsequent activism. Robert Sobukwe
himself told the journalist Benjamin Pogrund in September 1959 that the
membership included 'a certain amount of dead wood' and they were finding
it difficult to collect monthly subscriptions.[81] When asked about membership
in the Western Cape, the regional secretary, Philip Kgosana, estimated that it
was around 950, this being one of the PAC's strongest centres.[82]

In Natal, while the PAC may have had several thousand names on their
membership lists in 1959, in the run up to their inaugural meeting they
found it difficult to fill a hall for a public meeting addressed by Madzunya.
On this occasion Pan-Africanists were outnumbered by ANC members and
Madzunya, still wearing his trademark overcoat despite the Durban heat,
was shouted down halfway through his denunciation of Congress multi-
racialism as 'multiplied racialism'. After the local Special Branch man,
Detective Sergeant Swanepoel, had failed to restore order by calling for
calm, SACTU's Moses Mabhida seized the microphone and silenced the
hall.[83] Sergeant Swanepoel had beeen monitoring the local Pan-Africanists:
while Abednego Ngcobo was confident they had a local following of 2,000,
according to Swanepoel 'You could tell they weren't going to be much
trouble—there were only about 20–25 of them.' He felt he could speak
with authority for he knew them well: 'one of their top local people was an
ex-Special Branch black cop'.[84]

What is true is that in certain centres, the Pan-Africanists had emerged as a popularly influential group. In the freehold township of Alexandra, north of Johannesburg, traditionally a key centre of African militant working-class politics, local ANC leaders later conceded that Josias Madzunya was 'a very powerful leader...a powerful public speaker...a simple type, not the sophisticated urban type', with a appeal 'not just to the younger generation, but the ordinary man in the street'.[85] Through 1956 and 1957, in Alexandra the Africanists were capable of filling a square with their public meetings, preventing the 'Charterist' ANC from assembling in their favourite venues. Indeed the PAC's evident reluctance to include Josias Madzunya in their leadership prompted a rift between the Alexandra Africanists and the new organization that would detach from it a significant number of potential supporters.

Aside from their own attempts to build a membership-based organization, the Pan-Africanists also sought to extend their influence less directly through seeking trade union affiliation. Among the personalities elected to its first executive was an experienced trade unionist, Jacob Nyaose, the secretary of the African Bakers' and Confectioners' Union. In October 1959, Nyaose announced the formation of a new trade union grouping, the Federation of Free African Trade Unions of South Africa (FOFATUSA). Nyaose's trade union experience dated back to the Second World War in which he led a baking workers' strike and subsequently represented his union at wage board hearings. At various points between 1942 and 1951 he was elected to serve terms as secretary-general of the Council for Non-European Trade Unions, SACTU's predecessor. FOFATUSA's eighteen affiliates included a group of quite well established unions including the Bakers' and Confectioners', the Laundry Workers', and the African women's section of the Garment Workers' Union. The Bakers' Union was strong enough to secure a closed shop agreement with employers in 1948: an unusual achievement for an African union.[86] Most of the unions had belonged to SACTU but disaffiliated in 1958 after objecting to the 1958 strike call. Many of the trade unions' officials who were to constitute FOFATUSA also opposed SACTU's links with the left-wing World Federation of Trade Unions. Jacob Nyaose claimed that FOFATUSA was loyal to the PAC but this was not a view that was shared by all the leaders of the affiliates. Lucy Mvubelo, the Garment Workers' secretary had a general objection to any party political affiliations and as far as she was concerned FOFATUSA 'was never a movement of any political organization'. She resisted Nyaose's proposal that the unions should merge their bank accounts and that 'we should educate our members to take part in demonstrations'.[87] Indeed there were strong incentives for the FOFATUSA unions not to embrace political affiliation with the PAC for they had been promised £31,000 by the International Confederation of Free Trade Unions (ICFTU) provided they began working more closely with the ANC-linked South African Congress of Trade Unions, a condition that would be very difficult for an active ally of the Pan-Africanists to fulfill.[88] Jacob Nyaose, though, succeeded in convincing his fellow PAC executive members and, possibly himself, that they could count upon the support of FOFATUSA affiliates. As far as he concerned 'When he joined [the PAC], FOFATUSA became part of the PAC.'[89]

Robert Sobukwe's inclination was to build a following through activism and through inspirational behaviour from leadership. 'Show the light and the masses will find a way', he had assured the outgoing students at Fort Hare in 1949. His own understanding of the shape such a programme of public education would assume was very much to the fore in his proposal for a 'status campaign', which he proposed at a meeting that the PAC held at the beginning of August 1959 for 'Heroes' Day', the anniversary of Anton Lembede's death. Sobukwe was convinced that a prolonged process of preparatory 'nation-building' was necessary before the PAC could hope to summon large groups of followers in a confrontation with the authorities. Sobukwe envisaged that a succession of consumer boycotts that targeted enterprises whose staff habitually treated African customers abruptly or rudely would attract publicity and augment popular political confidence, while at the same time such a venture would not represent the kind of threat to public order that would attract official repression. The project was to be directed at overcoming individually internalized feelings of racial inferiority that Sobukwe and other leaders believed were such an important brake on protest mobilization.[90] However, though PAC warnings to businesses that they would mount pickets or boycotts if African customers continued to be treated badly attracted press publicity there is no record of any serious effort to follow these warnings with any activism. Within the ranks of the PAC's committed following, the young men who constituted its activist community clearly had little enthusiasm for what Sobukwe envisaged as a low-key patient process of instilling politically assertive inclinations among people hitherto unaffected by organized campaigning.

Instead of a process of carefully phased 'consciousness-raising', the PAC decided on a more dramatic course. On 15 September, national PAC leaders held an executive meeting in Bloemfontein, midway between the two concentrations of the movement's support in the Transvaal and in the Western Cape. Here they agreed to propose a campaign against the pass laws to the upcoming national conference in December in Johannesburg. Between the September meeting of the executive and their national conference, PAC leaders helped raise expectations by telling journalists that they were drafting plans for 'positive action'. By the time delegates representing 153 branches and 31,053 members[91] assembled, Sobukwe himself seems to have set aside his original rationale for embarking on a low-risk preparatory venture. After listening to complaints from the floor about inaction, the PAC president asked for support for a mandate to launch a 'decisive final' action against passes. Not surprisingly, he received an overwhelming endorsement. Delegates agreed, though, that they would need to undertake 'intensive organization', so as to 'get the nation ready for action at the very earliest time'. Leadership would announce their call to action, 'at any moment, as from now', without any further consultation. The PAC would remain committed to the status campaign—Leballo actually circulated a memo to employers on 25 January telling them to address Africans by 'their proper aboriginal name' or face a 'total boycott',[92] but now the action against the pass laws would be assigned 'top priority'.[93]

The ANC also had plans for a pass campaign and it announced these at its annual conference, ten days after the PAC's. As we have noted it had in fact been committed to an anti-pass initiative since its curtailment of the women's protests in 1958. The ANC chose 31 March as the day on which it would open the first phase of its campaign. Its conception was for a programme that would begin with demonstrative kinds of protest and which would only later engage with the authorities in civil disobedience and labour stay-aways. The Pan-Africanists' proposals for 'positive action' therefore were partly shaped by an immediate political necessity to outbid the ANC[94] but in a more profound way their decision to embrace action was shaped by their more generalized understanding of the political environment in which they lived and worked.

How detailed a conception of their campaign Robert Sobukwe and the other leaders had developed in December is not clear. By February, though, they were ready to discuss their strategic intentions publicly. The immediate aim was to achieve the abolition of the pass laws and to secure a minimum wage of £35 a month. On the chosen day, African men should leave their passes at home and surrender themselves for arrest at police stations. Women would not actively participate, Sobukwe decreed; later they would be assigned 'their historic role' but for the time being, 'they must see to it that all men go to jail'. The organization's leadership would be in the forefront of this civil disobedience: they would be the first to present themselves for arrest. After their arrest they would engage no defence lawyers nor would they take out bail nor would they pay fines as an alternative to imprisonment, they resolved. As part of their preparations for the campaign, organizers should prepare subordinate layers of leaders at every level to replace those under arrest. The anti-pass campaigning would be strictly non-violent, Sobukwe emphasized in his public addresses. However, positive action would continue after the abolition of passes. It would be an 'unfolding programme', Sobukwe predicted, though even quite senior leaders inter-viewed nearly ten years later remained vague as to what would have been the next steps after Pan-Africanists had secured the abolition of the passes.[95] The programme, 'a never ending stream' of militant campaigning, would ulti-mately lead to a major confrontation with the South African authorities— what kind was never clearly specified—that would result in a change of regime, 'independence', as Sobukwe put it. This climatic final phase would begin after a three-year-long struggle. 'In 1960 we take our first step', a PAC circular announced, 'in 1963 our last'.[96] The date echoed a call by the 1958 All African People's Conference in Accra for continental freedom by 1963.

This longer-term perspective was widely understood among rank and file activists. Aubrey Mokoape was a sixteen-year-old schoolboy when he joined the PAC. Interviewed in 1984 he remembered that 'basically as I understood the plan and identified with it':

> ... it would bring the country to a halt, that we would have large numbers of people surrendering themselves to prisons and that the effect of this would be to clog the legal machinery, secondly, perhaps in an indirect way, to bring industry to a halt ... Actually what we foresaw was numbers upon numbers, day after day, continuing to do this.[97]

So, public statements by PAC leaders and the texts of their leaflets suggested that their movement would achieve 'independence' by 1963. At a certain stage, they predicted, repression by the authorities might engender violent insurgency. In the initial phases of positive action, though, Sobukwe be-lieved, any public advocacy of violence would alienate potential support as well as of course exposing their still vulnerable organization to police action. In fact, even privately it seems, Pan-Africanist leaders did not engage in any serious strategic discussion about the use of violence against the authorities. The Trotskyite, Baruch Hirson, then a disaffected member of the Congress of Democrats later recorded in his autobiography a meeting of PAC members that was arranged at his home in Johannesburg in mid-1959:

> The group of men who arrived were introduced as the Central Committee. With them were a (white) and woman whose names I did not know. Discussion followed on PAC policy and I questioned them on a number of issues. One point became prominent. After they agreed that they wanted to take over the state, I asked them how they were going to win over the army or at least neutralize it. I also suggested that their declaration that Africans must rule would give the white army little inducement to stay neutral (if they could be won over at all). There was no answer. The PAC had not considered the question, and obviously knew little about the role of the army at times of unrest. It was late and they had to go.[98]

Benjamin Pogrund wrote a slightly different report on this meeting. In his version, after the discussion of how the PAC would deal with the South African military, Baruch Hirson then 'pointed out that in any event a change in South Africa's society by military means was out of the question. This sort of thing went out with the French revolution.' At this stage, Myrtle Berman, one of the other whites present and named in Pogrund's report, observed 'that economic pressure was the only answer, but even then, one would have to face the possibility of the authorities deliberately seeking opportunities to cause violence'.[99]

Certain PAC leaders did make casual references to the inevitability of violence but Sobukwe both at the time and later acknowledged that in 1960, black South Africans were not 'in any position to launch violence or that our people were prepared for it'. Sobukwe was critical of non–violent passive resistance but he drew a distinction between primarily demonstrative passive resistance as it had been deployed in the past in South Africa and what he called 'the potential power of massive non–collaboration'. As he admitted ten years later, 'I sincerely believed that determined non-collaboration could do the job, since the whole economy rests upon us.'[100] Just how massive such non–collaboration should be before it could achieve major administrative disruptions Sobukwe did not explain. According to Potlake Leballo, Sobukwe did not think that at this stage the PAC should actively prepare for violence. The issue seems to have arisen when the Pan-

Africanist leaders met in Bloemfontein, in September 1959. As Leballo recalled:

> ... at the meeting some of us felt that we should engage ourselves in violence. We should collect as many weapons as we can, and it should be the beginning of a violent struggle. But the president and a few others also had a view that we were not yet prepared for a violent struggle, for an armed struggle. It would take us a long time before we can reassert the minds of our people to make them understand that the regime there of the white man, really the white man was nothing insofar as we were concerned. It was just another ordinary human being like ourselves. And so we felt that, however, the question of armed struggle should not be completely excluded, but this should not be the basis from which we start. That's right.[101]

Leballo himself was much readier to embrace the likelihood of violence. Indeed, he told Gerhart, it was he that proposed 'the idea of violence' at the Bloemfontein meeting, prompted, he said, 'because I was more in contact with the youth myself'. Gerhart also interviewed others present at this meeting and they suggest that Leballo's account was very exaggerated, though there may have been some loose talk of 'fighting' the 'enemy'.[102] Pan-Africanists habitually used heroic apocalyptic language. For example, a regional conference in Cape Town in January 1960 included in its agenda items the issue of whether 'individual leaders' were ready 'to sacrifice when the hour of death struck'.[103] The PAC's most zealous followers would have probably shared Leballo's perceptions. Ten years later Leballo claimed that he believed in 1960 that an armed insurgency would encounter much less resistance than might be supposed: 'Historically, we know the Boers, how they are. They are outwardly become so strong and terrifying, and yet we know inwardly they are weak. And therefore we felt that at the time when we would be taking an armed—taking arms—it would not take us very long.'[104]

Elliot Magwentshu, in 1960 a member of the Western Cape PAC's regional executive, has supplied the most detailed recollection of how PAC principals understood the likely trajectory of their campaigning. In 1970 he told Gail Gerhart that when the Cape Town leaders met Sobukwe and Leballo in mid-February 1960, they extracted from their visitors 'some explanation of what would take place first, and so on':

> We had been told that the first campaign would be that of going to surrender ourselves to the police and be locked up if the government decides to lock us up; and that this alone in the process would bring the government down, if it is properly organized. Because if the African people can completely stop going

to work, whether they are in prison or outside prison, this would force the government to come to some terms with the African people. If the government decides to proceed, which we thought they didn't have a chance of doing so, if they just felt to proceed with white labour and cut us off with an idea that we will starve and decide to go back to work, we felt that during that period when we are out, we will then organize ourselves into small groups that would destroy the bridges, destroy the rails, to make it impossible for their transport to move about. And this would unfold in more actions as the time proceeds ... But [Sobukwe] did make it very clear that they will be very ruthless from the onset, and that we should be prepared for the worst.[105]

A range of considerations helped to convince the Pan-Africanist leaders that 'the power of their example'[106] would engender a massive response to their call for action. First, within their own organization they tended to recruit disproportionately from young men, often unemployed school leavers, who were more likely than their elders to be predisposed in favour of aggressively assertive kinds of political action. Again and again, both in the recollections of PAC leaders and in their claims at the time, they emphasized their success in mobilizing 'the youth'. For example, Selby Ngendane told Benjamin Pogrund in December 1958 that in the Transvaal Africanists' paid up membership after their breakaway from the ANC 'was mainly from the youth'.[107] In certain localities PAC organizers attempted to build influence among *tsotsi* street gangs and indeed claimed successes: in Benoni, for example, a local PAC leader, Abel Chiloane, claimed that he had succeeded in bringing to a halt a turf war between rival groups of youthful gangsters.[108] In later conversations with Benjamin Pogrund, Robert Sobukwe insisted that 'the switch from status campaign to anti-pass campaign' was undertaken by leadership 'in response to direct demands from branches'.[109] Shortly after the conference, Leballo admitted to Pogrund that the main topic in closed sessions of the meeting 'had been criticism from the floor of the executive for lack of action'.[110] At the conference, Benjamin Pogrund noted 'the number of teenagers present— most of them poorly dressed and looking very much like ruffians'. Later he asked Potlake Leballo about them and Leballo told him that the PAC 'especially in the Orlando area had quite a large proportion of teenage members'.[111] Leballo also told Gail Gerhart that delegates at this meeting included 'particularly the youth of the Transvaal ... those who were in boxing clubs, football clubs, and a number of many others, even those they call *tsotsis* [hoodlums]'.[112] When he was interviewed ten years later, Elliot Mfaxa also maintained that the PAC's leadership deliberately directed their appeals at township gangs.[113]

So, it is likely that PAC leaders were faced with demands from their own youthful rank and file to embrace a confrontational strategy. For many of them, given their lack of experience in mounting mass-based protest, it was an easy step to draw general conclusions about the mood of the public from the sentiments they encountered among their own supporters. In Johannesburg, the PAC breakaway in 1959 had drawn well-known public personalities from key centres of militant political activity, not just in Soweto but in the freehold areas of Sophiatown and Alexandra as well. In Sophiatown, Pan-Africanists were led by a former ANC branch chairman, Z. D. Siwisa. In consequence, PAC leaders expected 'the whole of Johannesburg to respond'.[114] Underlying this belief was the confidence the PAC leaders derived from their alliance with FOFATUSA. The Pan-Africanists' principals took this very seriously. After all, Jacob Nyaose was an experienced trade unionist with an impressive record and FOFATUSA included relatively well-organized affiliates. Nyaose was accorded a prominent position in the PAC's hierarchy, grandiosely styled as 'secretary for labour'. Sobukwe believed that FOFATUSA would provide the anti-pass campaign in its opening phase with a disciplined corps of several thousand African workers, particularly along the Witwatersrand, giving the PAC's action a critical mass of support that would inspire wider participation. Meanwhile, Leballo may have also convinced himself that the PAC call would enjoy support among Basuto migrant workers affiliated to the Basuto Congress Party. Later, both he and BCP leaders would claim that the membership of both organizations overlapped,[115] though as we shall see, the evidence for this is weak. Other PAC leaders may have shared Leballo's assumption that they could count on the support of BCP members. Zephania Mothopeng was another former teacher who had worked at the Basuto High School in Maseru and who had also developed a friendship with Ntsu Mokhehle, and Robert Sobukwe himself appeared at the BCP's 1957 Congress as an invited speaker, delivering the opening address.[116]

A decade-long immersion in closed sectarian politics may have also reinforced the PAC leaders' organizational misconceptions. Sobukwe's remarks about 'determined non-collaboration' suggest that he believed that the authorities had never been called upon to arrest really large groups of politically motivated law-breakers. It is true that during the ANC's main effort to organize civil disobedience in the 1950s, the Defiance Campaign, volunteers always presented themselves for arrest in small groups—mass defiance was envisaged only for a later stage of the campaign. But when women protested against the issue of passes in 1958, on one single occasion on 27 October more than 900 intentionally courted arrest under the Criminal Law Amendment Act that prohibited breaking the law for political protest. It was true that the numbers arrested exceeded the local prison's holding capacity but as we shall see, in most centres the Pan-Africanists would struggle to match this number of voluntary law-breakers. Their assignment to women of an only auxiliary role in positive action is also surprising given the recent history of often very bellicose protest by African women to passes and suggests just how insulated from the wider political environment the Africanists had become as a consequence of their preoccupation with their battles with the 'Charterists'.

A final factor influencing the PAC's leadership may have been external sources of direction or inspiration. In general, the Pan-Africanists perceived themselves as constituents of a continental emancipatory movement. As they told their followers, 'we are on the side of history'.[117] Banners at all their major gatherings proclaimed that 'Africa [was] for the Africans, from Cape to Cairo, Morocco to Madagascar'. Even at this early stage, continental authorities may have supplied directives, not just encouragement. Jordan Ngubane, an African Liberal Party member who had become close to the PAC leadership (and who may have joined the organization, the evidence is unclear), claimed in his published memoir that the PAC was under external pressure; that a Ghanaian official who had met PAC leaders had criticized the status campaign as a waste of time.[118] There were contemporary press reports of meetings between PAC people and a Ghanaian diplomat in Lesotho in early 1960[119] and Aloysius Barden, the secretary of Kwame Nkrumah's African Liberation Secretariat was exchanging letters with Sobukwe and Leballo[120] through 1959, though PAC leaders insisted later that the Ghanaians did not actively shape their strategy.[121] What is true, however, is that the Pan-Africanists understood themselves as a constituent in a general tide of liberatory politics that had been sweeping across the African continent a 'Wind of Change' as the British prime minister, Harold Macmillan, had put it in his speech to the South African parliament in January 1960.[122] The manifesto that the Pan-Africanists had adopted at their founding convention devoted nearly half its content to a blow-by-blow narrative of 'the expulsion of the European imperialist exploiters from large tracts of Africa and the emergence of no less than nine sovereign and independent African states'.[123] Kwame Nkrumah's ascent in Ghana certainly supplied an attractive strategic model for the South African Pan-Africanists, as Leballo told Gerhart, that was why

'in our flag, you see it has got the star where Ghana is'.[124] Nkrumah's
Convention People's Party (CPP) split from the genteelly middle class United
Gold Coast Convention in 1949. After only a few months from its formation,
Nkrumah's new party announced a programme of 'positive action', demonstrations that would coincide with a general strike. The government detained
the CPP's leaders, their following expanded massively, and within two
years Nkrumah was released to become chief minister. For the South African
Pan-Africanists, the temptation to draw parallels between this history and a
likely scenario in their own country was irresistible. Like them, Nkrumah
had confronted an older generation of more conservative and more experienced politicians. His calls to action had caught the mood of the unemployed
semi-urbanized 'veranda boys', a hitherto despised political constituency. His
'positive action' had served as the catalyst for the emergence of an insurrectionary movement. A decade later, the wind of change that had swept
Nkrumah into power seemed to be shaping events in South Africa. On the
eve of the Sharpeville massacre, PAC speakers in Cape Town told their
followers that 'even Nkrumah is going to support us in this struggle'. Moreover, 'Macmillan was also here in South Africa. He also saw that things are bad
here.' If the tide of freedom could envelop the rest of Africa, then why not
here, where as everywhere else in Africa, as Macmillan had pointed out 'this
growth of national consciousness is a political fact'. 'We say', the Cape Town
Pan-Africanists insisted, 'in 1963, the new parliament will be opened by
Mr Sobukwe. Tomorrow we will make a history of the New Africa.'[125]

Despite their injunctions for an early campaign, the Orlando-based
leaders did not seem to recognize any immediate necessity for intensive
preparatory work to encourage wider participation in their 'positive action'
beyond their own committed adherents. Robert Sobukwe himself on the
day the conference ended travelled with his daughter to visit his family in
Graaff-Rienet, a long overdue domestic obligation, apparently, remaining at
his parents' house for the next three weeks.[126] Serious organizational work
began only after the Christmas holiday when Potlake Leballo convened a
workshop to train members of a Task Force that the PAC would deploy as
grass-roots mobilizers. The five day 'seminar' between 5-10 January was
held at the Donaldson Community Centre in Orlando and attended by 230
or so activists, chosen by the regions and branches, 'the best militant fellows
or good organizers', three or four from each branch, Leballo told Gail
Gerhart later. Most probably came from the Transvaal, for the PAC headquarters could not afford to pay transport costs for such a large assembly, the

branches had to pay. How much practical instruction they received is unclear: Leballo's recollections suggest that the fellows received 'indoctrination' mainly, 'so that there should be no deviation'. Their assigned duties, though, would be mainly organizational. A key priority was to communicate the PAC's intentions to the public. In certain centres, the PAC was able to hold mass meetings but even so leaders emphasized the necessity of door-to-door canvassing though the extent to which this happened was very uneven. The PAC leaders prepared texts for four leaflets. The intention was to produce 400,000, for house-to-house distribution. Jordan Ngubane undertook to have the leaflets printed in Durban but he failed to keep his word. Apparently Robert Sobukwe had intended to launch the pass campaign on 7 March but had to postpone after it became clear the leaflets would not arrive from Natal.[127] Instead the Pan-Africanists had to make do with home-made versions cranked out on the Gestetner roneo machine now installed on Potlake Leballo's kitchen table. Press reports do suggest that these roneod flyers circulated quite widely, though, and moreover, that they were available in several African languages.[128]

Meanwhile, in mid-February, Robert Sobuwke and Potlake Leballo embarked on a national tour, accompanied by Howard Ngcobo, the only national executive member who owned a motor vehicle, in this case an aged Volkswagen Kombi bus. The purpose was partly to elicit public enthusiasm for the impending campaign—they hoped that large crowds would greet their arrival in each centre. They also needed to hold discussions with regional leaders: for an organization without access to telephones such face-to-face communication was indispensable. As we shall see, they were not disappointed by the reception they encountered in Cape Town but events in East London set the tone for the rest of their circuit. East London was where the Pan-Africanists believed they had a major base, despite the decline of African political organization in this centre since the Defiance Campaign. Local leadership was in the hands of quite prominent personalities including Alcott Gwentshe, a shop assistant who as a saxophonist led his own jazz band. The East London Pan-Africanists tended to hold white-collar jobs: sales workers, draughtsmen, and attorneys' clerks for instance. C. J. Fazzie, the PAC's provincial secretary, ran a general dealership in Duncan Village and his store became the organization's operational base.[129] When Sobukwe and his companions arrived in East London, contrary to their expectations, there was no mass rally for them to address. The council had maintained a ban on political gatherings in African townships since

1952. Instead, the Special Branch had arranged their own welcome and the three visitors were arrested for entry into a location without the required permit. After paying their fines the best they could do was to speak to a discreet house meeting. Next in their itinerary was Engcobo but here their local contacts failed to keep appointments. In Aliwal North and in Durban, before their return to Johannesburg, they spoke to PAC members only.[130]

One of the main difficulties that the PAC experienced in its efforts to mobilize support for its campaign was self-inflicted. By common consent, the decision about the date when the 'positive action' would begin would be made by Robert Sobukwe alone, without requiring him to consult anybody else. With the exception perhaps of Potlake Leballo,[131] Sobukwe told no other leaders which date he favoured until very late indeed, only a few days before it become public knowledge.[132] He was anxious that the PAC's schedule should not be upstaged by the ANC bringing the launch of its campaign forward, apparently. During the national tour that he made with Leballo the date of the launch remained a secret. As we have seen, Sobukwe's original inclination was that militant activism would follow a lengthy phase of psychological preparation in which a 'black consciousness must be fostered'. He was dissuaded from this view in September 1959 and agreed upon a more rapid move to confrontation. Leballo probably played a significant role in helping Sobukwe change his mind. Sobukwe respected Leballo whom he saw, in contrast to himself, as a man of action. As he told Gail Gerhart, 'with a note of real admiration' (her comment), 'PK was a fighter. He was always for barging ahead.' He discussed Leballo with Benjamin Pogrund as early as 1958, maintaining that Leballo 'as an interesting person, who was not really a racialist, but was someone who had been greatly misunderstood'.[133] Ten years later, Sobukwe held to this view, telling Pogrund that Leballo was 'basically good' and moreover amenable; Sobukwe had succeeded during his association with Leballo in 'toning him down'.[134] In any case, Sobukwe liked Leballo's decisiveness partly because in his view, he felt he himself lacked a comparable certainty of purpose. 'Don't we all have a Hamlet in our personalities', he wrote to a friend in 1966, 'Don't we all require conferences, services, parties, talks, discussions, etc. to "whet our blunted purpose".'[135]

People like Leballo, Sobukwe perceived, could provide ordinary people with what they needed, 'clear cut answers, a year or two away'. His own predisposition was different, he confided to the same correspondent, six years later. He was much closer to the position of true liberals, who 'by definition, I think, cannot be consistent' for they must be 'open to new and convincing ideas all the time'. His private preference was to 'be intellectually honest and above all not to be dogmatic. We call it independence of mind. But this can be dangerous in politics.'[136] One revealing anecdote is told by Randolph Vigne, then a member of the small non-racial Liberal Party, who attended an informal encounter that Pretoria-based members of the Liberal Party arranged with PAC leaders who were attending a literary workshop in Atteridgeville. Sobukwe opened the conversation by providing a brief outline of the PAC's principles. He did this very hesitantly, Vigne noticed, and he 'kept looking at the other PAC people', as if to seek their sanction.[137] Mistrusting his own privately liberal predispositions, in his more public life Sobukwe decided to take his political cues from his mercurial colleague.

Robert Sobukwe made the first public announcement about the impending campaign on Friday 18 March. Sobukwe's final instructions, read out at PAC branch meetings on the 18th, emphasized that the campaign should conducted with 'absolute non-violence':

> There are those in our ranks who will be speaking irresponsibly of bloodshed and violence. They must be firmly told what our stand is. Result of violence: let us consider, for a moment, what violence will achieve. I say quite positively, without fear of contradiction, that the only people who will benefit from violence are the government and the police. Immediately violence breaks out we will be taken up with it and give vent to our pent up emotions and feel that by throwing a stone at a Saracen or burning a particular building we are small revolutionaries engaged in revolutionary warfare. But after a few days, when we have buried our dead and made moving graveside speeches and our emotions have settled again, the police will round up a few people and the rest will go back to the passes, having forgotten what our goal had been initially . . . This is not a game. We are not gambling. We are taking our first step in the march to African independence and the United States of Africa. And we are not leading corpses to the new Africa . . . The principal aim of our campaign is to get ourselves arrested, get our women remaining at home. This means that nobody will be going to work. Industry will come to a standstill and the government will accept out terms . . .[138]

That week Sobukwe had written to the commissioner of the South African police, General Rademeyer, asking him 'to instruct your men not to give impossible orders to my people' and reassuring him that if given adequate time the protestors 'if told to disperse we will'. However Rademeyer should not expect thousands people to 'run helter skelter' in obedience to 'the usual mumbling by a police officer of an order requiring the people to disperse within three minutes'.[139] Sobukwe did not include this commitment to obey reasonably delivered police requests in his instructions to the branch leaders quoted from above and it does not seem as if they received any other tactical advice. A particularly important omission from Sobukwe's message to his followers was what they should do in the event of the police refusing to make any arrests. Sobukwe may not have anticipated this problem, for like most of the PAC national leaders in 1952 he had not been a participant in the ANC's Defiance Campaign in which police were quite often reluctant to cooperate with civil disobedience by arresting law-breaking resisters.

Written records, though, may offer a very selective account of how the PAC organized its campaign and of what they told their followers. To an extent, imaginative individual enterprise may have helped to compensate for the absence of systematically orchestrated top-down preparation. Stanley Nkosi was a broadcaster employed in the SABC's language services as a Zulu announcer. With several of his colleagues he was also a PAC member. On Sunday morning on arriving for his shift he set aside the musical compilations prepared for him the previous day and instead chose to play every fifteen minutes for the next eight hours, Hamilton Masiza's anthem, *Vukani Mawethu* ('Arise my people'), interrupting the normal programme schedule to play and replay the recording. The song could be heard all over Soweto through the 'Msakazo' open air re-diffusion system. At the end of his shift in case any of his listeners had missed the point, Nkosi delivered an 'exit speech', reminding them that tomorrow, 21 March, would be a significant day.[140]

How many listeners would have understood Nkosi's signing off or the message implicit in his playing of Masiza's song we will never know. However, by mid-March 1960 most of the Pan-Africanist leaders had managed to persuade themselves that they had accumulated a substantial following. They were certain that amongst grass-roots supporters of organized African politics their own championing of an ascriptive 'aboriginal' African identity offered emotional and moral fulfilment. They believed that various ANC failures to win popular support through the decade were attributable to the ANC's leaders' reluctance to mobilize people on the basis of a racially essentialist nationalism. They were convinced that they could offer inspirational leadership not just to activists but to people who had hitherto held back from joining political organizations. Leaders needed to lead from the front, to set an example. As Robert Sobukwe told Gail Gerhart, 'ordinary Africans, like Madzunya, didn't believe we were prepared to suffer. We thought that, just as in the ANC, the people were willing to follow their leaders almost blindly, in our case they would also follow when we had given the example.'[141] Only then, the Pan–Africanists insisted, would it be possible to overcome the generalized 'indifference, fear, despair, and apathy',[142] the principally psychological restraints that had inhibited mass rebellion.

3

The Sharpeville Shootings

Robert Sobukwe was as good as his word. On Monday 21 March, the PAC top echelon would lead from the front. By dawn, most of the PAC's leaders had assembled, ready to hand themselves over for arrest at their nearest police station. Sobukwe himself woke up early, a few minutes before 5 o'clock, in time to heat water for a bath in the kitchen, to dress by candlelight, and to eat his normal breakfast of mealie meal porridge, eggs, and tea. He had said his goodbyes to his four children the night before; they were staying with his mother-in-law. At 6.30 am he left home to walk over to Tshabalala's store to meet the main leadership group from Orlando. As dawn broke, Sobukwe was leading his small band on a circuitous route, collecting other volunteers on the way. Benjamin Pogrund was among the journalists on the lookout, and he arrived in Soweto early enough to witness 'this small knot of men walking silently and determinedly, picking their way through the people hurrying to work and the peak hour buses and taxis'.[1] The youngest volunteer present, Aubrey Mokoape, remembered later that he had seen groups of people burning passes but no one else has offered any corroboration of this.[2] Pass-burning was a tradition associated with the ANC's history: the PAC had explicitly counselled against it. After about an hour's walking, three miles or so, they reached Orlando police station. The group numbered about a hundred and at the station they were welcomed by a similarly sized crowd of onlookers and additional volunteers. After drinking a cup of coffee, Sobukwe and Leballo walked through the station gates and entered the charge office. Sobukwe told the senior officer, Captain de Wet Steyn that he and his companions had no passes: they needed to be arrested. Captain Steyn replied dismissively. He was busy and they must wait outside. The volunteers settled down outside the police station, sitting on the grassy embankment below the fence. The numbers remained small. Wives and friends came to offer encouragement and re-freshments. At eight o'clock a few secondary school pupils arrived, dressed in their uniforms and carrying their satchels; PAC members at Orlando High School had rounded up a group of volunteers when the school gates opened. This initiative succeeded in prompting a police reaction. Captain de Wet Steyn telephoned the Orlando headmaster, Wilkie Kambule, sug-gesting that he should come and collect his truant pupils. Kambule agreed: no Orlando students would be locked up by the police that day.

Aubrey Mokoape's recollections suggests that within Sobukwe's group people felt disappointed at the ostensibly desultory response to the PAC's call. There were no massive crowds outside police stations that morning and most Soweto commuters boarded their buses and trains in the normal fashion. If any PAC Task Forces were present at bus terminals and train stations they made no efforts to discourage people from going to work. While they were proceeding to Orlando, Sobukwe's companions 'could see people streaming up to Dube station from Mofolo, all on their way to work despite our call'.[3] Mid-morning, one of Sobukwe's companions, Selby Ngendane, obtained a lift from one of the journalists in attendance at Orlando. They undertook a tour of Soweto's police stations and on his return Ngendane was able to report that small groups of PAC branch officials were detained in police cells in Pimville, Moroka, and in Newlands, next to Sophiatown, supposedly a major base for the Pan-Africanists.[4]

There already had been several advance signals that positive action might begin on a rather smaller scale than the more optimistic PAC leaders had anticipated. Interviewed a decade later, Potlake Leballo conceded that several members of the PAC's executive had urged postponement arguing that 'we had not done enough spadework' and that 'the organizational work had not been done'.[5] Leballo was later to find himself at odds with most of the personalities concerned and so perhaps we should disregard his subsequent contention in this interview that they had developed cold feet. Sobukwe himself could recall nobody raising such concerns when he was interviewed nor did he corroborate Leballo's recollection that on their way to Orlando, Sobukwe's group had to locate certain errant PAC leaders who were indisposed by sudden illnesses or who had gone into hiding. Jacob Nyaose also related a similar anecdote about a branch leader in Mofolo upon whom the Task Forcers had to work very hard to persuade to participate after they found him apparently crippled by a mysterious leg injury.[6] Leballo claimed as well that a group of two thousand volunteers had gathered on a football field in Orlando well before dawn to wait for PAC officials who failed to arrive and so members of this crowd had returned to their homes before Leballo and Sobukwe's group reached Orlando. This also sounds rather too much like a story intended to discredit Leballo's then rivals within the exile PAC community.

We have rather firmer evidence, though, of Josias Madzunya's defection from the PAC's cause. Police witnesses recorded his speech to his followers in Alexandra on Sunday. Here he explained that he disagreed with Sobukwe's proposed course of action: 'We are differing in our organization', he said:

> Some say that we should leave the passes at home and surrender ourselves at the police station, but I say that we should destroy the passes and go to work. If you leave passes at home and not go to work you shall still be possessing a pass ... We must first be organized fully well in order to launch any campaign in the same way as Banda did for Nyasaland ... The pass will never be abolished unless you organize and organize and organize.[7]

Madzunya later explained to Pogrund that he was convinced that Sobukwe's call was premature. 'We had to organize', he maintained, 'It wouldn't be for three years until we had 100,000.' Sobukwe's choice of date, Madzunya believed, was influenced mainly by his anxiety that the ANC's launch of their campaign would pre-empt the PAC's action. Madzunya had already warned Sobukwe that he would take this position earlier in the week.[8] It was a significant setback. Africanists in Alexandra, including substantial cohorts of disaffected youngsters, were largely constituted as Madzunya's personal following, and these followers took their cue from their local champion. On Monday there would be no positive action in Alexandra.[9]

While they were walking to Orlando against the tide of hurrying commuters, Robert Sobukwe encouraged his followers, reassuring them: 'Boys, we are making history.'[10] And so they were, though we remember their procession today because of events that were unfolding elsewhere, in communities which up to that time had mainly been bypassed by the main currents of organized political activism.

On the whole, as we have seen, the PAC's principals did not pay too much attention to the task of organizing a disciplined membership. Many agreed with their president, Robert Sobukwe, who maintained that 'All we are required to do is to show the light and the masses will find the way.'[11]

On the eve of its anti-pass civil disobedience, therefore, the PAC remained a relatively small band of enthusiasts, many of them clustered in or near the Soweto neighbourhood of Orlando where many of its leaders lived. The PAC's angry oratory attracted considerable press attention, but the new Congress's membership was generally confined to the ANC branches that had broken away to form the organization in 1958 and 1959.

In two vicinities, though, the PAC succeeded in attracting people previously unengaged in organized politics. The PAC developed a structured organization in Sharpeville and the other townships that surrounded the steelmaking centre of Vereeniging, thirty miles south of Johannesburg. The second area in which the PAC was successful in winning mass support was among the African communities that lived around Cape Town, 1,500 miles away.

In both these areas it was the PAC's initial success in persuading thousands of local residents to assemble in excited gatherings outside public buildings that was decisive in turning what would otherwise have been a minor protest into a major crisis. For elsewhere in South Africa that Monday, public responses to the PAC's call were generally desultory. Only in these two widely separated areas was the PAC successful in presenting a real challenge to local officials. In most of the other places in which the PAC organized pass protests, local police stations could easily accommodate the modest groups of activists who presented themselves early in the morning while most other people were boarding their buses and trains to travel to work. Accordingly, to explain the causes of the crisis we need first to explore the local dynamics that generated masses of determined protestors willing to remain standing for hours outside police stations in Sharpeville and in the townships of Cape Town. In Cape Town, the events of 21 March represented the opening act of a much more extended confrontation between the PAC's followers and the police that we will address in the next chapter. Here, though, we will consider the developments that led up to the police opening fire in Sharpeville.

Around Vereeniging, the PAC first established a presence in the sprawling settlement of Evaton, one of the oldest African urban communities in the Transvaal, twelve miles away from Sharpeville. There 'Africanists' had predominated in the local ANC branch for several years. One of them, Joe Molefi, was the proprietor of a printing press in Johannesburg, providing the Africanist group with a critical propaganda resource and enabling them to produce their own leaflets and flyers.[12] Local Africanist influence was also possibly attributable to the proximity of the prestigious Wilberforce Institute.

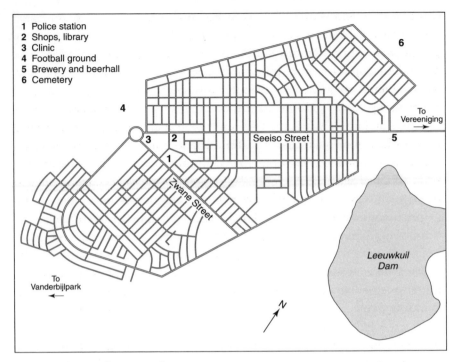

1 Police station
2 Shops, library
3 Clinic
4 Football ground
5 Brewery and beerhall
6 Cemetery

Map 2. Sharpeville street-plan

In the 1950s this school was under the headmastership of Victor Sifora, 'Black Savage' in the columns of *The Africanist*. His ascendancy at Wilberforce may have drawn other teachers with Africanist sympathies to work there.[13] Joe Molefi, one of the Evaton leaders, later maintained that Wilberforce high school students supplied a significant share of the local Africanist and Pan-Africanist support.[14] In 1956, the Evaton leaders had led a bus boycott that, after considerable violence resulting in fifteen deaths, succeeded in preventing the company operating the service to Johannesburg from raising fares. Through this experience, the Evaton activists had come to recognize the importance of organizing systematically. In nearby Sharpeville, considered by the authorities a 'model' township, seven thousand boxy dwellings arranged in orderly lines along a grid of neat streets concealed rising political tensions. These tensions created a receptive atmosphere for the PAC's first emissaries from Evaton.

Sharpeville was a relatively new settlement, three miles from the centre of Vereeniging. Its first dwellings were constructed in 1943 to accommodate the inhabitants of an old inner city 'location', Topville. Already a slum before the Second World War, Topville's population expanded during the early 1940s, a consequence of of Vereeniging's wartime boom as a steel producer. Living conditions in Topville became increasingly unhealthy and an epidemic of deaths from pneumonia persuaded the authorities to resettle its inhabitants in a modern planned township, named Sharpeville after Vereeniging's mayor, John Sharpe, located on a site originally intended for the building of white ex-servicemen's homes.[15] Sharpeville's original householders were willing settlers, for the first removals were voluntary and the houses in Sharpeville were relatively more spacious and some of them were supplied with electricity and running water. The removals stopped, though, in 1951 because of new planning regulations instituted by the Department of Native Affairs. The department's officials were concerned about the proximity of Sharpeville's boundaries to nearby white suburbs.

For the next seven years about 15,000 people would remain in Topville. Sharpeville's expansion resumed in 1958. Vereeniging's municipal managers finally succeeded in meeting the new regulations. They were keen to demolish Topville quickly, for inner-city land values has escalated through the decade and Topville's site was earmarked for new factories.[16] This time the resettlement of Topville's inhabitants was undertaken abruptly and its residents had no choice. Without warning they were ordered by armed police especially brought in from outside Vereeniging to pack their belongings into trucks and leave behind anything for which there was no room to be bulldozed along with their old houses. Nor could they expect to move into proper houses with lights and water: most of the 10,000 or so people who moved from Topville to Sharpeville between 1958 and 1959 were allocated plots in the Vuka site and service scheme. Each household was assigned to a patch of bare ground with a temporary hut assembled on a concrete platform with a toilet.

Not surprisingly, then, not everybody the authorities compelled to live in Sharpeville in this second resettlement welcomed the move there, and indeed five thousand of Topville's inhabitants moved elsewhere. Elderly people and illegal lodgers without the appropriate passes were despatched to Witzieshoek, a bleak rural reserve on the Basotho border.[17] Other people chose to move away, mainly to Evaton, where controls on settlement were less restrictive. The people who had remained in Topville included standholders who had made a living out of renting out rooms and shacks to tenants: Sharpeville did not allow such arrangements. There were other disadvantages to living in Sharpeville. The township was three miles from

Vereeniging's city centre and for many people the commuting journey to work was further still and in 1959 bus fares doubled. In Topville, residents often kept livestock, chickens, or goats, but this was prohibited in Sharpeville. A more general source of discontent was sharp rent rises in 1959 imposed because the Vereeniging council needed to recover its capital costs in extending the township. By the end of the year more than 2,000 householders were seriously in arrears with their rent payments, more than a third of Sharpeville's tenants. Those behind in their rent payments were threatened with eviction and punished in other ways: for instance, the township superintendent would not allow rent-defaulting families to bury their dead in the township cemetery.

As far as Vereeniging's city fathers were concerned, Sharpeville was a civic showcase, 'a modern Bantu town'.[18] They were proud of its orderly lay-out and of the amenities clustered in the township's centre: a stadium, a brewery, and beer-hall—a vital source of municipal revenue—administrative offices, a public library, a clinic, a creche, and, from 1959 a new police station. Indeed by contemporary conventions, Sharpeville was heavily policed, a reflection of civic anxieties that dated from very violent riots in Topville in 1937, disturbances sparked off by a liquor raid in which two policemen were killed. The violence followed a day of confrontations between police and a large crowd that had gathered at the public square. Before this protest public resentment of the police was at a peak as a consequence of the authorities' introduction of 'pick-up raids', motorized police patrols that trebled the rate of arrests for pass offences and other minor legal infringements.

After the riots, white politicians and editorialists called for action against the Communist Party, blamed for inciting the riots. The party denied that it had any presence in Vereeniging,[19] a disavowal that was subsequently confirmed in an official enquiry. A branch was set up by ex-members of the Industrial and Commercial Workers' Union which was busy in Vereeniging between 1927 and c.1930 but it became inactive during the factional strife that paralysed the national party at the beginning of the 1930s.[20] However in the early years of the Second World War Communists helped to establish five trade unions in Vereeniging's single worker compounds, among brick and tile workers, steel workers, power workers, timber workers, and the employees of a flour mill. They did not survive the decade: most were suppressed through sackings and the hiring of 'scab' labour after a wave of strikes at the beginning of 1946.[21] Meanwhile, the Communist Party itself re-established a presence in Top Location, in 1941 holding meetings to protest the 450 arrests made during the first local pass raids since the beginning of the Second World War.[22] Again, party organization seems to have petered out by 1945. Even so, amongst local officials, these developments provoked alarm which was reinforced by the national perception of wartime priorities. Within government, Vereeniging was considered a strategically important centre due to its concentration of heavy industry.

The presence of the new police station from 1959 brought with it additional manpower to enforce influx control and through that year municipal police were on the offensive, hunting out illegal residents, often relatives of householders, in night-time pass raids. From 1958, new restrictions on Basotho migrants encouraged a stricter enforcement of influx control in Vereeniging, a major employer of Basotho migrant labour. Often the raids took the form of house-to-house searches undertaken by armed policemen reinforced from outside the district.[23] The police were also on the lookout for illegal liquor distilling, reportedly on the rise in 1959 as householders sought to augment their incomes to pay the new rents. The municipal police's pass raids especially targeted young men who were particularly affected by very high local unemployment.

Youth unemployment had been a focus of official agitation since the early 1950s. Local industrialists preferred to employ Basotho migrant work-ers who could be paid less, accommodated near their workplaces in walled compounds, and who, they believed, were unreceptive to trade unionism. In any case, much of the industrial work available was heavy and menial, considered by relatively well-educated long-term residents as degrading.[24] By 1959 there were insufficient senior high school places in Vereeniging to accommodate African junior certificate holders: we can conclude then that Vereeniging's African teenage population was unusually well-educated.[25] Industrialists complained that those local youngsters they did hire were often 'cheeky' and 'insubordinate', predisposed to abusing or even assaulting their supervisors when reprimanded.[26] There were few alterna-tive jobs in Vereeniging to factory work, for the city was not a major commercial centre, and pass regulations made it difficult for school-leavers to seek work in Johannesburg even if they could afford the train fares. According to a report in the *World* newspaper, 'scores of youths roamed the streets' and in nearby Bophelong, affected by similar conditions, resi-dents had assembled to warn the authorities that the dangerous situation generated by the pass laws prevented their children from seeking work on the Witwatersrand and was helping to turn them 'into jailbirds and crim- inals'.[27] In Sharpeville itself, members of the Advisory Board warned, juvenile gangs were becoming more and more active and by 1959 had become a regular presence at the bus station, preying on commuting school pupils. In response, Vereeniging Council accorded to the Advisory Board the power to administer corporal punishment. The council itself attempted to impose a curfew and began expelling delinquent *tsotsis* to labour camps managed by the Native Affairs Department.[28]

Local official reactions to disaffected teenagers were unusually harsh. From Sharpeville's inception the authorities were determined to administer a tightly controlled community. They refused to sanction public meetings, even during Advisory Board elections, and at times of popular political assertion in other urban centres, during the Defiance Campaign in 1952 for example, they made sure that a conspicuously evident local police presence would discourage any local political activity. In 1955 the town clerk of Vereeniging noted approvingly that 'No organized trouble had been en- countered in Sharpe Native Township since its establishment in May 1943.'[29] This was not quite true. On 18 May 1953, the superintendent informed the Advisory Board that members of the Society of Young Africa (SOYA) had been holding secret meetings in Sharpeville. In fact SOYA has been busy in the township from the previous year and in September 1952 had claimed that it enjoyed a large local following.[30] Now in 1953, the group was planning to organize a boycott of the planned queen's coronation festivities. Board member Reverend Sethlatlose professed shock. He felt 'very small' at this news. These people, he said, were from elsewhere and they had attracted a following from local 'won't works', people 'who were prone to doing these things'. They should be ejected, he said.[31] Subse- quently the board was to hear that there had been no disorder.[32]

In 1958, the introduction of women's passes, widely contested elsewhere, proceeded smoothly in Vereeniging where the authorities were able to boast that 'so many presented themselves for registration that the number had to be controlled daily'.[33] In fact, despite an official ban on political groups, a branch of the ANC did exist, it had a membership of 200 or so,[34] but its genteel and middle-aged leadership behaved cautiously and refrained from active participation in most of the ANC's national campaigns apart from persuading its members to stop buying potatoes during the 1958 consumer boycott.

The absence of political assertion through the 1950s in Sharpeville certainly did not signify a lack of local associational life or social activity, though. Indeed, Sharpeville had a regional reputation as a centre of African cultural achievement, as the home of several prominent sports personalities as well as the Sharpetown Swingsters and the Satchmore Serenadors jazz ensembles, whose performances would attract hosts of weekend visitors from the more obviously politically animated community of Evaton. The trumpeter Hugh Masekela grew up in Sharpeville, where his father had a local reputation as a sculptor and carver: 'in those days Masekela's music was the main thing in Sharpeville'.[35] The Central Boys' Boxing Club supplied another attraction for visitors and local residents. The club nurtured a succession of local champions: John Mtimkulu in 1955 became the youngest ever South African amateur lightweight title holder.[36] For David Sibeko, a PAC leader who lived in Evaton, Sharpeville was a community invested with a rich diversity of cultural resources, 'a place close to my heart—I had friends there—artists, sportsmen—and social friends'.[37]

To summarize, in Sharpeville by the end of 1959 there was a combination of grievances that helped make sections of the community very receptive to fresh political direction. About a third of the township's residents had been forcibly resettled within the last year, losing their homes, various sources of income, and in many cases, their belongings. Also many would have been separated from those neighbours, friends, and kinsfolk whom the authorities refused to resettle in Sharpeville, forcing many of them to leave the region altogether to live instead in the Basotho reserve. More generally, Sharpeville's residents had recently experienced sharp increases in their rents as well as more and more frequent intrusions into their homes by abusive municipal policemen searching for illegal residents and illicit liquor. Finally, unemployed 'youth' constituted a growing share of the local population—nearly 21,000 out of an official population for the township of 37,000 were aged below eighteen.[38] Sharpeville's school-leavers were confined by an exceptionally restrictive local labour market. These youngsters were often relatively well-educated, unable to find anything but the most menial jobs locally, and were reportedly contemptuous of the existing social hierarchy.

The PAC established a branch in Sharpeville in July 1959, holding a formal inaugural meeting at the Anglican church, though local preparations for this began some months earlier. Its leaders were drawn from a group of young men, all factory workers but comparatively well-educated. Two brothers led the local organization. The branch secretary was Nyakane

Tsolo, described in his pass book as a 'labourer'. His brother, Job, was branch chairman. Nyakane and Job were the sons of Philemon Tsolo, a coal merchant and, reputedly, an important Basotho chief, well to do, by local standards, for he also owned a shop and brewed beer, illegally, running the family businesses with the help of his five sons, whom he expected to complete the daily coal deliveries before they went to school. It was an austere household, apparently. No electricity, just candles and piped water available in the yard, not indoors. The family occupied two houses, next door to each other, with Nyakane sharing the second house with his older brothers, Job and Gideon and Gideon's young family; this separate dwelling afforded the brothers a little independence. Father was a strict churchgoer and a harsh disciplinarian but by 1959 Nyakane, aged nineteen, was beginning to challenge paternal authority. Through their teens, the three brothers had been subjected to a household discipline that included the nightly bagging of coal, the morning deliveries, and regular church-going on Sundays. Philemon discouraged his sons from participating in Sharpeville's recreational life: they were forbidden from playing football, for example. This was a stricture that may have been engendered by protective concerns rather than moral disapproval, for Philemon's two older sons were dead, stabbed by *tsotsis* on their way back home from attending evening soccer fixtures. Philemon sent Job to Healdtown during the 1950s and, possibly influenced by the school's political life during one summer vacation, Job attempted to set up a branch of the Society of Young Africa, a Trotskyite group that had established itself in the elite Eastern Cape high schools. As we have seen, SOYA's activities in Sharpeville swiftly attracted official displeasure and in Sharpeville the SOYA branch from July 1953 was forbidden to hold meetings by the location superintendent.

Perhaps for this reason, Philemon sent Nyakane to the local high school in Sharpeville, Legoshang Secondary, which he attended until he secured his junior certificate in 1958. There was no money for him to remain at school, for proceeding to Standard 10 would have required him to leave Sharpeville and attend a boarding institution. After leaving school, all the boys attempted to find work outside the family businesses but decent jobs were hard to find around Sharpeville. Nyakane eventually settled for work on the factory floor at African Cables while Job obtained a post at Tozer's pipe factory. Gideon did a bit better: he worked as a cashier at the municipal bottle store. They would hand their wages over to their father every week but they received pocket money back and with this source of independent income there was an easing of the domestic constraints. Nyakane enjoyed a busy social life for he had been popular at school and maintained a considerable personal following from Legoshang Secondary: even at school, Gideon remembers, 'he would do anything to attract a following'. Nyakane's friends included several members of the Sharpeville Swingsters. Gideon also remembers that Nyakane kept his books after leaving school; they were on a shelf where he slept, including a frequently consulted volume of Shakespeare's collected works. He brought newspapers and magazines home: *Drum*, the Johannesburg *Sunday Times*, and, of course, *Bantu World*.[39]

It was from reports in the newspapers that Nyakane drew his inspiration when he turned to organizing his fellow workers at African Cables. Joining him on the shop-floor there was a whole group of recently recruited youngsters, school-leaving junior certificate holders who had reluctantly settled for factory work in the absence of anything better. They swiftly found an issue around which to focus their more generalized sense of frustration and disappointment. Management employed the workforce on a twelve-hour shift, five shifts a week. In fact, the men had to finish off at 5.15, twelve and a quarter hours after their work started, presumably to allow for them to change and clean up but they were not paid for the extra fifteen minutes. 'We need a union', Nyakane advised his former classmates. They began approaching other workers, cannily waiting until the end of the shift and engaging them as they were on their way to the bus stop. There was plenty of enthusiasm, apparently, not so much because of grievances within the factory but because people were exasperated by a recent upsurge of anti-pass raids by the municipal police. They would stop workers on their way to the bus terminal demanding to inspect their reference books and in this way often causing them to miss their transport and hence arrive late for work. Management did nothing to help. The union proved popular, drawing many members of the night shift to its weekend meetings on the soccer field. Accounts diverge: Gideon believes that the union persuaded its members to mount a sit-down strike mid-shift and that this succeeded in persuading the company to pay its workers for the extra quarter of an hour. Michael Thekiso, one of Nyakane's former school friends who belonged to the initial organizing group, remembers that they told management they would go to the 'Labour Court' if they were not paid for the overtime.[40]

Variations of this narrative have become an oral tradition in Sharpeville but the history of local trade unionism may be more complicated and

Nyakane Tsolo may not have played quite such a pioneering role. The 1980s trade union leader Petrus Tom joined Jacob Nyaose's Bakers' and Confectioners' Union—later a FOFATUSA affiliate—while working at a Vereeniging bakery in 1953. He was 'not active' as a trade unionist, though, when he left the bakery and started working at African Cables in 1956. There was no union there but he was one of a group of workers who downed tools one evening because management refused to pay them a night shift allowance. They returned to work but were charged with participation in an illegal strike. They received suspended sentences but in 1959 management conceded the allowance. It is possible that this incident may have supplied the original inspiration for forming the union.[41]

Whichever recollections are correct, we know that Tsolo's union began to attract attention from quarters outside the factory a few weeks after it began recruiting members. Pan-Africanists in nearby Evaton learned about the union's formation and seeking to extend the reach of their new organization, Evaton PAC leaders arranged a meeting with the Tsolo brothers and suggested they should set up a PAC branch. They invited Nyakane to attend PAC meetings in Orlando. Nyakane seems to have travelled to Orlando in April for the PAC's foundation conference where he encountered Sobukwe in the men's room. Not knowing who the person was washing his hands in the basin next to him, Nyakane told Sobukwe that he had organized many people and that Sobukwe should accompany him to the PAC function next door. Sobukwe laughed and said, 'No, let's go to the meeting together.'

In Sharpeville, Gideon remembers, Nyakane 'was *the* leader'. He was small and frail-looking but indomitable. In the township, the PAC constituted itself around Nyakane's peer group, young men in their late teens and early twenties, at the beginning about twenty or so junior certificate holders from the Legoshang classes of 1957 and 1958, mainly the same group that had set up the union at African Cables. They held their meetings in the house the Tsolo brothers occupied, late at night when they were on day shift, after Philemon had gone to sleep, a habitually clandestine method of organization that became entrenched as the PAC's style in Sharpeville. As Gideon observed, the organization needed to work silently, to 'keep secret'. Not secretly enough, though, to evade the attention of the various eyes and ears deployed within Sharpeville that reported untoward developments to the location's administration. One day, Nyakane returned home from work to find his father had visitors. Sitting in the best chairs in Philemon's front room was the superintendent, Mr Labuschagne, and Mr Ferreira, Vereeniging's director of native affairs. Labuschagne knew the family well, indeed officials considered Philemon to be a pillar of the community, law- abiding, devout, and industrious. All the more distressing then for the authorities to learn that his son was causing trouble, creating difficulties at African Cables and worse still, in contact with outsiders, political miscreants from Johannesburg. Nyakane was undismayed by this homily. He looked Ferreira in the eyes and he said: 'Mr Ferreira, you see where I am standing?' He gestured with his hand, waving it towards the window. 'This is my place. From Cape to Cairo. From Madagascar to Morrocco. This is my place. I do what I want to do.' He turned around and without another word left the room.

By the end of the year the PAC had enrolled less than 100 followers in Sharpeville, mostly very young men and women,[42] most of them residents of the Vuka site and service scheme. Philip Frankel suggests that women asserted themselves in playing a 'dominant role' in setting up the PAC in Sharpeville, a reflection of the very specific grievances that affected women particularly, the prohibition of brewing and distilling, for example. Even if this is so, for local organizers this was a disappointing total. Not enough, Tsolo and his comrades believed, not if the organization was going to meet its national target of 100,000 members, and, responding to this injunction, recruitment became less selective, making it easier for police informers to join the new organization.[43] The Tsolo brothers knew that there were police agents present at their meetings, they even knew their identities but they continued their efforts to extend their new organization's following. In fact, a local membership of even a hundred was impressive evidence of commitment and diligence, especially given the attitude of the authorities. Quite aside from his efforts to use family pressure to discourage Nyakane Toslo, Sharpeville's superintendent, Michael Labuschagne, cancelled the visitors' permits of two PAC men from Evaton, accusing them of infringing local regulations by 'talking politics'.[44] Thereafter, the Sharpeville Pan-Africanists remained in almost daily contact with Evaton's Z. B. Molete on the telephone, taking regular calls from Evaton on the public kiosk outside the post office. Despite all their efforts, though, in Sharpeville PAC membership remained quite modest, not more than 150, as Nyakane Tsolo later told the Commission of Inquiry,[45] and a tiny fraction of the PAC's Transvaal membership of around 12,000 or so. Its informal following may have been greater, though, particularly among teenagers, for the PAC in Sharpeville did not enrol as full members youths under the age of eighteen.

As we shall see, young teenagers were very much in evidence in the Task Forces the Sharpeville PAC leaders assembled to help them organize their protest on 21 March. The PAC men also tried to find allies among the more amenable local gangster leaders, an effort that provoked disagreements within the branch executive.[46]

Repressive local conditions certainly inhibited the movement's expansion in Sharpeville but it may have influenced the quality of its organization more positively. Nyakane Tsolo was exceptional among branch-level PAC leaders in the Transvaal in having any experience of organizing shop-floor action and this may have predisposed him to take a more systematic approach to organization than local-level PAC leaders elsewhere. In Orlando, for example, where the PAC attracted a youthful following, very similar to Sharpeville, amongst high school students and unemployed school leavers as well as *tsotsis*,[47] the local PAC leadership were often school-teachers or clerical workers, with no real experience of protest mobilization. At the Commission of Inquiry held after the massacre, police Special Branch Colonel 'Att' Spengler maintained that the PAC before the anti-pass protest seemed much more active in Johannesburg, conducting frequent open air meetings. In Sharpeville, he said, its activities were more 'underground' and it relied heavily on the distribution of propaganda leaflets.[48] Other police witnesses confirmed that in Sharpeville the PAC assembled people in small groups, holding 'secret' meetings in the evening in private houses.[49]

Preparations for the anti-pass campaign in Sharpeville as elsewhere had to be very hurried: Sharpeville organizers only learned about the date for the protest five days beforehand, at a meeting to which they were summoned in Evaton, along with other regional branch leaders. As we have noted, the first public announcement about the date of the impending campaign was on Friday 18 March, the day when Elizabeth Mabona remembers that her household received 'letters' in their post-box instructing them to stay away from work the following Monday. Quite how the organizers should mobilize and conduct the protest was never specified in any detail by national leadership: the Evaton meeting was disrupted by a municipal pass raid and there was no time for any detailed discussion. It does seem though, that there was some direct contact with the Orlando leadership. Gideon remembers Potlake Leballo visiting the Tsolo brothers at their home at least once.[50] Leballo himself claimed later that he commanded personal support in Sharpeville because of his earlier work in the vicinity among Basotho migrant workers, supporters of the BCP. This consideration may indeed

have motivated him to pay especial attention to Sharpeville but as we have
seen, the PAC's local organizers were young men who had lived all their
lives in Sharpeville, not people with strong links with the Basotho migrant
workers, who in any case tended to live in the single workers' hostels
maintained by employers and located on the edges of the township. Apparently, the Sharpeville leaders at the very last moment tried to persuade
Sobukwe or Leballo to lead their local protest. Leballo told Gail Gerhart
that on the evening of 20 March, he received visitors from Sharpeville:

> I was under heavy pressure, to the extent that the president didn't want to—to
> go to Sharpeville, to lead the demonstration there. The pressure was so much,
> and at Sharpeville where we had organized the youth there, they came and
> pleaded with the president. And when he refused I decided that I would
> escape and run away so that the day of the struggle there they (would) have
> already collected their weapons . . . (but) I had no one to back me in my
> argument . . .

Robert Sobukwe may well have decided that Leballo was best kept on a
tight rein, because, as Leballo recalled, 'on that day the president saw to it—
he sabotaged me because when these people we had arranged secretly with
the organizers in Sharpeville to come and fetch me. He also saw them
secretly and said that I would be coming, he will see to it that I get a car
there. And then he told me, no, well, you will get a car, and to my surprise
no car came. Instead he gave me another assignment and I never got to the
place there.'[51]

In the preceding weeks, though, Leballo had managed to maintain a good
supply of his roneod leaflets to Nyakane Tsolo and his confederates in
Sharpeville. Here a wide distribution of leaflets with the exhortation that
'Passes must go' at the beginning of March informed residents that an anti-
pass initiative was impending. Gideon recalls that the Pan-Africanists
distributed the leaflets on several nights, sliding them under people's
doors, 'working silently, not meeting the people'. Nyakane orchestrated
the leaflet distributions: for this purpose he borrowed a dress from Gideon's
wife to use as a disguise.

The PAC's summons to action also spread by word of mouth, undergoing modifications in the process. According to one local resident, Petrus
Tom, two decades later an important trade union organizer in the region,
many people seemed to think that they would be required to burn their
passes—a form of protest that the Communist Party had used locally in the

1930s. In the first week of March, perhaps prompted by the injunctions contained in the leaflets, a crowd of women assembled outside the super-intendent's office to demand rent reductions also carried placards denounc-ing the pass laws, which, as we have seen, had been recently extended to embrace women in this region.

On their return from Evaton, the Sharpeville PAC leadership went to work with a will. As Petrus Tom noted:

> In March that campaign became very hot. Everywhere people sitting in shebeens had those stickers ... It was the strongest campaign I've ever seen. Sometimes you saw people standing at bus stops asking people to burn their passes ... Some people started small fires at the bus stops and everyone would take out their passes and burn them.[52]

Either beforehand, or very quickly on Thursday and Friday, PAC activists assembled a large number of 'Task Forces. The teams were drawn mainly, it seems, from the PAC's informal following, not from the more disciplined signed-up membership. Many of the Task Force members Job Tsolo recruited were the truculent unemployed teenagers who congregated around the beerhall, reputedly a hooligan element whom most house-holders would have regarded with apprehension. Residents interviewed by Philip Frankel in 1999 recalled house-to-house visits by Task Force beginning on Friday in which activists told people to stay away from work on Monday and prepare themselves to march to the police station. Task Forcers probably exceeded their instructions in instructing people to burn their passes: no PAC leaders spoke about pass burnings. As the testimony quoted at the opening of Chapter One suggests, many of the people who attended the protest were uncertain as to whether they should leave their passes at home or bring them with them. The Task Forcers also referred to a demand for a £35 a month minimum wage, a last minute addition to the PAC's national agenda, intended to cement the Pan-Afri-canists' alliance with the Federation of Free Trade Unions. They distributed cyclostyled leaflets telling residents not to go to work on Monday and to hand in their passes. The police monitored all this activity closely through their informers holding PAC membership. During the course of Friday afternoon police called in their informants by the simple expedient of arresting them. Learning of these arrests and misinterpreting them as a preliminary to more widespread arrests of PAC officials, members of the branch executive decided to go into hiding. Freed of any restraint from the branch leaders, Task Force exhortations to householders swiftly degenerated into bullying.

Both contemporary and retrospective testimony[53] suggests that Task Force activity was often intimidating. According to Petrus Tom, he was woken up on Sunday evening because people were knocking at the door and on the windows: 'I peeped through the window and they shouted, "Come out, come out! If you don't get out we'll burn you in the house."'[54] Earlier that day, police began to receive complaints from women that gangs of youths had arrived at their houses, threatening to take away sons and husbands to the stadium where they would assemble in readiness for the protest.[55] Ikabot Makiti a member of one of the Task Force remembers that the instructions they gave to householders were explicit: the protest was for men only, women were meant to stay at home, though, as he conceded, in the event the next morning 'they came all the same'.[56] Parents were told that their children should not attend school the next morning.

Gideon joined one of the groups engaged in these visits. His memories remain discomfiting because for him, it was a fearful experience, 'a nightmare', in which the PAC's and other more self-appointed 'patrols' undertook their door-to-door canvassing nervously, dodging police patrols, but at the same time feeling compelled themselves to threaten people: 'Those who are not with us are against us', they informed householders. Some people were beaten, he thinks, though not by disciplined PAC members.[57] Helping to ratchet up local fears, pastor Mokotudi Nku, a local prophet, in her service that Sunday claimed that she had had a vision the night before: in her dream, she said, 'she had foreseen a black cloud. A lot of people would die on Monday . . . they would die in a camp of passes.' Threats from the protest organizers made their own contribution to communal apprehension.[58] In the testimony quoted in the opening chapter Elizabeth Mabona recalled people in her street telling her that anyone who tried to go to work would be killed.

How peremptory or frightening such warnings were may have varied, though it is quite evident that they were being issued indiscriminately without any careful direction from above. Task Force members even woke up SAP Sergeant Christiaan Nxumalo, someone who would have been well-known to Nyakane Tsolo and his fellow branch leaders. He claimed to the Commission that the Task Forcers told him to come out of his house, that if he did not accompany them that his windows would be smashed. He obeyed their instructions and walked with the team for a couple of blocks but then the group was broken up and dispersed by the arrival of some of Nxumalo's colleagues.[59] Nxumalo went back to his house to change into his uniform and then left home to walk to the police station to report for duty. During this journey he was first stoned and then stabbed by a group of teenagers.[60]

At least one PAC witness at the Commission, Simon Mashetedi, blamed such escapades on quite independent initiatives undertaken by groups of *tsotsis*, claiming that gangs of delinquents constituted that night 'another movement in Sharpeville and that movement was against us'.[61] This seems unlikely, because in fact as Frankel has suggested, Task Force activities through Sunday night appeared to have a broad strategic purpose in demoralizing and confusing the police by keeping people out on the streets, the Task Forces working in small mobile groups so that the police themselves would remain dispersed and disorientated. Between midnight and 3.00 am police broke up and scattered two quite large groups of 'young Africans carrying sticks and kerries', one hundred and five hundred strong respectively, baton-charging the one and firing shots at the other.[62] One of these groups probably woke up George Myubu, the African policeman we encountered in the opening pages of this book. Myubu dressed hurriedly and outside his house joined a large throng on its way to the police station. On arriving at their destination he encountered an intimidating spectacle: a large crowd had assembled and its leaders were shouting 'they'd tackle the police'. In Myubu's words, it was 'almost like a rehearsal'. Sensibly he decided he would be safer at home and discreetly detached himself from the group he had been accompanying and hurried back to his house, locking himself indoors for the rest of the night.[63]

Only two streets in Sharpeville had lighting and so for the most part the Task Forcers could work under the cover provided by darkness. Simon Mashetedi also mentioned a plan to assemble at the football stadium small groups of volunteers who would present themselves at the station in sequence demanding arrest under the pass laws: he thought this was abandoned after the police began halting such groups on their way to the stadium. Other witnesses did attend a meeting at the football ground that was interrupted by the police at midnight. The police broke up the meeting using their *sjamboks*, hurting some people quite badly. After midnight on Sunday, the branch leaders emerged from their hiding places and assumed a more active role in managing events. One key decision the PAC leaders took was to detain bus drivers, taking then to a house and keeping them there until sunrise, three hours after the first commuter buses normally left the depot. The drivers had in fact been approached at the depot on Sunday afternoon by 'PAC men with badges' who said to them:

> We beg you, our people, tomorrow we must be as one. We are not going to fight the Europeans. We just want them to alter this pass law because it is hard on us. If you run away you might get hurt. We will lay our hands on the one that does not want to join us.[64]

When the first commuters arrived at the depot at 3.30 am they were greeted only by PAC Task Forces: there were no buses. Subsequently the PAC posted pickets at the exit points out of the township as well as cutting the telephone wires connecting the administrative offices in the township with the wider world.[65] PAC officials later denied they were responsible for severing telephone links, attributing such activity to over-enthusiastic youngsters. It is tempting to speculate that Potlake Leballo might have drawn upon his own experiences in advising the Sharpeville group: the Lovedale College riot which he had helped to lead had featured severed telephone wires. Given that the Sharpeville Pan-Africanists knew that the local police were well-informed about their plans they had good reasons to try and impede any police effort to summon reinforcements. But we also know that the Sharpeville leadership did not expect to encounter substantial police opposition to their efforts. They had been told by the Orlando leaders 'that every township would be taking this action' and therefore they 'did not expect a large number of police officers from other townships to come to Sharpeville'.[66]

Leballo's advice may have also prompted the Pan-Africanists to try to ensure that the Basotho migrant workers would participate in the protest, though on the whole if they were legal residents immigrant Basotho workers were left alone by municipal police and so they would probably have been disinclined to join the protest. However, the Sharpeville organizers sent a Task Force to the Basotho workers' hostel, on the edge of the township. They stayed with the workers overnight but the success of their efforts to elicit support would remain untested: through the early morning the hostel's gates remained locked and the men would remain confined within their compound until late in the day.[67]

After a brief lull in the dawn hours, the Task Forces reappeared on the streets at around 6.00 am, this time directing people with their whistles to gather at the end of Seeiso Street, near the municipal buildings and the beer-hall, a few hundred yards from the police station. Nyakane Tsolo had spoken to local priests, and several added their own contributions to the Task Force's clamour with celebratory reveilles of church bells.[68] The first police detachments that appeared were greeted with a shower of stones that Task Forcers had been stockpiling. At this juncture the police attempted to disperse the crowd with a baton charge and firing their guns over people's heads. The police attempted to use tear gas to disperse the crowd but in the thin atmosphere of the highveld the gas dispersed too quickly. Not all the gunshots went high: a constable armed with a sten gun fired a round that killed two people and hurt four more. Later the police claimed that two shots were fired at them subsequently from a nearby house. People in the crowd far from being intimidated by these events reassembled and moved to outside the police station to await events, gathered on the edge of the station's perimeter fence.

The officer in charge of the group of policemen that had fired at the crowd radioed for reinforcements. Early efforts at reinforcing the station by bringing additional police across the township in open lorries had to be halted after the lorries were stoned. From 10.30 am three 'Saracen' armoured personnel carriers began a shuttle delivering extra police officers to the group lined up outside the station. Undeterred by these developments the gathering of 5,000 or so people remained in place for the next five hours, their numbers growing steadily through the morning so that by midday the police believed they were confronting a crowd of about 20,000.

For a better understanding of the subsequent developments, a description of the spatial dimensions of the protest should be helpful. The single-storey police station was located on the north side of Zwane Street, one of two major thoroughfares running through Sharpeville. Next to the south and west sides of the station were well-built-up residential neighbourhoods but there was open veldt on the north side of the station compound and in the area to the west open spaces separated a clinic, shopping centre, and library. The main gate of the station compound was on the west side, opening into a side street linking the Zwane and Seeiso thoroughfares. The main station building looked out on the south side where there was also a small gate in the low wire fence that ran along the border of the compound, about ten meters from the building. Behind the station on the north side were holding cells, large open walled-in courtyards with grill meshes as ceilings, sufficiently spacious to accommodate perhaps as many as thirty or so people for short periods. As the crowd gathered, its main body would become concentrated around the west and south entrances though through the morning smaller groups began gathering along the north fence. Only a scattering of people assembled along the east fence. Most of the police would be lined up along the west and south sides of the station. One of the Saracen vehicles would take up a position at the south west corner of the compound while the others, once the garrisoning of the station was complete, would station themselves along the north fence.

People right by the fence shouted at the police, calling to be arrested because they were without their passes. At mid-morning local PAC leaders had crossed the perimeter fence to negotiate with the officer commanding the station, Sergeant Wessels, but they left after he refused to arrest them or their followers. There was no room in the cells to hold such a huge number of offenders, he said, and he had no authority to make arrests: they should wait until someone more senior arrived.[69] In his evidence to the Commission, Tsolo claimed that had the police arrested people until the cells were full that would have been sufficient and his colleagues would then have asked the crowd to disperse. The campaign was intended to become a rolling sequence of protests in which the PAC would lead pass protestors repeatedly to stations.[70] An African constable present during this exchange confirmed Tsolo's recollection in its essentials but also remembered this exchange:

> [Sergeant Wessels] then asked Tsolo: 'You are a Pan-Africanist. In the event of a non-European getting the majority whether they will drive the European away or what are they going to do with the Europeans.' 'They are all Africans', Tsolo replied. 'They are as one; there is no difference.' The last words used by Tsolo were 'What the European eats, the non-European eats.'[71]

There were no further attempts during the morning to establish any lines of communication with the police command. Senior police officers did try and persuade people to move away from the station across the open ground to the north west, to gather instead in the football stadium but Pan-Africanist officials acted swiftly to discourage any such dispersal of their following. As we have seen, several witnesses decades later would testify that they were warned that if they went to the stadium they would be killed. Meanwhile, police officers claimed that after their initial parley with him, Nyakane Tsolo went home briefly for lunch, though this seems unlikely.[72] During his alleged absence the police did not make any effort to negotiate with any of Tsolo's comrades, though higher-ranking officers did reach the station at around eleven, along with reinforcements. Major Willem van Zyl, the Vereeniging district police commander who arrived at a still later stage to take control of the situation, explained this lapse by claiming it was difficult to identify who was leading the crowd:

> At Sharpeville there was not one leader. There were dozens of them. Every youngster from 25 to 16 was edging [sic] them on. They made no attempt to hand themselves over, no leader came forward to say 'I am here with my men to hand myself over', as I thought they would. No pass books were handed over, or any attempt was made to hand them over.[73]

This may have been what the later arriving police perceived but members of the crowd recalled a quite different scenario, one in which Nyakane Tsolo had 'the whole crowd in the palm of his hand because whenever he raised his hand, it enveloped the whole crowd, he would raise his hand for silence and for Afrika'.[74] Anyway, instead of actively seeking out the PAC leadership, Major van Zyl used his radio again to appeal for air support and at midday two airforce Harvard trainer aircraft flew low over the station. Their effect it seems only raised the feelings of excited anticipation experienced by many of demonstrators, evidence as it were of official acknowledgement of the scale and importance of their presence. Petrus Tom remembers 'the people were throwing their hats at the aeroplanes. They thought the aeroplanes were playing with them.' By this time, a belief was spreading that at 2.00 pm a senior official from the Bantu Affairs Department would make an important announcement about the passes, 'that some big boss was coming that would give them an answer'.[75] Several witnesses at the Commission recalled that they had been told this by Nyakane Tsolo and the testimony Philip Frankel collected in his interviews suggests that this belief was deliberately encouraged by PAC men active within the crowd with the aim of encouraging people to remain waiting outside the police station.[76] An alternative explanation of the source of this rumour was offered by Frederick Batkani's recollection of what people had been told when they were ordered to assemble at the football stadium. He remembers the police saying that their commissioner would arrive at the stadium at 2 o'clock to give 'the answer from Pretoria' about the pass laws.[77]

To judge from the evidence they offered at the Commission of Inquiry as well as at more recent investigations, most of the people present in the crowd were there to offer moral support to the protest, not to offer

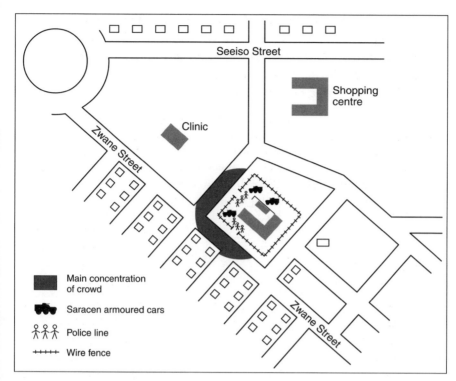

Map 3. Police deployment outside Sharpeville police station

themselves up for arrest. Though several witnesses to the Commission claimed they had been intimidated into joining the assembly others said they had attended out of curiosity. Many people in the crowd, whatever the reasons for their arrival outside the station, to judge from photographs and reports of their behaviour, had become emotionally engaged onlookers. Contrary to the instructions of the Task Forces, the crowd included plenty of women: they are conspicuously evident in the photographs.

By 1.00 pm outside the police station there were about 400 policemen: 200 were white and armed with guns and about 200 black, equipped with knobkerries (clubs). This was ten times the normal complement of personnel who worked at the station and many of the policemen present were reinforcements from outside the Vereeniging district. Most of the white police were holding .303 rifles, though a few of the officers transported in from outside had brought sten guns with them. Altogether the police were carrying 4,000 rounds of ammunition. In addition, the three armoured cars were equipped with heavy machine guns and additional ammunition. Some of the guns contained explosive 'dum–dum' bullets, obtained from an army depot earlier that morning.[78]

Afterwards, the police claimed they were surrounded by an obviously aggressive and hostile crowd. Lieutenant Colonel Pienaar told the Commission of Inquiry that his officers were surrounded by a 'frenzied mob of 20,000 natives'.[79] Several police witnesses at the Inquiry mentioned the behaviour of women that morning. Women they said were 'urging men on' with bellicose ululations.[80] Several women in the front row of the crowd spat at the police facing them.[81] A number of policemen testified that they had heard members of the crowd shout 'Cato Manor' at them: less than a month previously, nine policemen had been killed in Cato Manor outside Durban in riots sparked off by a liquor raid.[82] Many people in the crowd gave the thumbs-up 'Africa' sign used as a salutation by the ANC. Others shouted the PAC slogan '*Izwe lethu*', 'the land is ours'.[83] White policemen were usually unable to understand everything that was shouted at them from within the crowd but they were kept informed by those black police who could understand Sesotho and who were deployed to restrain the front rows of the crowd and keep them away from the fence. Black police reported their impressions to the white officers, one of whom recalled forty years later that 'we were told by the native police that the mob was dangerous . . . there was blood in the air'.[84] According to Superintendent Labuschagne, several of the African police had encountered women raising their skirts at them at different points in the township earlier that morning, a form of sexual mockery calculated as an insult to their manhood. With little love lost between black police and local residents they may well have been as prejudiced observers of the crowd as their white counterparts and they may have exaggerated the extent to which the crowd's mood was aggressive.

Participants and outsiders who moved among the protestors remember the atmosphere quite differently. All the evidence submitted in 1996 to the Truth and Reconciliation Commission suggested a pacific and celebratory multitude:

> At the police station we sat down, we were singing hymns, you know it was just a jolly atmosphere. We were singing those hymns as Christians because we were just rejoicing. And we didn't know what will follow thereafter. We were just joyous because we thought that same afternoon we would get a message. Everybody was taking his feelings out.[85]

Witnesses to the Commission insisted that there was no one present on their side of the fence who was armed, on this they were adamant: 'I didn't see anyone carrying any weapon, not even a stick and knobkerrie, not even a knobkerrie. I only saw umbrellas.'[86] More contemporary testimony also suggested that in general the crowd was good-humoured. Several witnesses at the Commission of Inquiry mentioned people singing 'Abide with me' and other hymns. Two claimed that most members of the crowd were 'happy' to be there that morning.[87] One of these witnesses, Bennett Griffiths, was the son of an African policeman, a Sharpeville resident who had been prevented from going to work that day. Robert Maja, a Presbytarian minister, also told the Commission that the people 'at the meeting' were 'in a happy mood', adding that they were mostly 'respectable people'. 'We never had those people called tsotsis' he said.[88] Maja was certainly overstating the case but it is also quite obvious that most people in attendance had no expectations of danger or violence: elderly people brought fold up chairs with them so they could sit while waiting in the sun. As we know, Lydia Mahabuke attended the gathering holding hands with her six-year-old sister. There were other witnesses present, journalists and photographers from *Drum* magazine and the *Rand Daily Mail* who arrived mid-morning. While attempting to make his way through the ranks of the crowd, the *Mail*'s Benjamin Pogrund encountered only goodwill: '...the demonstrators were completely friendly'.[89] Humphrey Tyler, the *Drum* reporter, also thought 'the crowd seemed perfectly amiable', loosely gathered, and not more than 3,000 in total, far smaller than the police believed, an impression that aerial photographs seem to confirm.[90] Even more telling was township Superintendent Labuschagne's evidence at the Inquiry at which he confirmed that he had walked through the crowd at around 1.00 pm and had stopped to chat with people who greeted him; for Labuschagne this was not a hostile gathering.[91] Sergeant Nkosi went off duty at the same time and walked away from the station, through the crowd, without any sense of being under threat.[92]

The photographic record offers corroborative evidence in support of the contention that on the whole the crowd was good tempered rather than aggressive. Lawyers used the sequence of photographs by Drum's photographer Ian Berry at the Official Inquiry to make this point. Berry's photographs were reproduced in the sequence in which they were taken in Ambrose Reeves's volume, *Shooting at Sharpeville*. Unfortunately copyright restrictions prevent their appearance in this book. Ian Berry began taking his photographs at about 12.00, ninety minutes before the shooting started. Generally his pictures suggest a fairly relaxed environment. One of the first pictures is of a Saracen personnel carrier making its way through the crowd.

People had evidently willingly moved aside to clear a passage for its progress. A group of young men are offering open palmed PAC salutes as the vehicle passes them and one of the police in the Saracen reciprocates with his own open handed greeting. In later photographs other onlookers offer the ANC's 'Africa' salute: raised arms, clenched fists and thumbs up. In several of Berry's pictures of the awaiting crowd taken within half an hour before the outbreak of shooting, white and black policemen are standing at ease often with their backs to onlookers, clearly unperturbed by any sense of threat. In Berry's pictures people turn away from the police station to look into the camera, to smile, and in other ways register their presence with the photographer. A few onlookers wave sticks they are carrying but these items do not look like weapons, rather the sort of supportive accessory a prudent person might bring in anticipation of having to wait standing for a long time. Other people are carrying fully unfurled umbrellas, shading themselves from the sun. The photographs show that at one o'clock the front ranks of the crowd were quite densely packed though other photographs indicate that after a few rows people could stand in their own space and even move around. The pictorial record confirms that the police had no difficulty in themselves driving their vehicles through the crowd. The aerial photograph taken presumably from the aircraft that overflew the station at midday supplies an at least approximate indication of the size of the crowd. At the very most the multitude of protestors on the west side of the police station is assembled in a gathering twenty rows deep, thinning out towards the north. Along the west side fence there would have been sufficient room for two hundred people at most standing very close to each other. The crowd on the south side is evidently smaller. In total, 4,000 would be a very generous estimate for the numbers of people assembled around the police station at midday. On Zwane Street people stand on the pavements and the central reservation, keeping the carriageways clear. When this photograph was taken, ninety minutes before the shooting this was an orderly enough assembly. It might have become larger within the next ninety minutes but this seems unlikely to judge from the dynamics evident in the picture. Many of the figures depicted in the streets around the station are walking away from not towards the crowd.

Why were the police so ready to perceive the crowd as so dangerous that they felt they needed to arm themselves with such lethal force? Certain senior police officers present that day had in fact kept themselves well-informed about the PAC's local progress and plans. Colonel 'Att' Spengler

of the Special Branch in Johannesburg had organized a network of informers who had joined PAC branches, including the PAC groups around
Vereeniging. An African Special Branch detective testified to the Commission about PAC meetings he had attended in Sharpeville: apparently he was
recognized to be a police agent but Job Tsolo told those present to leave him
alone and he was permitted to take notes.[93] From such sources Spengler and
his colleagues first heard about an impending pass protest as early as November, he claimed at the Commission of Inquiry. The Special Branch
officers learned of more definite plans at the end of February when they
organized a meeting with their Vereeniging area agents, who included two
of the Sharpeville PAC branch's executive members. Like everybody else,
even at that stage Spengler could only guess about the likely date for the
opening of the PAC's campaign. The Special Branch men were contemptuous of the local police and instead they depended upon the township
superintendent, Labuschagne, as a major source of local intelligence. Spengler knew enough about the extent of preparations in Sharpeville to perceive that it might be a major centre for the PAC's impending action but at
this stage, at the beginning of March, he did not share his knowledge with
the local police, nor did he anticipate that the protestors would behave
violently. There was plenty of time he believed, for his PAC informants
were telling him that the protest was likely to begin after Easter, in April.

Meanwhile the Vereeniging police were making their own plans. They
obtained copies of the anti-pass leaflet circulating in Sharpeville in early
March and on the 14th conferred with local officials, city councillors,
members of the Defence Force regional command, as well as with senior
colleagues from Johannesburg, including Lieutenant Colonel G. D. Pienaar,
divisional inspector of the Witwatersrand SAP, the regional head of the
regular uniformed constabulary. Only at this stage did the police begin
discussing the possibility that they would need to control large crowds but
they made no detailed plans for this contingency other than agreeing that
they would need to adopt a regionally coordinated approach in which the
different stations around Vereeninging should be ready to reinforce each
other. Lieutenant Colonel Pienaar and the local National Party councillors
argued that local police should be equipped and prepared to fire into
crowds: unlike the Special Branch men, certain local politicians had a
much more threatening picture of the likely developments, coloured partly
by their inexperience of mass protest as well as their fears that unruly protest
in Sharpeville might spill over into nearby white suburbs.

The police in Vereeniging undertook no more detailed planning before the first reports from their own informers started to arrive early on the 18 March, warning that protests outside police stations would begin on Monday. The PAC's Task Force only began to become noticeably active during the course of Sunday: an apparently normal start to the weekend persuaded the police to make no special provisions and the Sharpeville station was left with its normal complement of staff. The situation was similar in all the main centres of PAC activity around Vereeniging. A *Rand Daily Mail* reporter spent early Sunday evening with police patrols in Evaton and they told him everything was quiet and nothing was unusual.

A mounting mood of panic would influence the way the policemen at Sharpeville would view the crowd assembled in front of them. This was the product of events the night before. Task Forces began to mobilize groups on the streets in the course of Sunday night. Some of the people in the Forces the police encountered on their patrols threw stones at them and brandished iron bars. Police dispersed seventeen of such groups by 3.00 am on Monday morning, some of them numbering several hundred, they thought. Their estimates of such numbers may well have been exaggerated, as the police were patrolling in the dark for Sharpeville had no streetlights. While they were out in the streets the police convinced themselves that they heard shots being fired. This is possible because Sharpeville gangsters used firearms habitually. Indeed, three months previously in December 1959, municipal police had found an arms cache hidden in a house in which they were conducting a liquor raid. They arrested Geelbooi Mofokeng, a well-known petty offender whom they encountered near the scene of the raid and questioned him about the cache. After a severe beating in which the police suspended Mofokeng on a pole, spinning him around between blows, it was all too evident he knew nothing and they released him. Right now, in the early hours of Monday morning, after baton-charging one of the bands of protestors a police patrol discovered a pistol lying on the ground. Early attempts to call for additional manpower were held up because the telephone line at Sharpeville station went dead, deliberately sabotaged, the police believed. Additional men did start arriving at the station before dawn but they were to be affected by the apprehensive mood of alarm amongst the men already there, many of them demoralized, weary, and angry after several hours of confrontational encounters with the Task Forces. Whether they were actually frightened, though, is more questionable. Aside from Sergeant Nxumalo, only two other policemen had been hurt that night, both injured slightly by flying stones.[94]

Even so, by the time the crowd began assembling outside the police station, the constabulary within the perimeter fence had been on duty all through the night and many of them had encountered what seemed to them to be insurrectionary bands of armed insurgents. Task Forcers on the edges of the crowd had to keep quite busy in discouraging people from leaving through the morning but from the police perspective this assembly seemed immovable. Early efforts to prevent the crowd from gathering using tear gas and baton charges had failed and some of the police would have been aware of the lethal exchange of fire earlier in the morning. The failure of the aircraft to intimidate the crowd probably helped to accentuate police convictions that they were surrounded by an impassioned mob. By 1.00 pm most of the police present were reinforcements, brought in by Saracen armoured cars to support fellow officers supposedly under siege. These were the officers who had equipped themselves with automatic weaponry. They were young working-class Afrikaner men who in their routine dealings with black people were accustomed to ready obedience: for them even good-natured civil disobedience would have represented an affront and even a threat. As one contemporary commentator noted: 'many of the police expected unquestioned deference from Africans and when they did not get it at Sharpeville they interpreted this as riot and rebellion'.[95] Their perceptions of the crowd would have been selectively influenced by the expectations that accompanied them in their armoured passage to the station. They would not have experienced the affability encountered by the journalists, they would not have heard the hymn singing, and they would not have seen the old folk sitting in their deck chairs at the edges of the assembly. Instead of the hymns, the policemen lined up with their weapons outside the station registered the political slogans, shrill ululations, and what they thought were taunts about Cato Manor. Rather than the friendly citizens who greeted the journalists the policemen could only see people who appeared to be potential aggressors, many of them irresponsible youngsters, *tsotsis*.

Shortly after 1.00 pm Nyakane Tsolo decided to resume his efforts to negotiate. He approached Colonel 'Att' Spengler, who had arrived a few minutes before, driving his car behind a convoy of Saracens, together with Lieutenant Colonel Pienaar. Spengler and Pienaar had just had a conversation in which they had disagreed about how they should deal with the demonstration. Spengler thought they should make another attempt to persuade the PAC men to call off the protest. If that failed the police should fire their weapons over people's heads. Pienaar demurred, he felt that such a warning would be insufficient: the police should fire *into* the crowd.

Colonel Spengler may have favoured a more conciliatory approach but his style of negotiation was abrupt. When Tsolo started speaking, Spengler cut him short, ordering the PAC leader to instruct the crowd to go home. Tsolo refused, saying that only Sobukwe had the necessary authority for such a command. Spengler lost his patience and placed Tsolo under arrest. While constables escorted Tsolo inside the station through the main gate, Spengler began searching for other more amenable intermediaries. He recognized another member of the PAC's branch executive, Thomas More, and called out to him, inviting More to join him behind the fence. On entering the compound, More demanded to be arrested and as with Nyakane, turned down Spengler's request to bring the demonstration to an end. Spengler accompanied More to join Nyakane inside the station. Here a second altercation ensued. Special Branch officer Wessels asked More whether anybody else wanted to be arrested. More answered elliptically: his followers were all willing to die for their freedom, 'he did not mention passes at that moment'.[96] After this, Spengler gave up on Thomas More and walked out of the station intent on finding someone more cooperative. He proceeded slowly along the west fence searching for faces he might recognize.

A third PAC member, a man wearing a red shirt but who remains anonymous in the official record, thrust his way forward and spoke to Spengler. He too wanted to give up his pass and undergo arrest, he said. Spengler acceded to this request, seizing the man by the shoulder to bring him forward but the would-be-protestor appeared to have second thoughts and shrank back, pulling Spengler with him and causing him to stumble. Meanwhile people in the front row of the crowd along the west fence pushed forward to see what was happening, causing the fence to cave in towards the station. Lieutenant Colonel Pienaar ordered the police to load their weapons, though he insisted at the Commission of Inquiry that he told the men that they should not fire without a specific order from him. Pienaar then told the Commission that when the men 'formed up' after his command, a few people threw stones, conceding that these were the first stones thrown from within the crowd that morning.[97] He said at that juncture he was about to give the order to fire, though what he 'had in mind' was 'a few well directed shots at the leader' not what was to follow. At this critical juncture one of the few people in the crowd who really was armed decided to begin his own private offensive against the police. That morning, the man who was so harshly treated after the arms cache raid in December, Geelbooi Mofokeng, elected to revisit the Sharpeville police precinct, this time carrying a gun, joining the crowd gathered outside the station. By one o'clock he had worked his way to the front row, by the fence, his judgement still affected by a heavy night's drinking. He thought he saw one of his interrogators in front of him and raised his gun to shoot. One of his neighbours forced Mofokeng's pistol into the air but he fired two shots all the same.[98] Someone in the row of police now drawn up into a firing position shouted 'skiet' or 'n'skiet', either 'shot', or 'shoot' in Afrikaans. The policeman helping Spengler get to his feet heard the word as an order and fired his sten gun, triggering a lethal fusillade as 168 constables followed his example and discharged 1,344 rounds of ammunition into the crowd. Humphery Tyler, the *Drum* reporter was near enough to supply this vivid account:

> We heard the clatter of a machine gun, then another, then another. There were hundreds of women, some of them laughing. They must have thought the police were firing blanks. One woman was hit about ten yards from our car. Her companion, a young man went back when she fell. He thought she had stumbled. The he turned her over and saw that her chest had been shot away. He looked at the blood on his hand and said: 'My God, she's gone!'. There were hundreds of kids running too.
>
> One little boy had on an old blanket coat which he held up behind his head, thinking, perhaps, that it might save him from the bullets. Some of the children, hardly as tall as the grass, were leaping like rabbits. Some were shot too. Still the shooting went on. One of the policemen was standing on top of a Saracen and it looked as though he was firing his gun into the crowd. He was swinging it round in a wide arc from his hip as though he was panning a movie camera. Two other officers were with him and it looked as though they were firing pistols. Most of the bodies were strewn on the road running through the field in which we were. One man, who had been lying still, dazedly got to his feet, staggered a few yards and then fell in a heap. A woman sat with her head cupped in her hands.
>
> One by one the guns stopped.

The police fired their guns in two volleys, the first into the front rows of the crowd and the second volley aimed higher so that the bullets found their targets in the centre the crowd, mainly hitting people who had already turned to run away. The shooting began with the constables on the west side of the station discharging their .303 rifles but subsequently the men standing on the Saracens, armed mainly with sten guns, joined the fusillade. The first volley killed people who had been pressing up against the fence, including several members of the Pan-Africanists' activist following. The later shooting, directed from the Saracens found its targets in the mass of people fleeing northwards, across the open veldt towards the shopping centre. Several of the police fired twelve rounds each: they would have had to reload their weapons to achieve this and indeed *Drum*'s photographer managed to capture on film one constable reloading his revolver.[99] Most of the people who were killed were shot in the back, hit when they were running away. At least three times as many people were wounded as the number killed, many of them very severely.

After the firing stopped, there was a pause before policemen emerged through the gate in the perimeter fence. Photographs show them moving among the bodies occasionally using the tips of their rifles or the toes of their boots to turn them over to discover which people were still alive. Other officers began to collect the stones scattered across the square, throwing them behind the perimeter fence, already assembling the justificatory evidence they would need later to defend their actions. One witness whose testimony is quoted at the beginning of this book saw police placing stones and knives into the hands of dead people in a grotesque extension of the simulation. There are no reports of policemen offering support or help to any of the wounded, though one of the photographs depicts a black policeman apparently holding the hands of a seated woman. The police did supply grudging assistance to ambulance crews when these arrived twenty minutes after the shooting, helping to load bodies, dead and alive, into the vans. Shortly thereafter it began to rain, a gentle shower that in survivors' recollections would be mentioned again and again as the sole source of comfort available to them at that time, a momentary lifting of despair, a divinely ordained washing of the streets.

Philip Frankel's interviews with survivors, nearly forty years later, elicited accusations that black constables, deployed to move and load into vehicles the bodies of the dead, hurt and perhaps killed more people, mutilating wounded women with *assegais* and beating people with knobkerries.[100] Dutch students who interviewed eyewitnesses in 1999 recorded several testimonies in which 'in between all the bodies policemen were finishing off those still living'.[101] Witnesses to the Truth Commissions made similar charges. In 2001 another survivor, Solomon Lesito, named one of the policemen involved:

> Nearby, another policeman known as Kobuwe went about stabbing those who were still alive. By accident he stabbed a woman who was eight months pregnant. When the woman said to the policeman 'Pini, my child, how could you?', he discovered it was his mother. In his frustration he attempted to remove his uniform, but his white colleagues refused and said: 'Jy draai hom aan, nie so nie, ons gaan jou toesluit.' (Get dressed, not that way, we'll lock you up.)[102]

No such allegations surfaced in the official inquiry but people may well have been inhibited from reporting such activity at the time. It would not have been the first occasion when South African police behaved in this way: as noted in Chapter One, the victims of the police's suppression of 1930 anti-pass protests in Durban may have died from wounds they received after their shooting. Even the contemporary evidence, though, suggests that with respect to most of the police present their treatment of both the living and the dead ranged from extremes of vindictiveness to a merely callous disregard. Witnesses claimed that police spoke to some of the people who were dying, mocking them with inversions of the slogans they had listened to throughout that morning. 'Ja, nou gaan jy na Mayebuye-toe' ('Yes, now you are going to return') they told one man badly hurt in the leg, and to another: 'Daar het julle dit; vat dit; dit is julle Afrika daardie.' ('There you have it, take it, that is your Africa.')[103]

The Reverend Robert Maja was one of several Sharpeville residents who attempted to offer comfort to the wounded, bringing them water as they lay on the ground. He noticed the careless way in which the police were removing the bodies and remonstrated with one of ranking officers: 'I am asking you, if you take that corpse, please remove the brains as well.' A photograph presented at the Inquiry indicates the compliance with Maja's request: a policemen is using a spade to shovel up the brain tissue that had spilled into the dust.[104] By this point British television cameramen were filming events and their footage does suggest for the most part that the police offered no help to the people actively seeking to tend the wounded. Half an hour after the shooting, the film indicates, by the time the ambulances arrived they were still holding their weapons, both rifles and *sjamboks*. Several of the black constables that appear on the film are holding crudely made *assegais* (stabbing spears), though it is not clear whether these are their own weapons or evidence they had collected.[105]

In 1999, former police officers and retired medical staff at the Vereeniging hospital told Philip Frankel that when the first bodies arrived at the hospital police were already on hand to examine the bodies and remove those that had been very badly disfigured by wounds from explosive 'dum-dum' ammunition. These bodies—perhaps as many as two dozen—would later be buried secretly, near Parys, Frankel learned from his informants. They would not be subjected to the post-mortems that were reported at the Inquiry in which all the dead were considered to have died from ordinary bullet wounds.[106] If this is true, then, of course, the death toll from the massacre would have been substantially higher.

While the constabulary were engaged in these early efforts to reorder and tidy-up the carnage they had created, their commanders hurried away, losing no time in making the arrangements that would isolate the township behind an encircling barrier of patrols and roadblocks. There would be no more anti-pass assertions in the vicinity of Vereeniging after the gunfire outside Sharpeville police station, though the PAC's strike call would continue to immobilize the city's economic life for the rest of the week as traumatized people chose to stay at home. The police had already broken up smaller gatherings at Vanderbijlpark and at Evaton. They succeeded in dispersing a gathering of 9,000 with a baton-charge at Vanderbijlpark. Until the baton-charge, though, police 'mingled with the crowd' and maintained communications through the morning with local PAC officials, very different from the confrontational stand-off that developed so quickly at Sharpeville. Protestors at Evaton were intimidated into flight by fourteen low-flying Sabre jets.[107]

In Bophelong, local Pan-Africanists cooperated with the township manager, Mr Knoetze, in keeping the crowd orderly before surrendering themselves. Later though, in Bophelong, there was an exchange of stones and shooting between a reassembled crowd and the police which left one man dead. The PAC managed to register only token numbers of protestors in other centres. In Pretoria's Lady Selborne township, when a few local PAC officials appeared without their passes the sergeant on duty in the charge office simply took their names and sent them home.[108] In Soweto, the dawn-time procession of small bands of the PAC's national leadership to their various local police stations in Orlando, Pimville, Moroka, and New-lands attracted only a few onlookers. By the time the police opened fire in Sharpeville, Robert Sobukwe and his lieutenants had been locked up in police custody for several hours. In Durban, the PAC's treasurer, Abednego

Ngcobo, led a very small number of anti-pass protestors to present themselves at the central police station. Ngcobo was charged with 'failing to produce his pass book on demand' and merely fined £5 the next day.[109] In East London, despite quite an extensive programme of meetings and public addresses in Duncan Village, only a dozen or so Pan-Africanists volunteered themselves for arrest, though later more than twice that number were convicted for incitement.[110]

Back in Sharpeville, in the hours that followed the bloodshed, within the cordon they had established the police conducted a ferocious *ratissage*, investing the township in force, on the hunt for 'troublemakers' and 'ringleaders', searching even the hospital wards to which the wounded had been taken. In the next few days the police arrested up to several hundred people they suspected of complicity in organizing the protest, working with army units to cordon off the township. By the time the residents of Sharpeville were permitted to bury their dead, in two carefully managed ceremonies on 30 March and 2 April, in most cases there had been no opportunities to organize night-time vigils for the dead. Their bodies arrived in lorries, their coffins already closed and locked. This was a further affront to the bereaved. Johannes Sefatsa lost his brother at the massacre; the two brothers were both Pan-Africanist followers and Samuel Sefatsa, a promising young professional boxer was a close friend of the Tsolo brothers. Because of the closed coffin, Johannes could not see his brother for a final time.[111]

One of the funerals was filmed by a British television crew, and despite the massive attendance it was an orderly occasion. Those Pan-Africanists still at liberty signalled their presence and paid their respects with a lonely banner that they held up at the graveside. They did not speak, though. Through the services, only priests would address the mourners. As Gideon Tsolo observed, 'there was no more politics by that time'.[112] With uncharacteristic sensitivity the police remained out of sight.

Elsewhere in the Transvaal, news of the killings prompted rioting and more organized forms of protest in Soweto over the next few days. With most of the key Pan-Africanists now in prison after their arrest at various police stations, it was the ANC's turn to seize the initiative and its leaders announced that the following Monday, 28 March, would be a day of passburnings. Though a second echelon of PAC leaders had prepared themselves to assume command, in the Transvaal the PAC's pass campaign was eclipsed. But in Cape Town the PAC's protest was to succeed in prompting a much more sustained insurgency.

4

The Cape Town Marchers

On the night of Monday 21 March in Cape Town, police violence transformed a mostly peaceful campaign of civil disobedience into a popular insurrection.

Let us begin with an outline of the key events in the opening phase of the PAC's 'positive action' in Cape Town. On Sunday, 20 March, PAC leaders addressed large meetings in the main African townships outside the city, in Nyanga West and Nyanga East and in Langa, where a crowd of 5,000 assembled in the 'New Flats' district, an area inhabited by members of the city's migrant labour force. Here the mainly male audience listened to an address by Philip Kgosana, the PAC's regional secretary. Borrowing freely from Sobukwe, Kgosana warned that in their protest the following day, anti-pass protestors should absolutely eschew using any violence: 'We are not leading corpses to a New Africa.' He continued:

> We are not going to burn or damage any part of the Pass Book in any manner. We are not going to fight or attempt to fight, insult or attempt to insult, provoke or attempt to provoke the police in their lawful duties. We are not going to throw the stones at the police or do anything that is going to obstruct the police. Any person who does these things will be dealt with by the police of course, and we, as an organization, shall deal further with him. Nobody is carrying money, knives or any dangerous weapon with himself tomorrow. People are not going to join this struggle with evil personal interest in it. Nobody is going to burn any building, office, school or any property of the government. Nobody is going to burn any bus or threaten anybody. If anybody does these things and the police begin to shoot, any person who will die or receive injuries shall be demanded on the head of the mischief maker. The Gods of Africa shall pass judgement on such a person.[1]

After these meetings, the main PAC leaders, as in Sharpeville, went into hiding at pre-arranged safe houses while their Task Force volunteers began

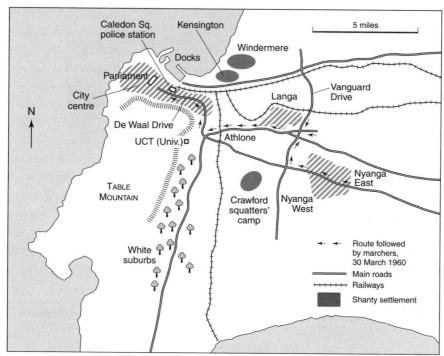

Map 4. African townships and shanty settlement around Cape Town

working the streets, moving from house to house. Again, as in Sharpeville, priests marked midnight by ringing their church bells, and in the early hours of the morning the PAC principals began to emerge. Philip Kgosana was woken very early by his comrades, eager to tell him that the portents were good for rain was falling, heavily. They 'were convinced spiritually that we had won before we had started', Kgosana wrote later. 'God has consented', they told Kgosana. As Kgosana explained, 'in certain African traditions, we believe that if rain drizzles just before a great event, the event will be a success because even the Gods show their consent by letting the rain fall. We believe that the rain washes off our tears.'[2] Encouraged by this excellent omen, the Pan-Africanist principals emerged from their quarters at around 4.30 am to find about 4,000 men had gathered at Langa Square, an open space next to the New Flats complex accommodating the migrant workers.

By 6.00 am this assembly had grown to 10,000 'excited men'. The local PAC organizers intended to lead this group to the police station to begin the process of handing themselves over for arrest, all of them. This move was thwarted, though, by the arrival of seven police vehicles. On disembarking from these, the constables lined up in front of the crowd with batons raised. Five senior PAC men were present, including Philip Kgosana. It was Kgosana who took the initiative to approach the police, introducing himself to Detective Head Constable Sauerman, and requesting that if the police wished to say anything to the crowd they should communicate through himself or any of the other leaders. They should not issue direct orders to the crowd. Kgosana then informed the police that the protestors would be marching to the police station to surrender themselves. The police warned Kgosana that they would 'defend the station': they should not march. Kgosana agreed that his followers would keep away from the station and he would post Task Force teams as pickets to guard the approaches to the station but the protest would continue, nobody would be going to work that day. Kgosana's conversation with Sauerman seems to have been characterized by mutual civility. As he told a reporter from *Contact*:

> The senior officer in charge of the police refused to arrest me. He wanted to know who would control the demonstrators when I was in gaol. I told him that our demonstration was opposed to violence. At this he shook my hand in congratulation.[3]

Both Kgosana and the Langa New Flats PAC branch secretary, Mlami Makwetu, addressed the crowd.[4] After warning that the police would interpret a mass procession to the police station as an attack, the PAC leaders asked their followers to reassemble in the evening. Witnesses at the subsequent Commission of Inquiry insisted that Kgosana also told the crowd that they would have news in the evening, that at six o'clock there would be 'word from national office'. Through the day, rather as had happened in Sharpeville, a rumour circulated that there would be an important announcement, an official response to their demands, that the police had undertaken to supply such a response that evening. As in Sharpeville, witnesses and participants disagree about the degree to which PAC officials deliberately encouraged this belief.

The crowd eventually broke up around 9 am and Philip Kgosana and the other regional PAC principals began a tour of the other locations in which their organization had undertaken preparations. At Philippi station near Nyanga, police had persuaded a large group to return to their homes after at least a thousand of its constituents had handed in their names to register their intention to defy the pass laws. The PAC officials then learned that several protestors had actually been arrested and were being charged in central Cape Town and they decided to take the train into the city to visit them. While in town, Philip Kgosana paid two important calls, to the offices of two locally published newspapers that addressed African readers, *Contact* and *New Age*. *Contact* was edited by members of the Liberal Party, with whom, as we will see, Kgosana was on familiar terms and Communists constituted the main editorial influence over *New Age*. During their absence the gathering outside the New Flats began to reassemble and by 5.30 pm different estimates suggest that there were between 6,000 and 15,000 people waiting to be addressed in Langa Square. In the police station nearby a group of about sixty policemen, thirty of them African constables, boarded a convoy of Land Rovers headed by a Saracen armoured personnel vehicle. Nine of the white officers carried sten guns.

Local PAC men opened the formal proceedings by calling for prayers. Their more senior colleagues had not yet arrived: Kgosana and the other regional executive members were still on the train, returning from Cape Town. The police convoy arrived at 5.44 pm. The policemen got out of their vehicles to confront a crowd that though orderly was exuberant, for the constabulary was greeted with a crescendo of slogans and cheers. After a few minutes the commanding officer, Captain Louw shouted through a loudhailer a three-minute ultimatum: the crowd should disperse before the police would take action. Louw did not try to seek out any PAC officials and officers rebuffed at least one offer from Elliot Magwentshu, the PAC branch secretary for Langa township, to function as an intermediary. As Judge Marius Diemont noted later in concluding his official enquiry, Louw's warning, even if it had been heard above the general din, allowed an unreasonably short time for dispersal and in any case would have bewildered people who were expecting an official announcement.[5]

Judge Diemont's report, itself unusually critical of the police, supplies a careful chronology of what happened next. At 5.56 pm Captain Louw ordered his men to line up and one minute later the police advanced, charging the crowd and using their batons. Diemont noted that most of the baton injuries sustained during these charges were head wounds concluding that the police had deviated from standard procedure in which officers were supposed to target lower parts of the body. Diemont's view was that the police behaviour was 'unlawful and undisciplined', for they had used 'indiscriminate and immoderate force' against people who were running away. Forceful action failed to intimidate most of the crowd, though, and indeed its front ranks surged forward after the second charge and what Diemont termed a 'barrage' of stones, half bricks, and bottles assailed the police. Officers and journalists who were present told the investigation that they heard cries of 'kill the whites' and police maintained that they had heard gunfire, apparently directed at them from the first floor of one of the migrant worker hostels. At this juncture, at 5.57 pm Louw ordered his men to use their firearms. The police shot their weapons individually, not in collective volleys, releasing 100 rounds of ammunition over a five-minute period, firing mainly into the front ranks of the crowd, wounding twenty-eight people and killing two. Protestors only began their retreat at 6.15 pm after another barrage of stoning engendered a final baton charge.

Far from quelling the tumult, police firepower succeeded only in ratcheting up the scale and intensity of communal rebellion. While the returning PAC regional leaders set about trying to reestablish their control over events, the Task Force assumed command of Langa's streets. Men lined up at the edge of the township and began stoning cars travelling along Vanguard Drive, the main arterial road into the city. Meanwhile the PAC's young Jacobins threw up road-blocks across the township's access roads and severed its telephone lines. At around 6.30 pm a group of protestors began advancing on the police station only to be driven off with batons and guns fired over their heads. At 6.30 pm 'a wave of incendiarism' (Diemont's words) enveloped the township. While looters attacked the houses of locally resident African policemen, Task Forcers set alight every official building they could identify, beginning, significantly, with the rent collection office and the complex of buildings accommodating the organization that managed the reception and return of migrant labourers. The arsonists also targeted municipal workshops, Langa High School, the public library, the civic hall, the post office, and Dutch Reformed, Methodist, and Apostolic churches. Fire engines were attacked at the road-blocks and were forced to withdraw; only later did they enter the township under armed police escorts. The aggression that night was directed at all outsiders, not just soldiers and policemen. A mob halted a company car owned by the *Cape Times*, destroying the vehicle and burning to death its coloured driver, Richard Lombard. At 8.00 pm South African Defence Force (SADF) Saracens entered Langa to station themselves around the police station and other official buildings but unrest was to sustain itself for several hours. It was only by midnight that rioting finally subsided. By then, Philip Kgosana recalled much later, 'Langa was an army camp, with wailing Saracens speeding up and down the streets.'[6] Despite this military presence within the township, the PAC's rebellion was only just beginning. It would develop into a challenge to South African authority that was without precedent.

Clearly this was a very different movement from the gatherings that PAC activists had managed to summon in the industrial heartland of the Transvaal. In the Transvaal, many of the people who stood outside police stations at the behest of the Pan-Africanists attended as onlookers, curious, even sympathetic, but not fully engaged. In Cape Town things were different: largely male crowds were constituted by thousands of mainly young men who intended to demand arrest, as the roll call at Philippi police station made clear. The following the PAC had attracted in Langa was evidently combative and animated by passionate political conviction. PAC membership statistics for Langa suggest a much deeper level of political organization than the PAC had achieved in Sharpeville. We need to explore the social setting in which the organization became rooted to understand why the Pan-Africanists were able to mobilize such determined adherents.

Cape Town was unique among South Africa's larger cities in that its one hundred thousand African inhabitants constituted a minority of the population, outnumbered by whites and coloureds. The government was committed to excluding Africans from the city altogether. In 1954, the region was designated as a coloured 'labour preference area': in future, government policy would be to aim for 'the ultimate extinction of natives from this area'.[7] From 1954, no more family houses were constructed in the main township, Langa. Langa had 25,000 residents, 19,000 of whom were adult men. Most of these men, 17,500, were contract workers who lived in dormitories in the single men's 'barracks' or the more recently constructed 'zones' or in eight multi-storey blocks of 'flats', dwellings that provided double rooms for people who wanted better accommodation than the dormitories in the barracks or the zones. 'Influx control' was implemented with doctrinaire severity and between 1959 and 1961 25,000 men and women were forcibly transported, 'endorsed out', to remote reserves in the Eastern Cape. Moreover, in the process of issuing African men with the new 'reference books', required by the 1952 Natives Abolition and Coordination of Documents Act, many of the 62,000 recipients of the new books had their status downgraded from permanent urban residents to transient contract workers, permitted to live in Cape Town only as long as they were employed.[8] A series of shanty encampments that had sprung up during the

1940s began to be demolished in the mid-1950s. A few of their inhabitants were lucky enough to be moved into proper family houses with 'tarred streets with signs and proper home addresses'.[9] The majority of the former shanty town residents, though, were either sent away from the Western Cape or they were re-housed in the dismal 'bachelor' hostels. One of these settlements remained intact, Kensington in the Windermere area. Around 3,000 families lived in Windermere but at the beginning of 1960 they were told that soon they would be moved to Nyanga. They would have to live in a squalid site and service scheme that had just been opened, in an area outside Cape Town's municipal boundary. This would mean that people who had held jobs in Cape Town might not be allowed in future to work in the city and they and their families would be at risk of 'endorsement out', resettlement in the Eastern Cape.

Anthropological research undertaken in Langa during the late 1950s supplies insights into the social distinctions within Cape Town's African population that are helpful in identifying the PAC's social following. Anthropologists perceived four groups to constitute Langa's population: migrant labourers, semi-urbanized, urbanized 'townees', and 'decent people'. In this conceptualization, migrant labourers, though working for a large part of their lives in an urban environment, remained socially and culturally oriented to rural life. Members of the semi-urbanized group would have originally arrived in Cape Town as migrant workers but now were aspiring to becoming townsmen while retaining connections with the countryside:

> The semi-urbanized man behaves very much as a townsman while he is in town, and seeks to move out of the barracks or zones into the flats or a room in a private house, but he does not cut his ties with the country. His wife may or may not be with him, but he still thinks of country life as better for an older, settled man. Many women remain semi-urbanized in their attitudes and values though they have lived in town for some years and their husbands have become real townsmen.[10]

The townees were distinguished from both the professional and lower-middle-class 'decent people' by their flashy clothes, youth, preference for certain types of factory work, violent 'wild' behaviour, and contempt for the rural conservatism of the migrants and for the middle-class 'respectability' of the decent people. In Langa the majority was constituted by the first category, the migrants. They lived in the barrack or zone dormitories with people from their home region. The aspirant townsmen tended in

Langa to concentrate in the double-roomed 'flats' but many too would have lived as lodgers in the few remaining shanty settlements such as Kensington because there was room only for 1,300 beds in the 'flats'. The townees and decent people of Langa lived in the family housing. The PAC's determined focus on pass laws would have had an especial appeal for groups denied permanent urban status, that is the migrant workers, particularly the aspiring semi-urbanized townsmen living in the Langa flats, as well as the people in shanty encampments threatened with resettlement. To these groups, the PAC appeared to share their concerns in a way that seemed quite new. As one of the hostel dwellers recalled more than four decades later: 'We used to think that the struggle was for the learned, but we were told by the PAC to come and join an organization that catered for all the people.'[11]

The regional ANC had a local history of strife between African nationalists and Communists. Over the previous two decades the Communist Party had developed a relatively strong presence in Cape Town and since its banning its members were assertively active within the white Congress of Democrats (COD). In 1955 Communists had assumed control in the Western Cape preparations for the Congress of the People and this provoked divisions within the ANC. As the Congress's national organizer, T. Tshunungwa, commented, 'a politically raw African who has been much oppressed, exploited and victimized by the European sees red when a white face appears'. In the Western Cape, Tshunungwa observed, 'extreme confusion resulted from the 'COD men taking a lead in the ANC meetings'.[12] This seems to have been especially the case in Cape Town where relatively weak local ANC leadership made COD's contribution to the direction of joint Congress Alliance campaigning very visible. The COD's national leadership itself expressed concern about this, noting in 1959 that the Cape Town branch seemed 'unnecessarily dependent' on ANC activity.[13] As Elliot Magwenthsu, one of the Cape Town Africanists explained, 'we felt that our branches were being run from Caledon Street, by the Congress of Democrats'.[14] Disagreements paralysed the ANC organization in the Western Cape after 1955. Most of the Cape Town branches effectively split into two, separately electing their own leaders and making rival claims for acknowledgment from the ANC's provincial executive, which itself was divided between Africanists and Freedom Charter supporters.[15] Social distinctions reinforced the ideological divisions, apparently. 'Charterists' tended to be older people who had lived all their lives in Cape Town, city born and bred. Many of these would have been involved in the trade unions Communists had been helping to lead in the region since the 1930s: they would have known the COD people as old comrades from that era. ANC loyalists embraced as well a more conservative group than the left-wing Charterists: people within the township's political elite—elected Advisory Board and Vigilance Association members. Elected Advisory Boards and the Vigilance Association had existed in Langa since the 1920s, their membership overlapping.[16] In 1960, the Association claimed 300 members and tended to represent 'more conservative rent-payers in the married quarters'.[17] Since 1936, Communists had successfully solicited the Association's support in their campaigning in Native Representative elections.[18] In contrast to Charterists and other loyalists, the Africanist dissenters tended to be relative newcomers to Cape Town, and country born.[19]

The ANC's Western Cape regional chairman, Thomas Ngwenya, although an ANC loyalist often found himself at odds with Communists active within the ANC. To strengthen his own position he began working closely with members of the Liberal Party who themselves were trying to build a township base in the Vigilance Committees, competing with the Communists in the 1954 Native Representative elections.[20] In the three largest ANC branches, in Langa, Nyanga, and Kensington, disaffected 'Africanists' began to build a following and in 1958 these groups seceded. There is detailed information about the activities within one of these branches because the minute books of the original dissident Africanist Committee in Kensington and the subsequent PAC branch executive have been preserved. These records shed a little light on the movement's character within the squatter community. It was led by a group of fairly experienced former ANC members; the two leading office-holders, Synod Madlebe and Peter Bomali, were described in a court record as 'labourers' aged in their forties and fifties respectively.[21] Apparently, until September 1959, the membership of the branch consisted entirely of 'old men',[22] though soon after the branch began to attract the 'youth'.[23] In common with other PAC branches in the area, most recruitment was undertaken through public meetings, though there was a plan to 'zone' Kensington for a 'door-to-door campaign' in order to construct a 'cell system'. This plan was only beginning to be put into effect in early 1960.[24] As well as organizing public meetings (held from February 1960 in conjunction with the Nyanga West branch, which was composed of people evicted from Kensington now living on site and service plots), Kensington's PAC activists travelled to Worcester, Somerset, and Stellenbosch to find new recruits for the movement. Their conception of the organization's ideal social character is revealed in this comment from the minute book:

> [Kensington PAC officials travelled] to Worcester with the intention of organizing. They arrived at 1 pm. They succeeded and left a promise to the effect that they would be coming and join all the parties they have lectured and <u>see to the intellectuals who would be eligible to take posts</u> (my emphasis).[25]

In the terms of the social categories used at the time by South African urban anthropologists, the background of the Kensington activists corresponds most closely with the 'semi-urbanized' group. Peter Bomali, for instance, the branch chairman, aged fifty-five, had worked on a farm in the Free State before arriving in Cape Town in 1940. He had received no schooling and he lived in great poverty with his diabetic wife and a son who suffered from epilepsy.[26] The Kensington branch was the largest of the Cape Town branches with a total strength in November 1959 of 154 members. Its membership was constituted by relatively urbanized people but this may not have been typical of the PAC's overall following in the Western Cape. From its establishment in July 1959 there was a flourishing PAC branch in the Langa Flats, home of the 'semi-urbanized' migrants. A special 'conference' was held in the Flats in January 1960 to encourage the affiliation to the movement of more migrants. The townee teenage 'youth' of Langa township contributed to the movement's socially heterodox character by forming an especially effective and energetic PAC Task Force. Ostensibly reformed *tsotsis* also helped to constitute Task Forces in Nyanga East and West.[27] According to the memoirs of one of the PAC leaders, the best organized branch was in Nyanga West, among the displaced squatters. Here again the Kensington minute book is revealing when it notes that 'Mr Mgweba saw this influence, no work, no passes, amongst the women in Nyanga West.'

The encounter within the PAC of semi-urbanized migrants and townees—groups that conventionally tended to be at odds with each other—is convincingly represented in Mxolise Mgxashe's 'activist' memoir. Orphaned as an infant, Mgxashe grew up in Parkwood shanty town, supported by his aunts who worked as domestic servants. The family was moved to a house in Nyanga in 1959 and in January 1960, Mgxashe began attending Langa High School. He could not afford to pay the bus fares between Nyanga and Langa and so he stayed with an old friend Gilbert Maqelane in the 'zones', the bachelor hostels. Maqelane had also lived in Parkwood, living next door to the Mgxashe household. He was fifteen years older than Mxolise, working on a

construction site. Mxolise helped Gilbert with his writing and reading assign-
ments that Gilbert brought back from night school. Now Gilbert could return
the favour, sharing his room and board in the bachelor flats with Mxolise. By
now Gilbert was a 'staunch' PAC member. On the evening of the 21 March,
Mxolise joined a group of his fellow students from Langa High School 'who,
driven by curiosity and passion for the objectives of the PAC anti-pass
campaign and in solidarity with the scores who had died at Sharpeville that
morning, walked to the Langa bus terminal where the rally was held'.[28]

The evidence available suggests that the PAC succeeded in evoking
support from a broad cross-section of the Cape Town African community:
the only group from which it did not attract a significant following was the
middle-class 'decent people', the 'intellectuals' mentioned perhaps rather
wistfully in the passage quoted above from the Kensington minute book.
The substantial number of migrant workers within its following made the
Cape Town Pan-Africanists socially distinctive. Certainly many of the PAC
speakers were addressing this constituency with their evocation of the spirits
of Makana, Hintsa, and Mghayi[29] and their references to the Xhosa deity:

> We should always remember our customs so that we should be lucky in what
> we are doing. Now we belong to different churches and have forgotten our
> God, Qamata. Why do we worship another God?[30]

Pan-Africanists were also specifically addressing the migrant workers' concerns in their frequent denunciations of 'the traitors, the African chiefs at the
reserves, that is why there was culling and selection of cattle'. As one of their
Cape Town leaders, Philip Kgosana, recalled later: 'In Cape Town we
inculcated a new spirit in the people. They had to renew their contact
with the African God and our ancestors. We believed, as we still believe
now, that we were oppressed largely because we had deserted our customs,
our traditions and our Gods.'[31]

Imaginative and assertive leadership was a key characteristic of the Pan-
Africanists in this region. What kinds of men presided over this movement
in Cape Town? We have very detailed biographical information about one
of the predominant personalities in these unfolding events, Philip Kgosana.

Philip Kgosana was brought up in Makapanstad, a rural settlement thirty
miles outside Pretoria, the second son of a unpaid priest in the Church of
Christ, an American mission. His father grazed cattle and earned a modest
living as a carpenter, a livelihood just about sufficient to send both his sons
to school. After several stops and starts in his formal education Philip joined

his brother Sam in Pretoria, enrolling at the age of seventeen at Lady Selbourne High school, one of the premier African schools in the Transvaal. He completed his matriculation exams four years later, meteoric progress. His parents could not afford the fees that he needed to attend a teacher training college, his chosen next stage. Instead he obtained a post as a clerk in a Coca Cola factory but was dismissed after a week and then worked as a messenger in the government department that administered Bantu education, delivering files to the offices of the then minister, Dr Verwoerd. His evident intelligence attracted support and sponsorship from Dr William Nkomo, Lady Selbourne's leading citizen and father of one of Kgosana's classmates. Dr Nkomo helped him to negotiate a scholarship from the Institute of Race Relations. The scholarship manager at the Institute telephoned the University of Cape Town on Kgosana's behalf and persuaded the authorities there to admit him to the Commerce Faculty, not Kgosana's preference, because he wanted to study pharmacy, but better than working as a clerical menial for Minister Verwoerd. Meanwhile, Bob Leshoai, his inspirational English teacher at Lady Selbourne High School, managed to secure for him a monthly stipend of £5 from a elderly white widow who was also willing to donate some of her son's cast-off clothes.[32]

For the teenage Kgosana, Bob Leshoai had been an important early mentor.

> I don't know whether I'd always admired Bob because he was an English teacher. He'd come in and simply say, 'To be or not to be, that is the question' and he would be quoting our prescribed text, *Hamlet*, and he would be pulling out from there, and he would spend the whole forty minutes adding so much meaning to 'To be or not to be' and relating it to our situation here in South Africa, whether we have to choose between the sorts of things Shakespeare was talking about; whether to surrender to a situation or take up arms against a sea of troubles, that is how Bob used to say.

For Leshoai, Kgosana may have stood out among his peer group. He published an essay by his pupil in the school magazine he edited. Philip had written about an occasion when he was walking to the cinema. He arrived too early for the film—it was an Elvis Presley feature, and he began 'just moving about Marabastad'. He saw two women who had evidently just completed their work in somebody's kitchen, 'you know, those Marabastad women with grass rings'. They were eating peanuts, tossing the shells away. As he recalled in his essay, 'here were these women, tossing peanuts, exploited and probably underpaid, and I am going to see a movie, Elvis's *Jailhouse Rock*, and I am going to see this movie. "I want to be free, like a bird on a tree", Elvis had sung for the film and I could relate to these women to what I was going to see.' After the film he returned home and wrote about how he felt as he saw these women, 'trudging the streets'.[33]

Leshoai himself contributed a tweed jacket, a sweater, and a pair of shoes and it was with a wardrobe of second-hand garments that Kgosana embarked on his third-class rail journey to Cape Town at the beginning of 1959. On arrival he had just enough money to pay for a week's lodging at a cheap hotel in the coloured neighbourhood of District Six, midway between the university and the city but he needed more affordable permanent accommodation quickly. The university registered only twenty Africans amongst its student body and made no arrangements for their boarding apart from excluding them from halls of residence.

On his first day on campus, after registering, Kgosana ran into Nana Mahomo, a fellow Transvaaler, 'whom [he] found, thought very much as I did about politics'. Mahomo, a founding member of the PAC, had registered at the university in 1957 as a law student with the deliberate intention of 'initiat(ing) political organization in the Western Cape': his university affiliation was simply a means to enable him as a Transvaaler to stay in Cape Town.[34] It was another African student, though, Archie Mafeje, who suggested a practical solution to Kgosana's accommodation problem. Mafeje told Kgosana that he should find a bed in the Langa New Flats: several UCT students, out-of-towners like Kgosana, had rented rooms there paying as little as £1 a month: meanwhile Mafeje would help with train fares. Also on Mafeje's advice, Kgosana wrote to Patrick Duncan, the editor of *Contact*, to ask for financial help. Duncan replied within a day. He was reluctant to offer charity, but he would like to meet Kgosana. Kgosana must have impressed Duncan for he emerged from the subsequent appointment he made at the *Contact* office with a generous sales commission, weekly payments that would enable him to pay fares and to buy stationery.

By the end of his first week in Cape Town, Kgosana had left his hotel room in District Six and acquired a bed in a room in Block C, Langa New Flats. During his first evening there he made friends with a PAC member, Ladebe Nxelewa, who on meeting him and hearing that he was from Pretoria asked Kgosana if he had ever met Robert Sobukwe. As it happened, Kgosana had recently attended in Lady Selbourne an evening house meeting that Sobukwe had addressed: even in this brief encounter Sobukwe had made a deep impression upon him. Nxelewa soon became a firm friend, asking Kgosana to share his evening meal and helping him out with money for his bus fares, though as Kgosana puts it, despite all the help he received, 'Money continued to be my constant plague.' Money difficulties help partly to explain Kgosana's poor academic progress—he could not afford all the textbooks for his economics courses but he was also distracted from his studies by his growing political engagement: by the middle of the year Kgosana was deputizing for Nxelewa as an assistant branch secretary. He was learning Xhosa fast in the Flats but making less progress with his formal studies at the university: he failed all but two of the subjects in his first year commerce exams. Undaunted he returned home for a brief Christmas holiday with his family. He was the sole Western Cape representative at the PAC's Orlando Conference: he had managed to obtain a lift with fellow students travelling to the Transvaal from the Cape and none of the other Cape Pan-Africanists could afford the fares, despite their efforts to solicit funds. Here at this pivotal meeting he was invited to join Sobukwe and other senior leaders on the committee that drafted the conference resolutions. Two weeks later Philip Kgosana returned to Cape Town, ostensibly to retake his exams, for he needed to maintain his university registration to qualify for continued residence in the Cape. In reality, though, Kgosana had become a full-time political activist, a commitment that was rewarded at the end of January when he was elected regional secretary of the Western Cape PAC.[35]

Philip Kgosana attracted sponsors and patrons very readily. Even from this short profile of his life up to this point it is evident that he impressed a range of older men, themselves strong personalities: Bob Leshoai, Patrick Duncan, Ladebe Nxelewa, and Robert Sobukwe were each cases in point. He was exceptionally bright and it was this intelligence combined with his appearance of innocent vulnerability that may have helped to arouse protective instincts, a capacity of which he himself was well aware and willing to exploit. He looked in fact even younger than he actually was, 'baby faced' as one acquaintance described him.[36] He was slightly built and he unintentionally accentuated his youthful appearance by habitually wearing a pair of blue shorts so that he could preserve his one pair of hand-me-down flannel trousers. As he recalled of his relationship with Nxelewa: 'When I needed money I just told him like a child and he gave it to me.'[37] But as well as filial charm, his patrons could also perceive promise, strength, and ambition. Philip Kgosana so impressed Sobukwe during the brief spell they worked with each other at the PAC conference that the PAC president advised the

Cape Town Pan-Africanists to make him the public face of their organization, partly, perhaps, to distract the authorities from paying attention to more experienced men but also because Sobukwe perceived that Kgosana possessed a range of leadership attributes: oratorical eloquence, decisive self-confidence, and, most importantly, the social empathy that enabled him to bridge the very disparate worlds of Pan-Africanist politicians and African intellectual life more generally on the one hand and on the other the lived daily experience of Ndebele domestic workers in Marabastad or Xhosa contract labourers in Cape Town.[38] In return, Kgosana looked up to Sobukwe. From his initial meeting with Sobukwe in Lady Selbourne in 1958, in his words, Sobukwe 'really stole my heart'.[39] Kgosana modelled his oratorical style on Sobukwe's example, reproducing his gestures and mannerisms, the inflections of his voice,[40] even picking up Sobukwe's conversational habit of emphasizing a point with the phrase, 'That's right', 'as if it were a punctuation mark'.[41] And amongst the students of Langa High School whom Kgosana addressed in February, even before the opening of the pass campaign, he had become a hero, a boy in shorts who could command in a world of men.[42]

Most of PAC top echelon in Cape Town were not the kinds of men who would later provide reflective autobiographical testimony for historians and so we know much less about their backgrounds and their personalities. Kgosana embodied the kind of 'intellectual' whom the Western Cape PAC sought so hard to recruit into its leadership. Yet another influential personality who was to help shape events in the next few days, Mlami Makwetu, was much more representative of the movement's semi-urbanized rank and file. Makwetu was the acknowledged leader of the PAC's following among the migrant workers in the Langa New Flats. Mgwashe's memoir supplies a brief pen portrait of Makwetu whom he recalls in the 1960s as 'articulate with a good command of Xhosa' in which he could give expression to his 'sophisticated rural outlook'. Makwetu was 'idolized' apparently, 'by immigrant worker elements in the branch most of whom came from his home village in Cofimvaba' among whom he worked sometimes as a casual labourer at the docks. He was a big man, exceptionally tall with a 'height that made him look even bigger than Sobukwe'.[43] One contemporary description from 1960 depicts him as 'a tall svelte young man of about 20, with the air of a university lecturer' who 'carried himself with quiet authority'.[44] Another source attests to Makwetu's gracious manners.[45] In more modern times, Makwetu again emerged on the national political stage when he led the PAC in the 1994 election and he supplied a terse summary of his life history for the compilers of a biographical directory. He was born into a peasant household in Cofimvaba district in the Transkei in about 1930. He attended mission schools in Stutterheim and Queenstown and matriculated through Lovedale College in 1946. He travelled to Cape Town to seek work in 1948. He joined the ANC while living in Cape Town, in 1952, during the Defiance Campaign and was a principal mover in the secession of Africanist branches in 1959. Through the 1950s he made a living as a hawker, 'on his own', selling 'soft goods', women's wear. Philip Kgosana remembers that he was 'always moving around, with a suitcase'.[46]

Trial records help us to sketch in details about the backgrounds of a few of the other key figures who directed the movement in Cape Town. Of the thirty-two men later put on trial for leading the PAC in Cape Town, all regional executive members or senior leaders in the PAC's main branches, all except Kgosana were described in the trial records as labourers. Twelve of the men were in their twenties, the others were older, most in their thirties and forties. Ten were residents of the migrant worker quarters in Langa. Several of the accused provided the court with autobiographical statements. They included Peter Bomali, the Kensington branch leader we have encountered already. Accused no. 17 was Twelve Siyadubiwa, aged thirty-eight. He had arrived in Cape Town in 1945 to set up trade as a herbalist, a practitioner of traditional medicine, constantly forced to shift his premises because of the expanding zone around the city from which Africans were excluded from renting shop-space. Algernon Sikiti, aged forty-eight, also stands out because he was relatively well-educated, the son of a court interpreter and a former schoolteacher but for the previous ten years employed as a checker in a dry-cleaning plant. Abel Gaberone, a resident of a Nyanga site and service plot, aged thirty, was more typical of the general PAC membership. He had failed to obtain a job 'to suit my education'—he had been schooled up to Standard Five—and worked as a gardener and domestic servant.[47]

The American researcher, Gail Gerhart, when interviewing Elliot Magwentshu in 1970 asked him to classify a list of PAC members from Cape Town, mainly branch level office-holders, using the social categories developed by the anthropologists Archie Mafeje and Monica Wilson. Of sixteen Langa PAC members, Magwentshu suggested that six were of the semi-urbanized *Ibari* group: 'a stereotype held by townsmen regarding the semi-urban young men: he is considered "a barbarian", wears flashy clothes, is uncouth and wild'. Three were full countrymen (*amaqaba*) and the

remaining seven Magwentshu considered as belonging to completely urbanized groups. In Nyanga, the *Topi* and the *ooscuseme* constituted the largest
grouping among the seventeen PAC officials Magwentshu identified and
categorized: six officials belonged to each of these groups. In the Mafeje–
Wilson classification, *Topi* are older respectable people, fully urbanized but
not very educated, often small businessmen, wholesalers' agents, taxi drivers, and the like. The *ooscuseme* group as depicted by Mafeje and Wilson are
educated middle class, often professionals, and speakers of English at home.
However it seems that Magwentshu applied this label rather more liberally
to include people who may have hoped to become middle class in this way.
Even so it seems sensible to conclude that the Nyanga PAC leaders and
members were less likely to be engaged with rural culture and less influenced by traditional customs and manners than their comrades in Langa.[48]
In the sections of Langa that were inhabited by migrant workers, the PAC
was most strongly established in the Flats, the buildings in which men shared
rooms, not dormitories, favoured by the aspirant townsmen—*Ibari*—and
the more established resident workers. Philip Kgosana's building, Block C,
was 'the power base' of the Langa PAC. From this base, the PAC began to
build its following among the single mens' communities, first in the other
Flats and then in the barracks and the zones.[49]

The trial documentation also helps to illuminate the PAC's preparations
for the anti-pass campaign in the Western Cape. By December 1959, the
original nucleus of ex-ANC members who had constituted the original
breakaway Africanist secession had augmented the new movement's
following by setting up fresh branches in the shanty settlements and the
bachelor hostels, hitherto unexplored territory for modern political organizations. Maybe as many as 7,000 new recruits had joined up. However, on
his return from the Transvaal, Philip Kgosana found that the resolutions he
had helped to draft at Orlando had engendered no fresh waves of activity in
Cape Town. Indeed, despite the national injunctions to prepare for 'positive
action' the regional executive had held no meetings since his departure
and was not due to reassemble until 20 January. On 24 January, PAC rank
and file dismissed the regional leadership and voted in an energetic new
executive, this time dominated by men from the bachelor quarters and by
ex-shanty dwellers. This body appointed Kgosana as its secretary, in deference to Robert Sobukwe's recommendation.

Increasingly in the Western Cape this was becoming a movement shaped
by the perceptions and preoccupations of semi-urbanized workers. This is

evident from the speeches that the ever-attentive police recorded at the various public meetings the PAC held in Langa and Nyanga between May 1959 and March 1960. At first, the most frequently reoccurring topics were issues that primarily concerned experienced town-dwellers rather than more recently arrived migrants from the Transkei. Sobukwe's instructions that the Pan-Africanists' first campaign should be aimed at businesses and shops that failed to accord Africans courteous treatment was interpreted by several speakers as a call for African entrepreneurial opportunities:

> The government boasted that it has given Africans their rights, but it is not so in practice. Let all white clerks leave the offices of Langa. Langa buses must be driven by African drivers. In railway stations tickets must be issued by Africans for Africans. Africans must be given the right to do business in African areas.
>
> The only remedy that will free you from slavery is racialism. Support your African business people.
>
> Let an African buy from another African.
>
> We want Africans to open businesses here at Langa. Here at Langa it is a black spot. An African cannot open a business at Athlone. This organization says an African's money must go to an African pocket from an African pocket

In this first phase, some of the fiercest invective was directed not so much at the authorities but rather at the ANC and its allies. A number of speeches reflect the social tensions that helped to fragment African nationalist politics in this region.

> The African National Congress is called the Congress of Sam Kahn. Sam Kahn pays his servant the same ages as van Wyk of Stellenbosch. If any European wants to join this Congress let him rub out his name as European.
>
> Today you are being misled by Trade Unions. You should cut your connection with any organization that has white people.
>
> We do not affiliate with Congress of Democrats. Do not think when you are oppressed by Europeans that other Europeans will come and free you.
>
> The 1952 Defiance Campaign was planned by our political oppressors. Who came to us as if they sympathized? Were any of these sympathizers shot at the time of the Defiance campaign?

After Christmas, though, the police records suggest that the PAC was directing its rhetoric mainly to a quite different audience constituted by people much more on the margins of urban life:

> The prophecy of Mqhayi is being fulfilled, that the governed shall govern and the rulers shall be ruled.

Why do we worship another nation's God? We have our own way of worship and customs.

We say why this country is so bad like this it is through the traitors, the African chiefs in the reserves that is why there is culling and selection of cattle.

Some people sleep in the bushes because of these passes. We are calling upon you Africans to come and work with us, because these passes are now all over also in the reserves[50]

Of course the Cape Town Pan-Africanists continued to try to win over a broad social spectrum. References to African deities notwithstanding, several of the Pan-Africanist speakers whose words appear in police records took care to stress that 'you must have nationalism for Christ had it in himself' or that 'Jesus was full of nationalism. Moses too.' 'We want all the churchmen' an audience in Nyanga West was reminded, 'We want a very strong leader from the church people.' Regional leaders themselves, though, were quite evidently aware that their new movement was socially distinctive, different from more established political organizations. Again and again, they emphasized that the PAC was a movement that welcomed 'illiterate' people. Moreover, 'in the old days an organization like this could not be controlled by such young people but this has happened', a regional leader told the meeting held in Langa on 14 February to formally launch the anti-pass campaign. Robert Sobukwe and Potlake Leballo were present on this occasion. Sobukwe himself directed part of his speech at the men from the single quarters: 'We have come here to Cape Town to find out from you whether it does not affect you, to work for low wages. It is something for you to leave your wives behind.' Leballo delivered a characteristically exuberant address to a crowd in Kensington. As Kgosana recalled:

Everybody felt the electricity as Potlake Leballo, National Secretary, climbed on to the platform and waved his pipe in the air. His powerful voice rang out in Sesotho: 'Ke Potlake wa ho Leballo u gu thweng oa bona leftasha es flno le thopile ka badischabo.' (This is Potlake of the Leballos, of whom it is said 'hold your shield lightly, your father's land has been looted by foreigners').[51]

Not all the Western Cape leaders were as impressed with Leballo. Elliot Magwentshu discussed Leballo's visit at some length when he was interviewed by Gail Gerhart ten years later. To be sure, he conceded, Leballo was an effective demagogue, he told his audience the kinds of things that they wanted to hear, he was good at 'what he calls the moving of the cows—crowds, he meant'. But when the regional leaders met him more privately, 'he never said anything very important'. As national secretary, Magwentshu suggested, Leballo 'should have briefed us about the strength of the party in the other areas'. But, he said, Leballo 'didn't do this thing. He never told us. He just told us that the party was very popular in the Witwatersrand, and that A. B. Ngcobo and others in Natal, they are doing very well, they are strong there, that was just all.' To the committee Leballo delivered the same 'type of talk' that he used in public meetings. Nor were all members of the committee happy with the language Leballo used in public. 'There was almost a row in the meeting', Magwentshu recalled, 'because the man was insulting the white people, telling them they would be destroyed. It does not matter what happens. They were "White Dogs." And all this and all this.' On one issue, though, the Cape Town leaders received quite explicit guidance. They asked Sobukwe how they should respond if the police used violence to suppress their protest. Should they reciprocate? According to Kgosana, Sobukwe at this stage was quite categorical. 'If I wanted you to use violence', he said, 'I would have to teach you to use it.' This he could not do with any integrity, he said, because he possessed neither the relevant knowledge nor the experience. For the Pan-Africanists, for the time being, he insisted, violence was simply not a plausible option.[52]

In their campaigning preparations the Western Cape Pan-Africanists did not confine themselves to speechmaking at open-air meetings. As we have seen, Philip Kgosana visited Langa High School in January and there seems to have been a concerted effort to direct the PAC's message at teenagers: 'Task Forces' constituted by children aged 10 to 17 years were much in evidence in the days before the campaign, pasting stickers and posters on telegraph poles through Langa and Nyanga. Kgosana wrote to all branch secretaries on 3 March to inform them that Nana Mahomo would be visiting each branch the following week to explain the work of the Task Forces, so it seems from this that these groups were already constituted well before the campaign launch. Kgosana also instructed the branch officials to send him the names of people who would constitute the next and successive 'layers of leadership', to replace the people arrested in the initial protests so that the campaign could sustain itself.[53] Local Pan-Africanists later claimed to members of the Liberal Party that in several of their branches they had in place 'their first, second, third and fourth layers of leadership'.[54] Branch leaders did not merely await orders for they were busily engaged in building up their auxiliary formations. In Nyanga, according to one contemporary observer, the Task Forces incorporated gangster networks.[55] The stickers the Task Forcers were pasting up were hardly very arousing. They featured a lugubrious image of a kneeling handcuffed man and the legend, 'Hlexe Silibale—Lest we forget', Sobukwe's idea, apparently, though they were printed locally. The picture may have been the work of Gerald Sekoto, to judge from later drawings which Sekoto provided for the PAC exiles.[56] The police tore them down as quickly as they were put up. More helpfully, through the weeks that preceded the campaign, older PAC officials conducted house-to-house visits and evening house meetings through the townships. With membership donations, the regional leaders bought for £16 a second-hand duplicator: 'it rattled all night to produce leaflets, pamphlets amnd other propaganda material'.[57]

As importantly, PAC men took care to speak to people within key sectors of the local workforce. They visited the docks on 19 March and after obtaining consent from sympathetic watchmen, they distributed leaflets and spoke to groups of the workers. Dockers in Cape Town had eluded efforts at trade union organization through the decade. The Pan-Africanists' support networks within the migrant worker hostels enabled them to access this hard-to-reach group. The PAC in Cape Town also invested considerable effort in winning over better-organized workers. Philip Kgosana later claimed that the PAC had established a strong following in Worcester.

Worcester, twenty miles from Cape Town, was an area in which the ANC-aligned Food and Canning Workers' Union had built up a robust organization. Here PAC speakers would capitalize on local feeling resulting from the harsh measures directed at rioters protesting the banishment of a local trade unionist, Elizabeth Mafikeng.[58] After 21 March it would be one of the few places in which both coloured and African workers heeded the PAC strike call. This may have been attributable to ANC influence but Kgosana claimed that 'Worcester was a triumph for us—but it took me four visits and many meetings.' Kgosana was not the only visitor, for the diary of a PAC organizer, Ralph Mbatsha, supplies a corroborative reference to his own visit to Worcester.[59] PAC members were also active in the apple orchards around Elgin; here too most of the African workforce went on strike from the first day of the campaign.[60] The regional executive compiled a list of 45 different workplaces assigning responsibilities for making contacts with employees and securing commitments to participation in the campaign.[61]

Less intentionally, perhaps, local PAC leaders attracted another vein of potential support when they established connections with key figures in the Liberal Party in Cape Town. In late 1959, Christopher Mlokoti, then the Nyanga branch chairman, had visited the Liberal Party's office to put the PAC's case, accompanied by his deputy and treasurer, Amos Matros.[62] Here they encountered Randolph Vigne, a member of the party's provincial executive. Vigne was impressed by his visitors. He introduced them to the provincial chairman Peter Hjul and, moreover, 'assured them of the Liberal Party's interest in discussing co-operation between the two organizations'.[63] Vigne kept his word, writing a memorandum arguing the case for the Liberals to offer support for the PAC's anti-pass campaign. This was considered by the party's executive in Johannesburg on 9 March which also had before it a letter from Potlake Leballo requesting help for any dependents of those who would be imprisoned in the campaign. Nana Mahomo had also approached the Black Sash for such assistance. The Black Sash was a liberal human rights group formed originally to protest against constitutional changes disenfranchising coloured voters. The Black Sash's representative at the Liberal executive meeting, Eulalia Stott, also spoke up in favour of cooperating with the PAC. It was decided 'to offer such assistance as the Party could afford'. Before his final departure from Cape Town, Nana Mahomo apparently told Western Cape PAC leaders 'that there were only two organizations to whom they should go for assistance, or with whom they should cooperate in the following campaign, and those organizations were the Liberal Party and the Black Sash'.[64]

Like Eulalie Stott, Randolph Vigne had also met Nana Mahomo, on several occasions it seems, indeed Mahomo did some work for Vigne's publishing house, copy-editing African language manuscripts.[65] Mahomo lived in lodgings in the house of Joe Nkatlo, one of the Liberal Party's most well-known African members, and formerly a key personality within the Cape ANC, and, possibly, by early 1960 a member of the PAC.[66] Several other African members of the Liberal Party in the Cape had joined the PAC.[67] By early February Mahomo had developed sufficient confidence in the goodwill of the Cape Town Liberals that he would visit the *Contact* office to tell Randolph Vigne and Patrick Duncan that he would be leaving and that after his departure 'another younger Cape Town University student would be in charge, Philip Kgosana'.[68] At that stage Mahomo intended to help lead the anti-pass campaign from the PAC's headquarters in Johannesburg as he had been instructed by Sobukwe, he told Gail

Gerhart, seven years later. If this is true, it was an odd decision by Sobukwe to withdraw from the PAC's strongest area one of the most experienced and senior Pan-Africanists, effectively leaving Mahomo's 'understudy' (Mahomo's expression), Philip Kgosana, in charge.[69] It suggests just how out of touch the Johannesburg leaders were with events outside their own region.

Kgosana, as we have seen, had already met Duncan and had been working as a *Contact* sales agent. Mahomo also wrote to Vigne from Johannesburg on 11 February, informing him about Robert Sobukwe's impending visit to Cape Town to suggest that he should arrange a meeting between the Liberals and the visitors. In the letter, Mahomo also promised that on his next visit he would 'be able to clear up some points raised in your last letter'. The letter is friendly and informal and closes with Mahomo thanking Vigne for his offer of transport during any future visit.[70] Vigne did not in fact meet Sobukwe in Cape Town though he had encountered him a year earlier at a writers' conference in Atteridegeville outside Pretoria.[71] Here one of the Pretoria-based Liberals, Colin Lang, arranged a special session on the evening after the conference so that Liberals could meet the 'top Africanists'. Vigne remembers Sobukwe speaking quite hesitantly, repeatedly looking at the other PAC people present as if to reassure himself of their approval of what he was saying.[72]

Patrick Duncan would make a key contribution to the history that was to unfold over the days that followed the Langa shootings. Among the radical white opposition to apartheid, Duncan's background (and manner) was unusually patrician. He was the son of a wartime South African governor-general, educated at Bishops, Winchester, and Balliol. Before going up to Balliol he spent a summer vacation in Nazi Germany, guests of Helmuth and Freya Von Moltke, family friends and subsequently leaders of the anti-Nazi Kreisau Circle. He attended an encampment of the *Reichsarbeitsdienst*—a Nazi youth service corps—for three weeks, an experience which he believed later to have been for him profoundly formative, a direct encounter with 'the evil stench of totalitarianism'.[73] After Oxford, the lingering effects of a childhood affliction with Osteomyelitis prevented his enlistment during the Second World War: instead he joined the colonial service in Basutoland. Here he became fluent in Sesotho and developed his first friendships with black Africans. He resigned from the service in 1952 to become a political activist, a move he had in fact been contemplating since the National Party's victory in 1948. He led a group of volunteers during the ANC's Defiance Campaign and served a short prison sentence, one of the first white South Africans to undergo conviction for participation in an African-led political campaign. Subsequently he worked as the Liberal Party's national organizer before taking up the editorship of *Contact* in Cape Town in 1958. Through the 1950s, Duncan drew his political inspiration from his reading of Gandhi's *Satyagraha in South Africa*. Two terms of argumentative tutorials with Harold Laski at the LSE on a 'refresher course' arranged by the Colonial Office helped to strengthen what had been an intuitive intellectual aversion to Marxism: in this South African setting this translated into strong antipathy to the Communist Party.

In joining the Liberal Party, Duncan hoped to help build it into a powerful mass non-racial opposition to apartheid, and an effective counter to the influence of the Communist Party within African nationalist politics. Under his editorship, *Contact* increasingly directed itself at an African readership and in its editorial offices a group of young Liberals who shared Duncan's vision of building a militant community that would rival the popular appeal of the Marxist Left gravitated around him. To this group, the PAC's appearance represented an intriguing prospect. In public the PAC was as rhetorically hostile to white liberals as it was to Communists. For example on 14 February Robert Sobukwe spent part of his speech in Langa directing invective against '*abelungu abasithandayo*'—'whites who like us',[74] referring to specific individuals, Kgosana recalls, including Pat Duncan.[75] As we have seen, though, in behind-the-scenes encounters with Liberals the Pan-Africanists were more conciliatory: they needed resources to support workers for a protracted strike—for at least two months Christopher Mlokoti envisaged,[76] and the Cape Liberals seemed to be sympathetic. On their side, Pat Duncan and other Western Cape leaders were anxious to develop close working relations with popular African organizations, in addition to building the Liberal Party's own black membership. To do this they were prepared to be receptive and diplomatic. As Duncan had noted in 1957, in any alliance with African-led movements, Liberals needed to 'realize the very difficult position with Africans that African leaders get into when they become dependent upon white support. There is trouble in the ANC at the moment over this issue.'[77]

Pat Duncan had first met Sobukwe in January 1958 and after this encounter he reported that he felt 'there was little common ground between his views and mine'.[78] Later, though, the relationship between the two men seems to have become warmer. Through Benjamin Pogrund in 1959 Duncan conveyed a message to Sobukwe that if 'his group ever wanted any articles published, *Contact* was at their disposal'.[79] Subsequently he visited Sobukwe in his office at Wits. Without any preliminaries, he announced: 'Robert, I am joining the PAC. I never want to hold office in the movement. I'll just be one of the rank and file. Can you stop me?'[80] How serious Duncan was at this point we cannot know. He may well have been trying to simply challenge Sobukwe's insistence that for the time being, the PAC would remain racially exclusive, a topic over which he had already had arguments with Pogrund.[81] Duncan's correspondence confirms that by this point he had met and liked several of the other PAC leaders: he was favourably impressed after a conversation with Z. B. Molete and Jacob Nyaose in November 1959,[82] only one month after Molete had called him in the columns of *Contact* a representative of 'a foreign national minority', accusing Duncan of attempting to 'cash in' on 'his so-called participation' in the Defiance Campaign.[83] He was on familiar terms with Nana Mahomo, too.[84]

Pat Duncan was a compelling and engaging personality: he would fix his vividly blue eyes on the face of whoever he was talking or listening to, and give the person his fully absorbed concentration, whatever the circumstances. Passionate in his anti-colonialism, he took pleasure in a large map of Africa pinned on the wall of the *Contact* offices; country by country he filled in with a black pen as each became independent. In the garden of his family home in the Cape Town suburbs he installed a swimming pool in the shape of the African continent.[85] His gift for friendship often transcended political affiliations. As the writer Es'kia Mphahlele recalled, 'I hated Liberals and their Party but there was something genuinely felt and unpatronizing about Patrick Duncan.'[86]

In Cape Town, as we have seen, the PAC had assembled an extensive following and in contrast to the efforts of its officials in other centres, its local preparations for the campaign were comparatively systematic and farsighted. This quality of organization and leadership is a critical consideration in understanding the way political protest intensified into communal rebellion in the aftermath of the Langa shootings. By the time the rioting had subsided in Langa during the night of 21 March, the township was the main focus of police operations. Police and army detachments organized a cordon of roadblocks around Langa, superseding the earlier efforts by the Task Force groups to establish their own controls over the key points of entry into Langa. In Nyanga, though, it seems as if the PAC managed to maintain its road-blocks, perhaps as a consequence of the police concentrating their deployment in

Langa. But as we shall see, whatever the variations in the police presence, from the night of 21 March for the next ten days moral authority in the townships would reside in a network of PAC committees.

In tracking the key developments through which this rebellion progressed we have an unusually rich range of first person testimonials, some of them written down very close to the time of this history. Philip Kgosana wrote his life story for *Drum* magazine in early 1961 and included in this account a detailed narrative of his role in the Cape Town movement. In 1963 he provided a second version of events which included fresh and highly critical references to his interactions with Patrick Duncan. Kgosana also supplied a third chronology in 1976 in response to a request for information from Patrick Duncan's biographer. In 1988 Kgosana published a book-length autobiography that supplied a detailed recapitulation of his recollections, based substantially on a manuscript that he wrote during the 1960s. In addition to Kgosana's memoirs the record also includes two day-by-day narratives written in the form of diaries, one written by Patrick Duncan, and another, possibly produced at Duncan's instigation, kept by Collingwood August, a coloured member of the Liberal Party who worked in the *Contact* office and who lived in Nyanga. Finally police records produced during court proceedings supplied verbatim transcripts of one of the crucial encounters between the principal personalities who shaped the events that succeeded the Langa shootings. There are discrepancies between the narratives presented in these different sources: these disagreements will be addressed and explained in what follows.

On Tuesday morning, very early, at 4.00 am, the police appeared in force at the Langa hostels and the New Flats, smashing open doors and breaking windows, and turning people outside. Police than marshalled the workers into columns and marched them to the railway station. At every intersection of their route the police parked Saracen armoured cars. Despite this effort to thwart the PAC's strike call employers' later estimates suggest that 50 per cent of the African workforce responded that week to the PAC's injunction that no one should go to work. The Athlone power station was entirely without labour and building contractors reported especially high rates of absenteeism of 70 per cent or so.[87] PAC leaders themselves were energetic in their efforts to counter the police's intimidation. Kgosana's 1988 narrative, the most detailed of the records available tells us that Kgosana himself and several of the other PAC principals had spent the night in hiding in a house near Langa High School. They emerged from this refuge to see the

Saracen cars on their way to the 'zones'. After learning about the police efforts at strike-breaking, Kgosana and his comrades walked to the railway station to board coaches 'packed to capacity with strikers, some of whom had baton wounds on their heads and arms'. The PAC officials moved along the train, telling the workers they should not go to their places of employment but should rather fan out through the town telling anybody they found in shops or other workplaces to stop work. Later that day Kgosana marched with a procession of 'chanting, jubilant people' to the dockyard: on their arrival several hundred stevedores left their ships and joined them on their train journey back to Langa. In his autobiographical articles published in *Drum*, Kgosana does not mention these efforts to keep the strike going: instead he spends the morning in hiding and only travels to Cape Town in the afternoon for a brief meeting of the regional leaders. The article shows signs of having been subjected to quite heavy editorial pruning, though, and clearly some of the differences between its chronology and the later narratives are a consequence of such excisions.

What neither of these two sources mention is a visit that Kgosana made to the *Contact* office on Tuesday afternoon. It is referred to in Duncan's diary, though this record is silent on what transpired between the two men on that day. The two men had met the day before, and Kgosana's 1988 autobiography refers to what became rather a fractious encounter at the *Contact* office that Monday. He visited the office, he suggests, at Duncan's invitation because Duncan wanted a first-hand account of the opening of the campaign. After giving Duncan his story Kgosana used Duncan's telephone to call Brian Bunting, *New Age*'s editor. Bunting had managed to get a message to Kgosana while he was on his way to Duncan's office requesting a meeting. When Duncan realized Kgosana was speaking to Bunting, Kgosana recalled, 'he grabbed the receiver from my hand and slammed it down in wild fury', warning Kgosana that he would have nothing more to do with him if he maintained any further contacts with Communists. According to this account, up until that weekend Duncan had no idea that Kgosana was a PAC official, he knew him only as a needy student earning a *Contact* sales commission. 'He was shocked to learn I was the PAC's regional secretary and asked why I had not sought his advice on the matter.' This encounter concluded with what Kgosana describes as an exchange of 'cheap apologies'. He then ignored Duncan's injunctions and called in at the *New Age* offices where Brian Bunting offered 'a car-load of food provisions for the strikers' which he accepted.

Kgosana did write about this meeting in a very different vein in one of his earlier statements. In his 1961 memoir he meets Duncan in the *Contact* office on Monday afternoon. Duncan was 'excited about the campaign' and offers Kgosana a friendly warning: 'You have poked the bees, but now you must be very careful. Anything can happen tonight.' Duncan's diary records the meeting in very positive language. He was obviously impressed with Kgosana's command of the situation. Duncan's confidence in Kgosana's sagacity at that stage is very evident in the entry: Kgosana 'understood the dangers of the situation and the ever present possibility of violence erupting'. Collingwood August's diary also suggests that this Monday meeting was generally friendly. Kgosana's impression that Duncan had only just learned that he was a PAC leader may be wrong: from the beginning of the year the Cape Liberal group had been keeping themselves informed about who was who in the local PAC and they had decided to help them. The weight of the evidence does seem to confirm that Philip Kgosana was warmly received when he visited the *Contact* office on Monday and there is no reason to suppose that this meeting with the *Contact* group the next day was any different. As we shall see, though, there did occur an altercation between Kgosana and Duncan about Brian Bunting but this happened on the 24th. Philip Kgosana's 1988 autobiography refers to no meetings in the *Contact* office or any other contact with Duncan on Tuesday, Wednesday, or Thursday. Randolph Vigne's memoir does contain a revealing reference to the meeting between Duncan and Kgosana on Tuesday. On this occasion Kgosana arrived at a time when the party's local leadership was meeting in the *Contact* boardroom. Kgosana was with several of his colleagues when he knocked on the door. At this point:

> Pat Duncan (this is to illustrate how few people in the party were aware of the importance of the campaign) said to Philip, 'Can't you see we are having a meeting. We can't see you now, I'll see you later', and sent him away.[88]

Rather taken aback by Duncan's abrupt dismissal of his visitor, Randolph Vigne and a couple of others left the room to join Kgosana to see what he and his companions needed. At this stage, Vigne's notes suggest, Kgosana's main concern was to make contact with the press because he felt that yesterday's events had been misrepresented in the main newspapers. It also seems likely that the two men discussed a proposal that the Liberals should collect food and organize its delivery into the townships. Later on, Duncan seems to have tried to make amends for his earlier snub: he invited Philip

Kgosana to a dinner party to be held at his home the following night. Kgosana may well have remained disconcerted by Duncan's initial brusque response to his arrival at the *Contact* office though and the initially unfriendly tone of this meeting seems to have overlaid any recollections of his earlier warmer encounter with Duncan on Monday.

After Tuesday morning's raids, in the week that followed the police made no further attempts to force a return to work. During the day the Nyanga Pan-Africanists exploited the concentration of police deployment in Langa to erect fresh road-blocks. Here the bus crews stayed at home. By Wednesday the strike had closed down municipal services and brought industry to a halt. Newspapers reported reprovingly that 5,000 chickens died after not being fed or watered. That day the PAC leaders in Langa were visited by the owner of an ice cream factory to offer them the uncollected stock in his factory: the Pan-Africanists accepted with alacrity. Kgosana's 1988 autobiography and earlier writings refer to free deliveries by a maize wholesaler and a bakery 'that supplied us free with 1,000 loaves of bread daily'.[89] Duncan's diary indicates that the Liberals were also beginning to orchestrate food deliveries to the PAC township leaders on Wednesday. Kgosana's memoirs do not refer to Duncan's efforts to organize food deliveries though he does acknowledge a £50 donation 'Patrick Duncan gave from his own pocket'.[90] In his 1988 autobiography he recounts how he and Eulalia Stott, the Black Sash president (and Liberal Party member), organized the delivery of 100 sacks of maize meal in Nyanga East, 'courtesy of the Black Sash'. Meanwhile PAC leaders continued to work hard to enlarge the protest: on Wednesday morning two members of the regional executive, Gasson Ndlovu and Elliot Magwentshu, addressed a meeting of workers in the township adjacent to the Simonstown naval base: they returned to Cape Town with encouraging news for their comrades: all the African workers at the base were now on strike.

At this stage, apparently, coordination between the Langa and Nyanga leaders was weak. A few days after the launching of the campaign, Randolph Vigne visited A. C. Jordan, Cape Town's leading African intellectual and a lecturer at the university. He found Christopher Mlokoti and other Nyanga PAC branch committee members assembled in Jordan's sitting room. They were trying to raise funds so that they could hire a car and drive to Johannesburg to get their orders from the national leaders still at liberty. They did not know what do, Vigne recollected. They were ignorant of events elsewhere in the country and 'they didn't know what was happening in Cape Town'. They seemed to have lost touch with Kgosana, 'not even knowing where to find him'.[91]

That evening Philip Kgosana attended Duncan's dinner party. This doesn't seem to have been a great success, though Duncan's diary reported 'a useful and friendly' occasion. The guests included Thomas Ngwenya of the ANC, Randolph Vigne, and Anton Rupert, head of the Rembrandt Corporation, a prominent member of the Afrikaner economic elite. Kgosana's 1963 recollections mistakenly dates this meeting as taking place on the 26th. On his arrival he found he had to tidy himself up: the Duncans dressed for dinner and Kgosana was not even wearing a tie.[92] At the dinner table, Kgosana remembered, he 'was subjected to nasty cross-questioning by Rupert who kept on discussing the African people as immature and that our campaign was aimless'.[93] Kgosana was also offended by the fact that Duncan's domestic servants were in attendance rather than being on strike. Randolph Vigne's recollections to an extent corroborate Kgosana's depiction of an uncomfortable evening: Rupert was heavily patronizing, and did indeed draw comparisons between what he took to be evidence of African political immaturity and unripe fruit. More presciently perhaps, Rupert went on to tell Kgosana that these days were likely to represent the great moments of his life and he should therefore make the most of them.[94]

Duncan had hoped that Rupert, whom he saw as a politically influential figure, might be as impressed with Kgosana as he was, and would then be open to persuasion to act on the PAC's behalf. After all, Kgosana himself was on public record as stating that one aim of campaign was to put pressure on industrialists who would in turn appeal to the government to repeal the pass laws.[95] Anton Rupert did shortly after his meeting with Kgosana issue a public statement in which he called for a 'revision of politics'.[96] In 1976, when asked by Duncan's biographer for his memories of the dinner party, Rupert claimed he could not recall dining at the Duncans that evening. In the 1990s, though, in a more relaxed political climate, Rupert managed to remember the evening. He told the historian Hermann Giliomee that 'he was shocked that a young man without laces in his shoes could bring out such a multitude'. He spoke to Hendrik Verwoerd the next day, telling him that he should consider offering concessions such as property rights to urbanized Africans.[97] A slightly different version of this story appears in Rupert's authorized biography.[98]

It is possible that at least on Kgosana's side, the evening may have prompted him to perceive his relationship with Duncan in a new and more guarded way, especially as the next day when he once again visited the *Contact* offices he received Duncan's ultimatum that he should refrain from any contact with Brian Bunting and *New Age*. Perhaps rather unwisely, Duncan reminded Kgosana that Sobukwe had stipulated in his speeches that his followers should have no contact with members of the Congress of Democrats, a perfectly true observation though Sobukwe's embargo on such contacts also referred to members of the Liberal Party. In any case, though Duncan received the impression that Kgosana agreed on this occasion to have no further dealings with Bunting, Kgosana reports in his book that he met Bunting after leaving the *Contact* office. When interviewed in 1976, Brian Bunting himself confirmed that he and Kgosana discussed the arrangements for the delivery of a truckload of food organized by the Congress of Democrats.[99] Meanwhile, that afternoon or evening—the records conflict over the time—a deputation of one hundred Task Force members presented themselves at the Cape Town police headquarters to demand arrest. They were detained and locked up in the police stations' cells. Writing in 1988, Kgosana explains that this protest was a reaction to an earlier raid on Langa, on Wednesday night, when the police arrested a member of the regional executive, Bam Siboto. In his 1961 account, Kgosana's recollection is different: he refers to a much wider effort by the police to search for the PAC leaders in the township in which they managed to undertake 'a great round up'. Whichever version is the more accurate, by Thursday evening, the PAC leadership seems to have decided to take the offensive with a major confrontation with the authorities.

On Friday 25 March, Philip Kgosana headed a demonstration of between 2,000 and 5,000 people outside Cape Town's police headquarters in Caledon Square. Most of the participants in this protest had travelled by train to the centre of Cape Town, rallying at Parade Square before taking different routes to converge upon the police station at 11.00 am. Duncan's diary records a telephone call to him at his office from Philip Kgosana at 9.30 am. Kgosana was then on his way to the police building. He told Duncan that a large group was on its way to the square to hand themselves over to the police: 'They have seen yesterday the police had room to arrest 101 men and they want to join them. Come quickly.'[100] In his memoirs Kgosana describes being roughly manhandled into the station together with Gasson Ndlovu, another regional official, leaving outside the other two PAC leaders of the demonstration, Mlami Makwetu and Ladebe Nxelewa. He was locked up in an upstairs room with a police sergeant. Shortly after Kgosana's detention

Duncan arrived at Caledon Square to encounter what he perceived to be a 'good humoured and relaxed crowd'. He noticed many dock-workers among the crowd and he noted approvingly that 'Task Force' runners were preventing demonstrators from blocking the pavement or disturbing the traffic. Duncan then persuaded the police chief, Colonel I. B. S. Terblanche, who was facing the crowd, to negotiate with those PAC leaders still at liberty. This he agreed to do and at 11.40 am five PAC men, Terblanche, and Duncan went into the building. Their subsequent exchanges were transcribed and appeared later in the record of the trial of the PAC leaders:

DUNCAN: These people have come to be arrested for failing to carry their passes. Is there no way in which you can satisfy them—even if it is just by taking their names? They are peaceful and the crowd is under the control of its leaders.
TERBLANCHE: But I am not going to arrest any of them.

A little later:

TERBLANCHE: Do you see any room here to accommodate all the people?
MAKWETU: But yesterday you have arrested 101 of our friends and we want them to be with us.
TERBLANCHE: But I'm telling you here and now that I do not want to arrest any African for not carrying a reference book. They will, as in the past, be warned to appear in court.
MAKWETU: This is not good enough for us. We will never carry passes again.

A little later:

TERBLANCHE: What will you do to get the people home?
MAKWETU: Let me tell them on your instructions that they need not carry passes any more.
TERBLANCHE: I cannot give you that permission but I'm willing to give instructions to my men that for a period of one month they will not ask for reference books.
MAKWETU: But Colonel, we never want to carry passes again.
TERBLANCHE: Look, this position cannot go on as it is at present, the locations are in disorder, road blocks have been put up to hamper the police in the execution of their duties, the people are hungry and children will die of hunger in the locations if this position is allowed to continue, but your men are responsible for it. Why are you bringing yourselves into disrepute?
MAKWETU: But Colonel, we are willing to go to work right now but we do not want to carry passes.
DUNCAN: Your problem is to get the people away from the street and back home.
DUNCAN: On what the Colonel has said, that he is willing to give you a month's time to sort this position out, will you not try to take your people home?

MAKWETU: Two of our friends are here, we do not know where and we cannot go back without them.

Duncan interceded again at this point and succeeded in persuading Terblanche of the wisdom of releasing the PAC leaders he had arrested. Philip Kgosana and Gasson Ndlovu were brought into the room after the substance of the agreement had been concluded: the PAC leaders would tell their followers to return home on the understanding that the police would stop enforcing the pass laws for a month, or in Duncan's words, until the 'position' was 'sorted out'. In Kgosana's 1963 and 1988 memoirs when he rejoins the other leaders he is taken aback by Duncan's presence and affronted at his 'usurpation' of leadership by 'negotiating with the police to consider suspending the pass laws—an uncalled for suggestion from an intruder'. Kgosana lost his temper, he recalls and told Duncan, 'to mind his own business'. In Kgosana's 1988 narrative, Duncan then withdrew from the discussion, later apologizing to Kgosana. Kgosana then turned to the most senior policeman present. General C. I. Rademeyer, the (national) commissioner of the police to tell him that 'the PAC demanded nothing less than a total abolition of the Pass Laws'. Rademeyer was disinclined to offer any further concessions. Instead:

> He tried, in his own stereotyped way, to convince me that pass books were needed for the identification of Africans and that without them there would be a total breakdown of 'native administration'. He then said that by organizing a demonstration against Pass Laws and actually marching into the city and creating so much tension, we had committed a very serious offence. He was, however, not going to order our immediate arrest but would let us go until we were charged. He promised to release the 100 Task Force members and Bam Sibito before the end of the day.

At this juncture the PAC leaders agreed to march their followers back to Langa.

Duncan's diary makes no reference to any disagreement or friction with Philip Kgosana during this encounter at Caledon Square. Kgosana's recollection that he was surprised to find Duncan present when he was released from confinement is at odds with the record of events in Duncan's diary and at least one other person present in the *Contact* office could remember Kgosana's telephoned invitation to Duncan to attend events at Caledon Square. However he may well have been disconcerted by Pat Duncan's assumption of an intermediary role and his earlier telephone summons to Duncan may simply have been motivated by his awareness of the importance of securing favourable press coverage. Even so, Philip Kgosana's accusation that Duncan intruded into the negotiations and raised the possibility of a suspension of the laws seems too harsh, though the transcript does indicate that he may have helped to overcome Makwetu's initial objections to the proposal before Kgosana's return. Kgosana was not present when the concession was initially negotiated and in his autobiography he may have been reproducing what the other PAC men present told him had happened. The police record of the dialogue indicates that the suspension was Colonel Terblanche's idea though, as we have just noted, Duncan's interjections were probably very important in helping to persuade Mlami Makwetu to accept the compromise. The transcript suggests that at best Makwetu's assent was reluctant. It is worth emphasizing at this point the key role played by Makwetu, the PAC's branch secretary at Langa New Flats, later extremely critical of the Mlokoti group's friendship with the Liberals. Makwetu was one of the main leaders of the PAC's migrant worker group, 'idolized' by members of this community.[101]

Certainly at the time, though, PAC leaders and followers interpreted the concession they had extracted as a triumph. Though Philip Kgosana may have been irritated or even angered by Duncan's assumption of an active role in the negotiations his 1988 memoir concedes that the suspension represented 'another major victory against the enemy'. As the PAC's followers marched away, chanting and singing, carrying Philip Kgosana shoulder-high, their mood was 'jubilant'. That evening Terblanche's *ad hoc* local suspension of the pass laws was confirmed and extended nationwide by General Rademeyer of the police and the minister of justice, F. C. Erasmus. According to Philip Kgosana when he was writing in 1988, Rademeyer's announcement, broadcast on the radio the next morning was 'an historical event'. Moreover 'That [the pass laws] were suspended—even for while—sent a wave of hysterical jubilation among our people, and the entire black population of the Cape Peninsula threw its weight behind the PAC campaign.'[102]

All the contemporary evidence as well as subsequent events suggests there was no serious rupture at this juncture between Pat Duncan and Philip Kgosana, that as far as Duncan was concerned at least, they were on friendly terms. After all, the PAC had won an important victory. They had succeeded in compelling the police to negotiate and offer concessions. Duncan's role in helping to create the relationship between the police and the PAC leaders was decisive. In the short term the stand-off between the police and the PAC helped to strengthen the PAC's hold on the townships. Peter Hjul, the Liberal Party chairman in the Cape, was working closely with Duncan through these events. Interviewed in 1976 he insisted that this was the intention of the *Contact* Liberal group:

The whole object of Pat's negotiations with Terblanche was to establish the PAC's responsibility, to enhance its importance, and to establish a de facto recognition of its control of the townships and of the police's exclusion from them.

To judge from the expanding response in the region to the PAC's strike call it seems likely that police harassment did lessen. An indication of the extent of the PAC's authority within the townships is supplied by the entry Collingwood August wrote in his diary on Saturday:

> I put in a brief appearance at the *Contact* office, I must leave soon. The permission given to me by the task force, the youths of the PAC who have complete control of the townships, is due to expire.

In Langa the PAC worked closely with the Langa Vigilance Committee: the two organizations together arranged the funeral of police victims and money was collected by PAC men on behalf of both groups.[103] Duncan's diary suggests that by 26 March 'PAC committees were completely in charge of Nyanga and partly in charge in Langa'. Duncan's perception that the PAC was in command in the two townships is confirmed by Kgosana's evident confidence in his recollection of a meeting he attended in Langa on the evening of Saturday 26th. Langa nurses were concerned because white doctors were reluctant to visit the township hospital to attend patients because they were frightened they might be molested. They also wanted to know if they should join the strike. Kgosana reassured them 'that theirs were essential services and could not be stopped' and, moreover, that he would guarantee the safety of the doctors.[104] Despite this impressive degree of internal control within each township, up until Monday 28th the three PAC committees in Nyanga East, Nyanga West, and Langa were unable to coordinate their activities. Patrick Duncan's diary entries include the claim that on Monday the *Contact* group succeeded in creating liaison between them.[105] Meanwhile the PAC's influence was consolidated over the weekend when the organization assumed command of food supply distribution. Pat Duncan had canvassed energetically, raising money from businessmen and goods from wholesalers. Black Sash women assembled and drove a column of lorries which Task Forcers escorted into Langa and Nyanga. Duncan's support was not altogether uncritical, though:

> The Nyanga East Committee came into the offices of *Contact* . . . They asked us to introduce them to the police . . . Before the committee went off to see

Terblanche I told them I had sensed, on the Wednesday, that the police were very worried about the road blocks that had been build in Nyanga. I said it was difficult to see the point of them, that the police could only regard them as a provocation and as a challenge to their authority and that it might be wiser to pull them down. They claimed that they had been put up by *tsotsis* but that they would do what they could.

Mxolise Mgxashe's autobiography confirms that the PAC's activists in Nyanga East behaved especially aggressively, even allowing for the effects of anachronistic retrospection: 'In Nyanga East there was an "Intifada" in the making. Militant youths were throwing stones at the police and soldiers as they drove past in their armoured vehicles.'[106] Peter Hjul's description of the visit of the Nyanga East delegation and Duncan's subsequent communication with Terblanche suggests a more complicated set of exchanges, though. He was present when the Nyanga East delegation arrived at the *Contact* office. They told Duncan and Hjul that the previous night, African policemen dressed in civilian clothes had approached residents and given them the PAC salute. If people responded positively the police beat them up. This had happened several times: it was evidently a planned effort to intimidate strikers, or to discredit the PAC. Duncan telephoned Colonel Terblanche immediately. Terblanche denied any knowledge of such activities but he told Duncan he would like to hear about the assaults directly from the PAC men. Duncan accompanied the PAC deputation to Terblanche's office. After hearing their complaints, Terblanche said he would investigate and he 'would see that it did not happen again'. But, he said, he also had a complaint. People were putting up road-blocks, and these were causing confrontations with the police.

> The PAC then said that if the police would patrol the townships only in patrol wagons and not in Saracens which they felt were provocative, they would get the road-blocks removed. And they left on those terms. No other undertaking was made or given. The PAC undertook to remove the road-blocks, and the police undertook to remove the provocateurs. And that was that: the road-blocks were pulled up and the strong-arm squads disappeared.[107]

Terblanche at that juncture seems to have been rather impressed with the PAC. Apparently, in the same conversation with Duncan he had observed that crime in the township had dwindled 'to almost nothing'. Under the PAC's control, he noted, there seemed to be no crime, the townships were 'orderly', save for the confrontations between activists and the police.[108]

Contemporary sources confirm that by the beginning of its second week, on Monday 28 March, the strike affected 95 per cent of the African workforce, 60,000 workers, affecting especially the dockyards, construction, engineering, hotels, garages, and daily deliveries of bread and milk.[109] The strike may have received extra impetus from the ANC's call for a one-day stay-at-home to mourn the dead of Langa and Sharpeville. The Johannesburg *Star* reported that coloured people were blacklegging in Cape Town but at Worcester, home of the Food and Canning Workers' Union (FCWU) to which both African and coloured workers belonged, coloured workers joined the strike, possibly partly also as a consequence of the PAC presence there. In the smaller towns around Cape Town, ANC organization historically was more firmly established than in the metropolis, consolidated around FCWU branches. On the 28th and in the days that followed there were riots, marches, and the pass-burnings called for by the ANC's national leadership in a number of these smaller centres: in Stellenbosch, Simonstown, Somerset, and Hermanus. Meanwhile, in the townships around Cape Town food deliveries probably helped to maintain activist morale as well as enhancing the PAC's public prestige in their role as food distributors. *Contact* claimed that the Liberals raised £1,500 of food. In addition the South African Coloured People's Organisation sent food donated by Indian shopkeepers into Langa and the Congress of Democrats supplied a lorry-load. Politically these donations were important though the food could not have gone very far in meeting the needs of 60,000 workers and their families. In arranging food deliveries, the Liberals' intention was not simply humanitarian: their aim was to strengthen the PAC's authority, and on the whole their help was offered unconditionally. Peter Hjul stressed this point in an interview with Benjamin Pogrund:

> We came into this only after the campaign had started, and our attitude was that we had no right to instruct a group of people who seemed to be doing a perfectly good job on their own, just how they should be carrying out their campaign...where we did give advice and direction, was in the function where we agreed to perform. That is the supply of food. We supplied the food after we had arranged for its collection, and the collection of the money, where the PAC had no control whatsoever. Their control came when they came into our office and gave us the list of where it was needed and so on.[110]

Nyanga PAC had been rendered leaderless earlier in the campaign by the arrest of its chairman, Christopher Mlokoti. The committee sent a message to Duncan asking him to discover from Terblanche what had happened to Mlokoti. We do not have Terblanche's reply; Duncan does not mention in his diary what happened when he raised this matter. We do know that Duncan used this opportunity to assure Terblanche that the Liberals were behind the police so long as they kept the peace 'by reasonable and humane methods'.

Terblanche must have been suitably reassured because he helped Duncan and Kgosana persuade an electrical goods supplier to lend a public address system to the Langa PAC committee. The colonel also agreed that no uniformed police would be present at the funeral for which the electrical equipment was needed. In sharp contrast to the circumscribed proceedings the authorities would sanction later that week in Sharpeville, here political leaders would shape the programme. A cable from Jawaharlal Nehru was read out. In an opening speech, Lawrence Mgweba 'called for firm resistance against the enemy'. Philip Kgosana too addressed the mourners, warning them that it was likely that during the coming week they would 'see vicious action on the part of the racist government'. They would need strong determination 'to carry the fight through to the bitter end'. Kgosana's audience included well-known local ANC personalities. They joined in the singing of '*aphi no majoni?*' (Where is the soldier?), Kgosana leading the chorus in 'a remarkably pure and rounded tenor'.[111] The *Cape Times* reported that apart from sporadic stoning of cars on Vanguard Drive, the main highway out of Cape Town, the occasion was peaceful. People arrived from all parts of the Western Cape to be greeted with shouts of 'Afrika' and the clenched fist PAC salute. Estimates of the numbers ranged from 50,000 to 200,000. The *Cape Times* reporter observed that a small group of whites were seen enthusiastically joining in with these exchanges. PAC speakers told the crowd to stay out on strike and to refrain from violence. In spite of recent happenings, they said, Africans had no hatred for other racial groups.[112] The funeral represented the high watermark of cooperation between the Pan-Africanists and Liberal Party members. Randolph Vigne wrote an enthusiastic description of the event shortly afterwards:

> In our car were the Liberal Party representatives: Joseph Nkatlo, the Cape Vice Chairman and two provincial committee members, myself and Collingwood August, with Samuel Motsoasi of the PAC. Parts of Kgosana's address and the other speeches gave us Liberals reassurances about Africanist beliefs that we had not hoped for. We were not fighting Verwoerd, we are not fighting nationalism or the Afrikaners or the whites—we are fighting the set

up. Who would be such a fool as to look at another man and to say 'You must be a bad man because your skin is this colour or that colour.' Soldiers do not cry on the battlefield when their fellows are killed. We do not cry for our fellow Africans who died here. They are our soldiers. They have taught us what you now know: that you cannot buy freedom with pennies and that other people do not give it to you. You have to win it, to fight for it. We shall fight first *with absolute non violence* (the seven syllables repeated several times over). We must starve and suffer and die so that we can be free. The slow drive to the graveyard was excited, even happy. The shouting of 'Izwe Lethu'—the reply—'Afrika'. 'Inkululeku' and the reply 'Ngwethu' with the right hand raised, elbow crooked, palm open. The slogans were called hundreds of times by every man and women. Along the route to the graveside outbursts of hope and celebration were expressed in the PAC salute. Grief was held back for the graveyard. Here the proceedings were confused. Dozens of clergymen, one of the most eloquent a coloured priest. Difficulties with the coffins. Loudspeaker troubles as inexperienced speakers tried to shout into them. The heat of the afternoon. You could have said the burial service was an unworthy end to the day. Yet I can only recall a elderly stout Xhosa lady, in ancient black, leaning over our car bonnet and following the burial service with her finger tracing the lines in her prayer book, her thoughts on it and it alone. And I shall remember the singing of the hymns with the voices of the crowd ending sometimes several bars after the rest.[113]

Philip Kgosana's forecast of a government clampdown within the next few days was prophetic. In fact as he was speaking, parliament was engaged in enacting legislation that would prohibit the PAC and the ANC. On the day of the funeral police raided several houses in Langa, firing shots at people trying to escape. During Tuesday, PAC leaders noted the arrival of police reinforcements to support the officers already stationed in the cordon surrounding Langa. At around 9.30 on the morning of Wednesday 30th, the police descended in force upon the New Flats and the zones in Langa, that is the areas in which the migrant workers lived and in which the strongest commitment to the strike was likely to be located. Simultaneously with this raid in Langa, a nationwide process of detentions began: that day over 1,500 people would be arrested as the government declared a state of emergency. Most of the detainees would be members of the ANC or allied organizations: outside Cape Town the PAC's national leadership was already mostly behind bars.

The police action in Langa was in Pat Duncan's words 'a really savage affair'. The constables broke down the doors of the dwellings they visited and started using their truncheons to drive the people they found sleeping inside out into the street. Near the zones, buses were lined up on to which the police forced some of the workers. Strikers retaliated with sticks and stones. It was this police assault that prompted the most remarkable event in this ten-day drama, the disciplined exodus of 30,000 residents from Langa and Nyanga and their march on Cape Town.

The extent to which this development was the effect of any premeditation or the degree to which it was spontaneous varies according to different accounts. The Langa PAC Committee had been planning a major demonstration that would take the PAC's following into town, but this was projected for Thursday, not Wednesday, and it would not begin with a march, rather the intention was that protestors would travel to Cape Town in pairs or in small groups. In his 1961 account, Kgosana refers to a discussion he had with one of the Langa PAC officials early on Wednesday, before he had learned of the police raid, in which 'we should surrender the next day with the whole of the Cape Peninsula—a mammoth plan'. In this narrative he tells us that while he was having this conversation he was alerted that 'a long line of marching men' was already on its way, supposedly intent on surrounding Caledon Square. In his later accounts, Kgosana suggests that the march was the outcome of a leadership decision: he joined it late, he maintained, only because his appearance needed careful timing if he was to evade arrest, not because he had been taken by surprise. Certainly there are indications of some preparatory work: the 'stewards' marshalling 'the crowd with wonderful control' observed by the *New Age* correspondent, as well as the fact that the Langa column was shortly going to be joined by a large procession of protestors from Nyanga. Mgxashe's memoir quotes Meshack Mampunye, one of the Western Cape regional executive leaders who, like Kgosana, was still at liberty. That morning, on his way to hospital to arrange for the admission of his wife, then in labour, at Bonteheuvel, he encountered a huge group of people emerging from Kensington, led by a fellow executive member, Sisa Mhambi. Mhambi told Mampunye that they were on their way to Langa to discover how the PAC was going to react to the police raids.

> Just when we were arguing among ourselves about what to do, whether we should march to the Athlone police station or not, we were joined by another massive crowd, and that was when we decided to march to Cape Town, with Kgosana at our head.

Subsequently, Mgxashe remembers, the marchers were joined by thousands of people from Nyanga East and West who disembarked from trains on to which the police had forced them so that they would go to work that morning.

Whatever the reasons for his absence from the procession at its beginning, Kgosana quickly found his way to its head, arriving as the marchers crossed the Athlone/Pinelands railway line. He had obtained a lucky lift from the *Christian Science Monitor*'s correspondent. This enabled him to assume control of events in the front ranks of the crowd, wearing his frayed brown second-hand jacket, now spattered with yellow brown mud, and his trademark blue shorts. At this juncture, Kgosana was determined that the marchers' objective should not be Caledon Square but rather the parliamentary buildings where they could find the minister of justice, Erasmus. When the marchers were fully assembled on De Waal Drive, a dual carriageway into the city by Groot Schuur Hospital, Kgosana addressed them, emphasizing the need for discipline and telling them they 'should obey [his] commands implicitly'. 'His control of the crowd was faultless', one observer confirmed.[114] By this stage the army and the police were busy garrisoning the city: during their halt on De Waal Drive, the marchers were overtaken by lorry-loads of naval ratings.

In his 1988 memoir, Kgosana claims that his objective was to deploy his massive following to enact 'a final showdown with the white rulers of South Africa' but this seems to be an exaggeration. Kgosana's choice of route hardly suggested such an appetite for confrontation: 'I decided we should go by way of De Waal Drive, so as not to block the traffic on the main road.' And indeed from time to time the procession would halt to allow the passage of cars with white passengers and 'unwieldy double decker buses were waved through the crowd'.[115] Most witnesses suggest that the mood of the marchers was peaceful, orderly, 'almost joyful' and that the column proceeded in 'total silence'.[116]

At the foot of the unfinished Athlone power station, looming larger than Table Mountain from the Cape Flats, came the first of the men from Langa. In their workclothes, tribesmen fresh from the Transkei and newspaper boys, university students and domestic servants, builders and schoolteachers, the crowd was a whole: the men from Langa marched in peaceful informal formation, unarmed and unarrogant, towards Cape Town. They came to tell their troubles, trusting and still friendly, believing that non-violence could not provoke violence, and that they would be heard. Police had driven them from their homes in the early morning and spontaneously the men came together, walking towards Cape Town. This was no organized demonstration — PAC plans had been to move in twos and threes on the next day, 31st March, meeting in front of Caledon Square Police Station, to wait in silent protest until their leaders were arrested.[117]

A British Independent Television News film that has survived helps to confirm these impressions. The film first shows what seem to be vanguard groups of marchers in an orderly procession walking along the road between Langa and the Athlone power station. In the film all the marchers are men and as they pass the camera crew many of them offer the open palmed Pan-Africanist salute. The film focuses briefly on faces: many of the men appear to be smiling and some of them wave their hats in greeting. They march about five abreast, keeping to the left-hand side of the road. They part to allow cars proceeding in the opposite direction and a double-decker bus carrying passengers to the township is also allowed to pass by unhindered. Overhead the marchers progress is being monitored by a Coastguard helicopter.[118]

The marchers seem to have assented good humouredly to a second change of direction. When the they were still outside the main built-up area, Eulalia Stott, the Black Sash president, had approached Philip Kgosana and on learning his objective she had implored him not to lead his followers to parliament: the reaction, she warned, would be quite ruthless. Kgosana refused to reassure her, the decision, he said, was out of his hands. Shortly afterwards, though, Kgosana changed his mind. An English journalist, Ken Blumberg, was watching as the marchers approached the final slope that would take them into the built-up city area:

> ... at the top of the slope, Kgosana halted his column and persuaded them to sit down at the side of the road and under the trees. After a conference with his lieutenants, Kgosana came over to the group of journalists. 'We do not want to have these people shot', he said. 'And I am thinking it might be better if I left all these people here and just went with about ten people to see Mr Erasmus. I could tell him I have all the others at my back. That's right?' We told him we thought this was a very responsible decision, that it seemed the only way to prevent complete disaster. 'That's right,' he said. So about ten Africans, five photographers and a handful of journalists separated themselves from the crowd and began walking towards the Houses of Parliament ...

The ITN film supplies a visual record of these developments, showing a large group of marchers resting and waiting, sitting on the verge of the road under a clump of pine trees. There is footage of Philip Kgosana in his jacket and shorts walking away from the group with his companions.

A meeting with Detective Head Constable Sauerman at the Rowland/Buitenkamp Streets intersection prompted another change of plan. Sauerman grasped Kgosana by the arm and urged him to turn back and proceed instead to the crowd's originally intended destination, Caledon Square.

Kgosana may not have needed much persuading: as soon as the naval ratings overtook his procession on their way into town he could be certain that parliament in particular would be strongly garrisoned. He thinks now that this consideration certainly helped to shape his subsequent decisions.[119] Blumberg's account corroborates Sauerman's recollection of this meeting with Kgosana, offered in his court testimony:

> I met you and I spoke to you first. I said to you that there will be a crowd of people gathered at the police station and that they were not willing to disperse before they had seen their leaders and that you'd better come down and speak to them with the object of getting them dispersed. You said to me that you were on your way to the House of Parliament to see the Minister. I advised you against that and said, 'No, you must first come down to the police station with me.' Then you continued and you said that you will come with me but you insist on seeing the minister as your people refuse to carry passes in the future and that you want the Minister to abolish the pass laws.[120]

Sauerman was ready to honour this undertaking. As the open space in front of the police headquarters began to fill up with this massive assembly, General Rademeyer, Colonel Terblanche, and a number of other senior officers appeared in front of the main entrance. The first to speak to Kgosana was Colonel Terblanche. 'What's wrong now, Kgosana?', he asked. Kgosana then told Terblanche that the march was a spontaneous reaction to his officers' assault on Langa that morning. Then, addressing Rademeyer, Kgosana demanded the immediate release of all imprisoned leaders 'since it was obvious that without responsible leadership, violence was inevitable'. Moreover he wanted an interview with the minister of justice, 'to put our demands to him'.

General Rademeyer's first response was to prevaricate. That would not be possible, he told Kgosana. The minister was unavailable. He was out for lunch, he said. Kgosana was unmoved: he needed to see the minister. Colonel Terblanche said he would try and contact the minister on the telephone, and hurried inside the building. Terblanche spoke to Erasmus who told him to disperse the crowd with no further concessions. Many years after his retirement, Terblanche described his subsequent exchanges with the minister. 'I said to the minister, "Please sir, I'm in full control" and he said "Carry out my order." ' Terblanche 'bowed his head in prayer'. 'Dear Lord', he entreated, 'I'm not capable of handling this situation. I'm handing over to you.' He then went outside. The minister would meet a small delegation later that afternoon, he told Kgosana.[121] Moreover the police would not use force again to break the strike.[122] These concessions were sufficient for Kgosana and his comrades:

This was another historic breakthrough for the PAC...to people outside South Africa, it might sound funny to describe an appointment with a minister as 'historic', but given the apartheid situation in the country, where a black man is regarded as sub-human, it [was] unthinkable that 'an agitator' can force an appointment with a minister. Such pressure had never been exerted on an official of the white government before.

Borrowing a loudspeaker from the police, Kgosana then called for silence. 'The murmuring of thousands of voices stopped.'[123] Kgosana then told the multitude his good news. He had secured an appointment with the minister: now they should return to the townships. In Kgosana's words, on hearing his command, 'the 30,000 demonstrators turned as one man and made their way home'. As he told Joseph Leyleveld nearly thirty years later, 'When I ordered them to go quietly, they went back quietly', the procession allowing itself to be led by a police van all the way out of the city centre.[124]

Terblanche's accounts of his encounter with Kgosana on the 30th varied slightly over the years. The final version supplied in interviews he gave to journalists in 1987 suggests that he had his conversation with the minister before meeting Kgosana. Indeed, he recalled, at first it was very difficult to find any PAC leader to speak to. It was only after he was recognized by one of the Pan-Africanists in the crowd that he would make any progress in negotiating. A man came up to him, he told journalists in 1987, who had once worked as a cook in the police station in which he had been a commander. As station commander he had disciplined a constable who had assaulted this individual. 'I will never forget you', he now promised Terblanche and moreover, he would lead him to their leader, Philip Kgosana. Terblanche's memory may have confused his encounter with Kgosana on the 30th with earlier meetings, though, for in this interview he suggests that he had never met Kgosana before the 30th whereas we have a range of contemporary evidence to the contrary. Terblanche thought that his conversation with Kgosana on this occasion lasted about half an hour but he supplied no real details about their exchanges.[125]

At 5 o'clock Philip Kgosana trustingly presented himself for his interview with the minister. He was arrested. Soldiers, sailors, as well as policemen then laid siege to Langa and Nyanga. Not enough police or military units were available locally and sailors and soldiers were flown in. Four regiments and hundreds of sailors were deployed in the Langa cordon and the army command issued officers and NGOs with sten guns.[126] The cordon could only be extended to Nyanga three days later but from the moment Langa was cordoned off, the Pan-Africanists lost their capacity for coordinated action.

Before Nyanga was totally surrounded, on 2 April, 1,000 men tried to march into Cape Town, but the police forced them to return to the township. That day the government announced it was mobilizing reserve army units. On Tuesday, 4 April, the police advanced beyond their cordons, into Langa and Nyanga. The day before they had halted a food delivery organized by the Liberal Party whose food deliveries had actually increased in the first days of April in a concerted effort to sustain the strike after Kgosana's arrest.[127] Now men were beaten without restraint in the streets. It took the police four days to break the strike. They used sticks, batons, *sjamboks*, crowbars, and Saracen armoured cars to comb through the Langa hostels and force a return to work. In certain cases, the degree of police violence was extraordinary. One man whom journalists encountered in hospital had been bayonetted in the face in Nyanga on the 4th. In Nyanga, policemen told residents that if they found them again without their passes, or with their passes in disorder, they would to beat them some more, 'men, women, children, all'.[128] By Saturday, in both townships, when making their food deliveries, Liberals were encountering the fourth or fifth layers of PAC leadership: the earlier echelons had been arrested.[129] On 6 April a defiant PAC spokesman told journalists visiting Nyanga that the strike would continue until Robert Sobukwe gave the word that it should end. Nyanga's resistance was especially protracted partly because here it seems the PAC's organization had been unusually systematic and deep-seated.

On Saturday, 2 April, a detachment of police entered Nyanga West site and service scheme, the area inhabited by people removed from Kensington squatter settlement and reputedly a PAC stronghold. The police were acting as escorts for sanitation workers whose entry into the township had been resisted by residents for the previous two weeks. In addition to overflowing latrines, the officials were startled to discover that 'most of the shacks were stacked with food including sacks of mealie meal as if the inhabitants had prepared for a siege'.[130] On Thursday 7 April, the siege of Nyanga was finally broken when the police took the township by storm, arresting 1,500 people and detaining 250. The following Monday, employers reported an almost total return to work. Cape Town's rebellion was over.

Could its outcome have been different? Did Philip Kgosana capitulate too easily? Should he have insisted on keeping his supporters in Caledon Square until he met the minister? Might he have extracted more significant concessions than such a meeting? What would have happened if he had refused to disperse his followers? Kgosana's critics do suggest, to cite R. W. Johnson's phrase, that his decision to turn back the crowd was one of those historical moments when 'extraordinary "chances" were missed'[131] and that the 'gullible' Kgosana failed to realize 'that his only bargaining power lay in his ability to keep the crowd behind him'.[132] Members of the Trotskyite Non-European Unity Movement argued that Kgosana's 'surrender' of his power amounted to a betrayal, one that they blamed on his Liberal friends who, they alleged, had persuaded Kgosana to negotiate and to tell his men to go home.[133] The belief that members of the Liberal Party were present and in contact with Kgosana in front of Caledon Square on the 30th has found its way into several of the published accounts of events[134] but though it may have reflected rumours circulating at the time it is untrue: all the authoritative sources, including Kgosana's memoirs and Patrick Duncan's diary, make it clear that no members of the Liberal Party were present, that Philip Kgosana made his decision on his own. As Vigne notes, on that day the Liberals 'stood by', watching the marchers 'as spectators of something taking place'. Actually, to their credit, the ITN film shows what are evidently Liberal Party members standing on the pavement holding hastily written banners exhorting onlookers to 'Join the Protest' and 'Stop Police Terror'. The arrival of the marchers in Cape Town's centre interrupted a meeting Liberal Party executive members were having with a group from the Nyanga PAC committee, who were still evidently out of touch with the main Langa-based leadership group.[135] Commenting more generally on the relationship that had developed between members of the Liberal Party and the local Pan-Africanists, Robert Sobukwe told Benjamin Pogrund in 1968:

> A number of whites had given clear proof of their willingness to work as equals with Africans in a completely disinterested spirit. One example, he said, was that of the Liberals in Cape Town. He agreed with me that they had not attempted to control of the PAC campaign, and had merely given full assistance as requested.[136]

Some PAC members were even more generous. In prison, on Robben Island, several of 'his men', apparently, had confided to Sobukwe that 'they were so impressed with what the Liberals did, that they would have been willing to accept the amalgamation of the PAC and the Liberal Party, had the situation arisen'.[137] Joe Molefi told Gail Gerhart in 1969 that 'the white Liberals gave us tremendous support during the Langa and Sharpeville disturbances' and that moreover this support was disinterested, that the Liberals 'hadn't tried in any way to influence policy'.[138]

It is likely that had Kgosana decided to remain outside the police building his followers would have stayed with him. In particular rural black South Africans shared a moral conception of how just authorities should behave and this may have explained the determination of the marchers 'to wait in silent protest'. These beliefs may help to explain the enduring patience with which crowds were willing to maintain their vigils outside official buildings that characterized the PAC's protests in the Transvaal as well as in Cape Town. As the social anthropologist, John Blacking, has noted:

> Kgosana invoked the traditional idea of a peaceful protest in which the numeri-
> cal strength of people and their implied threat of non-cooperation should have
> been sufficient to produce a just response; but he did not follow the idea
> through by waiting patiently until their demands had been satisfied, as did for
> example a famous Venda chief and his followers, who surrounded the govern-
> ment's administrative offices with an orchestra of three hundred reed-pipes and
> accompanying drums, and also the followers of a head women who resisted
> another chief's autocratic attempt to replace her with a favoured rival. . . . his
> fault was rather that in dealing with whites, he invoked the idealized knowledge
> of European thought and society that he had learnt at school and university . . .
> rather than following the logic of traditional African politics which had started
> the march and moving no further than he could see clearly.[139]

And indeed in Colonel Terblanche Kgosana may well have met an unusually amenable and conciliatory adversary who was predisposed in favour of
further negotiation. Terblanche himself conceded much later that:

> I could not see my way clear to using force in the heart of Cape
> Town . . . I was determined to find a peaceful solution and I was prepared to
> stand there and argue for days if necessary to avoid bloodshed.[140]

Evidently Ignatius Terblanche was a very different personality from the aggressive officials who helped shape police responses to the crowd at Sharpeville. Indeed the relative sophistication of police tactics during the events that preceded the great march to Caledon Square deserves emphasis and needs to be explained. When the police launched their final strike offensive in Nyanga, Patrick Duncan telephoned Colonel Terblanche to express his outrage at the violence the police were using. Terblanche told Duncan that 'the whole matter' had been taken out of his hands. Duncan then said he would demand that the police's behaviour be raised in parliament. Terblanche's reply to this was as consistent in its civility as he had been in his earlier dealings with the Liberals: 'Mr Duncan', he said, 'you will not be doing me a disservice if you do that'.[141] Margaret Ballinger, one of the Liberal Party's native representatives, did indeed reprimand the minister and, Liberals believe, effectively so, because the beatings ceased after her encounter with him and General Rademeyer in the corridors of the House of Assembly.

Terblanche's relative restraint may have been attributable to his experiences the previous year. He had directed police operations during the riots in Worcester that occurred after Elizabeth Mafeking's banishment in which the police shot several people and he may well have been anxious to avoid a repetition of such bloodshed. Peter Hjul thought that Colonel Terblanche was a policeman of the 'old school', not politically partisan in the narrow sense, unlike officers who had benefited from the sectional promotions that had affected the police's senior command during the 1950s, political interference that had less impact upon the police hierarchy in the more liberal Cape than in the Transvaal. Hjul noticed that Terblanche was unusually deferential in his dealings with Pat Duncan, behaviour that he attributed to a story he had heard that the colonel owed an early promotion to Duncan's father, Sir Patrick, from a time when he had been in command of the police guard assigned to the governor-general's official residence.[142]

Whether this anecdote is true is impossible to confirm but Terblanche's own comments about his early career suggest he was identifiably a United Party supporter. In the 1950s he was opposed to the cessation of black voting rights, 'not the act of a Christian' he said. In 1950 he had been stationed at Witzieshoek and was almost killed there during the resistance against cattle culling, an experience that helped to strengthen his aversion to using violence against protestors, he told interviewers in 1987.[143]

In any case, Terblanche's actions during these events contrast sharply with those of his colleague at Sharpeville, Lieutenant Colonel Pienaar, who was ultimately responsible for the police there loading their weapons in readiness to fire. In the planning before the event, Pienaar, together with National Party politicians in Vereeniging with whom he had conferred, favoured a show of force and his views were eventually to prevail over his Special Branch colleague, Colonel Att Spengler. Spengler was inclined in favour of negotiation, and he was better informed than Pienaar by local intelligence. This knowledge enabled him to gauge the intentions of the local PAC leaders. In Cape Town, too, Special Branch detectives were ready to negotiate with PAC officials: Sauerman's intercession just before the marchers arrived in Cape Town's city centre was an especially critical instance of such predispoitions. In the end, though, it was Colonel Terblanche's defiance of his minister that was decisive. His willingness to disobey Erasmus was a telling and courageous demonstration of political independence.

However if Philip Kgosana had opted for intransigency it is quite probable that more senior authorities might have over-ruled Terblanche and chosen a more confrontationist path. The government was already under attack from its parliamentary opponents for the concessions it had offered to the Pan-Africanists five days previously. The leader of the United Party in Natal, Douglas Mitchell, called the suspension 'a shocking exhibition of weakness in dealing with the matter'.[144] An embarrassed minister of justice had felt compelled to explain in the House of Assembly that the suspension of the pass laws was needed 'to avoid a congregation of people at police stations and possible bloodshed and so as not to tie the hands of the police in combating riots, as well as giving protection to the public at those places where it is most essential'.[145] On the 30th Minister Erasmus was in no mood for further concessions, apparently. In anticipation of Kgosana's initial resolve, parliament was ringed with soldiers armed with automatic weaponry[146] and even if it was not the case that Erasmus had ordered the soldiers to fire on any demonstrators that approached the buildings as Kgosana himself believed,[147] the detachments who were deployed in front of parliament were nervous enough to act upon their own initiative. As Helen Suzman recalled:

> I well remember looking out of the below-the-ground level window of my small office and seeing the trembling, booted feet of a soldier, part of the military detail sent to guard parliament.[148]

The ITN film has captured a group of young serviceman holding their rifles in hands that are visibly shaking. The film indicates that the force drawn up outside the House of Assembly included armoured cars equipped with heavy machine guns with officers in radio communication with their commanders. There were armed policemen equipped with sten guns at the police station too, though they were out of sight by the time Kgosana's followers arrived.[149] Much later Terblanche told reporters that inside the building there were two hundred armed policemen, though at his orders these men were locked in an inner courtyard; only senior officers were allowed outside the building.[150]

Colonel Terblanche was later disciplined, apparently for being so ready to bargain with Kgosana and for countermanding Erasmus's instructions, though it also seems likely that he was being scapegoated for his superior officer's, General Rademeyer's, handling of the exchanges with the Pan-Africanist leader. Promotion to which he was entitled was withheld by the minister and as he recalled much later, 'I was blamed for not using force, I was an outcast even among my colleagues.'[151] Minister Erasmus later lost his cabinet post and was despatched to South Africa's embassy in Rome, a demotion that was interpreted at the time as a penalty for his management of events. Frans Erasmus was widely derided amongst his colleagues for his ebullient stupidity and boorish manners; one anecdote has him abusing his ministerial prerogatives in riding in an army helicopter while on a game hunting expedition in the Kruger Park: in the story, possibly apocryphal, the minister takes pot shots at a rhinoceros with a sten gun. J. P. J. Coetzer, then a senior official in the Department of Justice and later the department's director-general supplies a pen portrait of Erasmus in his memoirs. Erasmus's bellicosity that day may well have been reinforced by uncertainty and hence a determination to appear decisive to his colleagues. Coetzer notes that Erasmus, though a qualified barrister, had never practised and from the day of his cabinet appointment remained well out of his depth in his efforts to manage his portfolio.[152]

What might have happened if police had shot into the crowd can only be a matter for speculation. In Sharpeville it took less than a minute's firepower to disperse a crowd of several thousand. Arguably—and the case has been argued in this vein—Kgosana's followers may have reacted differently to gunfire, and those who survived might have been prepared to retaliate violently on a massive scale. But to judge from the various descriptions of the marchers supplied by eyewitnesses as well as the film and photographic evidence available this was not an assembly constituted by people who anticipated a violent confrontation, however outraged they may have been by the police's brutality that morning. The London *Observer*'s Africa correspondent interviewed Langa Pan-Africanist marchers afterwards. One of them told Legum that the march was primarily 'a protest against beatings' but that moreover, the 'reason for coming to town is there's no shootings [in town]'. Indeed, Legum noted, many of the hostel dwellers wanted to march out of the township with their blankets and sleep in town where they would feel safe from any further police assaults.[153]

Erasmus's command to Terblanche that he disperse the crowd suggests that at the highest level, this was an administration prepared to use force to win back control of public space. There is still a need for systematic comparative research that addresses the reasons why normally aggressive authoritarian states on occasions refrain from employing violent methods of mass repression.[154] Even so, it is likely that the crowd assembled in central Cape Town on 30 March did not represent the sort of challenge in which one large-scale act of civil disobedience would have been likely to extract durable concessions. Successful non-violent action normally depends upon simultaneous challenges in a number of spaces and places. It works when 'political opportunities' are present, opportunities that result from the long-term withdrawal of external support for a regime and because of divisions within it, 'destabilizing environmental conditions'.[155] Most critically, the kind of symbolic force Kgosana had at his command works best in a setting in which a civilian population that normally supports authority becomes disaffected by brutal excesses. In fact white civilians did object quite vociferously to the tactics the police used to suppress the strikes in Nyanga and Langa between 4–6 April. Apparently, so many white bystanders phoned in to complain about the attacks to Cape newspapers the switchboards were jammed. C. F. Regnier, president of the Cape Chamber of Commerce made a personal appeal to Terblanche to halt the assaults. Earlier events had already prompted Anton Rupert to urge the prime minister to offer concessions and, as we shall see, there was dissent within Verwoerd's cabinet.

Not all white civilians were as morally troubled as the people who phoned Cape Town's newspapers, though. The prime response among many white South Africans was simply fear. Press reports referred to sharp increases in firearm purchases nationwide, but especially pronounced in the Vaal region, around Vereeniging.[156] In the week after the Sharpeville massacre, a journalist recorded the comment of a white women working behind a shop counter: 'They should shoot all those bloody kaffirs dead and then they'll come back to work tomorrow.'[157] This perception may have been quite generalized among Vereeniging's white citizenry. As Segametsi Makhanya recalled in 2000:

> I was working as a maid for a white women in Vereeniging at the time, and the first time I went back to work after the shootings she said she was disappointed with the number of people shot. She even stated that she wouldn't have minded if I had been shot as well. I quit my job the day after, that was too much.[158]

Mrs Makhanya's employer may have been influenced by Carol de Wet, who was the NP MP for neighbouring Vanderbijlpark, and who allowed himself to be quoted that 'It is a matter of concern to me that only one person was killed'—this was before the full scale of the massacre became evident.[159] It is not so unlikely that similar sentiments may well have prevailed among those officials and politicians responsible for deciding how the police might have responded to a crowd that refused to leave Caledon Square. Elsewhere in South Africa, the tide of protest was receding. As Kgosana had realized during his progression along De Waal Drive, the authority could concentrate their coercive resources in Cape Town.

Philip Kgosana was right. Though the Sharpeville killings did trigger rioting and demonstrations across South Africa in the succeeding week, much of this was spontaneous or dependent upon very localized initiatives, usually from ANC leaders, not Pan-Africanists. Outside Cape Town there was no evidence anywhere else of any efforts by successive layers of PAC leadership to mobilize further anti-pass campaigning despite William Jolobe's press statements from the PAC office that forecast that the campaign would continue 'with added vigour'.[160] Outside Cape Town, the most concerted protest activity after the massacre was on Monday 28 March, when the ANC called for a stay-away to mark 'a day of mourning': according to press reports this affected about 80–90 per cent of the African workforce in Johannesburg and Durban as well as almost all African workers in Cape Town. In Worcester on 28 March, the strike affected both coloured and African workers, an effect of the strong presence of the Food and Canning Workers' Union, an affiliate of the South African Congress of Trade Unions. In the African township in Worcester crowds of rioters burned down clinics, churches, schools, and the homes of African police constables. On Tuesday 29th, though, in the other main centres, in contrast to Cape Town, the previous day's strikers were back at work.

On 31 March, though, at Cato Manor, the large shanty town on the edges of Durban, pickets at bus stops stopped Africans from going to work and subsequently a large detachment of policemen halted a crowd of 5,000 men from marching to the city. The next day separate groups of marchers from different points again attempted to assemble in Durban's city centre and police shot three men while intercepting these groups. Trade Union shop stewards and ANC officials in Durban called for a second stay at home on the 4 April and subsequently there were clashes between strikers and workers returning to their hostels not just on 4 April but on the 5th and 6th as well. The 31st March had been the original day on which the ANC had planned to launch its pass campaign and this evidently coordinated protest in Durban reflected the ANC's local preparations there: the PAC's presence in Durban was very slight. There was a 30 per cent effective stay-at-home in Germiston on 30 March and on 1 April several hundred protestors burned their passes at the Bloemfontein bus terminal.

In East London there was no discernable response to the ANC's stay-away call nor any active support for a local call for a stay-away made by PAC officials in mid-April though through late March and the first half of April police reported a succession of arson attacks on public buildings. Police action might well have inhibited other more politically directed insurgency. Between 21 March and mid-April the police arrested 1,433 people, mainly 'natives with no passes, *tsotsis*', after five raids that deployed Saracen armoured cars, soldiers as well as policemen, and on one occasion, a light aeroplane. The purpose of the raids, police local commanders explained, was to remove potentially politically volatile people from the locality.[161] How much of this unrest can be attributed to the PAC's influence is difficult to judge. In Port Elizabeth, though there were no reports of PAC anti-pass activity on 28 March, Pan-Africanists distributed leaflets in the main townships in the days before 28 March instructing residents to ignore the ANC's stay-away call: these leaflets were later repudiated by PAC officials in Johannesburg.[162] In Johannesburg on 28 March a large crowd, mainly composed of teenagers surrounded two African policemen on patrol in Soweto's Meadowlands. The teenagers demanded their passes and upon being handed over, they were burned. The men then ran away but the youths caught one and stabbed him to death. They then successively attacked the municipal offices in each of Meadowlands' six zones, burning them down. According to onlookers, the youths shouted Africanist slogans, though press reports suggested that criminal *tsotsis*, 'boy thugs' were the main assailants, using political slogans cynically. As we have seen though in the PAC's recruitment of youngsters in the Task Forces, the distinctions between politically motivated mobiliza-tion and the sub-culture of youthful gangster activity were not clear-cut, and political mobilizers tapped into existing social networks.[163]

As theorists of non-violent action argue, 'struggles for political change should not depend on a single event, however momentous, but should rather focus on the process of shifting the balance of power through a range of mutually supporting actions over time'.[164] Arguably such a process was unfolding in Cape Town during the days that preceded Philip Kgosana's great march. In the days that followed, though, police action would halt this movement in its tracks. As Kgosana himself had predicted, in the fearful aftermath of these upheavals, 'emotions settled' and 'people went back to passes' in conformity with the laws that were quickly reimposed.

5
Aftermath: Effects and Consequences

In Sharpeville the local authorities lost no time in retaliating. At dusk on the 21 March, police patrolled the township assailing and arresting anyone they encountered who was out of doors. On Tuesday, uniformed men scoured the streets and lanes around the police station, collecting every stone, stick, and any other object they could find that might be represented as a weapon. In front of the station the police constructed two formidable pyramids of 'sticks, clubs, bottles, knives, iron pipes, assegais, pangas, needle swords and other weapons'.[1] Photographs of this alarming display later appeared in newspapers. As noted in the testimony quoted in earlier chapters, according to one eyewitness, the fabrication of such evidence even extended to 'police officers putting knives and stones indeed into dead people's hands to make it look like they had been armed and violent'.[2]

As we have seen, Nyakane Tsolo and Thomas More, the main local PAC leaders, were inside the station before the shooting started. While the dead and wounded lay in the street outside the station, Tsolo and More were taken to the men's holding cell and beaten up by apoplectic constables. During the next twenty-four hours the police rounded up and arrested most of the other key PAC activists as well as many other people who had joined the crowd outside the police station. Police commanders issued to their patrols a list of a hundred or so known PAC members, including the 'ringleaders'. They managed to identify seventy-six of these supposed culprits among the several hundred or so people they arrested. Captured Pan-Africanists included most, though not all, the members of a second layer of leadership that Tsolo and More had nominated.[3] The detainees weretaken to Boksburg prison. There from the first day of their incarceration, prison warders inflicted a punitive regime. Bandaged wounded survivors from the shooting who were still wearing their bloody clothes were forced to undergo a brutal cleansing from power hoses.

One patrol arrived at the Tsolo household in the evening of the 21st to search Nyakane's room for papers. Failing to discover anything obviously incriminating, the search team confiscated Nyakane's modest library of schoolbooks, including his volume of Shakespeare. The police even visited hospitals in the weeks that followed to apprehend patients who had been treated for gun-shot wounds, detaining them on public violence charges.[4] These detainees were released in batches as the police withdrew charges: most did not undergo trial. After a year, five of the Sharpeville leaders were convicted and jailed for incitement and public violence. Nyakane Tsolo would have been among them but shortly after obtaining bail in March 1961 he absconded, crossing the Basotho border to rejoin the Pan-Africanists at their new headquarters in Maseru. Most of his companions who had succeeded in evading the police fled to Lesotho leaving behind a tiny group to reconstruct a PAC network in Sharpeville. Within the township, arrests of suspected troublemakers and raids on their houses continued for a year or so after the massacre. Many of these incursions, it appeared to local residents, seemed to be targeted completely randomly. They were still occurring—sometimes at night—when the last of the detainees returned to Sharpeville from prison in early 1961.[5] The exodus to Lesotho included people who were badly hurt: as far as the police were concerned gunshot wounds were obvious evidence of complicity. In Maseru there are several graves of Sharpeville residents who died shortly after their arrival.

All this activity probably succeeded in obtaining its desired effects. The first of these was the rapid creation of an intimidating atmosphere that would inhibit any local witnesses offering evidence at the official Commission of Inquiry that was announced in the week following the shootings. In the longer-term, though, the fearful climate police activity engendered ruled out any continuation of open political activity. Many years later residents would tell visitors that 'for a long time, nothing happened in Sharpeville; we were afraid to speak'. Through the next months, Sharpeville's inhabitants had to obey a strict curfew. 'The days after the shootings the township was like a grave. There was a strict curfew, people weren't allowed outside after six.'[6] Local testimony suggests that in the days that followed the massacre many new recruits were drawn into the police's informer networks:

A lot of people acted as spies for the police. Because they were so poor, they needed those few Rands they were paid. As a result you couldn't say anything anymore because those sell outs would get you arrested.

All this helped to break down any vestiges of communal solidarity that might have survived the killings. Gideon Tsolo remembers that he and his family began to encounter hostility even from neighbours living in the same street. 'They are the people who put us into trouble', the neighbours said.

Robert Sobukwe and the other leaders that had assembled outside Orlando police station had to await the arrival of security police before they could be arrested. At first the police only wanted to detain the ten most senior Pan-Africanists, but eventually following much argument they consented to arresting of all the Positive Action volunteers present. After accompanying the police to conduct searches of both his house and his university office Sobukwe was confined with other top echelon Pan-Africanists at police headquarters in Marshall Square. Over the next few days, Sobukwe and his fellows were kept in the holding cells but they were allowed visitors and were able to receive and send out occasional messages, keeping in touch in this way with William Jolobe's office. They were all charged on 23 March and then they were imprisoned in the Johannesburg Fort. A week later Robert Sobukwe and twenty-two others were remanded under the 1953 Criminal Law Amendment Act which carried a maximum five-year prison term. True to their principles, they refused to plead, Sobukwe speaking for the group with his customary courtesy, reassuring the magistrate that in rejecting the court's authority they were 'not impugning his personal integrity'. Again in conformity with their undertakings, the Pan-Africanist principals engaged no lawyers and in the forthcoming trial they cross-examined police witnesses, mainly to contest the accuracy of transcripts of the proceedings at PAC meetings. Sobukwe elected to give evidence and he also spoke after conviction and before sentence. 'If we are sent to jail there will always be others to take our place' he told Magistrate J. K. du Plessis. Du Plessis was unmoved. He pronounced sentences that he said should serve 'as a deterrent to others similarly minded':[7] three years for Sobukwe, two years for Leballo and three others, and eighteen months for the rest. They started their terms in Pretoria's Central prison before joining 160 or so sentenced Pan-Africanists in Boksburg. Subsequently they were transferred to a farm prison at Stofberg where they were put to work uprooting trees, clearing land, and building an irrigation dam. Sobukwe would finish his term once again in Pretoria but on its completion in May 1963 he would then be detained under a special law, an amendment to the Suppression of Communism Act, renewed annually, 'the Sobukwe clause', as the measure came to be known. He was taken to Robben Island, the former lepers' colony offshore from Cape Town that now accommodated a maximum security prison. He would live confined in a small warders' cottage, separated from the other prisoners, for the next six years.

Meanwhile in Cape Town, Philip Kgosana and his companions arrived at Caledon Square late in the afternoon of 30 March for their expected meeting with Minister Erasmus. They were arrested under state of emergency regulations. A heavily armed detachment of policemen escorted them under gun point to the charge office where they underwent a strip search. They remained for five days in police cells. On 2 April, Kgosana received a visit from the secretary of justice, C. J. Greef. Kgosana 'repeated the PAC demands which would have to be fulfilled before the campaign could be called off and warned of widespread violence unless campaign leaders were released'. Greef dutifully wrote down in his notebook everything Kgosana said and promised he would report back to the minister. The Cape Town leaders were then transferred to proper prison cells, isolated from each other to be interrogated by Special Branch officers. Their trial began in May. Unlike the Johannesburg group, Kgosana and his fellow-accused engaged defence lawyers. In November, before a lengthy adjournment, they succeeded in obtaining bail. The month before, Mlami Makwetu, who had remained at liberty, visited Johannesburg. He returned to Cape Town with the news that Sobukwe had issued a command that young PAC followers should leave South Africa for military training. This, Kgosana explains in his autobiography, prompted his decision to break his bail conditions and leave South Africa. On route for Pretoria, Kgosana visited Z. B. Molete and Joe Molefi in Evaton. The two men were at liberty because on 21 March they had been unable to persuade the police at Evaton to arrest them. Molete was then acting-president in place of Sobukwe. While the two were critical of his decision to bail himself out, they showed him a letter from Sobukwe that confirmed what he had had been told by Mlami Makwetu.[8] Obliged to report daily to the police station near his parents' home, Philip Kgosana took advantage of a relaxation of this reporting requirement during the Christmas holiday to cross an unguarded and unfenced Swazi border. If he had remained he might well have been acquitted for in May 1961 the magistrate dismissed the charges against all his co-accused finding the police transcripts of PAC speechmaking too unreliable to serve as a safe basis for conviction.

Between 30 March and mid-May, nationwide the police arrested nearly 10,000 people under state of emergency regulations, 2,000 in the first few days. Most of the detainees would not be released until the end of August. Their numbers included a major proportion of the most effective leadership of the ANC and the Communist Party. Several days before their detention, in anticipation of an impending ban on their organization, ANC leaders began planning a new organizational structure that could function more easily under clandestine conditions but the state of emergency arrests pre-empted its implementation.[9] Two days earlier, the government had intro-duced a parliamentary bill to ban both the ANC and the PAC. Again with United Party backing the bill became law and the two organizations were declared illegal on 8 April. That day the authorities once again beganarrest-ing people under the pass laws. In the next two months 20,000 Africans were convicted for Urban Areas infringements, an unprecedented level of enforcement compared to conviction statistics from previous years.[10] Effec-tively for the next six months organized protest was immobilized by the removal of its most assertive leadership.

★

For many of apartheid's opponents, the Sharpeville massacre and the repres-sion in its wake signalled a new epoch. In the words of Joe Slovo, an influential strategic thinker for the South African Communist Party, Shar-peville was a 'strategic turning point', a time 'when the ruling class made clear its intention of smashing black opposition totally . . . when it finally sealed off the avenues for effective opposition without the element of armed force'.[11] By the time he was writing this, in the mid-1970s, Slovo's argu-ment represented a doctrinaire orthodoxy. In the Communist Party's offi-cial history, after Sharpeville, among 'the masses of oppressed people' the 'exposure of the police-state' confirmed 'that the days when resistance could be confined to non violent and legal methods had gone forever'.[12] This was written more than a decade after the event but, as we shall see, it is likely that Slovo and other leaders within the Congress Alliance began to think in this way during the state of emergency. Pan-Africanists shared this understanding of the Sharpeville crisis as a watershed. For the Evaton PAC activist, David Sibeko, the events 'proved that the South African regime was vulnerable'.[13] Nyakane Tsolo also believed that on 21 March and in the days that followed, 'we defeated a paralysing fear of the white man . . . Nothing like that had happened before.'[14] Many academic commentaries have echoed these perceptions: 'half a century of non violence had failed',[15] the massacre and its immediate aftermath constituted 'the breakpoint of South African liberalism',[16] the moment that effectively ended any realistic prospects of political amelioration and reformist change. This was the event above any other that confirmed 'themarginalization of liberalism',[17] when it became clear that that 'the majority of white South Africans would never accept a liberal solution to the colour problem'.[18] In a similar vein, Sharpeville marked the beginning of 'a period of repression, which, at greater or lesser intensity, was to last for nigh on three decades'.[19]

More generally, arguments about Sharpeville's significance divide into two camps. First, taking their cue from the activist perceptions cited above, a school of radical historiography would emerge that projected the crisis as a critical staging point in a journey towards revolutionary change. This kind of writing became especially influential during the mid 1970s, though subsequently its arguments would become progressively more subtle and complicated. Second, in a more gradualist vein, more ameliorationist perceptions shaped a parallel course of liberal scholarship both within and outside South Africa: for its constituents, Sharpeville's 'epoch-making significance' was in making the 'reality' of black urbanization and industrialization obvious to white South Africans. As an editorial in *Contact* suggested two weeks after Philip Kgosana's march, 'the very quietness of the vast throng of 30,000 was its greatest strength'. In the face of this giant power, the editorial continued, 'the guns in the hands of the police, their very armoured cars and machine guns, looked as if made of cardboard', for they represented sources of coercion that the government was unwilling to use.[20] Through the 1970s and 1980s, liberal analysts of South African politics would insist that Sharpeville was the beginning of a cyclical historical process in which urban insurgency, some of it violent, would engender responses from authorities that would balance or alternate repression with reform.

Today, fifty years after Sharpeville and nearly twenty years after South Africa's rulers' decision to begin a negotiated transition to democracy, it may be rather easier to assess the historical consequences of Sharpeville than it was during the decades when the prospects of a lasting political settlement still seemed so uncertain. The remainder of this chapter will address the consequences ofthe Sharpeville massacre and the events we associate with it. First it will consider the very broad ways in which South Africa changed, socially and politically, after the Sharpeville crisis. To what extent can we understand these changes as the effects, both direct and indirect, of the Pan-Africanists' protest and of its suppression? Then, against this backdrop of sociological and institutional change we will explore the way in which Sharpeville decisively altered the trajectory of black political organization. We will do this through following the PAC's attempts to direct insurrectionary warfare from exile bases. We will also trace the parallel progress undertaken by its parent organization, the ANC, which was certainly as deeply affected by what happened at Sharpeville. The final section of this chapter will investigate the ways in which the events at Sharpeville affected South Africa's international relations. In particular we will discuss the crisis' impact upon external perceptions of South Africa, and the resulting ways in which the government's international authority weakened.

★

In the short-term, in the weeks and months following the massacre and amid the tide of political disorder that gripped South Africa's towns there were plenty of signals that political confidence was eroding among white South Africans and among other groups who had a vested interest in South Africa's stability. This was evident at the highest level of leadership in the government when the acting prime minister, Paul Sauer, normally the minister of lands, suggested that 'the old book of South African history was closed at Sharpeville'. South Africans needed to rethink 'in earnest' the policies that addressed 'the Native question'.[21] Sauer was deputizing for Verwoerd who at the time was recovering from an attempt on his life. On 9 April in Johannesburg, Verwoerd had been delivering an ebullient address to those present at the opening of the Rand Show. 'We shall not be killed' he told his rapturous listeners, 'we shall fight for our existence and we shall survive.' At this juncture, a man walked up to the dais upon which Verwoerd was standing and fired two shots from one metre away. Verwoerd was rushed to hospital. The police arrested David Pratt, a smallholder who farmed just outside the city and who had succeeded in obtaining a VIP card. Pratt would later undergo psychological assessment and he would not stand trial. He would die in prison. Though the authorities emphasized Pratt's history of nervous illnesses, the handwritten notes he left in his room at the mental hospital in which he would be confined confirm that his motives were most certainly political. His decision to shoot Verwoerd was triggered, he explained, by a spectacle he had witnessed a few days before. He had seen a group of pass offenders being roughly manhandled into a police van.

By the next morning, he explained, 'the feeling became very strong that someone in this country must doing something . . . and it better bloody well be me, feeling as I do'. Pratt felt he had a divine mandate to undertake his mission, comparing himself to a biblical prophet. He was not alone in invoking divinity. Many of Verwoerds's admirers perceived in their icon's rapid recovery from the head injuries he sustained from Pratt indications of higher purpose. As one Senator Malan observed a few days later: 'A grateful *volk* has bowed its head in gratitude at the miracle that their leader was saved so that he can continue his work. The Father himself must be thanked for his recovery.'[22]

Verwoerd himself, both before and after Pratt's attack, was very obviously disdainful of any suggestions that the events at Sharpeville and the subsequent happenings constituted a crisis that required fresh approaches of the kind that Anton Rupert was urging him to undertake after Rupert's encounter with Philip Kgosana. Sauer had originally raised his concerns in cabinet and the leaders of the Cape and Transvaal wings of the National Party, Ben Schoeman and Eben Donges, had joined him in urging that 'serious consideration should be given' to replacing African pass books.[23] Paul Sauer's relationship with Verwoerd was never close, though, and he was a minor member of cabinet. In his speech he called for better wages, changes in the pass laws, more development in the reserves and legalizing liquor sales to blacks—he was himself a wine farmer and their representatives had been lobbying for reform over this issue for some time. The government needed to create a new spirit of trust between whites and blacks, he said. Before he spoke he consulted at least two colleagues who warned him that though they were sympathetic they would be unable to offer him support. Ben Schoeman, another member of Verwoerd's cabinet was sitting next to Verwoerd in parliament when the prime minister was handed a note with the news about the shootings, Verwoerd showed the note to Schoeman. 'Now we shall have big trouble' he observed laconically.[24] One contemporary source, the Progressive Party MP Jan Steytler told journalists that Verwoerd was so shaken by the initial reports from Sharpeville that he needed to be dissuaded from resigning. This seems unlikely. Verwoerd's son remembers that he and his family joined Verwoerd for lunch every Sunday. He cannot remember his father ever discussing Sharpeville.

Verwoerd may have been comparatively unmoved by events, stoically resolved from the moment he heard the news from Sharpeville to maintain an uncompromising adherence to existing policies. He certainly had no reason to worry about his administration's capacity to contain any rebellion. In fact he and his colleagues had undertaken early preparations to enable them to manage political disorder on a national scale. In 1958, in anticipation of the disruption that might have resulted from the ANC's stay-away call, special arrangements were instituted to prevent the breakdown of key services. An inter-departmental committee was set up to plan such arrangements constituted by the secretary for labour and including soldiers, policemen, and officials from prisons and Native Affairs departments.[25] Even so, Verwoerd's language at the Rand Show suggests that he was very aware that a fresh sense of vulnerability was affecting his own supporters. As we have seen, firearm sales peaked in the following few weeks. Even *Die Kerkbode*, the weekly newspaper of the Dutch Reformed Church, published an editorial that suggested rulers should consider fresh solutions to the problems confronting South Africa. Meanwhile, though, members of their congregation should 'remain steadfast in their faith'.[26]

Not all white South Africans were so determined to survive through prayer and fortification, though. For the first time since the Second World War, there was a net outflow of white migrants; that is the number of immigrants was exceeded by emigrants from 1960 through to the end of 1963. In fact the trend of sharply increasing emigration began in 1959 when 2,000 people left for Britain, nearly double the average for the preceding decade, their departure spurred certainly by the increasing visibility of violent or at least forceful disaffection among black South Africans: the Cato Manor riots were important in this respect. Four thousand people travelled to Britain in 1960 and 5,000 in 1962. Then the number of British-bound immigrants levelled off at 3,000 a year until the end of the decade.[27] The overall number of emigrants was greater, of course, but Britain was the main destination partly because South Africans enjoyed open entry into Britain until 1962 and even after that date they received preferential treatment from the British immigration authorities. They were mostly people who were English-speaking even if they were not of British descent. Some of these exiles would have been people leaving because of their political commitments, people who had experienced or who might expect official persecution because of their engagement in extra-parliamentary opposition. But their numbers were small and the majority of immigrants from South Africa in the 1960s were people whose decision to leave was influenced by more utilitarian considerations: they were worried about a future in which the social order seemed to be under threat. In fact as we shall see net inflows of migrants after 1963 would lead to a very rapid increase in the white population, accounting for about half of its growth between then up to 1976, but those who left usually belonged to a socially influential group of successful professionals; their departure probably had a disproportionate effect on public perceptions.

Economic reactions to the Sharpeville emergency helped to reinforce perceptions that South Africa was in a state of crisis, though it is likely that foreign investors were also influenced by the subsequent break-up of the Rhodesian federation and Congo's chaotic decolonization. Immediately after the massacre, share prices plummeted and an exodus of capital would continue until late 1961 at a monthly rate of R12 million.[28] In 1960 alone, the total net outflow of private capital was R194 million.[29] Foreign reserves fell from R312m to R153m between June 1960 and May 1961.[30] Capital flight was checked in May 1961 by stricter controls on capital exports and fresh restrictions on the convertibility of the Rand. Even the Anglo American corporation had to resort to foreign bank borrowing to obtain fresh capital.[31] Negative net capital flows between 1960 and 1964 represented the first real threat to South African economic progress for a very long time and halted a real GNP rate that had been increasing at around 5 per cent every year since the 1930s. Local businessmen, both English-speaking and Afrikaans represented in ASSOCOM, the Federated Chamber of Industries and the employers' bodies for the iron and steel and mining industries, signed a joint memorandum expressing their qualms about influx controls that promoted 'a feeling of insecurity among the Bantu'. The memorandum suggested that contravention of the pass laws should be decriminalized and reference books should be replaced at least for urban Africans with simple identity documents.[32] Certain business leaders were bolder. Colin Corbett, president of the Johannesburg Chamber of Commerce appeared on 11 April on an edition of the BBC's *Panorama*. He told Robin Day that there should be direct consultations between the government and 'responsible African leaders' such as Albert Luthuli, 'a man of sterling character'. South Africa was evolving into a 'multiracial state' he insisted, 'nobody can stop it'.[33]

The emergency's effect on South African relations with other governments might also have been expected to generate anxious forebodings among white citizens as well as more excited expectations among black South Africans. As Deon Geldenhuys has observed, the crisis represented 'a trial of strength in foreign relations', a moment at which 'the apartheid issue had arrived prominently on the world's agenda'.[34] In fact initial reactions from foreign governments that white South Africans would have regarded as friendly were fairly restrained. The Australian prime minister, Sir Robert Menzies, refused a call from his parliamentary opposition for trade sanctions or even a motion of censure. The Labour Party had been calling for a South African trading boycottfor more than a year, its own support for a whites-only Australian immigration policy notwithstanding. 'I had hoped', Menzies explained, 'it [the Labour party's call] was as dead as the dodo.' However now he felt compelled 'to act on our representative in South Africa to inquire into the matter and give us a close assessment of what happened'.[35] Menzies' restraint reflected his own anxieties about the possible parallels that might be drawn between South African apartheid and his own government's discrimination against Aborigines.[36] Meanwhile the Canadian premier, John Diefenbaker, told journalists his government could 'see no purpose' in diplomatic protest, though at the same time, he reminded them, Canadians had no sympathy for racial discrimination. In Australia political reactions extended well beyond any cabled exchanges between Menzies' office and officials at the embassy in Pretoria. In Sydney more than a thousand students engaged in a violent confrontation with police who were trying to control the most unruly student demonstration ever in their experience. A week later 1,200 people attended a rally in protest against apartheid at Sydney's Lyceum Theatre to listen to the superintendent of the Central Methodist Mission characterize the conflict between blacks and whites in South Africa as emblematic of a cosmic moral struggle.[37]

Meanwhile in New Zealand a comparable scale of mobilization occurred in a context in which New Zealand–South African relations were already a cause of political tension. South African refusals to allow entry to Maori All Black rugby players had been a source of discord since 1937 when Evarard Jackson was told to stay at home and not accompany his fellow team members on their South African tour. In 1959 when the news broke that an All Black side visiting South Africa would not be allowed to include Maori players the Citizens All Black Tours Association was formed in opposition to the proposed tour. The twenty branches of the association collected 153,000 signatures for its 'No Maoris—No Tour' petition and managed to assemble the largest demonstration witnessed in New Zealand since the depression era.[38]

Sir Robert Menzies' and Harold Macmillan's conservative administrations in Australia and Britain respectively were both anxious to avoid an open rupture with South Africa. Britain especially was keen to keep South Africa within the Sterling currency 'area' and officials were worried that a rupture over the Commonwealth might provoke a South African departure from the Sterling group.[39] In 1961, though, Canadians broke ranks with the other white dominions in helping to lead arguments that South African should leave the Commonwealth. At the 1961 Commonwealth Conference, an assembly that was now joined by the heads of governments from recently independent African and Asian governments, Verwoerd arrived with an application for South Africa's continued affiliation, a requirement of his country's adoption of a Republican constitution in place of its previous dominion status. He very nearly succeeded too, for contrary to popular beliefs, amongst the prime ministers assembled in London, there was no line-up against South Africa. As British officials noted afterwards, if Verwored had offered 'only one millimetre of concession the result might have been different'.[40] In particular the Indian, Malayan, and Pakistani leaders were keen to avoid a confrontation between new Commonwealth members and the older group of white-led dominions. Amongst African leaders, Kwame Nkrumah was inclined to be conciliatory though Nigeria's Abubaker Tafawa Balewa took a tougher line: allowing South Africa to remain a Commonwealth member would represent an endorsement of apartheid he insisted. Despite Nigerian misgivings Verwoerd was induced to approve of a statement that incorporated a set of blandly expressed Commonwealth principles that even he could subscribe to. The sticking point came when he was asked on the third day of the negotiations whether he would welcome to Pretoria diplomatic representatives from newly independent African governments. This concession Verwoerd could not countenance for as officials later explained on his behalf 'he could not have the capital crowded with so many embassies'.[41] Verwoerd was more tactful at Lancaster House, apparently. He told the other heads of government that 'more progress' was needed with implementing apartheid before black embassies could open without 'confusion' and 'incidents'.[42] It was at this juncture Australian and British diplomats advised the South African to withdraw his application: during the course of that afternoon it had become obvious that several of the premiers felt that too much had been conceded to South Africa in the statement drafted by Macmillan's officials.[43]

In effect South Africa had been nudged out of the Commonwealth. This was South Africa's first really significant set-back diplomatically, though Verwoerd was dismissive, suggesting that in reality South African's relationship with historic allies such as the British might become easier now that Britain no longer had to feel that it should try to achieve any agreement between South Africa and other Commonwealth members.[44] British officials had in fact reassured Verwoerd that close bilateral arrangements between his country and Britain would persist despite its withdrawal from the Commonwealth.[45] That year an inter-departmental cabinet committee was formed in Whitehall to ensure that relations with South Africa should not be disrupted: it would meet 26 times in 1961 alone.[46] However, British policy was multifaceted. Certainly, maintaining a good working relationship with Pretoria would remain important for successive administrations, but even in 1961 British officials were ready to offer certain kinds of help to apartheid's more radical opponents. In what was then Bechuanaland, colonial officials under the direction of the British Secret Intelligence Service (MI6) set up a system of secure transit enabling key South African refugees and other secret travellers to cross Bechuanaland and proceed in safety all the way to Dar es Salaam using a special air service funded by British intelligence and local businessmen. Passengers in 1961 included Philip Kgosana, Patrick Duncan, and Nelson Mandela.[47]

If 1960 represented a crisis of confidence for the South African government, for most white South Africans it was short-lived. Writing in the 1980s, the veteran liberal parliamentarian, Oscar Wollheim suggested that Sharpeville was a watershed in the 'beginning of a process' in which 'increasing numbers' of white South Africans began 'to question such things as the apartheid system, influx controls, the pass system' and to acknowledge 'the economic necessity for thepresence of black people in cities'. In fact, though this was very evidently the case when Wollheim was writing, in 1960 and in 1961, after momentary hesitations as far as most white South Africans were concerned the most obvious political dynamic was increasing electoral support for the government and the National Party. Rather than inducing liberal disaffection among white South Africans, black nationalist mobilization at the end of the 1950s encouraged a confluence in white politics that, arguably, helped South Africa to emerge 'as a stronger state and a more unified white nation'.[48] The government organized a referendum in October to seek support for a republican constitution, honouring a commitment it had made in 1959. On a high poll, the government won a narrow majority of 52 per cent, representing a small swing in pro-government voting from the previous election, possibly a reflection of the registration of younger voters, disproportionately Afrikaans-speaking, ostensibly a modest victory, but in fact the first time ever the National Party had obtained a majority of white votes. The 1961 election featured a slightly larger swing towards the government.

Five years later the 1966 general election results demonstrated accentuated swings towards the right among white voters, with the National Party beginning to make significant gains among English-speaking voters.[49] This was despite the 1959 defection from the opposition United Party of a group of eleven disaffected liberal MPs who constituted a new Progressive Party. In 1961 the Progressives retained only one seat in the constituency Helen Suzman defended against the United Party and not surprisingly they did not do better in 1966. Through the decade, in fact all the trends suggest more or less unbroken majority white electoral support in high turnout elections for the government. The National Party's more liberal opponents in the Progressive Party would have to wait until the 1974 elections before emerging as a significant force in parliamentary politics: that year they won seven seats.

White voters' behaviour through the decades reflected the prosperity that was the consequence of industrial boom as well as a result of the reassurance that arose from the government's effective if harsh containment of rebellions by its black subjects. Between 1960 and 1970 per capita incomes among whites climbed by nearly 50 per cent, from R22 389 (in constant 1995 Rands) to R32 779. Rates of increase for other groups were more modest but for whites this was a decade of unprecedented affluence[50] and by 1970, as Johnson suggests, they were rivalling Californians as the most wealthy community in the world.[51] Social mobility accelerated among Afrikaners especially: in 1960, 43 per cent of Afrikaner workers were in white-collar occupations whereas in 1977 the proportions had grown to 65 per cent.[52] This rising wealth was mainly a consequence of industrial expansion: between 1960 and 1966, for instance, the numbers employed in manufacturing grew from 957,000 to 1,181,000, an expansion of around 25 per cent.[53] Through the decade industrial growth exceeded 7 per cent a year.[54] Of the growth in the industrial workforce, white workers constituted a quarter, increasingly concentrated in supervisorial and managerial positions. Much of the additional skilled manpower was to arrive from outside South Africa. Between 1960 and 1970 the white South African population increased in size from 3.09 million to 3.77 million and it would expand at an even faster rate in the next decade reaching 4.53 million in 1980. Immigration was responsible for about half this increase.[55]

Industrial progress was partly a consequence of government policies that promoted import substitution, that is the relatively costly production of manufactured commodities directed at internal markets. Industry also benefited from massive inflows of foreign capital from 1962 onwards, partly from new sources of investment outside the traditional American and British capital markets, especially from Germany. German investment, especially by Siemans, for example, helped to build up a local telecommunications industry almost from scratch through the decade, so that by 1970 South Africans were making about half the components it used and employing 8,000 people in its factories, about half of them white.[56] Britain remained the main investor though and indeed between 1964 and 1966 South Africa was Britain's most important source of income from external investment.[57] American investment doubled during the remainder of the decade. Amongst foreign businessmen the risks that made South African investments so unattractive in 1960 were easily forgotten. A spokesman for General Motors, when announcing his company's decision to expand its assembly plant in Port Elizabeth by another 395 acres, admitted that his board 'ha[d] not given the racial situation any thought whatsoever, either in its short-term or its long-term planning'. The following year the chairman of the Norton Company appeared in Johannesburg to open a new factory. 'I think South Africa is going to remain a strong country, led by white people', he said.[58]

Black South Africans were also affected by this industrial advance. In manufacturing, black, mainly African, employment rose by 75 per cent between 1958 and 1968. In factories Africans increasingly undertook relatively skilled work, moving into the foundries and onto the assembly lines, a development acknowledged in the late 1960s by the administration's successive relaxations of job reservation as well as the efforts to direct new industry to the 'border areas' around homelands. In the Durban textile industry, for example, 90 per cent of the workforce was African by 1973 and of this workforce only 10 per cent was unskilled—nearly half were skilled machine operators, factory clerks, or needle setters, work that required quite extensive training.[59] Economic growth did not bring much prosperity to most black South Africans: their per capita income increased by only 23 per cent through the decade, a period in which inequality between blacks and whites became even more accentuated.[60] However the cultural changes that accompanied urbanization and industrialization—by 1968, 750,000 Africans read daily newspapers and African radio ownership doubled between 1966 and 1968—encouraged new awareness of injustice and prepared a fresh constituency for revolt.[61] Growth also expanded an African middle class—teachers, professionals, shopkeepers, civil servants, clerks, and so forth: between 1960 and 1970 this group grew from 144,000 to 264,000 nationally and trebled its size in Soweto.[62]

Economic expansion and diversification in the 1960s was partly an acceleration of trends that were already happening during the previous decade. In certain respects, though, the shock administered by the collapse of investor confidence prompted developments that both stimulated and profoundly altered the economy. Falling share prices after Sharpeville encouraged the movement of Afrikaner financial institutions into manufacturing and in general through the 1960s share ownership became increasingly domesticated, a change that helped to provide political support for government industrial policies. As already mentioned, the government imposed fresh controls on capital exports. Probably as important a factor in encouraging industrial investment as any fiscal policies though was the government's apparent capacity to maintain its political authority and its ability to impose political order. As we shall see, Sharpeville did not end black insurgency during the decade and in the next year both the Pan-Africanists and the ANC would mobilize their supporters in violent rebellions. However, except in isolated localities, neither of these efforts would represent a significant threat to the security of white citizens nor would they cause significant interruptions in the normal routines of economic activity and public administration. They were, though, sufficiently dramatic to provide the public political support the government would need to garrison its citizens with fresh defences.

First, and most obviously, Verwoerd's administration accorded new powers to the police. From 1961, a new minister of justice, B. J. Vorster, would begin a programme to consolidate police powers. New legislation including the so called 'ninety day law' suspended *habeas corpus* and extended police authority to detain and interrogate suspects held in isolation, without access to lawyers. From 1962 the police began torturing suspects held under the terms of the new Sabotage Act. The use of torture including the application of electrical shocks was quite common in routine criminal investigations during the 1950s[63] but now a judiciary that had been substantially reconstituted by politically motivated appointments was willing to rule against legal objections to any ill-treatment of detainees.[64] A new part-time Reserve Police Unit began recruiting white South Africans in 1961.

Under the direction of Vorster's old comrade in arms from the *Ossewab-randwag* fraternity, General van den Burgh, what was a small and focused special branch would begin its transformation into a formidable Security Police equipped and deployed as a counter-insurgency force. In 1963 a new radio network was instituted that would supply instant direct communications between more than a thousand police stations and police headquarters in Pretoria. By the end of the decade the size of the police budget was beginning to rival public expenditure on education, and the resources at its disposal included a fleet of eighty armoured personnel carriers and five hundred custom-built riot trucks.[65]

In parallel with the consolidation of police strength, through the 1960s the South African military underwent a major expansion. Between 1960 and 1966 budgetary allocations to the Defence Force rose from R44 million to R255 million. During this period there began to be sustained investment in a local armaments industry, R33 million in 1964, the year an Armaments Production Board was set up to coordinate public and private sector activity. In 1961, with government encouragement, local manufacturers negotiated 127 licences to produce foreign-designed military equipment. In 1968 the parastatal company Armscor was established as the body responsible for ensuring the procurement and production of South African weaponry needs. By 1964 South Africa was manufacturing its own automatic rifles and two years later the first Impala jet aircraft began to be assembled outside Pretoria. One decade later Armscor would preside over the tenth largest arms industry in the world. The state's backing for a local munitions industry encouraged other kinds of manufacturing, most obviously in telecommunications and transport. In other ways too, after Sharpeville, South Africa became progressively militarized. In 1960, national service became a universal obligation for young white men, before then the Citizen Force, the conscript component of the Defence Force, had been constituted through ballots. Through the 1960s military training would be lengthened in stages from three months to a year (in 1972).[66] Soldiers generally, and the command structure particularly, would change during the 1960s as the army became increasingly led by officers wholly trained in local military colleges in which indigenous military traditions associated with nineteenth-century frontier communities displaced the influence of imperial martial doctrine. In particular, as Philip Frankel has argued, the professional reflexes of the new graduates emerging from the Joint Defence College in the 1960s would at least partly be shaped by nostalgic recollections of the nation

'armed and in unity' expressed in the historic obligations of Boer commando citizen-soldiers.[67]

White security and—at least for the time being—prosperity was the effect
of other sources of coercive control as well. South African historians
perceive in the suppression of the PAC's protest at Sharpeville the decisive
action in breaking organized African resistance to the extension of pass laws
and the increasingly efficient implementation of these laws. Africans who
hitherto had been allowed to remain in town because they were urban-born
became progressively more vulnerable to expulsion from the cities if they
were unemployed, through legal changes introduced in 1964. The new
legislation was drafted initially by officials in the Bantu Affairs Department
together with members of the South African Agricultural Union in the
months after Sharpeville. Officials believed that in the atmosphere of alarm
that accompanied the emergency they could overcome objections from
local authorities and urban employers to their efforts to limit their dependence on black labour. Officials argued that the unrest following the
shootings 'took place especially in areas where the local authorities are
controlled by opponents of government policy' and this tendency they
argued was a good justification for reducing local government's power
over the management of influx control, and any other aspects of 'Native
administration'.[68] The argument may have been tendentious with respect to
Sharpeville itself, a township in which influx control had been very tightly
managed by the United Party and Independent controlled council but there
was plenty of evidence elsewhere that local authorities were seriously
threatened by popular tumult. In 1959 after the Cato Manor riots, the
manager of Durban's Non-European Affairs Department would inform
the minister of Bantu affairs that:

> . . . the authority of the Durban City Council—civil government authority for
> the area—has been challenged and overthrown. That statement is not an
> exaggeration of the facts, for it is true to say that the City Council has been
> defeated at Cato Manor, and cannot restore its authority without the fullest
> co-operation and most active assistance of the government.[69]

Even so, it would take four years for the central government to get its way
before it could overcome its opponents in organized industry and municipal
government and enact the legislation that would enable the Department of
Bantu Affairs to become the main source of civil authority for urban black
South Africans. Meanwhile, from the mid-1960s, increasing effort was

invested into compelling workers from the countryside to seek urban work
only through the labour bureaux that were set up in their home locations,
though many workers continued to defy and evade rural 'influx' controls.
Despite such evasion, one effect of the government's efforts to regulate
black people's lives was a sharp rise in the prison population: by 1970 it had
nearly doubled since 1960, a rate of expansion four times the pace of
population growth.[70] Another way in which the government tried to
check permanent African settlement in the main cities was in relocating
townships, where it was possible, to behind the frontiers of local homelands.
So though the government halted the growth of the African share of the
population within the official boundaries of the major cities, urbanization
was simply displaced to huge dormitory towns near the historic urban
centres: Kwa Mashu outside Durban, Mdantsane near East London, and
Mabopane and Garankua within daily commuting distance to Pretoria. In
these centres, industrial workers lived in massive state housing schemes,
hostels for single workers, houses for families, and as sociologists noted at the
time, increasingly they were likely to send their children to school and to
use public services, meagre as these were. Such relocations during the
decade increased the urban population of the ethnic homelands from
35,000 to 619,000.[71] Homeland populations were also swollen by the
enforced resettlement within them of a million labour tenants and farm
squatters, a development that accompanied the increasing mechanization of
commercial agriculture. Overall, homeland populations increased by 70 per
cent during the 1960s.[72] Eleven million out of fifteen million Africans in
1970 lived in the homelands to whose administrations all Africans, irrespective of their residence, were assigned as citizens that year.[73]

    Within the homelands, from 1961, political institutions were to become
more complicated with the introduction of electoral politics. As Deborah
Posel has observed, this was an important change of tack in government
policy, for during the 1950s, government had maintained its commitment to
an elaboration of older colonial indirect rule arrangements in which local
chiefs were invested with greater coercive power. Now the government
favoured the evolution of 'self-governing homelands', a policy that as
Verwoerd explained in 1961 represented a shift, 'not what we wanted to
see'. The homelands would now serve an additional purpose to their earlier
economic function of constituting labour reservoirs. They would become
the terrain for the enactment of ethnic self-determination for all Africans,
including people who lived in towns permanently, whom even National

Party politicians and officials during the 1950s were prepared to accept as 'detribalized'. From 1960, the authorities sought to deflect African political aspirations in the cities through the offer of 'the privileges of a free society' on a 'multi-national' basis in separate elected parliamentary governments in each homeland.[74] Beginning with the Transkei, all the homelands would be organized as separate statelets, each assigned with a separate ethnic identity that would more or less correspond with shared language and pre-colonial political configurations. From 1961 the intention was that in stages these territories would achieve progressive degrees of political autonomy before the final attainment of fully independent sovereignty. The Transkei was the first of the homelands to be set upon this road. Here a consultative and partly indirectly elected Territorial Assembly already existed. It would be transformed in 1963 into a legislative assembly with 110 members. Sixty-five of these would be chiefs and only forty-five of the new Transkeien parliamentarians would be elected directly through a popular franchise.

This kind of arrangement would ensure that political authority in the Transkei and in other homelands would remain heavily patrimonial. Local chiefs already had considerable power—their functions included the payment of pensions, land allocation, and the appointment of teachers—but in addition, through serving as electoral officers they could help to ensure that even the more democratic dimensions of parliamentary government would not subvert their authority. Even so, in the first round of elections, in 1963, tensions between Transkei's three paramount chieftaincies opened up political space for a Democratic Party as well as local supporters of the Liberal Party to offer vigorous competition to the pro-independence Transkei National Independence Party headed by Chief Kaiser Matanzima. The Democratic Party won thirty-eight of the forty-five elected seats, though Kaiser Matanzima was able to assemble a parliamentary majority from most of the non-elected chiefs. Matanzima's regime would depend primarily on coercive powers: for its first decade it would govern under the terms of a state of emergency, but the government's strategy to deflect the course of modern African nationalism through the promotion of politicized ethnicity was not inconsequential for it would have long-term effects on black South African political affiliations. The nine homeland administrations would each increasingly accumulate the equipment and resources of full statehood and with these they would receive *de facto* day to day recognition from their citizens as the locally effective authority. In those regions in which homeland leaderships could animate communal nostalgia for pre-colonial social arrangements they could even acquire moral legitimation: this happened in Kwa Zulu through the alignment of homeland leadership with a still widely respected Zulu royal house. Political support for ethnic nationalism was also available because through the 1960s, around the homeland bureaucracies, a group of beneficiaries and clients would accumulate.

In the Transkei, for example, even minor headmen and lower chiefs began to be paid salaries that afforded proper livelihoods so that they would no longer need to migrate to find work. Here, before 1960, aside from chiefs and headmen, only a handful of Africans were employed permanently in public service. After 1963, a new civil service was instituted to administer schools, public health, and the judicial service. It employed 2,446 Transkeien residents that year and 3,673 in 1970. It grew very fast indeed during the 1970s, for by the end of the decade its establishment numbered nearly 20,000. Its members were relatively highly paid as were teachers, whose numbers expanded from 4,844 in 1962 to 13,984 in 1978. One of the first acts of the new administration was to relax the previous strict limitations on the issue of trading licences. There were 361 African traders in 1963. Every year thereafter the authorities would issue around 150 new licences. The new Xhosa Development Corporation would acquire through the decade more than 500 previously white-owned stores and it would also administer the transfer to Transkeien ownership of white farms. Not everybody who benefited from these developments would offer support for homeland nationalism. In the Transkei, teachers provided vigorous backing for the Democratic Party's opposition to Matanzima between 1962 and 1965. Certain chiefs would also oppose the introduction of the new authorities, resisting the bureaucratic incorporation of their offices. Soon, though, public servants, teachers, parliamentarians, and chiefs through the award of licences and farming leases would acquire their own stakes in the Transkei's commercial and agricultural economy and such rewards inevitably would help foster political conformity.[75]

On the basis of all these developments, South African historians represent Sharpeville as a crisis in South Africa's political economy. Their argument is complicated and it has several stages. In contrast to earlier generations of both liberal and more radical critics of South Africa's racial order who generally agreed that the advance of industrial capitalism would weaken ruling group support for racial segregation, a 'revisionist' Marxist school of historiography that emerged in the 1970s maintained that the progress of industrial capitalism in South Africa was unusually dependent upon cheap labour and that methods of 'extra-economic coercion' were needed to keep wages low. Before 1960, the Revisionists maintained, capital accumulation in South Africa had benefited from the retention of pre-capitalist small-holder agriculture in the African reserves as delineated in the 1913 land legislation. Household production helped to support the dependents of African workers on commercial farms, mines, and factories. By the 1960s, though, farming operations in the reserves were increasingly unproductive and for big business the main function of the reserves had become to serve as settlement areas for surplus population. In 'the face of the disintegration of the pre-capitalist economy', though, an increasingly well-organized and sophisticated system of controls, that is, a system of 'extra economic coercion', was needed to keep unemployed workers and migrant workers and their families in the reserves, away from the main population centres where they might combine to challenge public order.[76] It would moreover help to 'differentiate' or 'segment' African labour between more skilled permanent-ly urbanized workers and unskilled migrants, fragmenting their collective capacity to exert leverage.[77] At the same time, while pre-capitalist house-hold production was crumbling, factory production was becoming increas-ingly mechanized and so mass unemployment was becoming more deeply entrenched. From this perspective, the intensification of resistance to the pass laws through the 1950s reflected 'a crisis of reproduction' in the countryside. The Sharpeville massacre was decisive because it was then that the anti-pass campaign was broken and influx control could be fully systematized. Now a second phase of apartheid could begin in which the state would invest huge effort in reversing urbanization.[78] In other words, 'only in the 1960s, with the re-establishment of greater political unity among capital . . . and with the defeat and the repression of the mass political movement, was there rapid and sustained implementation of the policies which constituted the Bantustans as the major site of the surplus population of the reserve army'.[79] Settled in the homelands, masses of unemployed people would constitute less of a threat to social order than if they continued to live in the cities. Hence, Sharpeville was 'a political defeat' that created the conditions for massive economic expansion and 'was thus a crucial turning point in South Africa history'.[80]

With the advantage of hindsight unavailable to the Revisionists it is quite easy to pick holes in this argument. For example even through the 1960s, the period of very rapid manufacturing-led growth, the degree to which the government would succeed in creating the conditions in which all sectors of business would prosper is questionable. By the end of the decade, for manufacturing the limitations imposed by the domestic market for consumer goods and national skill shortages were very evident. In any case, unskilled labour was not necessarily cheap, especially when the costs of maintaining influx controls are taken into consideration.[81] As we will see, the proposition that the Revisionists were attacking, that increasingly the requirements of industrial prosperity would conflict with the maintenance of racial exclusion, would in the long-term turn out to be true. Even among the Revisionists themselves, the contention that the most advanced key business sectors were among apartheid's beneficiaries and that the repression of the 1960s facilitated industrial development was to become increasingly qualified especially after it became evident by the mid-1970s that the South African economy was in serious difficulties. At the time, though, their views became almost an orthodoxy at least in English language South African universities and, more surprisingly perhaps, they had a profoundly radicalizing impact upon the course of popular politics, supplying the intellectual foundations for its increasingly anti-capitalist orientation.

In the 1960s, though, most middle-class white South Africans lived in a socially insulated world in which it was easy to ignore long-term threats to their prosperity and security. Even during the immediate aftermath of the Sharpeville massacre many white South African were too socially distanced from events to feel emotionally affected by them. Myrna Blumberg for example observes that in the days that followed the PAC's rebellion in Cape Town:

> Daily white suburban life seemed to have changed hardly at all. One or two of
> my neighbours had sacked their African servants for taking part in the strike,
> or as one put it, 'It might not have been her fault, staying away, but we've got
> to think of ourselves, haven't we? We simply had to take on someone reliable
> in her absence.

Certainly, several thousand—possibly tens of thousands—of white South Africans were sufficiently alarmed or disaffected enough in other ways to leave South Africa in the year that followed the emergency, but they would rapidly be replaced by immigrants, and in certain cases, as Bill Johnson observed sardonically, 'some emigrants would trickle back, complaining as only South Africans could, that there were no servants in Australia'.[82] In Vereeniging, white politics followed national trends. Its local MP, Blaar Coetzee, a senior figure in the United Party, crossed the floor to join the

Nationalists. Meanwhile National Party councillors would secure control of the municipal administration. Coetzee's eventual successor in his seat would be F. W. de Klerk. He arrived in Vereeniging in 1961. In his autobiography he recalls that when he opened his attorney's practice, 'the trauma had subsided and the economy was booming. It was a good place for a young lawyer to set up his practice.' De Klerk specialized in company law and his firm prospered. Soon 'we could afford to move out of the flat we had been living in . . . We built a lovely home on an acre of ground on the banks of the Vaal River in a beautiful neighbourhood.' These suburbs were well-secluded from the sprawl of black townships, where brown smoke from the steel works would 'lay like a pall' during the cold winter mornings.[83] Even here, though, industrial expansion appeared to bring modest comforts for certain residents. In 1967 on the anniversary of the shootings, the local newspaper published a special supplement on Sharpeville. 'Not a week goes by' without British, American, French, Dutch, Greek, and even Japanese tourists 'making a beeline for the township'. Many of these visitors, apparently, found it hard to believe 'that some of the lovely homes owned by local businessmen, and that would do justice to a Paris or London suburb, are owned by non-Europeans'. Since the massacre, among the many new facilities constructed in the township, the community now had 'its own garage—with uniformed women petrol attendants—for about 2,000 motor vehicles owned by Sharpeville residents'.[84] Other amenities included a swimming pool, 'paid for by the white community through the Round Table', as well as, one official proudly informed a reporter from the *Rand Daily Mail*, 'the best designed Bantu post office I have ever seen'. Crime rates too, the police were happy to 'readily admit', were now well below average.[85]

Was the unruffled tranquillity these reports suggest so generalized among white South Africans? The social environment they inhabit in South African fiction published during the 1960s and early 1970s is more troubled, certainly. For those people that chose to read serious books there were plenty of disconcerting prophetic reminders about the eventual likely fate of their world. In one of her early novels, Nadine Gordimer represented the major contours of white South Africa's social geography as a 'Late Bourgeois World', materially vigorous but spiritually enervated. In *The Conservationist*, her main protagonist, the prominent industrialist Mehring, is a representative of the new elite whose wealth and power are the product of South Africa's economic modernization. Each weekend Mehring travels to his farm. 'Mehring was not a farmer', and his weekend property was a sentimental hobby:

> Many well-off city men buy themselves farms at a certain stage in their careers—the losses are deductible from income tax and this fact coincides with something less tangible it's understood they can now afford to indulge: a hankering to make contact with the land. It seems bred of making money in industry. And it is tacitly regarded as commendable, a sign of having remained fully human and capable of enjoying the simple things of life that poorer men can no longer afford.[86]

Usually his visits were solitary but sometimes he would arrive with friends. 'They said what a marvellous idea, we adore to get away, and—when they debouched from their cars (the children who opened the gate at the third pasture richer by a windfall of cents)—how lovely, how lucky, how sensible to have a place like this to get away to. There would be a sheep roasted on a spit rigged up over the pit and turned by one of the boys from the compound, and bales of hay to sit upon, lugged down on instructions over the phone to Jacobus.' Mehring's main purpose in owning this farm was not sociable, though: he saw himself as a conservationist, a restorer of the landscapeto its pristine pastoral condition. Into this ordered refuge, though, there appears and reappears at various stages in the narrative a dead body, a murder victim, probably one of the residents of the over-crowded black location that bordered Mehring's uninhabited holding. The police had allowed the body to be buried illegally on Mehring's land to save the bother of a proper investigation of whatever casual act of violence ended its life.

In the novel's narrative Mehring experiences a cumulative emotional and moral disintegration, encapsulated in a series of exploitative sexual encounters, episodes in which he derives his main enjoyment from the relish of possession. As in so much of Gordimer's writing, sexual behaviour is an analogy for the expression of wider sorts of power. As in his effort to maintain in his farm a conserved 'natural' space, a place emptied of human sociability, so too in his encounters with women Mehring replaces emotional exchange with increasingly one-sided forms of debased self-fulfilment. Most vividly this is enacted in an episode on a transcontinental flight 'at an hour between the hour of Europe and the hour of Africa', when Mehring is induced into caressing the 'subdued' teenage girl sitting next to him, a late arrival joining the flight in Lisbon, 'someone who never got her

own way, resigned to any objections as she approached the seat'. In the end
Mehring will eventually sell his farm but not before his unwanted visitor
receives a seemly burial from Mehring's workers. At the funeral 'there was
no child of his present but their children were there to live after him'. In
place of Mehring, Gordimer's prophetic final sentence reads, 'at last, he had
come back. He took possession of this earth, theirs, one of them.'

It might be objected, though, that however perceptive, Nadine Gordimer's understanding of the social world she inhabited was hardly typical. By
the early 1960s her work was subject to banning and censorship and in her
friendships and political affiliations she belonged to the small minority of
whites whose opposition to apartheid had drawn them into engagement or
sympathy with the ANC's clandestine activism. But unlike her earlier
novels, *The Conservationist* became a bestseller *inside* South Africa after its
publication in 1974. And Gordimer's depiction of the socially confined
hermetic world inhabited by Mehring in which resourceful power is eroded
by moral decay is also the subject of satirical attack from a very different
political perspective, by the Afrikaans writer, Etienne Leroux.

Leroux's *Seven Days at the Silbersteins* tracks the progress of Henry van
Eeden, the prospective bridegroom of the lovely Salome, selected to become the eventual master and heir of the Welgevonden wine estate, the
domain of the Silbersteins, a wealthy Jewish family. In the novel's narrative
the gauche Henry is drawn into the extravagant world of the Silbersteins
through a series of nightly entertainments, Bacchanalian feasts, while in the
days inbetween he is introduced and initiated into the less frenzied if equally
sybaritic routines of everyday life at Welgevonden. The Anglo–Jewish
Silbersteins are self-professedly bearers of a Cape-based liberal tradition,
and one critical reading of Leroux's text suggests that the novel is a
expression of alarm about the degrading and corrosive effects of privileged
consumption and 'demonic liberalism' upon Afrikaner innocence. This is
an interpretation that infers very direct parallels between the commentary
that appears in *Seven Days* and anti-liberal polemics published during the
1960s by conservative Afrikaner theologians.[87] This seems unfair, though,
for van Eeden as a character in the novel hardly invites any sympathy or
engagement and his supposed innocence is the product of mechanical
deference to higher authority. Meanwhile the Silbersteins themselves,
Cape liberal pretensions notwithstanding, are contented citizens of Verwoerd's new republic. Jock Silbertstein shows Henry around his wine-
making enterprise. 'The building had been designed by a Cape Town

architect whose object had been to retain the spirit of the Cape Style in modern factory design.'

> At the side where the white wine was being bottled there was a row of Coloured girls in white; and on the other side a row of White girls in brown uniforms. It was not quite clear what they were doing. Their hands moved; they touched the bottles, they manipulated instruments and were very busy doing something, the exact nature of which escaped the notice of the uniformed observers. But their hands moved to a specific rhythm—sure and competent—that implied practice.
>
> 'Apartheid', said Jock Silberstein. 'Complete apartheid. In spite of world opinion, it is nearer the spirit of our time than people think. It's an individual contribution to the whole; a protection of the underlying identity in order to attain the common purpose'. He smiled cheerfully at Henry. 'I find it poetic.'[88]

In Welgevonden, though, disruptive challenges to the common purpose are never far away. Even within the boundaries of the estate 'order was fragile'. The previous night, a riot had erupted in the village Jock had constructed for his African workers, the inhabitants persuaded by 'agitators' led by one of Jock's guests to play their role in an all too familiar repertoire to anyone living in the Western Cape in the early 1960s. Arsonists had attacked the Catholic church and various administrative buildings and these were reduced to 'charcoal drawings of frameworks'. That morning while a thin line of workers was winding its way to the factory under police escort:

> A few Saracens were drawn up in V-formation at the entrance to the village. A few soldiers with Bren guns across their knees sat on the armoured vehicles and looked, amused and bored...And then there were the faces of the assembled: the African faces that look alike to whites, the lips and eyes that according to individual experience, looked pleasant or crafty or cruel. The motionless faces that simply stared: that perfectly passive now were waiting for a call to further demonstrative outbursts – or waiting for the order: To work! Or, the next moment, would burst out laughing at someone who tripped over a beam and broke his leg. Or that merely hated.[89]

In contrast to Gordimer's novel, here black characters are represented through stereotypical perceptions, as passive members of 'a herded multitude' or mercurial bearers of chaos, rather than as embodiments of a rationally attractive alternative to existing South African society. In Leroux's dark comedy, the concept of a rationalized social order is under attack and all the characters that inhabit his degenerate Arcadian landscape are absurd grotesques, including those who seek its destruction.[90]

Etienne Leroux belonged to a loose grouping of avant-garde Afrikaner writers who became known as *Die Sestigers*, named after a magazine in which they published their work. Other members of the *Sestiger* group included Breyten Breytenbach, Ingrid Jonker, Andre Brink, and the co-loured poet, Adam Small. The *Sestigers* were united mainly by their self-conscious willingness to challenge orthodox literary conventions within Afrikaans language writing and they were deliberately iconoclastic, especially in confronting religious and sexual taboos. Jonker's poem on a 'Child what was shot dead by soldiers at Nyanga' remains the most powerful literary reference to the events at the heart of this book:

> The child is not dead
> not at Langa nor at Nyanga
> not at Orlando nor at Sharpeville
> nor at the police post in Philippi
> where he lies with a bullet through his brain.

> The child is the dark shadow of the soldiers
> on guard with their rifles, Saracens and batons
> the child is present at all assembles and law giving
> the child peers through the windows of houses and into the hearts of mothers
> this child who only wanted to play in the sun in Nyanga is everywhere
> the child grown into a man treks through all Africa
> the child grown into a giant journeys over the whole world
> Without a pass.[91]

Jonker was atypical even among the *Sestigers* in her feelings of alienation from the community she had grown up within, but more generally, by the middle of the decade, a rift had opened up between Afrikaner writers and the political leadership, very evident in Verwoerd's attack on N. P. van Wyk Louw, author of a play the government had commissioned for the fifth anniversary of the Republic. *Die Pluimsaad Waai Ver* presented a disconcertingly complicated picture of the Boer nation, fractured by political disagreements and differences of morale and, moreover, as contentiously, a national community that embraced its coloured Afrikaans-speaking servants. This was a startlingly revisionist history, very different from the kind of literary tribute that had been expected in which, according to Verwoerd, a national laureate, 'in accordance with the fixed pattern of paying homage to his own people, could push aside what is carnal and ugly and see the spiritual, the beauty and the greatness . . . and sing their praises'.[92]

That as eminent a literary personality as N. P. van Wyk Louw could disappoint political officials on this score is a telling indication of the way in which moral and political uncertainties were beginning to shape white South African high culture, but disaffection within the literary elite probably did not resonate widely among the general public. A potentially more disruptive theological revolt was nipped in the bud at the beginning of the decade when delegates from the Nederduitse Gereformeerde Kerk (NGK) endorsed the declaration adopted at a gathering convened at the Witwatersrand University's Cottesloe residence. The declaration called for the replacement of migrant labour and job reservation and condemned the political exclusion of Africans. The NGK delegates' qualified endorsement of the Cottesloe declaration provoked an angry condemnation from Verwoerd and, subsequently, after a process of energetic lobbying by Broederbond branches, the repudiation of the declaration by each of the NGK's four provincial synods. Meanwhile the errant editor of *Die Kerkbode* was replaced. A few individual churchmen refused to acquiesce to such pressure including Beyers Naude, moderator of the Southern Transvaal synod, but really deep-seated political dissent within Afrikaner churches would take much longer to develop.

Despite the absence of extensive religious tumult among Afrikaners, Verwoerd's own charismatic authority was a telling indicator of white South African deepening dependence on the invocation of metaphysical sources of social reassurance. Certainly, in his day-to-day governing, Verwoerd sought to embody dispassionate rationality. As *Die Burger*'s Piet Cillie noted, 'Dr Verwoerd'sspiritual make up was overwhelmingly intellectual: ordered thoughts, clear doctrines, fixed future patterns . . . Obstacles in human nature must give way to regulation and systemisation. The ideal must be imposed upon society.'[93] After 1960, though, he allowed and even encouraged the development of a sentimental cult around his personality that would assume tragic dimensions of martyrdom after David Pratt's assassination attempt. Orchestrated displays of mass homage—including the 50,000 enraptured admirers the National Party mobilized to welcome Verwoerd home from the 1961 Commonwealth Conference—would alternate with the publication of evidence of the *Volksleier*'s homely simplicity. For even though 'in the harsh world of politics' Verwoerd projected the necessary qualities of heroic fortitude, 'like granite, hard, austere and cold' in 'real life' he was friendly, warm, and kind. He 'loved nothing more than putting on old clothes to do some chores around the farm' and when he and his wife decided to build a beach-side holiday home, 'he designed it himself down to the last built-in cupboard'.[94] To generations of South African schoolchildren, the Verwoerds' servant-free home-life was represented as a domestic idyll, its wholesome practices encapsulated in Mrs Betsie Verwoerd's handbook on embroidery. Meanwhile evidence of divine purpose became increasingly evident in South Africa's lonely political trajectory. As he explained to the assembly that greeted him at Cape Town's DF Malan airport on his return from the Commonwealth Conference, he had attended the meeting 'ready to concede' continuation of Commonwealth membership in deference to the inclinations of English-speaking South Africans, 'but a higher hand had intervened and the Republicans had achieved complete freedom'.[95] In the young Republic, civic rituals were now endowed with sacramental portent. To the 20,000 participants at a special ceremony of thanksgiving for the Republic assembled at the Voorterkker Monument on 15 October 1961, Verwoerd suggested that newly unified English and Afrikaans speaking South Africans were 'like bride and groom entering life in love to create together and live together as life's partners'.[96] 'The God of our fathers' was comfortingly at hand at a birthday dinner on 8 September 1962, 'he is not forsaking us, he is still leading us by the hand, and, in that faith, the Republic will, in years to come, take its place in the world'.[97]

When Verwoerd succumbed to a second assassination attempt, on 6 September 1966, once again he was the victim of an assailant with a history of psychiatric illness, Dimitri Tsafendas. In the findings of the official commission that investigated Verwoerd's death, Tsafendas' story included an alarming catalogue of official ineptitude, bureaucratic bungling that was partly the effect of Verwoerd's own policies. Tsafendas was the illegitimate son of a black Mozambican mother and a Greek father. Despite a history of bad behaviour that had finally persuaded the minister of interior to sign a deportation order in 1964, Tsafendas managed to secure a post as a parliamentary messenger, the occupation that brought him into such fatal proximity to Verwoerd. The commission would learn that his employment in such a trusted position was a consequence of a labour policy that made such a post reserved for unskilled whites. Tsafendas concealed his mixed race parentage and managed to convince his prospective manager in the House of Assembly that he represented 'the best of the loose spineless applicants'.

In a setting in which the manager 'had already lost all my good boys', the official decided to dispense with the normal requirement of a security clearance. A subsequent trial confirmed Tsafendas' schizophrenia: in the words of the court judgement his actions were those of 'a meaningless creature', incapable of calculated premeditation.

Notwithstanding the inevitable references to higher purpose that would accompany the eulogies at Verwoerd's funeral—Betsie Verwoerd herself maintained that 'die here maak nie 'n fout nie' (God doesn't make a mistake)—even the Commission of Inquiry would struggle hard to find sacrificial significance in an almost accidental death. In this vein, Deborah Posel has suggested that in assassinating Verwoerd, Tsafendas 'arguably killed off an element of the hubristic certitude that Verwoerd had inserted into the Apartheid project'.[98] More widely, Posel suggests, the incompetence of the officials who had sanctioned Tsafendas' employment reflected a more general picture of inefficiency as the public service expanded. By 1965, managers were admitting that skills shortages were 'crippling' the administration, partly as a consequence of preferential employment of Afrikaans speakers, appointed because of their perceived loyalty rather than through qualification-based criteria. Amongst English-speakers, public awareness of the civil service's shortcomings was expressed in the popularity of ethnically condescending 'Van der Merwe' jokes that caricatured officials as buffoons.[99]

*

What about black South Africans? A widely shared view is that the killings and subsequent political repression resulted in terror and demobilization with oppositional politics confined to clandestine conspiracies and individualized acts of 'informal resistance'. Understandably, popular historical accounts of black South African politics in the 1960s emphasize the heroic activities of an unusually combative minority. In this exciting story, Nelson Mandela and his generational cohort of ANC leaders are depicted as the main instigators of decisive events. But really the history of black politics during the 1960s is more complicated. For many black South Africans in this decade the state's authority rested upon certain kinds of legitimacy. As was the case in the increasingly autonomous world of homeland politics this was manifest through support for officially constituted 'tradition' as well as trade-offs inherent in patron–client politics. Moreover, the rapid social changes that accompanied industrial growth helped establish new cultural bases and new institutional spaces for new kinds of political assertion.

We will refer in more detail to these developments later. But even in a more simple way the retrospective significance accorded to the ANC's activities in this period is a simplification. In the first few years or so after the Sharpeville massacre the Pan-Africanists remained a formidable rival to its parent organization.

Certainly, outside the Western Cape, before its banning, PAC organization was generally shallow. In Cape Town, however, the PAC enjoyed substantial support and it was here that its efforts to build a clandestine movement were most successful. The PAC's rhetorical militancy, its warlike language, the references in its oratory to conquest, dispossession, and restitution, and its identity as an indigenous African movement were going to make it increasingly attractive to those migrant workers who were still strongly influenced by rural culture. In the last months of 1960, local journalists based in Cape Town began to hear reports of a struggle between two different factions of PAC adherents. On the one hand there was a group dominated by the better-educated and more politically experienced members of the former regional executive, most of them from the older established squatter camps or the family housing in Nyanga. As we have seen, this was the strongest PAC base in March 1960, organized down to several layers of leadership. It was people from this group who had developed the initial contacts with the Liberal Party described in the last chapter. Christopher Mlokoti was one of the best known personalities in this group. These people, partly because of their friendships with white Liberals were now perceived by their opponents as '*Katangans*', a prejorative label that referred to the regional secessionists in the Congo who had been backed by Belgian settlers.[100]

The opposed faction was based in the Langa New Flats among the single male workers and, as might be expected, they were led by Mlami Makwetu. Makwetu's followers used the term *Poqo*—Xhosa for 'pure' or 'alone'—to describe themselves. After Philip Kgosana's departure in November 1960 Makwetu's faction was in the ascendant. This faction was increasingly influenced by the perceptions and values of barracks- or dormitory-based rural migrants, rather then the semi-urbanized men who had prevailed in March 1960. From their headquarters in the Langa Flats, the *Poqo* men began constructing 'cells' of between ten and a hundred men, first in the other migrant hostel communities and then amongst migrant workers living in smaller outlying towns and on farms inthe Boland. The cellular structure tended to overlay existing associations; workers usually lived with people from the same district or locality in the Transkei, and hence the *Poqo* cells drew on the networks, solidarities, and loyalties supplied by 'home-boy' groups and other mutual aid bodies to which migrants belonged.[101]

Makwetu's men had no difficulty in finding new recruits. Their message was stated in simple, direct terms. In December 1961 a leaflet in Xhosa appeared in Langa. It read:

> We are starting again, Africans ... we die once. Africa will be free on January 1st. The white people shall suffer, the black people will rule. Freedom comes after bloodshed. Poqo has started. It needs a real man. The Youth has weapons so you need not be afraid. The PAC says this.[102]

Sometimes the exhortations were more specific. Farm workers were told that *Poqo* intended to take the land away from whites and give it to Africans.[103] Fruit packers in Wellington were told that one day they would throw away their passes and take over the houses of whites. All who did not join *Poqo* would be killed 'along with the white bosses'. Men in Paarl were told there was no need for whites; the factories and the industries would carry on as usual, for was it not the black people who worked in them? Chiefs would be killed, for it was they who were responsible for endorsing out Africans from the Western Cape.[104] As the messages spread, they lost many of the distinctive attributes of the PAC speeches delivered before the pass campaign: there were fewer references to Pan-Africanism, Communism, or Socialism and no careful clarifications of the movement's attitude with regard to the position of racial minorities. Africanist ideology was reduced to a set of catchphrases, those which resonated most strongly with the experience and preoccupations of men who had been forced off the land, whose families were subjected to all sorts of official harassment, whose children lived on the margins of starvation, and who experienced every relationship with authority in terms of conflict, whether at the work place, in the compound, or in the reserve. To these people *Poqo* said: 'We must stand alone in our land'; 'freedom—to stand alone and not be suppressed by whites'; 'AmaAfrica Poqo'; 'Izwe Lethu' ('Our land').[105]

The language used by *Poqo* activists increasingly featured the idea of a general uprising within these communities. Local cells began to act out the opening phases of the insurrectionary narrative that had always been implicit in the PAC's strategic discourse. In June 1962, for example, twenty-one farm workers from Stellenbosch were convicted of plotting to attack a farm manager and his family, to destroy farm equipment, and then to march to town firing at buildings along the way. For weapons, the men sharpened old car springs into pangas.[106] Meanwhile, in the Paarl bachelor hostels at Mbekweni, *Poqo* cells underwent military drill, collected money to buy guns, and attended parades in a nearby plantation. A succession of murders of suspected informers attracted police attention and on the night of 18 November, the hostels were surrounded by police, and inmates were dragged out of their rooms forcibly. Those whom the police believed to be *Poqo* members were herded into a single block. Interrogations began and by the 21st three of the murder culprits had been identified. These men were taken away to the police station in the centre of Paarl. This event set in motion the uprising which the men had been working towards the previous months. In the early morning of 22 November, 250 insurgents carrying axes, pangas, and various homemade weapons marched on Paarl. After being repulsed in an attack on the police station, the men retreated into a suburban street and raided three houses, killing two of the sleeping occupants and wounding four others. In another incident, in December, a band of thirty *Poqo* members boarded a train in Cape Town, with the intention of assembling with other groups near Qamata and launching a coordinated attack on the palace of Chief Matanzima. Matanzima was the paramount chief of Emigrant Tembuland, and his assigned subjects generally blamed him for tougher influx control. He was also held responsible for the fencing of common land and the resettlement measures that were part of the Qamata Irrigation Scheme, a programme directed by white officials in the Native Rehabilitation Trust. As speakers told one *Poqo* group in Langa:

> The first thing Matanzima did was to introduce fencing and now he is moving huts and kraals to some other place. It appears that he has sold the plots where the kraals were to the Europeans because there are huts there. Now he is assaulting us . . . Chief Matanzima has sold our land; we are going to kill him.[107]

The initiative and planning for these conspiracies was probably local: most of the national PAC leadership was still in prison. But by late 1962, to judge from trial evidence, many *Poqo* members were conscious of a plan for a nationally coordinated uprising, the directives for which would come from above. Before mid-1961 those national leaders still at liberty were inclined to mend fences with the ANC: Z. B. Molete and Joe Molefi at first represented the PAC in an ANC-dominated campaign for a national constitutional convention. Similarly, Nana Mahomo who had left the country just before the Sharpeville shootings, helped ANC officials set up an exiled South African United Front (SAUF). The first PAC men who emerged from prison in March 1961 put an end to this conciliatory trend. Under the direction of Matthew Nkoana, a former journalist on the *Golden City Post*, underground PAC activists distributed leaflets on 28 May opposing a three-day strike that ANC leaders had called for. The Pan-Africanists decision to oppose the ANC's stay-away call would be a source of considerable acrimony between the two organizations. Nelson Mandela had actually invited Matthew Nkoana to a meeting to ask for his organization's support. 'When we parted', Nkoana recalled, 'he was in no doubt as to where we stood'. A three-day demonstrative strike would represent a reversion to pre-1960 tactics, Nkoana told Mandela, and in any case the PAC was not interested in a constitutional convention: 'it was philosophically incorrect from our point of view'.[108] Not all the Pan-Africanists agreed with this view. At Fort Hare, PAC members joined their ANC classmates in boycotting lectures for the three days.[109] Matthew Nkoana printed his leaflets with help from Liberal Party members, apparently. He had secured this assistance, he said in an interview in 1975, after meeting Pat Duncan and Jordan Ngubane at the *Drum* magazine offices. Nkoana's recollection may be wrong. Duncan would support the strike in a *Contact* editorial but perhaps he had a change of heart after being approached by Mandela. It is true that Liberals felt sidelined in the supposed coalition of organizations that planned for the strike, the National Action Council, 'a rubber stamp for decisions already taken by the Congress group'.[110]

Outside South Africa, disagreements about the United Front helped engender the first round of the corrosive infighting that would characterize the PAC's history in exile. Philip Kgosana was an early casualty. After leaving South Africa, despite a chilly reception from PAC officials in London and Accra, he had succeeded in obtaining personal audiences with Julius Nyerere, Kwame Nkrumah, and Haile Selaisse. Such favours did not protect him. Kgosana was expelled from the PAC at the beginning of 1962 'for acting outside the structures of the party'.[111] Nana Mahomo may well have perceived in his former protégé's new celebrity status a threat to his own position.[112] Kgosana would spend the rest of the decade in Ethiopia, attending a military academy and then completing a degree in economics at the University of Addis Ababa.

During the following months PAC leaders began to assemble in Maseru. Here they would find a warm ally in the Basuto Congress Party which in

1960 had become a fierce opponent of the ANC. The party's president, Ntsu Mokhehle believed he had discovered a plot against him by BCP members who also belonged to the ANC. Subsequently he would turn down a request from top ANC leaders for help in the months running up to the May strike. In August 1962 the Maseru Pan-Africanists were joined by Potlake Leballo and most of the other men who had been imprisoned alongside Sobukwe. Leballo was allowed to travel to Basutoland by the South African authorities on a one-way exit permit. He brought with him a fresh source of authority. Before his release Robert Sobukwe had given him a letter, naming him as acting president and instructing the rest of the executive to constitute a 'Presidential Council' under Leballo's authority. At this point preparations for a popular insurrection began in earnest.

The Maseru headquarters now represented the hub of quite an extensive network of PAC supporters, though its authority was contested by other geographical centres of exile activity. Leballo's extended family in Maseru helped with hospitality until more long-term accommodation was arranged for the refugees by the Basuto Congress Party.[113] At least fifty-eight clusters of PAC or *Poqo* adherents existed between April 1961 and April 1963. There were twenty-two local PAC groups in the Transvaal and sixteen in the Western Cape, eleven in the Eastern Cape and fourteen in the Transkei as well as smaller numbers in Natal and the Free State. In the Transvaal and the Eastern Cape, subsequent trials suggested that the PAC was a very youthful organization composed largely of teenagers and men in their early twenties, with teachers and clerical workers often assuming leadership functions. The Eastern Cape organization included three fifteen-member cells, each a separate hall of residence at Fort Hare. Here for the previous four years, Pan-Africanists had struggled to 'capture' the campus from the ANC's Youth League, entrenched there through the 1950s.[114] In these two regions, the Transvaal and the Eastern Cape, it was a movement of the urbanized and lower middle class; noticeably in the Transvaal very few industrial or service workers joined the clandestine PAC. The survey evidence from Johannesburg described in Chapter Two suggested that around Johannesburg the PAC had a special appeal for the young and comparatively well-educated; this seemed to be supported by the social background of people accused of *Poqo* activities in this region. In the Western Cape and in the Transkei, though, the movement's social composition was in sharp contrast: in both areas it was a movement of migrant labourers, men who lived, for most of their working lives, in hostels and employers' compounds on the premises of factories or farms, but whose homes and families were in Tembu districts of the Transkei.

These sociological differences were reflected in organizational distinctions. In the Transvaal and the Eastern Cape cities, a fairly elaborate hierarchical structure imposed itself on the movement with regional leaderships, branches, and cells, each with its own officials, all linked with Maseru ina written communication system featuring female couriers and amateurish codes. In the Western Cape and Transkei the structure was less bureaucratic and much less subject to any central authority. In mid-1961 when Matthew Nkoana was trying to exert his own leadership over the movement he visited the Cape and returned to Johannesburg with the 'feeling that the PAC was going to be unable to control our chaps there'.[115] As we have seen, organization was influenced by the pre-existing social networks supplied by 'home-boy' groups, burial associations, and rural resistance movements formed in the wake of the Bantu Authorities Act, independent of national political organization. These included the Dyakobs, the Jacobins, and the Makhuluspan. Such bodies served to transmit information and ideas between the Western Cape and Transkei. It seems likely that in Transkei itself the *Poqo* groups were started by migrant workers from Cape Town, but they could expand to embrace all the men in a single village. The more autonomous character of the movement tended to protect it from police interference. A final distinguishing feature of these migrant rurally-oriented *Poqo* groups was their resort to magical protective measures.

This last point testifies to the main difference between the two kinds of movement. In the case of the relatively urbane Transvaal and Eastern Cape groups, PAC followers deferred to the organizational conceptions and strategic directives of their leaders in Maseru, exercising very little independent initiative. Their main activity was to attend meetings where they were alternately harangued or exhorted to make themselves ready for the great day of the uprising. In the case of migrant worker and rural groups, the movement developed organizationally from the bottom up. It adapted itself to the social institutions it found around it, generating its own ideas. It was inspired to a much greater extent by locally relevant beliefs and preoccupations, particularly those emanating from the countryside.

As Clifford Crais has noted, *Poqo* was a very different kind of movement to the modern political organizations that had predominated in African politics until the 1960s, organizations usually led by well-educated middle-class men, graduates of the missionary institutions that had established themselves in the wake of the nineteenth-century imperial conquest. Arguably, even Robert Sobukwe committed himself to a politics 'that scripted the African as a bourgeois individual with inalienable rights in a political world in which the state was conceived of as neutral arbiter'.[116] The PAC after 1960 and in particular its Western Cape offshoot had travelled a long distance from the liberal democratic foundation of African elite politics. Its perception of South Africa as a colonial society was to lead it to embrace a Manichean struggle in which it opposed the 'forces of darkness', terminology actually used in speeches addressed to the migrant workers in 1960.[117] In this undertaking, violence would cleanse society of foreign sources of corruption, and restore a purer social order in which the 'sons of the soil' would once gain hold power over their own lives. Accordingly, *Poqo* fighters began to undergo rituals while preparing for their attacks, procedures that were unprecedented in the history of organized politics in South Africa, though they were a familiar enough accompaniment to the various rites of passage that youngsters from the countryside experienced in their journeys to manhood. In preparing for combat, *Poqo* fighters had small incisions cut on their heads and upper backs, a precaution normally undertaken for protection against the mythical *impundulu*, the lightning bird, a bearer of witchcraft and sickness. In this setting they believed these wounds would immunize them to the bullets of white men. Returning migrant workers would customarily renew these protections on returning home for their annual leave. As one of the accused in the trial of the men who were convicted for their attempt to kill Paramount Chief Matanzima told the court, 'whenever I leave home I get incisions, when I leave my place of employment going home I get incisions to drive away evil spirits'.[118] These men blamed Chief Matanzima, recently elected as head of the Transkei Territorial Authority, for tougher influx control as well as land rehabilitation and resettlement schemes.

From September 1963 PAC branches began receiving a series of written commands from Maseru. They were advised to divide into cells. Once again, younger members should constitute Task Forces. While branch and cell leaders stepped up recruitment—each cell had to enlist up to 1,000 adherents—the Task Forces were to gather materials and assemble weapons. The weapons they manufactured were crude. Bombs were improvised from petrol-filled bottles and tennis balls filled with bearings, glycerine, permanganate of potash, and match heads. Swords were fashioned from filed-down pieces of metal. Recruitment methods were no more sophisticated and often

echoed the proselytizing approaches that the Orlando Africanists had
employed through the 1950s. A group in Port Elizabeth was told:

> We must organise right through the towns and in the buses. When you sit in a
> bus, the man next to you, you must tell him about this organisation.[119]

Perhaps to compensate for the rudimentary quality of these preparations,
many Task Force members were encouraged to believe that on the great
day, help would arrive from outside: Russia had promised guns, the African
states would supply 'aeroplanes and various war vehicles', and Ben Bella
would send soldiers, they were told. Branches and cells were expected to
submit lists of their members to emissaries from Maseru. Some of the more
prudent local leaders refused:

> I remember that a certain man was sent from Maseru, to us here in the Eastern
> Cape. He was sent to Fort Hare to ask for the list of PAC members. I refused.
> I told him I could not give him the list of the men I'd organised into the
> organisation because I wouldn't like ... I knew that he was being followed
> somehow. I wouldn't like to be arrested while he had that list on him. The
> people I had brought into the organisation would blame me for that. That was
> obviously carelessness. There was no need for him to carry about a list of
> people at College.[120]

Promises of external aid was a recurrent theme in Potlake Leballo's briefings
to branch leaders who were summoned in groups to Maseru in February
and March of 1963. Here they also received their operational orders: on the
chosen day, in each city, chairmen should divide their forces into groups
assigned to attack police stations, important government buildings, telephone exchanges, and so forth. After overcoming these targets, the Task
Forces should turn their attention to the white civilian population, killing
for four hours before halting to await instructions. Moses Dhlamini's
memoir captures the hectoring tone of these briefings.

> Leballo was in a fighting mood as he gave us a speech about the situation inside
> South Africa. 'This is the position,' he kept on concluding after each ha-
> rangue. Time and time again he kept on holding his pistol and lifting it up as
> though he were going to shoot it at the ceiling. He would put it down and
> begin puffing at his pipe which on many occasions he forgot to light. And
> then, suddenly, he began telling the others about how we had swum across the
> Caledon river while the police were chasing us ... After this he reminded us
> that we were at war and we had to fight against the Boer police and soldiers.
> He wanted to know why we had not fought against the policemen who were

chasing us. Why did we instead decide to flee? . . . He told us that when we
arrive in Soweto we should not stay in our houses. It was stupid of us to stay in
our homes when we knew quite well that we were going to lead a revolution.
All those who had been arrested, he said, had been caught napping in their
homes. 'When you are a revolutionary you must not sleep in your home. You
must carry a spade and at night you just go to the veld dig a hole and sleep
there for the night and when the enemy discovers that hole you can go and dig
another hole. In that way you will never be discovered. You can even use that
spade in armed combat when discovered. And why don't you make use of
those many disused mines?' He picked up his pipe and lit it and began puffing
the smoke. 'That is the position,' he repeated, 'that is the position.'[121]

Leballo would not specify a date for the uprising; this would follow in letters
to each branch chairman. These letters were duly written in late March
setting 7 April as the insurrectionary day, and couriers took them across the
frontier for posting in Bloemfontein. The police arrested one of the couriers. Potlako Leballo helped to answer any further questions the police may
have had about the Pan-Africanists' intentions by organizing a press conference on 24 March at which he told his audience that 100,000 insurgents
were awaiting his signal to stage an uprising. Leballo's indiscretion may have
been a consequence of suggestions by Hans Lombard, a white South African
journalist resident in Maseru with whom he had become friendly and
who had joined the PAC: later Lombard was confirmed to be a police
informer.[122] With the help of an address list assembled from the intercepted
correspondence, the South African police started detaining hundreds of
PAC supporters—within a month 3,246 *Poqo* suspects had been arrested.
On 1 April the Basutoland police raided the PAC offices and confiscated
membership lists. Later the police also found a diary kept by Leballo that
indicated that after his officially-sanctioned departure from the Republic
Leballo had revisited South Africa on several occasions to speak to the
PAC's regional leaders.[123] These they later allegedly handed over to their
South African colleagues. Leballo's uprising was over almost before it began.

By the second week of April only three groups of insurgents remained
willing to follow his orders. On 8 April, in King William's Town, 60 *Poqo*
combatants armed with homemade incendiary bombs assaulted the police
station. Meanwhile in East London armed groups began marching on the
city before being intercepted by police. The following night, arsonists from
Orlando attempted to burn down three buildings in Johannesburg city
centre.

While the *Poqo* conspirators were being interrogated, tried, and convicted—1,162 of them were eventually jailed—Leballo sensibly went into
hiding. He re-emerged in September 1963 to help put his stamp on an
ambitious scheme for a protracted guerrilla struggle which would use a
couple of trading posts as training bases and command centres. The trading
posts were owned by Patrick Duncan. Duncan had maintained his friendships with Pan-Africanist leaders in Cape Town, through the emergency
and beyond, so much so that when the *Poqo* networks began planning their
rebellion a spokesman for the Langa group visited Duncan to ask him to
help them buy guns. Duncan refused: at this stage he still felt committed to
Gandhi's non-violent philosophy. In the course of 1961 he would change
his mind. He may have been influenced by his continuing contacts with
PAC personalities but we also know that while visiting the United States
that year he tried to raise money to enable the South West African People's
Organisation (SWAPO) to establish a refugee settlement in Botswana to
serve as a base for clandestine organization in Ovamboland. SWAPO had
yet to fully commit itself to insurgent warfare but less ambiguously Duncan
alsohelped the Angolan leader Holden Roberto obtain maps for his rebellion
after meeting him in Kinshasa. Duncan finally left South Africa in May 1962
after receiving a banning order confining him to Cape Town for five years.
He bought the two stores one month later, subsequently applying for
licences to run them as businesses. His original conception was that the
stores would supply command centres from which political networks could
be extended across the Transkei, a region that through 1962 was a focus for
Liberal Party organization. He left the Liberal Party in February 1963, by
this juncture convinced that absolute adherence to non-violence was mis-
taken. He joined the PAC in Maseru shortly thereafter.[124] Duncan left
Basutoland in April, several days after the police raided the PAC's office,
never to return, leaving the stores under the stewardship of his old political
associate Joe Nkatlo. The remaining Pan-Africanists did use the stores in the
way that Duncan envisaged: in November 1964, the Basutoland police
conducted a search of the two premises finding firearms, ingredients for
explosives, and home-made pangas.[125]

Potlake Leballo's plans included off-loading arms on the coast of Transkei, this time using a second-hand motor torpedo boat purchased in Europe
by Nana Mahomo. While trained PAC soldiers would build support structures amongst the rural population around the borders of Lesotho, support
for the movement would be generated by an urban-focused campaign of

terrorism, which would include assassinations, kidnappings, sabotage of symbolically important buildings, and the seizure of gold bullion, money, arms, and ammunition. Whether the PAC's leaders really took this plan seriously is difficult to judge. Certainly it helped to persuade members of the Organisation of African Unity's African Liberation Committee (ALC) to hand over R100,000 to Potlake Leballo in 1964. The PAC's boat actually set sail but ended up in Madagascar where it was mysteriously sold. There is some evidence of efforts to implement the plan: surviving Cape Town *Poqo* groups were delegated the task of reconnoitring the Hex River railway tunnel with a view to derailing the Blue Train, as well as searching for guerrilla hiding places in Namaqualand and the mountainous area near Paarl. Leballo himself, though, journeyed north from Maseru in August 1964, three months after surviving an assassination attempt in which an unknown assailant detonated explosives in his Land Rover, one of a succession of violent incidents that local police attributed to PAC infighting. In May 1965 those of his colleagues who remained in Maseru were arrested by the Basuto police and thereafter put on trial. The trial failed to secure convictions but it gave full exposure to the PAC's war plans. Most of the presidential councillors subsequently joined Leballo in Dar es Salaam. John Pokela, acting national secretary, remained in Maseru and was later kidnapped by the South Africans and imprisoned on Robben Island after conviction for his role in the Blue Train plot. Meanwhile Patrick Duncan's stores continued to trade, innocently enough it seems, providing Joe Nkhatlo with a livelihood for at least the next decade or so.

Sporadic revivals of the *Poqo* movement occurred in the small towns of the Border region and the Karoo until 1967. Here the conspiracies followed the earlier insurrectionary model; the participants seemed to be functioning independently of each other and with no lines of communication with the exile leadership. They mostly involved farm workers, though leadership was supplied by teachers, ministers, and lay preachers. One example must suffice. In 1966 a lay preacher, R. Ndoylo, appeared at a Bible meeting attended by the workers from one farm and chose a passage from Lamentations as his text: 'Our skin was black like an oven because of the terrible famine.' He went on to explain to the workers 'that it was difficult to get food and water and that our land was being taken away from us. At Vleiland [the farm] we got very little money. We were paid 70 cents a week and that was very little . . .'. He said that according to *Poqo* they should be paid 70 cents a day. Ndoylo later told his followers that after the arrival of weapons

Robert Sobukwe at an outdoor PAC meeting in Alexandra, Johannesburg, late 1959. Sobukwe has his arm outstretched. Josias Madzunya, wearing his heavy woollen over coat – despite the evidently warm weather – stands beside Sobukwe.

Sobukwe leads PAC anti-pass protestors into the Orlando police station precinct, 21 March 1960. Note the badges the protestors are wearing on their lapels and their open palm salutes. A relaxed detachment of African constables are on standby.

(*left*) Sobukwe patiently awaits arrest outside the Orlando charge office, Soweto.

(*below*) All Africans had to carry one of these passbooks or, if not, certificates of exemption. Within the passbooks people needed to have endorsements or permits that detailed their employment status, their entitlement to live in town, and a range of other authorisations. Africans were required to show these documents to police and were arrested and charged if they failed to produce them.

Police inspect the dead and wounded after the shootings at Sharpeville. White officers are wearing the peaked caps whereas African police wear sun helmets.

Zwane street, Sharpeville, after the shootings.

Police load bodies into a Land Rover pick-up, Sharpeville.

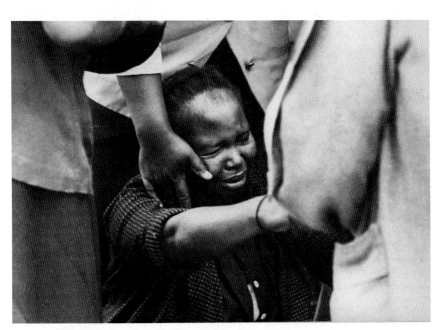

Mourning the victims of the massacre, Sharpeville, 30 March 1960.

Burying the dead, Sharpeville cemetery, 30 March 1960.

PAC supporters hold up their banner by the graveside; meanwhile an aircraft monitors proceedings.

Pat Duncan and Manilal Gandhi lead ANC volunteers into Germiston location, 8 December 1952. Pat Duncan is using crutches after breaking a leg during a road accident.

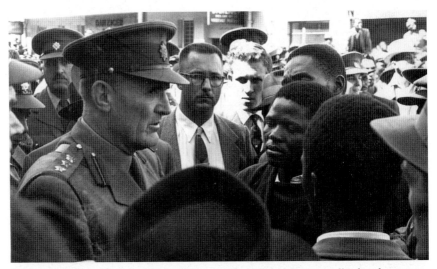

Philip Kgosana and Colonel Terblanche outside Caledon Square police headquarters, 30 March 1960.

Philip Kgosana carried by his supporters after leaving Caledon Square, 25 March

The marchers on De Waal Drive as they near Cape Town's city centre. They keep to the right, leaving plenty of room for traffic.

Philip Kgosana, in his shorts, with companions on their way to Caledon Square. They are accompanied by Detective Head Constable Sauerman.

from the Congo they would participate 'in an uprising which would take place simultaneously all over the country on an appointed day'. Ndoylo would tell the people at Vleiland when the day was to be.[126] Such testimony is a striking indication of the considerable popular sympathy the PAC's apocalyptic project engendered. The migrant workers, the farm labourers, the Tembu peasants, the school children, the location teachers, and the lay preachers who constituted the base of the *Poqo* movement transformed the improbable scenarios conceived by the PAC headquarters into ideas and narratives grounded in everyday experience, local traditions, and folk imaginings. That was the movement's strength as well as its limitation.

Most political movements find exile difficult, but by any comparison, the PAC's history as a refugee organization was an unusually troubled one. The story began quite promisingly with the rapid construction of a network of diplomatic offices in London, Accra, Cairo, Francistown, Dar es Salaam, and Leopoldville in 1962. Much of the initial work was achieved by Nana Mahomo who was joined by Patrick Duncan in June 1963. Ostensibly, the patrician Duncan was an unlikely recruit to the Africanist cause, but as we have seen he had worked closely with PAC people during the Sharpeville crisis, as a Liberal Party member he had been outspokenly committed to majority rule, and, unusually amongst white radicals, he spoke fluent Sesotho, a result of his career as a district officer in Basutoland. His Sesotho fluency really did mark him out even among Pan-Africanists who maintained reservations about the organization's admission of white members. For Abednego Ngcobo who encountered him for the first time in London, Duncan had a 'better attitude' and speaking Sesotho was part of this. Ngcobo was a native Zulu speaker but he enjoyed conversing in Sesotho and relished his meetings with Duncan for this reason.[127] Duncan also had an unrivalled range of friendships and connections within the British and American political establishments. In June 1963 he and Mahomo began a two-month tour of the United States, securing an interview with Bobby Kennedy and a small donation from the American Federation of Labor and Congress of Industrial Organizations (AFL–CIO). Afterwards, while Duncan based himself in Britain, Mahomo travelled to the Congo where he persuaded Holden Roberto's *Frente Nationale de Libertacao de Angola* (FNLA) to share their military training facilities at Kinkuzu. Fourteen PAC recruits arrived in November 1963. They were joined by a second group one month later. Unfortunately camp conditions were poor, the FNLA was already a fairly degenerate organization, and without a busy routine, the PAC men swiftly grew demoralized. Mahomo left them to their own devices; though in theory he was meant to be in charge of the trainees he was back in his London office by December. In subsequent years very few PAC leaders routinely visited their training camps, nor did they undergo military instruction themselves. Most of the Kinkuzu trainees either deserted or were returned to Dar es Salaam in 1964, though a few remained, serving with the FNLA forces from time to time until the late 1970s.

By 1964, however, Mahomo had more pressing matters than the fate of the Kinkuzu trainees to preoccupy him. Robert Sobukwe had invested Potlake Leballo with 'absolute authority' but this was not welcomed by the more competent and independent-minded of his fellow executive members. In Dar es Salaam, a feud broke out over the control of funds. Since 1962 Mahomo and Peter Molotsi had been raising funds on behalf of the PAC; Molotsi had conducted the negotiations with the OAU's African Liberation Committee (ALC) and had banked ALC money in an account for which he was the sole signatory. Mahomo had followed the same procedure with the funding he had extracted from American donors. On his arrival in Dar es Salaam, PAC treasurer, A. B. Ngcobo, found he had no direct control over any funds. Meanwhile rank and file PAC adherents were complaining that they were destitute and subject to frequent bullying by Tanganyikan officials. Peter Molotsi's assistant, Gaur Radebe, was being held by the police, suspected of complicity in an attempted *coup d'etat*. Leballo ordered Patrick Duncan to travel to Dar es Salaam to investigate. Duncan and Ngcobo persuaded the Tanganyikan government to freeze Molotsi's bank account and withdraw his travel documents. Molotsi was suspended from PAC membership. In London, Mahomo was then asked to hand over the funds he administered to Ngcobo; he refused and was also suspended. Patrick Duncan was subsequently entrusted with the task of representing the PAC in Algiers; he was uniquely qualified as the organization's only French speaker. Duncan succeeded in obtaining Algerian training facilities for 100 aspirant PAC guerrillas; the training was of somewhat better quality than the drill offered by the Angolans in Zaire or the Ghanaians, who also started helping the Pan-Africanists in late 1964. Patrick Duncan only held his post in Algiers for a year. In June 1965 he was dismissed by Leballo, for, amongst other reasons, being engaged in 'a one-man crusade against the People's Republic of China'.[128] Duncan denied doing any such thing but privately he conceded that 'his middle class way of life was out of line with the movement's ideas', a

typically self-effacing concession.[129] He died two years later in a London
hospital from aplastic anaemia, still loyal to his PAC comrades, but mourned
much more widely.

Leballo's charges against Duncan were quite unfair, but in truth, by mid-
1965, from the PAC leadership's point of view, the skills, resources, and
social connections which Duncan had placed at the disposal of the organization were superfluous. In August 1964 Potlako Leballo left Maseru to
establish his headquarters in Dar es Salaam. His departure followed a
succession of attacks on his leadership; he was widely blamed for the *Poqo*
arrests of April 1963. Shortly before his departure, PAC rebels had blown up
his house after Leballo had expelled nine of his local critics. After confirming his authority in Dar es Salaam, and deciding upon a new name for South
Africa—Azania—unwittingly borrowed from Evelyn Waugh, Leballo
travelled to China which had recently entertained its first PAC delegation.
Bernard Leeman suggests that Leballo's Chinese experiences were of epoch-
making importance. Leballo, apparently:

> . . . attended the Nanking Military academy and worked as a labourer building
> the Yangtse Bridge . . . Leballo later took part in the Cultural Revolution and
> openly acknowledges his debt to Mao in connection with his own military
> writings, which still remain the most important Azanian work on revolution-
> ary warfare . . . [130]

Overcoming their earlier aversion towards Marxism as a 'foreign ideology',
PAC leaders began employing Maoist strategic language. Guerrilla trainees
were told to prepare for a protracted people's war in which the PAC's lack
of resources and its rural support base would become major assets; a self-
sufficient movement active within a mobilized peasantry would encourage
its followers to 'seize the land'. People within the PAC who opposed this
sort of thinking were 'rightwing deviationists' or 'elitists'; such tendencies
within leadership would be curtailed by periodic bouts of healthy 'rigorous
self-criticism'. A. B. Ngcobo and Peter Raboroko, until then the PAC's
chief ideologue, were among the first to fall victims to this new line when
they were expelled after calling for international action against South Africa
at an anti-apartheid conference held in Brasilia in August 1966. Subsequently, Ngcobo and Raboroko denounced Leballo's leadership at an OAU/ALC
meeting and attempted to install themselves in the PAC's Dar es Salaam
office. After some factional scuffling, the office was shut down on the orders
of the OAU Liberation Committee.

These events helped to prompt a 'Leadership Conference' at Moshi, Tanzania. Here Leballo succeeded in confirming the expulsions and suspensions of Raboroko, Ngcobo, and most of his other opponents on the National Executive—Ngcobo and Raboroko were condemned for conducting a slanderous offensive against Leballo's leadership 'with the two small voices of evil cherubim'.[131] The meeting also resolved that in future the 'people's war' would take priority over diplomacy, and authorized Leballo to set up a 'Revolutionary Command' in Lusaka to supervise infiltration efforts by the newly designated Azanian People's Liberation Army (APLA). By now the PAC was under considerable pressure from the OAU/ALC to commence military operations. About two hundred APLA members had received training in Congo, Algeria, and Ghana. From this group, PAC commanders assembled a team of a dozen APLA soldiers to accompany Comite Revolucionario de Mocambique (COREMO) guerrillas into Mozambique; in return for helping to sabotage the Beira oil pipeline they would be escorted to a safe crossing point on the South African frontier. The PAC/COREMO group survived for two months before encountering a Portuguese patrol at Villa Piri. Most members of the expedition were killed or captured but two survivors returned to their Zambian base, Senkobo. At this point Leballo's National Executive opponents, led by Ngcobo, descended upon the camp hoping to capitalize on the dissatisfaction arising from the failure of the Mozambican expedition. Instead, they were locked up; one of their members, Z. B. Molete, was believed to have stolen OAU money intended for equipping future expeditions.Meanwhile, the Zambian authorities learned that PAC officials were implicated in anti-Kaunda plotting; the Revolutionary Command centre was closed and the APLA troops were returned to Tanzania, to be accommodated by an exasperated Tanzanian government, weaponless, in Zimbabwe African National Union (ZANU) camps. For a year, the OAU withdrew its recognition of the PAC as an officially sanctioned liberation movement. The guerrillas were idle until 1970, when Potlake Leballo managed to win back official approval by appearing as a state witness in the Oscar Kambona trial. Invited to join a conspiracy against Nyerere, he had attended the early discussions and then betrayed the other participants to the police. In 1970 APLA resumed training, under Chinese instruction, at Chunya camp. Both at Chunya and in Dar es Salaam for many exiled Pan-Africanists conditions of daily existence could be very dispiriting. Henry Isaacs supplied this revealing vignette of the PAC's torpid office routine during the 1970s:

> Each morning, the chief representatives and other assistants opened the office at 7.30. Senior PAC officials trooped in later to read the incoming mail, scrutinize invitations to conferences and, if necessary, nominate (normally from their own ranks) delegates to such conferences. Occasionally, they discussed problems or read the *Tanzania Daily News*. In the course of the day, PAC members filed into the office, individually or in some groups. By noon the sparsely furnished office resembled a pass office in South Africa, with inert humans everywhere, waiting. They waited for the PAC's director of finance to approve expenditure for 100 shillings for firewood at a PAC residence in Dar es Salaam; they waited for 30 shillings for dry-cleaning, or for hospital fees. There was never any bustle of activity, or any signs of serious business. At 2.30 p.m. everybody spilled out of the office, dispersed to the PAC residences in various parts of Dar es Salaam where Tanzanian domestic workers had lunch ready. Eating, like most activities was communal. After the meal, almost everyone retired for an afternoon siesta.[132]

In the following years the PAC made several efforts to send APLA units back to South Africa. The Zambians relented between 1971 and 1973 and allowed the PAC to operate from their territory in collaboration with SWAPO and the *Uniao Nacional para a Independencia Total de Angola* (UNITA). In 1973 a PAC member was arrested in Lusaka for assault and once again the Zambians withdrew their hospitality. Denied the possibility of using UNITA and SWAPO facilities, the PAC then turned to its old allies in the Basuto Congress Party with whom it still maintained affectionate relations, a link that Leballo had nurtured sedulously during his stay in Maseru between 1962 and 1964 when once again he became active within the party.[133] In January 1974 the BCP's leaders had led an unsuccessful armed uprising against the government of Leabua Jonathan which had been returned to power through a military coup after losing the 1970 elections. Ntsu Mokhehle, the BCP leader (and, as we know, an old classmate of Robert Sobukwe at Fort Hare), fled to Lusaka and began planning a guerrilla insurgency. Because they were contesting the authority of a continentally recognized African government, the BCP partisans could not appeal for OAU assistance. Lacking money and weapons, they nevertheless enjoyed strong support among refugee Basuto communities in the Transkei and the Qwa Qwa homeland as well as the Libyans. The PAC had just received an offer of training from the Libyan government; to the embarrassment of the Revolutionary Command it could only muster 25 APLA volunteers. Most of the Chunya veterans were unwilling to leave Tanzania—some of them had started up households with local women and begun farming in the vicinity of the camp. Nearly 200 Basuto mine workers, mostly from the Welkom area, made up the first consignment of recruits which the PAC sent off to Libya. Gradually the PAC replaced the BCP members with its own men as, from 1975, APLA ranks started being replenished by the first exiles from the Black Consciousness Movement. The association with the BCP was maintained, though, and PAC combatants seem to have partici-pated in Lesotho Liberation Army units in the 1980s.

Some of the fresh arrivals at Chunya were recruited by a reconstituted PAC network in South Africa, led by Zephaniah Mothopeng, a sixty-six-year-old farmer and teacher and, alongside Sobukwe and Leballo, a leading figure amongst the Africanists in Orlando during the 1950s. Mothopeng began reconstructing an organized base for the PAC from 1974 immediately after the expiry of a banning order he had lived under in Witzieshoek after his release from prison in 1967. He formed a Young Christian Movement in Kagiso township outside Krugersdorp to serve as a front for PAC recruit-ment networks. Other groups assembled under the leadership of released prisoners in East London and Pretoria and were visited by a courier, ex-Robben Islander Isaac Mafatsha despatched by APLA's High Command in 1975.[134] Clarence Makwetu was amongst other ex-prisoners Mafatsha visit-ed. Mafatsha wanted Makwetu to accompany him back to Dar es Salaam. He found Makwetu 'in the fields' on his farm in Cofimvaba. Makwetu refused to go but later it seems Makwetu made contact with Mothopeng and helped foster a revival of Pan-Africanist networks in Cape Town.[135]

Meanwhile, the new Frelimo administration allowed a group of APLA soldiers to travel across Mozambique to Swaziland where they began a programme of military instruction directed at displaced members of the Mgomezulu tribe, a community straddling the South African–Swazi border which was at that time divided by a succession dispute. In May 1976 the South African police captured the three PAC instructors. One year later Mothopeng was apprehended and sent to prison for fifteen years, his third jail sentence since 1960. Despite these setbacks, the PAC was at last able to demonstrate a degree of activity within South Africa: the flow of recruits continued after Mothopeng's arrest and the return home of the first fresh graduates from Chunya was signalled when three PAC insurgents were convicted in 1978 of establishing an arms dump in Krugersdorp. The PAC's readiness to begin guerrilla operations inside South Africa seemed to be confirmed when the Transkei police captured five APLA soldiers who had crossed the border from Lesotho and managed to remain operational for four months. In August a group of three or four insurgents fought a running gun battle with South African and Bophuthatswana police at Witkleigat, near the Botswana border. Police captured one of the insurgents whom they identified as a youth who had fled South Africa after the Soweto riots and who had been despatched across the border to play his role in the PAC's 'Operation Homecoming'.[136]

The ostensible rural emphasis in APLA's programme probably reflected the strategic priorities spelled out by Potlake Leballo at the PAC's consultative conference held in Arusha, Tanzania, in 1978. The 'Azanian revolution', Leballo told his followers, 'can develop from a guerrilla type of war in the countryside, extending its authority and then surrounding and taking over the cities'. It would be 'from the ranks of the peasants in the reserves' Leballo predicted, 'that the guerrilla forces [would] find their most eager support'.[137] Several of the training programmes APLA recruits underwent encouraged this strategic orientation: in 1981, twenty-one cadres returned from South East Asia where under Khmer Rouge instruction they had 'joined Cambodian peasants in the fields, and tended pigs, goats and rabbits'.[138] The content of military indoctrination varied from country to country. In Guinea, Letlapa Mphahlele began six sweltering months of infantry drill in 1981, parading every morning in full battle order with helmets, MP44 rifles, trench-digging spades, gas masks, and water bottles.[139]

After Mozambican independence in 1975, South African borders had become more accessible and recruitment should have become much easier for the PAC. However, at this juncture, the organization fragmented in a murderous leadership conflict. In February 1978 Robert Sobukwe died of cancer in Kimberley. Potlake Leballo swiftly acted to assert his authority as Sobukwe's titular successor. He journeyed to Botswana and Swaziland, requesting the authorities in both countries to detain a number of potentially disloyal PAC members who were reportedly critical of his performance as acting president. Leballo's supporters then summoned a 'consultative conference' at Arusha, Tanzania, where he succeeded in winning the sympathy of most of the delegates, many of them recent exiles from South Africa. At the conference, Leballo was opposed by the APLA commander, Templeton Ntantala, and afterwards Leballo used his new authority as PAC president to expel Ntantala. Ntantala was one of the original leaders of ther PAC in the Western Cape, aligned with Makwetu in the divisions that developed during the 1960 emergency and he later fought with Zimbabwean guerrillas in the opening stages of their operations in 1966 after training at Nanking.[140] He enjoyed the support of older men in Chunya and these deserted the camp after the news of his expulsion reached them to form a short-lived Azanian People's Revolutionary Party. They left behind them the APLA encampment largely populated by the younger post-Soweto uprising recruits who favoured Leballo's bellicose language and martial manner. The prospect of conflict between two rival groups of PAC soldiers alarmed the authorities in Dar es Salaam. The Tanzanian army began patrolling the perimeter of Chunya.

Leballo managed to persuade the Swazi and Botswana governments to imprison a number of potentially disloyal APLA soldiers within their borders, and some of Ntantala's supporters in Botswana were subsequently handed over to the South African police by the authorities in Gaborone. In May 1979 Leballo needed to travel to London for medical treatment; before his departure OAU and Tanzanian officials helped to persuade him to resign from office and hand over authority to a presidential troika made up of David Sibeko, Vus Make, and Elias Ntloedibe, the first two being leading PAC diplomats. In June 1979 three young APLA soldiers, supporters of Leballo, assassinated Sibeko in Dar es Salaam. The culprits were put on trial. Sibeko's colleagues claimed later that the murder was instigated by South African agents but they produced no evidence to sustain this accusation and Vus Make may have been complicit in the killing.[141] Vus Make assumed the role of president. APLA commanders refused to accept his accession and after a skirmish with the Tanzanian army, which left nine APLA soldiers dead and 40 wounded, the remaining 500 Chunya inmates were disarmed and scattered among several settlements under close Tanzanian military supervision.[142] Reports of APLA mutinies continued through 1982 and 1983 and more than a hundred PAC members defected to register as refugees or to join the ANC in Tanzania.[143] The resumption of military operations inside the Republic had to wait until 1986, although a few APLA soldiers did participate in operations of the Lesotho Liberation Army, the BCP's military wing. In May 1985, twenty-three PAC members were expelled from Lesotho after a skirmish in March between an APLA group and Lesotho security forces, in which six of the South Africans were killed.[144]

The responsibility for the PAC's disarray can be attributed partly to poor leadership; here Leballo's personal failings were especially telling. Though he was courageous and dedicated, Sobukwe's chosen substitute was also intolerant, dishonest, foolish, and quarrelsome. The PAC's traditional disregard for organizational matters and its origins as a mutinous and doctrinaire sect within the ANC helped to make it very vulnerable in the demanding circumstances of exile. Under such conditions tight discipline and philosophical pragmatism are crucial ingredients of survival. Its loose structure and its strategic emphasis on charismatic authority invited irresponsible and corrupt behaviour amongst its principal personalities, few of whom had administrative skills or activist experience before they left South Africa. Finally, the lack of dependable and generous patrons compelled the PAC to choose weak and unreliable allies and to entangle itself in the domestic political conflicts of its host territories. By this stage, the Pan-Africanists had lost most of their political following inside South Africa. Leadership replacement would help a modest recovery in their fortunes through the 1980s. We will refer to their subsequent history later in this book. At this juncture, though, we need to consider the parallel transformation of the ANC into an exile-led clandestine insurgency.

★

ANC leaders agreed to commit themselves to using at least limited violence in mid-1961. Nelson Mandela's autobiography suggests the decision to use violent tactics followed the state's forcible suppression of a three-day worker 'stay-at-home'.[145] The ANC intended that this protest should demonstrate popular support for its call for a constitutional convention. Turn-out was impressive but for Mandela and his colleagues it was the government's reaction that mattered. For Mandela,ten thousand arrests under new detention laws and a massive army and police deployment in the main African townships 'raised the question of whether we can continue talking peace and non-violence'.[146]

In fact, discussion of at least the possibility of the ANC and its allies embarking upon an 'armed struggle' began a year earlier. Members of the South African Communist Party (SACP) began considering the adoption of violence in mid-1960. Some of them claimed later that a party conference in December 1960 authorized preparations for guerilla combat.[147] SACP delegates attending an international conference in Moscow in July 1960 extracted a Chinese promise to provide military training. The next month the party's leading theoretician, Michael Harmel, circulated a paper entitled 'What is to be done?' which asked whether the era of non-violent protest was over. In banning the ANC after the Sharpeville massacre, Harmel contended, the state 'had created an entirely new situation, leading inexorably to the use of violence'.[148]

From time to time during the 1950s, ANC-led campaigns had featured a violent undertow: for example, in Natal, ANC rural activists opposed to the government's coercive land conservation programme set fire to sugar cane fields in 1957.[149] By 1961, ANC leaders believed they could harness such rebellious predispositions and that if they did not they might be supplanted by their more aggressive Pan-Africanist rivals. Moreover, as we have seen, the events that occurred in the wake of the Sharpeville massacres encouraged ANC leaders as well as the Pan-Africanists to perceive that the state was unprepared for confrontation and vulnerable in other ways as well. That the shootings were followed by protests in every major town encouraged them to believe there was a generalized predisposition towards rebellion. The exodus of foreign investment that followed the declaration of the emergency also appeared to confirm the precariousness of the existing order: as the *Economist* observed at the time 'Only a madman would buy South African shares.'[150]

Several ANC leaders, including Nelson Mandela and Walter Sisulu, had at least speculated about launching an armed offensive against apartheid for several years, but they encountered considerable opposition to such a course. In mid-1961 at meetings of the ANC's leadership, Mandela had to work hard to overcome objections. Chief Luthuli maintained his moral reservations about using arms and the SACP's secretary general, Moses Kotane, was also sceptical, believing that violence was premature. Eventually and with mixed feelings, the ANC's principals consented to sanction the establishment of a new military organization, *Umkhonto we Sizwe* (Spear of the Nation). It would function separately from the ANC and would be cosponsored by the SACP.

Chief Luthuli's objections deserve attention for they suggest a quite different set of perceptions about the implications of the Sharpeville massacre. Luthuli did not agree that the crisis constituted a turning point that required a strategic switch. Chief Luthuli had presided over the ANC since the Defiance Campaign. His engagement with organized politics before then had been quite brief and his main organizational involvements had been with religious bodies and the ideas derived from these would have an enduring influence on the ways in which he thought politically. Luthuli belonged to the Congregationalist Church of the American Board Mission, a member of the Methodist family. Congregationalism 'defined [Luthuli's] home, school, vocation and spiritual life' to an extent that marked him off even from other mission-educated ANC leaders.[151] His family were Congregationalist converts from the 1840s. From the time he spent as a teacher at Adams College, Luthuli retained as advisors a key group of lay Christian mentors including Senator Edgar Brookes and the American Congregationalist, John Reuling. These were people with whom he remained in contact through his ANC presidency, and who retained influence on his political thinking. Luthuli was elected as chief of Groutville Reserve in 1936, and it was through this experience 'that he acquired the role of public leader'.[152] He remained active in missionary associations and travelled to India, and was elected chair of the Natal Missionary Conference in 1941. He won a seat on the Native Representative Council in 1946, just in time to join the vote forits adjournment in reaction to the suppression of the miners' strike. By this stage he had become a member of the ANC. An address delivered on Gandhi at Howard University in Washington shows the strong imprint on his thinking of *Satyagraha* tenets at this time. Though he expressed private reservations about 'extremist' trends in African politics, Luthuli was elected as president of the Natal ANC in mid-1951 as a consequence of Youth League support. Youth Leaguers viewed him as more democratic and more radical than the incumbent W. G. Champion. His acceptance of high office within the ANC brought about his dismissal from the chieftancy. Luthuli's response to the authorities was grounded in theological authority. 'Through politics', he argued, 'one implements faith', the one was an extension of the other, inseparable.[153]

Though he enjoyed immense respect from his peers, during the 1950s Chief Luthuli was often on the sidelines of key decisions made by the top ANC leaders who were mostly Johannesburg-based. A succession of bans had confined him through much of the decade to his home in Groutville, twenty miles north of Durban. But it was also true that his own conviction that the white minority 'would ultimately surrender to constructive pressure' was increasingly leading him to direct his appeals to white audiences.[154] During the state of emergency, Luthuli became ideologically estranged from the main group of ANC leaders, partly as a consequence of his enforced isolation from them but also because his continuing social associations with white Christian liberals and the behavioural and strategic cues he drew from such relationships: 'While Luthuli prayed and meditated, Mandela and others planned and decided.'[155] Luthuli's conciliatory testimony to the Treason Trial, offered just several days after the Sharpeville massacre, shows just how wide a gulf had developed between his views and those of Walter Sisulu and Nelson Mandela. These two men were beginning to convince themselves that violence against a violent antagonist was the only option.

From Chief Luthuli's point of view, though, international reactions to Sharpeville opened up fresh opportunities for non-violent activism—and for winning 'non-racial' support for the ANC acrosshistoric racial lines. He was encouraged in such a perspective by the kind of personal support he received from white South Africans and influential foreign visitors during the state of emergency, support that effectively insulated him from the ideological radicalization that affected most of his fellow ANC leaders. Again and again over the next year, Chief Luthuli would insist that 'the non-violent method' remained 'the most effective and practical in our situation', and that in South Africa conditions had never been sufficiently tested to disprove its efficacy.[156] By mid-1961, though, such arguments had lost favour among the members of the ANC's top echelon, though they may well have continued to resonate among sections of the ANC's rank and file. Even to certain leaders, the 1961 strike had been a success: Govan Mbeki, a witness to a 75 per cent response to the strike in Port Elizabeth was 'dumbfounded' by the decision to call it off.[157] In Natal, most of the ANC's provincial leadership disapproved of the turn to violence, if we are to believe Bruno Mtolo's admittedly tendentious account.[158]

For the time being, though, *Umkhonto* would engage only in very carefully controlled sabotage operations avoiding any casualties. This restraint may have been partly in deference to Luthuli's reservations, but Mandela writing thirty years later recalls that all were in agreement that non-lethal sabotage 'offered the best hope of reconciliation afterwards'.[159] This may even have extended to South African Communists. Michael Harmel as late as 1959 could argue that in South Africa a non-violent road to revolutionary change remained open[160] and though in his case visiting Moscow may have helped to change his mind, others remained worried that guerilla warfare could degenerate into racial *jacquerie*.[161]

The ANC began sabotage operations on 15 December 1961. More than 200 attacks followed in the next three years. Targets varied—railway signal systems, electrical sub-stations, official buildings—but in general the actions were planned to avoid bloodshed, though on their own initiative local units did kill or try to kill policemen and informers. On 16 December, an important nationalist anniversary for Africans and Afrikaners, *Umkhonto* distributed a leaflet expressing the hope that the sabotage would 'bring the government and its supporters to their senses before it is too late ... before matters reach the desperate stage of civil war'.[162] The police arrested most of *Umkhonto*'s national command in August 1963 though they had apprehended Nelson Mandela one year earlier, shortly after a journey he had made across Africa to Europe to raise foreign support. Several African governments together with China and the Soviet Union agreed to provide training facilities. Preparations for guerrilla warfare began early with the recruitment and despatch of men for military instruction.

In early 1962 members of the High Command drafted a strategy for 'protracted war'. This clearly took its inspiration from Castro's victory in Cuba and from Guevara's *foco* theory in which a limited guerrilla offensive in a remote rural vicinity can manufacture the conditions that are needed for a revolutionary upheaval. In *Umkhonto*'s '*Mayibuye*' scheme, military operations would begin with the landing in rural locations 'by ship and air' of four guerrilla bands, each numbering thirty men. These would combine with locally recruited auxiliaries who would be armed through sea-based deliveries. The plan envisaged 'massive assistance ... from the whole of the African continent and the Socialist World'.[163] Effectively it assumed the willingness of sympathetic Eastern Bloc governments to supply naval support.

Though *Umkhonto* encountered no difficulties in recruiting potential trainees and sending them abroad, other aspects of the plan were woefully impractical. The fully trained guerrillas were meant to find in each of the four areas initially chosen for operations 'at least 7,000 men ready to join the guerrilla army'.[164] In fact, as with the ANC, *Umkhonto* was mainly an urban organization, and ANC organization was non-existent in each of the four localities in the countryside targeted for the first phase of the campaigning. In any case, even governments that in the early 1960s were prepared to arm the ANC were most unlikely to themselves intervene militarily in the region in the manner envisaged in '*Operation Mayibuye*'. Most of the recruits who underwent training in China, Eastern Europe, and Africa were going to remain outside South Africa for a very long time. Meanwhile by 1965 about 800 or so ANC and *Umkhonto* members were serving prison terms alongside Nelson Mandela on Robben Island or in Pretoria Central, probably a majority of the *Umkhonto* membership that remained inside South Africa.[165] Togther with the 2,000 or so Pan-Africanist and *Poqo* followers this represented a removal of a major proportion of the black South African

activist community and their white sympathizers. The effects of this exci-
sion of leadership were amplified by the passage into exile of between 900
and 5,000 people in the four years after Sharpeville.[166] The exiles included
most of the significant office holders in the ANC and the Communist Party
that were not imprisoned, many of the more experienced trade unionists,
and a substantial share of the Liberal Party's membership. Almost an entire
generational echelon of writers, journalists, artists, and musicians accompanied the politicians into exile: Denis Brutus, Bessie Head, Alfred Hutchinson, Keorapetse Kgositsile, Mazisi Kunene, Alex La Guma, Lindiwe
Mabuza, Arthur Maimane, Miriam Makeba, Hugh Masekela, Todd Mat-
shikiza, Bloke Modisane, Louis Moholo, Zakes Mokae, Ezekiel Mphahlele,
Selby Mvusi, Nat Nakasa, Matthew Nkoana, Lewis Nkosi, Cosmo Pieterse,
and Can Themba. Their departure effectively depopulated urbane black
South Africans of their most influential public intellectuals for a decade.

For the next ten years, the political lineages the ANC embodied would
have virtually no organized presence within South Africa. Various efforts
were made by surviving activists to rebuild the ANC. Between 1966 and
1969, Nelson Mandela's wife, Winnie Mandela, led a group of cells that
planned arson attacks on a railway shunting yard, a conspiracy that from its
inception had been watched closely by the police. The external ANC made
several efforts to infiltrate organizers through merchant shipping, some of
them foreign passport holders. In 1967 and 1968, joint *Umkhonto*–Zimbabwe African People's Union operations attempted to infiltrate groups
across the Wankie Game Park in Rhodesia.

A few ANC networks composed of 1950s veterans, and augmented by
released political prisoners, continued to function, recruiting younger people and circulating photocopied leaflets. From 1974 contact resumed between these groups and the ANC's external organization through ANC
officials stationed in Botswana, Swaziland, and Lesotho. By the mid-1970s
there were ex-prisoner-led groups in Cape Town, Port Elizabeth, Johannesburg, and Durban, perhaps totalling 150 activists altogether. In 1975 the
Johannesburg and Durban groups began transporting to Swaziland recruits
for military training in the Soviet Union.

Rudimentary as these arrangements were, they were just about sufficiently developed to enable the ANC to assume an auxiliary role in a massive
rebellion inside South Africa that erupted the following year. For in 1976,
nationwide riots by schoolchildren put South Africa's rulers on the defen-
sive. Important social changes after 1960 helped to create a new political

environment that altered the political opportunity structure for black South Africans. These changes affected urban people most sharply. By 1970 African town-dwellers were increasingly likely to have been urban born: surveys and census statistics indicate that adult Africans who had lived in Johannesburg for thirty years represented 60 per cent of the local population in 1967, twice the proportion five years before. City and rural dwellers were much more likely to be literate than a decade previously—two-thirds of African adult city dwellers could read in 1970. More and more African children were attending high school: in Soweto in 1975, three out of every four households accommodated secondary schoolchildren. Increasing literacy and high school enrolment was becoming normal among working-class people, in contrast to the 1950s when among Africans it was confined to a social elite. Overall, African school enrolment expanded from 1.5 million in 1960 to 3.7 million in 1970. Working-class Africans were increasingly newspaper readers, more than 1.1 million in 1975: that year in Soweto three out of four adult male residents read a daily newspaper, mostly favouring the tabloid *World*, which enjoyed a six-fold increase in readership between 1962 and 1975. With government replacing churches as the chief agency of African education, the geographic location of the African elite shifted, from the Eastern Cape to the Transvaal. As the town-born generation grew and became educated, African membership of mainstream Christian churches expanded rapidly: for the Anglicans, Catholics, and Methodists, African congregations began to outnumber whites and African ministers began to move up the church hierarchies.[167] A leisure industry emerged in the 1960s directed at black working-class consumers, focused on football, foreign-derived rock and local *mbaqnaga* music, and theatre, and helping to 'forge new identities and values distinct from older more particularistic ones'.[168]

These changes ensured that political activity would evoke a much wider popular response than hitherto. Craig Charney cites fieldwork by Philip Mayer conducted in 1971 among urbanized Africans. In his interviews, Mayer discerned evidence of a new pride and a fresh social confidence, his informants telling him that they 'were made of strong stuff', that they were people who were 'surviving under the worst suppression'. One respondent claimed he had 'proved my black power, which is in fact internal'. Another noted that 'I do not feel inferior whatever insults I am confronted with. I am keeping my black pride and don't react with violence.'[169] Such sentiments contrast very sharply with the 'cultural shame' discernable a generation earlier, when middle-class Soweto residents often appeared to believe that 'Europeans' were 'superior to us in all fields' and 'close imitation' of 'the Western style was required 'for us to become truly civilised'.[170] In a context in which people lacked confidence, politics had been dominated through much of the 1960s by the vertical relations of patronage, in which 'big men' supplied protection and benefits in return for support. In such circumstances clientalism could supply a surprisingly substantial popular base for home-land-centred political organizations. By the early 1970s, though, in the wider public domain created by literacy and urbanity, there was room for a different kind of politics in which ideology and camaraderie would to an extent replace deferential personalized loyalties directed at patrimonial leaders.

It is this setting that helps us to understand the expanding influence of the Black Consciousness Movement after its foundation as the South African Students' Organization (SASO) in 1969. Certainly, Black Consciousness (BC) remained organizationally frail with very restricted formal member-ship. A Black People's Convention established in 1972 could muster a modest forty-two branches a couple of years later. SASO's newsletter circulated among 4,000 subscribers. To become a social movement, though, Black Consciousness did not need legions of disciplined activists. Teachers, priests, and journalists spread its messages. These were the graduates from the universities, colleges, and seminaries in which the movement incubated. Seminaries were especially important, and the twenty local chapters of the University Christian Movement with 3,000 members, mainly black by 1968, was probably the most influential agency of Black Consciousness during the early 1970s.[171]

For this new community 'blackness' was a state of being that represented the reversion of oppression. Being black was not narrowly a matter of race, indeed the new movement's founders were self-conscious in their refusal to accept 'any assumptions about the innate characteristics attributed to race'.[172] All the oppressed groups—Africans, Indians, coloured—could become black. Becoming black was a process that involved creating a new identity, an identity that might draw upon older pre-colonial memories—though few Black Consciousness thinkers showed much interest in histo-ry—but that would mainly be the product of challenges to and inversions of the dominant values and norms in an oppressive society: in South African, white norms, values, and standards. To a degree BC writers drew upon *negritude* sources of inspiration—Leopold Senghor and Aime Cesaire, particularly. Julius Nyerere's *Ujamaa* principles supplied another source of textual authority especially in the BC efforts to establish producer cooperatives. But it was the American Black Power movement that impressed most deeply, particularly in its emphasis on the need for a separatist black politics, isolated from the enervating influences of white liberals, if blacks would one day achieve their own liberation and build a society without races. For Steve Biko and other principals in the movement, mass activism would be the outcome of a systematic process of cultural transformation, a shift in consciousness. This could be promoted by organizations that attempted to alter the beliefs that structured ordinary day-to-day life through cultural activity, welfare, and educational projects.[173] South African Black Consciousness writers borrowed most freely from their American contemporaries. Stokely Carmichael's dictum that 'before a group can enter the open society it must first close ranks' was almost replicated in the SASO manifesto: before the 'black people should join the open society, they should close ranks'.[174]

By 1972 Black Consciousness organization began to embrace school children. The first branches of an African Students' Movement grew out of youth clubs at three schools in Orlando and Diepkloof in 1968. As with SASO, the University Christian Movement was a key agency in the establishment of the new organization.[175] In 1972, a name change to the South African Students' Movement (SASM) signalled its embrace of Black Consciousness. Acknowledged as part of the BC family by the annual *Black Review*, SASM branches now began to proliferate beyond Soweto as it drew upon the resources and networks of allied formations. SASM's programmes regularly featured speakers from the wider movement and as with the older organizations its activities emphasized leadership training, the fostering of a politically advanced intelligentsia. In contrast to SASO and Black Community Programmes, though, from 1974 certain SASM groups also began organizing in a conspiratorial cellular fashion, prompted to do so by ANC 'elders', former activists from the 1950s and ex-Robben Island prisoners.[176] In 1976 a trial in King William's Town brought together SASM members with an ex-prisoner, accused of inciting each other to undergo military training.[177] By then SASM was well-established across the schools of the Eastern Cape; it also enjoyed a following in the smaller towns of the Free State and the Transvaal as well as in the main centres.[178] As Black Consciousness ideas percolated downwards they lost much of their subtlety. The movement's leaders were careful to avoided racist phraseology; their teenage followers were less fastidious; as one of them remembered later: 'in

1976, Soweto students . . . used emotional images, describing the clenched fist salute as crushing the white in our palms. They said white coffee is weaker than black.'[179] Encouraging the self-confidence reflected in such statements were external events that suggested a new vulnerability in authority. The black press reported extensively South African military reversals in Angola after its failure to prevent the entrenchment of a Soviet-backed *Movimento Popular de Libertacao de Angola* (MPLA) in Luanda, asking its readers 'Would you fight for South Africa if we were invaded from Angola?' In Soweto, the anthropologist Philip Mayer encountered among his informants during fieldwork conducted in 1975 a generalized 'belief that things were moving in their favour and giving them fresh bargaining power'. 'If Frelimo can achieve Freedom in Mozambique', Mayer was told, 'then ours is not far behind'.[180]

When the ideas of the Black Consciousness Movement percolated down to secondary schools, they found ready adherents. The enforcement of a regulation that half the curriculum should be taught in Afrikaans provoked the Soweto Students' Representative Council (SSRC) into launching demonstrations on 16 June 1976. The police fired into a crowd of 15,000 children, killing two. In the following days, the revolt spread to fifty towns. In a year of street battles, strikes, and classroom boycotts, at least 575 protesters died. Several thousands more left South Africa, many of them to join the ANC, not through any particular ideological preference but simply because the ANC was better organized to receive them than the Pan-Africanists. Though before the revolt the ANC had begun to recruit amongst the students who were to constitute the leadership it did not exercise any real influence over the direction of the revolt. However, *Umkhonto* units fresh from their Soviet training began operations in Soweto during the rebellion.

The government's response mixed reform with repression. In 1979, legislation conceded rights to black trade unions. Other measures attempted to solicit support from urban Africans. By the 1980s, though, urbanized Africans were more likely to acknowledge the authority of the ANC exiles. In Africa the ANC had constructed a formidable bureaucracy including an army. Presided over by Oliver Tambo and based in its headquarters in Lusaka, the organization was still led by the generation who had predominated in the 1950s. The Communist Party was still decisive in shaping the ANC's strategic ideas. Communists perceived themselves to be engaged in a struggle for 'national democracy', itself a transitional phase in the advance to a fully Socialist society. They understood 'national liberation' as a profound systemic alteration of a kind that could only follow their seizure of power. How to achieve this objective became clearer in the late 1970s. Events in Soweto suggested fresh prospects for the kinds of legal activities that had seemed impossible in the 1960s. A visit to Vietnam underlined the importance of building an organizational base through a non-violent political struggle in which the general population could participate. In turn, this political movement would later provide a platform for a 'people's war'. So, for the time being, the ANC should foster a broad front from existing legal organizations to promote the widest kinds of political struggle.

Meanwhile *Umkhonto* 'armed propaganda' would make the ANC visible. From 1976 the guerrillas became increasingly conspicuous. Operations were directed at targets chosen for their psychological impact on the general population. On the whole, the campaign was concentrated in the Johannesburg–Pretoria area and in Durban. A successful rocket attack on the Sasolburg synthetic fuel refinery in June 1980 represented *Umkhonto* operations at their most elaborate and dramatic. Despite such spectacles the warfare was essentially symbolic. Up to 1985, *Umkhonto* mounted fewer than a hundred attacks a year. Command structures remained external and there were never more than 500 *Umkhonto* soldiers deployed inside South Africa. The insurgents' conduct reflected the nature of their training. In particular, cadres were warned of the dangers of 'militarism', the isolation of military from political activity. ANC leaders opposed indiscriminate terrorism and up to 1984 the basic intention of *Umkhonto*'s activity was not to represent a serious military challenge but rather to enhance the ANC's popular status and win for it inside South Africa a loose mass following. By the end of 1983, such a following was beginning to assume organizational coherence with the formation of a United Democratic Front (UDF), an ostensibly new organization that included many ANC veterans in its topechelons. The UDF's formation would prompt the final and decisive anti-apartheid rebellion, an insurrectionary movement that would begin in September 1985, in the townships of the Vaal, around Vereeniging, in Sebokeng, Zandela, Boipetong, and Sharpeville.

We will return to the Vaal rebellion and the events that accompanied it in the closing chapter of this book. From the developments addressed in this chapter so far the dynamics and trends are clear enough. They can help us identify the consequences inside South Africa of the Sharpeville massacre. But before we can complete any assessment of whether the crisis can really be considered a turning point historically, we need to consider the effect of the confrontation upon South Africa's external relations.

★

As we have seen, the shootings did not lead to any serious break in diplomatic ties between South Africa and her most important Commonwealth allies. Indeed, South African politicians were able to persuade themselves that their enforced departure from the Commonwealth would help to strengthen relations with Britain. And it is true that Britain's Conservative administration maintained a protective posture towards South Africa. On 30 March 1960, the United Nations Security Council assembled for a special session to discuss the Sharpeville massacre. Bernadus Fourie, South Africa's United Nations representative would address its members. He offered an unapologetic defence of police conduct, claiming that officers 'were attacked with a variety of weapons: pangas, axes, iron-bars, knives, sticks and firearms'. Indeed, he insisted, 'shots were fired at the police before the police returned fire in order to defend their own lives and also to forestall what might have been greater and more tragic blood-shed'.[181] The British delegate at the Security Council warned other members that he would have to veto any proposition for sanctions. In the end the Security Council agreed upon a weak expression of concern about the violence, a resolution that the American representative could support but on whichboth the British and French abstained from voting. Even so, the fact that the Security Council focused on South Africa in this way did signify an advance in the United Nations' opposition to apartheid. Two years later, though, Britain would follow the American lead and assent to a Security Council call for a non-mandatory arms embargo. Britain would stop selling any arms to South Africa that might be used against domestic political opponents, though British firms would still be allowed to export to South Africa the more ambitious sorts of equipment needed for external defence. For instance, Britain agreed in early 1964 to the supply of sixteen Buccaneer strike aircraft, a contract that the new Labour Party administration agreed reluctantly to honour in early 1965. Thereafter, though, for the remainder of the decade, British arms manufacturers were compelled to stop any contact with the South Africans, leaving the field clear for their French competitors. In 1971, the policy was rescinded. Edward Heath's Conservative government ended the embargo, announcing its decision to sell South Africa a fleet of helicopters at the 1971 Commonwealth Conference, referring to potential Soviet threats to the Cape sea route as well as its legal obligations under the terms of the Simonstown naval agreement. In other commercial areas, the Labour government of the 1960s followed its predecessor, refusing, for example to end South Africa's Commonwealth preferential trade tariffs. Harold Wilson would assure John Vorster in 1967 that 'Britain would not seek an economic showdown.'[182] At this stage the British government was being advised by its diplomatic representatives in South Africa that it should work to retain leverage with the South African administration; if it supported sanctions or helped such organizations as Defence and Aid it would lose any influence it had.[183]

For the South Africans, aside from Britain, their most important diplomatic exchanges during the 1960s were with the Americans. As with the British, initial American diplomatic reactions to the crisis would be cautious. After Sharpeville, an 'unusually strong statement' from Joseph Satterthwaite, President Eisenhower's assistant secretary of state for Africa, may have persuaded Verwoerd to act against his original predisposition and appoint Commissions of Inquiry into the Sharpeville and Langa shootings, but the statement remained unpublished.[184] At the beginning of 1961, the incoming Kennedy administration was keen to signal to key groups of black American voters its commitment to African causes. The new assistant secretary of state, George 'Soapy' Mennan Williams, a former governor with a strong track record for supporting civil rights appointed as his deputy Wayne Fredericks. Fredericks had worked for Kelloggs and had opened and managed one of its factories in South Africa. In South Africa Fredericks had formed friendships with a range of liberal and anti-apartheid personalities. Within Kennedy's administration, Fredericks became an early advocate of sanctions calling for an arms boycott at the beginning of 1963, anticipating the United Nations Resolution later that year to which the Americans would commit symbolic support. Fredericks' and Williams' appointments would continue after Kennedy's assassination. Williams would resign finally in 1966 after addressing the House Committee on Africa to argue the case for halting American investment in South Africa, an issue on which official policy remained studiously non-committal.

Ultimately, the Kennedy administration's engagement with Africa was tempered by strategic considerations. Even so, when Martin Luther King visited the White House on 17 December 1962 the president was ready to spend three hours with the civil rights leader listening to King's advocacy of sanctions against South Africa. On 15 August 1963, Robert Kennedy received Patrick Duncan in his attorney-general's office. This meeting prompted an expression of 'amazement and dismay' from the South African foreign minister, Eric Louw. After hearing Duncan's proposal for launching action against South Africa from bases in Basutoland Robert Kennedy asked Duncan to submit a memorandum outlining his plans in more detail.[185] The Kennedy brothers' courteous reception of Luther King's and Duncan's representations were in fact to represent high watermarks of the Kennedy administration's commitment to the cause of anti-apartheid. During the final year of Eisenhower's administration, the South Africans had agreed to the establishment of an American missile tracking station outside Pretoria. The construction of this installation went ahead under the Kennedy presidency and indeed in June 1962 a fresh set of negotiations committed the Americans to new arms sales inreturn for South African cooperation, acquiescing even to a South African stipulation that no black American aircraftmen should be stationed at the base.

Kennedy's successor, Lyndon Johnson, would in fact take an ostensibly tougher line on arms sales, supporting the United Nations calls and cancelling an agreement to supply submarines as well as stopping the export to South Africa of heavy metalworking equipment. In 1965 American warships ceased using the Simonstown docks after Verwoerd had responded to a formal request for the refuelling of an aircraft carrier by demanding that black sailors obey apartheid laws while on shore-leave. More generally, though, the Johnson administration would find itself in alignment with South Africa on key African issues, in 1965 supplying the Portuguese with twenty B52 bombers for use against insurgents in Angola. When Bobby Kennedy visited South Africa in 1966 at the invitation of the National Union of South African Students (NUSAS) despite concerns that the former attorney-general would 'try to get ahead of you on the question of political liberty for negro Africans',[186] Lyndon Johnson's speechwriters confined themselves in what was billed as a major public address in Africa to a bland statement of support for African self-government which avoided any direct reference to South Africa or Portugal. From 1969, under a new Republican administration a major review of American foreign policy ordered by Henry Kissinger resulted in yet further downgrading of black South African rights in favour of realist imperatives of national interest. Most of the bans on military equipment exports were relaxed and even rhetorical condemnations of apartheid softened. Nixon's electoral dependence on US southern conservatives helped to accentuate and confirm the shift.

It is true that from 1960 onwards, even foreign powers that could still be considered South African allies now needed to be more apologetic than had been the case before in conducting their official relations with Pretoria. On the most important economic and strategic issues for Britain and the United States, South Africa remained a key African partner, awkward certainly and sometimes a source of political embarrassment but indispensable. South African consciousness of this indispensability wasvery evident. Verwoerd's inhospitable attitude to visiting American sailors was one example of this confidence as was his appointment of Carel de Wet as his ambassador in London. De Wet was the former parliamentarian who had complained that the police had killed insufficient numbers at Sharpeville.

More globally, it is true, South Africa's diplomatic status deteriorated during the 1960s.[187] A succession of set-backs at the United Nations began with the special session of the Security Council on 30–31 March 1960, summoned in reaction to the massacre. In 1962 the UN's General Assembly set up a Special Committee on Apartheid. One year later, as we have noted, the United Nations would adopt its first call for non-mandatory sanctions against South Africa. In fact, though, from its inception, the United Nations had supplied a sympathetic forum for condemnation of South African race policies. Both the Communist Party and the ANC sent delegations to the United States to help the Indian delegation prepare a resolution attacking South Africa at the first meeting of the General Assembly at Lake Success in 1947. Through the 1950s South Africa began to be excluded from the UN's specialized agencies and in 1955 South Africa temporarily recalled its mission from New York. More serious for South Africa in its immediate effects was the contraction of its formal connections with other African countries. In 1961 diplomatic exchanges with Egypt ended and the South Africans closed their consular office in Nairobi just before Kenyan independence. The Ghanaians became the first African country to prohibit South African ships and aircraft from using harbours and ports, a ban that would become general through independent Africa after the formation by the OAU of an African Liberation Committee (ALC). The Ghanaians also ended trade with South Africa. After the ALC's decision to outlaw South African overflights, the South Africans were compelled to invest R3.8 million on constructing an airport at the Isla do Sol so that their aircraft could refuel in their journeys to Europe. South Africa's African isolation was partly self-inflicted, however. Verwoerd's administration itself went out of its way to court

Pan-African hostility and itself took the initiative in curtailing its African diplomatic contact.

There was another more decisive way in which the Sharpeville emergency affected South Africa's international relations, though. That Martin Luther King was ready in 1962 to use a rare appointment at the White House for a discussion with his president of the merits of using sanctions against South Africa is a telling indication of the way in which anti-apartheid lobbying had acquired a significant social constituency in the United States. In the United States and elsewhere, organized labour helped to constitute this constituency, and even before 21 March, a movement to isolate South Africa economically had begun but the events at Sharpeville were decisive in enabling this movement to acquire velocity. Robert Massie has compiled a list of boycott initiatives in 1960 across the world. It includes:

> Liverpool, England. Municipal Council votes to support Union goods to protest apartheid (7 January 1960); London rally to back one month economic boycott of South Africa (28 January 1960); Swedish labour leaders black plans for international boycott of South African goods to protest apartheid (2 February 1960); AFL-CIO executive council urges boycott of South African exports to US (14 February 1960); West German Trade Union Federation backs boycott of South Africa (12 March 1960); ICFTU sets 2 month boycott of South Africa (6 April 1960); ILWU urges boycott on all trade with South Africa (11 April 1960); US economic boycott of South Africa urged on Africa Freedom Day, 14 April 1960; Survey shows boycotts of Union cost \$1 million loss to US exporters in last 2 months (30 June 1960); Ghana sets total boycott of South African goods, 30 July 1960; Kenya leader Tom Mboya urges all African states to join boycott (4 August 1960).[188]

One explanation for the extent of such protests is the way in which 'Sharpeville' became a global 'media event', indeed, to use Hakan Thorn's phrase, the 'dominant way of framing apartheid in the international media'.[189] For the first time, news from South Africa received headline coverage on the front pages of newspapers and television networks in Europe and North America. Television was especially important in prompting new kinds of trans-national engagement with remote political events: the British ITN film crews who travelled to Sharpeville and Langa helped to promote this kind of engagement. In the United States, reportage on television merged with impassioned editorializing, NBC commentaries provoked the irascible South African foreign minister Eric Louw to request Caltex, NBC's main advertising sponsor, to exercise its influence to persuade the presenter Chet Huntley to tone down his remarks about South Africa.[190] Media treatment of the massacre and subsequent events reflected their accessibility to international audiences. *Drum*'s photographer certainly made a critical contribution in amplifying Sharpeville's impact, his pictures playing a critical function in transforming opposition to apartheid into an international public cause.

This transformation of anti-apartheid into a global concern would not have happened so easily, though, if the organizational and institutional underpinning for such an offensive was not already partially assembled. In the next chapter we will be addressing the ways in which a global social movement against apartheid constituted itself. At this stage the American experience will suffice to illustrate the point. Through the 1950s, decolonization stimulated fresh public interest in the United States in Africa, especially, though not exclusively among African-Americans. In 1958 an American Negro leadership Conference on Africa brought together the principal figures in six important black organizations, including the trade unions in which African-Americans predominated. From 1955 the American Committee on Africa (ACOA), founded by George Houser, a Methodist minister and former Freedom Rider supplied a focal point for anti-apartheid solidarity. After his return from managing Kelloggs in South Africa, Wayne Fredericks worked for the Ford Foundation, establishing its Africa Program. Amongst elected politicians, John Kennedy was unusual in his interest in African affairs, itself prompted by his more general sympathy for anti-colonial politics that he developed while visiting Vietnam in 1952. In 1958 the Senate's Foreign Relations Committee formed a new sub-committee on Africa and Kennedy became its first chairman. When Kennedy appointed his key foreign policy advisor in January 1960, he chose Chester Bowles, author of *Africa's Challenge to America*. Hence, by March 1960, a network of individuals and associational activities in the United States were already available to supply direction and cohesion to the wider social movement to oppose apartheid that began to mobilize after the reports from Sharpeville.

★

To recapitulate: was the Sharpeville emergency really a crisis? Did the massacre and the events that followed it truly constitute a watershed, a moment when, in the words of Paul Sauer, 'the old book of South African history' finally closed? Was Sharpeville followed by profound political changes that it helped to cause?

At the time many people believed this to be so. The disorder that followed the shootings impacted powerfully on white political morale. This was evident in the calls for major reforms, urgings that emanated even from within Verwoerd's cabinet. Faltering faith in regime stability persuaded significant numbers of whites to leave their homeland and, for a while, such concerns discouraged other people from arriving to settle in South Africa. This was the first time South Africa had experienced net migration flows since the Second World War. There were conspicuous economic reactions as well: imploding share prices and a massive capital flight.

These were short-term consequences of political panic. They had themselves certain long-term effects. For example, falling share prices enabled Afrikaner financial firms to acquire very cheaply a significant stake in local industry. Eventually, through the 1960s, this social development helped to bring business closer to government. But Verwoerd was swift to reassert his authority over his cabinet and more broadly to impose his will within key institutions such as the NGK. The government's readiness to use overwhelming force to contain black protest encouraged a rapid reconstruction of confidence in regime efficacy among white South Africans. In 1961 the ruling party obtained an unprecedented electoral majority. Within a few years, large-scale white immigration into South Africa would resume, at a higher rate than ever before. Political repression and the state's own industrial policies were both important considerations in inducing a tide of foreign investment into manufacturing. Ten years later, to many observers Sharpeville would be remembered as a significant challenge to the state's authority certainly, but a challenge from which the government had emerged more robust than ever. During the 1960s only a minority of white citizens would be troubled by the moral disaffection that was beginning to be so evident among a new generation of writers, working both in Afrikaans and English.

To an extent, even radical critics of minority rule shared the more general perceptions about South African power and prosperity. At the beginning of the 1970s a new 'revisionist' school of Marxist political economy constituted itself among South African exiles at British universities. Its members would argue that the South African state's containment of black political resistance at Sharpeville was decisive. It would represent the fulfilment of a necessary condition for the further development of an industrialized society based upon a system of 'extra-economic coercion'. In this view, the systemization of influx control, the enforced limitation of black urbanization, the expansion of police powers, and the build-up of military capacity were all dictated by the major imperatives of the kind of capital accumulation that was fuelled by foreign investment. This was an argument that discounted objections to certain features of apartheid from local industrialists confronted with skill shortages and from commercial enterprises that sought an expansion of black consumption. Later, the revisionists' central contention that confining black unemployment to relatively remote rural 'homelands' was an indispensable condition for industrial progress would appear increasingly questionable. Apartheid's modernization in the 1960s would introduce or strengthen major economic inefficiencies.

Even so, there is a strong case for maintaining that the repression engendered by the Sharpeville protest did change South African politics fundamentally, and that it facilitated a particular kind of industrialization and in doing this widened existing social inequalities very sharply. Moreover, if the shootings had not happened, if there had been no crowds to confront the policemen at Sharpeville and Langa, and if there had been no state of emergency, the government may well have lacked the political support amongst white voters and elites that it needed to promote import-substitution, extend police powers, and limit black urbanization. It probably would not have been so ready to concede statehood to the nascent homeland administrations. In this undertaking South Africa's rulers created institutional settings and social support for a conservative patrimonial politics that would have very long-lasting effects.

For black South African leaders, the massacre and the nationwide tumult it engendered as well as the subsequent suppression of their organizations made violent strategies directed at regime overthrow seem very compelling. It was true that before Sharpeville both within Pan-Africanists' and among the ANC's top echelons there were influential people who already believed that a violent confrontation with the authorities was inevitable and that they should prepare for it. But if the PAC's protests had not mobilized such a massive response and if Robert Sobukwe's protest had been confined to the small numbers who had accompanied him to Orlando police station, then advocacy of guerrilla warfare might have remained a minority view. Sobukwe himself was ambivalent about the necessity for an armed insurgency and within the ANC in 1960 Chief Luthuli's principled objections to violence were still widely shared.

But even in the setting that actually prevailed after Sharpeville, there remained plausible political alternatives to sabotage and guerrilla warfare. As

ANC leaders later admitted, in opting for conspiracy and sabotage, the ANC neglected other essential activities. Mandela himself was to make this point. He wrote in prison in the mid-1970s that in establishing *Umkhonto* 'we ... drained the political organizations of their enthusiastic and experienced men, [and] concentrated our attention on the new organization'. In this reasoning, the ANC had allowed itself to abandon the work of political organization, substituting it with sabotage operations in which most of its followers were reduced to the role of spectators.[191] Academic critics of the decision to adopt violent strategies take the argument further to contend that many rank and file political activists were unready for armed confrontation and that the repression it would invite would discourage any other political assertion. One of Mandela's friends and contemporaries, the social psychologist Fatima Meer, a few years after Mandela's arrest suggested that generally black South Africans were politically immobilized. This, she explained, was a consequence of the structural characteristics of the South African social system: the measure of economic security it offered, the government's willingness to employ police repression against its opponents, and the migratory labour system. For many African men, the experience of an oscillatory labour system created contending focuses of loyalty between town and countryside and deflected their aggression inwards so that it became 'irrationally dissipated in the neighbourhood and family'.[192] In a similar vein, Edward Feit has argued that to succeed in its first campaign, *Umkhonto* would have needed to disrupt order on a much wider scale, 'beyond a level the government could control'.[193] On the whole, Feit suggests, for many black South Africans even the authoritarian order maintained by the government represented a form of security.

More sympathetic analysts of black politics at this time suggest that there remained opportunities for industrial organization, and that in particular the ANC's insurgency deployed, and in so doing removed from the factories a whole layer of experienced trade union leadership.[194] Recent research on shop-floor organization in the years immediately preceding and following Sharpeville supports this argument. In the period before Sharpeville, trade unionists, despite the restrictions of the 1953 Native Labour (Settlement of Disputes) Act, enjoyed increasing success in extracting concessions through strikes and subsequent negotiations with employers. In the aftermath of Sharpeville, Ben Schoeman's Department of Labour, in a deliberate effort to institute a safety valve for the expression of worker grievances, encouraged the wider formation of elected workers' committees that the 1953 legislation had sanctioned in the hope of providing a more easily controlled alternativeto trade unions.[195] In at least one case, local SACTU trade unionists succeeded in infiltrating one of these committees[196] and it is possible that after Sharpeville the committees may have offered sheltered accommodation for militant trade unionists elsewhere. At least two of Nyakane Tsolo's fellow members of the union he helped to set up at the African Cables factory in Vereeniging later joined the officially sanctioned works' committee at the plant.[197] For many activists, though, commitments to insurrectionary violence closed off other strategic options, at least for a decade. Even later when organized black opposition resurfaced, as we shall see, the 'armed propaganda' supplied by guerillas continued to shape popular political expectations, especially among young people. In the 1960s, insurgent militarism helped to demobilize black South Africans politically and it removed from any attempts at active engagement with the mass of urban South Africans an entire generation of black leadership.

More positively, one effect of the dispersal of black political leadership and its exodus was the contribution this diaspora would bring to the formation of an international social movement that would oppose apartheid and itself help to shape post-apartheid settlement. This was the final way in which Sharpeville would change South African history, in altering South Africa's relationship with the rest of the world. This change would be manifest not so much in the *realpolitik* of formal diplomacy: here as we have noted, South Africa's most important foreign alliances would remain unbroken. The new networks of anti-apartheid activism that began to assemble across the world in reaction to Sharpeville would themselves influence with their own expectations and values strategic decisions by South Africans. They would also help to reconstruct politics in their own national settings as well as more globally. We will explore their experiences in the next chapter.

6

The Anti-Apartheid Movement

After 1960 'anti-apartheid' became a global preoccupation. In the United Kingdom, organized opposition to apartheid would develop into 'Britain's biggest-ever international solidarity movement'.[1] More generally, international anti-apartheid campaigning is acknowledged to have built 'one of the most influential post-war social movements'.[2] This may have happened anyway, even if the police had not fired their guns at Sharpeville. It seems less likely, though. Perceptions of crisis generated by the shootings at Sharpeville and the accompanying tumult elicited strategic shifts by the state and its most important opponents. These altered the course of South African politics.

As we shall see, a diaspora of socially assertive South African exiles arrived in their host societies in Europe and North America just at a time when a fresh constituency for an idealist 'politics of conscience' was under assembly, itself a product of social change and in particular a consequence of a massive expansion of higher education. If the exiles had arrived later they may well have made less impact, their cause overtaken by others. Moreover, the massacre and in particular the media images that depicted it generated an emotional public response. This was so especially in countries that were connected to South Africa by kinship affinities and political alliances.

Networks of organized activity in four countries constituted the core dynamics of global public opposition to apartheid. The movement was wider as we shall see but these national networks were the most enduring and the best organized. These networks were located in the United Kingdom, Sweden, the Netherlands, and the United States. In each of these countries anti-apartheid movements would succeed in enlisting public sympathy and popular activism on a large scale and from time to time they would help to shape official decision making.

In their national settings anti-apartheid movements constituted them-selves more or less independently of each other, each emerging at the end of the 1950s out of earlier efforts to support ANC campaigning in South Africa. In 1952 in Britain, Christian Action, a Christian socialist pressure group founded in 1945 by a former Anglican chaplain in the Royal Air Force, John Collins, raised money to help the families of Defiance Campaign volunteers and would later supply the organizational base for anti-arpartheid activity in Britain. In the United States in the same year Americans for South African Resistance undertook a similar role and the following year would rename itself the American Committee on Africa (ACOA). Christian Action would later raise £50,000 for the defendants in the 1956–61 Treason Trial and for this purpose established the Defence and Aid Fund in 1958. A Swedish branch of this organization was set up in 1959. Meanwhile in the Netherlands the *Comite Zuid-Afrika* (CZA) constituted itself in 1957, again with the initial purpose of raising money for the Treason Trial defence. In these settings, early anti-apartheid organization was strongly church-based and nurtured by clerical contacts with black South African leadership that had developed over decades of missionary activity. The influence of churchmen in building the foundations of the internation-al Anti-Apartheid Movement was significant, as Robert Skinner has sug-gested, in promoting 'a moral reading of international politics' and in representing apartheid as a 'fundamental wrong', a framing of the issues that made them especially emotive.[3]

In Britain, missionary traditions would be particularly important in helping to root the Anti-Apartheid Movement in British society. Over the next three decades the movement would find some of its strongest support on Scottish university campuses, and indeed Scottish organized student protest at South African racial discrimination first occurred in 1947, the year of the royal visit to South Africa. Scottish universities had a particular African orientation that they developed through their role in the training of Scottish Presbyterian missionaries, especially at Glasgow and Edinburgh. The Glasgow Mission Society began establishing schools and colleges in South Africa's Eastern Cape in the 1840s. Elsewhere, both the Norwegian and the Swedish governments supported missionary pro-grammes in Southern Africa from the mid-nineteenth century and a history of contacts between missionaries and black South African leaders helps to explain the presence of senior churchmen in Nordic anti-apartheid groups. Of these, Dean Gunnar Helander, a Church of Sweden missionary posted to Johannesburg between 1938 and 1956, would assume an authoritative role from the start, helping to establish Defence and Aid.

Canon Collins's decision to transform Christian Action into a South African solidarity project was inspired by meetings with Michael Scott and Trevor Huddleston, both charismatic Anglican priests, who had been sent by their orders to South Africa. Scott had initially worked in London's East End where for a while he had become friendly with Communist Party leaders. In 1946 he participated in the Natal Indian Congress's passive resistance and served a three-month jail term. Trevor Huddleston's politics were initially inspired by 1930s' Christian socialism. Huddleston was a member of the Anglo-Catholic Community of the Resurrection, by 1950 the main agency in training black Anglican priests in South Africa. Until his enforced departure from South Africa in 1956 Huddleston ministered to the African freehold township of Sophiatown in West Johannesburg.

Collins had also recently read Alan Paton's *Cry the Beloved Country*, shortly after its publication in 1949. For Collins the book's effect was 'a call to arms',[4] its effects accentuated by a meeting with its author, who visited Britain on a speaking tour in 1950, an encounter that rapidly developed into an enthusiastic friendship. Paton's novel, a best seller and book club choice as soon as it appeared helped to animate empathy with black South Africans among millions of international readers through the 1950s. It was adapted into a musical on Broadway in 1949 and filmed with Sidney Poitier in 1951. In Britain, Trevor Huddleston's *Naught for your Comfort* was also very influential, selling out and undergoing reprinting within a month of its publication in March 1956. It's author's well-publicized return to Britain elicited a fresh wave of public interest in South Africa, with Huddleston addressing a series of crowded public meetings and receiving over a hundred letters a week from admirers.[5] Meanwhile the *Sunday Times* nominated *Naught for your Comfort* as 'The most influential book of the year.'[6] In Holland, another literary priest would build fresh extensions of anti-apartheid concern. The Dutch *Comite*'s founder, J. J. Beukes, was a protestant pastor who visited South Africa in 1955 and who subsequently published a book about his experiences there. Beukes was deeply impressed with Chief Albert Luthuli, and CZA's first undertaking was to attempt to collect endorsements to nominate Luthuli for the Nobel Peace prize.

Across the world public reactions to the Sharpeville massacre were most demonstrably evident in London where a meeting on 27 March organized in Trafalgar Square by the Labour Party succeeded in drawing a crowd of 15,000, one of the biggest open-air gatherings in the vicinity since VE day in 1945. The assembly included 4,000 people who had marched from Marble Arch behind the banners of the British Boycott Movement committee, the body that on 30 March would re-title itself as the Anti-Apartheid Movement (AAM). The Boycott Movement had been formed three months earlier, with the support of the Labour Party and representatives of a range of different groups including Christian Action as well as Michael Scott's African Bureau and, most importantly, South African émigré bodies, including the South African Freedom Association, whose adherents were mainly Indian South African students. In anticipation of the South African government's imposition of racial restrictions on admission to the main English language universities, significant numbers of black South Africans began enrolling in British universities, especially in London, towards the end of the 1950s. South Africans joined up with other African ex-patriates in London who were active in anti-colonial pressure groups and the Committee of African Organizations to begin organizing a consumer boycott of South African products in mid-1959. The Boycott Movement was a response to both ANC and South African Liberal Party (SALP) calls for an international trade boycott and the British Boycott Movement committee included Tennyson Makiwane and Patrick van Rensberg as ANC and SALP representatives. The boycott organizers summoned an impressive collection of celebrity patrons and prepared two million leaflets to circulate in a 'Boycott Month' of events planned for March 1960.

The Sharpeville massacre created a receptive political setting for the British Boycott Movement: if it had not happened it is unlikely that so many thousands of people would have attended the Boycott meeting at Trafalgar Square on 30 March. Press commentaries during the months before Sharpeville were hardly encouraging. As the London *Spectator* noted, 'the number of Conservative supporters... will be small. Nor is it likely that hardcore Labour voters are going to pay any attention to the campaign: most of them supported Suez, and care very little what happens to a bunch of wogs.'[7] Sharpeville created a fresh mood of public outrage. As the AAM itself conceded, the massacre 'brought about a new consciousness of apartheid'.[8] A Gallup poll taken shortly afterwards indicated that among its respondents 99 per cent had read about or heard about the killings and 80 per cent were now opposed to apartheid.[9] The event received front page lead story coverage in the British press and featured conspicuously in television news. On BBC television, for example, between March and May 1960 there were fifty-six film reports on South Africa, responding almost daily as the crisis unfolded. This extent of coverage compares with an average of about 15 South African focused stories a year through the preceding decade.[10] External media treatment of South Africa changed qualitatively too: for the first time in these reports black South African political leaders appeared speaking directly to the cameras.

Civic outrage, even when expressed through well-orchestrated public demonstrations, only occasionally becomes sustained into long-lasting orchestrated agitation. It was the presence in London of at least several hundred South African exiles that supplied the critical agency in turning momentary public protest into a social movement that would sustain itself over three decades. In most cases, their arrival in London was a consequence of the Sharpeville crisis and the government's subsequent repression of the Congresses. Exiles, though, were present in much smaller numbers in and around the formation of organized anti-apartheid movements in Sweden, the Netherlands, and the United States and even in Britain the presence of South African exiles is insufficient by itself to explain the success of an externally preoccupied solidarity movement in mobilizing public support.

During the 1960s the Anti-Apartheid Movement in Western Europe developed in tandem with a broader family of single-issue-oriented social movements, movements that mobilized significant followings, predominantly drawn from middle-class communities and particularly active on university campuses. They were distinctive because their followers were engaging with rights-based concerns in which they had no direct or material self-interest. In Britain for example, Anti-Apartheid leadership and followers at the time of the movement's inception overlapped to a certain extent with the Campaign for Nuclear Disarmament. In Britain and elsewhere during the later part of the decade, anti-apartheid as a cause was embraced in a wider wave of generational revolt in universities. To take another example, this time outside Europe, in the United States student sympathy with the civil rights movement helped to prompt Students for a Democratic Society (SDS) to instigate the South African divestment campaign in 1966 in New York when students from Columbia University and the Union Theological seminary staged a sit-in outside the Chase Manhattan bank to protest against loans to South Africa. Subsequent protests at shareholders' meetings helped to generate further publicity and account withdrawals worth $30 million.[11]

So, why were middle-class radicals and student activists during the 1960s so ready to embrace anti-apartheid as a political cause? One set of explanations focuses on social and cultural changes that made certain groups particularly susceptible to political appeals that emphasized participation in global struggles for emancipation and justice. Higher levels of consumption and welfare in Western industrial countries freed people from material concerns and hence weakened earlier narrow bases of class solidarity while simultaneously broadening the scope of their social empathy. Decolonization, immigration, and the increased provision and accessibility of international air travel each in different ways made it more likely that middle-class political preoccupations would be affected by events in the 'Third World', a term that itself was coined in the 1960s. By 1960, photojournalism and television had helped to create a new 'visualized transnational media space'[12] and new global audiences for political events that this new media projected. Subsequent technological developments in the 1970s helped to enlarge this space, particularly the advent of cheap and rapid photocopying and off-set litho printing. The Sharpeville massacre's visual projection was critically important in the mass media's 'framing' of apartheid as an issue of global political concern.

Expansion of university education—in Britain its provision doubled over the 1950s and it was to rise even faster in the next decade—and the availability of financial support for students—fostered an assertive sense of distinctive social identity among young people more generally. More specifically, with respect to the students themselves, as their numbers increased during the 1960s, there was more and more 'discrepancy between the elitist training offered by the university and the increasingly meagre prospect of attaining elitist roles' after graduation, arguably a major source of campus disaffection.[13] Even more importantly, through the 1950s and 1960s, young people became the prime target markets for the music and fashion industries. Through their consumption choices teenagers and people in their early 20s began to emphasize their own generational separateness, a separateness accentuated by a growing knowledge gap between them and their parents, the product of post-war acceleration of technological change. Access to much easier and safer contraception underlay new challenges to established sexual conventions, instituting a new set of challenges to adult authority.[14]

Meanwhile amongst older adults, growing middle-class predispositions to embrace altruistic or radical politics may have been the effect of changes in the way the middle class itself was constituted. Its growing proportional size and social weight and a shift in its internal composition as a consequence of the expansion of 'public professions' accompanying the build-up of the welfare state both promoted adherence to egalitarian and socially responsible values.[15] In his study of the middle-class base of CND, Frank Parkin argued that in contrast to the mainly materialist concerns of working-class political movements, middle-class radicalism was 'directed mainly to social reforms which are basically moral in content', in which the main rewards of political success were payoffs of 'an emotional or psychological kind' rather than any sectional benefit.[16] Anti-Apartheid appealed to what certain social scientists characterize as a 'conscience constituency', unaffected by personal grievances.[17]

By 1960, then, broad kinds of social and cultural change had fostered a fertile political environment for an anti-authoritarian activist politics that often found its expression in identification with heroically conducted and emotionally captivating struggles for freedom and justice. Amongst a range of such struggles, identification with South African opposition to apartheid was a consequence of the arrival in Europe after 1960 of a cohesive community of middle-class and socially mobile South African political exiles, easy for their host society to assimilate because of their professional qualifications and their cultural familiarity. The evolution of Anti-Apartheid activism into an international community in which participant morale was strengthened by their own perceptions of global camaraderie was also helped by a unique source of institutional support, the United Nations Special Committee against Apartheid set up by the General Assembly in November 1962. In particular through its own programmes of sponsored meetings, workshops, and conferences the committee provided the encounters through which national anti-apartheid groups could build connections with each other and inspire each other, functioning as a key agency in the creation of 'an imagined community of solidarity activists'.[18]

There were special reasons specific to particular countries, though, why anti-apartheid became one of these causes. In Britain public interest in Africa generally and South Africa specifically had quickened just before Sharpeville as a consequence of press coverage of Macmillan's continental tour and his 'Winds of Change' speech in Cape Town. Also it seems the boycott campaign really did succeed in affecting the everyday behaviour of significant numbers of shoppers. Gallop polls conducted between December 1959 and March 1960 discerned significant and increased support for the boycott and the effects of the boycott were also evident in a £2 million contraction in trade and falling prices for South African produce. Public interest in South Africa may also have been affected by patterns of emigration, for between 1945 and 1960 South Africa was a major destination for British emigrants. Of course, this trend helped to encourage sympathy and identification with the white minority but it may also have had the more general effect of making South Africa more visible and accessible to British citizens than other parts of the world.

In the Netherlands, Dutch post-war emigration to South Africa, second in volume only to Britain's for much of the 1950s, prompted warm diplomatic relations with Pretoria and even a well publicized royal tour in 1954. As in Britain, a generalized acknowledgement of 'kinship' with the white minority may help to explain the emotional public response to the Sharpeville massacre. Dutch parliamentarians discussed South Africa for the first time and adopted a motion appealing to their South African counterparts to exclude racial domination. Anti-apartheid activism in the Netherlands remained restricted to very small groups, however, until the 1970s when they were invigorated by new arrivals from South Africa, mainly Afrikaans-speaking university students. Institutional and public support for anti-apartheid movements would only really develop during the 1970s, a consequence of the emergence of a 'new left' within the Labour movement, and the build-up of sympathy within the Protestant Reformed churches, especially after Reverend Beyer Naude's emergence in 1963 as a major critic of apartheid from within the Reformed Ecumenical Synod's South African congregations.

Sweden had no significant flows of migration towards South Africa though quite strong trading and tourist linkages between the two countries developed during the 1950s. Earlier connections forged by the Swedish Lutherans may also have helped to engender a morally critical public awareness of South African events. There were other historical linkages between Sweden and South Africa. In 1900, a pro-Boer movement despatched a group of Swedish volunteers to join the defence of Kruger's republic. In 1960, Swedish trade unionists were assertive in the leadership of the International Confederation of Free Trade Unions (ICFTU) and this may help to explain the comparatively vigorous trade union and cooperative society participation in the boycott movement as well as the initiatives undertaken after 21 March by local trade union branches to hold meetings in factories and building sites to acknowledge the Sharpeville massacre.

Popular journalism instilled public familiarity with South Africa: the novelist Per Wastberg's two books about his experiences while visiting the subcontinent in 1959 were published in 1960, each containing sympathetic profiles of the main African political personalities, including Robert Sobukwe. Their content had appeared earlier in Stockholm's main daily newspaper, *Dagens Nyhter*, and Wastberg's publishers sold 170,000 copies.[19] In 1960 Wastberg was the latest of a series of influential Swedish public commentators who visited South Africa in the 1950s; his editor at the *Dagens Nyhter*, Herbert Tingsten, had himself published a series of twenty articles after travelling to South Africa in 1953.

A very particular anti-colonial orientation within the Swedish student movement also helps to explain public engagement with anti-apartheid at the beginning of the 1960s. This was partly a consequence of successive Swedish social democratic governments maintaining a strategic foreign policy of 'third way' alignment that committed them to active support for decolonization, a choice connected to Swedish efforts to project an international attractive alternative to Cold War ideological polarities.[20] The Swedish *Forenade Studentkarer* (SFS) joined forces with the National Union of South African Students (NUSAS) in 1950 to gather funding for scholarships for black students at Wits who had just been deprived by the government of their entitlement to state bursaries. In 1957 Nordic students found a fresh African preoccupation in the cause of Algerian self-determination and through an exceptionally well-organized web of youth organizations, the Social Democratic Student Federation managed to achieve a significant shift in official policy with the Swedish government's decision to welcome an official representative of the Algerian insurgency. In a highly consensual political system in which political institutions were organized to facilitate public accessibility, student unions exercised comparatively stronger influence in mainstream politics than in other western democracies: as Thorn acknowledges, 'the allies of the Swedish anti-apartheid movement were closer to state power'.[21]

In the United States through the 1960s and even through most of the 1970s, anti-apartheid remained a cause that was confined to lobbying rather than activist mobilization, though this would change with the entrenchment of the divestment movement on college campuses during the 1980s. One reason for this limitation, as we have seen, was the comparatively sympathetic posture adopted by the Kennedy administration at the opening of the decade as well as the willingness of civil rights leaders to incorporate opposition to apartheid among their concerns, as was the case with Martin Luther King. The growth after the 1965 civil rights legislation of a Congressional Black Caucus also helped to strengthen the ACOA's lobbying predispositions: it opened a Washington office in 1967. In contrast to Britain, the Netherlands and Sweden, despite the ACOA's efforts, consumer boycotts of South African products were unlikely to prompt much public interest, for South African exports to the United States were negligible and hardly conspicuous in shops.[22] Anti-apartheid solidarity networks spread through church groups—especially Methodist and Episcopal congregations, and through these capillaries reached into university campuses, but really until the mid-1970s, American generational rebellion focused mainly on civil rights and opposition to the Vietnam War.

Western European student solidarity with anti-colonial movements during the 1960s was partly guided by doctrinal considerations, at least among leadership groups. Strategists of student rebellion during the 1960s believed that their activism on and off the campuses was not simply a consequence of the stresses and strains that higher education institutions were experiencing because of their expanded intake. Rather, the sharp growth in student numbers in advanced industrial countries during the 1960s reflected a 'colossal transformation of the productive forces'.[23] Students were undergoing training to perform new roles assigned to 'intellectual labour', roles that subjected them to contradictory demands, on the one hand requiring the development of creative and critical capacity and on the other hand confining such skills within narrowly defined vocational disciplines. Accordingly:

> ... there is a permanent contradiction within the universities and colleges of advanced capitalist countries today. On the one hand, these societies have an absolute functional need of a mass of intellectual workers. On the other hand they cannot tolerate the realization of the critical potential of this mass.[24]

Widening rifts during the 1950s between student leaders and European Labour and Communist parties strengthened convictions that, for a time at least, campuses were 'red bases' of anti-capitalist insurgency in advanced industrial countries, capable occasionally of disrupting 'the memory repression of organized labour'.[25] Increasingly cut off from the mainstream of working-class organization, theorists of student rebellion identified anti-colonial movements as students' natural allies, in the words of Herbert Marcuse, finding the 'class base' for their rebellion in the 'external proletariat' of the Third World.[26] In France especially, student support for the Algerian rebellion between 1957 and 1962 helped to isolate students from the conventional left, Socialist and Communist, and strengthen commitments to solidarity activism, commitments that spread from the Sorbonne through the Western European student movement, as we have seen in the way that Nordic students adopted the Algerian revolt as a special concern. In particular national settings, these strategic predispositions influenced students to identify anti-apartheid as a symbolic cause through which they could express a wider repudiation of authority.

This happened in Britain in 1969 and 1970 when the Stop the Seventy Tour (STST) committee mobilized a following of 50,000 people in various forms of direct action that disrupted the programme of the visiting Springbok rugby players and actually succeeded in generating sufficient pressure to compel the authorities to cancel a series of test matches it had arranged for South African cricketers. STST was set up by Young Liberals acting in conjunction with local branches of the Anti-Apartheid Movement. Peter Hain, the son of South African Liberal Party members who had made their home in London from 1964, himself a leading personality in the (British) Young Liberals, was conspicuous as the committee's main public figure. The committee organized marches on twenty-two sports grounds as well as directing pitch invasions and mounting pickets of the hotels used by the Springboks, a programme that lasted over three months and which attracted sufficient support and attention to persuade the government that the impending cricket tour should not take place, not least because Labour Party politicians were worried that opposition to the visitors might prompt racial clashes in British cities.[27] Though the STST had succeeded in enlisting support from establishment quarters it very obviously grew out of a student activist milieu, so much so that within the Anti-Apartheid Movement reservations were expressed that the high profile tactics the committee favoured might animate against the movement 'the allegedly widespread prejudice against students'.[28]

STST success helped to foster stronger commitments to anti-apartheid campaigning within the National Union of Students (NUS) under Jack Straw's presidency and, during the 1970s, the NUS would succeed in mobilizing students over one issue in which they possessed critical leverage, disinvestment in South Africa by British high-street banks. As with the efforts to stop South African sports tourists, student activism during the 1960s and early 1970s could from time to time succeed in mustering sufficient public commitment to their cause to engender official reactions, however anti-apartheid's encounter with the 1960s student movement was important in another way too. For student leaders like Jack Straw and Peter Hain, who later became members of political elites, anti-apartheid solidarity was a formative experience. Stop the Seventy Tour was not a unique case of anti-apartheid being taken up as a cause in the late-1960s student revolt. In Sweden as well, in May 1968, the University of Lund-based Swedish South Africa Committee broke up the Swedish Davis Cup match with Rhodesia with a sit-in action and the throwing of oil bags into the court. This protest, Hakan Thorn observes, was 'the closest the Swedish student movement would get to 1968-type activism'.[29]

Anti-Apartheid only from time to time elicited mass participation. At the heart of the movement in each of its national settings was an overlapping cluster of quite small organizations. For example, the British Anti-Apartheid Movement had an office in London, but in the 1960s could only afford one full-time administrator: at the peak of its influence, in the 1980s, it employed twenty-three staff. Its influence partly depended on the presence of organizational representatives on its national committee, many of them delegated by a range of bodies, including the Labour, Liberal, and Communist parties, eleven trade unions, and the British Council of Churches as well as representatives of local anti-apartheid committees, of which there were a fluctuating number: twenty-one in 1965, ninety in 1987. It also acquired social respectability from a formidable line-up of well known sponsors: prominent politicians and other public personalities, a feature bringing the British movement much closer to the mainstream of institutional politics than its counterparts elsewhere.

The organization recruited members individually from 1962 as well as from affiliate organizations. For most of its history, individual membership was modest, around 2,500 through the 1960s and 1970s, rising to nearly 20,000 at the end of the 1980s and at any time active membership, that is people regularly attending monthly local meetings and participating in pickets and other campaigning, was around ten per cent of these totals. AAM published a regular monthly newsletter. Its circulation during the 1960s rose to 7,000 and then remained roughly at that level for the next decade but in the 1980s it rose to around 20,000 and with one issue reached 85,000.[30]

By the 1980s affiliates included 200 or so constituency Labour parties, 708 trade union branches, and ninety-one student unions. Individual members

were chiefly white and middle class: the British AAM never really succeeded in enlisting enthusiastic support within British black or immigrant
communities, South Africans aside, partly because its leaders blocked any
efforts to draw the movement into wider anti-racist activities for fear of
losing their mainstream appeal. During the 1980s, newspapers directed at
London's West Indian community did encourage their readers to engage
with the Anti-Apartheid Movement but there was also an assertively racially
separatist group of organizations that tended to be more sympathetic to the
PAC.[31] And despite the presence of trade unions in Anti-Apartheid's
affiliate structure, trade union support for a long time was half-hearted,
largely because of trade unionist concerns about the impact of South African
economic sanctions on British jobs. In the 1980s, trade unions gave stronger
backing to divestment and together with local Labour Party branches they
played a decisive role in persuading local authorities to divest pension fund
investments in South African connected companies.[32] The Communist-led
technicians union, AEUW, was Anti-Apartheid's most reliable British trade
union supporter but in the 1980s, NALGO, the local government union,
supplied especially critical backing for the divestment campaign. At that
time NALGO's hierarchy included former student leaders of the Anti-
Apartheid Movement.

One of these was Hugh Bayley, a former vice-president of the National
Union of Students who became a district organizer for NALGO after
completing a master's programme in South African studies at the University
of York. As an NUS official Bayley had assumed responsibility for liaison
with the Anti-Apartheid Movement, joining its executive. He had a long-
standing interest in Africa, dating back to a childhood curiosity sparked by
letters from his godmother who lived in Durban. From the mid-1970s
Hugh Bayley helped lead AAM's trade union committee. Persuading
trade unions to adopt Anti-Apartheid resolutions at their annual conferences was not so difficult and such actions had a certain merit in promoting
general sympathy within their membership but engendering more decisive
action was more challenging, he recalls. Bayley represented the NALGO
staff on the investment committee of the union's own pension fund. Here
he succeeded in persuading the fund's trustees to withdraw its pension
investments in companies with South African holdings. With members of
the union's executive committee he worked out a protocol that would
allow the actuaries to weight the risks of South African investment. In 1980
Bayley succeeded in wining a local council seat in Camden and he then

persuaded the council to adopt a similar disinvestment policy, a pioneering step that would be followed by other local authorities through the decade.

Hugh Bayley's role as a British anti-apartheid activist is very representative of the cross currents that helped the movement resonate across such a cross-section of British social life. His initial interest in South Africa was a consequence of family connections—an effect of emigration to the sub-continent. He was politically socialized through an increasingly internationalized student politics in an intellectual setting in which universities were themselves diversifying their curricula, adding fresh fields such as African area studies. He joined the labour movement at a time when British trade unions were undergoing profound transformations as they constructed an expanding membership among white-collar workers, traditionally members of a 'middle class'. Later Bayley would become a parliamentarian and a minister.[33]

Throughout its history, the British anti-apartheid community was pulled between the competing and potentially conflicting dynamics of influencing policy-making circles through lobbying and the more confrontational and less easily controllable politics of militant action. Between these two tactical repertoires the movement sought to elicit broader public participation: through such undertakings as demonstrations, fundraising, consumer boycotts, and pickets outside high-street banks. Encouraging supporters to write letters to their MPs was another way to engender broader public involvement. For Defence and Aid, its roster of 700 letter-writers supplied it with a critically important channel through which it could send money and other kinds of support to the dependents of political prisoners in South Africa. Shopping boycotts and letter-writing, or even wearing a badge or a T-shirt offered to movement sympathizers emotionally rewarding 'every-day action possibilities'.[34] Politicized choices about lifestyle could bind anti-apartheid supporters ever more closely in what Hakan Thorn has identified as the 'individual networks of everyday life' that were so important in sustaining the movement.[35] It was these opportunities that helped Anti-Apartheid to transcend the limitations of formal organization to become a social movement, capable as it was in the late 1980s of summoning hundreds of thousands of people to attend rock concerts and demonstrations. Of course these levels of mobilization were not simply the consequence of Anti-Apartheid's preceding activism for they were also affected by the coverage that mass media and especially television assigned to South African events after the onset of the 1984 township insurrection. In this decade too, when British politics was especially polarized, Anti-Apartheid campaigning became a focus for more generalized antipathy to Margaret Thatcher's government.[36]

In the United Kingdom, in Sweden, in the Netherlands, and in Ireland, though there were no formal affiliations, the main anti-apartheid organizations tended to align themselves and work closely with the ANC and in doing so, they added significantly to its authority. There are several reasons for this alignment. In Britain, Holland, and Sweden, the churchmen who played such an important role in establishing the early organizational incubators for Anti-Apartheid had developed close friendships with ANC leaders: this was particularly the case with Trevor Huddleston, Canon Collins, and Gunnar Helander. Huddleston in particular was important in this respect for in Johannesburg he had helped to organize ANC opposition to Bantu education. As we have seen, many anti-apartheid movements were led by exile ANC members or people in host countries who were sympathetic to the ANC, and this certainly helped to boost the ANC's international status.

Outside Africa, the Pan-Africanists were much less successful in engendering public or official support. This was partly a consequence of their origins as a sectarian movement that they never altogether succeeded in transcending. It was also true that many of the first 'multiracial' wave of exiles who constituted ANC communities in European countries found it easy to assimilate. They often possessed professional qualifications and benefitted from networks of kinship and friendship. Less socially assured PAC exiles found themselves at a comparative disadvantage. Significantly, the PAC had more standing among African-American anti-apartheid activists than it ever acquired among South African solidarity groups in Europe. It also drew some backing from those British black activists who were disenchanted with the British Anti-Apartheid Movement's reluctance to challenge domestic, that is, British-based, instances of racism. Because of its general success in eliciting sympathy from the political establishment, the British Anti-Apartheid Movement was particularly careful to avoid taking up local political concerns that might have alienated sectors of their support. In the 1980s, this policy would engender internal tensions with the formation of a militant faction within the AAM, the City of London Anti-Apartheid Group, itself linked to the Trotskyite Revolutionary Communists.[37]

More generally, though, the PAC did not draw much strength from the international solidarity that the Sharpeville shootings were so decisive in generating. This was all the more notable given that the anniversary of the massacre remained such a symbolic date in the anti-apartheid calendar. Because of its neglect or failure to mobilize support networks in the communities that hosted its exiles, the PAC remained a needy organization. Though its African and Middle Eastern allies from time to time donated significant sums—$150,000 and $50,000 from Iraq and Nigeria respectively in 1982—the PAC's income from such sources was a fraction of what the ANC was obtaining from its allies.[38] Part of the explanation for the imbalance between the Anti-Apartheid Movement's treatment of the ANC and the PAC is to do with the early friendships between European activists and ANC-affiliated black South Africans in the 1950s. Also the ANC's 'multi-racialist' message was easy to project in language that could match the ideological predispositions of British and other European liberals. For one reason or another, ANC exiles and their allies were able to convince their hosts that they were more representative. From his experience of working with South Africans in anti-apartheid committees in the early 1970s, for Hugh Bayley the main considerations were pragmatic as much as they were principled: 'Ideology mattered, but on its own it wouldn't have won the race. No, it was simply clear to us that the ANC could lay claim to broader support.'[39]

In the early 1960s, though, as well as these social and cultural considerations, there were very particular developments that helped to distance the Pan-Africanists from anti-apartheid solidarity. ANC members resident in Britain played key roles in helping to found the Anti-Apartheid Movement and for the first few years South African exiles who either belonged to the ANC or who were sympathetic to it were conspicuous on its national committee. No PAC members belonged to the national committee as founder members. However from its inception the AAM accorded recognition to the Pan-Africanists, a notional neutrality which would often exasperate London ANC officials. The AAM invited the Pan-Africanists to send their own representatives to its national committee meetings as observers, a courtesy which it also accorded to the ANC. For the first two years, between June 1960 and March 1962, Nana Mahomo, as the PAC's London representative, could attend AAM meetings on behalf of the South African United Front (SAUF), an alliance of the two liberation organization formed in Dar es Salaam at the behest of African leaders.

National committee minutes, though, suggest that attendance by SAUF representatives was infrequent and that when it occurred it was mainly ANC spokesmen for the SAUF who were present.

When SAUF members spoke at AAM national committee meetings they tended to register concerns connected with ANC activities inside South Africa: the 1961 campaign for a constitutional convention, for example.[40] Even so, the documentary evidence in the Anti-Apartheid Movement archive suggests that for a while the SAUF functioned fairly harmoniously and PAC and ANC participants cooperated quite effectively in campaigning for trade sanctions. They worked together to draft a resolution passed at the second Conference of Independent African States in Addis Ababa in July 1960 calling on African countries to prohibit South African ships and aeroplanes from using their port facilities. In September 1960 Nana Mahomo and Yusuf Dadoo (of the South African Communist Party) represented the SAUF as speakers on a national tour organized for them by the Anti-Apartheid Movement. Subsequently Mahomo and Dadoo would make a succession of formal visits to London embassies together. The SAUF disbanded in March 1962 after an escalation of rhetorical hostilities between the two organizations in the wake of the PAC's opposition to the 1961 stay-at-home strike. The documentation in the AAM archive suggests that the dissolution was not a consequence of any tensions between the London-based participants in the SAUF, though. After the SAUF's dissolution the PAC retained observer status on the AAM's national committee but its representatives attended meetings very infrequently.[41]

Meanwhile liaison arrangements between the AAM and the ANC became increasingly institutionalized. Even so, the AAM would sometimes take up issues on the PAC's behalf, reproving the colonial secretary for the conviction in 1965 in Basutoland of Pan-Africanists involved in planning military operations in the Republic[42] or urging the British government to protest against the execution of *Poqo* members in 1967, for example, but in reality the relationship between the AAM and the PAC was mutually disdainful. Even British AAM officials often found the PAC's Africanism 'repugnant'[43] and PAC members believed that the AAM supported the ANC 'to the exclusion' of their organization.[44] More unfairly, they were also heavily critical of Canon Collins' International Defence and Aid Fund (IDAF) claiming it withheld welfare funding from the dependents of imprisoned Pan-Africanists. This was untrue though IDAF did discriminate in the ANC's favour when it came to directly supporting exile political activity.[45]

All the same, Pan-Africanists in London and in other 'Western' countries might have been more successful in eliciting solidarity and assistance from their host communities if they had really wanted to. As we have seen, from the mid-1960s the PAC's African-based leaders had committed their followers to a 'protracted people's war' that they claimed they would pursue through a strategy of 'self reliance'. In this project there was no point in attempting to persuade Western governments to exercise diplomatic pressure or impose economic sanctions on South Africa: much more than the ANC, Pan-Africanists opposed any prospect of a negotiated political settlement. 'We are not a civil rights movement', PAC leaders would sometimes observe.[46] From their perspective, AAM's emphasis on a liberal rights-based set of claims missed the point:

> It misrepresents the nature of the struggle by concentrating on 'Anti-Apartheid'. The struggle is not for the ending of enforced racial segregation. It is for the national liberation of oppressed Black peoples.[47]

In 1981, Pan-Africanists in London helped set up a parallel solidarity organization to AAM calling itself 'Azania Solidarity' which provided rhetorical backing and platforms at public meetings for the PAC as well as a later generation of Black Consciousness exiles and disaffected ANC factions. Azania Solidarity was openly critical of the AAM not just for its 'one-sidedness' with respect to its relationships with South African organizations but also for its strategic moderation: 'The struggle in Azania was for the restoration of the land and its wealth, not just a civil rights issue or minor concessions, as depicted by AAM.' Indeed, apartheid itself was a creation of 'British Imperialism' at the beginning of the century, subsequently Afrikaner nationalists 'merely touched it up', hence the struggle for Azania had to be an anti-imperialist struggle so there was no point in trying to win over British politicians.[48] The PAC office in London hedged its bets, however, maintaining formal contact with the AAM, and PAC members sometimes attended local AAM meetings. PAC officials also continued to seek help, sometimes successfully, from individual Labour Party MPs. In 1981, for example, Andrew Faulds tried to help the PAC secure British asylum for activists expelled from Zambia.

At the beginning of their exile, though, Pan-Africanist officials assumed a much more diplomatic posture with respect to the British and American political establishments. Nana Mahomo especially invested considerable effort in trying to secure funding from trade unions and other potential donors in Britain, Europe, and North America, with some success. In 1963 Patrick Duncan joined him in London and through his friendships and contacts was able to obtain funding to support London office expenses.[49] Duncan could bring to the PAC unusually privileged access to powerful people and during a visit to the United States that year he was able to meet both the Kennedy brothers—Bobby and Teddy—as well as Chester Bowles, an undersecretary of state for Africa, and Wayne Fredericks. In a series of private meetings with these people he argued the case for the United States to at least acknowledge the PAC's status as a decisive agency in South African politics. He would advance the same arguments through his journalism, in, for example, substantial invited contributions to *The Times* and *Foreign Affairs* and in appearances in May and June 1963 on the BBC's *Tonight* and *Panorama* programmes. Both Duncan and Mahomo were able to elicit sympathetic interest in British non-Communist left and liberal circles, and here too, Duncan's personal friendships were helpful: he was on first-name terms for example with Denis Healey and the *Observer*'s editor, David Astor. He managed to persuade Barbara Castle to table questions in the House of Commons about South African police operations in Basutoland.[50] The South African exile community also included significant numbers of ex-Liberal Party members, some of whom were active in AAM and supportive of the PAC, for example the ex-diplomat, Patrick Van Rensberg, one of the AAM's founders.

Mahomo would quickly fall out with Potlake Leballo and lose his designation as the PAC's London representative. Duncan at his own request would move to Algiers to run the PAC's mission to the Algerian government, a sensible enough appointment as he could speak French fluently and would indeed represent his organization very effectively, persuading the Algerians to extend their guerrilla training programmes to the PAC. The Algerian-based Pan-Africanists would also benefit from a swift decision by Duncan to 'recognize' the new administration after Boumedienne's coup against Ben Bella: local ANC officials delayed, waiting for sanction from higher authority. Mahomo would remain based in London and with the help of the Tribune group within the Labour Party would edit a magazine, *Crisis and Change*. Later he directed a powerful documentary film on South African resettlements, *Last Grave at Dimbaza*, which itself became widely shown at AAM public meetings.

Relations between the PAC's London office and the organization's headquarters in Dar es Salaam were always troubled. The London office through its fundraising enjoyed resources independently of the officials in Dar, and Potlake Leballo in particular viewed London-based Pan-Africanists as a source of potential opposition to his own authority. The question of who should control funding supplied from British sympathizers was a constant source of tension between Pan-Africanists in London and Dar: Mahomo was dismissed because of his insistence on retaining in London the money he raised.[51] After Mahomo's expulsion, the PAC's representation in London would be downgraded. In November 1963, a PAC list of foreign representatives who qualified for national executive membership through their designation included no reference to a London office. It was only in the late 1970s that the PAC re-established a properly functioning office in London.[52] The Pan-Africanists' presence in other European capitals and in North America through the 1960s and early 1970s was similarly ephemeral: they preferred to concentrate their diplomatic efforts in Africa. From 1980 the PAC appointed a succession of capable London officials. As we have noted, through the 1980s, the PAC-based London representatives tried to remain on friendly terms with the Anti-Apartheid Movement while sponsoring its own supportive networks on the fringes of the British left. The AAM continued to send representatives to PAC-sponsored events when they were invited to do so, to Sharpeville commemorations for example.[53]

The American movement which became such a potent force in the 1980s as with British anti-apartheid also depended heavily on its campus-based following, but it also established a political base within African-American community organizations, especially churches. As we have noted anti-apartheid was confined generally to lobbying, conferences, and public educational activity by the ACOA and other small groups until the late 1970s. Through the 1960s, the ACOA remained very much a New York-focused organization with no organized connections with grass roots activism elsewhere.[54] The SDS action at the premises of Chase Manhattan in 1966 was exceptional and through the 1960s and early 1970s militant student activism was almost wholly focussed on opposition to the Vietnam war and civil rights. By the mid-1970s, though, the Vietnam war was over and the civil rights movement had achieved key goals. However for students enrolling at universities in the second half of the decade, the 1976 Soweto uprising projected a new morally compelling political drama that appeared to offer the prospects for a continuation of earlier student struggles for racial justice and the redirection of American foreign policy.[55] In 1978 the ACOA began to publish a campus newsletter and it hired a student organizer. Outside the campuses parallels between the struggle to win civil rights and opposition to apartheid were underlined by the emergence of Bishop Desmond Tutu as a familiar personality in American newspapers and television, for here was an culturally accessible hero, eloquent, brave, peaceful, and a man of God. Even before his Peace Prize award, for many African-Americans, Tutu had a special claim to leadership, as Jesse Jackson expressed it, 'the Martin Luther King of South Africa'.[56]

In Washington in 1978 a new pressure group, TransAfrica was formed, with the intention that it should promote African-American concerns in the shaping of African policy making on Capitol Hill. TransAfrica was more than a lobby, though, for it enrolled a membership of around 10,000.[57] Its director was Randall Robinson who had previously worked in the office of Charles Diggs, one of the leading Representatives in the Congressional Black Caucus after it was formed in 1971 and the first black chair of Congress's sub-committee on Africa. African-American legislator interest in Southern Africa was aroused by the Nixon administration's foreign policy emphasis on creating a closer relationship with the white minority governments from 1970 onwards. The formation of the Polaroid Revolutionary Workers' Movement (PRWM) by black employees at Polaroid's Cambridge, Massachusetts, headquarters signalled wider concern with US–South African connections: the PRWM was formed to stop Polaroid's processing of film for South Africa's passbooks. An 'uneasy' coalition began to evolve between elected African-American politicians and similar locally based community groups.[58] When it was established, TransAfrica would assume a position at the helm of this alliance. Together with the ACOA, TransAfrica would play a leading role in a campaign directed at corporate divestment of South African financial interests.

Through the late 1970s and early 1980s the divestment campaign directed itself at two principal targets, university shareholdings and pension funds and similar investments undertaken by city governments and state legislatures. From the autumn of 1977, beginning at Amherst and Princeton, on campuses students boycotted classes, occupied administrative buildings, and constructed symbolic shanty settlements in open spaces. Meanwhile public sector unions used their influence to persuade city and state legislatures to sell their South African interests: here the increase in African-American elected representation was a key factor in persuading more than forty state legislatures to enact divestment laws. The growing presence of black students on campuses—especially at elite colleges—may have been an important consideration as well.[59] In October 1983, the ACOA organized a National Student Anti-Apartheid Conference in New York at which half of the three hundred or so delegates were African-Americans.[60] Certain researchers contest this assumption, though. During the shantytown protests of 1985 to 1990, liberal arts colleges with relatively smaller enrolments of black students tended to have a higher rate of participation, and in general white students seem to have predominated in the student wing of the divestment movement.[61]

In 1984, Jesse Jackson's bid to win the Democratic presidential nomination supplied an important stimulation for community activism in African-American neighbourhoods. In Washington this supplied the political base for the Free South African Movement, a civil disobedience protest in which volunteers ignored local laws that prohibited gatherings within 500 feet of foreign embassies and participated in sit-ins outside the South African embassy. TransAfrica leaders helped to ensure that prominent personalities were among the picketers and among those arrested. They would include Stevie Wonder, Amy Carter, the former president's daughter, 'a large flock of youthful Kennedys',[62] as well as Coretta King. Much of the mobilization behind the Free South African Movement was undertaken by the Southern African Support Project. This was a group established by African-Americans who in 1974 had attended the Sixth Pan Congress in Dar es Salaam.

The American movement was less centrally coordinated than European Anti-Apartheid campaigning and depended upon a wider range of organizational initiatives. Religious organizations were especially important in creating a national following for anti-apartheid activism, in particular the Quaker American Friends Service Committee supplied a vital networking infrastructure. Chief Luthuli's daughter, Thandi Luthuli-Gcabashe led the Friends' peace education program, active across the US South. Though South African exiles were less visible in the American movement than in Britain, they, together with Americans with African experience, often supplied critical leadership. Neva Seidman, the daughter of an American economist who had grown up in Ghana and Tanzania where she made friends within the ANC community, arrived in Harvard as a freshman in 1974. Here she would establish a South African Solidarity Movement that would inspire a summer of unrest through April to June 1978 in which as many as 3,500 students would participate in protests against the university's portfolio holdings. Dumisani Khumalo, a journalist who had left South Africa in 1978, joined the ACOA and in 1981 coordinated a national conference on public investment that assembled all the major anti-apartheid groups as well as trade unionists, city officials, and state legislators.

The American movement was probably unique in the influence it exercised over legislators and shareholders. For African-American politicians during the 1980s, Anti-Apartheid became an extension of the civil rights movement. Largely because of the relative importance of universities as investors—very different from their less-endowed European counterparts—and because of the way in which decisions by these institutions could have a wider impact among stockholders. Among the movement's major achievements was Chase Manhattan's decision in July 1984 not to renew its $500 million loan to South Africa, a move that precipitated a sharp devaluation of the Rand. Chase Manhattan's chairman, Willard Butcher, denied his bank's decision was motivated by political concerns but in fact Chase Manhattan was facing the threat of divestment by New York City and other major shareholders. The movement's influence was evident in the various sanctions adopted by state legislatures. The Senate's 1986 Comprehensive Sanctions law was enacted after vigorous committee lobbying from members of the Congressional Black Caucus but this was not the whole story. Representatives and senators felt compelled to respond to pressure from within their constituencies. As one senatorial staffer recalled: 'Once the members began to hear about South Africa in their member districts, they began to figure out how to alter their position on sanctions.'[63]

In Britain, too, by the mid-1980s Anti-Apartheid campaigning had succeeded in establishing sanctions as a major political concern and in 1987 the government, also under pressure from the Commonwealth, would enact token sanctions legislation. In earlier decades, through its Labour Party connections, the Anti-Apartheid Movement had influenced British policy on arms sales in 1964 and 1967 and, of course, it could claim a victory in the cancellation of the 1970 cricket tour. The agitation directed at Barclays bank began to affect bank policy as early as 1972, more than a decade before Barclays' eventual withdrawal from South Africa. Within Sweden, public anti-apartheid sentiment was sufficiently developed by 1969 for Olaf Palmer's Social Democratic administration to begin granting official assistance to the ANC. Swedish government aid allocations to the ANC between 1977 and 1991 would total around \$200 million.[64] It was only in 1987, though, that the Swedish authorities ended trade linkages with South Africa.

In the Netherlands, in contrast to the Americans, the British, and the Swedes, the main Dutch anti-apartheid group did not develop such strong connections with mainstream politicians. Within the *Anti-Apartheid Beweging Nederland* the strongest political party connections were with the Dutch Communist Party. Even so, Dutch governments adopted a fairly sympathetic position early on. Under 'New left' leadership a Dutch Labour Party government began awarding grants to the ANC in 1977, a policy that was an outcome of parliamentary lobbying by the Labour Party-linked *Angola Comite*. Anti-Apartheid campaigning around the trade boycott probably helped to generate public acceptance of such transfers: in 1973 Boycott Outspan Action achieved a major impact on public opinion polling. After Angolan independence, the *Angola Comite* reconstituted itself as the *Komitee Zuidelijk Afrika* (KZA). In conjunction with the Reformed Church group, *Kairos*, KZA directed the energies of its national network of local activist groups at halting oil shipments to South Africa, picketing Shell facilities and setting up a Shipping Research Bureau to monitor Rotterdam's discreet oil traffic to South Africa, the main channel for South African supplies from the international spot market after the cessation of South African imports from Iran in 1979. *Anti-Apartheid Beweging Nederland*'s (AABN) preference, though was for 'hard action' and more radical kinds of campaigning. Of all the anti-apartheid groups across Europe and America, AABN's adherents were distinctive for their direct engagement with the ANC, engagement that extended to helping the ANC to establish logistical support for its Operation Vula between 1989 and 1991. AABN were not alone in their preference for hard action. Between 1985 and 1988 various clandestine groups began a succession of violent attacks, including the bombing of a prominent oil trader's house, arson assaults on Makro stores, and sabotage at Shell service stations. In contrast to the non-violent civil rights traditions that supplied the moral base for parts of the American movement or the liberal humanist lineage of British Anti-Apartheid, left-wing Dutch anti-apartheid activists seemed to take their historical cues from their parents' wartime resistance against German occupation.[65]

How extensive was the movement elsewhere, outside its four main national bases? Ireland was a lively theatre of anti-apartheid mobilization, though in the absence of really strong strategic and commercial connections

between Ireland and South Africa here activists had less leverage in compelling decisive action by their government or by local corporations. There
were busy anti-apartheid organizations in countries with much weaker
historical and cultural connections with South Africa including France,
Germany, Belgium, Italy, and Switzerland though here they failed to develop effective public constituencies or shape government policy significantly.
In East Germany, Hans-Georg Schleicher has argued that in certain respects
anti-apartheid solidarity activity embodied 'a genuine popular movement',
dependent on charity and individual initiative.[66] Certainly there was moral
pressure to participate in the Solidarity Committee's officially sponsored
ANC support activity: for example donations would be recorded on trade
union membership cards. However, East German Lutheran churches' donations to the ANC, Schleicher suggests, may well have expressed spontaneous
voluntary commitment within congregations. Outside Europe, Anti-Apartheid attracted support amongst students in Australia, indeed the protests after
Sharpeville in Sydney marked the beginning of a unprecedented wave of
student activism which would soon embrace aboriginal rights as well as
opposition to conscription for the Vietnam war.[67] In New Zealand, South
African pressure on the local rugby authority to drop Maori players in South
African test tours helped to foster general sympathy for black South Africans,
as well as possibly building and extending public opposition to domestic
racism. New Zealand's anti-apartheid movement would overlap closely with
Maori struggles against discrimination.[68] In both countries, post-Sharpeville
South African émigrés, mainly ex-Liberal Party, played important roles in
initiating organization.

Later on in this chapter we will consider the overall impact of Anti-
Apartheid in shaping South African politics. As will become evident there
are strong grounds for believing that its efforts did help to end minority rule
and induce democratization. But what about the effects of Anti-Apartheid
within the settings in which it mobilized its supporters? Did it leave in its
wake a significant imprint on the political culture of its host countries?
Answering these questions will become easier if we follow the course of
Anti-Apartheid in a single country in which it achieved a strong public
following. For this purpose the next part of this chapter will focus on the
case of Ireland and Irish Anti-Apartheid. Here there may be a particularly
strong case for proposing that Anti-Apartheid had domestically transformative effects, politically and culturally.

★

On Thursday 19 July 1984, Mary Manning, a cashier at Dunnes Stores in Dublin's Henry Street, told a customer she would not check out any Outspan grapefruits. A few minutes later she informed her managers she would not sell any South African fruit that day or any other. She was upholding a decision made by her trade union, the Irish Distributive Administrative Trade Union (IDATU). Three months before, the IDATU decided that its members would not handle South African goods, a decision that was initially prompted by an unusually discerning Limerick trade union official steward who had noticed the frozen broccoli he had bought in the local shopping centre had come from South Africa. Mary Manning was supported by her shop steward, Karen Gearon, who walked out of the store with her. Most of the workers at Dunnes in Henry Street went on strike that day and eight of them, mainly women in their early twenties, joined Mary Manning and Karen Gearon on the picket lines thereafter. They would stay on strike for the next two and a half years, surviving on strike pay of £21 a week, returning to work only after the Irish government prohibited the sale of South African fruit and vegetables in Irish stores.

Mary Manning and her colleagues' protest was exceptional—they were joined only by a single worker at another store—and the Irish Congress of Trade Unions withheld even rhetorical backing for over a year. At a time of rising unemployment there was no real solidarity action by other unions. For example despite IDATU complaints the Irish Transport and General Workers' Union (ITGWU) truck drivers continued their deliveries to the store. Even within their own union, though, the strikers received initial encouragement from IDATU's Dublin divisional organizer, Brendan Archbold, a long-standing Irish Anti-Apartheid Movement (IAAM) member, later their union's support for their action was subject to qualification. By January 1986 the union was ready to suspend pickets and was attempting to disband the strike support group.[69] This was after the government announced that it would ban the importation of any South African fruit or vegetables produced by prison labour. At first the protest did not seem to engender much sympathy from members of the public. The strikers' picket line outside the store entrances attracted derision and abuse from shoppers. People called the strikers 'nigger lovers' and even spat at them. One woman accosted Mary Manning and told her that she 'was right not to handle South African goods because she would not either if black people had handled them before her'. Two of the strikers received a visit from the Special Branch.[70]

Public perceptions of the strike were to change, though. There was growing support for the movement, partly a consequence of a meeting between the strikers and Archbishop Desmond Tutu while he was on his way to collect the Peace Prize in Oslo. Public interest quickened when the strikers' cause was taken up by the Labour Party's youth wing as well as by parliamentarians and even by the Catholic Church. The strikers succeeded in extracting supportive statements from Bishop Eamonn Casey and from the Conference of Religious Superiors and after these many priests stopped shopping at Dunnes Stores. Strike supporters participated in the protest in more assertive ways as well, filling their trolleys and leaving them at the check-out stands, a tactic that was later borrowed by protestors in South Africa. Later Mary Manning and her companions managed to raise £6,000 in street collections to pay for their air tickets so that they could visit South Africa. Dunnes remained obdurate, though, continuing to stock South African products and replacing staff in its Henry Street store with non-union labour.[71] The South African boycott was preceded by a history of tense relations between trade unionists and managers, partly a consequence of a particularly authoritarian dress code imposed on its younger staff as well as other kinds of humiliating restrictions.[72] As Karen Gearon recalled, this history of mistreatment by their supervisors was decisive:

> That was at Easter and we got the instruction down in July, about two days before the strike started. I was shop steward at the time, so I passed it on to everybody. At the time we were going through a lot of hassle at Dunnes. They treated us badly as employees, so we were really at our wits' end. Then this instruction arrived and at the time it could have been about anything. It could have been about selling milk in a carton and we would have followed it. We were so naïve we actually didn't know what goods in the shop were South African. We had to go around picking things off shelves and finding out. We found out that it was mainly fruit and vegetables that carried the South African label.[73]

In 1983, IDATU had fought a vigorous battle with Dunnes over recognition, correcting a reputation among shop-workers for being too ready to defer to management. Other firms had responded to the IDATU resolution by agreeing to join the boycott at its inception. In 1985 the minister of labour referred the strike to the Labour Court which delivered a report in which it proposed that the minister should assemble all supermarket owners to explore the possibility of drafting a code for managing conscientious objections among workers to handling South African goods. The minister held several such meetings and indeed did succeed in persuading all the major supermarket chains except for Dunnes to reduce their South African stocks.[74] At that time the Labour Party was in a coalition government and the minister, Ruari Quinn, was a Labour Party member and a one-time Anti-Apartheid supporter. Initially, though, the Labour Party leadership held back from engagement in a strike over a 'conscience' grievance that was so well outside the normal considerations of industrial relations.[75]

The Dunnes strike represented the high water mark of the Irish Anti-Apartheid Movement's (IAAM) public influence. By 1984 the IAAM had existed for twenty years. This was not the first time it had inspired militant kinds of activism. Halting Irish–South African rugby fixtures was a key preoccupation from the Movement's inception: in 1964, Secretary Barry Desmond wrote to every rugby club in Ireland.[76] In January 1970, for example, several hundred opponents of the Springbok rugby side had clashed with police while demonstrating outside the hotel accommodating the visiting players as well as demonstrating their concerns more sedately outside Lansdowne Park the following day, 10 January. The 9,000 or so Lansdowne Park marchers were led by a phalanx of public notables: Patrick Lynch, the chairman of *Aer Lingus* (and, indeed, at the time, the chairman of the IAAM), the author Thomas Pakenham, the National Farmers' Association secretary, Richard Deasy, as well as several senior parliamentarians. The protestors did not stop the game which was played in a half-empty stadium surrounded by police and which resulted in a draw. Later the Springboks encountered a similar reception in Limerick before their second fixture. There would be no further South African rugby tours of Ireland until after 1994, though this was a pragmatic decision by the rugby authorities rather than a principled switch in policy. More than a decade later, in 1981, Irish players toured South Africa as members of the British Lions, the Irish Rugby Football Union (IRFU) apparently undeterred by sharp condemnations by politicians across the political spectrum. The IRFU only decided to officially cease playing South African fixtures in October 1989, just a couple of years before the ending of the international boycott of South African sport.

The attitudes of members of the rugby fraternity notwithstanding, according to Nelson Mandela, the Irish ranked with the Dutch and the Scandinavians as leading western nations in the anti-apartheid solidarity movement. Mandela was visiting Ireland at the time he made this remark but the observation was not just prompted by his habitual courtesy to any of his hosts. As with the British and Swedish movement, from early on IAAM succeeded in obtaining easy access to people in powerful positions. It also combined lobbying with direct action. The Dunnes strike suggests that in its third decade, what had begun as a pressure group was beginning to develop into a more broadly appealing social movement. Mary Manning and her colleagues did not belong to the Irish Anti-Apartheid Movement and at the time they began their protest they were only vaguely informed about South African issues. Why did anti-apartheid become such an evocative cause in Ireland?

Historic connections between South Africa and Ireland may have helped to engender interest in South Africa, at least within elite circles. Sixty thousand people of Irish descent lived in South Africa by the 1960s, mostly the descendents of immigrants who had arrived between 1880 and 1910. Irish emigration to South Africa dwindled thereafter as the demand for skilled artisans slackened. Between 1899 and 1902 30,000 Irish soldiers had fought in the Anglo–Boer war in the Imperial forces. The first Roman Catholic bishop arrived in South Africa from Ireland in 1834. The largest single group of Catholic Irish missionaries worked in South Africa and Irish churchmen remained prominent in the Roman Catholic hierarchy in South Africa through the apartheid era. The South African Catholic Church retained strong links with Irish religious institutions. Both Archbishop Denis Hurley and Archbishop Owen McCann were the sons of Irish immigrants. Trained as a novice in Dublin during the 1930s in the Oblates of Mary Immaculate, Archbishop Hurley was to become a vigorous critic of the South African authorities. In 1984 he was arrested and charged with police defamation and subsequently his house was petrol-bombed.

The history of Irish and South African republicanism is quite closely intertwined. Arthur Griffith, the founder of Sinn Fein returned to Ireland in 1898 after working as a journalist and mineworker in the Transvaal. As in Sweden, a strong 'Pro-Boer' movement existed among nationalists in Ireland during the 1899–1902 war and in South Africa, Irish immigrants assembled two brigades that fought under Afrikaner command against the British. Tactics used by both sides in the Irish War of Independence were shaped by the Anglo–Boer war experience—and may themselves have been borrowed from the experience of bandit gangs of ex-Irish servicemen operating on the Highveld in the early 1890s who later helped to constitute the Irish Brigades.[77] In the 1922 Rand Revolt, an insurrectionary protest against the allocation of skilled work to Africans, the insurgents included an Irish commando unit. Meanwhile between the two world wars, the memory of historic solidarity helped to engender friendly relations between Free State politicians and the former Boer generals who now led the South African government. Ireland's own dominion status was partly modelled on South African precedent and General Jan Smuts played an active role in the Anglo–Irish settlement. General Louis Botha, the Union of South Africa's first prime minister, was married to a descendant of Robert Emmett.

South African diplomatic support for Ireland was especially important during the 1930s when South Africa backed Irish positions at inter-Dominion trade negotiations. Afrikaner nationalist support for Irish neutrality during World War Two helped to explain the initially sympathetic stance adopted by the Irish government after the National Party's accession to government. Sean MacBride, Irish foreign minister from 1948 to 1955, was the son of Major John MacBride, executed after the Easter uprising and a veteran of the Anglo–Boer War in which he had commanded the Irish Transvaal Brigade, holding a commission from the South African Republic. MacBride was later one of the most influential public figures associated with the IAAM, though in the 1950s, as with many other Irish nationalists, he was warmly predisposed to Pretoria. His later opposition to apartheid was partly the consequence of a history of emotional engagement with Southern Africa prompted by his own family history.[78]

The impetus to form an Anti-Apartheid Movement in Ireland was external in origin, though. The IAAM was initially an extension of the British movement. It was founded by Kader Asmal, shortly after his arrival in Ireland to take up an appointment as a law lecturer at Trinity College. Asmal was the son of a shopkeeper in a small rural centre, Stanger, twenty miles or so north of Durban. He was a third generation South African, a member of the Indian community that had been established in Natal as a workforce for the sugar plantations during the nineteenth century. He qualified as a teacher in the early 1950s and worked in various sugar cane company towns while taking correspondence courses for a university degree. His first contact with politics was a consequence of his opposition at school to the segregation of cricket clubs. In 1952, he was inspired by a meeting with Chief Albert Luthuli, president-general of the African National Congress and a Stanger resident, to join the ANC's Defiance Campaign of civil disobedience against 'Unjust Laws'. In London in 1959 he shared a house with other South Africans with ANC connections, and in conjunction with British students and members of Christian Action and the Labour Party he helped to launch the 'Boycott of South African Goods'. As we have seen, the organizational network created to promote the boycott in 1960 became the British Anti-Apartheid Movement.

As we know, British AAM benefited from public reactions to the Sharpeville massacre, but its influence was also attributable to long-standing associations between the South African Congress movement and well-connected anti-colonial lobbies in London. Thousands of South African political exiles would make their home in London and elsewhere in Britain and the British AAM supplied one obvious focus for their own activism. The Irish movement did not have a comparable social base nor could it exploit existing international associations between the ANC and a local left community. There was a small group of South African students in Dublin, enrolled mainly in the Royal College of Surgeons and they supplied early support for a boycott of South African goods instituted by the Irish Congress of Trade Unions in response to the ANC's appeal in 1959. A South African Circle met at Trinity monthly from about 1960.[79] Patrick Noonan, who from 1970 became the parish priest for Sharpeville's Catholic congregation, posted up boycott stickers in his father's grocery store on the River Liffey at the age of 17. His father had just received a consignment of Outspan oranges and he was unimpressed by his son's efforts. He tore the posters down. One year later, Noonan remembers:

> . . . .vivid photos splashed across Irish newspapers in the aftermath of the 1960 massacre at Sharpeville. Perhaps that ignited something in me. I was 18 at the time, not ever realising that I would be living in Sharpeville when the liberation struggle took another giant step forward in the 1980s into the future.[80]

Kader and Louise Asmal held the first meeting of a more formally constituted Irish Anti-Apartheid Movement in their own living room in 1964 and throughout its history the IAAM's committee would meet every other Monday night at the Asmals. The Movement's first undertaking was to collect signatures for a petition for the release of South African political prisoners. This campaign began with a parade and then a meeting at Mansion House addressed by the SACP's Michael Harmel, 'a South African of Irish parentage'.[81]

The Movement's success in attracting public support was largely a consequence of Kader Asmal's own energy and commitment as well as his growing professional distinction. He arrived in Dublin as a qualified British barrister. He obtained a Dublin MA in 1966 and became a barrister at law at King's Inn in Dublin ten years later. Early involvement in Irish civil liberties and civil rights campaigning, both in the republic and in the North helped to foster empathy for the anti-apartheid cause among Irish nationalist politicians. Asmal's own students were to represent another channel of influence—his first law classes at Trinity included Mary Robinson with whom he later formed the Irish Committee for Civil Liberties. Mary Robinson remained a sponsor of the IAAM after her election as state president. Asmal's intention was that, as with the British organization, Irish Anti-Apartheid should aim to acquire broad appeal with well-known local personalities at its helm.

Irish Anti-Apartheid's active leadership as well as names that appear among its sponsors help us to identify the particular networks through which it could project its appeals and advocacy most effectively. Labour Party parliamentary deputies contributed especially energetically to its leadership, for example, Barry Desmond and Conor Cruise O'Brien in the 1960s and 1970s and Joan Burton in the 1980s. From its inception the IAAM could count on active engagement from leading figures within the left republican movement. In particular Father Austin Flannery, a Dominican priest in North Dublin and a distinguished Latin scholar played a significant role in this respect, serving as IAAM's chairman and president through the 1970s. Anthony Coughlan of the Connolly Association and a key founding figure in the Northern Ireland Civil Rights Association also helped to strengthen the Irish left's presence within the Movement's early leadership. The trade unionist official Cathal MacLiam was an executive member throughout IAAM's history. Barry Desmond before his election to the *Dail* in 1969 was secretary of the Irish Trade Union Congress. Kader Asmal's academic colleagues at Trinity as well as lecturers at other Dublin higher education institutions supplied an important proportion of the IAAM's executives through the decades. Patrick Lynch, Trinity's professor of political economy and *Aer Lingus'* chairman through the 1970s, also served as the IAAM chairman during the 1970s as well as serving on a range of key government commissions. People holding senior academic positions at Trinity and elsewhere predominate in the Movement's leadership during the 1980s, many of them individuals who had direct experience of working in Africa. Kader Asmal's professional work as a law lecturer may have helped IAAM to enlist among its sponsors several leading Irish senior counsel. Essentially, then, IAAM's social connections were strongest with the liberal professions, with organized labour and labour politics and with left republicanism.

The conspicuous role of leading Trinity academics in its upper echelons—Mary Robinson would be a case in point—may have helped it to develop a somewhat patrician Anglo–Irish orientation and this too may have helped to set boundaries to its influence. Noel Lemass appears on the 1972 list of sponsors as a solitary if illustrious Fianna Fail TD and Fine Gael's Garret FitzGerald was a long-standing supporter until he resigned in 1984 during his second term as Taoiseach, but really IAAM's metropolitan and labour roots did not make for ready communication with the landowners, small town lawyers, publicans, and 'young Turks of business in mohair suits'[82] that constituted the groups from which the two main Irish national-ist parties recruited their parliamentary representation.

In 1969, IAAM despatched a questionnaire to all candidates in the upcoming general election to canvass their opinions about South Africa. This exercise supplied a useful barometer of the IAAM's influence within political parties at that time. The questionnaire attracted 74 responses, 38 from the Labour Party, 36 from candidates in Dublin, only eight from Fianna Fail candidates and only thirteen from incumbent deputies.[83] Even within the Labour Party, the IAAM could not count upon universal support. During the Springbok rugby tour when the Springboks visited Limerick, the local Labour deputy, Steve Coughlan, criticized the opposi-tion to the fixture and refused to cancel a civic reception for the visitors. In Ireland's rugby capital, where in contrast to other Irish cities rugby is a working-class sport, efforts to disrupt the games were reportedly widely viewed as the work of 'left-wing political perverts' and 'Maoists'.[84] There probably were Maoists among the Limerick demonstrators on the day of the match, for a body called the 'Irish Revolutionary Youth Movement' had just opened a bookshop in Limerick but local opponents of the visit included trade unionists, Labour Party officials, and several Jesuit priests. Desmond attributed Coughlan's hostility to the call for a match boycott to his involvement in a constituency selection row that threatened Coughlan's candidature in the previous election. The local deputy was also mayor of Limerick and he remained widely popular surviving a vote of no confidence within the Limerick Labour Party in the aftermath of the tour. The IAAM's efforts to picket the Springbok's hotel were disrupted by members of a right-wing group, the Irish National Party, who also organized a counter demonstration after the match. Five hundred *garda* were deployed outside the stadium in what the local newspaper called 'the siege of Limerick'. As the *Leader*'s rugby correspondent pointed out, the tumult accompanying the Springboks' progress across Ireland 'will almost certainly make it to be the last tour of a South African rugby team'.[85]

A Liaison Group between the Irish Congress of Trade Unions and the IAAM facilitated access to the labour movement. Local branches and school-based associations helped the organization to build its public following. By 1975, outside its Dublin stronghold there were branches in Cork, Belfast, Derry, Galway, Waterford, and Midleton. Six more branches would be formed in the next decade, including a branch for Irish-language speakers as well as 'twelve active student groups'.[86] The IAAM maintained a membership of round 2,000 for much of its history though the Asmals believe that altogether at one time or another about 30,000 people belonged to the organization.[87] To a greater degree than Britain, the IAAM's support base 'was anchored among Irish trade unionists' and its initial parliamentary connections were strongest with the Labour Party. From 1968 the IAAM's following in the *Dail* included the Labour Party's Conor Cruise O'Brien, whose public opposition to apartheid dated back to his condemnation of South African policies at the United Nations in 1957. In 1968 Conor Cruise O'Brien would lead a sanctions march through Dublin.

As with the British AAM, the Irish organization would extend its influence through affiliate membership, in Ireland mainly from trade unions and student organizations as well as political parties. In comparison to other Western European movements, the IAAM would enjoy especially widespread trade union endorsement and the Asmals confirm that organized labour supplied 'the backbone of the IAAM's work'.[88] The range of its affiliations would constitute the IAAM as 'the broadest coalition of national organizations in Ireland's history', apparently. However, in contrast to the Swedish and British anti-apartheid movements, the IAAM's political affiliations omitted the major political parties. Here its adherents included the Labour Party as well as the Socialists and Communists and the Northern Irish SDLP as well as Sinn Fein, a minor party in the South, though of course by the mid-1980s, a major force in Northern Ireland.

The two main Irish political parties, Fianna Fail and Fine Gael refrained from corporate affiliation though they did not discourage their own deputies from joining. As late as 1984 the executive reported that 'neither Fine Gael nor Fianna Fail have responded positively to requests to commit their

parties more actively'.[89] There were other gaps in the movement's affiliation. Despite the presence of clergymen within the organization's executive
and list of sponsors and despite assertive participation by 'hundreds' of
priests and nuns in a vigil in 1980 to protest against the Irish rugby tour of
South Africa[90] as well as in other IAAM public demonstrations, the IAAM
had to struggle to obtain affiliations from churches and religious organizations. As the 1977 annual report noted: 'Churches are slow to commit
themselves...The Churches have yet to be convinced of the need to
actively combat racism and apartheid.' The report suggested that congrega-
tional attitudes at the time might well have been influenced by the killing of
missionaries in the war in Zimbabwe.[91] In 1974, though, the IAAM did
succeed in persuading the Irish Jesuits to divest themselves of South African
related shareholdings.[92]

Even so, Asmal's growing stature at Trinity—he was appointed dean of
arts in 1980—and his sociability helped to ensure that the Movement's
individual membership crossed all party lines, from left to right, embracing
senior party notables in the *Dail* as well as novice politicians in local
government. Fine Gael's Garret FitzGerald was an early adherent and
continued to attend and even preside over IAAM conferences during his
term as foreign minister between 1973 and 1976. One of his much later
successors as foreign minister, Dermot Ahern, joined the IAAM as a Fianna
Fail city councillor. FitzGerald resigned from IAAM in 1984 after Kader
Asmal refused to prohibit Sinn Fein members from joining as did Bishop
Donal Lamont, the former Bishop of Umtali who had joined the IAAM on
his return to Ireland. Disagreements about Sinn Fein were one cause of the
rift between Asmal and Conor Cruise O'Brien. This rift became public in
1985 after O'Brien's repudiation of his earlier support for the academic
boycott and his acceptance of an invitation to lecture at the University of
Cape Town. Local student groups disrupted O'Brien's classes in both Cape
Town and Johannesburg, the first time that there had been any organized
opposition inside South Africa to academic visitors. Sinn Fein's affiliation
remained a sensitive issue within the IAAM and in 1985 Kader Asmal felt
the need to stress in a letter to a Limerick member his 'own revulsion at the
activities of Sinn Fein and its associates'.[93]

What was the impact of the Irish Anti-Apartheid Movement? Until the
1980s it failed to achieve definite changes in official policies. In 1986, the
Irish government closed its tourist office in Johannesburg, though *Aer
Lingus* which opened a South African office in 1968 maintained a presence

in South Africa throughout the remaining decades of the apartheid era, ending its flights to Johannesburg only in 1996. The government also maintained its reciprocal no visa agreement with Pretoria.[94] Mary Manning and her colleagues as well as trade unionists more generally could take the credit for Ireland's announcement in December 1986 that the government would halt South African food imports, about half the total of South African imports into the country. The Electricity Supply Board stopped buying South African coal, though imports to private customers were uninterrupted. South African textile imports also continued, however, and Irish food exports were unaffected and actually rose sharply through the 1980s, a reflection of the government's sensitivity to the interests of the Irish meat producers.

Farmers had a history of militant protest against threats to their often precarious livelihoods. For example a three-week demonstration by farmers outside parliament in Dublin in 1966 enjoyed very evident public sympathy.[95] Faced with a choice no Irish government would oppose farming lobbies. The lukewarm endorsement of the Dunnes strikers' actions by politicians and trade unionists may have reflected a consciousness of the growing significance of South African–Irish economic links during the mid-1980s recession. By 1983 Ireland had built up a positive trade balance with South Africa and Irish exports included significant sales of new industrial manufactures: computers and pharmaceuticals. Irish exports to South Africa rose steadily through the three decades of the IAAM's existence, reaching £57 million in 1988.[96] Additionally, through the 1970s South African firms had accumulated significant Irish investments, in certain cases receiving encouragement and inducements from the Irish Industrial Development Association, despite IAAM protests, and assurances from the government in 1972 that there would be no further visits to South Africa by IDATU officials.[97] Dunnes Stores' 'acting secretary' and main industrial relations trouble-shooter at this time, Noel Fox, served as the Irish contact person for a London based group 'Doing Business in South Africa'.[98]

During the 1970s and 1980s increasing numbers of Irish sportsmen, entertainers, and artists held back from visiting South Africa as a consequence of the IAAM's embargo. In 1986, Trinity College and University College refused to allow their staff leaves of absence to travel to South Africa, a policy also adopted by RTE, unusual instances of institutional employer support for the academic and cultural boycotts. Subsequently the Department of Education warned universities it would expect them to 'have regard to government policy in their approach to dealings with South Africa'.[99] Much earlier, in 1971, Trinity had also divested itself of any South African-connected shareholdings. In general, the IAAM was rather successful in persuading Irish intellectuals to support its embargo on cultural contacts of any kind with South Africa, as early as 1964 persuading twenty playwrights including Samuel Beckett and Sean O'Casey to refuse to allow performances of their work in South Africa. In 1986 South Africans were excluded from an international conference on information processing held in Dublin, the World Computer Congress, after trade unions threatened action if the South Africans attended. Throughout its history, the IAAM picketed or in other ways actively opposed any efforts by South African employers to recruit Irish workers. In 1975 with the help of trade unions the IAAM opposition persuaded the South African Electricity Supply Commission and Philips South Africa to abandon their Dublin interview schedules. Though the IRFU maintained its commitment to playing against South African teams until the late 1980s, the IAAM was rather more successful with respect to other sporting codes, including boxing, ploughing, cricket, tug-of-war, and golf. Trade union antipathy to particular events in which South Africans were scheduled to participate was often the decisive consideration. The 1989 announcement by the IRFU that they would cease sending teams to South Africa was after a computer company threatened to withdraw £500,000 sponsorship.[100]

Well before IAAM's formation, the Irish government had begun to move away from its historical affinities with Afrikaner nationalism. Whereas in 1953, Ireland was still willing to despatch an official representative to the tercentenary celebrations of white settlement in South Africa, by 1956 one year after its admission to the United Nations its representatives were voting in favour of General Assembly condemnations of apartheid. One year later, Conor Cruise O'Brien, as the Irish delegate, was actually willing to co-sponsor such a resolution. As in the case of Sweden and of several other small countries, by the 1950s, Ireland geared its foreign policy increasingly to supportive engagement with international organizations and this strategic orientation encouraged Irish UN delegates to align themselves with the Afro-Asian bloc in the General Assembly. Such an alignment was also understood as a corollary of Ireland's official perception of itself as a postcolonial society. As the head of the Irish UN delegation noted in 1958, South Africa could be perceived to be 'giving the coloured people the kind of treatment Cromwell gave the Irish'.[101]

Irish officials were predisposed to offer rhetorical condemnations of apartheid at the United Nations. As an IAAM report in 1972 conceded, 'Irish voting at the United Nations is far in advance of other Western nations.'[102] However official opposition to apartheid was subject to limits. Dublin was ready to host a South African trade mission in 1961 and through the rest of the decade Irish governments repeatedly reiterated their reluctance to adopt any economic sanctions against South Africa. Dublin re-negotiated a trade agreement with South Africa in 1967, the year it began to make regular annual contributions to the United Nations Trust Fund on South Africa. The initial purpose of these grants was to maintain the Irish delegation's standing within the General Assembly. The Department of External Affairs announced the donations in a public statement every year, on 21 March, Sharpeville Day, which, as in Britain, the Irish Anti-Apartheid Movement marked with annual commemoration.

Kevin O Sullivan's research in the Irish state archives indicates that IAAM began to have a serious impact on policymakers in 1969, during the rugby tour protests. In October 1969, Noel Dorr, an official with the Irish delegates at the United Nations, wrote home to his colleagues to warn them that 'recent developments in Dublin on the question of our attitude to Apartheid . . . [make the] question likely to be particularly sensitive this year'.[103] Such warnings notwithstanding, Jack Lynch's Fianna Fail government refrained from exerting any pressure on the Irish Rugby Football Union though President De Valera, normally a keen rugby fan, declined his invitation to Lansdowne Park. The following year, though, the minister of trade for industry and commerce, Conor Trachtaa, would announce that in future, the Irish Export Board would send no more missions to South Africa, the first official concession to IAAM lobbying.

From 1973, a Fine Gael–Labour coalition included five active members of Anti-Apartheid within its cabinet. Fine Gael's foreign minister, Garret FitzGerald, resisted appeals from the Labour Party caucus for his government to offer funding to liberation movements. Conor Cruise O'Brien, then the minister of posts and telegraphs, was especially opposed to such a move, influenced by his hostility to armed republicanism in Northern Ireland.[104] Even so, with Garret FitzGerald's appointment, Irish officials became freshly receptive to IAAM advocacy. FitzGerald himself entertained an IAAM deputation at Iveagh House. In 1973 he would overrule senior officials in his department and advise his colleagues in defence to withhold leave from a soldier who was proposing to join a hockey team touring South

Africa. The same year he also forbade entry into Ireland for the Rhodesian team that had been invited to attend the World Ploughing Championships. Ireland had recently joined the European Union and under FitzGerald's ministry, departmental officials developed a new strategic conviction that Ireland should use its 'special relationship' with ex-colonial territories to build bridges between Europe and the Afro–Asian block. One requirement of such an undertaking would be that Ireland should do what it could to discourage European policies that strengthened apartheid.[105]

Similarly, in the 1980s, another Labour and Fine Gael coalition, between 1982 and 1987, supplied Anti-Apartheid with fresh opportunities to influence official policy. In 1984 Barry Desmond, by now minister of health and welfare issued a circular to all the regional health boards instructing them to cease any purchases of South African supplies.[106] As we have seen, the Labour Party's Ruari Quinn, responding to public sentiment generated by the Dunnes strike, announced a partial embargo on agricultural exports from South Africa and later in 1986, the deputy foreign minister received a second IAAM deputation at Iveagh House, this time including two senators and three deputies. The 1986 legislation was the strongest explicit opposition to apartheid any Dublin administration would offer. After 1987 a new Fianna Fail government much more predisposed to local agricultural and business interests was unlikely to extend sanctions to embrace Irish exports. However Irish governments continued to channel overseas development aid to Southern African 'front-line' territories. This was a budgetary choice that its own officials acknowledged was an expression of official anti-apartheid commitment. Indeed former front-line states today constitute five of the seven African 'priority countries' to which the Irish government directs its aid programme. Today Irish official empathy for the developing world has become an important component of Irish public conceptions of national identity, explained as the historical outcome of a colonial past. Official solidarity with Southern Africa, beginning in the anti-apartheid era, is just the most recent in a succession of 'imagined appropriations' from the sub-continent that have helped to enrich and reinforce Irish nationalism since the Anglo–Boer War.[107]

The IAAM's influence within the Irish political establishment was partly a consequence of its skilful exploitation of traditions of republican affinity between Ireland and South Africa. As an early leaflet noted, 'the Irish people have always opposed oppression. As the first country in this century to take up arms for national freedom, the African people look especially to us for help.'[108] Its emergence out of a trade boycott prompted its initial emphasis on building relations with Irish trade unions. Shifts in Irish society resulting from the expanded provision of secondary education also helped the Movement, especially during the 1980s, as its following expanded on university campuses and within schools. In 1974, the inception of an Irish programme of development aid reflected growing prosperity and an increasingly export-oriented economy. As Ireland's official and commercial contacts with the developing world proliferated, its relations with Pretoria cooled. The association of a succession of important Irish diplomats and foreign policy makers with the IAAM was not coincidental

Overall, the Irish contribution to South Africa's growing international isolation though significant because of the extent to which it reflected political commitment within Ireland was hardly decisive. Trade between the two countries represented a small share of both countries' imports and exports and, as we have seen, actually increased during the 1980s, the decade during which the IAAM enjoyed widest support. Certainly, the Irish government's willingness to impose (very selective) restrictions on South African trade after 1986 set it apart from the majority of European countries and in this respect the Irish joined the Dutch and the Nordic governments in helping to shape European Community policies. Sporting isolation certainly affected white South African morale, especially after the end of foreign rugby tours, and after a ban announced by the International Rugby Board in 1984.

Did the Anti-Apartheid Movement leave a long-term impact upon the politics and institutions of its host society? It certainly helped to open up previously fairly closed arenas of policy making. Foreign policy up to the 1970s was especially insulated from civic pressure and Anti-Apartheid's successes in obtaining access to ministers and other senior officials in this domain established a precedent. In the mid-1990s, the Department of Foreign Affairs established a standing committee in which its staff could assemble with NGO representatives to address human rights concerns in foreign policy, an institutional legacy of this breakthrough. Despite the qualifications in Irish government commitment to anti-apartheid measures, the public pressure that the IAAM mobilized probably encouraged Irish officials' perceptions of Ireland's diplomatic role as 'a mediator between Europe and the developing world'.[109]

In Ireland, Anti-Apartheid was an unusually sustained and vigorous protest movement. From time to time it succeeded in attracting large numbers of assertive supporters as well as more widespread public sympathy, as during the efforts to oppose the 1970 rugby tour or during the 1984–1986 Dunnes strike. It seems quite likely that such a long-lived and well-supported movement may have helped to incubate wider networks of civil society activism despite the determination of its ex-patriate South African leadership not to take up local causes. On a small island with a tightly knit community of public intellectuals different activist causes would draw upon the same group of notables for their leadership and sponsorship and in doing so must have helped to shape and reinforce each other. Especially obvious in this respect are the overlaps in leadership between Anti-Apartheid, the Irish Council for Civil Liberties (ICCL), and the Northern Irish Civil Rights Association (NICRA). Kader Asmal, a founder and chair of the ICCL was one of two main speakers at the foundation meeting that assembled the groups that would form NICRA, delivering an address on 'Human Rights: International Perspectives'.[110] Northern Ireland civic activists explicitly acknowledge the degree to which they were influenced by African-American struggles. As Bernadette Devlin has recalled: 'Many of us weren't even aware that we lived in ghettos until we discovered the black ghettos and said, that's our position.'[111] Asmal's presence at the Belfast meeting in November 1966 suggests that the external sources of inspiration through which Northern Irish activists were beginning to reinterpret their experiences may have been wider still. Today in Northern Ireland the exhibition display at the Museum of Free Derry suggests that the television and newspaper reports of the Sharpeville shootings helped to make local people 'increasingly alert to the wider world' and to similarities between their own grievances and those of other disenfranchized communities.[112] In the late 1980s and early 1990 NICRA veterans played a key role in promoting 'track two' diplomacy initiatives in South Africa, bringing together South African and Northern Irish politicians so that the Irish leaders could learn lessons from the South African experience of negotiations.[113]

Did the movement have further social and cultural consequences? Did it affect public attitudes? Irish commentators suggest that ever since Irish republican mobilization against the Anglo–Boer War, within Ireland 'civil society has been characterised by a remarkable level of awareness of international issues', attributing this predisposition to the global social connections fostered by successive waves of Irish emigration.[114] From this perspective Anti-Apartheid animated existing republican traditions of anti-colonial solidarity. There may have been more complicated dynamics at work, though. Just as Peter Hain's Stop the Seventy Tour became a focus for a wider generational rebellion on British student campuses, the cause of IAAM was sustained by and expressed broader kinds of social disaffection. In 1969 opposition to a cricket tour was directed not by the IAAM but rather by a Coordinating Committee Against Racialism, a coalition 'of various left wing groups'. It used much more aggressive tactics than the IAAM would have sanctioned: smoke-bombs and pitch occupations.

In 1970, anti-apartheid mobilization was nurtured by an iconoclastic current of Irish radicalism, a brief springtime for an Irish new left, 'when Cuba seemed a reasonable model to Irish intellectuals, and when the Front Square of Trinity College Dublin had been occupied by the Maoist Internationalists setting out their stall'.[115] Even the Labour Party contested the 1969 election of a left-wing manifesto predicting that 'the seventies would be socialist'. Disappointing electoral returns and subsequent coalition arrangements with Fine Gael turned the Labour Party rightwards ensuring that for the ensuing decades Irish left-wing politics would have no significant party bases. In this setting activist solidarity movements might have functioned as proxies for domestic radical politics, in the same fashion as happens today in the case of the Irish support for Palestinians. And from time to time such agencies could project an especially compelling appeal to groups whose interests during the 1980s were very likely to be neglected by mainstream political parties. This is what happened in the cases of the Dunnes strikers, mostly young women whose resolve not to handle South African fruit was prompted by their resentment of an especially intrusive managerial style. Their protest challenged existing patriarchal conventions in a society in which women were relatively recent entrants to the industrial labour force and were absent from most leadership echelons in public life. Significantly, the Special Branch officers who warned off Mary Manning called the strikers 'silly little girls'. In other ways too, anti-apartheid solidarity was an expression of and helped to reinforce changes in public conceptions of Irish social identity as the country began to embrace more inclusive and more egalitarian notions of a citizenship based on civic rights rather than ethnic essentialism.

★

In 1989, a few months before President de Klerk announced his willingness to un-ban the ANC and negotiate a transition to democracy, the Washington-based Investor Responsibility Research Centre (IRRC) conducted an assessment of the impact of sanctions. As we have seen, the economic isolation of South Africa was the primary purpose of the international anti-apartheid movement. In North America, the anti-apartheid movement played a critical role in persuading state governments and institutional investors to withdraw from South African financial engagement and without pressure from the movement the Western European and North American governments would probably not have adopted even the symbolic sanctions they enacted in the 1980s. As importantly, though the original British Anti-Apartheid Movement's first efforts to encourage a boycott of South African trade failed to reduce South Africa's foreign trade significantly, it performed an agenda-setting function for policy makers and it certainly prompted the South Africans to direct resources into costly evasive measures.

The IRRC investigation remains one of the most authoritative evaluations of the economic and political effects of sanctions. The economic assessment was based upon analysis of official South African foreign trade statistics. The IRRC's findings suggest that by 1989 sanctions or the threat of sanctions had imposed heavy costs upon the South African economy. From the 1960s onwards, the government had invested heavily to reduce South African dependence upon imported technology and oil, an effort that in the long-term imposed its own penalties, reducing growth significantly from the 1970s onwards. To an extent though, this effort had been successful. South Africa had become increasingly less dependent upon imports and meanwhile its main exports, precious and strategic minerals, were unaffected by sanctions and unlikely to be so. The South African products that were the focus of anti-apartheid trade boycotts—fruit and vegetables—were of minor significance. However through the 1980s it was becoming increasingly evident to South African business elites that the government's strategy of gearing manufacturing to local markets had led to technological stagnation. Moreover in this decade, particularly with the cessation of fresh American investment, replacing outmoded technology was becoming much more difficult. In this respect, therefore, Anti-Apartheid's targeting of divestment as a campaigning issue was decisive. South African heavy industry still depended upon imported machinery to manufacture its products. In 1989, then, the IRRC investigation concluded that sanctions were still a long way from imposing crippling effects on the South African economy—the economy actually grew by 3 per cent per annum in 1987 and 1988. However business leaders were increasingly alarmed about the future costs of economic isolation. In 1988 a report commissioned by one of the main mining houses noted how sanctions 'were beginning to have an adverse effect'. In particular, 'the expansion of the South African economy is being restricted by the continued absence of substantial capital inflows'.[116]

Awareness of sanctions' effects extended well beyond mining house boardrooms. The IRRC's opinion polling found that two-thirds of its white South African respondents agreed that sanctions would very likely have harmful effects upon the economy, though a rather larger majority also believed that despite the damage sanctions might inflict, the economy would 'cope'. However, sixty per cent favoured various kinds of reforms if these would result in the lifting of sanctions. Only a minority, it is true, 18 per cent, were ready to embrace the prospect of direct negotiations with the ANC. Nearly half of the white respondents supported power-sharing arrangements in which racial groups could still protect their 'lifestyles'. The IRRC's authors concluded that whites generally recognized the severity of external economic challenges but this recognition did not 'translate directly into a feeling of vulnerability'. How important, then, were sanctions in helping to bring about South Africa's democratization?

In his autobiography, F. W. de Klerk is dismissive about sanctions, conceding they damaged the economy but arguing that the costs they imposed were broadly accepted among whites. Even so, de Klerk distinguishes between the effects of formal sanctions and the consequences of divestment and capital flight and suggests that for his administration regaining access to foreign capital markets had become a priority.[117] The views of de Klerk's finance minister, Barend du Plessis, offer corroboration: in 1990 he told journalists that disinvestment played a critical role in the abandonment of apartheid.[118] Jan Heunis, a senior civil servant in the office of the presidency in his memoirs believes that the 'major reason' for de Klerk's embrace of transition politics was that 'the country... was about to be brought to its knees by the combined efforts of the international community'.[119] This may not have been a view de Klerk shared, though. Positive inducements or incentives for reform may have been more important than sanctions in persuading de Klerk to begin his liberalization. In particular he evidently believed that the fall of the Berlin Wall had weakened his adversaries decisively, enabling the government to negotiate from a position of strength.[120]

Focusing on de Klerk's perceptions might well be taking too foreshortened a view. During the later years of the Botha administration there was plenty of evidence of the limiting effects of sanctions in various fields. For example, the arms embargo had led to a shortage of spare parts for the airforce's Mirage ground attack fighters, half of which were grounded by the time of the battle of Cuito Cuanavale. In this confrontation in Southern Angola, South Africa's declining air superiority was very evident.[121] With respect to finance, a refusal in 1983 by the International Monetary Fund to grant additional funding to South Africa was a consequence of legislation pushed through Congress by the Black Caucus and the consequent expansion of South African short-term debt probably prompted President Botha's repeal of the pass laws at the beginning of 1986, rewarded one year later with a comparatively lenient debt rescheduling. During the 1980s South Africans were certainly increasingly conscious of the threat posed by American sanctions. As one American observer noted: 'Every grunt, whisper or sneeze of the US Anti-Apartheid Movement is covered breathlessly—and derisively—by the South African media.'[122] Economic sanctions certainly helped to create domestic incentives for reform, especially when corporations seeking to deflect political pressures set their own terms for amelioration. This was the case with the Sullivan Principles, a code of conduct that many American companies adopted in response to campus protests across the United States in reaction to the Soweto rebellion. Even outside the domains of vital national interests, sports sanctions may have helped to weaken support for official segregationist policies among white South Africans.[123]

That the government in 1990 recognized that the ANC could exercise an effective veto over any prospects of reform acquiring local and international legitimacy was mainly attributable to its domestic popularity within South Africa and international prestige. The ANC's guerrilla offensive was largely an essentially symbolic or theatrical 'armed struggle', easily contained by the police and army but it was a major source of inspiration for more spontaneous and localized kinds of popular insurgency. On the whole, anti-apartheid movements offered little or no direct support for the ANC's military operations: in this respect the Dutch engagement in Operation Vula was exceptional. Indeed the arguments for sanctions were often projected by anti-apartheid activists in a way that suggested that sanctions might help to avert a large scale military confrontation, as indeed they did. Certain governments as a consequence of anti-apartheid lobbying helped to finance the ANC's welfare and educational activities. In particular the funding the

Swedish authorities supplied was on a scale comparable to the support the ANC received from the Soviet Union.

For those black South African political leaders who were significant beneficiaries of international civic opposition to apartheid, this opposition had significant effects on their own strategic predispositions. The degree to which South African leaders committed themselves to racial reconciliation during the negotiations and the extent to which they have maintained that commitment was very substantially the consequence of international solidarity for their cause. As Robert Price has noted, the sources of the most significant support that South African exiles could tap were mainly countries whose leaders were white Europeans. In such settings, as noted above, the ANC's 'multi-racialism' that it inherited from its alliances in the 1950s was an asset.[124] Support in western countries for the struggle against apartheid represented a key incentive in the ANC's retention of a secular open 'non-racial' vision of citizenship as well as helping to govern the organization's deployment of violence against civilians. The relatively open societies in which many ANC personalities were to establish new homeplaces may also have shaped their later political predispositions as well. Kader Asmal himself was to play a key role in both Mandela's government and its successor, first as minister for water affairs and later as minister of education. Asmal was also a major contributor to the ANC's acceptance of a liberal constitutionalism, joining the organization's negotiating team shortly after his return to South Africa in 1990. In his second career as a South African politician, Asmal continued to be influenced by his Irish experience, citing Irish constitutional legal precedents and the experience of rural electrification in the 1920s as sources of inspiration. Asmal is not exceptional: in Britain and Ireland, the United States and in Europe, the hospitality offered by anti-apartheid movements helped to nurture a reciprocal political civility that may yet be its most important legacy.

7

Sharpeville and Memory

I kabot Makiti was seventeen when he joined the crowd outside the police station in Sharpeville on 21 March 1960. He had just joined the Pan-Africanists, still a schoolboy. Subsequently, he came of age while serving a prison sentence on Robben Island between 1963 and 1968 for his contribution to clandestine efforts to rebuild the PAC in Sharpeville. Fifty years later he was interviewed by journalists in the week preceding the massacre's anniversary, one of the few remaining loyal Pan-Africanists still living in Sharpeville. Though he had joined the march early in the morning and so initially he was at the forefront of the assembly in Seeiso Street he was not present when the shooting began. He remembers being 'told that we would get our answer at 1.00 pm'. He was hungry and so he went home to eat, returning just in time to hear the police begin firing. 'We were not armed', he insists, 'so I didn't know what was going on. When I got closer I saw images that today still bring me pain.'

> There was blood everywhere. People were running, but they didn't know where to go because there were three helicopters circling above them. My legs could not move. People were falling, crying. Some tried to run but they were shot in the back and fell. They were helpless.[1]

Makiti mentioned helicopters in another of the interviews he gave. He recalled a red helicopter. 'All I heard', he recalled, 'was the rat-a-tat-a-tat of machine guns and the wailing of ambulance sirens, and a red helicopter which flew surprisingly low.'[2]

There are no contemporary reports of helicopters flying over Sharpeville that day. The police did not use helicopters until much later, in the 1970s. The only aircraft present were the military Harvard trainers that so signally failed to impress the crowd earlier that morning. Makiti's recollections are sufficiently precise to be persuasive, though. He definitely heard and saw helicopters. And indeed helicopters do feature in Sharpeville's violent history. Helicopters accompanied policemen and protestors in the open spaces of Sharpeville but not on that day in 1960. Rather they were in attendance on another day, nearly twenty-five years later, when the people of Sharpeville reassembled to take their protest to authority. That day there were helicopters and if Makiti's memories conflate the two occasions that is surely excusable, for in Sharpeville on Monday morning, 3 September 1984, history appeared to be repeating itself.

Over the weekend, teenagers—children even—were on the streets, visiting houses from door to door. They belonged to the Congress of South African Students (COSAS), a body which through its very name was intended to evoke historical memories for an earlier political generation. People should stay away from work on Monday, their young visitors urged householders. There would be a meeting and they would march to the administrative offices in nearby Sebokeng, they said, to demand that the authorities abandon the rent increases they had imposed recently. All the townships around Vereeniging would be joining the strike: Sharpeville, Sebokeng, Bophelong, Boipatong, and Evaton. A meeting in Evaton had made the decision to call for the stay-away the previous week, on 26 August. Subsequently, public assemblies in each of the five townships had acclaimed the decision. The rent increases would be stopped. People should pay only an affordable rent, thirty Rands a month. Councillors should resign. If they failed to then residents should boycott their businesses.

Before dawn on Monday there were pickets at the bus stops and the railway stations in the townships around Vereeniging, just as there had been nearly twenty-five years earlier, in 1960. Indeed on Sunday the door-to-door canvassers needed to address historically rooted apprehensions. During their house-to-house visits the day before:

> the older people advised the children that it is dangerous to confront people like this because we know what happened in 1960 when we were facing the police and they opened fire. They might open fire again. The children replied, 'No, this is not 1960, this is 1984. You can't talk about what happened in 1960. What we are doing now is different from that.'[3]

In Sharpeville that Sunday there were alternative sources of authority to supply guidance to young activists. If police evidence is to be believed, Tom Manthatha, a leader of the Soweto Civic Association, spoke to a group that had gathered in St Cyprian's Anglican church. It was now time, he told them, for the councillors to leave their posts. If they refused 'they should be attacked with stones and set alight'. 'You have the power', he continued, 'but you don't know how to use it. We must make the councillors resign. We asked them to resign, we asked them not to increase the rents but they did not listen.' In the subsequent trial, defence lawyers contested the veracity of this evidence though prosecutors countered such arguments by insisting that the evidence was based on a police report submitted immediately after the meeting before any subsequent events might have prompted the authorities to doctor the record.[4]

Despite the anxieties of older residents, large groups began to gather in the streets in each of the townships. People who attempted to board buses were stoned. Already at this stage, detachments of riot police were present in each of the townships around Vereeniging. During the night police fired upon and killed three teenage boys in Bophelong. In nearby Sebokeng there was an early morning confrontation between police and COSAS members when the activists tried to halt a yellow police personnel carrier, a 'Nyala' they mistook for a mobile ticket van. The police inside the vehicle opened fire but no one was hurt. In Sharpeville early in the morning a procession began to move through the streets, walking up the main thoroughfare, Seeiso Street, on its way to the municipal buildings where Sharpeville residents normally paid their rents. As one participant remembers, 'this was a march about rent, not politics', and the only symbols people carried were homemade placards bearing the single Zulu word, *asiminali*, we have no money.[5] Police attempted to disperse the procession with rubber bullets and tear gas but after scattering, the marchers reassembled into smaller groups. One of these groups chose a route that took them past the dwelling of Councillor Khuzwayo Jacob Dhlamini. As they reached his house the councillor appeared in his doorway. The marchers shouted at him. He must come out of his house, they called, he must join their protest. Dhlamini pulled out a gun and started firing his weapon. The police then arrived and the crowd dispersed but reformed after the police left. Dhlamini walked out of his house to confront his adversaries for a second time. A volley of stones brought him down to the ground. Soon Dhlamini's house was on fire. He meanwhile was forced inside his car and the vehicle too was set alight. He would die later from his burns and other wounds.

As the COSAS canvassers had assured the householders, this time it would be different, for this was not 1960 and two decades later neither repressive nor insurgent violence could be expected to have the same effect in demobilizing public protests as it had then. On 15 September, a COSAS guard of honour would escort forty-two coffins in a massive funeral, the biggest public assembly locally since 1960 to bury the casualties of various confrontations with the police in the five Vaal townships. The death tally that week was in fact higher for there was no public mourning for the murdered councillors. In Sharpeville, Petrus Tom suggests, Councillor Dhlamini's death engendered not shock but jubilation:

> We went to see what was happening. Dhlamini's corpse was lying outside in the street next to his car which had been overturned. His house was burning, his car was burning, and he was also burning beside his car. Everybody was ululating and shouting, 'Oh they've made a Kentucky Fried Chicken out of him'.[6]

In Tom's memoir the main agency in these events is supplied by children. It was children who set the houses alight and who killed Jacob Dhlamini. When the police fired tear gas and rubber bullets into the crowd 'we ran away'. The children also ran, Tom tells us, but in different directions, 'they went on to other places'. They burned bottle stores and official buildings, erecting barricades of burning tyres, 'to stop the police from getting through to the places that were burning'. At the mass funeral on the 15th, Father Patrick Noonan, Sharpeville's Catholic pastor observed how 'the service was . . . supercharged with youth practically dominating the whole proceedings'. After the service:

> Once again, as in all similar occasions, the large youth presence leads and controls the funeral procession. Teenage girls and young women with high-pitched voices in new rhythmic chants encourage their menfolk forward not only towards the cemetery but also in the struggle for liberation of every last black brother and sister.[7]

For the time being, though, older residents were willing to take their marching orders from the youngsters and were more occasionally ready participants in the carnage. A similar sequence of events affected each of the five black townships encircling Vereeniging. Acccording to another eye-witness report in Evaton the houses of both the mayor and his deputy were burned down. After the conflagration, the rioters rejoiced. Mayor Sam Rabotapi fled the township. His gown was worn by an elderly women. She now 'danced in the streets and called herself the first mayor'.[8]

Until the South African Defence Force deployed 7,000 soldiers and policemen in an invasion and occupation of the Vaal townships in

'Operation Palmiet' on 24 October, Sharpeville and its sister settlements would represent the epicentre for an insurrectionary rebellion that through the remainder of the decade would engulf South Africa. The revolt would continue despite initial concessions by authorities on 6 September. On this date 5,000 people assembled in front of a police cordon in Sebokeng. Behind the police there arrived a group of officials that included four cabinet members on a tour of riot areas. The assistant police commissioner accompanying this group persuaded local managers to meet a delegation chosen by residents and at a subsequent encounter Vereeniging's town clerk promised that the rent increases would be deferred. By now such measures were beside the point, for in the words of Patrick Noonan, 'it was in the streets, the homes and the churches of the Vaal triangle where arguably the final solution to the scourge of apartheid was hammered into place'.[9]

Once again we need to address questions about the local dynamics of rebellion. Why did South Africa's final decisive 'liberation revolution' begin 'in earnest'[10] in and around Sharpeville specifically? What considerations can explain the extraordinary authority that teenage activists could command here? And why did collective civic action slip so quickly into such brutally retributive killing? Finally, were events influenced by communal memory of the earlier confrontation between policemen and the residents of the Vaal townships, more than two decades before? Or was the location of what activists were swift to label 'The Second Sharpeville' simply coincidental, in no way a re-enactment shaped by historical engendered action repertoires?

★

Just as had been the case twenty-five years before, at the beginning of 1984 the authorities believed the Vaal townships to be orderly and disciplined communities. In 1976 during the Soweto students' uprising, the townships around Vereeniging experienced only occasional ruptures of routine. Altogether, the Cillie Commission of Inquiry noted seventy-five incidents in the Vereeniging magisterial district, most of them quite minor including twenty-four arson attacks on schools, public buildings, and councillors' homes. Of this total only eight occurred in Sharpeville including three school-burnings and a riot when disgruntled spectators were refused their money after a last minute cancellation of a football fixture. In his report, Judge Cillie noted that the unrest around Vereeniging was less severe than in most other affected centres. In Sharpeville 'most of the adult inhabitants . . . were not prepared to take an active part in the riots', in fact they cooperated in guarding local schools against attacks 'of their own accord'.[11] Parents did indeed keep their children at home, one local resident recalled later, explaining to them, 'No. They shot your father, they shot your uncle, don't tell me about the struggle, we saw it in 1960. No.'[12]

Amongst white South African officials, black communities the Vaal region enjoyed a reputation for political docility and orderly conduct. In the aftermath of the Soweto rebellion, the Vaal Triangle Community Council was the first of these bodies to be established following the enactment of the Community Council Act in 1977. Community Councils replaced the advisory Urban Bantu Councils and could enjoy executive powers that would be transferred to them from Administrative Boards at the discretion of the minister. In the case of the Vaal the elected council administered a R27 million budget and allocated accommodation and trading sites.[13] Local administrators were proud of their achievement in operating the new municipality's accounts on a profit basis, a record attributable to an 'economic rentals' policy requiring seven annual rent rises between 1978 and 1984 taking rents from around R12 a month in 1977 to R62 at the beginning of 1984. These increases helped to pay for electrification of the township's houses and for the construction of water-borne sewage facilities, undertaken after 1977, as well as the building of another six schools, bringing the total to fifteen. The Community Council was in turn replaced by the Lekoa Town Council (LTC) in elections in January 1984, the first fully fledged black local authority created under the 1982 Black Local Authorities Act. It was elected on a 14.7 per cent poll, low certainly but in fact indicating considerably more vigorous local participation in the elections than was the case elsewhere, especially in Sharpeville.

In 1977 the LTC's predecessor, the Vaal Triangle Community Council was also initially elected on an unusually high turnout, twenty per cent. Local officials and councillors were accustomed to political acquiescence and at the end of June 1983 they decided to begin the new council's term with the announcement of another rent rise, R5.50, maintaining that residents could easily afford this new imposition. Local workers, they believed, were comparatively well-paid. In fact, market research conducted in the following few months indicated that per capital incomes amongst black people living around Vereeniging were well below any national average and moreover the cost of living was rather higher and rising rapidly, by 13 per cent since the previous year.[14] A survey conducted in July 1983 by COSAS activists among 800 residents in the Lekoa townships suggested that 'high rents' was the prevalent grievance.[15] About half of the 60,000 black households in Lekoa were in rent arrears by the beginning of 1984.[16] Whatever else its causes, the apparent docility of Lekoa's new citizens had nothing to do with economic well-being.[17] But quite aside from the material hardship that the new rents imposed the succession of increases for older residents may well have represented a breach of faith and hence an injustice. Both in Sharpeville and in Sebokeng, residents recalled that twenty years earlier the authorities had promised that if they paid their rents for many years, after a time they would be expected to pay only for services. Then they would become owners of their houses and they would no longer 'be owing rent'.[18]

Below their surface calm, the politics of Lekoa's communities may well have been complicated by turbulent subterranean channels for quite a long time. In 1971 and 1972, an evidently lively cluster of youth organizations constituted themselves in Sharpeville, including the Vaal Youth Club, the Sharpeville Cultural and Health Club, the Sharpeville Youth Club, and the Sharpeville Students' Association. Though the Students' Association appears in the Black Community Programme's *Black Review* it was certainly not among the more rhetorically militant adherents of Black Consciousness. As well as seeking to promote 'a spirit of togetherness and brotherhood amongst the students of Sharpeville', the Association's aims and objectives included 'contact' with 'local bodies such as the Urban Bantu Council with a view towards establishing relations'.[19] Most Black Consciousness affiliates would have disdained any dealings with any of the 'sell-outs' represented in what they called derisively the 'Useless Boys' Club'. It is of course possible that Sharpeville's youth organizers hoped that through professing these aspirations they might deflect any hostility from the authorities. If this was the case they would soon encounter the limits of official tolerance. In 1973 the police detained five young South African Students' Organisation (SASO) activists for a month and later one of them, Nkutseou Matsau, was convicted under the Terrorism Act for publishing a poem and a newsletter, both considered by the court to be likely 'to engender feelings of hostility between black and white'.[20] Joyce Mokhesi thinks the SASO branch had been in existence at least since 1971: she attended an occasion when SASO members took young people to the cemetery to tidy the graves and to listen to a speech from the poet Don Mattera.[21]

This police action may have effectively decapitated local activism in the period immediately preceding the Soweto uprising. It is likely though that the PAC succeeded in re-establishing a presence in the Vaal townships in its aftermath if not before. Ikabot Makiti and a surviving group of the Tsolos' original recruits tried to reconvene the local branch as a clandestine organization. In 1960 Ikabot had originally joined the PAC while attending Kilnerton High School where he was a boarder: he was at home visiting his parents on the weekend before the massacre. He knew the Tsolo brothers well, though, and joined one of the local Task Forces canvassing support for the anti-pass protest on Sunday night. He was not among the local PAC supporters who were arrested after the massacre and he returned to school where he continued to attend secret PAC gatherings. In early 1962 pupils at Kilnerton went on strike over food grievances: the school closed down and students were sent home after refusing to return to class: in Ikabot's words 'We were young; we thought we could do anything.' Ikabot obtained a job at African Cables and rejoined a small cluster of Pan-Africanists still active at the factory, people who had constituted a second echelon layer of leadership, mainly classmates of Nyakane Tsolo. They heard about *Poqo* activities in the Transkei—specifically the Bashee Bridge murders—and in early 1963 resolved to travel to Maseru to obtain instructions from Potlake Leballo. Ikabot and four companions did indeed visit Lebello's headquarters and they received their marching orders but on their way back they were arrested, at the railway station in Bloemfontein. The police were checking the documents of passengers travelling from Maseru: 'they had a list and they knew who to arrest'. Ikabot and his comrades were escorted back to Vereeniging where they were questioned by local Special Branch officers after being identified by Sergeant Wessels from the Sharpeville police station, still the local officer in charge, as he had been before the massacre. As secretary of the clandestine branch, Ikabot had kept lists and records and these the police unearthed at his home, though luckily he had not identified individuals by their full names. Six young men, Makiti included, were convicted of continuing the activities of a banned organization, for which offence they would serve a five-year sentence on Robben Island. On the island, Makiti would finally encounter Robert Sobuwke. He and his fellow members of the labour span that worked outside the prison compound were escorted past Sobukwe's cottage each evening on their journey back to their cells. Once in response to their passing, Sobukwe emerged from his cottage. They could see him, fifty yards away, standing outside his door. He stooped down, reached for a handful of soil and then stood up again, letting the soil trickle through his fingers: 'Izwe Lethu' (Our Land).

On their release, three of the Sharpeville Pan-Africanists were banished to Witzieshoek, later the Qwa Qwa homeland, on the border of Lesotho. Makiti and the other two were allowed to return home. One of Makiti's comrades, Samuel Mokudubete, 'the small one', who returned to Sharpeville after serving his sentence, lived with his parents under strict police surveillance. He was stabbed to death at Park Station in Johannesburg in 1970.[22] Makiti himself found work at a factory and began once again to assemble support for the Pan-Africanists. In 1970 he began convening regular meetings every Sunday, using as a venue the old migrant workers' hostel on the border of the township. Amongst those who attended was a later PAC secretary-general, Thami ka Plaatjie, then a schoolboy in Evaton. Makiti remembers that his group kept themselves well separated from any emerging Black Consciousness affiliates. Through the 1970s and 1980s, though, it became increasingly difficult to enlist new recruits he recalls, especially when old rivalries between the ANC and the PAC resurfaced: 'People were worried about being called spies.'[23]

Resettlements in the 1960s may in any case have helped to disperse many of the remaining Pan-Africanists in Sharpeville, for from 1967 a significant proportion of residents of the site and service scheme as well as young married couples and sub-tenants were re-housed several miles away in the new township of Sebokeng in its zones 11 and 13. The chief director of the Sebokeng Development Board was John Knoetze, the same John Knoetze who in 1960 had so effectively helped Pan-Africanists in Bophelong contain the crowd on the day of the anti-pass protest. According to Father Noonan, Knoetze was the primary agent in the Vaal townships' pacification in the 1960s. In particular, 'the cumbersome relocation of communities to Sebokeng tended to have a palliative effect'.[24]

In June 1978 the police claimed that they had unearthed a nationwide conspiracy implicating members of an organization called Young Christian Workers (YCW). In their round-up the police arrested thirty young men and women, several of them residents of Sharpeville, Evaton, and Sebokeng. Police may have seen the YCW as an offshoot of the Young African Christian Movement, an interdenominational welfare organization set up in December 1975 'to bring youth back to the church and keep them away from drink', though the original YCW was a Roman Catholic youth movement, active in Soweto in the 1950s.[25] Court evidence suggests that this body supplied an organizational front for Zephania Mothopeng's efforts to begin a Pan-Africanist renaissance in Kagiso outside Krugersdorp.

According to Patrick Noonan, one of YCW activists detained at Vereeniging, Cosmos Thokoa, after his release and on his return home to Sebokeng became 'a secret member' of the PAC.[26] In 1978, two Krugersdorp women were convicted of undertaking arson attacks on the homes of state witnesses in Zeph Mothopeng's trial: they were active in a body called Christian Youth Workers.[27] The similarities in nomenclature indicate that each of these bodies may have accommodated Pan-Africanist revivals. However the arrests may well have shifted the balance of ideological affiliation among young activists, for it was a well-attended meeting of the Young Christian Workers in Sharpeville in March 1980 that hosted invited COSAS speakers enacting a local launch for 'Charterist' ANC-oriented activity.[28]

These developments seemed to have remained quite confined in their influence, though. As one resident observed in 1980 to Craig Charney, an unusually inquisitive visiting journalist from The Star, 'people are passive here' though any eruption of submerged anger if it came to the surface could be 'twice as bad as Soweto'. But people kept such feelings well hidden. Local residents told the same visitor that what kept Sharpeville quiet was the memory of 1960, reinforced by a strong police presence. 'People are afraid', a priest explained. To underline his point, one of the people Charney interviewed was questioned about the encounter by Administration Board officials the next day. During his day in Sharpeville, the Star's correspondent could find no one 'who would admit to being present at the 1960 shootings, though the crowd ran to 1000s'.[29] He also encountered grudging approval of some of the local councillors, perhaps a reflection of the local personal popularity of soccer manager George Thabe, leader of the Lekoa People's Party, a former personnel manager at African Cables, and first mayor of Lekoa. After his displacement as mayor in 1981, Thabe started to oppose rent increases, a factor that may well have helped to sustain his reputation amongst older people.[30] Lingering local endorsement of 'system' politics in Sharpeville was evident in the 1983 poll when ward number 27 attracted a 42 per cent turnout, by far the highest throughout the Lekoa townships.[31]

By 1982, though, a fresh set of local associations appeared to signal a reawakening and realignment of political activity in the Vaal townships, in conformity with national trends, bringing activists in the region into the broad church of organizations that would soon affiliate into the United Democratic Front. In certain respects, though, Sharpeville's parochial politics represented resistance to the regional trend. In his memoir, Patrick Noonan recalls that 1982 was an 'incubation period' of 'new political thinking'. In particular, he suggests, the ANC's Radio Freedom broadcasts were finding a receptive local audience. Using the relatively sheltered venues supplied by churches, his own premises in Sharpeville among them, new organizations began to assemble: indeed as he puts it, 'the churches became sites of political dissent in the Vaal'.[32] Amongst teenagers and younger men and women, it seems, any residual Pan-Africanist and Black Conscious networks of affiliation were eclipsed by the new sources of political inspiration supplied by the COSAS, established in the Vaal region in October 1980 and by 1983 drawing a following of 400 pupils at six schools. The Vaal Civic Association (VCA) held its launch in October 1983, holding a public meeting at the Nyolohelo Catholic Church in Evaton, simultaneously announcing the local inception in the Vaal region of the UDF—constituted by the Civic Association, COSAS, and a Vaal Organisation of Women. The Civic Association would be joining the UDF as a 'first level organization . . . because we have the same ideologies': the terminology used by the spokesmen of 'first level' and 'second level' suggests quite close familiarity with the strategic perceptions of top-echelon UDF leadership in which struggles around local grievances would build support for more ambitious 'national democratic' political assertions.[33] At its formation the Civic Association identified the principal grievances to which it would direct opposition: 'continuous increases in rentals, students turned away for failing at school, and too few pension pay out days'.

The Lekoa Council's announcement in June of another rent increase occurred in an increasingly excitable political climate. In January 1984 a decision by local education authorities to prohibit reenrolment at schools of pupils over-age as well as a succession of lock-outs of rent defaulters supplied fresh sources of grievance, as well as, in the case of the over-age pupils, a new cohort of disaffected unemployed youths, recently politicized through COSAS's classroom crusade. In Sharpeville, the blame for the rent increases was especially easy to personify for Jacob Dhlamini announced the increases at a mass meeting summoned for the purpose. Dhlamini was already an unpopular personality, mainly because of the way he used his control over local housing allocation: 'Dhlamini would get people out and get you a house if he liked you.' At the meeting a women tried to remonstrate with Dhlamini, wagging her finger at him. 'He became very angry and told her never to do that again, or else.'[34]

In Sharpeville, though, the Vaal Civic Association's 'area structures' competed for neighbourhood leadership with an organizationally autono-

mous Sharpeville Anti-Rent Committee (SARC) initiated by members of
the Black Consciousness-oriented Azanian People's Organisation. One of
SARC's leaders was the Anglican priest Tebogo Moselane, a friend of Steve
Biko when he attended university and also active in a local branch of SASO
in the early 1970s. SARC held weekly meetings on Sundays through August
at the Anglican church. Later the Sharpeville Anti-Rent Committee would
rename itself the Sharpeville Civic Association (SCA). By the end of August
the Sharpeville Civic Association had emerged as the most influential
organization within the township and its leaders decided to join the Vaal
Civic Association's protest by leading a march to Sebokeng so that Sharpeville residents could participate in the more generalized protest that was to
be undertaken by the Vaal Civic Association. Despite their willingness to
work with the wider civic body, the Sharpeville leadership was politically
different, connected with or engaged in Black Consciousness trade unions
and political organizations.[35] Several of the Sharpeville trade unionists,
Petrus Tom included, were veterans of the shop-floor organization that
the Tsolo brothers had helped to build at African Cables in 1959 which had
supplied the Pan-Africanists with their original local organizational nucleus.
In 1974 Tom became a shop steward at African Cables for the Engineering
and Allied Workers' Union (EAWU), taking all the other members of the
Liaison Committee with him into the union. EAWU adhered to a black
leadership line that by 1980 put it in the Black Consciousness labour camp,
though its origins in the Urban Training Project might have inclined it
earlier to eschew political activity. In 1982, though, the Metal and Allied
Workers' Union (MAWU) won over most of the EAWU branches around
Vereeniging, including at African Cables. MAWU was affiliated to the non-
racial Federation of South African Trade Unions, at that stage also still
holding back from any political alliances. Councillor Dhlamini, incidental-
ly, worked at African Cables as a personnel manager and in May 1984 he was
widely blamed in the township when a hundred workers were dismissed,
unfairly people believed. Dhlamini as a member of the council's housing
committee subsequently sanctioned the eviction of some of these workers
from their houses for rent arrears.[36]

The relatively strong presence of experienced trade union leaders in
Sharpeville both Black Consciousness predisposed and otherwise may help
to account for the relative independence of the Sharpeville Civic leadership.
For increasingly it was to find itself at odds with the other UDF affiliates.
From its inception the Sharpeville leadership disagreed among themselves

about whether they would undertake court action against the rents, a route that might have been suggested by the local history of successful ligation by trade unionists, or oppose them through 'peaceful protest', that is through boycotts and demonstrations. In November 1984 the police detained the more militantly predisposed SCA leaders including Tebogo Moselane, leaving the way clear for the advocates of litigation who in March 1985 were reportedly still collecting funds to pay the legal costs of fighting the rental increases in court. They were also engaged in meetings with the town clerk, in defiance of a VCA proscription of any negotiations until the police released the eighty or so activists arrested during Operation Palmiet. The SCA leaders were unabashed. Those who were detained, they said, were being held because of their politics: 'we are not political, we are not affiliated to any political organization'. For good measure they expressed disapproval of the COSAS 'agitators' who were preventing their children from going to school.[37]

Let us try and make sense of these political cross-currents in Sharpeville. After 1960, surviving networks of political activity were disrupted by dispersal of part of the township's population to their new homes in Sebokeng. Ten years later, a fresh cohort of politically conscious youngsters constructed a dense cluster of Black Consciousness organizations but these were speedily suppressed by the police. Though the Vaal townships remained relatively calm during the 1976 Soweto rebellion, Sharpeville became a key location in the PAC's efforts to revive its presence in South Africa between 1975 and 1978: these were again curtailed by the police. By this stage within the community a group of trade unionists, mostly men in their thirties and forties, probably embodied the most respected and experienced source of community leadership. Some of these had a history of earlier engagement with the Pan-Africanists but by the late 1970s the trade unionists were divided in their organizational and political affiliations. Memories of the 1960 massacre as well as more recent police activity had an especially inhibiting effect on older generations of residents in Sharpeville and consequently when civic leadership emerged they disagreed among themselves over tactics. A dominant faction within the SCA was disinclined to embrace wider political solidarities and preferred litigation to 'mass action'. These considerations would certainly have made it very difficult for passively predisposed older leaders to exercise any kind of disciplining influence over the aggressive behaviour of COSAS's teenage fraternity. A significant proportion of COSAS's following in the Vaal townships was constituted by the 'push outs', people who had been forced to leave school. Inevitably membership of the 'comrade community' would have over-lapped with a locally entrenched criminal gang sub-culture.[38]

Sharpeville's politics then was organizationally incoherent. There was more obvious unity of purpose between the older generation of civic leaders and politicized youth in other Vaal townships—or at least whatever latent differences that may have existed never found their way into newspapers and, as we shall see, Sharpeville remained unusually divided as a community compared to its neighbours, divisions attributable to the absence of decisive leadership. But even in the other Vaal townships, civic leadership was comparatively new and inexperienced, and by September it was shallowly rooted in the communities it purported to represent. In March 1985 the VCA only had around 100 activist members—six months earlier it was no more than a network of committees, one in each of the five townships. The Vaal's vanguard position in South African insurrectionary politics in the mid-1980s was not a consequence of especial organizational preparedness. Rent protests were widespread across the country in earlier months through 1984 and Tom Manthatha's speech suggests that excitable language was unexceptional but only here did such protests culminate in such a violent confrontation.[39] As in 1960, it was a combination of especially aggravating local conditions, politically animated youngsters, and the relative absence or weakness of older more cautious communal leaders that was to prove to be so combustible on 3 September 1984.

What were these local conditions? There were the issues identified in the protest: a succession of unusually steep rent charges in a setting in which household incomes were below average and in which other living costs were comparatively high. These concerns are important but probably insufficient to explain the scale and ferocity of protest. After all, as Noonan points out, despite their poverty at this time, members of his congregation in Sharpeville willingly paid increases in their parish dues. If the increases had been imposed by an impersonal Administration Board they might have engendered a more resigned reaction. After 1977, though, the rentals were imposed by locally elected councillors rather than white civil servants. These councillors moreover were very evidently beneficiaries of their office. In 1983 for example nine out of the twelve liquor licences awarded by the Orange-Vaal Administration Board were given to community councillors. The rewards for incumbency multiplied after the election of the Lekoa Town Council in January 1984. The new mayor of Lekoa, Esau

Mahlatsi, secured another twelve licences for himself and members of his extended family.[40] Corruption seems to have peaked in the months before the Vaal uprising for in early 1984 discontented councillors not aligned with the dominant faction attempted to pass two motions of no-confidence in the Lekoa Council based on complaints about corruption.[41] Petty venality was not a new feature of South African township administration but it does seem that the new powers accorded by the 1982 Black Local Authorities Act allowed councillors to breach the boundaries of local public tolerance of official rent-seeking. Meanwhile rapid expansion of secondary schooling in the previous few years was followed by the exclusion of over-age pupils and their subsequent expulsion into a sharply contracting local labour market, for a nationwide manufacturing recession imposed an especially heavy toll on the heavy-industry-based Vereeniging economy. In this situation, unemployed youngsters were very ready to perceive rental increases as personal infringements. As one teenager in nearby Tumahole told a researcher:

> I was washing clothes in the yard when I saw many people marching in the next street. I went to see what was going on . . . I joined the march because I saw the placards against high rents. I though it was better if my parents spent that money on me. We had very little money to buy clothes and things. That is what encouraged me to join the rent issue.[42]

As had been the case in 1960 a sense of relative deprivation helped to ratchet up an appetite for confrontation among teenagers politicized by classroom-based nationalist organization. This kind of sociology was not unique to the Vaal townships. What was unusual though is the degree to which 'children' were in command of events during the opening days of the rebellion, a reflection of a particular local propensity amongst elders to abdicate political leadership, itself a consequence of an especially politically repressive local history. To an exceptional extent, though, and for very understandable reasons, older people in Sharpeville were 'afraid'.

These considerations may help to explain why civic indignation escalated into collective passion when Councillor Dhlamini pulled out his gun. In the aftermath of the uprising the authorities charged six Sharpeville residents who participated in the protest with 'common purpose' complicity in the killing of Dhlamini. The charge was based on a legal doctrine which finds its argumentative parallel in theories of collective violence that suggest that crowds behave unreflectively, that when people join crowds they lose their

individuality and become intellectually degraded while at the same time
through the emotional 'contagion' engendered by physical proximity they
are empowered to undertake actions they would normally shrink from.[43]
Moreover, 'aroused groups need certainty, not doubt' so the decisions taken
by groups are often more extreme than many might have taken as individuals.[44] Activist accounts of Dhlamini's killing seem to share these assumptions about the way in which when people are gathered in a crowd 'the
effect of numbers is to impart to all a sense of their sudden, extraordinary
and uncontrollable power . . . [an] awareness that leads them to commit acts
that would individually condemn'.[45] As the correspondent for SASPU
National reported: 'What happened then was a result of people's anger,
they were closed out, they couldn't get any solution to their problem, let
alone communication.'[46] Anger of this kind could still be discerning,
however. As Joyce Mokhesi, sister of one of the 'Sharpeville Six', observes:
'If the people of the Vaal were merely a mindless mob, not only would the
violence have been random, and scores of people murdered amid rumours
of individuals informing for the system, but residents would never have
organized themselves to clean up the debris and rubbish created during the
uprising.'[47]

   There is testimony, though, to suggest that not every member of the
assembly gathered in front of Dhlamini was uniformly predisposed to
violence and that not everybody underwent the kind of emotional transformation that arguably encourages people in a collective to abandon normal
moral restraints. One of the 'Sharpeville Six' defendants, Duma Khumalo,
later told his story. He said he 'followed' rather than joined the procession
to Councillor Dhlamini's house. This statement is different from his trial
testimony in which he maintained he was coerced into participating in the
demonstration. He believed that the intention was to frogmarch the councillor to the administrative offices. On approaching the councillor's house,
Duma Khumalo saw Dhlamini firing his gun. People ran for cover and he
tried to help someone who had been wounded in the foot by a rubber
bullet. Later in his trial one witness testified that he had seen Duma pouring
petrol through a window of the councillor's house. Another claimed that he
had witnessed Duma pushing Dhlamini's car out of the yard before the fires
started. But Duma throughout would insist on his innocence. He told the
court that he tried to save Dhlamini's car when the house was already
burning, an action that probably helped to incriminate him.[48] Dhlamini
was a kinsman of Duma and 'he had no quarrel with him' he told the court

in his evidence.[49] Dhlamini was killed through being repeatedly 'hacked and stabbed'.[50] None of the Sharpeville Six accused of complicity in his death were seen carrying weapons before the violence and there was no creditable evidence implicating them directly in Dhlamini's murder. Obviously, though, Dhlamini's assailants were armed at least with knives.

Jeremy Seekings has suggested that in South African townships during 1984 increasing levels of conflict 'provided opportunities for, and attracted, chronically violent people' and that increasingly 'youth politics began to engage "undisciplined" non-student groups including street criminals who often armed themselves with knives. For especially marginalized young men violence was compensatory, a means through which they could assert power and acquire status.'[51] Subsequent events would indeed demonstrate that in Sharpeville networks of youth activism embraced criminal syndicates and it is likely that the 'push-out' on to the streets of over-age school students helped to accelerate this process.

In which ways did Sharpeville's history shape events that day? Is there any sense in which the confrontation between crowds and authority can be represented as a reenactment? Did collective memories of the massacre and accompanying events shape these developments more than two decades later? It is possible. Position-holders in activist echelons in the Vaal in 1984 and afterwards may have been inspired or influenced in their commitments by their own family history. At least a few had parents who had belonged to the PAC's local leadership or following in 1960. For example, Thami Zondo worked for the Detainees' Parents' Support Committee when he was himself detained in Sharpeville in 1985. In prison he was visited by Captain Steyn, 'the one', Zondo recalls, 'who had kept my father Michael under surveillance ever since the 1960 massacre'. Then his father, Michael Zondo, had belonged to the Pan-Africanists.[52] One of the Vaal Civic leaders, Lazarus More, was a kinsman of Thomas More, the Sharpeville PAC's secretary in 1960. The exiled Pan-Africanists worked hard to construct an association between their organization and participants in the 1984 rebellion, for a while recruiting Joyce Mokhesi, sister of Francis Mokhesi, one of the Sharpeville Six, to issue a condemnation in their name of International Defence and Aid (IDAF) for failing to support legal representation. In fact IDAF did pay for the lawyers as well as helping the families of the accused, though Joyce Mokhesi may not have known this.[53]

It is more likely, though, that if the PAC enjoyed any local influence it was through more subliminal kinds of recollection. In the ways in which activists tried to build their movement and elicit public support for it in 1984 there are many similarities between their tactical repertoire and the methods used by their fathers nearly twenty-five years earlier. As in 1959 and 1960, organizers in Sharpeville initially adopted a discreet style of operation: 'Our strength, our base, is built more by house meetings than mass meetings.'[54] In 1984 the SCA held its first public meeting in the Anglican church, the same venue used for the launch of the PAC's branch in Sharpeville. On the morning of 3 September, a first concern of the activists was to stop the buses just as it had been among Sharpeville Pan-Africanists on an earlier Monday morning. Of course these tactical echoes could be coincidental, the common sense dictated by activists' local knowledge of the particular configurations of their lived in setting, but they may also have been the effect of local folk memories or less consciously transmitted ritualized patterns of behaviour.[55] What we do know is that the outbreak of rebellion itself created a setting in which previously hidden memories could be given public expression.

Outside Patrick Noonan's sacristry in Sharpeville in the days that followed the rioting one of his parishioners 'had graciously installed' a patio: this was now Noonan noted in his diary, 'the first ever illegal memorial to the Sharpeville dead of 1960 and the Vaal dead of 1984'.[56] Four years earlier, as we have seen, no one in Sharpeville was willing to speak to visiting journalist Craig Charney about the massacre, he could encounter no one who had witnessed the event. Now there was a new climate in which people could once again communicate with the dead. On Christmas Day 1984, thousands of residents from Sharpeville and the other Vaal townships heeded an appeal from COSAS and the Youth Steering Committee to visit the cemetery and help clean the graves of victims of the massacre.[57] Thereafter, the observation of 21 March as an anniversary date became a communal reflex. On 20 March 1988, for instance, police disrupted an 'illegal gathering' at Sebokeng Methodist church, held to remember the Sharpeville massacre and to launch the Vaal Student Congress.[58]

The subsequent history of the townships around Vereeniging was to be punctuated by explosive cycles of confrontation between heavily armed policemen and protestors. Funerals often supplied flashpoints for further confrontation as on 24 October 1984 when mourners returning home from Sharpeville's cemetery after burying Lenny Isolene, a sixteen-year-old shot dead by police the previous week, were themselves ambushed by a detachment of *sjambok*-bearing policemen. The police pursued the mourners back to their homes beating them. Detentions and the authorities' intermittent deployment of soldiers to support the police in house-to-house searches helped to prevent major instances of coordinated protest for the remainder of the decade: the last ambitious civic undertaking was an 'Operation Clean-Up' in which residents collected refuse and loaded it onto specially hired lorries, a measure to compensate for the authorities refusal to maintain the normal schedule of rubbish collections, a penalty imposed for the rent boycott. The boycott itself continued: no rents would be paid in Sharpeville and its sister townships for another decade. As well as the six bystanders under prosecution for common purpose, the authorities charged another seven local residents with treason, alongside members of the national UDF leadership ensuring the removal and isolation of the strongest civic leadership from local developments.

In 1987, the authorities felt sufficiently confident about the degree of local order they had re-established to arrange a special visit to Sharpeville by the state president, P. W. Botha. Local residents remained indoors, though, and children from farm-schools in outlying vicinities were bused in to constitute a welcoming reception. This was despite efforts by Military Intelligence to establish pro-government loyalist Eagle Youth Clubs through the Vaal townships: in Sharpeville apparently the various inducements offered to local organizers only succeeded in a modest enlistment of around twenty people.[59] More adult groupings proved to be equally ephemeral: for a while a body calling itself 'Concerned Residents of Sharpeville' circulated pamphlets attacking priests and trade unionists for deceiving the people.[60] Independent survey research in fact indicated impressive levels of support for civic activism and trade unionism. A random sample of 1,155 adults in Lekoa's townships, 314 of them Sharpeville residents, indicated that two-thirds of the respondents belonged to a trade union or a community organization, that 27 per cent had attended a meeting of the Vaal Civic Association, and that more than half of them supported it. One quarter of the sample confirmed that they lived in a neighbourhood in which the VCA had organized Street Committees.[61] Meanwhile the PAC's insurgents were returning to their historic bases. Indeed in 1986, PAC publications claimed that in that year alone APLA units killed ten policemen in Sharpeville alone, in five operations.[62]

Richard Wilson, a British social anthropologist who conducted fieldwork in Sharpeville, supplies a bleak portrait of the township's development during the years that followed Nelson Mandela's release in 1990 and the unbanning of the ANC and the PAC. Both movements reestablished organized followings around Vereeniging but the Pan-Africanists were soon to be eclipsed by their old rivals. In particular, ANC-sponsored 'Special Defence Units' (SDUs) seized command of Sharpeville's streets, with local units sometimes naming themselves after liberation heroes— Slovo, Samora, and Castro—but also taking their titles from local gangs: the Germans, the Italians, and the Untouchables, whose networks and membership they absorbed into their own ranks. Originally intended to function as an anti-crime militia, the SDUs were swiftly drawn into armed political hostilities, first with the local Pan-Africanists and then more significantly with hostel-based branches of the Inkatha Freedom Party (IFP), which at that stage was setting up its own armed units among Zulu-speaking migrant workers in the Vaal with the help of the police and the army. IFP members at the KwaMadala hostel killed forty residents in a single massacre in neighbouring Boipatong on 17 June 1992, probably assisted by local police.

SDUs would also find themselves at odds with *Umkhonto we Sizwe* cadres, two hundred of whom returned to their homes around Vereeniging in late 1990. Understandably they were disinclined to defer to the political authority of delinquent teenagers. Wilson describes a conflict that accelerated during 1993 into an 'all-out war' between the homecoming soldiers and the feral 'Young Lions' in the SDUs, the latter blamed for thirty-six murders, eighty-four robberies, and twenty-one rapes in Sharpeville alone between May and October 1992. In the course of 1993 *Umkhonto* members eventually forcibly disarmed the errant SDU group, by this stage organized into a sixty-strong gang, the Germans.

Richard Wilson undertook his fieldwork in Sharpeville in 1996 in an environment still polluted by the lingering hatreds generated by these hostilities. Despite the Germans' enforced demobilization, 'Sharpeville was still a "no-go area" where no one organization, and certainly not the ANC, had complete control.'[63] In this vein, Wilson narrates the harsh story of the murder of Dennis Moerane, a former Sharpeville street criminal who to avoid family sanctions took refuge in the KwaMadala hostel helping IFP groups to carry out attacks on his former associates in the SDUs. Later he gave evidence against the IFP at the Goldstone Commission and joined the ANC while living at the YMCA in Johannesburg. In 1996 he started visiting his family with the permission of the Germans who controlled the section of Sharpeville where he lived. The protection they offered was insufficient, though. On Christmas Day he was found tied to a lamppost in front of Sharpeville's public library, his body stabbed and riddled with bullets. Two years later Dennis Moerane's killer was convicted, a soldier in the new Defence Force and an ex-*Umkhonto* combatant. In Sharpeville, national liberation had brought little comfort, and as Wilson was reminded by one his informants, here 'there are no politics any more: all that is left is political grudges'.[64]

★

Hundreds of grim local histories that parallel Sharpeville's troubled intro-duction into the era of South Africa's enfranchized democratic polity supply the underpinnings of the grand narrative of South Africa's insurrectionary political transition between 1984 and 1994. We traced the preceding stages of this history in Chapter Five, breaking it off at the time of the formation of the United Democratic Front.

Reforms prompted the UDF's establishment. In 1982 the Black Local Authorities Act extended the powers of elected African municipalities. The following year a new constitution replaced the existing exclusively white House of Assembly with a 'tri-cameral' legislature in which coloured and Indian voters would be represented in separate chambers. Africans remained excluded from central government. On 8 January, Oliver Tambo an-nounced 1983 to be 'The Year of United Action'. All democratic forces, Tambo urged, should merge 'into one front for national liberation', a call that was echoed by internal leaders in the weeks that followed. Eight months later, the UDF assembled. The UDF's leadership included many veteran ANC notables and increasingly it assumed the authority of an internal ANC surrogate. A federal hierarchy of committees linked a net-work of 600 or so organizations. These included local 'civic' organizations that had recently mushroomed in black townships in struggles to win improvements in services. The UDF's proclaimed purpose was to challenge the constitutional reforms. Soon, though, its affiliates were swept up in a tide of often violent insurrectionary opposition to the extremely corrupt local governments in African townships, sparked by heavy rent increases for public housing.

As we have seen, the rebellion began with rent strikes in the townships around Vereeniging. In the Vaal military occupation curtailed activism, but the rebellion spread. The movement's explosive energy was attributable to the combination of inflation and unemployment. Of black eighteen–twenty-four-year-olds, 80 per cent were unemployed in 1986 and inflation was accelerating. Economic downturn fatefully coincided with the govern-ment's efforts to legitimize its authority. The rent strike remained one of the UDF's more effective weapons, enduring through a state of emergency that between 1986 and 1988 succeeded in halting most of the open forms of militant politics. As the ANC's strategists had hoped, the UDF's activist culture was informed by a rediscovery of Congress traditions and inspired by the martial theatre of *Umkhonto*'s armed struggle. At the ANC's Consultative Conference, held in Zambia in June 1985, ANC leaders announced it was time to move to a 'Peoples' War' that would conclude in the 'seizure of power'. Now, 'the risen masses' would be turned 'into organised groups of combatants' while an externally trained 'core' would function as an 'officer corps'.[65]

In the eighteen months following the conference, *Umkhonto* stepped up operations. In 1986 guerrillas struck 228 times. Almost 160 guerrillas were killed or captured, one-third of *Umkhonto* losses since 1977. The escalation probably reflected wider weapon distribution: at the beginning of 1987 for example, teenage 'comrades' protecting rent boycotters often possessed sidearms, evidence that guerrillas were indeed equipping local 'mass combat units'. This may help to explain attacks on targets such as shopping arcades, though in October 1988 the ANC released a statement forswearing attacks on civilians. In 1989, the final year of *Umkhonto* operations, the number of attacks peaked at three hundred.

By then the ANC's commitment to arms had a long history. Early on, prospects for a generalized rebellion in South Africa appeared remote. Between 1964 and 1975, the year it began to rebuild its internal organization, the ANC's survival depended upon the quasi-official status it received from certain African governments, a 'representative' authority that enabled it to maintain base facilities in Tanzania and Zambia. In 1976, as organized anti-apartheid resistance expanded in the wake of the schoolchildren's uprising, it became easier for the ANC to build a disciplined following inside South Africa but even so up until the end of armed operations, most of the ANC's organization was located outside South Africa.

To a very large extent, then, externally derived resources sustained the ANC's revolt. These resources included accommodation from African governments. Between 1977 and 1989 Angola supplied military facilities. Angolan willingness to provide camps was especially important because it was exceptional. Until 1969 the Tanzanians had hosted *Umkhonto* but were dissuaded from further hospitality of this kind by South African pressure, though the Tanzanian government then granted land for the ANC to construct a training college. Meanwhile, Mozambique allowed the ANC to supply and reinforce guerrillas across its territory and until 1984 *Umkhonto*'s operational command located itself in Maputo. The Botswana authorities tacitly allowed guerrillas to cross its territory on the way to South Africa. Without this sort of cooperation, the ANC would have been unable to develop a significant presence inside South Africa.

Soviet support was also crucial. The Soviet Union provided the main training facilities for *Umkhonto* from 1969 until the opening of the Angolan camps in 1977. Soviet aircraft also transported *Umkhonto* units from Angola to Tanzania and Uganda after the closure of the Angolan facilities in 1989.[66] Soviet advisors helped train soldiers in African camps as well. The Soviet government began giving the ANC substantial financial help from 1963, $300,000 that year and tens of millions over the next three decades.[67] As importantly, the Soviet Union supplied weaponry at a time when no other governments were willing to do so though as we have seen Nordic governments funded the ANC's Tanzanian college and the Dutch joined them in financing educational and welfare work. Soviet assistance was probably partly prompted by great power competition in Africa, though Southern Africa was never a region of particular concern to Soviet strategists, South African official claims to the contrary notwithstanding. During the 1980s, public sympathy for the ANC in Western Europe and in North America became increasingly important, not so much because of voluntary financial contributions, though these were substantial, but mainly because public opinion persuaded governments and corporations to impose financial sanctions upon South Africa. As we know, the British Anti-Apartheid Movement, growing out of an early trade boycott campaign that began in 1959, was the first base of what was to develop into a remarkable pan-European new social movement, often drawing into its national leaderships key members of political and social elites.

ANC exiles often played a major role in setting up anti-apartheid groups, particularly in Britain and Ireland, the two countries where the movement was strongest. Here, the existence of a South African diaspora, often white, generally well-educated, and comfortably established in elite professions, helped the ANC make useful connections. The ANC's commitment to 'multi-racial' politics in the 1950s ensured that when its members went into exile they would be accompanied by people with ready access to middle-class occupations and influential social networks. In 1969, the ANC allowed whites, Indians, and coloureds to join the external organization, formalizing what was already a very close association between its own leadership and non-African allies. White, Indian, and coloured members of the Communist Party had joined *Umkhonto* at its inception. The Anti-Apartheid Movement represented an important base of support for the ANC during its insurgent phase but as a generally liberal constituency it may have also influenced the ANC to limit the scope and intensity of violence, through eschewing terrorism for example.

The 1976 Soweto uprising created new opportunities for organizing armed insurgency. Because of the range of resources available to the ANC, its leadership was able to exploit these opportunities much more effectively than any of its rivals. Equally important, though, in helping to sustain the rebellion were broader structural developments. Arguably, in the 1960s armed rebellions failed to elicit widespread public participation because even black South Africans experienced a measure of economic security. By 1980, for the South African authorities, ensuring security and order was very difficult. In contrast to the 1960s, when real GDP growth averaged around 6 per cent, by the 1980s GDP growth had contracted to around 1 per cent a year. Stagnant employment meant that every year increasingly large numbers of school leavers joined the unemployed: by 1986, among economically active Africans living outside the homelands, one in five was unemployed.[68] Most of these unemployed were relatively well-educated young people, for secondary education had expanded very quickly through the 1970s, more than trebling its enrolments between 1975 and 1984.[69] Among sixteen–twenty-four-year-olds it is likely that only a small minority succeeded in finding work. This generation was more open to modern political ideas than their parents' and less likely to find authority intimidating. They were less respectful not just of the authorities but of older people in general and among them sociologists encountered a ready propensity to use violence as 'a means of procuring scarce material resources'.[70] They had no personal memories of the political repression of the 1960s. It was the disaffected youthful cohorts that grew up in this setting that supplied the ANC with its recruits. More widely this generation's rebellion was expressed by a rising tide of violence that accompanied most instances of political protest (whatever the intentions of the UDF's political leadership) and which, as in Sharpeville, could also express itself in criminal violence. Between 1976 and 1994, around 24,000 people died as a consequence of politically motivated violence. Only a few hundred of these deaths could be directly attributed to insurgent guerrilla activity.

At its peak, guerrilla warfare scarcely represented a serious threat to South African security.[71] In October 1986, the ANC circulated to its national command centres a sober assessment. 'Despite all our efforts,' it argued, 'we have not come anywhere near the achievement of the objectives we set ourselves.' ANC structures inside South Africa remained too weak to supply reliable support for *Umkhonto*.[72] South African police continued to anticipate with precision the arrival of trained guerrillas from across the border, an indication of their success in infiltrating *Umkhonto* command structures, especially in Swaziland.[73] In the field the average survival period for guerrillas was six months, according to an *Umkhonto* officer's estimate.[74] Meanwhile South African 'destabilization' of neighbouring countries made it increasingly difficult for the ANC to maintain supplies and reinforcements. In April 1989 the ANC was compelled to move its guerrilla training facilities back to Tanzania from Angola, a consequence of the Namibia–Angola Peace Accord. By this time it was obvious to most ANC leaders that, in Secretary-General Alfred Nzo's words, the ANC did 'not have the capacity to intensify the armed struggle in any meaningful way'.[75]

From 1986 onwards, ANC spokesmen began to refer to the prospect of a negotiated accession to power. In September 1985, a meeting between ANC leaders and South African businessmen in Zambia represented an encouraging signal that powerful interests inside South Africa were willing to contemplate a change of regime. Here Thabo Mbeki, the head of the ANC's international office, explained the ANC's nationalization policies to the South African visitors: 'monopoly capital', including the press, would fall under public control but 'beyond that private capital would exist'. However nationalization might be Zambian style, with a 51 per cent state holding, leaving plenty of room for big companies. Within a few months, ANC references to negotiations were implying a very different form of political transition to the 'seizure of power' envisaged in the ANC 'Peoples' War' strategy. By January 1986, a senior ANC leader was telling the London *Observer* that the objective of the 'offensive' was 'breaking up the power structure'. 'We are not talking of overthrowing the government', he conceded, 'but [of] turning so many people against it that it would be forced to do what Ian Smith had to do'.[76] With a proliferation of contacts between the ANC and representatives of different interest groups within South African civil society, the likelihood of such a scenario was becoming more and more plausible.

In December 1985, from prison, Nelson Mandela initiated an increasingly ambitious schedule of talks with members of the government shortly after
the first contact between the external leadership and South African officials.
In mid-1986, ANC leaders offered a qualified endorsement of a negotiating
framework developed by the British Commonwealth's Eminent Person's
Group. The first meetings between the ANC and the British and American
governments in 1986 and 1987 and the embrace of sanctions by American
policy makers similarly encouraged perceptions that negotiations represented a viable route to 'national democracy'. 'National democracy' itself
began to be reframed so that it represented a much less alarming prospect for
white South Africans than the transitional order envisaged by Communists
as late as 1986.[77] Kader Asmal helped draft a set of constitutional guidelines
and economic principles. This was published by the ANC in mid-1988 and
suggested a political system that would retain many existing laws and
personnel. Economic prescriptions omitted any specific commitments to
nationalization.

Shifts in the ANC doctrine were matched by a sharp turnabout in South
African government strategy prompted by the mounting costs of backing an
insurgent movement in Angola and defending a quasi-colonial administration in Namibia. South African soldiers withdrew from southern Angola in
1988 after an internationally brokered agreement in December by Pretoria
to cease supplying and reinforcing UNITA in return for the removal of
ANC bases from Angola. Shortly afterwards, Namibian politicians began to
negotiate a constitutional settlement that would bring into power the
ANC's ally, SWAPO. Meanwhile, the implementation of sanctions by
formerly friendly governments as well as the Republic's exclusion from
financial markets appeared much more immediately alarming than the
increasingly untenable vision of a Soviet-sponsored revolutionary advance
enveloping the sub-continent, the major threat traditionally perceived by
official South African strategists. By 1989, as we have noted, with the
blocking of South African access to international capital markets, the government was in severe financial trouble. In 1989 a 21 per cent budget
increase was to be funded by raising taxation; by 1989 individual mainly
white tax payers were supplying sixty per cent of government revenue.

New leadership brought fresh vision. On 2 February 1990, President
F. W. de Klerk opened parliament with a speech he had written out by
hand. In composing his address, de Klerk was influenced by at least three
considerations. He knew from the recent election that most whites favoured

political reform that would incorporate black South Africans as fellow citizens. Secondly, the fall of the Berlin Wall 'created an opportunity for a much more adventurous approach than had previously been conceivable',[78] in particular an ANC without any further prospect of Soviet support might be a much weaker adversary, one that the government and its allies might realistically compete with in open electoral competition. Friendly exchanges with conservative administrations in London and Washington helped convince de Klerk that liberalizing South African politics would win him strong diplomatic support. Accordingly, in parliament he announced a series of measures that effectively reversed history. The government would legalize all prohibited organizations. Political prisoners not guilty of violence would be freed. The authorities would release Nelson Mandela without conditions. Nine days later Mandela walked through the gates of Victor Verster prison. Within three months, the first formal talks between the government and the ANC secured indemnities for returning exiles and in August the ANC agreed to a 'suspension' of its armed struggle 'in the interest of moving as speedily as possible to a negotiated political settlement'.

For the ANC, immediate pragmatic considerations were important in shaping its conciliatory response to de Klerk. Its leaders were aware of the limitations of what it could achieve militarily and they were in any case under pressure to negotiate with Pretoria from their African hosts, particularly in Zambia, who had their own reasons for favouring a South African settlement[79] as well as from their Cuban and East European allies.[80] But there were longer-term and more subtle considerations that affected the ANC's willingness to negotiate. The extent to which ANC leaders ever really believed that an insurrectionary seizure of power could be accomplished—or even wanted it—was questionable. When senior ANC officials encountered sympathetic North Americans and Western Europeans they often used a liberal language that contrasted rather sharply with the uncompromising phraseology that characterized the organization's internal strategic propositions. For example, the American researcher Steve Davis was told by one 'top ANC veteran' in Tanzania that before the arrival of the 1976 activists, 'we were tolerant, non-violent, convinced we could reason with whites'. The older generation, Davis learned, 'committed only to a controlled armed struggle' and was fearful of younger militants' vision: 'This is our fear: the whole-scale burning of the country. We want to avoid that. We are not mad. It's easy to destroy, much harder to rebuild.'[81] Nelson

Mandela's reassertion of leadership over the movement after his release certainly reinforced moderate sentiment within the ANC Executive: by the mid-1990s, Mandela was arguing that 'the purpose of armed struggle was always to bring the government to the negotiating table'.[82]

Reservations about violence may have strengthened with the progress of the ANC's insurgency. Its own success in exerting its political leadership over the rather wider rebellion orchestrated by the UDF meant that increasingly it was allied to groups that were dismissive about the prospects of guerrilla warfare. Certain key UDF leaders were unconvinced that guerrillas could capture power[83] and their own vision of a massive mainly non-violent movement compelling the government to concede change seemed increasingly plausible as the black trade unions became better organized and more politically assertive. Finally, of course, the ANC's success in animating through the Anti-Apartheid Movement a liberal constituency of supporters and sympathizers in Western countries including the United States meant that its allies included powerful groups predisposed in favour of a peaceful constitutional settlement.

In a 'hurting stalemate' ANC leaders found compelling reasons to end guerrilla warfare: as one contributor to its journal, *Sechaba*, noted, 'we are confronted with conditions in which an absolute victory is impossible.'[84] Their decision was unpopular with *Umkhonto* rank and file, though, and political violence did not end with the 'suspension' of armed struggle. Indeed it intensified: most victims of political conflict between 1976 and 1994 were killed after the ANC's agreement to halt operations. In the next four years, 14,000 people were killed in so-called 'black on black' violence. Most of these deaths were in Natal province and were a consequence of a lethal competition for territorial control between UDF/ANC supporters and adherents of the Inkatha Freedom Party. Founded in 1975, Inkatha was a movement constructed around the patrimonial politics of the Kwa-Zulu homeland. Presided over by Chief Mangosuthu Buthelezi, the movement benefited from Buthelezi's lineage within the Zulu royal house. The Zulu kingdom still retained considerable moral authority and this helped Inkatha to build a strong following in the countryside as well as among Zulu migrant workers. Buthelezi, an ex-ANC Youth Leaguer, initially maintained a courteous relationship with exiled ANC leaders but hostilities developed between Inkatha and Congress supporters in 1980 after Inkatha's brutal suppression of a school boycott in Kwa Mashu outside Durban. Bloody feuding between Inkatha and UDF supporters began shortly after the UDF's establishment in

1983. After 1990, the prospect of universal suffrage elections supplied fresh incentives to control territory both in Natal, the one province in which the ANC was likely to encounter serious competition for African support, and in areas in which Inkatha could claim the loyalty of sizeable communities of Zulu migrants, in the hostels around Vereeniging, for example.

★

As was the case with their contribution to local developments in Sharpeville during this period the Pan-Africanists' role in the national drama was as a disaffected auxiliary, busy in sideshow arenas rather than functioning as a decisive force shaping events on the central stage. Certainly, during the 1980s new leaders helped to inspire a recovery in the PAC's fortunes but many of its organizational vulnerabilities remained. Vus Make rapidly proved to be ineffectual and was replaced in the new office of chairperson in January 1981 by John Pokela who had recently emerged from confinement on Robben Island. Pokela arrived in Dar es Salaam with strong credentials; he had taught with Robert Sobukwe in Standerton and had played a key role in the *Poqo* revolt. Modest and conciliatory, Pokela managed to induce Ntantala and his followers back into the fold, though establishing his authority within the mutinous APLA proved more difficult. Two years after Pokela's accession, Potlake Leballo remained popular in the guerrilla camps and Tanzanian soldiers had to restore order after internal strife as late as 1983. Social relations within camps were further complicated by the manipulation of ethnic identities which both Leballo and Ntantala had used to mobilize support, Leballo amongst Sesotho-speakers and Ntantala amongst Ngunis.[85]

Leballo also enjoyed a degree of support from politicians in Zimbabwe and Libya, as well as from clusters of PAC members in London and Harare. The Libyans were annoyed with Pokela because in return for a donation of $50,000 from the Iraqis, Pokela issued a statement supporting Baghdad in its war against Iran.[86] Adding to Pokela's problems was the continuing venality of his colleagues. Former SASO president Henry Isaacs resigned from his post as the PAC's United Nations representative in April 1982 and distributed a detailed indictment of the shortcomings of members of the central committee to journalists. One year later, Assistant Administrative Secretary Benny Sondlo was murdered, leaving a legacy of rumours about his ostentatious lifestyle. There were five other people who were killed during Pokela's presidency, their murders justified with references to their activities as 'dissidents'.[87] This was followed by corruption accusations levelled at Sondlo's superior, Joe Mkwanazi, by rivals on the central committee. Despite these difficulties, Pokela managed to restore a measure of self-confidence to the organization. In this he was assisted by the capable Gora Ebrahim, foreign affairs secretary from 1983, who presided over an impressive revival of the PAC's diplomatic representation in Europe and an energetic mending of fences in Africa.

Indications of a renaissance of PAC networks inside South Africa also helped to improve morale. In 1983 a journalist and three trade unionists were convicted of possessing PAC literature. Though the men were later acquitted on appeal, the court proceedings indicated the existence of local PAC recruitment structures and Africanist sentiment within the Black Municipal Workers' Union. In 1981 the first of a new generation of Africanist organizations appeared with the formation of Azanian National Youth Unity (AZANYU) in the former PAC stronghold of Orlando East. In later years AZANYU claimed improbably large numbers of adherents but it certainly had significant support in the Western Cape, especially in Paarl's Mbwekeni township. Trials suggest that by 1985, AZANYU was functioning as an effective transmission belt for APLA recruits. By then a variety of other organizations were using the Africanist symbolic repertoire—a cluster of trade unions, the African Women's Organisation, and the Pan-Africanist Student Organisation. When Pokela died in July 1985, the PAC was able to claim that it had 'forged a firm link between the internal and external wings'.[88] Leballo managed to outlive his successor only briefly. In 1984 he settled in London, where despite illness and poverty he remained politically active, attempting to organize a BCP-sponsored military take-over in Lesotho through the post. He died in January 1986.

Under the new chairmanship of Johnson Mlambo, another *Poqo* survivor, the Pan-Africanists succeeded in reintroducing a steadily increasing number of APLA insurgents into South Africa. Their progress could be traced in a succession of trials. The PAC began claiming responsibility for specific attacks in 1986. Before that time their spokesmen had explained the absence of armed activity with immodest evasiveness. 'Peoples' war' Chairperson Mlambo had explained to the *Zimbabwe Herald* in 1985, 'is not waged by a few guerrillas from outside South Africa . . . only the Azanian masses had the exclusive right, the power, and the will to determine the struggle'. After 1986, such obfuscation was unnecessary. In 1986 the police admitted to killing or capturing thirty-eight APLA insurgents, by the end of the following year this number had risen to eighty-five. Courtroom testimony suggested a number of characteristics that distinguished the APLA insurgents. They continued to be Libyan-trained, though several had attended courses in Lebanon and Yugoslavia as well. They were generally young and recruited from inside the country, chiefly from the larger towns. Their tactical priority appeared to be attacks on the security forces rather than sabotage, and they were usually equipped with grenades and machine pistols, not limpet mines. Finally, in the Western Cape, a loose alliance had been formed between APLA and *Qibla*, an Islamic fundamentalist grouping.

The link with *Qibla* was not the only indication that the PAC was beginning to find a coloured popular constituency. As was evident during the 'March Days' in 1960 the PAC failed to attract significant coloured support in the Western Cape. In 1966 though, prominent members of the Coloured People's Congress joined the PAC in London after being denied full membership in the ANC. One or two coloured notables in Cape Town followed their example, including the Imam Haroun, an Islamic priest popular among students at the University of the Western Cape. Haroun was killed in detention in 1969. These developments may have helped to enhance the PAC's appeal within the coloured community in the 1980s. The strong showing amongst Africanist unions of white-collar organizations also helped to bring coloured labour activists into the PAC. Patricia de Lille and Benny Alexander were two modern PAC leaders to represent this trend. Both grew up in households in which Robert Sobukwe was a venerated role model. De Lille helped to establish a clandestine Africanist network in the Western Cape in 1982.

By the end of the 1980s guerrilla warfare, student activism, and ideological alignments within the labour movement entitled the Pan-Africanist exiles to claim a modest but significant following within South Africa. In December 1989 this internal presence of the PAC was given organizational expression with the formation of the Pan-Africanist Movement (PAM). At the helm of the PAM executive was Clarence Makwetu, for twenty years since his release from Robben Island a farmer in Qamata, Transkei. But surrounding him and testifying to a reinvigorated movement were student organizers, urbane professionals, and NACTU trade unionists. Against all odds, the PAC had endured the trauma of banishment and succeeded in rallying new forces.

It took several years for new PAC leaders recently arriving in Tanzania from South Africa, veterans of the *Poqo* movement and subsequent long prison sentences, to restore morale and discipline among mutinous APLA units. No APLA attacks were recorded in the first half of the eighties and the police arrests of APLA soldiers totalled fourteen between 1980 and 1985.[89] By the mid-1980s, though, the PAC's fortunes were reviving. Within South Africa a new generation of Africanist organizations had appeared, including trade unions, a youth movement, Azanian National Youth Unity, and the Pan-Africanist Students Organisation. As we have seen, trial evidence suggested that from 1985, one of these at least, AZANYU, was serving as an effective APLA recruitment agency. Reports of APLA guerrilla operations began appearing quite frequently in the South African press the following year. As noted above, PAC publications claimed that in 1986 APLA had been targeting policemen in Sharpeville. The first APLA attacks to be confirmed and identified as such by the police were four actions attributed to the 'Alexandra Scorpion Gang' between December 1986 and February 1987, in which two soldiers and two policemen were wounded and a café owner shot dead during a robbery.[90] Responsibility was attributed to three APLA guerrillas killed after a car-chase through the Johannesburg suburb of Bramley.[91] The leader of the Bramley group, Tshepo Lilelo, was a former AZANYU regional treasurer while living in Sharpeville. Two of the dead men had been members of AZANYU before joining APLA in 1983. The police claimed that they had arrested or killed altogether thirty-eight APLA insurgents in 1986[92] and by the end of 1987 the annual total had risen to eighty-five.[93] In 1987, APLA's journal reported twelve 'enemy' killed and another sixty-seven wounded.[94] Most of the casualties were from a grenade attack on two municipal police platoons drilling at the Soweto Police Training College. Eleven of the men killed were shot in or near Alexandra township. In general, the PAC's insurgents focused their attacks on policemen and soldiers, mainly in the townships around Johannesburg. They were usually equipped with grenades and machine pistols, not limpet mines, Umkhonto we Sizwe's weapon of choice. In the Western Cape, APLA had formed a loose alliance with Qibla. By 1988, APLA operations had extended to smaller towns in the Western Transvaal. In July, an encounter between APLA soldiers and police left four PAC members dead and twelve policemen wounded.[95] At the close of the decade APLA had become a significant participant in South Africa's fledgling guerrilla war.

Sceptical South African journalists sometimes characterized APLA's exile establishment as 'two men with a fax in Dar es Salaam'.[96] Police sources, however, tend to confirm the impression suggested by APLA's own propaganda of a rather more complex organization which by the 1990s had begun to move part of its command structure within South African borders. APLA's command arrangements attempted to embody the guerrilla doctrine of a unified political and military leadership. Right down to the three to eight person local field units or platoons, dual authority rested with field commanders and political commissars, the latter holding notional seniority. APLA's nine person military commission, a sub-committee of the PAC, included several civilian leaders in its membership and up until 1992 APLA's commander in chief was PAC chairman (from 1990, deputy president) Johnson Mlambo. The post of commander-in-chief fell vacant with the return to South Africa of the PAC's main politicians in 1992; this probably increased APLA's effective autonomy. APLA's high command had twenty-nine members, including in the 1990s six regional commanders based in South Africa. The most important posts in the high command were those of APLA commander, held by Sabelo Phama, chief political commissar, Romero Daniels Mofokeng, and the chief of staff, Barney Hlatswayo.

The APLA headquarters at Dar es Salaam was divided into a number of specialized departments responsible for operations, infiltration, security, propaganda, logistics, political education, training, and so forth, the directors of which also belonged to the twenty-nine member high command. APLA maintained three base camps in Tanzania. Here recruits underwent preliminary training and here they stayed before their despatch on operations in South Africa. In the Transkei, APLA's internal command structures were most developed, with the division of the territory into four zones under separate command and a regional political/military council whose officers included a chief of logistics, a chief of security, and a commander of training and operations. The planning of specific operations would be undertaken by local commanders, each of whom would control several APLA units within a particular area. Their tactical decisions were subject to general guidelines emanating from the more senior leadership echelons.[97] Supply of guerrilla units was organized separately from operations and specialized military supply units were functioning inside South Africa from 1987,[98] APLA's 'Year of Arming the Azanian Masses'.

How much of this rather impressive sounding organizational scheme actually functioned is difficult to assess from the evidence available. PAC strategists looked forward to a time when 'it will be necessary to organize large mobile units to operate in specified regions', when it would become imperative 'as armed struggle intensifies to expand our armed forces to regular divisions'.[99] Perhaps in anticipation of this development much of the training offered to PAC recruits in their Libyan camps in the late 1970s was conventional infantry drill.[100] In the 1980s, though, APLA was rather a small force and therefore many of the bureaucratic distinctions between specialized functions may have been more theoretical than real. We know that certain individuals often held more than one post: Romero Daniels Mofokeng, for example, political commissar, and after Phama the most senior APLA functionary, also served as director of the PAC's Intelligence and Security Department. The very rapid accession through the ranks to the directorates that some officers enjoyed also suggests that the APLA's 'Rear Command' was really quite a modest establishment. Directors were sometimes directly involved in military operations. For example, Themba Ncapayi, APLA's director of ideological education between 1991 and 1992, joined APLA in 1983 as a platoon commander at the age of twenty-two. He became a camp commander in 1988 and attended in 1989 a political training course in China. Shortly after his appointment as director of ideological education he went to South Africa 'to reinforce a team of fellow top APLA officers who were already at work in the country'.[101] He was killed in a clash with South African police in February 1992. The deployment of senior officers in combat roles seems to have been a well established convention in APLA. Director of operations, Enoch Zulu, was captured in South Africa in 1986 as was his deputy, Jan Shoba, one year earlier. Zulu's operational career began with his participation in the 1968 PAC/COREMO expedition. He served briefly, in 1980–1, as APLA commander. He was later convicted on charges which included involvement in *Poqo* activity in the Transkei in 1963 and was finally given amnesty in 1992.

As a consequence of the expulsion from the PAC in 1979 of Templeton Ntantala and his followers, who represented at that time the more experienced and more senior APLA generation, the APLA Command was generally composed of quite young men. Sabelo Phama was one of the oldest officers. He was born in Umtata in 1949. He joined the PAC as a schoolboy in 1962. Matriculating in 1967, he studied at the University of the Witwatersrand and at Fort Hare, from which he was expelled in 1972. For three years he assisted his brother who ran a building firm and worked 'underground' for the PAC. During this time he became friends with Romero Daniels Mofokeng, six years his junior, an association which was to persist throughout the two men's later careers as guerrilla leaders. He left the country in 1975 and trained in China in 1976 at the Nanking Military Academy. For a while he served in the PAC's publicity department, helping to produce material for APLA soldiers. In 1978 he and four others infiltrated into the Transkei from Lesotho, and in the course of five months attempted to prepare the ground for guerrilla campaigning, establishing arms caches and setting up a network of safe houses.[102] Arrested by the Transkeien authorities in early 1979, the APLA men were released on bail two years later. Phama's absence from Dar es Salaam coincided with the worst period of internecine leadership strife and he returned at the point when the PAC's new chairman, John Pokela, was attempting to reconstruct APLA's command. Phama was elected to the PAC's central committee in 1982 and was shortly thereafter made defence secretary and APLA commander.[103]

Estimates as to the size of Sabelo Phama's army vary. In the 1980s, police sources suggested that the Tanzanian-based soldiers numbered between 300 and 750.[104] One hundred and fifty APLA cadres were thought to have trained in Libya between 1982 and 1986.[105] Barrell, in 1989, cited anonymous PAC sources indicating a guerrilla strength of less than 450 men and women.[106] By 1991, police-informed authorities suggested that APLA's external force was about 800 with up to 120 operational inside the country at any time. Three hundred and fifty trainees were believed to have just completed the Libyan course.[107] In 1993, the Goldstone Commission was told by police and military sources that APLA's Tanzanian establishment numbered 2,700 (including women and children) and again, that about 120 APLA soldiers were operational. *Azania Combat* reprinted the operational figure with apparent editorial endorsement arguing that it demonstrated that their active deployment was three times that of *Umkhonto*'s in the 1980s.[108] Sabelo Phama, in his 1993 New Year's message, boasted that APLA's strength had by then reached 10,000, including internally trained fighters. He might have been referring to Pan-Africanist Students' Organization (PASO) members who had undergone short one-week weapons-handling courses administered by APLA in Transkei and Botswana and who occasionally undertook operations under APLA direction. Not to be outdone, in the same issue that printed Phama's speech, *Azania Combat*[109] suggested that APLA's strength had reached 15,000. In 1994, though, only 6,000 candidates appeared on the list APLA submitted for enrolment into the South African National Defence Force (SANDF).[110] By August 1995, about 5,500 former APLA combatants were serving in the Defence Force.[111]

In the aftermath of its unbanning, the PAC held a meeting in Harare to which it invited members of its internal surrogate, Clarence Makwetu's

Pan-Africanist Movement. PAM agreed to merge with the PAC which itself decided to relocate to South Africa. At this point, though, the PAC was determined to keep its external structures intact. Zimbabwe's minister for political affairs, Edison Zvogbo, warned the meeting of the dangers of engaging in protracted negotiations with the South African authorities.[112] Disputes within the PAC over the merits of taking part in negotiations were to continue throughout the next two years. During this period the PAC's official position maintained that any constitutional reforms should be debated by a democratically elected constitutional assembly and that negotiations to establish such a body should be held outside South Africa. Growing pressure from African governments as well as fears among the PAC's leaders of the consequences of being left out of any political settlement, prompted them to begin attending preparatory meetings for a multi-party Conference for a Democratic South Africa (CODESA) in November 1991.

This was shortly after the formation of a United Front with the ANC and ninety other political organizations. One month later, the PAC withdrew from these talks angered by the 'bilateral' agreements between the ANC and the government. It announced a campaign of mass action against CODESA and in favour of an elected constitutional assembly. This undertaking petered out after a comparatively decorous march on parliament by a few hundred activists and a few anti-CODESA rallies. Meanwhile, the Pan-Africanist Students' Organisation began a programme of assaults on white teachers working in townships, forcing the closure of five Katlehong schools.

By April 1992, though, there existed strong compulsions to return to the talks. At the PAC's third national conference in Umtata, delegates heard arguments in favour of negotiation from both Major-General Holomisa, the Transkeien head of state, and from the Organisation of African Unity. A series of meetings began with South African government representatives and, in November 1992, the PAC announced its readiness to participate in the multi-party forum. The PAC announced its new president, Clarence Makwetu, was 'refocusing on the ballot as a route to power'.[113] This decision notwithstanding, the PAC's formal entry into the Kempton Park Conference was delayed by a four-month argument with the government over its refusal to suspend the armed struggle. In the end, with the ANC's help, the Pan-Africanists prevailed and they became negotiators while APLA units continued the armed struggle. The PAC's intransigence on this issue effectively diverted the attention of its militant followers from their leaders' abandonment of the original demand for an elected constitutional assembly.

These manoeuvrings took place against a backdrop of spiralling political violence. Between the unbanning of the liberation movements in February 1990 and the election of a Government of National Unity (GNU) in April 1994, 14,028 deaths were attributed to political conflict, much of it between ANC and Inkatha supporters in Natal. APLA's contribution to this carnage, though relatively minor, had a significant public impact because unlike most of the victims, the casualties inflicted by APLA were, in increasing numbers, white rather than black.

Precise and accurate statistics for APLA activity in this period are not available. Press reportage is incomplete and confusing: press attention to APLA was sporadic and, in any case, there were many other sources of politically motivated violence. Militarized criminality confused the picture still further. APLA and PAC communiqués were sometimes at odds with each other and were sometimes demonstrably untrue. APLA's journal, *Azania Combat*, when reporting military activity, usually confined itself to reprinting information from South African newspapers. South African reportage tended to rely on police statements. The following sketch of APLA activity in the 1990s in the Goldstone Commission's report reflects the limited information available

> In 1990 at least ten incidents were noted in the press, mainly attacks on police-men and police stations. These were widely dispersed geographically, occurring in Soweto, townships around Cape Town, in the Northern Transvaal, Mother-well in the Eastern Cape, Manguang (Bloemfontein), Bophuthatswana and Umbumbulu in Natal. No sources inside South Africa offered corroboration for Sabelo Phama's claim that APLA had killed 25 soldiers that year, an assertion which the police bluntly denied.[114] A similar pattern was evident in eight attacks attributed to APLA in 1992; these again were mainly directed at the police and located in black townships in different parts of the country. In April, through, as trial proceedings subsequently indicated, a Uganda trained APLA soldier, Steven Dolo, petrol bombed a farm at Lady Grey (as well as attacking police single quarters in the district).[115]

It does seem that from 1990 APLA expanded its operations, aided by easier access to South African territory as well as the inception of local training, both of which were facilitated by the PAC's legalization. In 1992, newspaper reports suggested that its members participated in forty-five attacks on, or exchanges of fire with, police. The police informed the Goldstone

Commission in January 1993 that APLA had carried out forty-one attacks in the previous two years. At that time court proceedings against several captured insurgents were still pending and police would subsequently confirm APLA responsibility for more attacks in the period. PAC claims became increasingly inflated: APLA's journal suggested that 200 security forces had been killed by PAC combatants by August that year[116] and in January 1993 Sabelo Phama boosted this figure to 500.[117] Official SAP statistics indicate that 481 policemen died in 1992, a figure which probably inspired Phama's claim,[118] but of these only 175 were 'killed in the execution of their duties' and many of these were probably murdered by ordinary criminals. Notwithstanding PAC exaggerations, though, 1992 was an eventful year for APLA. There was a shift in emphasis in favour of civilian targets, with twelve attacks directed against farmers and a succession of armed assaults on restaurants, clubs, and hotels, sometimes timed to coincide with special functions. An APLA unit was intercepted at a road-block near the Transkei border after mounting a bank robbery in Molteno and four insurgents were shot dead. A man claiming APLA membership held up staff at the Foschini fashion store in Germiston, escaping with R160,000. Letlapa Mphahlele, APLA's Mabopane-based director of operations from 1990 suggests that during the 1990s APLA 'suffered more casualties on "repossession missions" than on combat with the enemy'. With no systematic supply arrangements cadres were 'urged...to commit robberies to survive', Mphahlele concedes.[119]

In his New Year's address, Sabelo Phama promised that 1993 would be 'The Year of the Great Storm'. Police statements confirm a significant stepping-up of the scale of operations with reports of 142 attacks, the great majority of them, 128, directed at farms. Police blamed all the farm attacks on APLA although it is possible that some of them may have been undertaken by other groups of armed activists, acting independently, as well as criminals. Twenty-eight of these farm attacks were in the Eastern Transvaal, a region hitherto unaffected by APLA operations. In some of the attacks animals were mutilated, a tactic which recalled the style of Zimbabwe African National Liberation Army (ZANLA) operations in Zimbabwe during the Chimurenga. Other civilian targets included hotels in Fort Beaufort and East London, a pub in Cape Town and worshippers at St James' church in Cape Town, twelve of whom were killed and 148 wounded by an APLA unit during a service on 25 July. At least sixty-one people including thirty-five farmers and farmworkers and three policemen died. APLA operations remained widely dispersed with an increased incidence of attacks in the Transvaal: APLA combatants appeared in court in July charged with robbing an Irving and Johnston warehouse on the East Rand; in April, gunfire aimed at passing cars in Walkerville near Johannesburg, killing a mother and her child, was, it seems, originally intended for the occupants of a schoolbus. A four-man APLA unit had questioned local children in the vicinity about when the bus was due but had then failed to fire when it arrived, possibly because it looked empty.[120]

Several characteristics of APLA operations merit comment. First, they do suggest a relatively disciplined force, systematically deployed. Even the terrorist attacks of 1992 and 1993 were discriminating and methodical: APLA units used grenades and automatic weapons, preferring direct engagement with their targets rather than the more impersonal use of limpet mines which *Umkhonto* units favoured when attacking civilians. In contrast to *Umkhonto*, therefore, the majority of APLA's civilian victims were white, intentionally so. Until 1992 most APLA attacks were directed at policemen, or more rarely soldiers, and were usually confined to townships. In many APLA operations there was evidence of careful preparation and intelligent planning. For example, at dawn on 5 May 1993, a police minibus was ambushed in Dobsonville from both sides of the road while waiting at traffic lights. The bus was carrying twenty-three passengers, returning to barracks after a night shift. Clearly the vehicle's daily route and programme were known to the attackers who had made their plans accordingly. The hotels that APLA units selected were attacked after reconnaissance, and offensives were timed to coincide with special functions. In the case of the King William's Town golf club assault, APLA command claimed that the guest list at the banquet that night included off-duty security personnel. The occasion was in fact organized by a National Party MP, Ray Radue.

Police often commented on the evident sophistication of APLA operations.[121] These were frequently two-pronged affairs, with one group of men firing guns into the target area whilst other insurgents threw handgrenades from a different entrance. In rural operations, APLA soldiers appeared to have been taught to disguise their tracks, a level of fieldcraft suggesting training of a quite different order to that available to *Umkhonto* personnel in the 1980s.[122] APLA units were armed with quite a wide range of weapons, including material used by South African security forces. Some guns were obviously obtained locally, either stolen from farms or bought from *Umkhonto* personnel. Armed robberies represented another kind of self-sufficiency: PAC leaders in the Transkei in 1992 exhorted followers to raise money by any means.[123] With its heavy dependence upon OAU funding the PAC was always short of money, which may explain why senior APLA personnel were involved in mandrax-smuggling into Zimbabwe.[124] In the Eastern Cape, APLA units were based in the Transkei, where the Holomisa administration tolerated their presence in return for the use of APLA training facilities in East Africa by members of the Transkeian Defence Force.[125] Short training courses were offered at small encampments in forested areas along the Transkeian border. This helps to account for the concentration of APLA activity in the Eastern Cape but the national distribution of APLA operations suggested that APLA units could function quite effectively without protected havens in independent homelands. Finally, in 1992 and 1993, the great majority of APLA operations were located in the countryside, reversing the emphasis between 1986 and 1991 on township-based activity.

Through the decade APLA's operations inside South Africa were shaped by two competing strategic visions. APLA commanders publicly subscribed to Maoist guerrilla theory and were probably influenced by their historical alliance with ZANU, with whom they had shared training facilities in the late 1960s.[126] During the 1970s, inspired by Chinese and Zimbabwean models, the Pan-Africanists' military planning was premised upon the assumption that it would find its main support in the countryside amongst 'peasants' and that its initial targets should be isolated and lightly defended white farming communities. The adoption of a fresh strategic blueprint, the 'New Road to Revolution' reflected the ascendency within the PAC leadership of a new group of 'Marxist–Leninists' who began to predominate in the political leadership over Potlake Leballo's adherents. The 'New Road' suggested that the industrial working class would supply the cutting edge of any South African insurgency and hence the initial strategic emphasis should be urban guerrilla warfare, directed principally at the security forces, police, and soldiers. However both rank and file and APLA commanders remained divided over the merits of these respective approaches, and through the early 1990s, within the army, itself at odds with the non–military political leadership, once again the Maoists seemed to be setting the agenda.[127] Not all guerrillas were inclined to base themselves in the countryside, though. Mphahlele complained that in the Transvaal in this period 'our cadres were concentrated in urban areas and only went into the countryside when they were hunted . . . We were not stretching the enemy as we should have been.

Some cadres stayed with PAC members, and the majority built shacks in the shanty towns.'[128]

Whatever their strategic inspiration may have been, levels of APLA campaigning were not matched by proportional increases in militant political protest or industrial action, despite the existence of quite large trade unions and youth organizations sympathetic to, or affiliated with, the PAC. PASO supplied armed auxiliaries in APLA operations,[129] but in general the PAC's mass organizations did not undertake the kind of urban-based mobilization that might have enabled the Pan-Africanists to build a political following from people impressed by the bellicosity of their guerrilla operations. Even so, given the intensity of political violence instigated by ANC and Inkatha supporters in townships, APLA's rural activity did represent quite a significant challenge to already hard-pressed South African soldiers and policemen. The form of insurgency chosen by APLA's commanders made good sense if they wanted to maximize the impact of their quite limited firepower.

By 1990, top Pan-Africanists disagreed even about the ultimate purpose of guerrilla warfare. The aim of APLA's campaigning during the 1990s was quite simply stated by PAC secretary-general Barney Desai shortly after his return to South Africa when he wrote in the *Sunday Star* that 'we hold the simple truth that what has not been won on the battlefield will never be won at the negotiating table'.[130] In 1990, PAC leadership was ready to acknowledge that the movement had 'failed to overthrow the South African State through revolutionary means' and that 'the military force of the state [was] intact' and that furthermore the PAC itself did not at that time have the resources to offer a serious armed challenge.[131] *Star* journalist Kaizer Nyatsumba met Sabelo Phama in Harare in 1990. During this encounter, Nyatsumba recalled later, 'Phama emphasised that the PAC's armed struggle was not war for war's sake and a time would come when arms would be laid down to give peace a chance.'[132]

Subsequent PAC rhetoric suggested a rather different vision. Phama, for example, in 1992 appeared on Bop TV promising that APLA would 'continue striking until the regime is forced to hand over power to the indigenous African majority'.[133] At about the same time the PAC Youth Department issued a statement that suggested that the South African police and army could be 'wiped out of existence'.[134] 'True liberation will come about principally from the barrel of a gun', was another Phama maxim that appeared quite frequently in APLA propaganda. The bellicose sloganeering as well as the timing of major APLA operations—the attacks on restaurants and clubs began just after the PAC announced its willingness to participate in multi-party talks—encouraged press speculation that APLA's commanders were deliberately trying to undermine a negotiation bid led by their more moderate civilian comrades. It does seem as if Desai represented a pragmatic 'centrist' faction that emerged at the PAC's 1990 Consultative Conference and which disagreed with military leaders over the degree to which the Pan-Africanists should commit themselves to a negotiated settlement.[135] There was also a more right-wing 'liberal' grouping led by A. B. Ngcobo, the Sobukwe Forum, whose adherents were much more strongly predisposed to negotiation as 'a once in a lifetime opportunity'; the Forum's members favoured a strategic alliance with Inkatha.[136]

Ngcobo himself had preserved a friendship with Chief Buthelezi that dated to their escapades as fellow students in the early 1950s: they were once arrested together by the Railway Police in Durban for not paying their fares.[137] These differences help to explain the erratic course the PAC took over participating in the negotiations between 1991 and 1994. Even so, PAC pragmatists themselves favoured maintaining APLA's offensive. After all, APLA's activities helped to boost the PAC's popular stature at a time when it was undertaking a political manoeuvre that risked censure from its most assertive partisans: for the previous two years PAC leaders had insisted they would not negotiate for anything other than an elected constituent assembly. Benny Alexander insisted that such incidents as the King William's Town golf club attack reaped immediate political dividends: 'in the past nine days we have experienced an unusual surge of membership' he told journalists.[138] Opinion polling later suggested that a substantial minority of young people living in cities strongly approved of APLA's activities.[139] Secondly, PAC leaders apparently believed that APLA's killings of whites 'had forced those orchestrating conflict in the townships to retreat', pointing to a decline in political violence statistics in the first months of 1993.[140] This, though, may have been an *ex post facto* justification of such actions rather than their preconceived strategic purpose.

A statement by Sabelo Phama in July 1993, that he would find it acceptable to lose five million people as the price for true liberation,[141] suggests that reducing the numbers of black civilian casualties of political conflict did not rank very high amongst APLA's strategic priorities. PAC and APLA leaders usually justified killing white civilians by suggesting that in a militarized society they were indistinguishable from the security forces:

'even children are taught to shoot in school', Sabelo Phama asserted in an interview conducted with the *Sowetan* in December 1992. However, there were apparently limits to what the PAC's top leadership was willing to sanction. APLA information secretary, Johnny Majozi, disclaimed responsibility for the St James' church massacre[142] and Desai told reporters that the PAC was not to blame for the Walkerville shootings, offering condolences to those who had died; race war was counterproductive and not PAC policy, he added.[143] On the ground, PAC cadres were less circumspect. A man held up at an APLA road-block near Alberton was told by one of his assailants 'you must know that 1993 is the year of terror. Old white people and white children will be murdered.'[144] The PAC youth's subculture was distinctive for the brutality of its discourse. At an APLA anniversary rally in Cape Town children wore T-shirts bearing slogans reading: 'Kill them, APLA, butcher them'. PAC regional chairman, Theo Mabuselo, told his audience to expect harsh reprisals from the authorities 'just because a master has died', a reference to the recent murder of an American exchange student by PASO members.[145] Letlapa Mphahlele, APLA's director of operations, did indeed sanction the St James' church attack; later he met one of the survivors of the congregation, Charl van Wyk, and from this staged conciliatory encounter a remarkable friendship developed.[146]

Judged by narrow military criteria APLA cadres were really rather effective, though their military impact continued to be constrained by the logistical difficulties confronting an externally located command remote from operations.[147] Certainly, before 1990, the PAC's military made only a minor contribution to a guerrilla insurgency, the historical importance of which was to be chiefly symbolic. In the years that followed, though, their scale of operations and the political impact of these began to rival *Umkhonto*'s earlier deployment. APLA operations were distinctive for their rural emphasis, their careful targeting, and their ferocity. APLA soldiers were comparatively well-trained and disciplined for members of a guerrilla force, and in their preference for direct engagement they often showed considerable force and dedication. As far as we know, APLA's command structure remained free of high-level police infiltration, despite the involvement and capture of senior officers in the field.

Evaluating APLA's achievements within a broader political context suggests different and less favourable conclusions. In the 1990s, the politically critical consideration was no longer the successful mobilization of a militant activist minority but rather the garnering of electoral support. By the 1990s, opinion polls suggested that while guerrilla heroics pleased young militants they alienated the older voting majority. In the April 1994 election the PAC fared miserably, even in those areas in which APLA had established a continuous presence. By the early 1990s, the soldiers of the Great Storm were out of step with the main rhythms of political change. A decade before, APLA's battles might have been epoch-making, now they merely served as a harsh reminder of what might have been in the absence of a successful democratic transition.

Among the returning Pan-Africanists, Philip Kgosana had survived exile with his reputation and honour intact. After his expulsion from the PAC he completed his training at the Ethiopian Harar Military Academy. He then travelled to Lubumbashi, to take up a position as a training officer for Holden Roberto's National Front for the Liberation of Angola (FNLA). He became swiftly disillusioned with his new employer after becoming familiar with the 'half starved disorganised rabble' that inhabited the FNLA's base camp at Kolwezi. Instead he moved to Uganda, intending to register for a post-graduate qualification in public administration at Makekere University, unfortunately timing his arrival to coincide with Idi Amin's seizure of power. He lived through the full seven years of the Amin dictatorship helping to manage and eventually lead a desperately needed UNICEF programme that attempted to care for the growing legion of orphans roaming Kampala's streets. Subsequently he held senior UNICEF positions in Sri Lanka and Botswana before returning to South Africa, in time to appear on the PAC's electoral list in the 1994 election. Too far down the register to win a parliamentary seat he subsequently served on the Tshwane (Pretoria) city council, representing the ward containing his birthplace, Winterveldt. Here he still lives with his wife Alice, in his father's homestead, helping to organize cooperatives among local farmers. In 2004 he appeared on the provincial honours list of the premier of the Western Cape, Marthinus van Schalkwyk, recipient of the 'Order of the Disa', official acknowledgement of his 'courageous leadership and negotiating skills' in 'preventing a bloodbath' on 30 March 1960.

★

Today the Sharpeville massacre is commemorated as a public holiday. In South Africa 21 March is Human Rights Day. This year, the fiftieth anniversary of the massacre, older residents attended church services. Additional events were organized by the Sedibeng Municipality: a night vigil in Sharpeville on the 19th and on the 20th a gala dinner, 'to launch the

Sedibeng Reconstruction and Development Agency and strengthen the relationship between business and the municipality'. The occasion was also to be marked with an important visitation in which the state premier would receive the freedom of the city. Moreover the first lady, MaKhumalo Zuma would be appointed as the new agency's patron, 'as she is a symbol of strength, hope and commitment', Mayor Mahole Mofokeng explained.[148] As things turned out, the president, Jacob Zuma, had a more pressing commitment, for he needed to fly off to Windhoek in Namibia that day. In his place Deputy President Kgalema Motlanthe spoke to a modest crowd of several hundred gathered at the cricket ground, next to the long-promised and still incomplete and now derelict George Thabe football stadium. Before travelling to the stadium, Motlanthe met survivors and laid flowers at the Garden of Remembrance in the Sharpeville Human Rights Precinct. Motlanthe's address was more of a civic homily than a memorial eulogy, though. In the weeks preceding the protest the township had once again been beset by riots, this time orchestrated by a group calling itself the Concerned Residents of Sharpeville, a rather unlikely resurrection of the title of what had been a state-sponsored vigilante association. The Residents were protesting about backlogs in the provision of electricity and running water to shack dwellers. Some of the Concerned Residents erected barricades of burning tyres and set the township library alight. Motlanthe used part of his address to express his disapproval of this destructive eruption. 'The people of Langa and Sharpeville in 1960 did not voice protest by burning libraries and looting public facilities', he reminded his listeners. 'On the contrary, they left their passes at home and marched peacefully to the police stations to hand themselves over for arrest.' In today's democratic era people should use democratic institutions to hold their government accountable, Motlanthe urged. All South Africans should ensure that the lives lost that day were 'not in vain'; they should 'pledge to show the world our abhorrence to the heinous acts of racism, racial discrimination, xenophobia and related intolerance', the deputy-president added.

When it was announced, Pan-Africanist leaders perceived the naming of the anniversary as a political slight, the absence of an explicit reference to the massacre a maliciously tendentious omission, calculated to deny their own party's historical agency. Hence, they said, 'for many of us, the day will remain Sharpeville Day, the day on which we commemorate the death of sixty-nine people at the hands of the South African police'. Before this year's celebrations, Letlapa Mphahlele, now the PAC president, noted that he had been omitted from the Sedibeng Municipality's invitation list. 'There is a calculated move by the ruling party to de-link the day from the PAC', he said. 'The silence is about erasing memories of Sobukwe. It is unfortunate that they treat the day—the event—as something that happened spontaneously, like an earthquake', Mphahlele continued.[149]

The PAC's understanding of the motivations that influenced the naming of the day is probably unfair though it is quite likely that the choice of words reflected official concerns to emphasize unifying themes in a conciliatory revisionism that predominated in official historical narratives in the mid-1990s. Indeed, the day itself was initially left off the list of anniversaries that would be accorded the status of public holidays. In effect, whatever its intentions, the anniversary's anodyne change of name 'detached Sharpeville from the specificity of the anti-apartheid struggle and framed it as part of the quest for human rights'.[150] For certain commentators this was an encouraging development. For instance, Robert Sobukwe's friend and biographer Benjamin Pogrund elected to interpret the decision positively: 'Sharpeville's place in our history was firmly acknowledged . . . when it was chosen as the site for signing the new constitution into law', he wrote in 1997. However the commemoration of the anniversary as an occasion to celebrate the advent of a new human rights dispensation may have helped to encourage its cavalier treatment as a date for festive events, concerts, and 'cultural performances' rather than commemorations and ceremonies. For many local people, Sharpeville Day is now 'just another boring holiday'. According to Kgosi Manyathela, a member of the local PAC: 'The ANC hosts big parties this day at the George Thabe Stadium and there is never a mention of Robert Sobukwe.' The day has become a political celebration in which 'there is a continuous failure to reflect the truth'.[151] 'Are we missing the point somewhere? Do we remember what we fought for?', this year's newspaper reportage of the anniversary quoted Tsoana Mhlapo as saying. Mhlapo is the spokeswoman for Sharpeville First, a body constituted by 'descendants of those who witnessed the Sharpeville massacre'. Her organization is calling for material improvements, better houses, and jobs 'for the very people who fought for liberation'. But symbolic reparations are needed as well, Mhlapo believes, 'an apology from the state for what happened here'.[152] For older residents as well, the public anniversary has been robbed of meaning. As Vincent Leutsoa told his interviewer in 2000: 'We should commemorate and hold silent prayers instead of music concerts and parties. The way the 21st is corrupted pains me. Nobody has ever asked the victims what they want, how they think the shootings should be remembered. It. Pains. Me.'

Through the 1990s, PAC leaders maintained that 'Sharpeville's heroes' were not 'properly acknowledged'. Since then the authorities have compensated for any earlier neglect: the people whom the police killed in the massacre are now indeed memorialized and their names appear on a monument which we will visit later in this chapter. But it remains true that they are remembered chiefly as victims, passive casualties rather than as active participants in a politically decisive drama, not as 'heroes', to borrow the Pan-Africanists' preferred terminology, and that their projection in this fashion reflects ways of interpreting historical events that risks diminishing them. This kind of representation is partly a reflection of the projection of the event at the time it happened. Hakan Thorn's analysis of the main ways in which foreign newspapers reported the massacre suggests that even liberal newspapers depicted Africans in a manner that 'reproduced two dominant and contradictory stereotypes of Africans, deeply anchored in European colonial discourse and well established in the media at that time'.[153] Accordingly, newspapers often echoed uncritically the language of police statements that characterized a crowd outside the police station as animated by irrational collective passions—both the British *Guardian* and the *Svenska Dagbladet* reported that the police station was 'under siege' and the *Guardian* reproduced Colonel Pienaar's characterization of the assembly around the station as constituted by 'hordes of natives'. Shortly after the shootings, the South African high commissioner in London echoed the police's version of events in his press statement:

> According to factual information now available, the disturbances at Sharpeville on Monday resulted from a planned demonstration by 20,000 natives in which the demonstrators attacked the police with weapons including firearms. The demonstrators shot first and the Police were forced to fire in self defence and avoid even more tragic results.[154]

A similar exposition was delivered by the high commissioner's colleague at the United Nations. 'Extremists' managed to gather together crowds at Sharpeville and Langa. At Sharpeville when the police 'attempted to arrest some of the violators' the crowd became 'belligerent' and assaulted the police 'with a variety of weapons: pangas, axes, iron-bars, knives, sticks and firearms'.[155]

The alternate representation of the confrontation tends to project Africans as passive victims, denying them agency as historical subjects. In the case of Sharpeville, Thorn suggests, this representation is reflected in the photographic images used on newspaper front pages of dead people lying on the ground. Over time it was this landscape of the dead and dying that would become dominant in at least external depictions of the event. Inside South Africa, newspapers first carried photographs of the aftermath of the massacre, bodies photographed from a respectful distance rather than the remarkable series taken by *Drum*'s Ian Berry that supplied a sequential and personified narrative of the events that preceded the massacre as well as close-up photographs of the killing and the dying. Berry's pictures were published inside South Africa sparingly in the mainstream newspapers, after the end of the state of emergency. The second more impersonal group of photographs was taken by Peter Magubane and the pictures elicited an unfavourable reaction from his editor at *Drum*, Tom Hopkinson. He admonished Magubane:

> You have pictures but you don't have pictures that will sell the paper. I would have loved to see a picture going through one's bone. I would have loved to see a picture cracking someone's skull. I would have loved to see a picture of spectacles lying there, and in the background you have some of the dead people.[156]

Hopkinson's reservations notwithstanding, these were the pictures that appeared most frequently. One week later, Magubane returned to Sharpeville for the funeral. His pictures of this event appeared in *Life* magazine and they succeeded in capturing the complexity of emotions at this event but they were never republished.

The same dichotomy between representing local residents at the Sharpeville massacre as either the subjects of irrational passions or as innocent and almost accidental victims of the state's brutality was also evident in the conflicting interpretations that are evident in comparing official explanations of the massacre to the agitation that condemned it.

The official analysis was supplied by the Wessels Commission. Judge Wessels' findings were not wholly predisposed in favour of the police testimony that he listened to and he expressed mild criticism of Lieutenant Colonel Pienaar's deployment of the men he commanded. He noted that while 'the effect of Police evidence was that open hostility was displayed' by the crowd outside the police station and 'that violence was threatened and that a breaking point had been reached at 1.40 pm that obliged the police to fire', he acknowledged that he heard opposing evidence that was 'irreconciliable'. And certainly, during the hearing lawyers acting for the bereaved cross-examined Pienaar incisively. Could he not have tried harder to disperse the crowd with an order, counsel asked? He would have liked to, Piennaar replied, but there was no time. 'In the whole of that half an hour, you could not have spared a minute and a half in order to make this humane effort?' He could not, Pienaar affirmed:

COUNSEL: 'I am suggesting, Colonel, that you could have climbed onto a Saracen in your striking uniform and held up your hand for silence—and perhaps they would have been silence. And then you could have said, "Now, go home or you are going to be shot". You could have done that, couldn't you?'

PIENNAAR: 'The only explanation I can offer is that time did not permit that.'

COUNSEL: 'And your only excuse is that you were too busy doing the other things that you have told us about?'

PIENAAR: 'Yes.'

COUNSEL: 'Colonel Pienaar, you could have detailed some other officer to make that effort, couldn't you?'

PIENAAR: 'I could have, I did not think of that.'[157]

Despite the police's concessions during cross-examination, in his conclusion Judge Wessels refused to find anyone culpable nor could he decide whether the shooting was justified or not. On the whole, though, Wessels tended to agree with the police that they had been confronting a hostile assembly. 'There could not be the slightest doubt', he maintained, that the PAC's protest was preceded by a night of 'violence and threats of violence' directed at the township's inhabitants and that such acts of intimidation continued into the morning. His report recapitulated the police evidence in detail while referring only occasionally and perfunctorily to evidence from residents. Much of the residents' evidence in any case corroborated the police's version, hardly surprising given the fearful local climate in which witnesses had to live, particularly in the cases of those who were under detention when they appeared before the Commission, often as witnesses coached and prepared by the police's lawyers. Most of the residents who appeared before the Commission therefore professed that they had no knowledge of the Pan-Africanists' activities or intentions, and that they attended the gathering either because they were curious or because they had had been intimidated. Police submissions included the assertion that the crowd was 'armed, noisy and excited', that 'a bloodbath was inevitable' and that the atmosphere was extremely 'inflammable'. As Lieutenant Colonel Pienaar insisted at the Inquiry, 'The native mentality does not allow them to gather for a peaceful demonstration. For them to gather means violence.'[158] So, the crowd was constituted as 'a mob', a term that Wessels himself appeared to endorse by using it in his own commentary, and the members of this 'throng' were 'prancing about', 'massed together', in 'a frenzied state'. As far as the commissioner was concerned the opposed evidence that the crowd showed 'no real hostility . . . could not be accepted'. This was despite testimony from Colonel Spengler that he did not think the crowd was likely to attack the police station. Though the crowd 'could not be regarded as an armed one' the situation was indeed 'inflammable' because of the 'size and the mood of the gathering'. The police's shooting was at least partly prompted by the shots they heard from the crowd 'and a sudden flooding of the Bantu' across the boundary of the station compound and it might have prevented even greater bloodshed.

If not quite measuring up to a justification of the police action, Judge Wessels' assessment on the whole treated the police indulgently in his review of their evidence, disregarding photographs and reports that contradicted their testimony. For example the police denied carrying *sjamboks* though photographs taken after the massacre included pictures of policemen carrying these weapons. The police denied that any shots were fired by the constables from their vantage points on the armoured cars. If accepted, this denial would strengthen the argument that the shooting was by ground based personnel who were taking their cues about the crowd's mood from the people immediately in front of them. Ian Berry's photographs proved this denial to be untrue. Judge Wessels disregarded rumours about soft-nosed bullets and did not attempt to explore why the police reloaded their weapons and continued to fire them after members of the crowd had turned and fled.[159] In his report Wessels preferred the upper estimates of the crowd size though the photographic record makes them seem rather questionable. Philip Frankel conducted his archival research in 1999 at a time of unprecedented absence of any restrictions, before records had been moved from the Department of Justice into the State Archive. He found 'piles of unanalysed forensic evidence (bullets extracted from the dead and wounded)—neatly packaged in dusty brown paper envelopes and closed with red sealing wax—which were either unknown or unavailable to the Commission'.[160] Some of the strongest evidence about the mood of the crowd was from

Superintendant Labuschagne who had walked through the assembly without encountering any significant hostility: this evidence Wessels disregarded. More to his credit he also paid no attention to the piles of sticks and stones that the police constructed as evidence to incriminate the gathering after the shooting. Police brought a somewhat unimpressive selection of these to the Inquiry: twelve sticks, one knobkerrie, two hatchets, ten pieces of iron, two umbrellas, and a bicycle pump.

Wessels' final judgement was hedged about with qualifications and prevarications. It was the police version, though, that would prevail in the kinds of popular understandings of the event that became common currency among white South Africans. For example, a compendious *History of Communism in South African* appeared in 1988, published by a professedly 'conservative Christian' agency and drawing heavily upon police informants. In its treatment of events at Sharpeville, mass hysteria among the residents was initially fostered by 'professional agitators'. Their efforts were swiftly rewarded:

> Vast mobs of blacks assembled at Sharpeville—an estimated 10,000 shouting, screaming wild eyed Africans marched on the local police station. They were armed with sticks, clubs, bottles, knives, iron pipes, assegais, pangas, needle swords and other weapons. There was at that time, a standing order that police were permitted to open fire when the safety of police stations were threatened. The handful of officers in charge panicked and opened fire. Pandemonium broke loose! When the shooting stopped, about 69 Africans lay dead and approximately 178 were wounded.[161]

Much the same version of events appears in the senior Department of Justice official J. P. J. Coetzer's memoir The police station was surrounded 10,000 screaming black people ('skreevende swart mense'). The police were an isolated detachment, incapable of summoning reinforcements. Because of the violent climate of the times it was reasonable for them to assume they were under attack, though their continuation of fire after people began to flee was inexcusable, Coetzer concedes. However their fears were later vindicated, he suggests, when the police collected and built a stack of the weapons they found among the dead: 'stoke, kieres, messe, ysterpype, assegaaie, pangas, swarrde, gebreeke botels ander voorwerpe'. The shooting was in conformity with standing orders that police should fire if they had good reasons to believe they were about to be attacked.[162]

The converse of this kind of understanding of what happened at Sharpeville is discernable in Bishop Ambrose Reeves' book. As the Anglican
bishop of Johannesburg, Reeves made the first call for an investigation and
he raised the money needed to employ the lawyers who would cross-
examine the police. Without his courageous enterprise there would be no
archival record for historians to consult. His own reading of the evidence is
understandably selective, though, concerned as he was to refute a menda-
cious official version of events. Bishop Reeves was sympathetically predisposed to the ANC leadership and his book makes only the most cursory
references to the PAC and its plans. He suggests that the organization was
able to operate in Sharpeville only as a consequence of recent restrictions
imposed by the authorities upon the ANC's leadership; this meant that the
committed advocates of non-violence were restricted while a less experienced and less responsible group was allowed to operate 'unchecked'. In
Sharpeville a few days before the shootings local Pan-Africanists 'took over
whatever political organisation existed there', established presumably by an
earlier generation of ANC activism. The Pan-Africanists did not advocate
violence, though, but their efforts through the night of the 20th to mobilize
support for their protest by peaceful meetings were roughly broken up by
the police. There was no real concerted plan of action and after daybreak,
because the Pan-Africanists succeeded in stopping the buses, 'groups of
Africans drifted through the morning to various points' for 'few people
were sure of whether they were supposed to gather and where'. Eventually
a crowd constituted itself in front of the police station in anticipation of an
important announcement. As they waited 'an idle holiday atmosphere
prevailed'. The gathering was composed mainly of women and children
and its members 'were engaged in various peaceful occupations'. Nobody
was waiting very purposively for 'these were not dangerous agitators but for
the most part ordinary citizens who had come to see what was going on'.
The police's lethal action was attributable not to any aggressive behaviour
but was a consequence of the beliefs and prejudices that informed their
commanders, their equipment, and their deployment.[163]

Reeves' analysis is a lot closer to the truth then the rationalizations of
police behaviour offered by official sources including the Commission but it
represents a simplification of what occurred all the same. In his book the
Sharpeville massacre was the consequence of authoritarian reflexes; the
inevitable outcome of any collective challenge that might have happened
anywhere in South Africa to a political order animated by racial prejudice.

And indeed he prefaces his discussion of the developments at Sharpeville with a narrative of comparable confrontations between the police and African communities, in Zeerust, in Sekhukuneland, and in Windhoek in what was then South West Africa. As is argued earlier in this book, it was a particular combination of local circumstances in Sharpeville that helped to explain the Pan-Africanists' success in constituting a following and their organizational preparations in the townships were extensive and systematic and informed by intelligent calculation. By no means were the local leaders allowed to operate 'unchecked'. Reeves was quite correct to argue that crowd was not aggressive—the photographic evidence he used is especially compelling—but his narrative suggests that the assembly's constitution and membership was largely apolitical, prompted chiefly by sociability and curiosity. This seems at odds with eyewitness accounts—supplied by journalists for example—and it is a characterization that makes the gathering's resolution and commitment very difficult to understand and it does its constituents less than justice. Moreover while it is certainly true that police behaviour was shaped by beliefs and prejudices this is not the whole story. It was also influenced by a succession of hostile interactions between constables and activists through the night before the protest—as Wessels had argued, but which are also recalled by residents themselves. There were also specifically local political dynamics which influenced the perceptions of police commanders at Sharpeville. Elsewhere, even in close-by Bophelong as well as in far off Cape Town, the police managed comparable challenges to their authority more effectively, negotiating with local PAC officials and succeeding in persuading them to disperse their followers.

For the next four decades Reeves' book remained the most authoritative analysis of the Sharpeville massacre and its arguments provided the template for the perceptions of the event that prevailed within the Anti-Apartheid Movement. Sharpeville—adopted by the United Nations as the 'International day for the Elimination of Racism'—became the most significant symbolic anniversary in the Movement's annual calendar, though it was a commemoration in which Pan-Africanists appeared on public platforms very infrequently. In the historical narrative that prevailed on these occasions police fired into an 'amiable' crowd constituted largely by 'curious residents' rather than politically assertive citizens.[164] A standardized narrative became the received history among members of the exile ANC community and their sympathizers. In as much as the Pan-Africanists played any significant role as an agency precipitating events, their success in orchestrating protest was mainly a consequence of the efforts invested by the ANC in preparing for their own protest against the pass laws. The PAC opportunistically capitalized on these efforts by deciding to 'jump the gun' and announce their own plans with an earlier starting date, an 'ill-conceived and hurriedly organized protest'.[165] The repression of the protest was an expression of 'deliberate violence' by a police force deployed by a state itself crossing 'the frontier of terror' into fascism.[166]

Meanwhile, the exiled Pan-Africanist leadership developed its own characteristic way of telling the story of Sharpeville, 'a living monument in the annals of the struggle of the African people' in which martyred citizens become heroic embodiments of the 'growing spirit of resistance within the country'. The massacre was preceded by extensive preparations. The PAC's organizers, 'headed by the president himself proceeded 'from door to door, hut to hut, township to township, village to village' and 'spoke to the masses in the buses, in the trains' and at a range of public places, 'spreading the gospel of liberation and exciting the masses'. All this was done in secret. Even so, despite this precaution, at Sharpeville the police appeared as 'the forces of darkness their might unleashed':

> Machine guns rattled, crackled and whistled. Saracens roared with rancorous gusto. Tanks boomed and pummelled with ghastly staccato. Felons felled the scurrying scattered crowds. Darkness: deep darkness upon the children of Azania! There they lay motionless ... littered like debris on the soil they loved.[167]

This is not the kind of language that could conceivably have been used by anyone who had lived through these events or indeed by anyone who had learned about them from first-hand testimony. After the Commission of Inquiry, though, it would be a long time before any of Sharpeville's inhabitants would be able to offer their own testimony on how they thought about the experiences of that day. For at least two decades after the killing in Sharpeville there would be no public conversations about the massacre or about the events leading up to it. Indeed 'we were forced to forget about the shootings, because if you spoke about them you were arrested'.[168] In Joyce Mokhesi's account of growing up in Sharpeville during the 1960s, parents remained silent: 'Their silent grief smothered our knowledge' for 'They wished us free of the anger they would not feel ... They hoped that the path of forgetting would give us, their children, a peace they could not feel.' For three years after the massacre, a Catholic priest, Father Rudolph O'Flynn, held a memorial service on 21 March but he was then deported and after that there were to be no more special church services.

A vengeful local constabulary treated wounded survivors who were recovering in hospitals as criminal suspects, imprisoning them and investigating possible charges that could be directed against them. Later on, it is true, the state offered compensatory payments to people who had been disabled but the amounts were derisory, one-off payments of less than one hundred Rands. The Vereeniging Municipality paid for the funerals and for the costs of erecting headstones, but these offered only cryptic reminders of what happened. 'The inscriptions make no mention of the struggle or the sacrifice [and] the graves are like any others . . . It [was] as if none of the dead had been massacred, as if there had been no protest; and in this emptiness there was nothing, not even honour, for a family to cherish.'[169] Police successes in inhibiting resident testimony at the Commission of Inquiry and in bullying people into giving evidence on behalf of the authorities helped to consolidate a culture of mutual distrust that continued to inhibit social and political life in the township twenty years later, as journalists discovered when they tried during the 1980s to persuade people to speak to them about the massacre.

Even without the police's subsequent efforts it is quite likely that the sheer scale of the violence inflicted on the 21 March would have had morally and emotionally damaging effects for a very long time. As Ambrose Reeves pointed out, 216 families were affected by the deaths or serious wounding of breadwinners and parents—at least five hundred children would have experienced a disintegration of their family life. But the consequences would have been much wider. Social psychologists believe that people who witness or experience and survive extreme violations of normal civic conduct as in mass killings undertaken by officials have to cope with stigma and trauma. They live in a setting in which they encounter generalized attitudes of suspicion and distrust which help to reinforce their own feelings of psychological isolation: this was certainly the case in Sharpeville to judge from the survivors' experiences. Traumatic violent experience estranges people and for its victims their experience makes them feel vulnerable, helpless, and even ashamed.[170] When the Tsolo brothers were released they found that their family was socially ostracized, blamed by their neighbours for the calamity that had been visited upon the community and punished by officials through the withdrawal of their father's business licence. Still suffering from his leg wound, Lebitsa

Ramohoase's testimony was cited by the South African Truth and Reconciliation Commission as an emblematic case of post traumatic stress:

> My life changed. I led a miserable life. You know my feelings changed altogether. But I don't know what kind of help I could give myself and I was satisfied. I said I have to be satisfied because it is something that happened to me. I am helpless; I can't do anything for myself.[171]

Following Freud, theorists of the psychological effects of political violence suggest that survivors of such experiences 'inhabit a liminal space, both part of society and removed from society', existing on a bewildering threshold between the living and the dead,[172] arguably an effect likely to be all the more pronounced in a cultural setting in which, as Father Patrick Noonan discovered in Sharpeville, people 'see little division between the supernatural and the everyday details of life'.[173] Vincent Leutsoa lost two members of his family on 21 March. As he recalled when he was interviewed more than forty years later, 'I was alive, but it didn't feel that way. I was alone.' Over and over again, survivors refer to the 'pain' they live with, not just physical pain but the kind of protracted emotional anguish which can become unbearable, a torment that survivors liken to 'a pain in my heart'. 'Almighty God, this story pains me', Isaac Moeung told a visitor in 2000. Shot and subsequently detained he was 'still angry', he said.[174] In 1984, Sharpeville residents interviewed for a documentary film insisted to researchers that people who had lived through the massacre 'were still crying within' ('ne 'ntse ba lla').[175]

Whether individually experienced psychological disorders are experienced collectively in social groups is more contentious. Catherine Merridale's research on death and memory in Russia reminds us that the process of grieving can depend and be influenced by social convention so that in certain 'high mortality regimes' grief may have to be highly individualized, repressed, and hidden, not shared or ritualized.[176] The assumption that nations or groups possess collective psyches that can be healed by the same sorts of therapeutic processes that may restore individuals was a key premise in guiding the activities of the South African Truth and Reconciliation Commission but even quite cohesive social groups are unlikely to be uniformly affected by events that may have traumatic effects upon individuals. It does seem reasonable, though, to suggest that in small tightly knit communities in which significant numbers of people witness and experience horrific happenings that their own stressed state will have broader social effects. The ways in which violence might cause a shared communal trauma might work in the following way. Violence that appears to break normal rules ruptures ordinary suppositions about everyday life, weakening the moral fabric surrounding institutions and eroding people's own perceptions of moral and social responsibility, their personal autonomy and self confidence.[177] In a setting in which public violence is sanctioned through policy decisions—as in the authorities' justification of the police's behaviour at Sharpeville, a setting is created in which people have to accustom themselves to what ordinarily would be intolerable; they achieve a measure of personal security through developing a protective layer of social indifference. Hence collective fears colour social relationships discouraging imaginative empathy and social solidarity—as seems to have been the case with the collective rejoicings Petrus Tom describes in his memoir after 'the children' had burned Jacob Dhlamini, after they had 'made a Kentucky Fried Chicken' from him.

Obviously the severity of this sort of 'collective trauma' will be all the greater if the violations are unchecked and unpunished and unopposed by groups that might represent alternative sources of moral authority to the officials inflicting violence. In the unusually repressive environment Sharpeville represented—unusual even in a South African context of comparison—no such local sources of alternative authority could emerge for a very long time. Here in the mid-1980s, in the near absence of an adult generation prepared to exercise leadership—a consequence of the fearful situation in which young men and women grew up in the 1960s and 1970s—alternative political authority would be exercised through militarized echelons of youth. Richard Wilson encountered these in his fieldwork in Sharpeville in 1996, cohorts of youngsters socialized in criminal sub-cultures and nurtured also in an inherited 'culture of violence',[178] caught up in cyclical vendettas, mimicking again and again the sacrifices of earlier generations, or, to borrow Joyce Mokhesi's hauntingly vivid metaphor, 'breaking open the wounds of their fathers' bodies, staining the white future'.[179]

In such settings what is needed to restore community life so that people no longer inhabit such 'liminal' spaces? Are there procedures that can help the emotional and moral recovery of individuals as well as supporting the reconstruction of communities affected by both the direct experience of officially instigated killing and by locally transmitted memories of such violations. The public telling of their stories—'truth testimony'—may go some way towards achieving the kind of moral reintegration that is needed by people who inhabit a liminal world of the half dead if it can elicit expressions of empathy that lessen the stigma felt by the casualties of collective violence. Best of all would be if individual accounts of pain and loss can cohere into a collective memory, 'subscribed to and shared by a group'.[180] Very optimistically, South African truth commissioners believed that the public compilation of diverse memories about particular events— not one story, but many stories—could lead to 'a rich and inclusive memory, sometimes called a "thick memory", that can capture gradations of responsibility for the past' and in so doing build new kinds of social solidarity between former adversaries.[181] Especially important, though, in any reconstruction of social cohesion there must be clear acknowledgement of wrong-doing either by the original perpetrators or by convincing proxies for them, as Tsoane Mhlapo maintains, 'an apology from the state for what happened here'.

Ethnographic studies of the local politics of reconciliation in South Africa suggest that what may be needed is rather more than apologies, that before people can overcome the kind of trauma that destroys their own self-belief and their sense of social security they need a form of justice with retributive moral foundations. For the Israeli social psychologist, Daniel Bar-tal, there are strong grounds for believing that revenge addresses basic human needs, it 'loosens the taut feeling caused by the slaying or despoiling of one's self' and 'an expression of responsibility to the killed'.[182] At the very least, judicial or truth-telling procedures need to name perpetrators of violence before reconstruction of a reintegrated moral community can begin among victims and their sympathizers. The process of 'social healing' is possible only once the source of violence has been identified and even 'sacrificed' through punishment to atone for the original harm.[183] It is possible that alternately more conciliatory forms of 'transitional' justice may also help to address such needs, though this is contested by critics of the South African Truth and Reconciliation Commission. Reparations might also rebuild civic authority, as several survivors from the massacre interviewed in 2000 suggested. But in Sharpeville, forty years after the event, as Isaac Moeung observed, 'the victims were never compensated'. 'We are left here alone with our memories.'[184]

Storytelling, acknowledgement, and reparation were each aims of the South African Truth and Reconciliation Commission. The Commission visited the Vereeniging region in August 1996. For those people who offered their testimony to the Commission there may have been relief and comfort but to judge from the interviews that we have cited in this book, lingering local perceptions of injustice remained very widespread. With respect to many of the residents of Sharpeville, the Commission's visit failed to achieve the kind of ritual 'symbolic closure' that its proceedings may have obtained elsewhere. We do know that the television broadcast of the Sebokeng hearings affected one white community profoundly. Piet Meiring, the DRC's representative on the Commission was invited to a parish meeting in Randfontein (on the West Rand) to address members of the white congregation who were shocked and mortified by what they had seen: 'We really did not know! Can we be guilty of the misdeeds of a small group of criminals?'[185] In Sharpeville, though, the effect of the hearings may have been blunted by the continuation of conflict, for, as we have seen, violent rivalries between different militarized factions were still in progress at the time the Commission began its investigation in Sharpeville. The Commission itself heard about the killing of Molefe Phele, a Sebokeng Pan-Africanist who after his return from Tanzania to Sebokeng in 1992 had been the victim of a drive-by shooting, possibly an incident implicating the police because Phele's father later saw his son's assassin's car parked at the police station.[186] Only one year before the Commission opened its proceedings ANC supporters fired shots at a PAC commemorative meeting at the George Thabe stadium. The confrontation followed the cancellation of an ANC rally planned at a different venue for the anniversary after the non-arrival of leaders who were scheduled to address the gathering.[187] Violence affected the hearings directly for on the night of 7 August shots were fired on one witness's home. On the following day, a group of *Afrikaner Weerstandsbeweging* supporters gathered outside the Sebokeng College of Education chanting slogans: the only evidence of any local white interest in the hearings.[188]

The Commission held public hearings on Human Rights Violations over four days in the hall of the Sebokeng College of Education, from 5 August to 8 August 1996, one of fifty or so public hearings held all over the country. The proceedings addressed a sequence of violent events, beginning with testimonies about the 1960 massacre on the first day before considering the 1984 rebellion as well as the conflicts between ANC and IFP supporters in the 1990s. The Commission allowed only a day, then, for survivors to address the events of 1960. These hearings were organized around testimony from witnesses who were already selected. During the preceding months the Commission had employed statement-takers who had visited people who had indicated their willingness to tell their stories. The Commission had elicited forty-six such statements from a range of witnesses present at the massacre including people who had survived wounding, detention, prison sentences, and exile. The original deponents therefore included Pan-Africanist activists, one of whom, Sidwell Kasa, is identified in the report as a participant in the pass protest. He was later imprisoned for three years and subsequently banished from the Vaal. From the deponents the commissioners then chose the witnesses who would testify at the public hearing.

The public testimony was from non-activists, 'apolitical' people, in the language used in the Commission's *Report*, or in the words used by Archbishop Desmond Tutu at the hearings, 'ordinary people trying to abide by the law'.[189] When Elizabeth Mabona woke up that Monday morning she 'found out that it was bad outside'. People were 'all over the streets'. No one was to go to work, and anyone who disobeyed this instruction would 'be killed' She joined a group on their way to the police station. At the station, 'we sat down, we were singing hymns, you know it was a jolly atmosphere'. At a certain juncture 'people from the PAC approached' and told them they could 'disperse', return to their homes for dinner and after eating come back to the police station 'so that there can be another meting'. Mrs Mabona retuned home but when she arrived there she found the house empty, her husband was still at the station. She became worried and went out into the street where she encountered one of her husband's friends. She asked him where her husband was because she had earlier seen them together. 'He said, no, he is around, please go. Why do you involve yourself in issues involving men?' She started walking back to the station but she then heard gun shots and ran back to her home. Later she learned that her husband was dead. She subsequently visited the hospital but could not find his body so she then decided to visit the police station. At the station she saw that all 'the people that had been taken to the station were all dead'. The police confirmed that her husband's body was among the dead. On the next day and the following days they questioned her, again and again, five times altogether, because they thought her husband was a Pan-Africanist. He was not and nor was she: she was 'taking part just as an onlooker'. She did not believe in the protest but she and her friends were 'singing these hymns as Christians because we were just rejoicing'. They were expecting to receive a message that afternoon and they 'were just joyous'.[190]

David Ramohoase was on his way to work at the dry-cleaning factory that morning when he was stopped by a PAC picket line. Its members asked him to accompany them to the police station. 'We asked them what are you going to do there, they said no we are going to enquire about the pass.' He walked with them willingly enough, for he too 'wanted to go and listen to this issue about passes'. He joined the crowd on its fringes, sitting at the edge of the main body, awaiting developments for 'a long time'. It was a very sunny day, he recalled, and many people were sheltering themselves with umbrellas. Not one person was armed as far as he could see. 'Those who might have had guns, maybe they were hidden somewhere' but he could see no weapons, not even a stick. 'Not even a knobkerrie', he insisted, he 'could see only umbrellas'. Between one and two o'clock a small white car arrived and out of this car 'a man jumped . . . a white person, and he had a very short stick in his hand and he had a band on his head'. The man dropped his stick and then he said 'shoot'. Mr Ramohoase fell to the ground. Later he realized he had been shot in the leg. The person next to him told him to keep his head down for the police were now walking around inspecting the bodies. His neighbour said if he looked up 'they will come and finish us off'. He did see the constables turning bodies over, but 'we didn't actually know what they were doing'. 'According to our minds', though, 'they were doing something to the people.' Mr Ramohoase remained in hospital for three months. Even today his leg still hurt him, especially when the weather was cold. But emotionally too, he was not well.[191]

From these 'narrative truths' the Commission assembled its findings. The police deliberately opened fire on an unarmed crowd that had gathered peacefully. The police continued to fire after the crowd began to flee. The police did not open fire spontaneously, for the deponents to the TRC gave evidence that suggested 'a degree of deliberation'. The report cited David Ramohoase's original deposition in which he said that a white man 'gave a sign' before the shooting started. In his statement, David's brother, Lebitsa 'remembered a white man climbing into a Saracen and pulling the door shut above him, just before gun shots rang out'. As a consequence hundreds of people were shot in the back and sixty-nine were killed. Many of the people who were wounded or killed 'were apolitical, women and unarmed', the *Report* concluded.[192]

To those residents who read the *Report*, these findings may have supplied the solace of an official moral vindication. They appear, though, in a few fleeting paragraphs, four pages in a six volume report of several thousand pages, overlaid by similar reports and findings about scores of more recent and nearly as bloody encounters between armed officials and protesting assemblies. From this perspective the shootings at Sharpeville are reduced to just 'an ordinary atrocity', rather than a defining event. And indeed it is notably missing from the list of happenings that the Commission chose to address with special hearings. To a degree in other settings, the Commission could offer a semblance of justice through eliciting testimony and even, sometimes, expressions of remorse from killers or from those who gave them orders, especially when it addressed applications for amnesty. But none of the policemen who were present at Sharpeville that day were visited or summoned by the commissioners and none of them applied for amnesty. In the words of Mary Mantsho, secretary of Sharpeville's Khulu- mani group, 'At the TRC the police did not come for us. We are always talking about this.'[193] The *Report* names no individual policemen, not even Lieutenant Colonel Pienaar. Instead the Commission's condemnation is impersonal. 'The former state and the Minister of Police' were 'directly responsible for the commission of gross human rights violations.' Perhaps if the TRC had attempted to solicit police testimony it might have succeeded. Philip Frankel's interviews with policemen, conducted in 1999 and 2000, do indicate that many of the Vereeniging-based white police officers who participated were traumatized, still experiencing repetitive nightmares and flashbacks. Forty white policemen left the service in the Vereeniging district in the weeks following the massacre. In the same period others expressed sorrow and even contrition to the congregations of the churches they normally attended.[194]

Thabo Mbeki's successor state would indeed pay reparations several years later but it would be left to the young leader of the 'New' National Party, Marthinus van Schalkwyk, born just a few months before the massacre to express an apology. During the 1999 election campaign, van Schalkwyk visited Sharpeville and laid a wreath. This was one of two symbolic visits van Schalkwyk made to the area—the other was to the site where the Treaty of Vereeniging was signed at the end of the Anglo–Boer War. Both visits were hardly likely to win votes and, instead, seemed to be conceived as an effort to reposition the National Party morally and philosophically through emphasizing continuities between two different national liberation move- ments. 'It is only when white South Africans understand the struggle of black South Africans to be free that they will themselves really be free', van Schalkwyk told a small gathering of a hundred people assembled at the site of the massacre in Sharpeville.[195]

Nyakane Tsolo was not mentioned in the Commission's *Report* and he did not offer testimony. He had returned to Sharpeville at the end of 1991 after a thirty-year absence. When he jumped bail in 1961 he travelled to Lesotho. Later he underwent military instruction in Egypt as a commando, training with their special forces. Among his companions he became known as 'Transistor Man' because he was so small. Between 1963 and 1973 he lived in East Germany, he told journalists later. If this report is accurate it would have been unusual because on the whole the German Democratic Republic was inhospitable terrain for Pan-Africanists. In 1973, though, 'circumstances' forced Nyakane and his young family to leave Germany 'secretly' and take refuge in the Netherlands. He remained in Rotterdam for the rest of his exile, for a period designated as a PAC representative and working with local anti-apartheid bodies. He remained a Leballo loyalist through the 1980s maintaining that his mentor had fallen victim to an internal struggle within the PAC between genuine revolutionaries and reactionary reformists, losing his formal standing as the organization's Netherlands representative as a consequence.[196] When he re-appeared in Sharpeville in 1991 he was just visiting. Despite his inclusion on the PAC's electoral list in 1994 he maintained his home in Rotterdam through the rest of the decade. He only made his homecoming permanent at the end of 2001. One year later he was dead, from a stroke.[197]

★

Nyakane Tsolo lived long enough to be invited to the opening of Sharpeville's memorial, an architectural tribute constructed on behalf of the Gauteng regional government and the South African Heritage Resource Agency. Since its opening in 2002 the monument has been expanded to include a museum and will shortly incorporate the now-abandoned old police station. The police have moved to new premises, a bright, light building one mile away, surrounded by flower beds. Policing today in Sharpeville is very different from historical patterns, according to Inspector Manala, the station's commanding officer. Local officers deal mainly with 'social crime' and domestic strife. The gangster syndicates still make their homes in Sharpeville but they operate outside the township, further afield, he says. There is very little serious organized crime within the borders of the township, the inspector insists.

Visitors can walk through the empty rooms of the old station. The building's bleakly functional exterior is now softened with a pink wash painted over the band of plaster above the orange face-brick. Lawns, paths, and two rows of shrubs and trees supply a shady formal garden in the area where once the front ranks of the PAC's supporters pressed against the wire fence. Inside, though, the decor and furnishings have hardly altered over fifty years: a long hardwood counter in the charge office, shiny red-polished concrete floors, iron windows, rusty filing cabinets and battered Venetian blinds The holding cells in which the police detained the Pan-Africanist leadership remain: creaky armoured doors, a meshed-in courtyard, concrete furnishings, and high-up grated windows.

The building will soon be renovated, converted into an archive, administrative offices for the museum, and meeting rooms to accommodate community groups. One local association that hopes to make the old station an assembly point for its activities is the local Sharpeville branch of Khulumani—'Speak out'. Prompted by the impending establishment of the Truth and Reconciliation Commission, Khulumani established itself as a national association of survivors of human rights abuses between 1960 and 1992.[198] Its immediate aim was to supply advice and support for people who chose to offer testimony to the TRC. Since its formation it has enrolled a membership of 55,000. In Sharpeville an energetic local branch of Khulumani has existed since 1995 meeting every fortnight in the Catholic church hall. Khulumani has three hundred Sharpeville residents on its 'database', a membership that includes many of the survivors of the 1960 bloodletting but also people who were affected by more recent abuses, up to and including the 1992 massacre in nearby Boipatong. Its officers, elected every three years by a show of hands, include as deputy chairperson, Johannes Sefatse, one of the people gathered in front of the police line on 21 March 1960. Nationally, Khulumani has agitated for a special pension fund for survivors and it has also opposed various amnesty applications. In its local setting in Sharpeville the organization views its role as the continuation of the business left unfinished by the Truth Commission: the provision of a sympathetic setting in which people can tell and retell their stories, a supportive milieu within which 'if they come they will be healed', its officers believe.[199] The group includes a cadre of trained counsellors and indeed from time to time 'facilitates' such training from visiting specialists. Usually its meetings are attended by between fifty or a hundred people. They can participate in a range of activities including a handicrafts programme and fieldtrips to historical sites. They help people who come to mourn their loved ones: 'Always after 21 March we bury some of the families.'

On such occasions, people assemble in front of the monument and they weep for their dead.

By the side of the old station, across the road where there was once open veldt, the Sharpeville memorial takes up the ground where most of the massacre's victims died. The site is inhabited by a memorial garden in which the names of the dead each appear on a separate obelisk. The garden is planted with the acacia trees and the grasses and the flowers that once grew wild in the surrounding landscape, now mostly built over. The obelisks are arranged on each side of a channel of water that drains from a fountain, a symbolic representation of the cleansing function first performed by the rainfall that arrived after the massacre, washing away the blood of the dead. In front of the garden is a monumentally proportioned gateway, brown rendered plaster, vaguely Etruscan, the default genre when South African architects attempt to represent African building traditions, though in this region indigenous construction was stone-based. By the side of the gateway there is a plaque, commemorating Nelson Mandela's visit to Sharpeville, the location he chose for the ceremonial signing into law of the 1996 Constitution. It reads: 'In memory of those who gave their lives for a free and just South Africa'. The names of the dead appear again on four plaques fixed to the front wall of the gatehouse. Certain residents believe that there are names that are missing and indeed this is quite likely, for the monument makes no direct reference to people who died from their injuries sustained at the massacre or who may have been buried secretly, unacknowledged by any inquest. The victims of later political conflicts lie in a newer cemetery, Vuka, located next to the old site and service scheme. Here too, the Heritage Agency has been at work, restoring the graves and building pathways.

Separating the Memorial Garden from the adjacent exhibition hall is a tree-lined paved pathway, 'Constitution Walk' which one day will lead through to a reconstructed historical precinct in which the Sedibeng Council hopes to restore Maraneng, the official residence that used to accommodate the king of Lesotho during his visits to the Basotho migrant community, as well as the Community Hall, burned out during the 1980s and the long disused swimming pool. The exhibition hall at present relies heavily on Ian Berry's photographs as well as excerpts from survivors' testimony: these combine to make a powerful impression that is all the more effective because of the simplicity of the display and the emotionally understated aesthetics of the memorial. Indeed some local residents would prefer a less allegorical monumental style that made more direct visual references to the event.[200] The absence of these may have been intentional. Other commentators have drawn attention to the way that official commemorations of apartheid's history strive to maintain a consensual and even 'politically decontextualised' tone.[201] Hence 21 March is a day to celebrate the achievement of human rights rather than to recall the Sharpeville shootings. Local residents often seem nonplussed by this predisposition. Japhta Mokwena has lived on Seeiso Street for the past fifty-two years. From his home he can easily see the police station in front of which he stood on 21 March 1960. He feels that today outside the station 'there should be a statue of the army tank used at the massacre . . . as a reminder that innocent people were gunned down'.[202] The museum's curator, Sekwati Sekoane, has in fact asked the police authorities if they can supply a vintage Saracen. In the meantime residents must content themselves with an almost life-size sculptured papier mache rendition of a Saracen, the work of Moses Tsolo, grandson of Job Tsolo, brother of Nyakane, a Fine Arts graduate from the Vaal Technikon.

The Pan-Africanists have built their own monument. In Phelendaba Cemetary on the township's outskirts sixty-four of the people killed by the police are buried in a single row one hundred metres long. Originally their graves were marked with plain concrete tablets, erected and paid for by Vereeniging Council, marked only with names and dates. These have been replaced with polished scrolls. Below the biographical details of each of the dead, the inscription reads 'Robala ka Khotso' (Rest in Peace). The new headstones were installed by the Heritage Agency and they are mostly identical though here and there, some families have chosen to put up their own tributes. On many of the graves there remain flowers and empty bottles and vessels from the libations that mourners continue to offer. Philemon Tsolo rests in his plot in the preceding row of graves, for the final resting places of Sharpeville's citizens are located in the order of their demise and Nyakane's, Job's, and Gideon's father died shortly before the massacre. At the head of the row stands the PAC's memorial, three painted concrete tables, yellow, green, and black, the traditional national colours. On the central tablet there is a map of Africa with the rays of a star illuminating the continent. Next to the continent a legend reads: 'They died for freedom: lest we forget', a reminder of the contested interpretations that extend their claims even to the bodies of the dead.

Memorials aside, in appearance Sharpeville would still be quite recognizable to anyone returning after a fifty-year absence. Rows of mainly ochre and grey four room dwellings still line most of the roads and lanes, the standard 'matchbox' houses constructed in hundreds of thousands across South Africa in the 1950s, utilitarian brick cabins with asbestos roofs and outhouse toilets. Some have been subjected to improvements: concrete tiles on the roofs, painted and plastered walls, burglar bars and front *stoeps* and on a few stands residents have built over their plots, walling their gardens and replacing the matchboxes with suburban double storeys. There is a astonishing range of what are evidently still well-attended churches, several dating from the 1950s, red brick halls with short towers and shallow steeples. Television satellites, power lines, and mobile-phone masts reflect key changes in the way that people live their lives since the 1960s but there are not many signs of post-democratic affluence. The heavy industries that were once the economic staple of this region are now in decline and local unemployment levels are somewhat higher than the already steep national average. What might have been Sharpeville's new middle class now lives in Vereeniging or even further afield in the leafy neighbourhoods by the Vaal River, in the resort settlement of Vanderbijl-park. Government subsidies have helped to build several thousand new houses, though, in a new section of the township, 'Sephiso' (Promise) and Sharpeville's population is now around 100,000. Besides the Human Rights Precinct, the township's new infrastructure includes properly tarred roads and, more exceptionally, a well-resourced library, replacing the old building that stood near the police station. The new building accommodates a computer-equipped study room and a hospitable reading room with well-stocked bookshelves. Sharpeville's civic endowments are completed with a community health centre. Complaints of the Concerned Residents notwithstanding, the township seems to have received a fair measure of public investment from the Sedibeng Municipality and the provincial authorities. Its neighbourhoods now constitute just four wards of a local government that embraces all the major settlements across the Vaal region. Each of these wards has elected an ANC candidate since the inception of local polls for here as elsewhere the Pan-Africanists receive short shrift in the voting booths. In a quite different way, though, historical traditions shape electoral politics. One of the councillors is the son of Samuel Kolisang who sixty years ago headed the township Advisory Board.

On the eastern borders of Sharpeville, on the way out along the road that leads to Vereeniging there is a lake formed by the reservoir that has accumulated behind the Leeukuil Dam. The dam is fringed with willow trees and bull-rushes and it is surrounded by gentle parkland. In a harsh landscape of decaying heavy industry the lake and its serene surroundings are startlingly beautiful. South Africans normally enjoy such amenities but here there are no concrete benches and barbecue sites for picnickers, there are no children's swings and no places for fishing. The lake is deserted, overlooked only by the ruined shell of the building that once served as the municipal brewery.

This neglect is attributable to a persistent local belief. Sekwati Sekoana, museum curator and one time Treason Triallist can supply an explanation for this strange abstention. As he shows schoolchildren around the memorial he tells them about the meaning of the water that is made to flow through the garden. 'After the shooting started it began to rain', he says. 'The rain washed the blood away from the dead and wounded and the water drained away to flow into the reservoir at the township's edge. The dam was often empty before that day but since then it has always been full. The people used to like sitting by the lake. Always they used its water for washing and drinking. Not for fifty years. Nobody has used the water since. Nobody goes there. Never.'[203]

For so many of Sharpeville's inhabitants, their homeplace remains a vicinity of restless spirits, tormented ghosts.

Notes

FRONT MATTER

1. Christopher Saunders, 'The meaning remains elusive', *South African Outlook*, 1985.
2. Ambrose Reeves, *Shooting at Sharpeville*, New York: Houghton Mifflin, 1961, pp. 30–1.
3. Belinda Bozzoli, 'Class, community and ideology in the evolution of South African society', in Belinda Bozzoli (ed.), *Class, Community and Conflict: South African Perspectives*, Johannesburg: Ravan Press, 1987, p. 1.
4. Tom Lodge, *Black Politics in South Africa since 1945*, London: Longman, 1983.
5. Matthew Chaskalson, 'The road to Sharpeville', in Stephen Clingman (ed.), *Regions and Repertoires: Topics in South African Politics and Culture*, Johannesburg: Ravan Press, 1991. Chaskalson's thesis with the same title was submitted through the Wits Department of History in 1986.
6. Terri Shakinovsky, 'The Local State in Crisis: The Shaping of the Black Working Class, Vereeniging 1939–1949', BA Honours Dissertation, Department of History, University of the Witwatersrand, 1983; Ian Jeffrey, 'The Sharpetown Swingsters: Their Will to Survive', BA Honours Dissertation, Department of Social Anthropology, University of the Witwatersrand, 1985.
7. Petrus Tom, *My Life Struggle*, Johannesburg: Ravan Worker Series, 1985; Johannes Rantete, *The Third Day of September*, Johannesburg: Ravan Storyteller Series, 1984.
8. Philip Frankel, *An Ordinary Atrocity: Sharpeville and its Massacre*, New Haven: Yale University Press, 2001.

CHAPTER I

1. Elizabeth Mabona, Testimony at the Truth and Reconciliation Commission, Sebokeng, 5 August 1996, http://www.doj.gov.za/trc/hrvtrans/sebokeng/seb793.htm
2. Frederick Batkani's testimony in Jasper van der Bliek (ed.), *Sharpeville Scars*, Tilburg: Tilburg-Lekoa Vaal Association, 2000, p. 29.
3. Ruben Rapoetsoe's testimony, van der Bliek, *Sharpeville Scars*, p. 37.
4. George Myubu's testimony, van der Bliek, *Sharpeville Scars*, p. 17.

5. Segametsi Makhanya's testimony, van der Bliek, *Sharepville Scars*, p. 25.

6. Carlton Monnakgotla's testimony, van der Bliek, *Sharpeville Scars*, p. 19.

7. Sam Poletsi's testimony, van der Bliek, *Sharpeville Scars*, pp. 13–15.

8. Lebitsa Ramohoase, Testimony at the Truth and Reconciliation Commission, Sebokeng, 5 August 1996, http://www.doj.gov.za/trc/hrvtrans/sebokeng/seb901.htm

9. Lydia Mahabuke, interviewed by the author, Sharpeville, 7 November 2009.

10. Simon Mkutau's testimony, van der Bliek, *Sharpeville Scars*, p. 35.

11. Mrs Mguni's testimony, van der Bliek, *Sharpeville Scars*, p. 23.

12. Vincent Leutsoa's testimony, van der Bliek, *Sharpeville Scars*, pp. 26–7.

13. David Ramohoase, Testimony at the Truth and Reconciliation Commission, Sebokeng, 5 August 1996, http://www.doj.gov.za/trc/hrvtrans/sebokeng/seb901.htm

14. Puseloto Ziphara Malelo's testimony, van der Bliek, *Sharpeville Scars*, p. 21.

15. Isaac Moeung's testimony, van der Bliek, *Sharpeville Scars*, pp. 38–9.

16. Albert Mbongo's testimony, van der Bliek, *Sharpeville Scars*, p. 29.

17. Sam Kolinsang's testimony, van der Bliek, *Sharpeville Scars*, pp. 41–3.

18. Quoted in Howard Smith, 'Apartheid, Sharpeville and impartiality: the reporting of South Africa on BBC television, 1948–1961', *Historical Journal of Film, Radio and Television*, 13, 3, 1993, p. 261.

19. John Kane-Berman, *Soweto: Black Revolt, White Reaction*, Johannesburg: Ravan Press, 1978, pp. 232–3.

20. For argument of this kind, see Michael O'Dowd, 'South Africa in the light of stages of economic growth' and Norman Bromberger, 'Economic growth and political change in South Africa', both in Adrian Leftwich (ed.), *South Africa: Economic Growth and Political Change*, London: Allison and Busby, 1974.

21. Robert Edgar, *Because they Chose the Plan of God: The Story of the Bulhoek Massacre*, Johannesburg: Ravan Press, 1988, p. 32.

22. Edward Roux, *Time Longer than Rope*, London: Victor Gollancz, 1948, pp. 256–7.

23. Dawn Ridgway, Milly Jafta, Nicky Kautja, Magda Oliphant, and Kapoli Shipingana, *An Investigation into the Shooting at the Old Location on 10 December 1959*, Windhoek: University of Namibia, 1991, p. 26.

24. Daniel A. Gordon, 'World reactions to the 1961 Paris pogrom', *University of Sussex Journal of Contemporary History*, 1, 2000, p. 4.

25. For an early report of the Mueda massacre in which Portuguese soldiers may have killed as many as 500 villagers demonstrating over wage rates and other grievances, see Eduardo Mondlane, *The Struggle for Mozambique*, Harmondsworth: Penguin African Library, 1969, pp. 117–18.

CHAPTER 2

1. 'Congress Youth League Manifesto', in Robert Edgar and Luyanda ka Msumza, *Freedom in Our Lifetime: The Collected Writings of Anton Muziwakhe Lembede*, Athens: Ohio University Press, 1996, p. 68.

2. A. M. Lembede, 'Policy of the Congress Youth League', in Robert Edgar and Luyanda ka Msumza (eds.), *Freedom in Our Lifetime*, p. 91.

3. Gail Gerhart, *Black Power in South Africa: The Evolution of an Ideology*, Berkeley: University of California Press, 1978, p. 72.

4. Zolile Hamilton Keke, 'A Pan-Africanist speaks: the story of the Pan-Africanist Congress', 1989, unpublished typescript, Randolph Vigne Papers, BC 1328, University of Cape Town Libraries, Manuscripts and Archives, p. 15.

5. Peter Raboroko, interviewed by author, Johannesburg, 14 June 1993.

6. Albert Luthuli quoted in Scott Everett Couper, 'Bound by Faith: A Biographic and Ecclesiastic Examination of Chief Albert Luthuli's Stance on Violence as a Strategy to Liberate South Africa', Ph.D. Dissertation, School of Anthropology, Gender and Historical Studies, University of KwaZulu Natal, Durban, 2008, p. 144.

7. Julius Lewin, 'No revolution round the corner', originally printed in *Africa South* in 1959 and reprinted in Julius Lewin, *Politics and Law in South Africa*, London: Merlin Press, 1961, p. 114.

8. Ken Luckhardt and Brenda Wall, *Organize or Starve . . . The History of the South African Congress of Trade Unions*, London: Lawrence and Wishart, 1980, p. 354.

9. Dan Thloome, 'Lessons of the Stay-Away', *Liberation* (Johannesburg), 32, August 1958.

10. Peter Raboroko, interviewed by the author, Johannesburg, 14 June 1993.

11. Potlake Leballo, interviewed by Gail Gerhart, Nairobi, 11 September 1968, DISA/Aluka Topics # 320 and 321.

12. Benjamin Pogrund, notes on a conversation with Robert Sobukwe, 3 May 1958, Robert Sobukwe Papers, A2618 Cb, University of the Witwatersrand Library, Historical Papers.

13. Elliot Mafaxa and P. L. Gqobose, interviewed by Gail Gerhart, Maseru, 29 December 1969, Gail Gerhart Papers, A2422, University of The Witwatersrand Library, Historical Papers.

14. For more detail, see Tom Lodge, 'Political mobilization in the 1950s: an East London case study', in Shula Marks and Stanley Trapido (eds.), *The Politics of Race, Class and Nationalism in Twentieth Century South Africa*, London: Longman, 1987, pp. 321–5.

15. Nana Mahomo, 'The Rise of the Pan-Africanist Congress of South Africa', M.Sc. Dissertation, Massachusetts Institute of Technology, Boston, 1968, p. 44.

16. Bernard Leeman, *Lesotho and the Struggle for Azania*, London: University of Azania, 1985, p. 84.

17. Potlake Leballo, interviewed by Gail Gerhart, Nairobi, 11 September 1968, DISA/Aluka Topics # 320 and 321.

18. Joel Bolnick, 'Potlake Leballo—the man who hurried to meet his destiny', *Journal of Modern African Studies*, 29, 3, 1991, p. 411.

19. Leeman, *Lesotho and the Struggle for Azania*, p. 68.

20. Leeman, *Lesotho and the Struggle for Azania*, pp. 71 and 90. When they were interviewed by Gail Gerhart (Maseru, 29 December 1969) Elliot Mfaxa and Pearce Gqobose confirmed that Leballo was an influential figure within the BCP, indeed, Mfaxa maintained, the BCP president, Ntsu Mokhele 'couldn't hold a meeting in the Transvaal without letting Leballo speak because he was so popular'.

21. Jack Halpern, *South Africa's Hostages: Basutoland, Bechuanaland and Swaziland*, Harmondsworth: Penguin African Library, 1965, p. 27, suggested that Leballo's conviction was for 'fraud, forgery and uttering'.

22. Main sources for this profile: Bolnick, 'Potlake Leballo', Leeman, *Lesotho and the Struggle for Azania*.

23. Robert Sobukwe quoted in Gerhart, *Black Power in South Africa*, p. 155.

24. Thomas Karis and Gail Gerhart (eds.), *From Protest to Challenge: A Documentary History of African Politics in South Africa, Volume 3, Challenge and Violence, 1953–1954*, Stanford: Hoover Institution Press, 1977, p. 58.

25. Gerhart, *Black Power in South Africa*, p. 147.

26. Gerhart, *Black Power in South Africa*, p. 149.

27. Madzunya in Alexandra, 20 March 1960, *Regina vs Sobukwe and 20 Others*, Gail Gerhart Papers A2422, 60 3 169.

28. Moses Dhlamini, *Robben Island Hell-Hole*, Trenton NJ: Africa World Books, 1986, p. 48.

29. Jordan Ngubane, *An African Explains Apartheid*, New York: Praeger, 1962, p. 163.

30. Philip Kgosana, interviewed by Bob Hess, Addis Ababa, 15 August 1963, Gail Gerhart Papers, A2422/1.

31. Lewin, *Politics and Law in South Africa*, p. 112.

32. Mathatha Tsedu, 'Madzunya's flame burns brightly', *The Sowetan*, 13 October 1986.

33. Benjamin Pogrund, notes on a conversation with Robert Sobukwe, 27 September 1958, Robert Sobukwe Papers, A2618 Cb, University of the Witwatersrand Library, Historical Papers.

34. Umhlabeni, 'Africanists break loose', *Contact* (Cape Town), 15 November 1958.

35. Notes by Benjamin Pogrund on the ANC conference, 15 September 1958, pp. 4–5, Robert Sobukwe Papers.

36. Notes by Benjamin Pogrund on the ANC conference, 15 September 1958, p. 19.

37. Peter Rodda, 'The Africanists cut loose', *Africa South*, 3, 4, July 1959.

38. Zolile Hamilton Keke, 'A Pan-Africanist speaks', p. 37.

39. Leeman, *Lesotho and the Struggle for Azania*, p. 97.

40. Lieutenant Colonel Hendrik Pitout quoted in Benjamin Pogrund, *How Can Man Die Better? Sobukwe and Apartheid*, London: Peter Halban, 1990, p. 5.

41. *Pogrund, How Can Man Die Better*, p. 8.

42. Sobukwe, notes on an interview by Benjamin Pogrund, 18 March 1960, Robert Sobukwe Papers.

43. Pogrund, *How Can Man Die Better?*, p. 12.

44. Robert Sobukwe to Benjamin Pogrund, undated letter, Sobukwe Papers, Ba.3.5.

45. Pogrund, *How Can Man Die Better?*, p. 18.

46. Godfrey Pitje, quoted in Pogrund, *How Can Man Die Better?*, p. 29.

47. Godfrey Pitje, 'Robert Mangeliso Sobukwe', *South African Outlook*, August 1978.

48. Frieda Matthews quoted in Pogrund, *How Can Man Die Better*, p. 39.

49. Pogrund, *How Can Man Die Better?*, pp. 33–9.

50. Pogrund, *How Can Man Die Better?*, p. 39.

51. Dennis Siwisa, cited in Pogrund, *How Can Man Die Better?*, p. 33.

52. Pogrund, *How Can Man Die Better?*, p. 46.

53. Godfrey Pitje to Jordan Ngubane, 9 November 1949, Correspondence, South African Institute of Race Relations Papers, University of the Witwatersrand Library, Historical Papers.

54. Godfrey Pitje, 'Robert Mangaliso Sobukwe'.

55. John Pokela to Benjamin Pogrund, 24 December 1984, Robert Sobukwe Papers, A 2618 Cj.

56. Pogrund, *How Can Man Die Better?*, p. 53.

57. Letter of appointment, 13 April 1954, Robert Sobukwe Papers, A2618 Aa Personal.

58. Robert Sobukwe, *African Studies*, 1968.

59. Pogrund, *How Can Man Die Better?*, p. 59.

60. Pogrund, *How Can Man Die Better?*, p. 65.

61. Pogrund, *How Can Man Die Better?*, p. 66.

62. Hamilton Keke, 'A Pan-Africanist speaks' p. 29.

63. Robert Sobukwe to Benjamin Pogrund, 29 June 1966, Robert Sobukwe Papers, A2618, 4.44.

64. Pogrund, *How Can Man Die Better*, 68.

65. Sobukwe, 'Opening address', in Karis and Gerhart (eds.), *From Protest to Challenge, Volume 3*, pp. 512–17.

66. Kwandire Kondlo, *In the Twilight of the Revolution: The Pan-Africanist Congress of Azania (South Africa), 1959–1994*, Basel: Basler Afrika Bibliographien, 2009, p. 63.

67. Sobukwe, quoted in Gerhart, *Black Power in South Africa*, p. 196.

68. Philip Bonner and Noor Nieftagodien, *Alexandra: A History*, Johannesburg: Witwatersrand University Press, 2008, p. 151.

69. Robert Sobukwe, interviewed by Gail Gerhart, 1970, Gail Gerhart Papers, A2618.

70. Robert Sobukwe to Bessie Head, 20 February 1972, Robert Sobukwe Papers, A2618, BA10.

71. Kondlo, *In the Twilight of the Revolution*, p. 59.

72. Gerhart, *Black Power in South Africa*, p. 217.

73. E. A. Brett, *African Attitudes: A Study of the Social, Racial, and Political Attitudes of some Middle Class Africans*, Fact Paper No. 14, Johannesburg: South African Institute of Race Relations, 1963.

74. Transcript from police notes of a speech by Mlami Makwetu, 1 November 1959, Exhibit P in *Regina versus Synod Madlebe*, Cape Town Case no. 313/1960, Gail Gerhart Papers.

75. Gerhart, *Black Power in South Africa*, p. 196.

76. Dhlamini, *Robben Island Hell-Hole*, p. 41.

77. Gerhart, *Black Power in South Africa*, pp. 218–19.

78. 'Disciplinary Code' in Karis and Gerhart, *From Protest to Challenge, Volume 3*, p. 532.

79. Leeman, *Lesotho and the Struggle for Azania*, p. 99; Keke, 'A Pan-Africanist speaks', p. 58.

80. Potlake Lebello, interviewed by Gail Gerhart, Nairobi, 11 September 1968.

81. 'Bob Sobukwe, in Sept. 18', Robert Sobukwe Papers, A2618 CF K38.

82. Philip Kgosana interviewed by Bob Hess, Addis Ababa, 15 August 1963, Gail Gerhart Papers, A2422/1.

83. 'Africanist flop', *Contact*, 21 March 1959.

84. Petrus Cornelius Swanepoel, conversation with author, Pretoria, 2 November 2009.

85. Alfred Nzo quoted in Bonner and Nieftagodien, *Alexandra: A History*, p. 142.

86. Jacob Nyaose, interviewed by Baruch Hirson, Geneva 1976, transcript in author's files.

87. Lucy Mvubelo, interviewed by Gail Gerhart, New York, 5 November 1973, Gail Gerhart Papers.

88. Jacob Nyaose, interviewed by Baruch Hirson.

89. Jacob Nyaose, interviewed by Baruch Hirson.

90. Sobukwe made his first public proposal for a status boycott to a convention of the Basotho Congress Party in 1957. His address was reprinted in *The Commentator* (Maseru), August 1968.

91. 'PAC National Executive Committee Report to the Annual Conference, 19–20 December 1959', in Karis, and Gerhart (eds.), *From Protest to Challenge, Volume Three*, p. 548.

92. Potlake Leballo, 'To all Public and Private Institutions, Commercial and Industrial Enterprises', Johannesburg, 25 January 1960, Gail Gerhart Papers. The PAC issued further warnings through January and early February. See, 'PAC warns city stores', *The World*, 6 February 1960.

93. Resolutions, 19–20 December, Randolph Vigne Papers, BC 1328, A1.

94. Nana Mahomo told Gail Gerhart that the PAC's decision to launch a pass campaign was 'precipitated by the ANC's announcement' of its impeding plans for opposing passes. Nana Mahomo, interviewed by Gail Gerhart, New York, 2 July 1967, Gail Gerhart Papers.

95. Elliot Mfaxa and P. L. Gqobose, interviewed by Gail Gerhart, Maseru, 29 December 1969.

96. National Executiuve, Pan-Africanist Congress, 'Pass must go now', Johannesburg, March 1960, Gail Gerhart Papers, 60.3.38.

97. Aubrey Mokoape, interviewed by Benjamin Pogrund, Durban, 2 December 1984, Robert Sobukwe Papers.

98. Baruch Hirson, *Revolutions in My Life*, Johannesburg: Witwatersrand University Press, 1995, p. 291.

99. Benjamin Pogrund, Report: Africanists, Johannesburg, 25 May 1959, Robert Sobukwe Papers.

100. Robert Sobukwe, interviewed by Gail Gerhart, 1970, Gail Gerhart Papers.

101. Potlake Leballo, interviewed by Gail Gerhart, Nairobi, 11 September 1968.

102. Elliot Mfaxa and P. L. Gqobose, interviewed by Gail Gerhart, Maseru, 29 December 1969.

103. L. Mgweba, letter from the Cape Western Regional Secretary to Branch Secretaries, Windermere, 21 January 1960, Gail Gerhart Papers, 60.1.11.

104. L. Mgweba, letter from the Cape Western Regional Secretary to Branch Secretaries, Windermere, 21 January 1960.

105. Elliot Magwentshu, interviewed by Gail Gerhart, Nairobi, 18 June 1970, Gail Gerhart Papers.

106. Robert Sobukwe, interviewed by Gail Gerhart, 1970, A2618.

107. Benjamin Pogrund, Report on the Africanists, 22 December 1958, Robert Sobukwe Papers.

108. Keke, 'A Pan-Africanist speaks', p. 59.

109. Benjamin Pogrund, undated notes on a conversation with Robert Sobukwe, Robert Sobukwe Papers, A2618 Bc.

110. Benjamin Pogrund, Pan-Africanist Congress, 20 December 1959, Robert Sobukwe Papers, A2618 Cu.

111. Benjamin Pogrund, Pan-Africanist Congress, 20 December 1959. Robert Sobukwe Papers, A2618 Cu.

112. Potlake Leballo, interviewed by Gail Gerhart, Nairobi, 11 September 1968.

113. Elliot Mfaxa and P. L. Gqobose, interviewed by Gail Gerhart, Maseru, 29 December 1959.

114. Benjamin Pogrund, notes on a conversation with Z. B. Molete, Maseru, 4 November 1984, Robert Sobukwe Papers, A2618 Cl.1.

115. Leeman, *Lesotho and the Struggle for Azania*, 97.

116. For full text, Mangaliso Sobukwe, 'Facing fearful odds', *The Commentator*, Maseru, August 1968, pp. 16–19.

117. Pan-Africanist Congress, 'Alerting the Nation', Johannesburg, 1960, Gail Gerhart Papers.

118. Ngubane, *An African Explains Apartheid*.

119. *Sunday Express* (Johannesburg), 15 May 1960.

120. Any advice from Aloysius Barden was likely to be unhelpful. Potlake Leballo showed to Benjamin Pogrund a letter he had received from Barden in November 1959. The letter was dated 28 October and 'dealt at length with a South African Coloured teacher who has asked the Bureau for help, referring to him dismissively as "an Imperialist paid agent" and a "half breed".' Benjamin Pogrund, Memo dated 11 November 1950. Robert Sobukwe Papers, K46.

121. Nana Mahomo, interviewed by Gail Gerhart, New York, 2 July 1967; Benjamin Pogrund, undated notes on a conversation with Robert Sobukwe, Robert Sobukwe Papers, A2618 Bc.

122. Anthony Sampson, *Macmillan: A Study in Ambiguity*, Harmondsworth: Penguin, 1967, p. 185.

123. Karis and Gerhart, *From Protest to Challenge, Volume 3*, p. 518.

124. Potlake Leballo, interviewed by Gail Gerhart, Nairobi, 11 September 1968.

125. Police transcripts of speeches by PAC leaders in Nyanga, 20 March 1960, Gail Gerhart Papers, 60.3.170.

126. Z. B. Molete, *Defier of the Undefiable*, undated PAC pamphlet, Lusaka, Randolph Vigne Papers.

127. Memo by Benjamin Pogrund, headed 'Add to notes on p. 5 (b)', report on a conversation with Sobukwe, Robert Sobukwe Papers, A2618, 13c.

128. *The World*, 30 April 1960.

129. C. J. Fazzie, interviewed by Mark Swilling, East London, 1983.

130. Keke, 'A Pan-Africanist speaks', p. 68.

131. Leballo claimed in 1968 that he had known about Sobukwe's choice of date since mid-January (interviewed by Gail Gerhart, Nairobi, 11 September 1968). If so, uncharacteristically, he told no one. Elliot Magwentshu told Gerhart that when Robert Sobukwe visited Cape Town in mid-February he insisted to local leaders that he had told nobody the date of the launch, 'not even the headquarters' (Magwentshu, interviewed by Gail Gerhart, Nairobi, 18 June 1970.

132. Z. B. Molete wrote to Benjamin Pogrund in the 1980s suggesting that Sobukwe informed the National Executive about his chosen date on 16 March. Z. B. Molete to Benjamin Pogrund, undated, Robert Sobukwe Papers, A2618, 13c. Jacob Nyaose on several occasions has claimed that he made the key decisions about when the campaign should be launched, maintaining that Robert Sobukwe delegated to him the responsibility of 'working out the mechanics' of the campaign: nobody else has offered any corroborative testimony and it does seem quite unlikely. (Nyaose interviewed by Baruch Hirson, 1976.)

133. Benjamin Pogrund, notes on a conversation with Robert Sobukwe, 3 May 1958, Robert Sobukwe Papers.

134. Benjamin Pogrund, notes on a conversation with Robert Sobukwe, 3 April 1968, Robert Sobukwe Papers, A2618 Cb.

135. Robert Sobukwe to Nell Marquard, 5 October 1966, Robert Sobukwe Papers, A2618 Bd.

136. Robert Sobukwe to Nell Marquard, 9 May 1972, Robert Sobukwe Papers, A2618 Bd.

137. Randolph Vigne, interviewed by author, Cape Town, November 2009.

138. Pogrund, *How Can Man Die Better?*, pp. 126–7.

139. Pogrund, *How Can Man Die Better?*, pp. 123–4.

140. Z. B. Molefe, 'The day Stanley Nksoi broke all the PAC rules', *The Star* (Johannesburg), 21 March 2001.

141. Robert Sobukwe, interviewed by Gail Gerhart, 1970, Gail Gerhart Papers, A2618.

142. Pan-Africanist Congress, 'The dawn has come: the great awakening has started', Johannesburg, 1960, Gail Gerhart Papers.

CHAPTER 3

1. Benjamin Pogrund, *How Can Man Die Better?: Sobukwe and Apartheid*, London: Peter Halban, 1990, p. 131.

2. Aubrey Mokoape, interviewed by Benjamin Pogrund, December 1984, Robert Sobukwe Papers.

3. Pogrund, *How Can Man Die Better?*, p. 130.

4. S. J. Ngendane to Pogrund, 25 August 1988, Robert Sobukwe Papers.

5. Potlake Leballo, interviewed by Gail Gerhart, Nairobi, 1969.

6. Nyaose to Pogrund, 18 October 1988, letter, Robert Sobukwe Papers.

7. Evidence presented in *Regina vs. Robert Sobukwe and 22 Others*, 1960, Gail Gerhart Papers, 60 3 169.

8. Josias Madzunya interviewed by Benjamin Pogrund, Sibasa, 13 April 1985. Transcript in Robert Sobukwe Papers, A2618 Cl file 1.

9. Philip Bonner and Noor Nieftagodien, *Alexandra: A History*, Johannesburg: Witwatersrand University Press, 2008, pp. 152 and 179.

10. Pogrund, *How Can Man Die Better?*, p. 130.

11. Robert Sobukwe, speech at completers' social, Fort Hare, October 1949 in Gwendoline Carter and Thomas Karis, *From Protest to Challenge*, Volume Two, Stanford: Hoover Institution Press, 1973, p. 331.

12. Nana Mahomo, 'The Rise of the Pan-Africanist Congress of South Africa', M.Sc. Diss., Massachusetts Institute of Technology, Boston, 1968, pp. 47–8.

13. Karis and Carter Microfilm, Reel 14a, 2X5 24 96/2.

14. Joe Molefi, interviewed by Gail Gerhart, Maseru, December 1969.

15. Petrus Tom, *My Life Struggle*, Johannesburg: Ravan Press, 1985, p. 21.

16. Matthew Chaskalson, 'The road to Sharpeville', in Stephen Clingman (ed.), *Regions and Repertoires: Topics in South African Politics and Culture*, Johannesburg: Ravan Press, 1991, pp. 117–19.

17. Minutes of the Non-European Affairs Committee, Vereeniging, 12 January 1959.

18. Vereeniging Municipality, 'A few facts about Sharpe Bantu Town', 28 November 1961, Archives, Vaal Teknorama Museum, 03/5165. Bishop Ambrose Reeves observes that Sharpeville was 'one of the best-planned and most reasonably conducted' of South Africa's townships, 'a location of which any municipality might be proud' (Ambrose Reeves, *Shooting at Sharpeville*, NY: Houghton Mifflin, 1961, p. 31).

19. Communist Party of South Africa, *Vereeniging: Who is to Blame?*, Johannesburg: 1937.

20. Sheridan Johns, 'Marxism–Leninism in a Multi-Racial Environment: The Origins and Early History of the Communist Party of South Africa', Ph.D. Dissertation, Department of Government, Harvard, 1965, pp. 377–8.

21. Baruch Hirson, *Yours for the Union: Class and Community Struggle in South Africa, 1930–1947*, Johannesburg: Witwatersrand University Press, 1989, pp. 63–73.

22. 'Police in house-to-house raid, Vereeniging', *Inkululeko*, Johannesburg, 6 June 1941; 'Late news: Vereeniging charges withdrawn', *Inkululeko*, 7 August 1941.

23. Tom, *My Life Struggle*, p. 6.

24. Chaskalson, 'The road to Sharpeville', p. 120.

25. *Vereeniging and Vanderbijlpark News*, 13 February 1959.

26. Chaskalson, 'The road to Sharpeville', p. 130.

27. *The World*, 26 March 1960.

28. Chaskalson, 'The road to Sharpeville', p. 132.

29. Ian Jeffrey, *The Sharpetown Swingsters: Their Will to Survive*, BA Honours Dissertation, Department of Social Anthropology, University of the Witwatersrand, 1985, p. 31.

30. *The Torch*, Cape Town, 9 July 1952 and 9 September 1952.

31. Minutes of the Sharpeville Advisory Board, 18 May 1953 in Town Clerk's Office, Vereeniging, Advisory Board Agendas and Minutes, 130/5/4, Volume 4.

32. Sharpeville Advisory Board Minutes, 28 October 1953 in Town Clerk's Office, Vereeniging, Advisory Board Agendas and Minutes, 130/5/4, Volume 4.

33. *Vereeniging and Vanderbijlpark News*, 10 October 1958.

34. Chaskalson, 'The road to Sharpeville', p. 142.

35. Peter Kurube, 'Sounds to heal Sharpeville's wounds', *Mail and Guardian*, 19 March 1999.

36. M. van Zyl, 'Swart Verstedeliking in Vereeniging, 1923–1960', Ph.D. Dissertation, Vista University, Vanderbijlpark, 1993, p. 226.

37. David Sibeko, interviewed by the author, London, 3 September 1975.

38. Michael Labuschagne, evidence, *Proceedings*, Commission of Enquiry, Sharpeville (henceforth *Proceedings*), p. 425.

39. Gideon Tsolo, interviewed by author, Sharpeville, 5 November 2009.

40. Michael Thekiso, interviewed by author, Sharpeville, 6 November 2009.

41. Tom, *My Life Struggle*, pp. 14–20.

42. Nyakane Tsolo, evidence, *Proceedings*, p. 2500.

43. Frankel, *An Ordinary Atrocity: Sharpeville and its Massacre*, New Haven: Yale University Press, 2001, p. 49.

44. Labuschagne, evidence, *Proceedings*, p. 429.

45. Nyakene Tsolo, evidence, *Proceedings*, p. 2469.

46. Frankel, *An Ordinary Atrocity*, p. 49.

47. Clive Glaser, *Bo-Tostsi: The Youth Gangs of Soweto, 1935–1976*, Oxford: James Currey, 2000, p. 84.

48. A. T. Spengler, evidence, *Proceedings*, p. 1242.

49. Edwin Litelu, evidence, *Proceedings*, p. 2688.

50. Gideon Tsolo, interviewed by author, Sharpeville, 6 November 2009.

51. Potlake Leballo, interviewed by Gail Gerhart, 11 September 1968, Nairobi.

52. Tom, *My Life Struggle*, p. 24.

53. In 1996, witnesses to the Truth and Reconciliation Commission maintained they were 'forcibly prevented from going to work on the day of the march' (Truth and Reconciliation Commission, *Report, Volume Three*, Cape Town: Juta and Co. Ltd., 1998, p. 534).

54. Tom, *My Life Struggle*, p. 25.

55. Frankel, *An Ordinary Atrocity*, p. 75.

56. Ikabot Makiti, interviewed by the author, Sharpeville, 20 July 2010.

57. Gideon Tsolo, interviewed by author, Sharpeville, 6 November 2009.

58. Buhle Khumalo, 'Memories throb like open wounds', *The Star*, 20 March 2001.

59. Christiaan Nxumalo, evidence, *Proceedings*, p. 1065.

60. Nxumalo, evidence, *Proceedings*, p. 1067.

61. Simon Lukas Mashetedi, evidence, *Proceedings*, p. 2234.

62. Union of South Africa, *Report of the Commission, of Inquiry into Sharpeville, Evaton and Vanderbijlpark Location Riots*, Pretoria, Ann. 125–61, 1961 (henceforth Wessels Report), para. 48.88.

63. George Myubu, interviewed in Jasper van der Bliek (ed.), *Sharpeville Scars*, Tilburg: Tilburg–Lekoa Vaal Association, 2000, p. 17.

64. Joseph Motha, evidence, *Proceedings*, p. 1933.

65. Wessels Report, p. 48, para. 88.

66. Buti Mofokeng quoted in Kingdom Mabuza, 'Sharpeville people were betrayed', *The Sowetan*, 23 March 2009.

67. Samuel Tshabalala, interviewed by the author, 6 November 2009.

68. Nyakane Tsolo, interviewed by Tefo Mothibeli in 'The day that changed our history', *The Star*, 19 March 1999.

69. Moses Smit, evidence, *Proceedings*, p. 2048; Sergeant M. Nkosi, evidence, *Proceedings*, p. 2713.

70. Nyakane Tsolo, evidence, *Proceedings*, p. 2488. Corroborative evidence on this point was offered by Simon Mashetidi who told the Commission that 'the spokesmen would be arrested and maybe some of his followers . . . the plan was to march to the police station every day' (*Proceedings*, pp. 2235–7).

71. Sergeant M. Nkosi, evidence, *Proceedings*, p. 2713.

72. Captain H. G. Theron, evidence, *Proceedings*, p. 296; Lieutenant J. C. Visser, evidence, *Proceedings*, p. 491.

73. Major van Eyl, evidence, *Proceedings*, p. 215.

74. Ellen Lidia, evidence, *Proceedings*, p. 2324.

75. Tom, *My Life Struggle*, p. 27.

76. Frankel, *An Ordinary Atrocity*, p. 103; S. Dholefa, evidence, *Proceedings*, p. 1860.

77. Frederick Batkani, interviewed in van der Bliek (ed.), *Sharpeville Scars*, p. 29.

78. Frankel, *An Ordinary Atrocity*, p. 147.

79. George Pollock, 'Scapegoat of Sharpeville', *Reynolds News* (London), 1961, cutting in Randolph Vigne Papers, BC 1328, A1.

80. W. J. Wessels, evidence, *Proceedings*, p. 649.

81. Constable J. G. Heyl, evidence, *Proceedings*, p. 560.

82. J. Ooosthuizen, evidence, *Proceedings*, p. 1009.

83. S. Dholefa, evidence, *Proceedings*, p. 1851.

84. Frankel, *An Ordinary Atrocity*, p. 125.

85. Elizabeth Mabona, quoted in Truth and Reconciliation Commission, *Report, Volume Three*, p. 535.

86. David Ramohoase quoted in Truth and Reconciliation Commission, *Report, Volume Three*, p. 356.

87. Peter Molefi, evidence, *Proceedings*, pp. 1753 and 1785; Bennett Griffiths, evidence, *Proceedings*, p. 1943.

88. Robert Maja, evidence, *Proceedings*, pp. 2366–8.

89. Pogrund, *How Can Man Die Better?*, p. 133. Pogrund's car was stoned while driving out of Sharpeville after the shooting.

90. Humphrey Tyler, *Life in the Time of Sharpeville*, Cape Town: Kwela Books, 1995, p. 17; Reeves, *Shooting at Sharpeville*, p. 37.

91. Reeves, *Shooting at Sharpeville*, p. 39.

92. Reeves, *Shooting at Sharpeville*, p. 64.

93. Detective Malachia Menatong, evidence, *Proceedings*, pp. 2704–8.

94. Reeves, *Shooting at Sharpeville*, p. 36.

95. Reeves, *Shooting at Sharpeville*, p. 76.

96. Sergeant W. J. Wessels, evidence, *Proceedings*, p. 650.

97. Lieutenant Colonel G. D. Piennar, evidence, *Proceedings*, p. 1470.

98. Pienaar's evidence referred to the two shots though he did not mention Geelbooi Mofokeng by name. Philip Frankel elicited the details of Geelbooi's earlier arrest and his arrival and subsequent action at the police station from his interviews with police who had been present during Mofokeng's arrest and with surviving bystanders in the crowd. Mofokeng was among the people who were killed on 21 March but his gun was not produced at the inquest. In a review of Philip Frankel's book, Lwandile Sisilana was dimissive, noting that 'PAC veterans...regard his story as the purest fantasy' (Lwandile Sisilana, 'Review of *An Ordinary Atrocity*', *We Write*, Johannesburg, October 2004).

99. Tom Hopkinson, *In the Fiery Continent*, London: Victor Gollancz, 1962, p. 255.

100. From interviews conducted in 2000 and cited in Philip Frankel, *An Ordinary Atrocity*, p. 139.

101. Albert Mbongo, interviewed in van der Bliek (ed.), *Sharpeville Scars*, p. 29.

102. Khumalo, 'Memories throb like open wounds'.

103. Reeves, *Shooting at Sharpeville*, p. 133.

104. Reeves, *Shooting at Sharpeville*, p. 93.

105. Independent Television News film held at the Apartheid Museum, Johannesburg.

106. Frankel, *An Ordinary Atrocity*, pp. 148–9.

107. Evidence of Sidwell Kasa, vice-chairman of Bophelong PAC, *Proceedings*, p. 2572.

108. Hannah Stanton, *Go Well, Stay Well*, London: Hodder and Stoughton, 1961, p. 178.

109. 'Pan-Africanist treasurer fined', *Cape Times*, 23 March 1960.

110. *Daily Despatch*, 7, 11, and 16 May 1960.

111. Johannes Sefatsa, interviewed by author, Sharpeville, 7 November 2009.

112. Gideon Tsolo, interviewed by author, 6 November 2009.

CHAPTER 4

1. Philip Ata Kgosana, *Lest we Forget*, Braamfontein: Skotaville Press, 1988, p. 106.

2. Tom Karis, Notes from a manuscript by Philip Kgosana, Gail Gerhart Papers, 60.1.12.

3. *Contact*, 2 April 1960.

4. The full exchange is reported verbatim in Philip Kgosana's earliest published account of events, '30,000 obeyed me as one man', *Drum*, March 1961. Kgosana's report is confirmed in its essentials by police evidence cited in the Union of South Africa, *Report of the Commission on the Langa Location Riots*, Ann. 126–61, 1961 (henceforth Diemont Commission).

5. Diemont Commission, pp. 74–8.

6. Kgosana, *Lest We Forget*, p. 23.

7. Secretary of Native Affairs Eiselen quoted in Yvonne Muthien, *State and Resistance in South Africa, 1939–1945*, Aldershot: Avebury, 1994, p. 75.

8. Muthien, *State and Resistance in South Africa*, p. 68.

9. Bra Ace Mxolise Mgxashe, *Are you with us? The Story of a PAC Activist*, Cape Town: Tafelberg, 2003, p. 33.

10. Monica Wilson and Archie Mafeje, *Langa*, Cape Town: Oxford University Press, 1963, p. 15.

11. Sipheto Quina quoted in Brown Bavusile Maaba, 'The PAC's war against the state', in South African Democracy Education Trust, *Road to Democracy in South Africa, Volume 1*, Cape Town: Zebra Press, 2004, p. 260.

12. Muthien, *State and Resistance in South Africa*, p. 149.

13. Muthien, *State and Resistance in South Africa*, p. 115.

14. Elliot Magwentshu, interviewed by Gail Gerhart, Nairobi, 18 June 1970, Gail Gerhart Papers.

15. Elliot Magwentshu, interviewed by Gail Gerhart.

16. Christopher Saunders, 'From Ndabeni to Langa', in Christopher Saunders (ed.), *Studies in the History of Cape Town, Volume 1*, Cape Town: History Department, University of Cape Town, 1979, p. 190.

17. Wilson and Mafeje, *Langa*, p. 8.

18. Peter Hjul, interviewed by Gwendoline Carter, Cape Town, 26 January 1964, Transcript at http://www.disa.ukza.ac.za (pp. 3–4).

19. Elliot Magwentshu, interviewed by Gail Gerhart.

20. Peter Hjul, interviewed by Gwendolen Carter, pp. 3–7.

21. *Regina vs. Synod Madlebe*, list of accused, 31/11, Albie Sachs Papers, Institute for Commonwealth Studies, University of London.

22. Karis and Carter Microfilm, Reel 6b, 2 DP1 8911, PAC Secretary's Minutes, Kensington, entry for 10 March 1960.

23. PAC Secretary's Minutes, Kensington, entry for 31 October 1959.

24. PAC Secretary's Minutes, Kensington, entry for 22 February 1960.

25. PAC Secretary's Minutes, Kensington, entry for 7 July 1959.

26. *Regina vs. Synod Madlebe*, statements by the accused, 31/3.

27. Mgxashe, *Are you with us?*, p. 42.

28. Mgxashe, *Are you with us?*, p. 36.

29. Mqhayim chief of the Western amaNdlambe, 1828–58; Hintsa, chief of the Gcaleka, 1804–35; Makana, Xhosa diviner and general in the Fifth Frontier War, 1818–19. *Regina vs. Synod Madlebe*, police transcripts of speeches, File 31/6.

30. *Regina vs. Synod Madlebe*, 31/6, speech by Peter Bomali, 6 March, Nyanga West.

31. Karis and Carter Microfilm, Reel 1, a, 2XKG 77, Philip Kgosana, unpublished autobiographical manuscript, Institute of Commonwealth Studies, University of London, p. 60.

32. Philip Kgosana, 'The Burial of Uncle Bob Leshoai', speech delivered in Mafikeng, 18 February 1996.

33. Philip Kgosana, interviewed by the author, Pretoria, 2 November 2009.

34. Nana Mahomo, 'The Rise of the Pan-Africanist Congress of South Africa', M.Sc. Dissertation, Massachusetts Institute of Technology, Boston, 1968, p. 46.

35. This profile is drawn from Kgosana's *Lest We Forget* and Joseph Lelyveld's *Move Your Shadow* (London: Abacus, 1987, pp. 315–47).

36. Myrna Blumberg, *White Madam*, London: Victor Gollancz, 1962, p. 28.

37. Philip Kgosana, 'The Story of My Exciting Life', *Drum*, February 1961.

38. On the impression Kgosana made upon Sobukwe see Albie Sachs' introductory notes to his papers at the Institute for Commonwealth Studies, File F31, p. 6.

Joseph Lelyveld supplies a sympathetic assessment of Kgosana's personality in *Move Your Shadow*. See especially pp. 342–7.

39. Philip Kgosana, interviewed by the author, Pretoria, 2 November 2009.

40. Benjamin Pogrund's note on conversation with Randolph Vigne, Robert Sobukwe Papers.

41. For Kgosana, see Blumberg, *White Madam*, p. 28 and for Sobukwe, Pogrund, *How Can Man Die Better? Sobukwe and Apartheid*, London: Peter Halbarn, 1990, p. 68.

42. Mgxashe, *Are you with us?*, p. 51.

43. Mgxashe, *Are you with us?*, pp. 68–9.

44. Patrick Duncan, 'The Two Thousand', *Contact*, 16 April 1960, p. 3.

45. Randolph Vigne, interviewed by the author, Vishoek, 8 November 2009.

46. Kgosana, interviewed by author, Pretoria, 2 November 2009.

47. Court records, *Regina vs. Synod Madlebe and 31 Others*, case no. 313/60, statements by accused, File 31/3, Albie Sachs Papers.

48. Chart prepared by Elliot Magwentshu on PAC in Cape Town following categories of Wilson and Mafeje, June 1970, Nairobi, Gail Gerhart Papers, 60.1.27.

49. Philip Kgosana, interviewed by the author, Pretoria, 2 November 2009.

50. *Regina vs. Synod Madlebe and 31 Others*, Cape Town, Case No. 313/60, court record and related papers, Albie Sachs Papers, 31.17, 31.6.21, and 31.6.22.

51. Kgosana, '30,000 obyed me as one man'.

52. Philip Kgosana, interviewed by the author, Pretoria, 2 November 2009.

53. Philip Kgosana, 'We shall win', letter to all branch secretaries, Gail Gerhart Papers.

54. Peter Hjul, transcript of conversation, 18.1, Robert Sobukwe Papers, p. 4.

55. Mgxashe, *Are you with us?*, p. 42.

56. Typed notes by R. Vigne on the PAC in the Cape, Robert Sobukwe Papers, A2618 Ch.

57. Karis, Notes from ms. by Philip Kgosana. Gail Gerhart Papers, 60.1.12.

58. See transcript of Elliot Magwentshu's speech at Worcester—'We have been shot at by police at Worcester' in *Regina vs. Synod Madlebe*, Albie Sachs papers, File 31/6/19.

59. *Cape Times*, 12 May 1960.

60. Typed notes by R. Vigne on the PAC in the Cape, Robert Sobukwe Papers, A2618 Ch.

61. Untitled list beginning with 'Hume Pipes, Belville', Gail Gerhart Papers, 60.0.6.

62. Addresses in Randolph Vigne's handwriting of PAC leaders who visited Liberal Party offices in 1959, Randolph Vigne Papers, UCT BC1328 A1.

63. Randolph Vigne, *Liberals Against Apartheid: A History of the Liberal Party of South Africa, 1953–68*, London: Macmillan, 1997, p. 115.

64. Typed notes by R. Vigne on the PAC in the Cape, A2618 Ch.

65. Randolph Vigne, interviewed by the author, London, 20 August 1975.

66. Doreen Musson, *Johnny Gomas: Voice of the Working Class*, Cape Town: Buchu Books, 1989, p. 122.

67. Vigne, *Liberals against Apartheid*, p. 125.

68. Vigne, *Liberals against Apartheid*, p. 116.

69. Nana Mahomo, interviewed by Gail Gerhart, New York, 2 July 1967, Gail Gerhart Papers.

70. Letter from Nana Mahoma to Randolph Vigne, 11 February 1960, Randolph Vigne Papers, UCT BC1328 A1.

71. Hamilton Keke supplies an account of Sobukwe's address to the writers: 'The Prof made three striking points: (1) when society is rotten, writers should shock it, not conciliate; (2) sex is not a disease: it should be written of with honesty and reverence; (3) offensive language should not be shirked if it conveys the truth.' 'A Pan–Africanist speaks', p. 69, Randolph Vigne Papers.

72. Author's interview with Randolph Vigne, Vishoek, 8 November 2009.

73. Duncan quoted in C. J. Driver, *Patrick Duncan: South African and Pan-African*, London: Heinemann, 1980, p. 28.

74. Zolile Hamilton Keke, 'A Pan–Africanist speaks', unpublished manuscript, 1989, Randolph Vigne Papers, BC 1328 C, p. 67.

75. Kgosana, *Lest we Forget*, p. 17.

76. See speech transcript, *Regina vs Synod Madlebe*, Albie Sachs Papers, 31.6.25.

77. Patrick Duncan, 'Some thoughts on the 1957 Multiracial Conference', p. 7, typed ms., Patrick Duncan Papers, University of York.

78. Patrick Duncan to Jordan Ngubane, 23 January 1958, Patrick Duncan Papers.

79. Notes by Benjamin Pogrund on a conversation with Robert Sobukwe, 3 May 1958, Robert Sobukwe Papers.

80. Aelred Stubbs, 'Robert Sobukwe', *South African Outlook*, August 1978.

81. Robert Sobukwe, interviewed by Gail Gerhart, 1970, A2618.

82. Patrick Duncan to Benjamin Pogrund, 3 November 1959, Patrick Duncan Papers.

83. Z. B. Molete, letter to the editor, *Contact*, 31 October 1959.

84. Patrick Duncan to Julius Lewin, 2 December 1959, Patrick Duncan Papers.

85. I am grateful to Jonty Driver for this description drawn from his own memories of Patrick Duncan.

86. Driver, *Patrick Duncan*, p. 68.

87. 'Absent workers a blow to business', *Cape Times*, 23 March 1960.

88. Typed notes by R. Vigne on the PAC in the Cape, Robert Sobukwe Papers, A2618 Ch.

89. Karis, Notes on a Manuscript by Philip Kgosana, p. 5, Gail Gerhart Papers, 60.1.12.

90. Karis, Notes on a Manuscript by Philip Kgosana, p. 5, Gail Gerhart Papers, 60.1.12.

91. Typed Notes by R. Vigne on the PAC in the Cape, Robert Sobukwe Papers, A2618 Ch.

92. Kgosana, *Lest we Forget*, p. 30.

93. Philip Kgosana, 'Patrick Duncan and the Pan-Africanist Congress', ts. dated 7 September 1963, Claude Barnett Papers, Box 175.

94. Randolph Vigne, interviewed by the author, 1975.

95. *Natal Mercury*, 12 May 1960.

96. Anon, 'The nineteen days', *Africa South*, July 1960.

97. Hermann Giliomee, *The Afrikaners: Biography of a People*, London: Hurst, 2003, p. 530.

98. The occasion also appears in Rupert's authorized biography: Ebbe Domisse and Willie Esterhuyse, *Anton Rupert*, Cape Town: Tafelberg, 2009.

99. Brian Bunting, interviewed by the author, London, 1975.

100. Patrick Duncan diary, entry for 25 March 1960, Patrick Duncan Papers. See also Patrick Duncan, 'The two thousand', *Contact*, 16 April 1960, p. 3.

101. Mgxashe, *Are you with us?*, p. 69.

102. Kgosana, *Lest we Forget*, p. 30.

103. *Cape Times*, 12 May 1960.

104. Karis, Notes from a Manuscript by Philip Kgosana, p. 6, Gail Gerhart Papers, 60, 1. 12.

105. Entry for 28 March 1960.

106. Mgxashe, *Are you with us?*, p. 41.

107. Hjul, 18.1, p. 7, Robert Sobukwe Papers.

108. Hjul, 18, 1, p. 8, Robert Sobukwe Papers.

109. Muthien, *State and Resistance in South Africa*, p. 158.

110. Benjamin Pogrund, Notes on an interview with Peter Hjul, Robert Sobukwe Papers.

111. Kgosana, '30,000 obeyed me . . . ' and report by Randolph Vigne on the Langa funeral of three PAC members, 28 March 1960, ts., Randolph Vigne Papers, UCT BC1328 A1.

112. *Cape Times*, 29 March 1960.

113. Report by Randolph Vigne on the Langa funeral of three PAC members, 28 March 1960, ts, Randolph Vigne Papers, UCT BC1328 A1.

114. An eyewitness, 'The 30,000', *Contact*, 16 April 1960.

115. An eyewitness, 'The 30,000', *Contact*, 16 April 1960.

116. Helen Suzman, *Memoirs: In No Uncertain Terms*, Johannesburg: Jonathan Ball, 1993, p. 51.

117. An eyewitness, 'The 30,000', *Contact*, 16 April 1960, p. 6.

118. Independent Television News film footage of the Sharpeville crisis held at the Apartheid Museum, Johannesburg.

119. Kgosana, interviewed by the author, 2 November 2009.

120. *Regina vs. Synod Madlebe*, p. A510, Albie Sachs Papers.

121. Pogrund, *How can man die better?*, p. 144.

122. Blumberg, *White Madam*, p. 31.

123. *Cape Times*, 31 March 1960.

124. Leyleveld, *Move Your Shadow*, p. 326.

125. Sybrand Mostert, 'They've righted the wrong, says the new brigadier', *Sunday Times* (Johannesburg), 12 July 1987. Anthony Heard's eyewitness account, compiled when he was a journalist at the *Cape Times* and submitted as an affidavit to the Langa Commission of Inquiry corroborates Kgosana's version of events and is at odds with Terblanche's recollections. See, Anthony Heard, 'Assurance that averted a riot—unpublished facts now on record', *Cape Times*, 11 July 1987.

126. 'Bayonets glint around location', *Cape Times*, 1 April 1960.

127. Hjul 18.1 Robert Sobukwe Papers, pp. 14–16.

128. Notebook, dated March/April 1960, Colin Legum Papers, UCT BC 1329 F3.9.5.

129. Hjul, 18.1, Robert Sobukwe Papers, p. 16.

130. 'Officials amazed by negative Nyanga attitude', *Cape Times*, 5 April 1960.

131. R. W. Johnson, *How Long Will South Africa Survive?* Johannesburg: Macmillan, 1977, p. 19.

132. Gail Gerhart, *Black Power in South Africa*, Berkeley: University of California Press, 1978, p. 244.

133. Non-European Unity Movement, *The Pan-Africanist Congress Venture in Retrospect*, Cape Town: 1960.

134. For example, Janet Robertson, *Liberalism in South Africa*, Oxford: Oxford University Press, 1971, p. 216.

135. Typed notes by R. Vigne on the PAC in the Cape, Robert Sobukwe Papers, A2618 Ch.

136. Benjamin Pogrund, Notes on a conversation with Sobukwe, 3 April 1964, Robert Sobukwe Papers: A26Cb.

137. Benjamin Pogrund, Notes on a conversation with Sobukwe, 3 April 1964.

138. Joe Molefi, interviewed by Gail Gerhart, Maseru, December 1969.

139. John Blacking, 'The power of ideas in social change: the growth of the Africanist idea in South Africa', in David Riches (ed.), *The Queen's University Papers in Social Anthropology*, Volume III, Belfast: 1979, p. 127.

140. 'The man who stopped bloodbath is 80', *Cape Times*, 3 February 1980.

141. Hjul, 18.1, Robert Sobukwe Papers, p. 18.

142. Peter Hjul, interviewed by author, London, 22 January 1976.

143. Arlene Getz, 'Ignatius Terblanche: the man who stopped a bloodbath', *Sunday Star* (Johannesburg), 12 July 1987.

144. Anon, 'The nineteen days', *Africa South*, July 1960.

145. Joanna Strangwayes-Booth, *A Cricket in the Thorn Tree: Helen Suzman and the Progressive Party*, Johannesburg: Hutchinson, 1976, p. 179.

146. Tony Heard, *The Cape of Storms: A Personal History of the Crisis in South Africa*, Johannesburg: Ravan Press, 1990, p. 93.

147. This is what Kgosana told Mxolisi Mgxashe in 1992: Mgxashe, *Are you with us?*, p. 56.

148. Suzman, *Memoirs: In No Uncertain Terms*, p. 51.

149. Blumberg, *White Madam*, p. 28.

150. Mostert, 'They've righted the wrong, says the new Brigadier', *Sunday Times* (Johannesburg), 12 July 1987, p. 7.

151. 'The man who stopped the bloodbath is 80', *Cape Times*, 3 February 1983; Pogrund, *How can man die better?*, p. 144.

152. J. P. J. Coetzer, *Gister se Dade Vandag se Oordeel*, Pretoria: JP Van der Walt, 2000, p. 95.

153. Notebook, dated March/April 1960, Colin Legum Papers, UCT BC 1329 F3.9.5.

154. See comments about propensities to suppress non-violent protest in German-occupied Europe between 1939 and 1945 and in China's Tiananmen Square demonstrations in 1989: Ronald McCarthy and Christopher Kruegler, *Towards Research and Theory Building in the Study of Non-Violent Action*, Cambridge, MA: Albert Einstein Institution, 1993, p. 24.

155. Doug McAdam, 'The US Civil Rights Movement: Power from Below and from Above', in Adam Roberts and Timothy Garton Ash (eds.), *Civil Resistance and Power Politics*, Oxford: Oxford University Press, 2009, p. 61.

156. 'Rush to buy pistols', *Cape Times*, 23 March 1960; 'Big demand for guns', *Cape Times*, 25 March 1960.

157. Humphrey Tyler, *Life in the Time of Sharpeville*, Cape Town: Kwela Books, 1995, p. 20.

158. Segametsi Makhanya, interview transcript in Jasper van der Bliek (ed.) *Sharpeville Scars*, Tilburg: Tilburg–Lekoa–Vaal Association, 2000, p. 25.

159. Pogrund, *How can man die better?*, p. 135.

160. PAC press release, Johannesburg, 22 March 1960, Gail Gerhart Papers, 60.3.61. See also the statement by telephone by William Jolobe to journalists, 24 March 1960: 'We are telling people to stay at home and go to jail. They must return to their homes—stay there until we hear from Mr Sobukwe, there must be no work—so that employers will feel the pinch.' Sobukwe papers. A2618 Cg.

161. *Daily Despatch*, 19 April and 11 May, 1960.

162. *Rand Daily Mail*, 28 March 1960.

163. Clive Glaser, *Bo Tsotsi: The Youth Gangs of Soweto*, Oxford: James Currey, 2000, pp. 87–90.

164. Kurt Schock, *Unarmed Insurrections: People Power Movements in Non-Democracies*, Minneapolis: University of Minnesota Press, 2005, p. 166.

CHAPTER 5

1. See Henry R. Pike, *A History of Communism in South Africa*, Germiston: Christian Mission International in South Africa, 1988, p. 399.

2. Segametsi Makhanya quoted in Jasper Van der Bliek (ed.), *Sharpeville Scars*, Tilburg: Tilburg-Lekoa Vaal Association, 2000.

3. Philip Frankel, *An Ordinary Atrocity: Sharpeville and its Massacre*, New Haven: Yale University Press, 2001, p. 159.

4. Thabo Motaung and Lydia Mahabuke quoted in Van der Bliek (ed.), *Sharpeville Scars*.

5. Thabo Motaung in Van der Bliek (ed.), *Sharpeville Scars*.

6. Segametsi Makhanya in Van der Bliek (ed.), *Sharpeville Scars*.

7. Benjamin Pogrund, *How Can Man Die Better?: Sobukwe and Apartheid*, London: Peter Halban, 1990, pp. 153–4.

8. Philip Kgosana, *Lest we Forget*, Braamfontein: Skotaville Press, 1988, pp. 57–8.

9. Bernard Magubane, Philip Bonner, et al., 'The turn to armed struggle', in South African Democracy Education Trust, *The Road to Democracy in South Africa, Volume 1 (1960–1970)*, Cape Town: Zebra Press, 2004, p. 70.

10. *Cape Times*, 16 and 17 May 1960.

11. Joe Slovo, 'South Africa—no middle road', in Basil Davidson, Joe Slovo, and Anthony R. Wilkinson (eds.), *Southern Africa: The New Politics of Revolution*, Harmondsworth: Penguin, 1976, p. 171.

12. A. Lerumo, *Fifty Fighting Years: The South African Communist Party, 1921–1971*, London: Inkululeko Publications, 1987, pp. 94–5.

13. David Sibeko, 'The Sharpeville massacre: its historic significance in the struggle against Apartheid' in http://www.sahistory.org.za/pages/library-resources/aticles_papers/1990-sharpeville

14. Tefo Mothibeli, 'The day that changed our history', *The Star*, 19 March 1999.

15. Roland Stanbridge, 'Contemporary African political organizations and movements', in Robert Price and Carl G. Rosberg (eds.), *The Apartheid Regime*, Cape Town: David Philip, 1980, p. 77.

16. Paul Rich, *White Power and the Liberal Conscience: Racial Segregation and South African Liberalism, 1921–1960*, Manchester: Manchester University Press, 1984, p. 129.

17. Heribert Adam, 'The failure of political liberalism in South Africa', in Price and Rosberg, *The Apartheid Regime*, p. 49.

18. Janet Robertson, *Liberalism in South Africa*, Oxford: Oxford University Press, 1971, p. 204.

19. Robert Ross, *A Concise History of South Africa*, Cambridge: Cambridge University Press, 1999, p. 131.

20. Patrick Duncan, 'The power of non-violence', *Contact*, 16 April 1960, p. 4.

21. Lewis Sowden, *The Land of Afternoon: The Story of White South Africans*, London: Elek Books Limited, 1968, p. 219.

22. Max du Preez, *Of Tricksters, Tyrants and Turncoats: More Unusual Stories from South Africa's Past*, Cape Town: Zebra Books, 2007.

23. Dan O'Meara, *Forty Wasted Years: The Apartheid State and the Politics of the National Party*, Johannesburg: Ravan Press, 1996, p. 103.

24. O'Meara, *Forty Wasted Years*, p. 103.

25. Julius Lewin, *Politics and Law in South Africa*, London: Merlin, 1961, p. 115.

26. *Cape Times*, 26 March 1960.

27. Mark Israel, *South African Political Exile in the United Kingdom*, Basingstoke: Macmillan, 1999, pp. 5 and 91–2; Stephen Lewis, *The Economics of Apartheid*, New York: Council for Foreign Relations, 1989, p. 22.

28. D. Hobart Houghton, 'Economic development, 1865–1965', in Monica Wilson and Leonard Thompson (eds.), *The Oxford History of South Africa*, Volume Two, Oxford: Oxford University Press, 1975, p. 39.

29. Heribert Adam, *Modernizing Racial Domination: The Dynamics of South African Politics*, Berkeley: University of California Press, 1971, p. 29.

30. James Barber and John Barratt, *South Africa's Foreign Policy: The Search for Status and Security, 1945–1988*, Cambridge: Cambridge University Press, 1990, p. 97.

31. R. W. Johnson, *How Long will South Africa Survive?*, Johannesburg: Macmillan, 1977, p. 27.

32. Stanley Greenberg, *Race and State in Capitalist Development: South Africa in Comparative Perspective*, Johannesburg: Ravan Press, 1980, p. 202.

33. Howard Smith, 'Apartheid, Sharpeville and impartiality: the reporting of South Africa on BBC television, 1948–1961', *Historical Journal of Film, Radio and Television*, 13, 3, 1993, p. 286.

34. Deon Geldenhuys, *The Diplomacy of Isolation: South African Foreign Policy Making*, Johannesburg: Macmillan, 1984, p. 23.

35. 'Menzies says no to boycott', *Cape Times*, 24 March 1960.

36. Jennifer Clark, 'The wind of change in Australia: Aborigines and the international politics of race', *The International History Review*, 20, 1, 1998, p. 93.

37. Clark, 'The wind of change', p. 94.

38. Tom Cameron, *Apartheid is not a Game*, Auckland: Graphic Publications, 1970, pp. 23–6.

39. Ronald Hyam and Peter Henshaw, *The Lion and the Springbok: Britain and South Africa since the Boer War*, Cambridge: Cambridge University Press, 2003, p. 163.

40. Hyam and Henshaw, *The Lion and the Springbok*, p. 270.

41. Sowden, *The Land of Afternoon*, p. 227.

42. Geldenhuys, *The Diplomacy of Isolation*, p. 13.

43. Hyam and Henshaw, *The Lion and the Springbok*, pp. 268–9.

44. Barber and Barratt, *South Africa's Foreign Policy*, p. 83.

45. Krishnan Srinivasan, *The Rise, Decline and Future of the British Commonwealth*, Basingstoke: Palgrave Macmillan, 2005, p. 49.

46. Roger Fieldhouse, *Anti-Apartheid: A History of the Movement in Britain*, London: Merlin Press, 2005, pp. 39–42.

47. Neil Parsons, 'The pipeline: Botswana's reception of refugees, 1956–68', *Social Dynamics*, 43, 1, 2008, pp. 20–1.

48. Anthony Marx, *Making Race and Nation*, New York and Cambridge: Cambridge University Press, 1998, p. 108.

49. Kenneth Heard, *General Elections in South Africa, 1943–1970*, London: Oxford University Press, 1974.

50. Sampie Terblanche, *A History of Inequality in South Africa*, Pietermaritzberg: University of Natal Press, 2002, p. 393.

51. Johnson, *How Long Will South Africa Survive?*, p. 28.

52. Hermann Giliomee, 'The leader and the citizenry', in Robert Schrire (ed.), *Leadership in the Apartheid State*, Cape Town: Oxford University Press, 1994, p. 109.

53. Hobart Houghton, 'Economic development, 1865–1965', p. 48.

54. Terence Moll, 'Did the Apartheid economy fail?', *Journal of Southern African Studies*, 17, 2, June 1991.

55. Lewis, *The Economics of Apartheid*, pp. 22–3.

56. David Kaplan, *The Crossed Line: The South African Telecommunications Industry in Transition*, Johannesburg: Witwatersrand University Press, 1990, pp. 30–4.

57. Barber and Barratt, *South Africa's Foreign Policy*, p. 99.

58. Robert Kinlock Massie, *Loosing the Bonds: The United States and South Africa in the Apartheid Years*, New York: Nan A Talese, Doubleday, 1997.

59. Institute of Industrial Education, *The Durban Strikes*, Johannesburg: Ravan Press, 1974.

60. Adam, *Modernizing South Africa*, p. 97.

61. Adam, *Modernizing South Africa*, pp. 98–107.

62. Craig Charney, 'Civil Society vs the State: Identity, Institutions and the Black Consciousness Movement in South Africa', D.Phil. Dissertation, Yale University, 2000, pp. 137 and 234.

63. Patrick Duncan, *South Africa's Rule of Violence*, London: Metheun, 1963, pp. 39–48.

64. Albie Sachs, *Justice in South Africa*, Berkeley: University of California Press, 1973, p. 252.

65. Philip Frankel, 'The politics of police control', *Comparative Politics*, 12, 4, July 1980, pp. 483–5.

66. Philip Frankel, *Pretoria's Praetorians: Civil-Military Relations in South Africa*, Cambridge: Cambridge University Press, 1984, p. 91.

67. Frankel, *Pretoria's Praetorians*, p. 63.

68. Deborah Posel, *The Making of Apartheid, 1948–1961*, Oxford: Oxford University Press, 1997, pp. 247–9.

69. Posel, *The Making of Apartheid*, p. 237.

70. John Kane-Berman, *Soweto: Black Revolt, White Reaction*, Johannesburg: Ravan Press, 1978, p. 83.

71. Doug Hindson, *Pass Controls and the African Proletariat*, Johannesburg: Ravan Press, 1987, p. 72.

72. Alan Baldwin, 'Mass removals and separate development', *Journal of Southern African Studies*, 1, 1, 1974, pp. 215–7.

73. Terblanche, *A History of Inequality*, p. 360.

74. Posel, *The Making of Apartheid*, pp. 231–2.

75. Chapter 6, 'Class formation in a Bantustan' in Roger Southall, *South Africa's Transkei: The Political Economy of an Independent Bantustan*, London: Heinemann, 1982, pp. 172–201.

76. Harold Wolpe, 'Capitalism and cheap labour power in South Africa: from segregation to apartheid', *Economy and Society*, 1, 1972.

77. Hindson, *Pass Controls*, pp. ix–xi, 10.

78. Hindson, *Pass Controls*, pp. 9 and 1968.

79. Martin Legassick and Harold Wolpe, 'The Bantustans and capital accumulation in South Africa', *Review of African Political Economy*, 7, 1976.

80. Duncan Innes, *Anglo: Anglo American and the Rise of Modern South Africa*, Johannesburg: Ravan Press, 1984, p. 174.

81. Charles H. Feinstein, *An Economic History of South Africa: Conquest, Discrimination and Development*, Cambridge: Cambridge University Press, 2005.

82. Johnson, *How Long Will South Africa Survive?*, p. 28.

83. F. W. de Klerk, *The Last Trek—A New Beginning*, Basingstoke: Macmillan, 1998, p. 37.

84. 'Phenomenal development of Sharpeville', *Vereeniging and Vanderbijlpark News*, 21 March 1967.

85. Frank Day, 'Five years later it's still a model township', *Rand Daily Mail*, 19 March 1965.

86. Nadine Gordimer, *The Conservationist*, London: Jonathan Cape, 1974, p. 29. For this reading of Gordimer's novel I have been guided by Stephen Clingman's *The Novel's of Nadine Gordimer: History from the Inside*, Johannesburg: Ravan Press, 1986.

87. Vivienne Sheer, 'Etienne Leroux's Sewe Dae by die Silbersteins: A re-examination in light of its historical context', *Journal of Southern African Studies*, 8, 2, April 1982, pp. 172–86.

88. Etienne Leroux, *To A Dubious Salvation*, Harmondsworth: Penguin, 1969, p. 79.

89. Leroux, *To a Dubious Salvation*, p. 103.

90. For an exploration of Leroux's work as a Jung-inspired search for psychological integration, see Robert L. Berner, 'Apartheid and Leroux's Welgevonden trilogy', *World Literature Today*, 53, 2, Spring 1979, pp. 205–9. For Berner, Leroux's point is that made so frequently by Jung: 'that the Devil is also part of reality and must be taken into account if we are to avoid the hubris which has been the source of so much of the spiritual arrogance of the past'.

91. Jack Cope and Uys Krige (eds.), *The Penguin Book of South African Verse*, Harmondsworth: Penguin, 1968, p. 237.

92. David Welsh, *The Rise and Fall of Apartheid*, Johannesburg: Jonathan Ball, 2009, p. 175.

93. Quoted in David Welsh, 'The executive and the African population', in Schrire (ed.), *Leadership and the Apartheid State*, p. 158.

94. Jan Botha, *Verwoerd is Dead*, Cape Town: Books of Africa, 1967, p. 121.

95. Botha, *Verwoerd is Dead*, p. 82.

96. Botha, *Verwoerd is Dead*, p. 73.

97. Botha, *Verwoerd is Dead*, p. 107.

98. For the argument in this paragraph I have drawn upon Deborah Posel, 'The assassination of Hendrik Verwoerd: the spectre of Apartheid's corpse', *African Studies*, 68, 3, December 2009, 331–50.

99. Deborah Posel, 'Whiteness and power in the South African civil service: paradoxes of the Apartheid state', *Journal of Southern African Studies*, 25, 1, 1999, pp. 105–8.

100. Report of evidence submitted to the Snyman Commission by Frank Barton, Cape Town editor of *Drum* magazine, in *Cape Argus*, 12 March 1963; Howard Lawrence, 'Poqo—We go it alone', *Fighting Talk*, 17, 2, February 1963, pp. 4–6.

101. 'Sobukwe was Poqo leader', *Cape Times*, 4 March 1963.

102. *Rand Daily Mail*, 23 March 1963.

103. *Cape Times*, 28 June 1962.

104. Republic of South Africa, 'Commission of Inquiry into the events on 20–22 November 1962 at Paarl and the causes which gave rise thereto', Proceedings Transcript on Chicago Africana Microfilm Project, microfilm held at the University of York (henceforth Snyman proceedings), p. 348; Report on trial of men involved in Chief Matanzima assassination attempt, *Cape Times*, 4 March 1961.

105. *Cape Times*, 28 June 1962, Snyman proceedings, pp. 271, 297.

106. *Cape Times*, 5 July 1962 and 28 June 1962.

107. *State vs Ngconcolo and 19 Others*, pp. 579 and 581, Trial records held at the Borthwick Institute, University of York.

108. Matthew Nkoana, interviewed by the author, London, 7 August 1975.

109. Neshtadi Sidzamba, interviewed by the author, Maseru, 11 June 1976.

110. Randolph Vigne, *Liberals Against Apartheid*, London: Macmillan, 1997, p. 142.

111. Kwandiwe Kondlo, *In the Twilight of the Revolution: The Pan-Africanist Congress of Azania (South Africa), 1959–1994*, Basel: Basler Afrika Bibliographien, 2009, pp. 111–12.

112. Joseph Lelyveld, *Move Your Shadow*, London: Abacus, 1987, p. 344.

113. Kondlo, *In the Twilight of the Revolution*, pp. 102–3.

114. Neshtadi Sidzamba, interviewed by the author, Maseru, 11 June 1976.

115. Matthew Nkoana, interviewed by the author, London, 7 August 1975.

116. Clifford Crais, *The Politics of Evil: Magic, State Power and the Political Imagination in South Africa*, Cambridge: Cambridge University Press, 2002, p. 213.

117. By 1963 the phrase was used widely within the movement: Moses Dhlamini, a *Poqo* leader from Kliptown outside Soweto travelled to see Leballo in March 1963. His journey was 'hectic with the forces of darkness racing behind our heels' (Moses Dhlamini, *Robben Island Hell-Hole*, Trenton NJ: Africa World Press, 1986, p. 144).

118. Crais, *The Politics of Evil*, p. 215.

119. SAIRR trial records collection. *State versus Neconga and 4 Others*, 1965.

120. Neshtadi Sidzamba, interviewed by the author.

121. Dhlamini, *Robben Island Hell Hole*, p. 145.

122. Thami ka Plaatjie, 'The PAC's internal undergound activities', in South African Democracy Education Trust, *The Road to Democracy in South Africa, Volume 2 (1970–1980)*, Pretoria: University of South Africa, 2006, p. 684.

123. Arianna Lissoni, 'The PAC in Basutoland, c.1962–1965', *South African Historical Journal*, 62, 1, March 2010, p. 65.

124. C. J. Driver, *Patrick Duncan: South African and Pan-African*, London: Heinemann, 1980, pp. 185–224.

125. Lissoni, 'The PAC in Basutoland', p. 72.

126. *Cape Times*, 9 June 1967.

127. Abednego Ngcobo, interviewed by the author, London, 28 May 1975.

128. Driver, *Patrick Duncan*, p. 250. Apparently, Duncan had spoken privately to other PAC members about his concerns about Chinese purchases of South African maize and somehow reports of this had reached Chinese officials who complained to a PAC delegation (Abednego Ngcobo, interviewed by the author, London, 25 August 1975).

129. Patrick Duncan correspondence, Patrick Duncan Papers, Borthwick Institute, University of York, 8.48.67.

130. Bernard Leeman, *Lesotho and the Struggle for Azania: Africanist Political Movements in Lesotho and Azania: The Origins and History of the BCP and the PAC, Volume Three*, London: University of Azania Press, 1985, p. 9.

131. Pan Africanist Congress, *Official Statement of Expulsion and Repudiation of the Call for United Nations Intervention*, Dar es Salaam, 1967, Lionel Morrison Papers, Borthwick Institute, University of York.

132. Quoted in Thomas Karis and Gail Gerhart, *From Protest to Challenge, Volume 5: Nadir and Resurgence, 1964–1979*, Bloomington: Indiana University Press, 1997, p. 290.

133. Kondlo, *In the Twilight of the Revolution*, p. 125.

134. Stephen Davis, *Apartheid's Rebels: Inside South Africa's Hidden War*, New Haven: Yale University Press, 1987, pp. 32–3.

135. Plaatjie, 'The PAC's internal underground activities', pp. 690–3.

136. 'Border Terror Battle', *Sunday Tribune* (Durban), 6 August 1978.

137. Potlake Leballo, *PAC's Revolutionary Message to the Nation*, cyclostyled text of address delivered at the PAC's Consultative conference, Arusha, Tanzania 1978, p. 14.

138. Leltlapa Mphahlele, *Child of the Soil: My Life as a Freedom Fighter*, Cape Town: Kwela Books, 2002, p. 77.

139. Mphahlele, *Child of the Soil*, p. 85.

140. 'The gallant TM Ntantala', *Azania Combat* (Dar es Salaam), 13, 1991, p. 12.

141. 'SA in plot to murder Sibeko', *Sowetan*, 2 March 1982; Kondlo, *In the Twilight of the Revolution*, p. 143.

142. Leeman, *Lesotho and the Struggle for Azania*, Vol. 3, pp. 86–94.

143. Howard Barrell, 'The Outlawed South African Liberation Movements' in Shaun Johnson (ed.), *South Africa: No Turning Back*, Bloomington: Indiana University Press, 1989, p. 75.

144. 'Lesotho makes it hot for exiles', *New African* (London), July 1985, p. 32.

145. Nelson Mandela, *Long Walk to Freedom*, Randburg: MacDonald Purnell, 1994, p. 259.

146. Benjamin Pogrund, *War of Words: Memoirs of a South African Journalist*, New York: Seven Stories Press, 2000, p. 99.

147. Ben Turok, *Nothing but the Truth: Behind the ANC's Struggle Politics*, Johannesburg: Jonathan Ball, 2003, p. 123.

148. Turok, *Nothing but the Truth*, p. 115.

149. Magubane, Bonner et al., 'The turn to armed struggle', p. 53.

150. Helen Suzman, *Memoirs: In No Uncertain Terms*, Johannesburg: Jonathan Ball, 1993, p. 52.

151. Scott Everett Couper, 'Bound by Faith: A Biographic and Ecclesiastic Examination of Chief Albert Lutuli's Stance on Violence as a Strategy to Liberate South Africa', Ph.D. Dissertation, Department of History, University of Kwa Zulu Natal, November 2008, p. 55.

152. Couper, *Bound by Faith*, p. 88.

153. Couper, *Bound by Faith*, p. 111.

154. Couper, *Bound by Faith*, p. 150.

155. Couper, *Bound by Faith*, p. 231.

156. Couper, *Bound by Faith*, p. 265.

157. Couper, *Bound by Faith*, p. 283.

158. Bruno Mtolo, *Umkhonto we Sizwe: The Road to the Left*, Durban: Drakensberg Press, 1966, pp. 23–26.

159. Mandela, *Long Walk to Freedom*, p. 272.

160. Micahel Harmel, 'Revolutions are not abnormal', *Africa South* (Cape Town), 2, 2, January 1959.

161. Magubane, Bonner et al., 'The turn to armed struggle', pp. 81–2.

162. Karis and Gerhart, *From Protest to Challenge: A Documentary History of African Politics in South Africa*, Volume Three, Stanford: Hoover Institution Press, 1977, p. 717.

163. Karis and Gerhart, *From Protest to Challenge, Volume Three*, p. 762.
164. Karis and Gerhart, *From Protest to Challenge, Volume Three*, p. 764.
165. Fran Buntman, *Robben Island and Prisoner Resistance to Apartheid*, Cambridge: Cambridge University Press, 2003, p. 18.
166. Israel, *South African Political Exile in the United Kingdom*, p. 40.
167. Charney, *Civil Society vs. the State*, pp. 232–41.
168. Charney, *Civil Society vs. the State*, p. 243.
169. Charney, *Civil Society vs. the State*, pp. 250–1.
170. Charney, *Civil Society vs. the State*, p. 101.
171. C. R. Halisi, *Black Political Thought in the Making of South African Democracy*, Bloomington: Indiana University Press, 1999, p. 103.
172. Anthony Marx, *Lessons of Struggle: South African Internal Opposition, 1960–1990*, New York: Oxford University Press, 1992, p. 45.
173. Halisi, *Black Political Thought in the Making of South African Democracy*, p. 121.
174. Themba Sono, *Reflections on the Origins of Black Consciousness in South Africa*, Pretoria: Human Sciences Research Council, 1993, p. 40.
175. Nozipho Diseko, 'The origins and development of the South African Students' Movement, 1968–1976', *Journal of Southern African Studies*, 18, 1, March 1992, 43.
176. Diseko, 'The origins and development of the South African Students' Movement', 61–2.
177. Alan Brooks and Jeremy Brickhill, *Whirlwind before the Storm*, London: International Defence and Aid, 1980, p. 87.
178. Charney, *Civil Society vs. the State*, p. 565.
179. Marx, *Lessons of Struggle*, p. 65.
180. Charney, *Civil Society vs. the State*, p. 527.
181. Massie, *Loosing the Bonds*, p. 65.
182. Fieldhouse, *Anti-Apartheid*, p. 69.
183. Fieldhouse, *Anti-Apartheid*, p. 161.
184. Massie, *Loosing the Bonds*, p. 66.
185. Driver, *Patrick Duncan*, p. 229.
186. Massie, *Loosing the Bonds*, 201.
187. Geldenhuys, *The Diplomacy of Isolation*, p. 14.
188. Massie, *Loosing the Bonds*, p. 727.
189. Hakan Thorn, *Anti-Apartheid and the Emergence of Global Civil Society*, Basingstoke: Palgrave Macmillan, 2009, p. xiii.
190. Massie, *Loosing the Bonds*, p. 80.
191. Nelson Mandela, unpublished autobiographical manuscripts, 1976, Department of Correctional Services Files, Nelson Mandela A5, National Archives of South Africa.
192. Fatima Meer, 'African nationalism—some inhibiting factors', in Heribert Adam (ed.), *South Africa: Sociological Perspectives*, Oxford: Oxford University Press, 1971, pp. 140–3.

193. Edward Feit, *Urban Revolt in South Africa*, Evanston: Northwestern University Press, 1971, p. 75.

194. Martin Legassick, *Armed Struggle and Democracy—The Case of South Africa*, Uppsala: Nordiska Afikainstutet, 2002, p. 21.

195. Alex Lichtenstein, 'Making Apartheid work: African trade unions and the 1953 Native Labour (Settlement of Disputes) Act in South Africa', *Journal of African History*, 46, 2005, pp. 305–12.

196. Litchenstein, 'Making Aparthied work', p. 311.

197. Author's interviews with Michael Thekiso and Samuel Tshabalala, Sharpeville, 6 November 2009.

CHAPTER 6

1. Christable Gurney, 'In the heart of the beast: the British Anti-Apartheid Movement, 1959–1994', in South African Democracy Trust, *The Road to Democracy in South Africa, Volume 3, International Solidarity*, Pretoria: University of South Africa Press, 2008, p. 324.

2. Hakan Thorn, *Anti-Apartheid and the Emergence of a Global Civil Society*, Basingstoke: Palgrave Macmillan, 2009, p. 5.

3. Robert Skinner, 'The moral foundations of British anti-apartheid activism, 1946–1960', *Journal of Southern African Studies*, 35, 2, June 2009, p. 415.

4. Denis Herbstein, *White Lies: Canon Collins and the Secret War Against Apartheid*, Oxford: James Currey, 2004, p. 9.

5. Skinner, 'The moral foundations of British anti-apartheid activism', p. 41.

6. Ronald Hyam and Peter Henshaw, *The Lion and the Springbok: Britain and South Africa since the Boer War*, Cambridge: Cambridge University Press, 2003, p. 315.

7. From *The Spectator*, 26 February 1960 and quoted by Hyam and Henshaw, *The Lion and the Springbok*, p. 317.

8. Roger Fieldhouse, *Anti-Apartheid: A History of the Movement in Britain*, London: Merlin Press, 2005, p. 20.

9. Hyam and Henshaw, *The Lion and the Springbok*, p. 318.

10. Howard Smith, 'Apartheid, Sharpeville and impartiality: the reporting of South Africa on BBC television, 1948–1961', *Historical Journal of Film, Radio and Television*, 13, 3, 1993, p. 254.

11. George Houser, 'Africa's challenge: the story of the American Committee on Africa', *Issue: A Journal of Opinion*, 6, 2/3, 1976, p. 23.

12. Thorn, *Anti-Apartheid*, p. 16.

13. Frank Parkin, 'Adolescent status and student disaffection', *Journal of Contemporary History*, 5, 1, 1970, p. 155.

14. Helen Lefkowitz Horowitz, 'The 1960s and the transformation of campus cultures', *History of Education Quarterly*, 26, 1, 1986, p. 16.

15. Alistair Bonnett, *Radicalism, Anti-Racism and Representation*, London: Routledge, 1993.

16. Frank Parkin, *Middle Class Radicalism: The Social Bases for the British Campaign for Nuclear Disarmament*, Manchester: Manchester University Press, 1968, p. 2.

17. Donald Culverson, 'The politics of the Anti-Apartheid Movement', *Political Science Quarterly*, 111, 1, 1996, p. 132.

18. Thorn, *Anti-Apartheid*, p. 69.

19. Tor Sellstrom, 'Sweden and the nordic countries: official solidarity and assistance from the west', in South African Democracy Trust, *The Road to Democracy in South Africa, Volume 3*, p. 443.

20. Thorn, *Anti-Apartheid*, p. 60.

21. Thorn, *Anti-Apartheid*, p. 97.

22. William Minter and Sylvia Hill, 'Anti-Apartheid solidarity in the United States', in South African Democracy Trust, *The Road to Democracy in South Africa, Volume 3*, p. 767.

23. Ernest Mandel quoted in Gareth Stedman Jones, 'The meaning of student revolt', in Alexander Cockburn and Robin Blackburn (eds.), *Student Power: Problems, Diagnosis, Action*, Harmondsworth: Penguin, 1969, p. 31.

24. Stedman Jones, 'The meaning of student revolt', p. 32.

25. Herbert Marcuse, *An Essay on Liberation*, London: Allen Lane, 1969, p. 69.

26. Marcuse, *An Essay on Liberation*, p. 80.

27. Hyam and Henshaw, *The Lion and the Springbok*, p. 328.

28. Fieldhouse, *Anti-Apartheid*, p. 330.

29. Thorn, *Anti-Apartheid*, p. 145.

30. Fieldhouse, *Anti-Apartheid*, p. 428.

31. Elizabeth Williams' doctoral research at Birbeck, cited in Hilary Sapire, 'Liberation movements, exile, and international solidarity: an introduction', *Journal of Southern African Studies*, 35, 2, 2009, pp. 282–3.

32. Fieldhouse, *Anti-Apartheid*, p. 389.

33. Hugh Bayley, MP, conversation with author, York, 15 October 2010.

34. Thorn, *Anti-Apartheid*, p. 202.

35. Thorn, *Anti-Apartheid*, p. 89.

36. Gurney 'In the heart of the beast', p. 324.

37. For an insider's explanation of these tensions: Norma Kitson, *Where Sixpence Lives*, London: The Hogarth Press, 1987, pp. 263–97.

38. Kwandire Kondlo, *In the Twilight of the Revolution: The Pan-Africanist Congress of Azania (South Africa), 1959–1994*, Basel: Basler Afrika Bibliographien, 2009, pp. 177 and 193.

39. Hugh Bayley, MP, conversation with author, York, 15 October 2010.

40. Minutes of National Committee meetings, Anti-Apartheid Movement, 5 October 1960, 7 December 1960, and 3 May 1961, Anti-Apartheid Movement Archive, Bodleian Library, Rhodes House, Oxford, MMS AAM 43.

41. South African United Front folder, Anti-Apartheid Movement Archive, Bodleian Library, Rhodes House, Oxford, MMS AAM 974.

42. Arianna Lissoni, 'The PAC in Basutoland, *c.*1962–1965', *South African Historical Journal*, 62, 1, March 2010, p. 74.

43. Fieldhouse, *Anti-Apartheid*, p. 284.

44. Henry Isaacs, 'Struggles within the Struggle: An Inside View of the PAC of South Africa', unpublished manuscript, p. 67.

45. Herbstein, *White Lies*, pp. 291–4.

46. Gora Ebrahim, 'PAC now united', *Africa News*, 31 January 1983, Pan-Africanist Congress folder, Anti-Apartheid Movement Archive, Bodleian Library, Rhodes House, Oxford, MMS AAM 968.

47. Anon., 'Anti-Apartheid is out of date', *Azania Solidarity* (London), 1, 1, 1981, Pan-Africanist Congress folder, Anti-Apartheid Movement Archive, Bodleian Library, Rhodes House, Oxford, MMS AAM 968.

48. Pan-Africanist Congress Commemorative Meeting, Westminister Conference Centre, London, 21 March 1981, Pan-Africanist Congress folder, Anti-Apartheid Movement Archive, Bodleian Library, Rhodes House, Oxford, MMS AAM 968.

49. Letter from Patrick Duncan to John Blundell, 11 December 1965, Patrick Duncan Papers, Borthwick Institute, University of York, 6.36.14.

50. Letter from Barbara Castle to Patrick Duncan, 23 April 1963, Patrick Duncan Papers, Borthwick Institute, University of York, 6.32.69.

51. Nana Mahomo file, Patrick Duncan Papers, 8.47.41; 8.47.50; 8.47.54; Potlake Leballo to Nana Mahomo, 'Instrument of suspension from office', 10 August 1964, Anthony Steel Papers.

52. Kondlo, *In the Twilight of the Revolution*, p. 120.

53. Mike Try to Michael Muendane, 16 March 1981, Pan-Africanist Congress folder, Anti-Apartheid Movement Archive, Bodleian Library, Rhodes House, Oxford, MMS AAM 968.

54. Donald Culverson, *Contesting Apartheid: US Activism, 1960–1987*, Boulder, CO: Westview Press, 1999, p. 49.

55. Robert Kinloch Massie, *Loosing the Bonds: The United States and South Africa in the Apartheid Years*, New York: Doubleday, 1997, p. 429.

56. Massie, *Loosing the Bonds*, p. 557.

57. Steven Metz, 'The Anti-Apartheid Movement and the populist instinct in American Politics', *Political Science Quarterly*, 101, 3, 1986, p. 384.

58. Culverson, 'The politics of the Anti-Apartheid Movement', p. 137.

59. Massie, *Loosing the Bonds*, p. 428.

60. Minter and Hill, 'Anti-Apartheid solidarity in United States', in South African Democracy Education Trust, *The Road to Democracy in South Africa, Volume 3*, p. 791.

61. Sarah Soule, 'The student divestment movement in the United States and tactical diffusion: the shanty town protest', *Social Forces*, 75, 1997, pp. 862–4.

62. Massie, *Loosing the Bonds*, p. 560.

63. Minter and Hill, 'Anti-Apartheid solidarity', p. 801.

64. Sellstrom, 'Sweden and the nordic countries', p. 492.

65. Connie Braam, *Operation Vula*, Bellevue: Jacana, 2004, p. 29.

66. Hans-Georg Schleicher, 'GDR solidarity: the German Democratic Republic and the South African liberation struggle', in South African Democracy Education Trust, *The Road to Democracy in South Africa, Volume 3*, p. 1101.

67. Alan Barcan, 'Student activists at Sydney University, 1960–1967: a problem of interpretation', *History of Education Review*, January 2007, p. 70.

68. Peter Limb, 'The Anti-Apartheid movements in Australia and Aotearoa/ New Zealand', in South African Democracy Education Trust, *The Road to Democracy in South Africa, Volume 3*, pp. 914–15.

69. *Dunnes Strike Support Group Newsletter*, 21 January 1985.

70. Mary Dundon, 'Drops in the ocean that turned tide', *Irish Examiner*, 19 July 2004.

71. IAAM, *Annual Report, 1984–1985*, p. 10, Mayibuye Archives, MCH34, 3.21.

72. Eamonn McCann, 'Dunnes Stores in black and white', *Magill Magazine*, 4 April 1985, p. 27.

73. 'The two oranges that shook Apartheid', *An Phoblacht* (Dublin), 22 July 2004.

74. IAAM, *Annual Report, 1984–1985*, pp. 10–12, Mayibuye Archives, MCH34, 3.21.

75. McCann, 'Dunnes Stores in black and white', p. 30.

76. IAAM, Secretary's Report, 22.05.1965, Mayibuye Archives, MCH34, 1AA.

77. Charles van Onselen, *Masked Raiders: Irish Banditry in Southern Africa, 1880–1899*, Cape Town: Zebra Press, 2010, pp. 221–2.

78. Donal P. MacCracken, 'Collaborators or liberators? Irish race attitudes in the South African historical context', in Gudmundor Halfdanarson (ed.), *Racial Discrimination and Ethnicity in European History*, Pisa: Edizioni Plus, 2003, pp. 117–25.

79. Louise and Kader Asmal and Thomas Alberts, 'The Irish Anti-Apartheid Movement', in South African Democracy Education Trust, *The Road to Democracy in South Africa, Volume 3*, p. 355.

80. Patrick Noonan, *They're Burning the Churches*, Bellevue: Jacana Books, 2003, p. 230.

81. IAAM, *Secretary's Report, 22.05.1965*, Mayibuye Archives, MCH34, 1AA.

82. Gemma Hussey, *Ireland Today: Anatomy of a Changing State*, Harmondsworth: Penguin, 1995, p. 159.

83. Press reports cited in Kevin O'Sullivan, 'Ireland and Sub-Saharan Africa, 1955–1975', Ph.D. Dissertation, Department of History, Trinity College Dublin, 2008, p. 133.

84. Desmond Barry, *Finally and In Conclusion: A Political Memoir*, Dublin: New Island Books, 2000, pp. 158–9.

85. Charlie Mulqueen, 'The first and last Springbok', *Limerick Leader*, 17 January 1970. See various reports, *Limerick Leader*, 3 January to 2 February 1970.

86. IAAM, *Annual Report, 1981–1982*, Mayibuye Archives, MCH34, 3.18.

87. Asmals and Alberts, 'The Irish Anti-Apartheid Movement', p. 378.

88. Asmals and Alberts, 'The Irish Anti-Apartheid Movement', p. 380.

89. IAAM, *Annual Report, 1984*, Mayibuye Archives, MCH34, 3.20.

90. IAAM, *Annual Report, 1980–1981*, Mayibuye Archives, MCH 34, 3.17.

91. IAAM, *Annual Report, 1977–1978*, Mayibuye Archives, MCH 34, 3.14.

92. IAAM, *Annual Report, 1973–1974*, Mayibuye Archives, MCH 34 3.10.

93. Kader Asmal to Peter Doyle, 9 April 1985, Mayibuye Archives, MCH 34, 2.2.

94. IAAM, *Annual Report, 1984–1985*, Mayibuye Archives, MCH34, 3.21.

95. Michael Cronin, 'Ireland, globalisation and the war against time', in Peadar Kirby, Luke Gibbons, and Michael Cronin (eds.), *Reinventing Ireland: Culture, Society and the Global Economy*, London: Pluto Press, 2002, p. 59.

96. IAAM, *Annual Report, 1988–1989*, Mayibuye Archives, MCH 34, 3.25.

97. IAAM, *Annual Report, 1972–1973*, Mayibuye Archives, MCH34, 3.9.

98. McCann, 'Dunnes Stores in black and white', p. 31.

99. Asmals and Alberts, 'The Irish Anti-Aparthied Movement', p. 398.

100. IAAM, *Annual Report, 1989–1990*, Mayibuye Archives, MCH 34, 3.26.

101. Quoted from official files by O'Sullivan, *Ireland and Sub-Saharan Africa*, p. 82.

102. IAAM, *Annual Report, 1971–1972*, Mayibuye Archives, MCH 34, 3.8.

103. O'Sullivan, *Ireland and Sub-Saharan Africa*, p. 135.

104. O'Sullivan, *Ireland and Sub-Saharan Africa*, p. 218.

105. O'Sullivan, *Ireland and Sub-Saharan Africa*, p. 222.

106. IAAM, *Annual Report, 1984–1985*, Mayibuye Archives, MCH 34, 3.21.

107. I have borrowed this idea from Bill Schwarz's essay about the imperial contribution to British political culture: 'Empire: for and against', *Twentieth Century British History*, 6, 3, 1995, p. 359.

108. O'Sullivan, *Ireland and Sub-Saharan Africa*, p. 126.

109. O'Sullivan, *Ireland and Sub-Saharan Africa*, p. 2.

110. Northern Ireland Civil Rights Association, *'We shall overcome': The History of the Struggle for Civil Rights in Northern Ireland, 1968–1978*, Belfast: 1978.

111. O'Sullivan, *Ireland and Sub-Saharan Africa*, p. 125.

112. Exhibit text, Museum of Free Derry, 11 May 2010.

113. Paul Arthur, conversation with author, Magee Campus, University of Ulster, Derry, 13 May 2010.

114. Peadar Kirby, 'Contested pedigrees of the celtic tiger', in Kirby, Gibbons, and Cronin (eds.), *Reinventing Ireland*, p. 26.

115. Roy Foster, *Luck and the Irish: A Brief History of Change, 1970–2000*, London: Penguin, 2007, p. 95.

116. Chris Alden, *Apartheid's Last Stand*, Basingstoke: Macmillan, 1996, p. 242.

117. F. W. de Klerk, *The Autobiography*, pp. 70–1 and 183.

118. Asmals and Alberts, 'The Irish Anti-Apartheid Movement', p. 394.

119. Jan Heunis, *The Inner Circle: Reflections on the Last Days of White Rule*, Jeppestown: Jonathan Ball, 2007, p. 152.

120. Adrian Guelke, *Rethinking the Rise and the Fall of Apartheid*, Basingstoke: Palgrave Macmillan, 2005, pp. 160–1.

121. Neta Crawford, 'How embargoes work', in Neta Crawford and Audie Klotz (eds.), *How Sanctions Work: Lessons from the South African Experience*, New York: St Martin's Press, 1999, p. 65.

122. Mer Voorhest, 'The US divestment movement' in Crawford and Klotz (eds.), *How Sanctions Work*, p. 141.

123. David Black, 'The effects and effectiveness of the sport boycott', in Crawford and Klotz (eds.), *How Sanctions Work*, pp. 223–4.

124. Robert Price, 'Race and reconciliation in the New South Africa', *Politics and Society*, 25, 2, 1997, p. 159.

CHAPTER 7

1. Nivashni Nair, 'Man remembers Sharpeville ahead of anniversary', *Times* (Johannesburg), 18 May 2010.

2. Monako Dibetle, 'Sharpeville is still bleeding', *Mail and Guardian*, 19 March 2010.

3. Petrus Tom, *My Life Struggle: The Story of Petrus Tom*, Johannesburg: Ravan Press, 1985, p. 66.

4. Judgement, Delmas Treason Trial Records, University of the Witwatersrand, AK 217, L12.3, p. 322.

5. Peter Parker and Joyce Mokhesi-Parker, *In the Shadow of Sharpeville: Apartheid and Criminal Justice*, New York: New York University Press, 1998, p. 11.

6. Tom, *My Life Struggle*, p. 64.

7. Delmas Treason Trial Records. Papers prepared by the Defence. Patrick Noonan, 'The Vaal Triangle during the unrest in 1984–1985', University of the Witwatersrand Historical Papers, AK 217 S8 10. 20, p. 7.

8. Johannes Rantete, *The Third Day of September: An Eye Witness Account of the Sebokeng Rebellion of 1984*, Johannesburg: Ravan Press, 1984, p. 8.

9. Patrick Noonan, *They're Burning the Churches*, Bellevue: Jacana Books, 2003.

10. George Bizos, quoted on the cover of Noonan, *They're Burning the Churches*.

11. Republic of South Africa, *Report of the Commission of Inquiry into the Riots at Soweto and Elsewhere from the 16th June 1976 to the 28th February 1977*, Volume 2, RP55/1980, Pretoria: 1980, pp. 167–168.

12. Parker and Mokhesi-Parker, *In the Shadow of Sharpeville*, p. 25.

13. Simon Bekker, 'The local government and community of Sebokeng', Occasional Paper no. 3, Department of Sociology, University of Stellenbosch, June 1978.

14. Prakash Diar, *The Sharpeville Six*, Toronto: McClelland and Stewart Inc, 1990, p. xix.

15. Delmas Treason Trial Records. Papers prepared by the Defence. Emergence of the VCA. University of the Witwatersrand Historical Papers, AK 217 S8.4.1.

16. Delmas Treason Trial Records. Papers prepared by the Defence. Lisa Seftel. Events in the Vaal Triangle. University of the Witwatersrand Historical Papers, AK 217 S8.10.4.

17. 'Defiant Vaal boycott enters third year', *Work in Progress*, Braamfontein, September 1986, pp. 16–17. See also Noonan, *They're Burning the Churches*, p. 121.

18. Delmas Treason Trial Records. Papers prepared by the Defence. Notes on a discussion with Philip Masia, general secretary of the Orange Vaal General Workers' Union, 10 December 1985. University of the Witwatersrand Historical Papers, AK 217 S8.10.19.

19. B. A. Khoapa (ed.), *Black Review 1972*, Durban: Black Community Programmes, 1973, p. 184.

20. Alan Brooks and Paul Brickhill, *Whirlwind before the Storm*, London: International Defence and Aid Fund, 1980, p. 81.

21. Parker and Mokhesi-Parker, *In the Shadow of Sharpeville*, p. 25.

22. Moses Dhlamini, *Robben Island Hell-Hole*, Trenton NJ: Africa World Press, 1986, p. 199.

23. Ikaboth Makiti interviewed by the author, Sharpeville, 20 July 2010.

24. Noonan, *They're Burning the Churches*, p. 11.

25. 'Movement aimed at abstinence', *The Star*, 20 October 1978; Dhlamini, *Robben Island Hell-Hole*, p. 70.

26. Noonan, *They're Burning the Churches*, pp. 179–83.

27. 'Woman planned to set fire to house', *The Star*, 8 August 1978.

28. Delmas Treason Trial Records. Papers prepared by the Defence. Emergence of the VCA. University of the Witwatersrand Historical Papers, AK 217 S8.4.1.

29. Craig Charney, 'Sharpeville—20 years later . . .', *The Star*, 21 March 1980.

30. *Sowetan*, 15 July 1981.

31. *Sowetan*, 1 December 1983.

32. Noonan, *They're Burning the Churches*, p. 51.

33. 'Civics on the frontline', *SASPU National*, 5, 7, December 1984, p. 13.

34. Diar, *The Sharpeville Six*, p. xxv.

35. 'Defiant Vaal boycott enters third year', *Work in Progress*, September 1986, p. 17.

36. Diar, *The Sharpeville Six*, p. xxv.

37. *Speak*, 3, 1, March 1985, letter to the editor complaining about the Sharpeville Civic Association, p. 6.

38. Richard Wilson, *The Politics of Truth and Reconciliation in South Africa*, Cambridge: Cambridge University Press, 2001, p. 177; Clive Glaser, *Bo-Tsotsi: The Youth Gangs of Soweto, 1935–1976*, Oxford: James Currey, 2000, p. 189.

39. Ineke van Kessel, *'Beyond our wildest dreams': The United Democratic Front and the Transformation of South Africa*, Charlottesville: University of Virginia Press, 2000, p. 51.

40. Noonan, *They're Burning the Churches*, p. 109.

41. Jeremy Seekings, 'Political mobilisation in the black townships of the Transvaal', in Philip Frankel, Noam Pines, and Mark Swilling (eds.), *State, Resistance and Change in South Africa*, London: Croom Helm, 1988, p. 207.

42. Seekings, 'Political mobilisation in the black townships of the Transvaal', p. 219.

43. See, for examples, Elias Canetti, *Crowds and Power*, Harmondsworth: Penguin, 1981, pp. 15–17 and the various authorities discussed in James B. Rule, *Theories of Civil Violence*, Berkeley: University of California Press, 1988, chapter 3.

44. Paerker and Mokhesi-Parker, *In the Shadow of Sharpeville*, p. 174.

45. Scipio Sighele quoted by Rule, *Theories of Civil Violence*, p. 93.

46. 'Sharpeville's Second Rebellion', *SASPU National*, 4, 1987, p. 14.

47. Parker and Mokhesi-Parker, *In the Shadow of Sharpeville*, pp. 23–4.

48. Mtutuzeli Matshoba, 'Nothing but the truth: the ordeal of Duma Khumalo', in Deborah Posel and Graeme Simpson (eds.), *Commissioning the Past: Understanding South Africa's Truth and Reconciliation Commission*, Johannesburg: Witwatersrand University Press, 2002.

49. Diar, *The Sharpeville Six*, p. 155.

50. Truth and Reconciliation Commission of South Africa, *Report*, Volume Three, p. 603.

51. Jeremy Seekings, *Heroes or Villains? Youth Politics in the 1980s*, Johannesburg: Ravan, 1993, pp. 66–7.

52. Noonan, *They're Burning the Churches*, p. 188.

53. Al Cook, 'The International Defence and Aid Fund for Southern Africa', in South African Democracy Education Project, *The Road to Democracy in South Africa, Volume Three, International Solidarity*, Pretoria: University of South Africa Press, 2008. pp. 219–20.

54. 'Sharpeville's Second Rebellion', *SASPU National*, 4, 1987, p. 14.

55. David Chidester, *Shots in the Streets: Violence and Religion in South Africa*, Boston: Beacon Press, 1991, pp. 104–5.

56. Noonan, *They're Burning the Churches*, p. 100.

57. 'Vaal residents stand firm', *Speak*, March 1985, 3,1.

58. Noonan, *They're Burning the Churches*, p. 194.

59. Noonan, *They're Burning the Churches*, pp. 132–4.

60. Noonan, *They're Burning the Churches*, p. 136.

61. Delmas Treason Trial Records. Papers prepared by the Defence. Philip Frankel, 'Socio-economic conditions, rent boycotts and local government crisis', Confidential Report for Sullivan Code Signatories, Urban Foundation, June 1987, University of the Witwatersrand Historical Papers, AK 217 S8.10.11.

62. 'Commando Tshepo was a born leader', *Azanian Commando*, Supplement 2, 1987, p. 2.

63. Wilson, *The Politics of Truth and Reconciliation in South Africa*, p. 181.

64. Wilson, *The Politics of Truth and Reconciliation in South Africa*, p. 186.

65. Quotations in this paragraph are from African National Congress, 1985, *Documentation of the Second Consultative Conference*, Lusaka, pp. 10–12, 18; and 44; African National Congress, 1985, *National Consultative Conference, June, Report, Main Decisions and Recommendations of the Second National Consultative Conference*, Lusaka, p. 6.

66. Irina Filatova, 'South Africa's Soviet connection', *History Compass*, 6, 2, 2008, pp. 398–9.

67. Vladimer Shubin, *The ANC: The View from Moscow*, Belville: Mayibuye Books, 1999, pp. 327–8.

68. Stephen Lewis, *Economics of Apartheid*, New York: Council on Foreign Relations, 1990, pp. 26–8.

69. Seekings, *Heroes or Villains?*, p. 13.

70. Cited in Seekings, *Heroes or Villains?*, p. 15.

71. For comparative assessment of the threat represented by political violence in South Africa in the late 1980s, see Jeffery Herbst, 'Prospects for revolution in South Africa', *Political Science Quarterly*, 103, 4, Winter 1988, pp. 674–6.

72. '1987: What is to be done?', document distributed by the ANC Politico-Military Council to regional command centres, October 1986. Later released to South African journalists by the South African authorities at a press conference.

73. Stephen Ellis and Tshepo Sechaba, *Comrades Against Apartheid: The ANC and the South African Communist Party in Exile*, London: James Currey, 1992, pp. 168–9.

74. Howard Barrell, *MK: The ANC's Armed Struggle*, Johannesburg: Penguin, 1990, p. 60.

75. Quoted in the *New York Times*, 9 February 1990. By mistake, Nzo was quoting from an internal NEC document at a press conference.

76. *The Observer*, London, 2 March 1986.

77. In this year, in a commemorative volume about the Freedom Charter, the editors, both members of the SACP, noted that after national liberation, the state would still 'cater for' small traders such as shopkeepers or barbers, 'so long as they do not threaten to become big capitalists'. Larger private concerns, though, would be deemed 'incompatible' with national liberation (Raymond Suttner and Jeremy Cronin (eds.), *30 Years of the Freedom Charter*, Johannesburg: Ravan Press, 1986, pp. 178–9).

78. F. W. de Klerk, *The Last Trek—A New Beginning*, London: Macmillan, 1998, p. 161. See also Frederick Van Zyl, *The Other Side of History*, Johannesburg: Jonathan Ball, 2006, p. 36.

79. Johannes Rantete, *The African National Congress and the Negotiated Settlement in South Africa*, Pretoria: J L Van Schaik Publishers, 1998, p. 135.

80. Luli Callinicos, *Oliver Tambo: Beyond the Engeni Mountains*, Cape Town: David Philip, 2004, pp. 601–2.

81. Stephen Davis, *Apartheid's Rebels: Inside South Africa's Hidden War*, New Haven: Yale University Press, 1987, pp. 60–1. Kwandile Kondlo, *In the Twilight of the Revolution: The Pan-Africanist Congress of Azania (South Africa), 1959–1964*, Basel: Basler Afrika Bibliogrpahen, 2009, p. 174.

82. Nelson Mandela, *Long Walk to Freedom*, Randburg: MacDonald Purnell, 1994, p. 578.

83. Jeremy Seekings, *The UDF: A History of the United Democratic Front*, Cape Town: David Philip, 2000, p. 113.

84. Alex Mashinini, 'People's war and negotiations: are they fire and water?', *Sechaba*, August 1988, p. 27.

85. Kondlo, *In the Twilight of the Revolution*, p. 222

86. Kondlo, *In the Twilight of the Revolution*, p. 160.

87. Kondlo, *In the Twilight of the Revolution*.

88. Gora Ebrahim, 'John Pokela's Obituary', *Zimbabwe Herald*, 13 July 1985.

89. Herman Stadler, expert evidence in *State versus Phikwane*, Rand Supreme Court, 1988, p. 29.

90. Craig Kotze, 'Alex Scorpion gang hits Soweto', *The Star*, 20 February 1987.

91. Craig Kotze, 'Scorpion "terror" gang is linked with PAC', *The Star*, 28 February 1987.

92. *Citizen*, 3 September 1987.

93. *Citizen*, 1 June 1988.

94. Willie Mazambane, 'APLA operations increase as record 65 cops are hit in single PAC guerrilla attack', *Azania Combat*, 4, 1987, p. 3.

95. 'Police capture PAC suspect in Western Transvaal', *The Star*, 28 July 1988.

96. 'Apla's capability underestimated', *The Star*, 4 December 1992.

97. Jacques Pauw, 'Defence force raid on Apla scrapped', *The Star*, 5 February 1993.

98. 'Massive PAC arms programme succeeds', *Azania Commando*, 4, 1987.

99. Stadler, expert evidence in *State versus Phikwane*, p. 26.

100. 'Libyans trained me—terrorist', *The Star*, 12 August 1982.

101. 'To the great Themba Ncapayi', *Azania Combat*, 15, 1992, p. 11.

102. *Post* (Johannesburg), 23 March 1979.

103. Kaizer Nyatshumba, 'Apla's Phama dies in car crash', *The Star*, 10 February 1994.

104. Wim Booyse, 'The re-emergence of the PAC', *Freedom Bulletin* (Johannesburg), July 1987.

105. Gary van Staden, 'Return of the prodigal son: prospects for a revival of the Pan-Africanist Congress', *International Affairs Bulletin*, 1989, p. 42.

106. Howard Barrell, 'The outlawed South African liberation movements', in Shaun Johnson (ed.), *South Africa: No Turning Back*, Bloomington: Indiana University Press, 1989, p. 77.

107. John Perlman, 'Bullets outweigh words in propaganda battle', *The Star*, 12 December 1992.

108. Willie Mazambane, 'Pretoria now admits APLA operatives in SA outnumber those of MK', *Azania Combat*, 16, 1993, p. 18.

109. Mazambane, 'Pretoria now admits...', p. 18.

110. Norman Chandler, 'Apla to be integrated into army', *The Star*, 14 July 1994.

111. *SANDF Internal Communication Bulletin*, 86, 29 August 1995.

112. *The Star*, 9 March 1990.

113. Doreen Atkinson, 'Brokering a miracle? The multi-party negotiating forum in The Small Miracle: South Africa's negotiated settlement', *South African Review*, 7, Johannesburg: Ravan Press, 1994, p. 19.

114. Denis Cruywagen, 'Apla steps out of big brother MK's shadow', *The Star*, 8 December 1992.

115. Republic of South Africa, *Report to the Goldstone Commission of Inquiry, regarding the prevention of public violence and intimidation from the Committee conducting a preliminary investigation into the activities of the Azanian People's Liberation Army*, Pretoria, 15 March 1993, p. 7.

116. Muriel Dimpho, '200 security forces now killed as PAC guerrillas hit hard', *Azania Combat*, no. 15.

117. Bronwyn Wilkinson, 'Apla Great Storm message jars with PAC', *The Star*, 2 January 1993.

118. Republic of South Africa, *Annual Report of the Commissioner of the SAP*, 1992, RP67/1993.

119. Letlapa Mphahlele, *Child of the Soil: My Life as a Freedom Fighter*, Cape Town: Kwela Books, 2002, p. 144.

120. Jocelyn Maker and Nick Olivari, 'Cold blooded killers plot ambush', *Sunday Times*, 2 March 1993.

121. 'Apla's capability underestimated', *The Star*, 4 December 1992.

122. Chris Barron, 'Attackers were highly trained', *Sunday Star*, 27 December 1992.

123. 'Call to beg for Apla', *The Star*, 1 February 1993.

124. Lovemore Ngoma, 'PAC man gets 18 years in $40m mandrax case', *The Herald*, 25 October 1992; Norman West, 'Top PAC officials in drugs scandal', *Sunday Times*, 16 May 1993.

125. Edith Bulbring, 'Holomisa tells SA to go to hell', *Sunday Times*, 3 January 1993. Mphahlele's memoir, *Child of the Soil*, refers to the help the PAC obtained from Transkeien officials. In 1993, APLA soliders helped General Holomisa suppress a Transjeien Defence Force mutiny (pp. 149 and 158–9).

126. Willie Mazambane, 'Tribute to late ex-APLA chief the gallant T. M. Ntantala', *Azania Combat*, no. 13, 1991, p. 13.

127. Kondlo, *In the Twilight of the Revolution*, pp. 240–54.

128. Mphahlele, *Child of the Soil*, p. 145.

129. Dawn Barkhuizen, 'Bungle, bungle, bungle', *Sunday Times*, 6 December 1992.

130. Barney Desai, 'To negotiate now is to capitulate now', *Sunday Star*, 13 May 1990.

131. Kaizer Nyatsumba, 'Talks inevitable, says surprise PAC document', *The Star*, 11 June 1990.

132. Kaizer Nyatsumba, 'Phama: parallels with Hani', *The Star*, 11 February 1994.

133. Willie Mazambane, 'PAC defends APLA's attacks on police', *Azanian Commando*, 1992, p. 3.

134. Willie Mazambane, 'PAC defends APLA's attacks...'.

135. Kondlo, *In the Twilight of the Revolution*, pp. 186–7 and 264.

136. Kondlo, *In the Twilight of the Revolution*, p. 195.

137. Abednego Ngcobo, interviewed by the author, London, 25 August 1975.

138. Perlman, 'Bullets outweigh words in propaganda battle', *The Star*, 12 December 1992.

139. '10% of blacks back Apla', *The Star*, 1 July 1993.

140. 'Race war threat', *New Nation*, 26 March 1993.

141. Kaizer Nyatsumba, 'Life of every South African is precious', *The Star*, 3 July 1993.

142. 'Slaying attempt to derail talks', *The Star*, 21 July 1993.

143. *The Star*, 22 March 1993.

144. *The Star*, 22 March 1993.

145. *Sunday Times*, 12 September 1993.

146. Mphahlele, *Child of the Soil*, pp. 203–6.

147. In this respect it is instructive to compare the scale of APLA's military operations with other guerrilla armies of comparable size. For example, in Malaya in 1951, a 5,000-strong Communist People's Army was responsible for the deaths of 500 soldiers and policemen and undertook about 500 operations every month (Noel Barber, *The War of the Running Dogs*, Malaya, London: Fontana, 1972, p. 161). Here, though, leadership and rank and file were all inside the country and did not depend upon external lines of communication and supply.

148. Mayor Mahole Mofokeng quoted in 'Pass law shootings victims' legacy lives on', *The Sowetan*, 2 March 2010.

149. 'ANC wants to erase memories of Sobukwe', *Sowetan*, 2 March 2010.

150. Gary Baines, 'Remembering Sharpeville', *History Today*, 60. 3, March 2010, p. 35.

151. Sharpeville Resident Kgosi Manyathela quoted in Monako Dibetle, 'Sharpeville is still bleeding', *Mail and Guardian*, 19 March 2010.

152. Karen Allen, 'South Africa's Sharpeville recalls 1960 massacre', *BBC News*, 21 March 2010, website: http://news.bbc.co.uk/2/hi/africa/8577518.stm

153. Hakan Thorn, *Anti-Apartheid and the Emergence of a Global Civil Society*, Basingstoke: Palgrave Macmillan, 2009, p. 134.

154. Ambrose Reeves, *Shooting at Sharpeville: The Agony of South Africa*, Boston: Houghton Mifflin, 1961, p. 62.

155. Bernardus Fourie, 'The Ambassador's Stand', *Africa Today* (Bloomington), 7, 3, May 1960.

156. Darren Newbury, *Defiant Images, Photography and Apartheid South Africa*, Pretoria: Unisa Press, 2009, pp. 161–2.

157. Reeves, *Shooting at Sharpeville*, pp. 42–3.

158. Reeves, *Shooting at Sharpeville*, p. 77.

159. For more detail, see Philip Frankel's discussion of police evidence to the Wessels Commision in *An Ordinary Atrocity: Sharpeville and its Massacre*, Johannesburg: Witwatersrand University Press, 2001, pp. 190–9.

160. Frankel, *An Ordinary Atrocity*, p. 198.

161. Henry Pike, *A History of Communism in South Africa*, Germiston: Christian Mission International of South Africa, 1988, p. 338.

162. J. P. J. Coetzer, *Gister se dade Vandag se Ordeel*, Pretoria: J P Van der Walt, 2000, p. 96.

163. Reeves, *Shooting at Sharpeville*, pp. 34–46.

164. Mary Benson, *Nelson Mandela*, Harmondsworth: Penguin, 1986, p. 84.

165. Bernard Magubane, *The Political Economy of Race and Class in South Africa*, New York: Monthly Review Press, 1979, p. 312.

166. Brian Bunting, *The Rise of the South African Reich*, Harmondsworth: Penguin, 1964, pp. 9 and 175.

167. Elias L. Ntloedibe, *Here is a Tree: Political Biography of Robert Mangaliso Sobukwe*, Mogoditshane, Botswana: Century-Turn Publishers, 1995, p. 76.

168. Jasper van der Bliek (ed.), *Sharpeville Scars*, Tillburg: Tillburg-Lejoa Vaal Association, 2000, p. 42.

169. Parker and Mokesi-Parker, *In the Shadow of Sharpeville*, p. 24.

170. Ridwan Nytagodien and Arthur Neal, 'Collective Trauma, Apologies and the Politics of Memory', *Journal of Human Rights*, 3, 4, 2004, p. 467.

171. Truth and Reconciliation Commission of South Africa, *Report, Volume 5*, Cape Town: Juta and Co., 1998, p. 133.

172. Brandon Hamber and Richard Wilson, 'Symbolic closure through memory, reparation and revenge in post-conflict societies', *Journal of Human Rights*, 1, 1, 2002, p. 37.

173. Noonan, *They're Burning the Churches*, p. 27.

174. van der Bliek, *Sharpeville Scars*, pp. 27 and 39.

175. Delmas Treason Trial Records. Papers prepared by the Defence. 'Rent grievances, Sharpeville, interviews from residents: transcript from movie', University of the Witwatersrand, Historical Papers, AK 2117, 8.10 17.

176. Catherine Merridale, *Night of Stone: Death and Memory in Russia*, London: Granta, 2001, p. 57.

177. Elizabeth Lira, 'Violence, fear and impunity: reflections on subjective and political obstacles for peace', *Peace and Conflict: Journal of Peace Psychology*, 7, 2, 2001, pp. 13–14.

178. Daniel Bar-Tal, 'Collective memory of physical violence: its contribution to the culture of violence', in E. Cairns and M. D. Roe (eds.), *The Role of Memory in Ethnic Conflict*, Houndsmill: Palgrave Macmillan, 2003.

179. Parker and Mokhesi-Parker, *In the Shadow of Sharpeville*, p. 26.

180. Wisman Chirwa, 'Collective memory and the process of reconciliation and reconstruction', *Development in Practice*, 7.4., 1997, p. 482.

181. Charles Villa Vicencio, 'Restorative justice: dealing with the past differently' in Charles Villa-Vicencio and Wilhelm Verwoerd, *Looking Back, Reaching Forward: Reflections on the Truth and Reconciliation Commission of South Africa*, Cape Town: University of Cape Town Press, 2000, p. 71.

182. Bar-Tal, 'Collective memory of physical violence', pp. 8–9.

183. Michael Humphrey, 'Form terror to trauma: commissioning truth for national reconciliation', *Social Identities*, 6. 1, 2000, p. 15.

184. van der Bliek, *Sharpeville Scars*, p. 39.

185. Piet Meiring, *Chronicle of the Truth Commission*, Vanderbijlpark: Carpe Diem Books, 1999, p. 63.

186. 'Commission hears of slaughter after Hani's assassination', *The Star*, 9 August 1996.

187. 'ANC, PAC supporters clash on Sharpeville Day', *Vaalster*, 27 March 1995.

188. Mzimane Ngudle, 'TRC not a toothless dog', *The Citizen*, 9 August 1996.

189. Kevin O'Grady, 'Sharpeville victims get less than R150', *Business Day*, 6 August 1996.

190. Case number 793, Konsatsama Elizabeth Mabona, Sobokeng, 5 August 1996, http://www.doj.gov.za/trc/hrvtrans/sebokeng/seb793.htm

191. Case number 902: David Ramahanoe, Sebokeng, 5 August 1996, http://www.doj.gov.za/trc/hrvtrans/sebokeng/seb902.htm

192. Truth and Reconciliation Commission of South Africa, *Report, Volume 3*, p. 537.

193. Mary Mantsho, secretary, Khulumani Support Group Sharpeville, interviewed by author, Sharpeville, 20 July 2010.

194. Frankel, *An Ordinary Atrocity*, pp. 128–30.

195. Bob Jones (ed.), *South African Election '99 Update 1–15*, Johannesburg: Electoral Institute of South Africa, 1999, p. 203.

196. Henry Isaacs, 'Struggles within the Struggle: An Inside View of the PAC of South Africa', unpublished ms. p. 218.

197. Miongedi Mafata, 'The struggle was his life', *The Sowetan*, 4 December 2002.

198. For a salutary discussion of Khulumani's aims and activities: Tshepo Madlin-goza, 'On transitional justice: entrepreneurs and the production of victims', *Journal of Human Rights Practice*, 2,2, 2010, pp. 208–28.

199. Mary Mantsho, secretary, Khulumani, Sharpeville, interviewed by the author, 20 July 2010.

200. Residents' critical aesthetic reactions to the monument are documented in: Ereshnee Naidu, *Empowerment through Living Memory: A Community-Centred*

Model for Memorialisation, Research Report, Johannesburg: Centre for the Study of Violence and Reconciliation, 2004, pp. 5–6.

201. Chana Teeger and Vered Vinitzky-Seroussi, 'Controlling for consensus: commemorating apartheid in South Africa', *Symbolic Interaction*, 30, 1, 2007, pp. 57–73.

202. Tokiso Molefe, 'Sharpeville—the struggle goes on', *City Press*, 21 March 2010.

203. Sekwati Sekoane overheard in the Memorial Garden, Sharpeville, 6 November 2009.

Bibliography and Sources

DOCUMENTATION AND ARCHIVES

African National Congress, '1987: What is to be done?', document distributed by the ANC Politico-Military Council to regional command centres, October 1986. Later released to South African journalists by the South African authorities at a press conference, author's files

Anti-Apartheid Movement Archive, Bodleian Library (Rhodes House), Oxford

Delmas Treason Trial Records, University of the Witwatersrand Library, Historical Papers, AK 217

Patrick Duncan Papers, Borthwick Institute, University of York

Gail Gerhart Papers, University of the Witwatersrand Library, Historical Papers, A2422

Independent Television News film footage of the Sharpeville crisis held at the Apartheid Museum, Johannesburg

Irish Anti-Apartheid Movement Papers, Mayibuye Archives, University of the Western Cape, Bellevue, Cape Town, MCH34

Henry Isaacs, *Struggles within the Struggle: An Inside View of the PAC of South Africa*, unpublished manuscript, author's files

Karis and Carter Microfilms, South African Political Materials, held at the University of the Witwatersrand Library, Historical Papers

Philip Kgosana, unpublished autobiographical manuscript, Institute of Commonwealth Studies, University of London

Philip Kgosana, 'The Burial of Uncle Bob Leshoai', speech delivered in Mafikeng, 18 February 1996, copy given to author

——, 'Patrick Duncan and the Pan-Africanist Congress', typescript, dated 7 September 1963, Claude Barnett Papers, University of Chicago, Box 175

Potlake Leballo, *PAC's Revolutionary Message to the Nation*, cyclostyled text of address delivered at the PAC's consultative conference, Arusha, Tanzania 1978, author's files

Colin Legum Papers, University of Cape Town Libraries, Manuscripts and Archives BC 1329

Nelson Mandela, 1976, unpublished autobiographical manuscripts, Department of Correctional Services Files, Nelson Mandela A5, National Archives of South Africa Lionel Morrison Papers, Borthwick Institute, University of York

Robert Sobukwe Papers, University of the Witwatersrand Library, Historical
    Papers, A2618
Randolph Vigne Papers, University of Cape Town Libraries, Manuscripts and
    Archives, BC 1328
Regina vs. Synod Madlebe, 1960–1961, Court Records and Related Papers, Folder 31,
    Albie Sachs Papers, Institute for Commonwealth Studies, University of London
Republic of South Africa, *Commission of Inquiry into the events on 20–22 November
    1962 at Paarl and the causes which gave rise thereto*, Transcript of Proceedings of
    Chicago Africana Microfilm Project, microfilm held at the Borthwick Institute,
    University of York
South African Institute of Race Relations Papers, University of the Witwatersrand
    Library, Historical Papers
State vs. Neconga and 4 Others, 1965. South African Institute of Race Relations Trial
    Records Collection, University of the Witwatersrand, Historical Papers
State vs. Ngconcolo and 19 others, trial records held at the Borthwick Institute,
    University of York
State versus Phikwane, Rand Supreme Court, 1988
Transcript of Proceedings, Commission of Enquiry, Sharpeville, Borthwick
    Institute, University of York
Vaal Teknorama Museum Archives, Sharpeville Files 03/5165
Vereeniging Municipality, Town Clerk's Office, Minutes of the Non-European
    Affairs Committee, Vereeniging and Sharpeville Advisory Board Minutes (these
    records are now under the administration of the Sedibeng District Council and
    are no longer accessible to researchers)

INTERVIEWS AND ORAL TESTIMONY

Paul Arthur, conversation with author, Magee Campus, University of Ulster,
    Derry, 13 May 2010
Hugh Bayley, MP, conversation with author, York, 15 October 2010
Brian Bunting, interviewed by the author, London, 1975
C. J. Fazzie, interviewed by Mark Swilling, East London, 1983
Jacob Nyaose, interviewed by Baruch Hirson, Geneva 1976, transcript in author's
    files
Peter Hjul, interviewed by Gwendoline Carter, Cape Town, 26 January 1964.
    Transcript at http://www.disa.ukza.ac.za
——, interviewed by author, London, 22 January 1976
Philip Kgosana, interviewed by Bob Hess, Addis Ababa, 15 August 1963, Gail
    Gerhart Papers, A2422/1
——, interviewed by the author, Pretoria, 2 November 2009
Potlake Leballo, interviewed by Gail Gerhart, Nairobi, 11 September 1968, DISA/
    Aluka Topics # 320 and 321

Elizabeth Mabona, Testimony at the Truth and Reconciliation Commission, Sebokeng, 5 August 1996, http://www.doj.gov.za/trc/hrvtrans/sebokeng/seb793.htm

Elliot Mafaxa and P. L. Gqobose, interviewed by Gail Gerhart, Maseru, 29 December 1969, Gail Gerhart Papers, A2422, University of the Witwatersrand Library, Historical Papers

Elliot Magwentshu, interviewed by Gail Gerhart, Nairobi, 18 June 1970, Gail Gerhart Papers

Lydia Mahabuke, interviewed by the author, Sharpeville, 7 November 2009

Nana Mahomo, interviewed by Gail Gerhart, New York, 2 July 1967, Gail Gerhart Papers

Ikabot Makiti, interviewed by the author, Sharpeville, 20 July 2010

Mary Mantsho, secretary, Khulumani Support Group Sharpeville, interviewed by author, Sharpeville, 20 July 2010

Aubrey Mokoape, interviewed by Benjamin Pogrund, Durban, 2 December 1984, Robert Sobukwe Papers

Joe Molefi, interviewed by Gail Gerhart, Maseru, December 1969, Gail Gerhart Papers

Lucy Mvubelo, interviewed by Gail Gerhart, New York, 5 November 1973, Gail Gerhart Papers

Abednego Ngcobo, interviewed by the author, London, 25 August 1975

Matthew Nkoana, interviewed by the author, London, 7 August 1975

Peter Raboroko, interviewed by the author, Johannesburg, 14 June 1993

David Ramohoase, Testimony at the Truth and Reconciliation Commission, Sebokeng, 5 August 1996, http://www.doj.gov.za/trc/hrvtrans/sebokeng/seb901.htm

Lebitsa Ramohoase, Testimony at the Truth and Reconciliation Commission, Sebokeng, 5 August 1996, http://www.doj.gov.za/trc/hrvtrans/sebokeng/seb901.htm

Petrus Cornelius Swanepoel, conversation with the author, Pretoria, 2 November 2009

Johannes Sefatsa, interviewed by the author, Sharpeville, 7 November 2009

David Sibeko, interviewed by the author, London, 3 September 1975

Neshtadi Sidzamba, interviewed by the author, Maseru, 11 June 1976

Robert Sobukwe, interviewed by Gail Gerhart, 1970, Gail Gerhart Papers, A2618

Michael Thekiso, interviewed by the author, Sharpeville, 6 November 2009

Samuel Tshabalala, interviewed by the author, 6 November 2009

Gideon Tsolo, interviewed by the author, Sharpeville, 5 November 2009

Randolph Vigne, interviewed by the author, London, 20 August 1975

——, interviewed by the author, Vishoek, 8 November 2009

OFFICIAL AND ORGANISATIONAL REPORTS

African National Congress, *Documentation of the Second Consultative Conference*, Lusaka, 1985

Republic of South Africa, *Report to the Goldstone Commission of Inquiry, regarding the prevention of public violence and intimidation from the Committee conducting a preliminary investigation into the activities of the Azanian People's Liberation Army*, Pretoria, 15 March 1993

Republic of South Africa, *Report of the Commission of Inquiry into the Riots at Soweto and Elsewhere from the 16th June 1976 to the 28th February 1977*, Volume 2, RP55/1980, Pretoria, 1980

Republic of South Africa, *Annual Report of the Commissioner of the SAP*, 1992, RP67/1993

Truth and Reconciliation Commission, *Report, Volume Three*, Cape Town: Juta and Co. Ltd., 1998

Union of South Africa, *Report of the Commission on the Langa Location Riots*, Ann. 126–61, 1961

Union of South Africa, *Report of the Commission, of Inquiry into Sharpeville, Evaton and Vanderbijlpark Location Riots*, Pretoria, Ann. 125–61, 1961

BOOKS AND SCHOLARLY ARTICLES

Adam, Heribert, *Modernizing Racial Domination: The Dynamics of South African Politics*, Berkeley: University of California Press, 1971

——, 'The failure of political liberalism in South Africa' in Robert Price and Carl G. Rosberg (eds.), *The Apartheid Regime*, Cape Town: David Philip, 1980

Alden, Chris, *Apartheid's Last Stand*, Basingstoke: Macmillan, 1996

Atkinson, Doreen, 'Brokering a Miracle? The multi-party negotiating forum in The Small Miracle: South Africa's Negotiated Settlement', *South African Review*, 7, Johannesburg: Ravan Press, 1994

Baldwin, Alan, 'Mass removals and separate development', *Journal of Southern African Studies*, 1, 1, 1974

Asmal, Louise, Asmal, Kader, and Thomas Alberts, 'The Irish Anti-Apartheid Movement', in South African Democracy Education Trust, *The Road to Democracy in South Africa, Volume 3, International Solidarity*, Pretoria: University of South Africa Press, 2008

Baines, Gary, 'Remembering Sharpeville', *History Today*, 60, 3, March 2010

Bar-Tal, Daniel, 'Collective memory of physical violence: its contribution to the culture of violence', in E. Cairns and M. D. Roe (eds.), *The Role of Memory in Ethnic Conflict*, Basingstoke: Palgrave Macmillan, 2003

Barber, James and John Barratt, *South Africa's Foreign Policy: The Search for Status and Security, 1945–1988*, Cambridge: Cambridge University Press, 1990

Barber, Noel, *The War of the Running Dogs*, Malaya and London: Fontana, 1972

Barcan, Alan, 'Student activists at Sydney University, 1960–1967: a problem of interpretation', *History of Education Review*, January 2007

Barrell, Howard, 'The outlawed South African liberation movements', in Shaun Johnson (ed.), *South Africa: No Turning Back*, Bloomington: Indiana University Press, 1989

——, *MK: The ANC's Armed Struggle*, Johannesburg: Penguin, 1990

Barry, Desmond, *Finally and In Conclusion: A Political Memoir*, Dublin: New Island Books, 2000

Bekker, Simon, 'The local government and community of Sebokeng', Occasional Paper no. 3, Department of Sociology, University of Stellenbosch, June 1978

Benson, Mary, *Nelson Mandela*, Harmondsworth: Penguin: Harmondsworth, 1986

Berner, Robert L., 'Apartheid and Leroux's welgevonden trilogy', *World Literature Today*, 53, 2, Spring 1979

Black, David, 'The effects and effectiveness of the sport boycott', in Neta Crawford and Audie Klotz (eds.), *How Sanctions Work: Lessons from the South African Experience*, New York: St Martin's Press, 1999

Blacking, John, 'The power of ideas in social change: the growth of the Africanist idea in South Africa', in David Riches (ed.), *The Queen's University Papers in Social Anthropology*, Volume III, Belfast: Queen's University, 1979

Blumberg, Myrna, *White Madam*, London: Victor Gollancz, 1962, p. 28

Bolnick, Joel, 'Potlake Leballo—the man who hurried to meet his destiny', *Journal of Modern African Studies*, 29, 3, 1991

Bonner, Philip and Noor Nieftagodien, *Alexandra: A History*, Johannesburg: Witwatersrand University Press, 2008

Bonnett, Alistair, *Radicalism, Anti Racism and Representation*, London: Routledge, 1993

Botha, Jan, *Verwoerd is Dead*, Cape Town: Books of Africa, 1967, p. 121

Bozzoli, Belinda, 'Class, community and ideology in the evolution of South African society', in Belinda Bozzoli (ed.), *Class, Community and Conflict: South African Perspectives*, Johannesburg: Ravan Press, 1987

Braam, Connie, *Operation Vula*, Bellevue: Jacana, 2004

Brett, E. A., *African Attitudes: A Study of the Social, Racial, and Political Attitudes of some Middle Class Africans*, Fact Paper No. 14, Johannesburg: South African Institute of Race Relations, 1963

Brooks, Alan and Paul Brickhill, *Whirlwind before the Storm*, London: International Defence and Aid Fund, 1980

Bromberger, Norman, 'Economic growth and political change in South Africa', in Adrian Leftwich (ed.), *South Africa: Economic Growth and Political Change*, London: Allison and Busby, 1974

Bunting, Brian, *The Rise of the South African Reich*, Harmondsworth: Penguin, 1964

Buntman, Fran, *Robben Island and Prisoner Resistance to Apartheid*, Cambridge, Cambridge University Press, 2003

Callinicos, Luli, *Oliver Tambo: Beyond the Engeni Mountains*, Cape Town: David Philip, 2004

Canetti, Elias, *Crowds and Power*, Harmondsworth: Penguin, 1981

Carter, Gwendoline and Thomas Karis, *From Protest to Challenge*, Volume Two, Stanford: Hoover Institution Press, 1973

Chaskalson, Matthew, 'The road to Sharpeville', in Stephen Clingman (ed.), *Regions and Repertoires: Topics in South African Politics and Culture*, Johannesburg: Ravan Press, 1991

Chidester, David, *Shots in the Streets: Violence and Religion in South Africa*, Boston: Beacon Press, 1991

Chirwa, Wiseman, 'Collective memory and the process of reconciliation and reconstruction', *Development in Practice*, 7, 4, 1997

Clark, Jennifer, 'The wind of change in Australia: Aborigines and the international politics of race', *The International History Review*, 20, 1, 1998

Clingman, Stephen, *The Novels of Nadine Gordimer: History from the Inside*, Johanesburg: Ravan Press, 1986

Coetzer, J. P. J., *Gister se Dade Vandag se Oordeel*, Pretoria: JP Van der Walt, 2000

Communist Party of South Africa, *Vereeniging: Who is to blame?*, Johannesburg: Communist Party of South Africa, 1937

Crais, Clifford, *The Politics of Evil: Magic, State Power and the Political Imagination in South Africa*, Cambridge: Cambridge University Press, 2002

Crawford, Neta, 'How embargoes work', in Neta Crawford and Audie Klotzn (eds.), *How Sanctions Work: Lessons from the South African Experience*, New York: St Martin's Press, 1999

Cronin, Michael, 'Ireland, globalisation and the war against time', in Peadar Kirby, Luke Gibbons, and Michael Cronin (eds.), *Reinventing Ireland: Culture, Society and the Global Economy*, London: Pluto Press, 2002

Culverson, Donald, 'The politics of the anti-apartheid movement', *Political Science Quarterly*, 111, 1, 1996

Davis, Stephen, *Apartheid's Rebels: Inside South Africa's Hidden War*, New Haven: Yale University Press, 1987

De Klerk, F. W., *The Last Trek—A New Beginning*, Basingstoke: Macmillan, 1998

Dhlamini, Moses, *Robben Island Hell-Hole*, Trenton NJ: Africa World Books, 1986

Diar, Prakash, *The Sharpeville Six*, Toronto: McClelland and Stewart Inc, 1990

Diseko, Nozipho 'The origins and development of the South African students' movement, 1968–1976', *Journal of Southern African Studies*, 18, 1, March 1992

Domisse, Ebbe and Willie Esterhuyse, *Anton Rupert*, Cape Town: Tafelberg, 2009

Driver, C. J., *Patrick Duncan: South African and Pan-African*, London: Heinemann, 1980

Du Preez, Max, *Of Tricksters, Tyrants and Turncoats: More Unusual Stories from South Africa's Past*, Cape Town: Zebra Books, 2007

Duncan, Patrick, *South Africa's Rule of Violence*, London: Metheun, 1963

Edgar, Robert, *Because they Chose the Plan of God: The Story of the Bulhoek Massacre*, Johannesburg: Ravan Press, 1988

—— and Luyanda ka Msumza, *Freedom in Our Lifetime: The Collected Writings of Anton Muziwakhe Lembede*, Athens: Ohio University Press, 1996

Ellis, Stephen and Tshepo Sechaba, *Comrades Against Apartheid: The ANC and the South African Communist Party in Exile*, London: James Currey, 1992

Feinstein, Charles H., *An Economic History of South Africa: Conquest, Discrimination and Development*, Cambridge: Cambridge University Press, 2005

Feit, Edward, *Urban Revolt in South Africa*, Evanston: Northwestern University Press, 1971, p. 75

Fieldhouse, Roger, *Anti-Apartheid: A History of the Movement in Britain*, London: Merlin Press, 2005

Filatova, Irina, 'South Africa's Soviet connection', *History Compass*, 6, 2, 2008

Foster, Roy, *Luck and the Irish: A Brief History of Change, 1970–2000*, London: Penguin, 2007

Fourie, Bernardus, 'The ambassador's stand', *Africa Today* (Bloomington), 7, 3, May 1960

Frankel, Philip, 'The politics of police control', *Comparative Politics*, 12, 4, July 1980

——, *Pretoria's Praetorians: Civil–Military Relations in South Africa*, Cambridge: Cambridge University Press, 1984

——, *An Ordinary Atrocity: Sharpeville and its Massacre*, New Haven: Yale University Press, 2001

Geldenhuys, Deon, *The Diplomacy of Isolation: South African Foreign Policy Making*, Johannesburg: Macmillan, 1984

Gerhart, Gail, *Black Power in South Africa: The Evolution of an Ideology*, Berkeley: University of California Press, 1978

Giliomee, Hermann, 'The leader and the citizenry', in Robert Schrire (ed.), *Leadership in the Apartheid State*, Cape Town: Oxford University Press, 1994

——, *The Afrikaners: Biography of a People*, London: Hurst, 2003

Glaser, Clive, *Bo Tsotsi: The Youth Gangs of Soweto, 1935–1976*, Oxford: James Currey, 2000

Gordimer, Nadine, *The Conservationist*, London: Jonathan Cape, 1974

Gordon, Daniel, 'World reactions to the 1961 Paris pogrom', *University of Sussex Journal of Contemporary History*, 1, 2000

Greenberg, Stanley, *Race and State in Capitalist Development: South Africa in Comparative Perspective*, Johannesburg: Ravan Press, 1980

Guelke, Adrian, *Rethinking the Rise and the fall of Apartheid*, Basingstoke: Palgrave Macmillan, 2005

Gurney, Christable, 'In the heart of the beast: the British Anti-Apartheid Movement, 1959–1994', in South African Democracy Trust, *The Road to Democracy in South Africa, Volume 3, International Solidarity*, Pretoria: University of South Africa Press, 2008

Halisi, C. R., *Black Political Thought in the Making of South African Democracy*, Bloomington: Indiana University Press, 1999

Halpern, Jack, *South Africa's Hostages: Basutoland, Bechuanaland and Swaziland*, Harmondsworth: Penguin African Library, 1965

Hamber, Brandon and Richard Wilson, 'Symbolic closure through memory, reparation and revenge in post-conflict societies', *Journal of Human Rights*, 1, 1, 2002

Heard, Kenneth, *General Elections in South Africa, 1943–1970*, London: Oxford University Press, 1974

Heard, Tony, *The Cape of Storms: A Personal History of the Crisis in South Africa*, Johannesburg: Ravan Press, 1990

Herbst, Jeffery, 'Prospects for revolution in South Africa', *Political Science Quarterly*, 103, 4, Winter 1988

Herbstein, Denis, *White Lies: Canon Collins and the Secret War Against Apartheid*, Oxford: James Currey, 2004

Heunis, Jan, *The Inner Circle: Reflections on the Last Days of White Rule*, Jeppestown: Jonathan Ball, 2007

Hindson, Doug, *Pass Controls and the African Proletariat*, Johannesburg: Ravan Press, 1987

Hirson, Baruch, *Yours for the Union: Class and Community Struggle in South Africa, 1930–1947*, Johannesburg: Witwatersrand University Press, 1989

——, *Revolutions in My Life*, Johannesburg: Witwatersrand University Press, 1995

Hobart Houghton, D., 'Economic development, 1865–1965', in Monica Wilson and Leonard Thompson (eds.), *The Oxford History of South Africa*, Volume Two, Oxford: Oxford University Press, 1975

Hopkinson, Tom, *In the Fiery Continent*, London: Victor Gollancz, 1962

Horowitz, Helen Lefkowitz, 'The 1960s and the transformation of campus cultures', *History of Education Quarterly*, 26, 1, 1986

Houser, George, 'Africa's challenge: the story of the American Committee on Africa', *Issue: A Journal of Opinion*, 6, 2/3, 1976

Humphrey, Michael, 'From terror to trauma: commissioning truth for national reconciliation', *Social Identities*, 6, 1, 2000

Hussey, Gemma, *Ireland Today: Anatomy of a Changing State*, Harmondsworth: Penguin, 1995

Hyam, Ronald and Peter Henshaw, *The Lion and the Springbok: Britain and South Africa since the Boer War*, Cambridge: Cambridge University Press, 2003

Innes, Duncan, *Anglo: Anglo American and the Rise of Modern South Africa*, Johannesburg: Ravan, 1984

Institute of Industrial Education, *The Durban Strikes*, Johannesburg: Ravan Press, 1974

Israel, Mark, *South African Political Exile in the United Kingdom*, Basingstoke: Macmillan, 1999

Johnson, R. W., *How Long Will South African Survive?*, Johannesburg: Macmillan, 1977

Jones, Bob (ed.), *South African Election '99 Update 1–15*, Johannesburg: Electoral Institute of South Africa, 1999

Kane-Berman, John, *Soweto: Black Revolt, White Reaction*, Johannesburg: Ravan Press, 1978

Ka Plaatjie, Thami, 'The PAC's internal undergound activities', in South African Democracy Education Trust, *The Road to Democracy in South Africa, Volume 2 (1970–1980)*, Pretoria: University of South Africa, 2006

Kaplan, David, *The Crossed Line: The South African Telecommunications Industry in Transition*, Johannesburg: Witwatersrand University Press, 1990

Karis, Thomas and Gail Gerhart (eds.), *From Protest to Challenge: A Documentary History of African Politics in South Africa, Volume 3, Challenge and Violence, 1953–1954*, Stanford: Hoover Institution Press, 1977

——, Thomas and Gail Gerhart, *From Protest to Challenge, Volume 5: Nadir and Resurgence, 1964–1979*, Bloomington: Indiana University Press, 1997

Kgosana, Philip Ata, *Lest we Forget*, Braamfontein: Skotaville Press, 1988

Khoapa, B. A. (ed.), *Black Review 1972*, Durban: Black Community Programmes, 1973

Kirby, Peadar, 'Contested pedigrees of the celtic tiger', in Peadar Kirby, Luke Gibbons, and Michael Cronin (eds.), *Reinventing Ireland: Culture, Society and the Global Economy*, London: Pluto Press, 2002

Kitson, Norma, *Where Sixpence Lives*, London: The Hogarth Press, 1987

Kondlo, Kwandire, *In the Twilight of the Revolution: The Pan-Africanist Congress of Azania (South Africa), 1959–1994*, Basel: Basler Afrika Bibliographien, 2009

Leeman, Bernard, *Lesotho and the Struggle for Azania: Africanist Political Movements in Lesotho and Azania: The Origins and History of the BCP and the PAC*, 3 volumes, London: University of Azania Press, 1985

Legassick, Martin and Harold Wolpe, 'The Bantustans and capital accumulation in South Africa', *Review of African Political Economy*, 7, 1976

——, *Armed Struggle and Democracy—The Case of South Africa*, Uppsala: Nordiska Afikainstutet, 2002

Lelyveld, Joseph, *Move Your Shadow*, London: Abacus, 1987

Leroux, Etienne, *To A Dubious Salvation*, Harmondsworth: Penguin, 1969

Lerumo, A., *Fifty Fighting Years: The South African Communist Party, 1921–1971*, London: Inkululeko Publications, 1987

Lewin, Julius, *Politics and Law in South Africa*, London: Merlin Press, 1961

Lewis, Stephen, *The Economics of Apartheid*, New York: Council for Foreign Relations, 1989

Lichtenstein, Alex, 'Making Apartheid work: African trade unions and the 1953 Native Labour (Settlement of Disputes) Act in South Africa', *Journal of African History*, 46, 2005

Limb, Peter, 'The Anti-Apartheid movements in Australia and Aotearoa/New Zealand', in South African Democracy Education Trust, *The Road to Democracy in South Africa, Volume 3, International Solidarity*, Pretoria: University of South Africa Press, 2008

Lira, Elizabeth, 'Violence, fear and impunity: reflections on subjective and political obstacles for peace', *Peace and Conflict: Journal of Peace Psychology*, 7, 2, 2001

Lissoni, Arianna, 'The PAC in Basutoland, *c.*1962–1965', *South African Historical Journal*, 62, 1, March 2010

Lodge, Tom, *Black Politics in South Africa since 1945*, London: Longman, 1983

——, 'Political mobilisation in the 1950s: an East London case study', in Herbert Luckhardt, Ken and Brenda Wall (eds.), *Organize or Starve... The History of the South African Congress of Trade Unions*, London: Lawrence and Wishart, 1980

Marcuse, Herbert, *An Essay on Liberation*, London: Allen Lane, 1969

Marks, Shula and Stanley Trapido (eds.) (1987), *The Politics of Race, Class and Nationalism in Twentieth Century South Africa*, London: Longman

Maaba, Brown Bavusile, 'The PAC's war against the state', in South African Democracy Education Trust, *Road to Democracy in South Africa, Volume 1*, Cape Town: Zebra Press, 2004

MacCracken, Donal P., 'Collaborators or liberators? Irish race attitudes in the South African historical context', in Gudmundor Halfdanarson (ed.), *Racial Discrimination and Ethnicity in European History*, Pisa: Edizioni Plus, 2003

Madlingoza, Tshepo, 'On transitional justice: entrepreneurs and the production of victims', *Journal of Human Rights Practice*, 2, 2, 2010

Magubane, Bernard, *The Political Economy of Race and Class in South Africa*, New York: Monthly Review Press, 1979

——, Philip Bonner, et al., 'The turn to armed struggle' in South African Democracy Education Trust, *The Road to Democracy in South Africa, Volume 1 (1960–1970)*, Cape Town: Zebra Press, 2004

Mandela, Nelson, *Long Walk to Freedom*, Randburg: MacDonald Purnell, 1994

Marx, Anthony, *Lessons of Struggle: South African Internal Opposition, 1960–1990*, New York: Oxford University Press, 1992

——, *Making Race and Nation*, New York and Cambridge: Cambridge University Press, 1998

Massie, Robert Kinlock, *Loosing the Bonds: The United States and South Africa in the Apartheid Years*, New York: Nan A Talese, Doubleday, 1997

Matshoba, Mtutuzeli, 'Nothing but the truth: the ordeal of Duma Khumalo', in Deborah Posel and Graeme Simpson (eds.), *Commissioning the Past: Understanding South Africa's Truth and Reconciliation Commission*, Johannesburg: Witwatersrand University Press, 2002

McAdam, Doug, 'The US Civil Rights Movement: power from below and above, 1945–70', in Adam Roberts and Timothy Garton Ash (eds.), *Civil Resistance and Power Politics*, Oxford: Oxford University Press, 2009, p. 61

McCarthy, Ronald and Christopher Kruegler, *Towards Research and Theory Building in the Study of Non-Violent Action*, Cambridge, MA: Albert Einstein Institution, 1993

Meer, Fatima, 1971, 'African nationalism—some inhibiting factors', in Heribert Adam (ed.), *South Africa: Sociological Perspectives*, Oxford: Oxford University Press, 1971

Meiring, Piet, *Chronicle of the Truth Commission*, Vanderbijlpark: Carpe Diem Books, 1999

Merridale, Catherine, *Night of Stone: Death and Memory in Russia*, London: Granta, 2001

Metz, Steven, 'The Anti-Apartheid Movement and the populist instinct in American politics', *Political Science Quarterly*, 101, 3, 1986

Mgxashe, Mxolise Bra Ace, *Are you with us? The Story of a PAC Activist*, Cape Town: Tafelberg, 2006

Minter, William and Sylvia Hill, 'Anti-Apartheid solidarity in the United States', in South African Democracy Trust, *The Road to Democracy in South Africa, Volume 3, International Solidarity*, Pretoria, University of South Africa Press, 2008

Moll, Terence, 'Did the Apartheid economy fail?', *Journal of Southern African Studies*, 17, 2, June 1991

Mondlane, Eduardo, *The Struggle for Mozambique*, Harmondsworth: Penguin African Library, 1969

Mphahlele, Letlapa, *Child of the Soil: My Life as a Freedom Fighter*, Cape Town: Kwela Books, 2002

Mtolo, Bruno, *Umkhonto we Sizwe: The Road to the Left*, Durban: Drakensberg Press, 1966

Musson, Doreen, *Johnny Gomas: Voice of the Working Class*, Cape Town: Buchu Books, 1989

Muthien, Yvonne, *State and Resistance in South Africa, 1939–1945*, Aldershot: Avebury, 1994

Naidu, Ereshnee, *Empowerment through Living Memory: A Community-centred Model for Memorialisation*, Research Report, Johannesburg: Centre for the Study of Violence and Reconciliation, 2004

Newbury, Darren, *Defiant Images, Photography and Apartheid South Africa*, Pretoria: Unisa Press, 2009

Newnham, Tom, *Apartheid is not a Game*, Auckland: Graphic Publications, 1970

Ngubane, Jordan, *An African Explains Apartheid*, New York: Praeger, 1962

Non-European Unity Movement, *The Pan-Africanist Congress Venture in Retrospect*, Cape Town: Non-European Unity Movement, 1960

Noonan, Patrick, *They're Burning the Churches*, Bellevue: Jacana Books, 2003

Northern Ireland Civil Rights Association, *'We shall overcome': The History of the Struggle for Civil Rights in Northern Ireland, 1968–1978*, Belfast: Northern Irish Civil Rights Association, 1978

Ntloedibe, Elias, *Here is a Tree: Political Biography of Robert Mangaliso Sobukwe*, Mogoditshane, Botswana: Century-Turn Publishers, 1995

Nytagodien, Ridwan and Arthur Neal, 'Collective trauma, apologies and the politics of memory', *Journal of Human Rights*, 3, 4, 2004

O'Dowd, Michael, 'South Africa in the light of stages of economic growth' in Adrian Leftwich (ed.), *South Africa: Economic Growth and Political Change*, London: Allison and Busby, 1974

O'Meara, Dan, *Forty Wasted Years: The Apartheid State and the Politics of the National Party*, Johannesburg: Ravan Press, 1996

Parker, Peter and Joyce Mokhesi-Parker, *In the Shadow of Sharpeville: Apartheid and Criminal Justice*, New York: New York University Press, 1998

Parkin, Frank, *Middle Class Radicalism: The Social Bases for the British Campaign for Nuclear Disarmament*, Manchester: Manchester University Press, 1968

——, 'Adolescent status and student disaffection', *Journal of Contemporary History*, 5, 1, 1970

Parsons, Neil, 'The pipeline: Botswana's reception of refugees, 1956–68', *Social Dynamics*, 43, 1, 2008

Pike, Henry R., *A History of Communism in South Africa*, Germiston: Christian Mission International in South Africa, 1988

Pogrund, Benjamin, *How Can Man Die Better? Sobukwe and Apartheid*, London: Peter Halban, 1990

——, *War of Words: Memoirs of a South African Journalist*, New York: Seven Stories Press, 2000

Posel, Deborah, *The Making of Apartheid, 1948–1961*, Oxford: Oxford University Press, 1997

——, 'Whiteness and power in the South African civil service: paradoxes of the Apartheid state', *Journal of Southern African Studies*, 25, 1, 1999

——, 'The assassination of Hendrik Verwoerd: the spectre of apartheid's corpse', *African Studies*, 68, 3, December 2009

Price, Robert, 'Race and reconciliation in the new South Africa', *Politics and Society*, 25, 2, 1997

Rantete, Johannes, *The Third Day of September*, Johannesburg: Ravan Storyteller Series, 1984

——, *The African National Congress and the Negotiated Settlement in South Africa*, Pretoria: J L Van Schaik Publishers, 1998

Reeves, Ambrose, *Shooting at Sharpeville*, New York: Houghton Mifflin, 1961

Rich, Paul, *White Power and the Liberal Conscience: Racial Segregation and South African Liberalism, 1921–1960*, Manchester: Manchester University Press, 1984

Ridgway, Dawn, Milly Jafta, Nicky Kautja, Magda Oliphant, and Kapoli Shipingana, *An Investigation into the Shooting at the Old Location on 10 December 1959*, Windhoek: University of Namibia, 1991

Robertson, Janet, *Liberalism in South Africa*, Oxford: Oxford University Press, 1971

Ross, Robert, *A Concise History of South Africa*, Cambridge: Cambridge University Press, 1999

Roux, Edward, *Time Longer than Rope*, London: Victor Gollancz, 1948

Rule, James B., *Theories of Civil Violence*, Berkeley: University of California Press, 1988

Sachs, Albie, *Justice in South Africa*, Berkeley: University of California Press, 1973

Sampson, Anthony, *Macmillan: A Study in Ambiguity*, Harmondsworth: Penguin, 1967

Sapire, Hilary, 'Liberation movements, exile, and international solidarity: an introduction', *Journal of Southern African Studies*, 35, 2, 2009

Saunders, Christopher, 'From Ndabeni to Langa', in Christopher Saunders (ed.), *Studies in the History of Cape Town, Volume 1*, Cape Town: History Department, University of Cape Town, 1979

Schleicher, Hans-Georg 'GDR solidarity: the German Democratic Republic and the South African liberation struggle', in South African Democracy Education Trust, *The Road to Democracy in South Africa, Volume 3, International Solidarity*, Pretoria: University of South Africa Press, 2008

Schock, Kurt, *Unarmed Insurrections: People Power Movements in Non-Democracies*, Minneapolis: University of Minnesota Press, 2005

Schwarz, Bill, 'Empire: for and against', *Twentieth Century British History*, 6, 3, 1995

Seekings, Jeremy, 'Political mobilisation in the black townships of the Transvaal', in Philip Frankel, Noam Pines, and Mark Swilling (eds.), *State, Resistance and Change in South Africa*, London: Croom Helm, 1988

——, *Heroes or Villains? Youth Politics in the 1980s*, Johannesburg: Ravan, 1993

——, *The UDF: A History of the United Democratic Front*, Cape Town: David Philip, 2000

Sellstrom, Tor, 'Sweden and the nordic countries: official solidarity and assistance from the west', in South African Democracy Trust, *The Road to Democracy in South Africa, Volume 3, International Solidarity*, Pretoria: University of South Africa Press, 2008

Sheer, Vivienne, 'Etienne Leroux's Sewe Dae by die Silbersteins: a re-examination in light of its historical context', *Journal of Southern African Studies*, 8, 2, April 1982, pp. 172–86

Shubin, Vladimir, *The ANC: The View from Moscow*, Belville: Mayibuye Books, 1999

Skinner, Robert, 'The moral foundations of British anti-apartheid activism, 1946–1960', *Journal of Southern African Studies*, 35, 2, June 2009

Sisilana, Lwandile, 'Review of *An Ordinary Atrocity*', *We Write*, Johannesburg, October 2004

Slovo, Joe, 'South Africa—no middle road', in Basil Davidson, Joe Slovo, and Anthony R. Wilkinson (eds.), *Southern Africa: The New Politics of Revolution*, Harmondsworth: Penguin, 1976

Smith, Howard, 'Apartheid, Sharpeville and impartiality: the reporting of South Africa on BBC television, 1948–1961', *Historical Journal of Film, Radio and Television*, 13, 3, 1993

Robert Sobukwe, 'A Collection of Xhosa Riddles', *African Studies*, 30, 1, 1971

Sono, Themba, *Reflections on the Origins of Black Consciousness in South Africa*, Pretoria: Human Sciences Research Council, 1993

Soule, Sarah, 'The student divestment movement in the United States and tactical diffusion: the shanty town protest', *Social Forces*, 75, 1997

Southall, Roger, *South Africa's Transkei: The Political Economy of an Independent Bantustan*, London: Heinemann, 1982

Sowden, Lewis, *The Land of Afternoon: The Story of White South Africans*, London: Elek Books Limited, 1968

Srinivasan, Krishnan, *The Rise, Decline and Future of the British Commonwealth*, Basingstoke: Palgrave Macmillan, 2005

Stanbridge, Roland, 'Contemporary African political organizations and movements', in Robert Price and Carl G. Rosberg (eds.), *The Apartheid Regime*, Cape Town: David Philip, 1980

Stanton, Hannah, *Go Well, Stay Well*, London: Hodder and Stoughton, 1961, p. 178

Stedman Jones, Gareth, 'The meaning of student revolt' in Alexander Cockburn and Robin Blackburn (eds.), *Student Power: Problems, Diagnosis, Action*, Harmondsworth: Penguin, 1969

Strangwayes-Booth, Joanna, *A Cricket in the Thorn Tree: Helen Suzman and the Progressive Party*, Johannesburg: Hutchinson, 1976

Suttner, Raymond and Jeremy Cronin (eds.), *30 Years of the Freedom Charter*, Johannesburg: Ravan Press, 1986

Suzman, Helen, *Memoirs: In No Uncertain Terms*, Johannesburg: Jonathan Ball, 1993

Teeger, Chana and Vered Vinitzky-Seroussi, 'Controlling for consensus: commemorating Apartheid in South Africa', *Symbolic Interaction*, 30, 1, 2007

Terblanche, Sampie, *History of Inequality in South Africa*, Pietermaritzberg: University of Natal Press, 2002

Thörn, Hakan, *Anti-Apartheid and the Emergence of a Global Civil Society*, Basingstoke: Palgrave Macmillan, 2009

Tom, Petrus, *My Life Struggle*, Johannesburg: Ravan Worker Series, 1985

Turok, Ben, *Nothing but the Truth: Behind the ANC's Struggle Politics*, Johannesburg: Jonathan Ball, 2003

Tyler, Humphrey, *Life in the Time of Sharpeville*, Cape Town: Kwela Books, 1995

Van der Bliek, Jasper (ed.), *Sharpeville Scars*, Tilburg: Tilburg-Lekoa Vaal Association, 2000

Van Kessel, Ineke, *'Beyond Our Wildest Dreams': The United Democratic Front and the Transformation of South Africa*, Charlottesville: University of Virginia Press, 2000

Van Onselen, Charles, *Masked Raiders: Irish Banditry in Southern Africa, 1880–1899*, Cape Town: Zebra Press, 2010

Van Zyl Slabbert, Frederick, *The Other Side of History*, Johannesburg: Jonathan Ball, 2006

Vigne, Randolph, *Liberals Against Apartheid: A History of the Liberal Party of South Africa, 1953–68*, London: Macmillan, 1997

Villa-Vicencio, Charles, 'Restorative justice: dealing with the past differently', in Charles Villa-Vicencio and Wilhelm Verwoerd (eds.), *Looking Back, Reaching Forward: Reflections on the Truth and Reconciliation Commission of South Africa*, Cape Town: University of Cape Town Press, 2000

Voorhest, Meg, 'The US divestment movement', in Neta Crawford and Audie Klotz (eds.), *How Sanctions Work: Lessons from the South African Experience*, New York: St Martin's Press, 1999

Welsh, David, 'The executive and the African population', in Robert Schrire (ed.), *Leadership and the Apartheid State*, Cape Town: Oxford University Press, 1994, p. 158

——, *The Rise and Fall of Apartheid*, Johannesburg: Jonathan Ball, 2009

Wilson, Monica and Archie Mafeje, *Langa*, Cape Town: Oxford University Press, 1963

Wilson, Richard, *The Politics of Truth and Reconciliation in South Africa*, Cambridge: Cambridge University Press, 2001

Wolpe, Harold, 'Capitalism and cheap labour power in South Africa: from segregation to Apartheid', *Economy and Society*, 1, 1972

JOURNALISM

Allen, Karen, 'South Africa's Sharpeville recalls 1960 massacre', *BBC News*, 21 March 2010, website: http://news.bbc.co.uk/2/hi/africa/8577518.stm

An eyewitness, 'The 30,000', *Contact* (Cape Town), 16 April 1960

Anon., 'Police in house to house raid, Vereeniging', *Inkululeko* (Johannesburg), 6 June 1941

Anon., 'Late news: Vereeniging charges withdrawn', *Inkululeko*, 7 August 1941

Anon., 'Africanist flop', *Contact*, 21 March 1959

Anon., 'PAC warns city stores', *The World* (Johannesburg), 6 February 1960

Anon., 'Absent workers a blow to business', *Cape Times*, 23 March 1960

Anon., 'Rush to buy pistols', *Cape Times*, 23 March 1960

Anon., 'Pan-Africanist treasurer fined', *Cape Times*, 23 March 1960

Anon., 'Menzies says no to Boycott', *Cape Times*, 24 March 1960

Anon., 'Big demand for guns', *Cape Times*, 25 March 1960

Anon., 'Bayonets glint around location', *Cape Times*, 1 April 1960

Anon., 'Officials amazed by negative Nyanga attitude', *Cape Times*, 5 April 1960

Anon, 'The nineteen days', *Africa South* (Cape Town), July 1960

Anon., 'Sobukwe was Poqo leader', *Cape Times*, 4 March 1963

Anon., 'Phenomenal development of Sharpeville', *Vereeniging and Vanderbijlpark News*, 21 March 1967

Anon., 'Border terror battle', *Sunday Tribune* (Durban), 6 August 1978

Anon., 'Woman planned to set fire to house', *The Star*, 8 August 1978

Anon., 'Movement aimed at abstinence', *The Star*, 20 October 1978

Anon., 'The man who stopped bloodbath is 80', *Cape Times*, 3 February 1980

Anon., 'SA in plot to murder Sibeko', *Sowetan*, 2 March 1982

Anon., 'Libyans trained me—terrorist', *The Star*, 12 August 1982

Anon., 'Civics on the frontline', *SASPU National* (Johannesburg), 5, 7, December 1984

Anon., letter to the editor complaining about the Sharpeville Civic Association, *Speak*, 3, 1 March 1985

Anon., 'Vaal residents stand firm', *Speak*, 3, 1 March 1985,

Anon., 'Lesotho makes it hot for exiles', *New African* (London), July 1985

Anon., 'Defiant Vaal boycott enters third year', *Work in Progress* (Braamfontein), September 1986

Anon., 'Commando Tshepo was a born leader', *Azanian Commando*, Supplement 2, 1987

Anon., 'Sharpeville's Second Rebellion', *SASPU National*, 4, 1987

Anon., 'Massive PAC arms programme succeeds', *Azania Commando*, 4, 1987

Anon., 'Police capture PAC suspect in Western Transvaal', *The Star*, 28 July 1988

Anon., 'Apla's capability underestimated', *The Star*, 4 December 1992

Anon., 'To the great Themba Ncapayi', *Azania Combat*, 15, 1992

Anon., 'Call to beg for Apla', *The Star*, 1 February 1993

Anon, 'Race war threat', *New Nation* (Johannesburg), 26 March 1993

Anon., '10% of blacks back Apla', *The Star*, 1 July 1993

Anon., 'Slaying attempt to derail talks', *The Star*, 21 July 1993

Anon., 'The two oranges that shook apartheid', *An Phoblacht* (Dublin), 22 July 2004

Anon., 'ANC, PAC supporters clash on Sharpeville Day', *Vaalster* (Vereeniging), 27 March 1995

Anon., 'Commission hears of slaughter after Hani's assassination', *The Star*, 9 August 1996

Anon., 'Pass law shootings victims' legacy lives on', *The Sowetan*, 2 March 2010

Anon., 'ANC wants to erase memories of Sobukwe', *Sowetan*, 2 March 2010

Barkhuizen, Dawn, 'Bungle, bungle, bungle', *Sunday Times*, 6 December 1992

Barron, Chris, 'Attackers were highly trained', *Sunday Star*, 27 December 1992

Booyse, Wim, 'The re-emergence of the PAC', *Freedom Bulletin* (Johannesburg), July 1987

Bulbring, Edith, 'Holomisa tells SA to go to hell', *Sunday Times*, 3 January 1993

Chandler, Norman, 'Apla to be integrated into army', *Star*, 14 July 1994

Charney, Craig, 'Sharpeville—20 years later...', *The Star*, 21 March 1980

Cruywagen, Denis, 'Apla steps out of big brother Mk's shadow', *Star*, 8 December 1992

Day, Frank, 'Five years later it's still a model township', *Rand Daily Mail*, 19 March 1965

Desai, Barney, 'To negotiate now is to capitulate now', *Sunday Star*, 13 May 1990

Dibetle, Monako, 'Sharpeville is still bleeding', *Mail and Guardian*, 19 March 2010

Dimpho, Muriel, '200 security forces now killed as PAC guerrillas hit hard', *Azania Combat*, no. 15

Duncan, Patrick, 'The two thousand', *Contact*, 16 April 1960, p. 3

——, 'The power of non-violence', *Contact*, 16 April 1960

Dundon, Mary, 'Drops in the ocean that turned tide', *Irish Examiner*, 19 July 2004

Ebrahim, Gora, 'John Pokela's obituary', *Zimbabwe Herald*, 13 July 1985

Getz, Arlene, 'Ignatius Terblanche: the man who stopped a bloodbath', *Sunday Star* (Johannesburg), 12 July 1987

Harmel, Michael, 'Revolutions are not abnormal', *Africa South* (Cape Town), 2, 2, January 1959

Heard, Anthony, 'Assurance that averted a riot—unpublished facts now on record', *Cape Times*, 11 July 1987

Kgosana, Philip, 'The story of my exciting life', *Drum*, February 1961

——, '30,000 obeyed me as one man', *Drum*, March 1961

Khumalo, Bhule, 'Memories throb like open wounds', *The Star*, 20 March 2001

Kotze, Craig, 'Alex Scorpion gang hits Soweto', *The Star*, 20 February 1987

——, 'Scorpion "terror" gang is linked with PAC', *The Star*, 28 February 1987

Kurube, Peter, 'Sounds to heal Sharpeville's wounds', *Mail and Guardian* (Johannesburg), 19 March 1999

Lawrence, Howard, 'Poqo—we go it alone', *Fighting Talk* (Johannesburg), 17, 2, February 1963

Mabuza, Kingdom, 'Sharpeville people were betrayed', *The Sowetan*, 23 March 2009

Mafata, Mongedi, 'The struggle was his life', *The Sowetan*, 4 December 2002

Maker, Jocelyn and Nick Olivari, 'Cold blooded killers plot ambush', *Sunday Times*, 2 March 1993

McCann, Eamonn, 'Dunnes stores in black and white', *Magill Magazine* (Dublin), 4 April 1985

Mashinini, Alex, 'People's war and negotiations: are they fire and water?', *Sechaba* (London), August 1988

Mazambane, Willie, 'APLA operations increase as record 65 cops are hit in single PAC guerrilla attack', *Azania Combat* (Dar es Salaam), 4, 1987

——, 'The gallant TM Ntantala', *Azania Combat* (Dar es Salaam), 13, 1991

——, 'PAC defends APLA's attacks on police', *Azanian Commando* (Dar es Salaam), 1992

——, 'Pretoria now admits APLA operatives in SA outnumber those of MK', *Azania Combat*, 16, 1993

Molefe, Tokiso, 'Sharpeville—the struggle goes on', *City Press*, 21 March 2010

Molete, Z.B., Letter to the Editor, *Contact*, 31 October 1959

——, 'The day Stanley Nksoi broke all the PAC rules', *The Star* (Johannesburg), 21 March 2001

Mostert, Sybrand, 'They've righted the wrong, says the new brigadier', *Sunday Times* (Johannesburg), 12 July 1987

Mothibeli, Tefo 'The day that changed our history', *The Star*, 19 March 1999

Mulqueen, Charlie, 'The first and last Springbok', *Limerick Leader*, 17 January 1970

Nair, Nivashni, 'Man remembers Sharpeville ahead of anniversary', *Times* (Johannesburg), 18 May 2010

Ngoma, Lovemore, 'PAC man gets 18 years in $40m mandrax case', *The Herald* (Harare), 25 October 1992

Ngudle, Mzimane, 'TRC not a toothless dog', *The Citizen*, 9 August 1996

Nyatsumba, Kaizer, 'Talks inevitable, says surprise PAC document', *The Star*, 11 June 1990

——, 'Life of every South African is precious', *The Star*, 3 July 1993

——, 'Phama: parallels with Hani', *The Star*, 11 February 1994

——, 'Apla's Phama dies in car crash', *The Star*, 10 February 1994

O'Grady, Kevin, 'Sharpeville victims get less than R150', *Business Day*, 6 August 1996

Pauw, Jacques, 'Defence force raid on Apla scrapped', *The Star*, 5 February 1993

Perlman, John, 'Bullets outweigh words in propaganda battle', *The Star*, 12 December 1992

Pitje, Godfrey, 'Robert Mangeliso Sobukwe', *South African Outlook*, August 1978

Rodda, Peter, 'The Africanists cut loose', *Africa South*, 3, 4, July 1959

Sibeko, David, 'The Sharpeville Massacre: its historic significance in the struggle against Apartheid' in http://www.sahistory.org.za/pages/library-resources/aticles_papers/1990-sharpeville

Sobukwe, Mangaliso, 'Facing fearful odds', *The Commentator* (Maseru), August 1968

Stubbs, Aelred, 'Robert Sobukwe', *South African Outlook*, August 1978

Thloome, Dan, 'Lessons of the Stay-Away', *Liberation* (Johannesburg), 32, August 1958

Tsedu, Mathatha, 'Madzunya's flame burns brightly', *The Sowetan*, 13 October 1986

Umhlabeni, 'Africanists break loose', *Contact* (Cape Town), 15 November 1958

Van Staden, Gary, 'Return of the Prodigal Son: prospects for a revival of the Pan-Africanist Congress', *International Affairs Bulletin* (Johannesburg), 1, 1989

West, Norman, 'Top PAC officials in drugs scandal', *Sunday Times*, 16 May 1993

Wilkinson, Bronwyn, 'Apla great storm message jars with PAC', *The Star*, 2 January 1993

UNPUBLISHED DISSERTATIONS

Charney, Craig, 3, 'Civil Society vs. the State: Identity, Institutions and the Black Consciousness Movement in South Africa', D.Phil. Dissertation, Yale University, 2000

Couper, Scott Everett, 'Bound by Faith: A Biographic and Ecclesiastic Examination of Chief Albert Luthuli's Stance on Violence as a Strategy to Liberate South Africa', Ph.D. Dissertation, School of Anthropology, Gender and Historical Studies, University of KwaZulu Natal, Durban, 2008

Jeffrey, Ian, 'The Sharpetown Swingsters: Their Will to Survive', BA Honours Dissertation, Department of Social Anthropology, University of the Witwatersrand, 1985

Johns, Sheridan, 'Marxism–Leninism in a Multi-Racial Environment: The Origins and Early History of the Communist Party of South Africa', Ph.D. Dissertation, Department of Government, Harvard, 1965

Mahomo, Nana, 'The Rise of the Pan-Africanist Congress of South Africa', M.Sc. Dissertation, Massachusetts Institute of Technology, Boston, 1968

O'Sullivan, Kevin, 'Ireland and Sub-Saharan Africa, 1955–1975', Ph.D. Dissertation, Department of History, Trinity College Dublin, 2008

Shakinovsky, Terri, 'The Local State in Crisis: The Shaping of the Black Working Class, Vereeniging 1939–1949', BA Honours Dissertation, Department of History, University of the Witwatersrand, 1983

Van Zyl, M., 'Swart Verstedeliking in Vereeniging, 1923–1960', Ph.D. Dissertation, Vista University, Vanderbijlpark, 1993

Index